CORPORATE RESTRUCTURING LAW IN FLUX

This book analyses recent developments in English corporate restructuring law from a range of comparative and theoretical perspectives, exploring some of the most difficult aspects of the design of domestic restructuring laws and their application in cross-border cases. The author team draw on their expertise in a wide range of jurisdictions to reflect critically on choices made in the Corporate Insolvency and Governance Act 2020 (UK) and on aspects of restructuring laws and restructuring law reform initiatives elsewhere, including in the EU, the US, and in various jurisdictions in Africa.

Corporate Restructuring Law in Flux

Edited by
Jennifer Payne
and
Kristin van Zwieten

•HART•
OXFORD • LONDON • NEW YORK • NEW DELHI • SYDNEY

HART PUBLISHING

Bloomsbury Publishing Plc

Kemp House, Chawley Park, Cumnor Hill, Oxford, OX2 9PH, UK

1385 Broadway, New York, NY 10018, USA

Bloomsbury Publishing Ireland Limited, 29 Earlsfort Terrace, Dublin 2, D02 AY28, Ireland

HART PUBLISHING, the Hart/Stag logo, BLOOMSBURY and the Diana logo are trademarks of Bloomsbury Publishing Plc

First published in Great Britain 2025

A catalogue record for this book is available from the British Library.

A catalogue record for this book is available from the Library of Congress.

Library of Congress Control Number: 2025936838

ISBN: HB: 978-1-50997-838-0
ePDF: 978-1-50997-840-3
ePub: 978-1-50997-839-7

Typeset by Compuscript Ltd, Shannon
Printed and bound in Great Britain

For product safety related questions contact productsafety@bloomsbury.com

To find out more about our authors and books visit www.hartpublishing.co.uk. Here you will find extracts, author information, details of forthcoming events and the option to sign up for our newsletters.

FOREWORD

Every insolvency lawyer who has – or hopes to have – an insolvency case with an important international component will want to have this book. It will also sit on the shelves of all academics and judges interested in this increasingly global field. It offers description and insights at the practical, policy, and theoretical levels. The authors of the chapters are well-known to their colleagues in the insolvency field in their home countries and around the world, and have obviously been chosen both for their expertise and for the clarity with which they describe the English system and compare it to other regimes in the United States, the European Union, and Africa.

Jennifer Payne and Kristin van Zwieten, the well-known Oxford scholars who organised and edited the book, also provide the first chapter. That chapter provides a really clear and useful summary of the newly augmented English system that, for many of us, would be worth the purchase of the book all by itself. The English apparently never repeal an insolvency law, but just add a new one. The authors provide a helpful map to a complex menu of choices for counsel to the Management and Insider Parties in Possession (MIPPs) of restructuring companies in England and around the world. In Chapter eleven, Anthony Casey (Chicago) gives an outline of the reasons that an English proceeding might be more attractive to a MIPP than filing a US Chapter 11 case.

The remaining chapters are a stimulating mix of theory and comparative law. Comparative examples are found throughout the book. For example, in Chapter three there is a really nice comparison and analysis of priority rules and their function in various systems. The comparative illustrations help readers from a variety of jurisdictions to understand other systems more clearly as well as stimulating consideration of useful reforms. One of its best features are its regular reminders that transplanting an insolvency system requires careful attention to national differences in context, including the surrounding legal and business cultures, from one jurisdiction to another.

On the policy side, Chapter four illustrates how the book provides some important insights about the fairness of various systems and rules, permitting the reader to contemplate how to judge systems from that moral/legal point of view. It even develops a test for 'fair allocation of restructuring surplus' (FaiRS). We will no doubt see that concept both asserted and debunked in the literature and in briefs.

We must be grateful for this important contribution to the global literature about a subject of increasingly global function and effect.

Jay Lawrence Westbrook
Benno C Schmidt Chair of Business Law
The University of Texas School of Law

PREFACE

In 2022, we launched a research project under the auspices of the Commercial Law Centre at Harris Manchester College, Oxford, called 'Corporate insolvency and restructuring law after CIGA'. The project was directed to evaluating the permanent changes made to UK restructuring and insolvency law by the enactment of the Corporate Insolvency and Governance Act 2020 (CIGA). CIGA added a new corporate restructuring procedure to the Companies Act 2006 (the Part 26A restructuring plan), and made significant changes to the Insolvency Act 1986, including the introduction of the new Part A1 moratorium, which can be used in combination with the new restructuring plan, or with other previously available procedures, or on a 'freestanding' basis. The overall aim was to ensure the availability of a legal framework that would facilitate the achievement of a binding restructuring as an alternative to a realisation (forced sale to a third party) for the treatment of a corporate debtor's expected inability to meet its fixed obligations.

With the support of the Oxford Law Faculty, we brought together a small group of academics and senior practitioners to meet for an initial workshop at Harris Manchester College. Some of our project members were experts in UK law, but others were experts in the restructuring laws of other jurisdictions; we felt that much could be learned by asking those with expertise in other jurisdictions to critically examine the design of the new UK rules, having regard to their experiences elsewhere. We were also very eager to hear from practitioners experimenting with applications of the new UK framework, either on its own, or in combination with restructuring frameworks abroad (through the proposal of parallel restructuring plans in cross-border cases).

Four points emerged quite clearly from this initial workshop. The first was that the exceptionally slender Part 26A provisions have left it to the judiciary to address the legal position on a wide range of difficult issues that have been addressed through the provision of detailed statutory rules in other jurisdictions. The second was that, although participants generally hoped for greater certainty on these issues, there were a variety of views as to how this would best be achieved, and what form the clearer rules would optimally take. Thirdly, it was agreed that whilst much could be learned from examining the approach taken to these issues in other jurisdictions, there was a real danger (as in all comparative work) in singling out particular components of a foreign legal framework for comparative analysis, without a proper understanding of the role of that component in the overall framework, and of the broader institutional context in which the framework is applied. The fourth point was that the utility of the new UK framework would depend not only on how these issues were resolved, but also on how the new forms of UK procedure would be received by foreign courts. In relation to restructuring plan proceedings in particular, participants expected that there would be significant variation in the way in which such proceedings would be received in applications for recognition and relief abroad, both within and outside the EU.

This book is a response to, or perhaps more accurately an elaboration of, these four points. In a series of chapters contributed by project participants, authors reflect on some of the most contentious and difficult issues arising from the CIGA reforms, and on restructuring law reform processes elsewhere (including in the US, in EU law, in selected EU Member States, and in selected jurisdictions in Africa), from a range of perspectives. Each of these chapters can stand alone, but we have sought to draw together the themes and ideas elaborated by the authors in the introduction to this book. Several chapters are co-authored by experts working in more than one jurisdiction and feature the kind of contextualised comparative analysis that was recognised in the workshop as being critical in a project of this kind. All chapters benefited from further discussion at a conference held in January 2024 in Oxford, again supported by the Oxford Law Faculty, at which drafts were probed by senior practitioner and academic discussants from a range of jurisdictions. We are very grateful to all those who contributed to the discussion at this conference, and at the initial workshop: the author team, of course, but also many others, including Wai Yee Wan, Jennifer Marshall, Katharina Crinson, Janis Sarra, Nick Segal, Felicity Toube, Inga West, Roy Goode, Horst Eidenmüller, Paul Davies, Gerard McCormack, Jonathan Harris, Louise Gullifer, Vasile Rotaru, Richard Salter and Jay Westbrook.

The book does not offer a comprehensive treatment of all the legal issues arising from the 2020 UK reforms (still less those arising in restructuring law reform exercises elsewhere). But it does offer a rigorous treatment of some of the most complex of these issues, informed by theory and comparative evidence, along with many insights into the processes and pitfalls of corporate restructuring law reform more generally. We believe that the book offers much of value to those interested in understanding and evaluating the current trajectory of UK law, as well as those engaged in similar evaluative work elsewhere. We would like to express our warm thanks to Roberta Bassi and Verity Stuart at Hart Publishing for supporting this book, and to all those in the production team who have helped to deliver the finished product. We hope it will prove to be a valuable contribution to policy debate, both in the UK and abroad, in this highly dynamic area of the law.

Jennifer Payne
Kristin van Zwieten
Oxford, November 2024

CONTENTS

LIST OF CONTRIBUTORS

Reinhard Bork, University Professor (Emeritus) for Civil Procedure Law and General Procedural Law, University of Hamburg, and Senior Research Fellow, Harris Manchester College, Oxford

Anthony J Casey, Donald M Ephraim Professor of Law and Economics, Faculty Director, The Center on Law and Finance, University of Chicago

Philip Hertz, Partner, Clifford Chance

Edward J Janger, David M Barse Professor of Law, Brooklyn Law School

Stephan Madaus, Professor of Law, Martin Luther University Halle-Wittenberg

Irit Mevorach, Professor of International Commercial Law, University of Warwick

Riz Mokal, Barrister South Square, London, Honorary Professor, University College London, and Honorary Research Fellow, University of Aberdeen School of Law

Natalie Mrockova, Career Development Researcher and Lecturer in Law at Merton College, Oxford

Sarah Paterson, Professor of Law, London School of Economics

Jennifer Payne, Warden, Merton College, Oxford and Professor of Corporate Finance Law, University of Oxford

Gabrielle Ruiz, Senior Lawyer, Clifford Chance

Felix Steffek, Professor of Law and University JM Keynes Fellow in Financial Economics, University of Cambridge

Sjur Swensen Ellingsæter, Associate Professor at the Department of Law and Governance, BI Norwegian Business School

Winifred Tarinyeba Kiryabwire, Associate Professor, Makerere University

Ignacio Tirado, Secretary General UNIDROIT and Professor of Law at the Universidad Autónoma de Madrid

Kristin van Zwieten, Clifford Chance Professor of Law and Finance, University of Oxford and Gullifer Fellow in Law, Harris Manchester College, Oxford

Adrian Walters, Professor of Law, Director of the Program in Business Law, Chicago-Kent College of Law

Jay Westbrook, Benno C Schmidt Chair of Business Law, University of Texas

TABLE OF CASES

UNITED KINGDOM

AUSTRALIA

CANADA

GERMANY

HONG KONG

NETHERLANDS

REPUBLIC OF IRELAND

SINGAPORE

SOUTH AFRICA

UNITED STATES

TABLE OF LEGISLATION

UNITED KINGDOM

STATUTES

STATUTORY INSTRUMENTS

AUSTRALIA

CHINA

EUROPEAN UNION

FRANCE

GERMANY

INTERNATIONAL

KENYA

LESOTHO

MALAWI

NETHERLANDS

NIGERIA

REPUBLIC OF IRELAND

ROMANIA

RWANDA

SINGAPORE

SOUTH AFRICA

SWEDEN

UGANDA

UNITED STATES

ZAMBIA

ZIMBABWE

1

Introduction

JENNIFER PAYNE AND KRISTIN VAN ZWIETEN

The past five years in Europe have been characterised by crisis and, unquestionably relatedly, by extensive reforms to corporate restructuring laws. In the EU, the Preventive Restructuring Directive was enacted in 2019 with a view to ensuring that viable enterprises in financial difficulty had 'access to effective national preventive restructuring frameworks' across the Union;[1] the Directive stipulates 'substantive minimum standards' for the design of restructuring procedures at the Member State level.[2] Many Member States have introduced entirely new forms of restructuring procedure in the process of transposing the Directive, which are being gradually added to Annex A of the European Insolvency Regulation,[3] so as to be eligible for the privileges that the Regulation confers in relation to recognition across the Union.[4] The UK withdrew from the European Union shortly after the enactment of the Directive, and long before the expiration of the time given by the Directive for its transposition, but restructuring law reform was already firmly on the policy agenda here, and by mid-2020, the UK had enacted a statute, the Corporate Insolvency and Governance Act 2020 (CIGA), which, among other things, introduced an entirely new restructuring procedure (the 'restructuring plan procedure') to the statute book.

These reforms, and reform initiatives being conducted in parallel in many other regions of the world, reflect an emerging consensus as to the importance of corporate restructuring laws, both as a complement to macroeconomic stabilisation tools in times

[1] Directive (EU) 2019/1023 of the European Parliament and of the Council of 20 June 2019 on preventive restructuring frameworks, on discharge of debt and disqualifications, and on measures to increase the efficiency of procedures concerning restructuring, insolvency and discharge of debt, and amending Directive (EU) 2017/1132, OJ L 172, 26.6.2019, Recital 1.

[2] ibid, Recital 12.

[3] Regulation (EU) 2015/848 of the European Parliament and of the Council of 20 May 2015 on insolvency proceedings (recast) OJ L 141, 5.6.2015. Annex A determines which Member State proceedings fall within the Regulation's scope (Art 1(1)).

[4] Including automatic recognition of the opening of proceedings by the courts of other Member States, such recognition carrying with it, in the case of main proceedings (ie those opened in the place of the debtor's centre of main interests: Art 3), the extension of the effects provided by the law of the state of opening across the Union, except to the extent that the Regulation otherwise provides or where secondary proceedings have been opened: Art 20(1). The Regulation limits the opening of proceedings falling within its scope through the provision of rules of jurisdiction.

of extraordinary crisis, and as a determinant of investment conditions in more ordinary times. But it is one thing to recognise the importance of such laws in the abstract, and quite another to work out precisely how a restructuring procedure should be designed. At their heart, restructuring laws are concerned with facilitating the striking of a new bargain between a debtor and its existing claimholders, so that the debtor's expected inability to meet its fixed obligations in full is resolved through a reorganisation of claims, rather than a realisation of assets. There are, however, many different ways to bring claimholders 'to the table', and the costs and benefits of these legal techniques will depend on a range of contextual factors that vary across jurisdictions. Recognising this, the EU Directive leaves much to Member States to determine when designing their preventive restructuring frameworks,[5] as does the best practice guidance issued by the World Bank in its *Principles for Effective Insolvency and Creditor/Debtor Regimes.*[6] This helpfully enables rules to be tailored to the context in which they will be applied, but leaves many hard choices to be made by those responsible for designing restructuring law rules at a granular level.

This book explores some of the most complex aspects of designing restructuring law rules, both substantive and procedural. It does so primarily through the close analysis of the UK's 2020 restructuring law reform experiment, although chapter authors draw extensively on examples from elsewhere to critically analyse choices made in the UK, and in some cases offer separate evaluation of aspects of restructuring law reform processes outside the UK. Given the centrality of the UK story to the book, we begin by introducing the 2020 CIGA reforms, before providing a detailed overview of each chapter of the book; we then conclude by identifying some themes that emerge from the collection of chapters.

I. The Changing Corporate Restructuring Landscape in the UK

The enactment of CIGA represented the biggest change to English corporate insolvency and restructuring law since the implementation of the Cork Report[7] recommendations in the Insolvency Acts of 1985–86. CIGA introduced a number of powerful new tools into the armoury of financially distressed companies wishing to restructure their obligations. Specifically, CIGA introduced a new bespoke restructuring procedure, the Part 26A restructuring plan,[8] which contains the option of a 'cross-class cram-down' whereby the restructuring can be imposed on one or more dissenting classes

[5] See further Reinhard Bork, 'Pre-insolvency frameworks: Developments in the European Union' (2024) 33 *International Insolvency Review* 6.

[6] World Bank, *Principles for Effective Insolvency and Creditor/Debtor Regimes* (2021) https://documents.worldbank.org/en/publication/documents-reports/documentdetail/391341619072648570/principles-for-effective-insolvency-and-creditor-and-debtor-regimes.

[7] *Insolvency Law and Practice: Report of the Review Committee* (1982) (Cmnd 8558).

[8] Contained in Part 26A of the Companies Act 2006, following the provision for schemes of arrangement in Part 26 of that Act.

of stakeholder, a new restructuring moratorium[9] (which can be used on a standalone basis or in combination with some other procedures, including the Part 26A procedure), and broad constraints on the exercise of rights to terminate or modify contracts for the supply of goods and services on the commencement of various insolvency and restructuring proceedings, including Part 26A plan proceedings.[10]

There were three main drivers of these legislative changes. The first was a desire to respond to perceived weaknesses in the existing regime. This is not to suggest that prior to CIGA the UK restructuring regime was unsuccessful. On the contrary, practitioners and the courts had developed powerful tools to deal with financially distressed companies.[11] In particular, they utilised the scheme of arrangement,[12] either as a standalone device or in combination with other mechanisms,[13] and schemes became an effective tool for restructuring not only the debt of English companies, but also of overseas companies that have sought to make use of the English court's jurisdiction.[14] However, the law lacked certain elements, including a formal cross-class cram-down mechanism, and a statutory stay to prevent creditors from enforcing their debt while the debtor negotiated the terms of the plan.[15]

The second driver was regulatory competition. The Great Recession of 2007–09 sharpened the focus of governments across Europe on corporate restructuring laws, prompting work by the European Commission that would eventually culminate in a proposal for a restructuring directive.[16] In the UK, there was also some political concern about the UK's ranking in the World Bank's *Doing Business* report.[17] A change in the methodology for the 'Resolving Insolvency' component of *Doing Business* meant that jurisdictions would be assessed not only by reference to outcomes in practice, but also by reference to whether the law 'on the books' exhibited the features suggested in best practice guidance issued by the World Bank and by UNCITRAL;[18] UK law did not exhibit all of these features.[19] By the time that the UK Government had finalised its proposal

[9] Contained in Part A1 of the Insolvency Act 1986.

[10] Contained in s 233B of the Insolvency Act 1986.

[11] For the distinction between financial distress and economic distress see DG Baird, 'Bankruptcy's Uncontested Axioms' (1998) 108 *Yale Law Journal* 573.

[12] See Companies Act 2006, Part 26.

[13] See eg *Re Bluebrook Ltd* [2009] EWHC 2114 (Ch) and Chapters 3 and 4 of this book.

[14] See eg *Re Rodenstock GmbH* [2011] EWHC 1104 (Ch).

[15] See Insolvency Service, *A Review of the Corporate Insolvency Framework: A Consultation on Options for Reform*, May 2016; Department for Business, Energy and Industrial Strategy (BEIS), *Insolvency and Corporate Governance: Government Response*, 26 August 2018.

[16] For the background, including the Commission's Recommendation of 12 March 2014 on a new approach to business failure and insolvency, OJ L 74/65 14.3.2014, see Chapters 2 and 3 of this book. In the UK, the first consultation on reform following the financial crises of 2007–2008 was in 2009: see Insolvency Service, *Encouraging company rescue – a consultation*, June 2009.

[17] See 'Conservative Party Manifesto 2015': https://ucrel.lancs.ac.uk/wmatrix/ukmanifestos2015/localpdf/Conservatives.pdf, 17.

[18] See World Bank, 'Resolving Insolvency methodology', available at: https://archive.doingbusiness.org/en/methodology/resolving-insolvency, and in particular the 'Strength of Insolvency Framework Index'.

[19] For example, in relation to the treatment of executory contracts in insolvency: see ibid, 'Management of the debtor's assets index'. On the role of the *Doing Business Report* in the UK reform process more generally, see S Frisby, 'Of rights and rescue: a curious confluence' (2020) 20(1) *Journal of Corporate Law Studies* 39. More recently, there have been difficulties with the *Doing Business* project. After data irregularities pertaining to *Doing Business 2018* and *Doing Business 2020* were reported, World Bank management paused *Doing Business* and initiated a series of audits and reviews of the Report's methodology: see https://www.worldbank.

for restructuring-related law reform in 2018, the EU was inching closer to settling the final text of a restructuring directive that would require Member States to put in place restructuring frameworks with provision for cross-class cram-down, supported by a statutory stay.[20] That meant that the UK was poised to leave the EU at a moment at which various Member States were expected to introduce procedures with features that the UK regime was recognised to lack. Outside of the EU, other jurisdictions, such as Singapore, were also moving to make similar changes.[21] As others have argued,[22] there can be little doubt that the UK Government's 2018 proposal was motivated in part by a desire to ensure the continuing attractiveness of London as a restructuring forum in the post-Brexit world.

The third driver was the Covid-19 pandemic. Although the Government had articulated a clear plan for corporate restructuring law reform in 2018, this did not gain legislative traction until the onset of the pandemic. Like other governments around the world, the UK Government responded to the pandemic by restricting trade across many sectors of the economy, issuing 'stay at home' orders, and by writing a business relief package designed to avoid a wave of business insolvencies.[23] At the same time, the Government also anticipated that some businesses would need to restructure in order to 'weather the storm'.[24] The Government therefore looked to 'dust off' the 2018 plan and proceeded to implement its recommendations for facilitating the rescue of financially distressed companies.

This dusting-off process was rapid: CIGA came into force on 26 June 2020, just over three months after the announcement of the first Covid lockdown in the UK. The upside was the introduction of a number of restructuring tools that the Insolvency Service had been advocating for some time. The downside, however, was a very limited period for any broad or meaningful consultation on the detail of the legislative provisions. This lack of consultation, while understandable in the circumstances of the pandemic, was problematic given that the legislation departed from the 2018 proposals in ways that were by no means all minor and incidental. For example, whilst the Government had previously indicated that a form of (flexible) absolute priority rule would be provided to

org/en/news/statement/2020/08/27/doing-business---data-irregularities-statement; https://www.worldbank.org/en/news/statement/2020/12/16/world-bank-group-statement-on-doing-business-data-corrections-and-findings-of-internal-audit; and https://thedocs.worldbank.org/en/doc/791761608145561083-0050022020/original/DBDataIrregularitiesReviewDec2020.pdf.

[20] See European Parliament, 'Report on the proposal for a directive of the European Parliament and of the Council on preventive restructuring frameworks, second chance and measures to increase the efficiency of restructuring, insolvency and discharge procedures and amending Directive 2012/30/EU' (21 August 2018), A8-0269/2018.

[21] See the Insolvency, Restructuring and Dissolution Act 2018 (Singapore), ss 64–66.

[22] See Frisby (n 19).

[23] See further K van Zwieten, 'Mid-Crisis Restructuring Law Reform in the United Kingdom' (2023) 24 *European Business Organization Law Review* 287, section II, and on the choices available to policymakers in the design of Covid-19 business relief policies more generally, K van Zwieten, H Eidenmüller, and O Sussman, 'Bail-outs and bail-ins are better than bankruptcy: a comparative assessment of public policy responses to Covid-19 distress' (2021) 15(2) *Virginia Law and Business Review* 199.

[24] 'Business Secretary's statement on coronavirus (COVID-19)' 28 March 2020. For an analysis of the case for restructuring compared with forced sales in the context of an industry-wide crisis, see A Shleifer and R Vishny, 'Liquidation Values and Debt Capacity: A Market Equilibrium Approach' (1992) 42 *Journal of Finance* 1343, and, making the case for deferring restructuring on the onset of the Covid-19 crisis, van Zwieten, Eidenmüller and Sussman, ibid.

address minority protection issues in a cross-class cram-down,[25] the final text contained no priority rule. The scope of the moratorium was also materially changed.[26] Some other important issues were left unaddressed.[27] The combination of material changes and statutory silence on some important questions has had repercussions, creating uncertainty for debtors and their creditors and for the market more generally. Some of this uncertainty is likely to resolve over time as courts have the opportunity to consider these provisions. This will happen more rapidly in those areas (such as restructuring plans) which have an embedded court oversight function. Where court oversight is not automatic and/or where the use of the mechanism is low, this will happen more slowly. It is notable, for example, that to date there have only been two court cases examining the provisions of the new restructuring moratorium.[28]

A. Restructuring Plans

While Part 26A restructuring plans are a new restructuring mechanism introduced by CIGA, they are based to a large extent on the pre-existing scheme of arrangement in Part 26 of the Companies Act 2006 (which remains available). As a result, a restructuring plan is an 'arrangement' or 'compromise' between the company and its creditors and/or shareholders or classes thereof[29] and may be proposed by the company or its creditors or shareholders.[30] It requires voting of creditors and shareholders in classes; the majority approval is 75 per cent by value of that class voting in favour.[31] As with schemes of arrangement, it is possible to exclude creditors from the plan if those creditors' claims will be paid in full, ie where they are unaffected by the plan.[32] In common with schemes of arrangement, two court hearings are required: the first to order the required meetings of creditors/members[33] and the second to sanction the restructuring plan.[34] There is a requirement to provide information to creditors/members and disclosure obligations are placed on directors that closely mirror the requirements in a scheme of arrangement.[35]

However, Part 26A contains a number of changes from the provisions governing schemes of arrangement in Part 26 of the Act. One important difference is that in order to be eligible for a restructuring plan, the company must satisfy a financial eligibility test:

[25] See BEIS, *Insolvency and Corporate Governance: Government Response*, 26 August 2018, paras [5.163]–[5.165], and see further Chapter 3 of this book.

[26] See van Zwieten (n 23) and Chapter 8 of this book.

[27] See, for example, those discussed in Chapters 5 and 6 of this book.

[28] *Minor Hotel Group MEA DMCC v Dymant* [2022] EWHC 340; *Re Grove Independent School* [2023] EWHC 2546. For discussion of the limitations of the moratorium, which may be linked to its low take-up, see Chapter 8.

[29] Companies Act 2006, s 901A(3)(a).

[30] ibid, s 901C(1)(2).

[31] ibid, s 901F(1). This is distinct from a scheme of arrangement which requires both 75% by value to vote in favour and a majority in number: Companies Act 2006, s 899(1).

[32] Although the court may scrutinise this decision when deciding whether the discretion to sanction the plan should be exercised: *Virgin Active Holdings Limited* [2021] EWHC 1246 (Ch) [226]–[266].

[33] Companies Act 2006, s 901C(1).

[34] ibid, s 901F(1).

[35] ibid, ss 901D and E.

it must have encountered or be likely to encounter financial difficulties that are affecting or will or may affect its ability to carry on business as a going concern, and the purpose of the compromise or arrangement must be to eliminate, reduce, prevent or mitigate the effects of any of the company's financial difficulties.[36] The restructuring plan is therefore focused on companies in financial distress. Perhaps the most significant difference between the two mechanisms, however, is that the court is empowered to sanction a restructuring plan in the presence of one or more dissenting classes.[37] A scheme of arrangement alone cannot enable a restructuring to be imposed on a dissenting class; all classes have to assent for a scheme to be sanctioned by the court.[38] The ability to impose a restructuring on a whole class of creditors is a more powerful tool for debtors. Such a tool has been available within Chapter 11 of the US Bankruptcy Code (Chapter 11) for decades, and is increasingly available elsewhere,[39] including in the EU, where the minimum standards imposed by the Preventive Restructuring Directive include provision for class-based voting and cross-class cram-down.[40] Creating a more powerful tool for debtors does, however, also necessitate the introduction of stronger creditor protection, so as not only to protect the minority creditors in any given company, but also to bolster the market for capital, since the risk of expropriation ex post will be factored in by professional investors ex ante.

In a scheme of arrangement, two forms of creditor protection are in place: the fact that the creditors meet in classes to vote on the restructuring (and all classes must vote in favour in order for the restructuring to go ahead); and that the court must sanction the scheme, and in making this decision the court will take account not only of whether the statutory provisions have been complied with, but more broadly, will apply a fairness test, and will consider, for example, whether the majority have voted bona fide in the interests of the class as a whole.[41] These forms of protection are appropriate when the court is only considering whether a restructuring should be imposed on dissenters *within* a class,[42] but are insufficient when the question is whether the restructuring should be imposed on a dissenting *class*, for in that case the question is not whether a minority can be bound to a plan supported by a similarly situated majority, but whether some classes can impose a plan on differently situated classes.

As explored in more detail later in this book,[43] many jurisdictions provide protection for the dissenting class through two types of rules: a 'best-interests-of-creditors' test, which requires the court to be satisfied that dissenters will not be left worse off

[36] ibid, ss 901A(2) and 901A(3)(b).

[37] Other changes include that an application can be made to exclude classes of creditors/shareholders from voting where the court is satisfied that 'none of the members of that class has a genuine economic interest in the company' (s 901C(4)).

[38] Combining a scheme with other restructuring tools could create a de facto cross-class cram-down, see J Payne, *Schemes of Arrangement*, 2nd edn (Cambridge, CUP, 2021) section 5.4.3; see further Chapters 3, 4 and 6 of this book.

[39] eg in the Singaporean scheme of arrangement: see Insolvency, Restructuring and Dissolution Act 2018 (Singapore), s 70.

[40] See Arts 9–11 of the Directive. However, Member States can opt to relax the requirement for class-based voting for SMEs. See Art 9(4), Recital 45, and below, Chapter 3, text to fns 137–138.

[41] See J Payne, *Schemes of Arrangement*, 2nd edn (Cambridge, CUP, 2021) section 2.4.3.

[42] For discussion see J Payne, 'The Role of the Court in Debt Restructuring' (2018) 77(1) *Cambridge Law Journal* 124.

[43] See Chapters 2, 3 and 5.

under the plan, and a priority rule for the treatment of complaints by the dissenting class that the plan distributes 'too much' value to other classes.[44] As to the latter, US Chapter 11 stipulates a rule of absolute priority.[45] The EU Restructuring Directive offers a choice between a 'relative priority rule' and two versions of absolute priority.[46] Part 26A contains a form of 'no-worse-off' rule (the court must be satisfied that, if the restructuring plan were to be sanctioned, none of the members of the dissenting class would be any worse off than they would be in the event of the relevant alternative).[47] There is, however, no statutory priority rule in Part 26A. This relatively 'light touch' approach has left a great deal to be determined by the courts.[48]

B. The Restructuring Moratorium and Constraints on *Ipso Facto* Clauses

The new restructuring moratorium and constraints on the exercise of rights to terminate or modify contracts for the supply of goods and services (so-called '*ipso facto* clauses') are intended to complement Part 26A. Whereas the cross-class cram-down power is available to facilitate the finalisation of a binding agreement between the debtor and its creditors as to their future relationship, the moratorium and constraints on *ipso facto* clauses are directed to ensuring that the debtor can continue to trade while that agreement is negotiated.

A moratorium is designed to address the fact that, left to their own devices, minority creditors can derail a debt restructuring not only by withholding their agreement (where unanimity is required) but also by exercising their rights to enforce the debt or initiate insolvency proceedings or some other legal process. A moratorium is effectively a legal intervention designed to promote the rescue of a company or business by enabling the debtor to keep operating as a going concern during this period. The intention is to provide a breathing space for the debtor within which it can reach agreement with its creditors and keep the business together long enough for a reorganisation to be effected.[49] It has become common for jurisdictions to include broad moratoria

[44] See further pp 12, 94 below.

[45] See US Bankruptcy Code §§ 1129(b)(1), and (2)(B). This is the rule that applies with respect to a dissenting class of unsecured claims. See further Chapter 5 of this book.

[46] Art 11 of the Directive; see further T Richter and A Thery, *INSOL Europe: Guidance Note on the Implementation of Preventive Restructuring Frameworks under EU Directive 2019/1023: Claims, Classes, Voting, Confirmation and the Cross-Class Cram-Down*, April 2020, available at: https://www.insol-europe.org/publications/guidance-notes, and Chapter 3 of this book.

[47] Companies Act 2006, s 901G(3). The 'relevant alternative' for these purposes is 'whatever the court considers would be most likely to occur in relation to the company if the compromise or arrangement were not sanctioned': s 901G(4). There is also a requirement that the compromise or arrangement has been accepted at a class meeting of at least one class of creditors/members who would receive a payment, or have a genuine economic interest in the company, in the event of the relevant alternative: s 901G(5).

[48] As illustrated most recently by the decision of the Court of Appeal in *Re AGPS Bondco Plc* [2024] EWCA Civ 24 (*Re Adler Group*). See further Chapters 2–6 of this book, all of which explore aspects of the cross-class cram-down power.

[49] See eg T Jackson, 'Bankruptcy, Non-Bankruptcy Entitlements, and the Creditors' Bargain' (1982) 91 *Yale Law Journal* 857.

provisions within their restructuring frameworks.[50] Until 2020 in the UK, while a moratorium was available in administration proceedings under the Insolvency Act 1986,[51] the only restructuring mechanism that featured a statutory moratorium was the company voluntary arrangement procedure, as it applied to small companies,[52] which was almost never used in practice. Debtors wishing to protect themselves during plan negotiation therefore sought various alternatives, the most common being to utilise a contractual standstill arrangement, whereby the creditors voluntarily commit to refrain from exercising their contractual rights. This can work well where the creditor body is small and relatively homogenous.[53]

The restructuring moratorium introduced by CIGA to Part A1 of the Insolvency Act 1986 can be used in conjunction with restructuring mechanisms such as schemes of arrangement or restructuring plans, but it can also be used on its own.[54] In contrast to the position in administration, the restructuring moratorium is a 'debtor-in-possession' procedure in the sense that directors retain powers of management, subject to the appointment of a licensed insolvency practitioner (the monitor, who is responsible for verifying the company's continuing eligibility to use the procedure, including verifying that it is likely that the moratorium will result in the rescue of the company as a going concern[55]) and certain other restrictions. There is an in-court and out-of-court procedure for obtaining a moratorium. The out-of-court process will usually only be available to a company if it is not subject to an outstanding winding-up petition and is not an overseas company.[56] It involves directors filing relevant documents at court and is similar to the process for appointing administrators out of court, but unlike in administration, no prior notice is required to be given to floating charge holders before the directors file for a moratorium.[57]

The effect of the moratorium is to impose a constraint on the ability of creditors to assert their debt claims against the company and a constraint on initiating insolvency proceedings and other legal processes.[58] A company subject to a moratorium will obtain the benefit of a payment holiday from certain pre-moratorium debts.[59] However, some pre-moratorium debts, including the obligation to pay debts or liabilities arising

[50] See eg the US Chapter 11 regime (see 11 USC §§ 362, 365(e) and 541(c)), the Singaporean restructuring regime (Singapore Insolvency, Restructuring and Dissolution Act 2018, ss 64–66); and the EU Restructuring Directive 2019/1023, Arts 6–7.

[51] Insolvency Act 1986, Sch B1, paras 42–43.

[52] Insolvency Act 1986, s 1A and Sch A1. These provisions were repealed by CIGA. See further van Zwieten (n 23).

[53] For discussion, see S Paterson, 'Rethinking the Role of Corporate Bankruptcy Theory in the Twenty-First Century' (2016) 36 *Oxford Journal of Legal Studies* 697.

[54] See generally CIGA ss 1–6 and Schs 1–8. For discussion, see J Payne, 'An Assessment of the UK Restructuring Moratorium' [2021] *Lloyd's Maritime & Commercial Law Quarterly* 454.

[55] Insolvency Act 1986, Part A1, s A38(1); see also s A6(1)(e).

[56] ibid, Part A1, s A3.

[57] For the position in administration, see K van Zwieten (ed), *Goode on Principles of Corporate Insolvency Law*, 5th edn (London, Sweet & Maxwell, 2018) para [11-45].

[58] Insolvency Act 1986, Part A1, Chapter 4.

[59] Pre-moratorium debts are: (a) any debts or liabilities to which the company becomes subject before the moratorium comes into force; or (b) any debt or liability to which the company has become or may become subject during the moratorium by reason of any obligation incurred before the moratorium: ibid, s 53(1), subject to (3). Section A18(3) sets out which pre-moratorium debts have a payment holiday.

under financial contracts,[60] are still required to be paid, and the monitor must bring the moratorium to an end if they think that the company is unable to pay pre-moratorium debts without a payment holiday that have fallen due.[61] The inclusion of debts under financial contracts in this category is striking, and significantly reduces the scope and utility of the procedure.[62] The other category of debts that must be paid as they fall due is moratorium debts; that is, any debt or other liability to which a company becomes subject during the moratorium other than by reason of an obligation incurred before the moratorium came into force, and any debt or other liability to which the company has become or may become subject after the end of the moratorium by reason of any obligation incurred in the moratorium.[63] Any unpaid moratorium debts and some pre-moratorium debts without a payment holiday, described as 'priority pre-moratorium debts', then get super priority in an insolvency occurring within 12 weeks of the end of the moratorium.[64]

The period of the moratorium is just 20 business days initially, which can be extended for a further 20 days without creditor consent or a court order.[65] There are constraints on the sorts of companies that can utilise the moratorium.[66] Some of these restrictions are entirely as you might expect, such as the exclusion of banks, which are subject to their own resolution regimes,[67] but others are more surprising and function to further limit the moratorium's utility. For example, the consequence of excluding any company that is party to a capital market arrangement (defined to include arrangements of more than £10 million which involve a party providing security to a trustee or agent or guaranteeing or providing security in respect of the performance of another party under a capital market investment, including rated/listed bonds)[68] is to remove many large corporates from the ambit of the provisions. There are also eligibility requirements before a moratorium can be put in place, including that the directors must state that, in their view, the company is, or is likely to become, unable to pay its debts.[69]

The new constraint on the exercise of *ipso facto* clauses in contracts for the supply of goods and services to the debtor is contained in section 233B of the Insolvency Act 1986. The provision applies to companies subject to a 'relevant insolvency procedure', defined so as to include administration, the new Part A1 moratorium, and companies for whom an order has been made summoning a meeting to vote on a

[60] Amounts payable in respect of 'debts or other liabilities arising under a contract or other instrument involving financial services' are excluded from the provision for a payment holiday in respect of pre-moratorium debts that have fallen due before the moratorium, or which fall due during the moratorium: see Insolvency Act 1986, Part A1, s A18(3)(f). A 'contract or other instrument involving financial services' has the meaning given by Schedule ZA2 (s A18(7)), which covers inter alia 'financial contracts' as defined.

[61] ibid s A38(1)(d)(ii).

[62] See further Chapter 8 of this book.

[63] Insolvency Act 1986, Part A1, s A53(2), subject to (3).

[64] ibid s 174A. Certain debts are excluded from this super priority, however, such as 'relevant accelerated debts': s 174A(3), (4), as to which see further Payne (n 54) and van Zwieten (n 23).

[65] ibid, Part A1, s A9.

[66] ibid, Sch ZA1.

[67] See the Banking Act 2009 (UK).

[68] Insolvency Act 1986, Sch ZA1 paras 13–14.

[69] ibid, Part A1, s A6(1)(d), and as to the meaning of 'unable to pay its debts', ss A54(1) and 123.

proposed Part 26A restructuring plan.[70] Prior to CIGA, the statutory regulation of rights to terminate or modify executory contracts by reason of the debtor's insolvency was very limited, being focused on preserving the supply of facilities such as gas, water and electricity and 'essential supplies' such as IT services.[71] Section 233B is much wider, applying to contracts for the supply of goods and services generally, subject to certain exceptions.[72] The provision has two main effects.[73] First, a supplier's contractual right to terminate, or 'do any other thing', because the company has entered the relevant procedure, ceases to have effect.[74] This would encompass any contractual provision for an alteration of terms (for example, as to price, or the terms of payment[75]) because of the commencement of the proceedings. Secondly, a supplier's contractual right to terminate because of an event occurring before the company becomes subject to the relevant procedure (any pre-insolvency events of default, whether or not related to the debtor's financial condition[76]) is temporarily suspended until the procedure comes to an end.[77] This is a material policy shift,[78] albeit one that is restricted to certain forms of executory contract.

II. An Overview of the Chapters of the Book

In Chapter two, *Gabrielle Ruiz* and *Philip Hertz* situate the Part 26A restructuring plan against the backdrop of restructuring law reforms that have taken place across the European Union as part of the transposition of the Preventive Restructuring Directive. They unpack the drivers of reform on either side of the Channel and then turn to explore how the restructuring plan procedure compares with new procedures in three 'restructuring hubs' in the Union – the Netherlands, Germany and France – having regard to the formal law (both substantive and procedural) and to evidence of the early use of each procedure in each jurisdiction. From a practitioner's perspective, they argue, the three most important factors or 'variables' that will drive selection from an ever-expanding menu of restructuring procedures across Europe are: certainty of outcome (including, in a cross-border case, in relation to recognition abroad); the expected time to achieve this; and the direct costs associated with doing so. Of course, as they emphasise, there will also be legal constraints on selection,[79] including rules of jurisdiction,

[70] ibid, s 233B(2). The list of relevant procedures does not include schemes of arrangement.

[71] ibid, ss 233, 233A.

[72] ibid, s 233B(10) and Sch 4ZZA. Excluded contracts include loan agreements, hedging agreements and other types of financial contracts. There is also a carve out for any set-off, netting arrangements or capital market investments. See Parts 3 and 4 of Sch 4ZZA.

[73] ibid, s 233B(3) and (4).

[74] ibid, s 233B(3).

[75] Separate provision is made to prohibit the supplier from making continued supply conditional on the payment of arrears: ibid, s 233B(7).

[76] Critiqued in van Zwieten (n 23).

[77] Insolvency Act 1986, s 233B(4) and see s 233B(8).

[78] See J Sarra, J Payne and S Madaus, 'The Promise and Perils of Regulating *Ipso Facto* Clauses' (2022) 31(1) *International Insolvency Review* 45.

[79] In this regard, particular attention is paid to the so-called 'rule in *Gibbs*' (*Antony Gibbs & Sons v La Société Industrielle et Commerciale des Métaux* (1890) LR 25 QBD 399; for a description of the rule, drawing on Ian Fletcher's *The Law of Insolvency*, 5th edn (London, Sweet & Maxwell, 2017), see *Re OJSC International Bank of*

which may differ markedly depending on whether or not the European Insolvency Regulation applies in a particular case.[80] The authors emphasise the relatively relaxed jurisdictional threshold for use of the scheme of arrangement and restructuring plan procedures in the UK.

The UK procedure is argued to have benefited significantly from the legislature's decision to model Part 26A on the scheme of arrangement procedure in Part 26 of the Companies Act 2006, which has enabled courts to draw readily on the schemes jurisprudence in interpreting parallel provisions in Part 26A. The authors suggest that this may have helped to encourage large case Part 26A filings from the outset, by enabling parties to rely on a body of precedent that will be absent in a jurisdiction introducing a scheme-like procedure for the first time, or in a jurisdiction that chooses to add to a scheme-like procedure by drafting a *sui generis* alternative to sit alongside it. The English courts are praised for taking the opportunities presented by the early restructuring plan cases to clarify, through the delivery of cogently reasoned judgments, those parts of the Part 26A framework that were initially more uncertain (either because they were novel, as with the cross-class cram-down power, or because there was doubt as to how novel parts of the framework were intended to interact with those carried over from Part 26).[81] Some persisting areas of uncertainty are also acknowledged, as are gaps in the legislative framework. The authors particularly highlight the absence of a stay in Part 26A,[82] and note cases in which English restructuring plan proceedings have been run in parallel with a Member State's restructuring process featuring a stay.

A major theme of the authors' analysis is the impact of procedural rules on the three variables of interest. Rules on disclosure, and on standing and cost risk for those seeking to challenge a plan, are identified as highly relevant to the 'time/cost calculus'. Some procedural choices made by the Dutch legislator when introducing the legislation for its restructuring scheme (the Wet homologatie onderhands akkoord, or WHOA) are also highlighted, including the decision to have a single court hearing and to make the decision on a plan non-appealable. It is suggested that fewer court hearings, together with the possibility of confidential proceedings, may make this procedure particularly attractive to smaller debtors, and the authors note that in its first years of operation the WHOA procedure has been used overwhelmingly by such debtors. Importantly, however, the authors also recognise that the frequency of use of the procedure to date (ten times the number of UK restructuring plan proceedings over the same period) has enabled a body of case law on the interpretation of core provisions, including the

Azerbaijan [2018] EWCA Civ 2802, [23] et seq). The rule is characterised elsewhere in this book as an 'aberration' (Chapter 4, fn 17 below).

[80] Which requires both that the procedure appear in Annex A of the EU Insolvency Regulation and that the debtor has its COMI in a Member State other than Denmark, which is a precondition to the Regulation's application in any particular case (Regulation 2015/848 (n 3), Recital 25).

[81] See in particular (in Chapter 2, section III.A.(iv).(a) below) the treatment of the *obiter* discussion in *Re AGPS Bondco Plc* (n 48) as to whether a Part 26A plan can provide for the cancellation of claims for no consideration, given the statutory language of 'compromise' and 'arrangement' that has been carried over from Part 26.

[82] The authors note, of course, the possibility of commencing administration proceedings, but do not identify the new freestanding moratorium in Part A1 of the Insolvency Act 1986 as a suitable alternative, presumably for the reasons identified above (text to nn 60–69).

Dutch absolute priority rule, to emerge very quickly. There may be different pathways, then, to embedding a new restructuring framework quickly, with a view to increasing certainty.

Next come a series of more granular chapters that examine and critically analyse particular components of the new UK restructuring law landscape. The first four all consider, from a range of comparative and theoretical perspectives, aspects of the power to bind a dissenting class to a plan in Part 26A, including the approach to ensuring that the dissenting class is not worse off than it would be in the 'non-plan world', and to regulating complaints by a dissenting class that the plan would unfairly distribute 'too much' value to an assenting class (Chapters three and four), and applications of the power to two particular creditor constituencies: creditors with rights *in rem* (Chapter five), and landlords under unexpired leases (Chapter six). These are followed by chapters on directors' responsibility in relation to the initiation of restructuring proceedings (Chapter seven), and the freestanding moratorium (Chapter eight). We highlight various aspects of these chapters, before turning to the final set of three chapters (Chapters nine to eleven).

In Chapter three, *Kristin van Zwieten* and *Sjur Swensen Ellingsæter* begin by distinguishing between rules requiring a dissenting class not to be left 'worse off' as a result of the sanctioning of a restructuring plan (often termed 'best-interests-of-creditors' rules, but which in the chapter are termed rules of 'baseline protection') and rules that regulate the distribution of value over and above this baseline (what the authors term 'rules of priority'). They chart the historical evolution of the absolute priority rule in US law, and explain why, in theory, it appears desirable for the lawmaker to supply a clear priority rule of this kind to regulate the exercise of a power to bind a dissenting class to a plan. The authors define a clear rule for this purpose as one that, following the work of Douglas Baird, specifies 'with precision' the relative entitlement of the dissenting class to value over and above the baseline.[83] The authors are largely agnostic as to the particular form that such a rule should take, but do argue that, under certain conditions, there may be benefits to non-adjusting creditors in writing a rule of absolute priority of the kind that they observe in US law.

This discussion then forms the backdrop for a detailed analysis of recent experiments with the design of priority rules in the EU, and of the position in the UK under Part 26A. In their EU law analysis, the authors first consider the requirements of the Preventive Restructuring Directive, before analysing the approach taken by three Member States – Germany, the Netherlands and Sweden – in transposing the Directive into national law. All three have settled on a form of 'absolute priority rule with exceptions', but with variation in the scope of the rule, in the specificity of the exceptions, and in the design of related rules. This survey suggests to the authors that jurisdictions confront a common set of questions when approaching the design of priority rules, which can sensibly be answered in more than one way, and that the significance of the choices made in the design of such rules will depend on choices made elsewhere in the restructuring

[83] See letter from Douglas G Baird to Rolef J de Weijs, 7 March 2019, referring to the priority rule that Baird had previously proposed (as to which, see Douglas G Baird, 'Priority Matters' (2017) 165 *University of Pennsylvannia Law Review* 785, and further Chapter 3, text to fns 85–94 below) as one that 'defines entitlements of the players with precision'.

framework, including in relation to the design of expenses rules, rules on class composition, and rules of baseline protection. In their UK analysis, the authors begin by setting out the approach taken historically in the limited categories of case where a de facto cross-class cram-down was previously possible, for it is to these cases that the English courts have, unsurprisingly, looked to develop the principles to guide the exercise of the new statutory power. The authors chart the emergence of a form of priority principle in the early restructuring plan case law, and characterise this as being, at least in its present form, vaguer than even the vaguest of options given by the Directive in relation to priority rules (which the authors term 'European relative priority'). The authors argue that neither professional investors nor less sophisticated players have been well-served by Parliament's decision to decline to stipulate a clear priority rule at the outset.

In Chapter four, *Riz Mokal*, *Stephan Madaus*, *Irit Mevorach*, and *Ignacio Tirado* focus in more detail on the UK position and analyse this from a different perspective. Whereas in Chapter three, *van Zwieten* and *Ellingsæter* are agnostic as to the form that a priority rule should take, at least as it will apply to professional investors, in Chapter four, *Mokal et al* concern themselves directly with the normative question of what it means to take a 'fair' approach to the distribution of the value expected to be derived from restructuring. Fair approaches are defined as ones where the 'distribution of a resource can be shown to be adequately supported by appropriate reasons and … is not marred by inappropriate reasons'. Taking this as their starting point, and drawing on their own extensive prior contributions to the literature, the authors construct a framework, which they refer to as the 'fair allocation of restructuring surplus' (FaiRS) approach, to guide the exercise of a cross-class cram-down power.

Four categories of appropriate reasons to distribute value are identified (prior entitlement, consent, desert, and need), and two categories of inappropriate reasons to distribute value are discussed (nepotism, as defined, and discrimination on improper grounds). This analysis is then integrated with insights from bargaining theory to produce the FaiRS approach. In this approach, the value that the restructuring is aimed at achieving is distributed as between dissenting and more junior classes 'in proportion to their respective contributions to the creation of such surplus'. The 'restructuring surplus' is defined by the authors as 'the cooperative surplus at issue in the restructuring'. A proxy is suggested for identifying relative contributions to the surplus. Permissible exceptions to this rule, which is characterised as a version of European relative priority, are then introduced. As in Chapter three, the authors of this chapter are concerned with enabling parties to bargain to reach a consensual solution that avoids the need for cross-class cram-down, but they take a far more pessimistic view as to whether an absolute priority rule provides the appropriate set of incentives. Finally, the authors turn to evaluate the developing UK jurisprudence against this framework. Some aspects of the jurisprudence are found to be aligned with the FaiRS framework, and others inconsistent with it. In the latter cases, the authors offer some prescriptions designed to better align the law with their suggested framework, with a view to ensuring the production of normatively defensible outcomes in Part 26A cases.

In Chapter five, *Ted Janger* analyses the entitlement of a dissenting secured creditor class in a US Chapter 11 or UK Part 26A plan case, and in particular the ability of such a class to claim an entitlement to the 'going concern increment', a concept equivalent to that of the restructuring surplus in the previous chapter. This project is motivated by suggestions in the literature and commentary that it is possible as a matter of English law to obtain security over all available value, giving rise to 'floating charge envy'. The author carefully unpacks this idea, beginning with an analysis of the extent to which assets can be encumbered in each jurisdiction, with a view to ascertaining whether either jurisdiction enables a 'blanket lien' to be obtained, before turning to the treatment of security interests on the commencement of Chapter 11 or Part 26A plan proceedings, and in the rules governing cross-class cram-down in each procedure.

Some differences in the scope of available assets are identified, although it is argued that these are easily overstated. As the author explains:

> while there is no such thing as a 'blanket lien' *per se*, a functional lien on substantially all of the debtor's property can be created with a combination of real estate mortgages, common law pledges, and an Article 9 security interest.

Matters become more complicated, however, once regard is had to the effect of the commencement of US Code proceedings. Commencement, the author explains, will 'stop floating liens from floating' and prevent new assets from falling within the scope of after-acquired property clauses. At plan confirmation stage, Chapter 11 limits the priority of a dissenting secured class to the 'allowed amount' of their claims (a rule which is, the author emphasises, to be clearly distinguished from the absolute priority rule that governs the entitlement of a dissenting unsecured creditor class vis-à-vis more junior classes, as discussed in Chapter three).[84] The author suggests that the absence of equivalent rules under UK insolvency law is the real source of 'floating charge envy', and the best argument for suggestions that the lender can obtain priority over enterprise value. This is argued to be 'deeply inequitable', on the basis that the value of the firm (measured by the capitalised value of the firm's future earnings) will not be attributable exclusively to the property over which the lender has collateral. The author concludes, however, that the precise entitlement of a dissenting secured class in Part 26A proceedings, and its ability to capture the going concern increment, will depend on the court's assessment of the relevant alternative to the plan.

In Chapter six, *Adrian Walters* and *Sarah Paterson* analyse the treatment of unexpired leases in Part 26A plan proceedings. The treatment of unexpired leases in UK restructuring law is an issue that has come to the fore in recent years, with debtors facing what the authors term an 'existential threat' whereby a bundle of unexpired leases of serial sites needs to be renegotiated or surrendered in order for the debtor-tenant's entire business enterprise to survive. As the authors explain, as a matter of English law, a tenant cannot compel the landlord to accept surrender without a continuing liability for the full amount of the rent for the remainder of the lease, but 'through ingenious lawyering and judicial acquiescence' the company voluntary arrangement procedure in Part I of the Insolvency Act 1986 was used to achieve something close to a surrender. Some doubts about the continuing viability of this technique, however, suggest to the authors that it is increasingly likely that debtors will instead turn to Part 26A to achieve this result.

[84] See § 1129(b)(2)(A) of the US Bankruptcy Code.

The authors compare the treatment of unexpired leases inside and outside of Part 26A along a range of dimensions, and identify dramatic differences. They analyse the ability to obtain something close to the functional equivalent of surrender in Part 26A, while surrender remains unavailable under the general law. They explain how a debtor-tenant can bundle together leases it wishes to modify in a specific way, put the proposal to the landlords as a group, and ask the court to impose the modification via the cross-class cram-down power if the statutory majority of landlords do not agree. It is suggested that this would be more difficult to achieve in Chapter 11, and the authors comment that it is remarkable that little consideration was given to the interaction between the cross-class cram-down power and unexpired leases, in the introduction of Part 26A. It is noted that, whilst Chapter 11 appeared to significantly influence the introduction of Part 26A, no attention appears to have been paid to the statutory provision for the treatment of unexpired leases in Chapter 11.[85] It is suggested that this may reflect a lack of attention by US bankruptcy scholars to the subject, and that this may in turn be a consequence of scholars working within 'silos', so that there is insufficient collaboration between real property and bankruptcy specialists.

As a result of their close analysis of the UK and US regimes, the authors conclude that there are reasons to be concerned about the position in the UK. In particular, it is argued that the attractiveness of the Part 26A plan as a vehicle for (functionally) surrendering or modifying unexpired leases means that debtor-tenants may opt for a restructuring plan exclusively to address unprofitable leases (a risk that, they explain, is far less acute in the Chapter 11 context), and that restructuring plans used in this way will have the effect of driving the rental market for healthy firms. More generally, they conclude that the use of restructuring plans in this way amounts to an ex post re-characterisation of the nature of a lease without any apparent reference to property law. The authors' view is that these concerns are more acute in Part 26A than they are in Chapter 11. They advocate further discussions across the silos of restructuring and property law, and across jurisdictions, in order to appropriately address these concerns.

In Chapter seven, *Felix Steffek* turns to the foundational question of how to secure the commencement of restructuring proceedings at the correct time. The starting point is the risk of value-destructive decisions being made by controllers at times of financial distress. The overall goal, the author explains, is to modify arrangements for the governance of the firm 'at the right point in time in order to maximise the expected value of the assets', and, in particular, to make such modifications as are necessary to produce a governance structure appropriate for achieving a restructuring or liquidation (as the case may be). In short, a shift from shareholder-oriented to creditor-oriented governance is required. Various legal mechanisms or strategies are identified as relevant to achieving this, but the author focuses particularly on the design of rules for the initiation of restructuring and liquidation proceedings, considering choices in relation to (i) who has the right to open proceedings, (ii) which kind of proceeding is opened, and (iii) the financial condition for opening. These choices are then analysed by reference to

[85] See § 365 of the US Bankruptcy Code.

what is termed the 'residual claimant principle', defined as the notion that the governance of the firm at any one time should follow the residual claimant.

In relation to the opening of proceedings, the author finds that the rights that are typically enjoyed by creditors around the world in relation to the commencement of restructuring or liquidation proceedings are consistent with the residual claimant principle. However, he finds deviations from the principle in relation to the other two dimensions of the design of initiation rules (which kind of proceeding is opened, and the financial condition for opening). Taking the financial condition point first, it is suggested that English law deviates from the principle by permitting directors to continue to trade after the onset of balance-sheet insolvency, but that this can be rationalised by reference to the differing incentives of shareholders and creditors to maximise value at this time. This discussion then lays the foundation for an analysis of the issue of when restructuring (as opposed to liquidation) proceedings should be commenced. It is argued that the costs of late restructuring are greater than those of late liquidation. If in doubt, restructuring ought to be opened 'too early' and liquidation, on the other hand, and for the reasons given, 'too late'. The remainder of the chapter focuses on how directors can be incentivised to act promptly through the imposition of legal duties. English law is found to broadly comply with the author's prescriptions, although it is recommended that some points be clarified in a statutory enactment, given the uncertainties around the interpretation of some existing duties.

In Chapter eight, *Natalie Mrockova* analyses the introduction of the new freestanding moratorium into UK law. She examines the genesis of the moratorium, explaining its origins and aims, and the rounds of law reform proposals that preceded it. The author compares the freestanding moratorium with other relevant procedures internationally, in particular Chapter 11 and the Chinese reorganisation regime (acknowledging, however, the differences in the goals of these procedures), and with relevant provisions of the Preventive Restructuring Directive. In assessing the success of the new moratorium, the author considers the final legislative product against the goals which were identified for the moratorium during the consultation process. On some of these criteria, she accepts that the moratorium has largely succeeded, particularly in terms of the desire to enact a low-cost restructuring tool which can operate to encourage early intervention when a company is experiencing financial distress. Other aspects of the new moratorium, however, are argued to be more problematic.

As the chapter documents, there has to date been a relatively low take-up of this restructuring tool. A government-commissioned review published in 2023 accepted that the use of the new moratorium has been 'considerably lower than expected'.[86] The author sets out a number of reasons for this: that the scope of the moratorium both in terms of debts covered and eligible companies is too narrow; that insolvency practitioners are often reluctant to take on the statutory role of monitor, who has responsibility for verifying the debtor's continuing eligibility to use the procedure and must bring the moratorium to an end in stipulated circumstances;[87] that the moratorium may be

[86] Insolvency Service, *Post Implementation Review of the Corporate Insolvency and Governance Act*, at para [3.2] published on 21 February 2023, available at: https://www.legislation.gov.uk/ukia/2023/69/pdfs/ukia_20230069_en.pdf.

[87] Insolvency Act 1986, ss A35, A38 and above, text to nn 55 and 61.

too short to provide the necessary breathing space to find a way forward, especially in larger cases, although some extensions are available; that the debtor-in-possession model gives considerable control to debtors, which may give rise to fears of abuse for creditors, some of whom, as a result of the moratorium's design, may be well-positioned to discourage recourse to it; and that the exclusive focus on the rescue of the company[88] limits the usefulness of the moratorium in practice. Some of these, such as creditors' fear of abuse, may dissipate over time as the market becomes accustomed to the operation of the new moratorium. A number of others, however, such as the scope of the moratorium and its length, are structural and could only be altered by legislative intervention. While the author gives a cautious welcome to this new tool of English restructuring law, she accepts that, absent legislative change, its practical utility is likely to continue to be limited.

In Chapter nine, *Winnie Tarinyeba Kiryabwire* returns to the more 'macro' perspective of Chapter two, but whereas Chapter two focuses on Europe (analysing developments in the UK against the backdrop of developments in the EU), in this chapter the author focuses on restructuring law reforms in Africa. Many of these reforms, the author explains, have been closely modelled on aspects of the law of jurisdictions outside of the regions of Africa, including the laws of France, the US and the UK. Borrowing from well-established legal frameworks elsewhere is, of course, a feature of insolvency law reform almost everywhere, and the early chapters of this book highlight sources of inspiration for a range of new EU and Member State restructuring rules, including the US Bankruptcy Code. But at least some of the reform initiatives analysed in this chapter involve something closer to the wholesale transplant of primary legislation, or at least substantial components thereof, suggesting that the risk of 'problems of fit' that all legal transplants are vulnerable to may be particularly acute.[89] Taking four categories of restructuring-related procedure in five jurisdictions (South Africa, Zimbabwe, Kenya, Uganda, and Nigeria), all of which involved reasonably substantial transplantation, the author explores the appropriateness of these procedures as tools for the resolution of financial distress in the contexts in which they apply.

The author concludes that many of the rules she surveys are a poor fit for their context. Some rules are premised for their application on the presence of some background institution that is simply absent in the transplanting jurisdiction. Other rules can be applied in the transplant jurisdiction, but differences in institutional frameworks are expected to significantly increase the costs of applying the rule (compared to those in the jurisdiction of origin), or to prevent the realisation of an expected benefit. In this regard, the author is also troubled by evidence that some transplants occur without regard to the fate of very similar attempts elsewhere, even though such prior initiatives could provide valuable insight into problems of fit. More generally, the author questions the suitability of many of the procedures she surveys for the firms that they are intended to treat, and in particular for firms whose external finance is concentrated in the hands of a small number of secured bank lenders. It is argued that this financing pattern

[88] See above, text to n 55.

[89] As other chapters of this book demonstrate (see eg Chapters 3, 5 and 6 below), difficulties may also arise where selected rules are borrowed from a foreign code whilst other features of the code that qualify the scope of that rule, or are otherwise essential to understanding the place of that rule in the code, are left behind.

probably provides the best explanation for evidence of non-use of many of the procedures in practice. Non-use is not identified as a problem *per se*; what is to be regretted is the missed opportunity that failed transplants present, namely the opportunity to meet some societal need through the supply of a more appropriate legal framework.

In the penultimate chapter of the book (Chapter ten), *Reinhard Bork* returns to a question identified as of critical importance in Chapter two, namely whether the effects of a restructuring being undertaken in one state, under the laws of that state, will be recognisable in another state. The term 'effects' here is important: the author argues that it is essential to separate recognition of the effects of a foreign restructuring procedure from recognition of the procedure itself, or of a court decision handed down in that process to produce the relevant effects. A decision might be recognised 'as such, meaning that the recognising courts treat the decision as existing and valid without further review', but this does not necessarily mean that all of its legal effects will be recognisable, as the author explains. In practice, he argues, it is with the latter that a recognition application will be concerned, an analysis that very much aligns with that of the authors in Chapter two.

Chapter ten focuses on the issue of securing recognition of the effects of an English law restructuring process abroad. To mirror the structure of EU law, and thereby enable some comparisons to be drawn between the position where EU law would apply and where it does not, the author considers recognition under cross-border insolvency law, cross-border civil procedure law, and private international law. He analyses recognition under national versions of the UNCITRAL Model Law on Cross-Border Insolvency,[90] considering the position in relation to Part 26A restructuring plans, schemes of arrangement, and moratoria under Part A1 of the Insolvency Act 1986. All three are shown to be recognisable forms of proceedings under the Model Law, but it is emphasised that, unlike under the European Insolvency Regulation,[91] recognition under the Model Law carries with it little relief. Additional relief is only available as a matter of discretion, and in any case might (depending on the approach taken in national law to the scope of available relief) fall short of ensuring that the restructuring is effective in the relevant state. The position is argued to be even more precarious under national cross-border insolvency laws that are not based on the Model Law, where the English procedures may not meet the criteria for recognition at all, and similarly under national cross-border civil procedure law, although in this case the author suspects that such laws will in any case be a poor fit for the objective. The author finds somewhat more promise in the application of rules of private international law, but not in a case in which adjustments are necessary across a company's capital structure.

In Chapter eleven, *Anthony Casey* completes the book with an analysis of the attractions of the UK scheme of arrangement and restructuring plan procedures as alternatives to Chapter 11 for a US-based firm. Many of the preceding chapters highlight how aspects of Chapter 11 have inspired the design of restructuring procedures elsewhere,

[90] UN, UNCITRAL Model Law on Cross-Border Insolvency (1997) available at: https://uncitral.un.org/en/texts/insolvency/modellaw/cross-border_insolvency.

[91] Regulation (EU) 2015/848 (n 3) and as to the extension of the effects of main proceedings under the Regulation, see above n 4.

and some[92] suggest that, at least in the UK context, closer attention might fruitfully have been paid to the granular features of the US Code in the design of Part 26A. In this chapter, however, the focus is on the relative *advantages* of the UK framework by comparison to Chapter 11, now that cross-class cram-down is available on both sides of the Atlantic. The author notes the high direct costs associated with recourse to the US regime, and argues that it is restricted in a number of ways that the UK regime is not. The author particularly highlights the restrictiveness of the US Code in relation to third-party releases,[93] and the fact that Chapter 11 plan proceedings are designed to be comprehensive in scope, while UK scheme and restructuring plan proceedings can be highly selective, targeting only a subset of creditors and/or shareholders. The author also notes increasing doubts about how early Chapter 11 can be accessed consistently with the requirement to file in good faith,[94] and about the ability of a debtor to select their US bankruptcy court venue; the latter factor might, it is argued, lead to greater global forum shopping: 'If debtors worry that US filings will be funnelled to less experienced courts, they will look for alternatives'. The combination of these factors suggests to the author that US-based firms might increasingly look to the UK procedures as an alternative to the US regime.

This kind of 'manoeuvre', as the author puts it, would be premised on the English courts having jurisdiction to open proceedings of the relevant kind, and on recognition by the US courts, and he offers detailed analysis of both points. As to jurisdiction, the author follows the analysis in Chapter two by characterising the English jurisdictional rules as permissive, although he notes earlier in the chapter that the equivalent rules for accessing the US Code are even more relaxed. It is questioned, though, whether English courts will necessarily be comfortable with filings by US-based firms that are designed to circumvent restrictions in the US regime that have been developed in the context of mass tort restructurings; this, the author explains, is true of recent case law developments in relation to both third-party releases and good faith filing.[95] On recognition, the author examines the approach of the US courts to recognition under Chapter 15 of the US Code, and how such recognition may, under certain conditions, be sufficient to give effect to the foreign restructuring process in other jurisdictions, because of the ability of a US court to restrain creditors with US assets and operations from enforcing against assets elsewhere. The mere fact of differences between the law governing the foreign restructuring process and the provisions of the US Bankruptcy Code does not mean that the US court ought to decline recognition on the basis that it would be 'manifestly contrary to the policy of the United States', but the author speculates that the US court may be more willing to apply this public policy exception in cases involving the restructuring of non-consensual creditor claims by a US-based firm in a foreign process. The author queries how US courts will respond to the absence of an absolute priority rule in Part 26A, and to uncertainty in the approach to priority in English law more generally, building on the analysis in Chapter three.

[92] Particularly Chapters 3, 5 and 6, but also to some extent Chapter 8.
[93] Following *Harrington v Purdue Pharma LP*, 144 S Ct 2071 (2024).
[94] Following *In re LTL Management, LLC* 64 F 4th 84 (3d Cir 2023) (*LTL I*).
[95] *Harrington v Purdue Pharma* (above n 93) and *LTL I* (ibid) both involving mass torts.

III. Some Common Themes and Implications

Despite the variety of subjects addressed in this volume, and the variety of methods deployed by the authors, there are a number of themes that run through the chapters. One is that it is not particularly illuminating to simply ask whether a jurisdiction has a restructuring framework that complies with (say) the EU Preventive Restructuring Directive's minimum standards, or with best practice guidance developed by international non-governmental organisations. It is, of course, important to know whether the law of a particular jurisdiction makes provision for class-based voting on a restructuring plan, for dissenting classes to be bound by such a plan, and for a moratorium on enforcement action and constraints on the exercise of *ipso facto* clauses during negotiations on the plan, but much more information is required about the design of each of these components, and the institutions responsible for their application, before any attempt at evaluating the framework can sensibly be embarked upon. It will come as no surprise to the legally trained reader to discover that the finer details matter, but the contributors to this volume also explain which details matter, and why they matter, and in so doing offer many insights for policymakers engaged in restructuring law reform around the globe.

A second theme is that certain questions common to the design of frameworks of these kinds everywhere can sensibly be answered in a range of ways, provided that the lawmaker is attentive to how the particular rule will interact with other aspects of the restructuring framework, and to institutional constraints that make some rules a better fit for some contexts than for others. This implies that there should be divergence, rather than convergence, at the level of rule-design that really matters: that is, in the detail. Ultimately, however, the efficacy of the lawmaker's framework will also turn on how it will be received by foreign courts in applications for recognition (a third theme), and here it is divergence in rule design that complicates the task of ensuring that a restructuring carried out in one jurisdiction is effective in another.

As to the UK in particular: the book makes clear that while the changes made to the law 'on the books' by CIGA were indeed seismic, the full contours of the reformed UK framework are yet to be revealed, because Part 26A is so sparse in its design, and silent on many important questions. Three (interrelated) factors will inform the development of the framework: the uses attempted by market participants, guided by restructuring professionals; the reception of these cases by the domestic courts; and, in turn, their reception by foreign courts. In some respects, then, it is premature to attempt to evaluate CIGA, and yet, the analysis in this volume suggests that much can already be valuably learned from the early chapters of this UK restructuring law reform story.

2

The UK Restructuring Plan in the New European Context

GABRIELLE RUIZ AND PHILIP HERTZ[1]

I. Introduction

This chapter considers how the UK restructuring plan available pursuant to Part 26A of the Companies Act 2006 sits within the new European context, and compares its progress against a landscape of reforms taking place across the European Union. Generally speaking, these reforms have been concerned with promoting rescue outcomes, in particular by facilitating the achievement of a binding compromise or restructuring as an alternative to an immediate realisation and distribution. The chapter is written from a practitioner's perspective and seeks to examine the development of the different procedures from that standpoint, looking at how each works from the legal and procedural angle.

Increasingly, where businesses operate across borders, participants involved in distressed situations seek practical restructuring solutions and are in most respects agnostic as to where (ie in which legal jurisdiction) the restructuring takes place. Instead, motivations might be driven by legal and practical effectiveness ie whether the plan binds relevant parties as a matter of domestic law and will be recognised as such by relevant courts abroad, and whether the costs are proportionate to the expected benefit. Where certainty of outcome is paramount, time and costs constraints are high on the agenda. We focus our considerations on recent trends in the UK, the Netherlands, France and Germany, drawing on insights from practitioners in each of the relevant jurisdictions. In particular, we consider how the UK restructuring plan compares in practice against the Dutch Wet Homologatie Onderhands Akkoord (WHOA); the French Accelerated Financial Safeguard (Safeguard) and the German Unternehmensstabilisierungs- und restrukturierungsgesetz (StaRUG).

The four procedures have some common features. For example, the procedures are all debtor-in-possession procedures and are initiated by the debtor in the sense that

[1] Insights and expertise has been provided by Clifford Chance colleagues Ilse van Gasteren and Evert Verwey (Amsterdam); Stefan Sax, Joseph Saed and Diana Schoch (Frankfurt); and Delphine Caramalli and Louis Nerson (Paris).

control rights during the proceedings do not pass automatically from directors to an insolvency practitioner;[2] a majority within a class has the ability to bind a minority, and the court has power to confirm a plan in the presence of a dissenting class (subject to certain conditions); and provision is made for debtors incorporated outside the restructuring jurisdiction to have access to the procedures and techniques alongside debtors incorporated within the restructuring jurisdiction. There are also some differences. For example, in the UK, there is no moratorium within the restructuring plan procedure itself. The lack of automatic recognition afforded to UK restructuring plans across EU Member States is another distinction when compared to the French, Dutch and German proceedings which, in their public form, benefit from an established automatic recognition framework by reason of their inclusion in Annex A of Regulation (EU) 2015/848 of the European Parliament and of the Council of 20 May 2015 on insolvency proceedings (recast) (the EU Recast Insolvency Regulation).[3] However, interestingly in practice, the UK restructuring plan has been used in some significant cases to deal with entities not incorporated in the UK, whereas the initial use cases for the new procedures in each of the Netherlands, France and Germany, appear to have a more domestic focus. There are also significant practical differences across the jurisdictions that affect the speed of proceedings – for example the number of hearings and time it takes to get a final decision – and, relatedly, direct costs. In this chapter we explore some of these differences and some early evidence of trends and use cases in our four chosen jurisdictions.

We begin with a brief overview of the reform landscape, contextualising the English reform against the backdrop of reforms in the EU (section I), before exploring the UK restructuring plan in some detail, and then turning to the new Dutch, French and German restructuring procedures (section II). We conclude with preliminary remarks on trends to date (section III).

II. The Reform Landscape in Europe

Within the European Union, the legal landscape for the treatment of distressed debtors has developed significantly over the past decade, influenced by economic forces including a desire to level the playing-field against the backdrop of the global financial crisis creating early access to restructuring frameworks[4] and more recently the drive towards achieving greater access to capital markets across the European Union. For present purposes, the most important of these are the Directive EU (2019/1023) on preventive restructuring frameworks (the EU Restructuring Directive), which most EU Member

[2] It should be noted that certain procedures do include the appointment of an administrator or expert to assist with the process. See further below.

[3] Proceedings falling within the scope of the Regulation are of course also subject to its rules on jurisdiction, which limit opening to cases in which the debtor has its centre of main interests (COMI), or an establishment, in the Member State. The Regulation applies only when a debtor has its COMI in a Member State.

[4] See Horst Eidenmueller and Kristin van Zwieten, 'Restructuring the European Business Enterprise' (2016) 16 *European Business Organization Law Review (EBOR)* 625, an article that was written in response to the Recommendation (ie before the EU Restructuring Directive was proposed).

States have now implemented into their domestic legislative frameworks,[5] and the EU Recast Insolvency Regulation, which in its recast form (2015/848) has an expanded scope designed to accommodate debtor-in-possession restructuring procedures of the kind contemplated by the EU Restructuring Directive, so as to render them eligible for automatic recognition and, in the case of main proceedings, the extension of their effects across the Union. The focus on facilitating restructuring ex post is intended to facilitate more cost-effective access to finance ex ante and forms part of the objectives of the European Commission's Capital Markets Union action plan.[6]

The early adopters of the EU Restructuring Directive include the jurisdictions which we have selected as the focus for this chapter, namely Germany, the Netherlands, and France.[7] These jurisdictions are often perceived as key restructuring hubs and influential in terms of their economic standing within the Europe. They have the advantage of not only the legislative framework, but a growing body of case law. These factors – together with the fact that in a number of respects the new procedures in these jurisdictions may have been influenced by the development of the UK restructuring plan – make them ideal candidates for comparing against the UK restructuring plan and contributing to the analysis of the European context. The pace of change underscores the dynamic nature of our subject matter: the European landscape will continue to be developed further, as initial use cases are extended and the current limits of each institutional offering are revealed, and parties adapt in the light of this.

The relationship between the reforms in the UK and those in our three other jurisdictions under focus is not entirely straightforward. The timing of the UK reform (2020, before the German, Dutch and French procedures were introduced, and well after the Brexit decision in 2016: see Appendix II) and of the EU Restructuring Directive, which was the main driver of the German, Dutch and French developments (June 2019, six months before Brexit), might seem to suggest that developments in the UK were quite separate from those on the Continent. In fact, the EU Restructuring Directive was the culmination of work on insolvency law harmonisation in the Union that began around 2010,[8] which led to a Recommendation in 2014[9] inviting Member States to ensure they had in place a 'preventative restructuring framework' complying with certain 'minimum standards'. This work was part of a trend, taking place against the backdrop of

[5] National implementation measures of the EU Restructuring Directive (Directive (EU) 2019/1023 of the European Parliament and of the Council of 20 June 2019) as communicated by the Member States to the EU Commission are available at: https://eur-lex.europa.eu/legal-content/FR/NIM/?uri=CELEX:32019L1023.

[6] For example see paragraphs (1), (6) and (8) of the preamble to the EU Restructuring Directive.

[7] In the interest of brevity we have limited our chapter to four jurisdictions. Of course other jurisdictions offer a number of different options to companies looking to restructure. For example, we have not included Ireland in our analysis, which of course is often considered a favourable jurisdiction for restructuring purposes. It should be noted that there exists the option to pursue a scheme of arrangement pursuant to the Irish Companies Act 2014 on a standalone basis and within the examinership regime; for example see *Re Ballantyne plc* [2019] IEHC 407; *Re Nordic Aviation Capital DAC* [2020] IEHC 445; and *Re EFW 21 Renewable Energy Limited* [2023] IEHC 690.

[8] With an INSOL Europe report commissioned by the European Parliament, which was followed by a Communication from the European Commission: see Horst Eidenmueller and Kristin van Zwieten, 'Restructuring the European Business Enterprise' (2015) 16 *EBOR* 625.

[9] Commission recommendation of 12 March 2014 on a new approach to business failure and insolvency (2014/135/EU).

the global financial crisis, to develop corporate rescue-style procedures designed to assist distressed businesses to restructure early and thus avoid terminal insolvency proceedings. In the UK, domestic law reform discussions commenced at around the same time as work in the European Union, albeit with a more limited scope,[10] and the UK was involved in negotiations on the text of the EU Recast Insolvency Regulation, which was intended to complement domestic restructuring law reforms across the Union. The UK reforms can therefore be said to share some foundations with the Continental reforms we will explore in this chapter. At the same time, there are also some important differences between the objectives of the UK reforms and the European Directive, which reflect the Brexit context in which the UK reform was enacted, and the different starting points in each jurisdiction. A quick survey of the EU Restructuring Directive and the materials accompanying the passage of the UK Corporate Insolvency and Governance Act 2020, which amended the Insolvency Act 1986 and the Companies Act 2006, makes this clear.

Starting first with the EU Restructuring Directive, its objectives are clearly set out in paragraph 1 of its preamble, which indicates that it is designed to 'harmonise procedures', with a view to 'improving efficiencies' and providing distressed entities with 'access to effective preventive national restructuring frameworks' that allow them to 'continue operating', all with an eye on promoting access to finance. These objectives have some similarities to the objectives articulated in the UK government's response to consultations from 2016[11] and 2018 on Insolvency and Corporate Governance – 26 August 2018:

> An efficient and equitable insolvency system that contains efficient procedures to allow for the financial rehabilitation of a company in distress is key to a modern economy. This should include a range of transparent rescue procedures to allow companies to restructure or seek new investment to give companies every chance of not failing, as well as ensuring fair and efficient procedures to protect the interests of creditors where companies do become insolvent. In response to stakeholder engagement and consultation, the Government will implement a number of significant reforms to ensure that the UK's insolvency regime retains its world-leading position including re-invigorating its rescue culture.

The end of that quotation, however, points to perhaps where the UK procedures differ most from the objective of its EU counterparts. While the EU Restructuring Directive was aimed at harmonising procedures with a view to encouraging rescue instead of liquidation and making investment across borders more accessible as a consequence of 'levelling the playing field', the UK, whilst emphasising the promotion of rescue-style procedures and efficiencies in much the same way as its EU counterparts, was also seeking to ensure that the UK remained competitive in its offering as a forum for international restructurings, or (put differently) to ensure it remained 'fit for business'

[10] Insolvency Service, 'Encouraging company rescue – a consultation', June 2009; Insolvency Service, 'Proposals for a restructuring moratorium – a consultation', July 2010. See Kristin van Zwieten, 'Mid-crisis restructuring law reform in the United Kingdom' (2023) 24 *EBOR* 287. As Payne notes, the UK reported itself to be compliant with the 2014 Recommendation's prescriptions (J Payne, 'Debt Restructuring in the UK' (2018) 15(3) *European Company & Financial Law Review*, but these did not extend to cross-class cram down, which the Directive provides for (see Kristin van Zwieten and Sjur Swensen Ellingsaeter in Chapter 3 in this book) and which is now possible in the restructuring plan procedure.

[11] See https://www.gov.uk/government/consultations/a-review-of-the-corporate-insolvency-framework.

on an increasingly international stage in a post-Brexit world. Consistently with this, the reform proposals referenced international 'best practice' in the design of restructuring frameworks, including the World Bank's *Doing Business* report and the UNCITRAL Legislative Guide on Insolvency Law.[12]

In the end, the UK reforms were ultimately enacted in an accelerated legislative process in the context of the COVID-19 pandemic amidst widespread concern that businesses would need assistance in the light of economic pressures. The UK restructuring plan was very much front and centre of the Government's business rescue package, and was promoted as a rescue tool that would be much needed and relied upon. Whilst some aspects of the 2020 reforms have received somewhat mixed reviews, reflecting perhaps the way in which they were enacted,[13] a 2022 evaluation concluded that the restructuring plan, while not yet greatly used in terms of frequency, was nonetheless a successful enhancement to the UK offering and satisfied the policy objectives, with their emphasis on rescue.[14] We have since seen more instances of the plan procedure being used.

III. New French, German, and Dutch Restructuring Procedures, Viewed against the UK Restructuring Plan

We focus on three EU jurisdictions which have had the benefit of new restructuring procedures since 2021 and are arguably the most developed of the Member State national frameworks transposing the EU Restructuring Directive. The procedures that we focus on are the Accelerated Financial Safeguard (sauvegarde accelérée) in France, the StaRUG in Germany and the WHOA in the Netherlands.[15] We begin with the UK plan and then turn to these three procedures. A table summarising some key features of the four procedures can be found in Appendix I.

We have based our analysis on our expertise and industry knowledge and/or on the reported decisions in each jurisdiction where information is available but limited.[16] In

[12] Insolvency Service, 'A review of the corporate insolvency framework: a consultation on options for reform', May 2016.

[13] See van Zwieten (n 10 above) arguing that the pandemic context distorted some design choices.

[14] See Corporate Insolvency and Governance Act 2020 – Final Evaluation Report November 2022, published in December 2022: see https://www.gov.uk/government/publications/corporate-insolvency-and-governance-act-2020-evaluation-reports/corporate-insolvency-and-governance-act-2020-final-evaluation-report-november-2022.

[15] Accelerated Safeguard (France): Ordinance No 2021-1193 of 15 September 2021 amending Book VI of the Commercial Code. Decree No 2021-1218 of 23 September 2021 amending Book VI of the Commercial Code – published 24 September 2021. StaRUG (Germany): Sanierungs- und Insolvenzrechtsfortentwicklungsgesetz – SanInsFoG (Recovery and Insolvency Law Further Developments Act) – published 29 December 2020. WHOA (the Netherlands): Wet implementatie RI 2019/1023 preventieve herstructurering-sstelsels, Kwijtschelding van schulden en efficientere insolventie published 23 November 2022.

[16] Eurostat: Statistics Explained published on 16 May 2024 provides annual bankruptcies in absolute figures as the sum of the quarterly reports for each country, on the whole there has been an increase in levels when compared to pre-pandemic levels, see: https://ec.europa.eu/eurostat/statistics-explained/index.php?title=Quarterly_registrations_of_new_businesses_and_declarations_of_bankruptcies_-_statistics#Annual_bankruptcies_in_absolute_figures (Figure 6). For example for Germany <30, France <50, The Netherlands <75 from Q3 2022 to Q3 2023 of reported bankruptcy cases.

terms of data on the use of these procedures, the data that will be required by the EU Restructuring Directive (see Article 29) is not yet generally available, but it is interesting to note that Member States will have to report, at minimum, on the following: (i) the number of procedures opened and closed (according to debtor type/size); (ii) the duration of procedures; (iii) the number of procedures ruled inadmissible, withdrawn, or rejected, before being opened. In addition, other data that 'may' be collected and reported on by Member States in respect of their insolvency and restructuring procedures includes average costs, recovery rates (for secured and unsecured creditors) and job losses linked to such procedures; these factors are reminiscent of the World Bank's *Doing Business* 'Resolving Insolvency' criteria. The usage data will provide some measure of whether the procedures are considered to be successful in practice. However, it should also be noted that in the case of each of France, Germany, and the Netherlands, the processes may not always be public, though we assume aggregate numbers ultimately provided will include the confidential proceedings. Of course, usage of the formal procedures is also only one part of the picture, since parties may reach a consensual solution in the shadow of the formal law.

A. UK Restructuring Plan

(i) Introduction

In the context of the cases to date (around 30 to date), UK practitioners have benefitted from some excellent judicial analysis[17] on the operation of the UK restructuring plan. This guidance has been strongly welcomed by practitioners, given the absence of a detailed statutory framework. It has helped that the courts have been able to draw significantly on jurisprudence on the scheme of arrangement procedure in Part 26 of the Companies Act 2006, which was certainly the intention of the legislature when it promulgated the restructuring plan in Part 26A. Courts have, of course, also recognised differences between the two procedures, most obviously in relation to the availability of the cross-class cram down power in Part 26A,[18] and have provided guidance on these differences. Perhaps the high-water mark in this respect to date has been the decision of the Court of Appeal in *Re Adler* in 2024 on the factors relevant to the exercise of the cross-class cram-down power.[19] Other issues on which considered and well-reasoned

[17] eg *Re Virgin Active Holdings Ltd and Others* [2021] EWHC 1246 (Ch); *Re Gategroup Guarantee Ltd* [2021] EWHC 304 (Ch) and [2021] EWHC 755 (Ch); *Re Smile Telecoms Holdings Ltd* [2021] EWHC 685 (Ch); *Re DeepOcean 1 UK Limited and Others* [2021] EWHC 138 and *Re Prezzo Investco Ltd* [2023] EWHC 1679 (Ch). The leading restructuring plan case is now *Re Adler* (*In re AGPS Bondco Plc* [2024] EWCA Civ 24 (23 January 2024) (*Re Adler*)) where the Court of Appeal set aside the first instance court's judgment sanctioning the plan. It did so on the basis that in exercising its discretion, the judge had wrongly applied the fairness test. Permission to appeal to the Supreme Court was granted in *Re Adler* on 28 May 2024, but following a recent restructuring of the same group, using a consent solicitation process, it is unlikely that the appeal will proceed. Other cases following *Adler* include *Re Project Lietzenburger Straße Holdco Sárl* [2023] EWHC 2849 (Ch) (*Project Furst/Re Aggregate*) and *Re CB&I UK Ltd* [2024] EWHC 398 (*McDermott International Ltd*) have also provided some valuable insights.

[18] See s 901G of the Companies Act 2006.

[19] *Re Adler* [2024] EWCA Civ 24.

judgments have been given include disclosure, valuation and costs. Overall, these judgments, together with the scheme jurisprudence on which they draw, have generated a high degree of confidence among practitioners as to the application of the restructuring plan procedure.

Practitioners wasted no time in putting the UK restructuring plan to work. The first time it was employed was at the height of the pandemic and within 38 days of the legislation being introduced, when the plan was used to restructure the behemoth Virgin Atlantic Airways in relation to its £1.2 billion recapitalisation.[20] Since then, the court has in some instances refused to exercise its power to sanction a plan, the highest profile failure being *Re Adler*. In this respect, the process has demonstrated that it is subject to the robust scrutiny of the English court and, as with its approach with schemes of arrangement, the court will not act as a 'rubber stamp', even in cases where the restructuring plan is not contested or reliant upon the exercise of the cross-class cram-down power.

In the examples of successful plans to date, the UK restructuring plan has demonstrated that it is a flexible procedure and one that deserves its place not just within the domestic restructuring market but on an international stage, with its application being used to restructure international groups either on a standalone basis or as seen employed in 2023 and 2024 in conjunction with parallel processes elsewhere. The low jurisdictional threshold in England and Wales, based upon a 'sufficient connection' with the jurisdiction, also no doubt assists in its potential application to groups of debtors with interests across a diverse geographical range, as does the preponderance of English law-governed finance documents. It is also worth noting that for the English court to exercise its jurisdiction to sanction a restructuring plan, it needs to be satisfied that the plan is likely to have substantive effect in the relevant jurisdictions outside of the UK.[21] This is evidenced to the court by way of expert reports; to date there has been positive treatment of this question including in relation to key jurisdictions such as Germany and the Netherlands. The dominance of English law-governed finance documentation within Europe may also assist when it comes to recognition based upon private international law, eg Article 12 (1)(d) Rome I.[22] Of course, over time the relative attraction of the English court's jurisdiction compared to others may change; certainly the rise of similar frameworks within the EU, including those surveyed below, and other European jurisdictions (such as Switzerland) means there will be greater competition for restructuring business.

One critical factor for the competitiveness of the plan will be the efficiency of the plan process itself, when viewed in relation to the time it takes and attendant costs it brings. One positive signal as to cost effectiveness has been the use of the plan procedure

[20] *Re Virgin Atlantic Airways Ltd* [2020] EWHC 2376 (Ch).

[21] eg *Re Gategroup Guarantee Limited* [2021] EWHC 775; *Re Adler* [2024] EWCA Civ 24; *Re CB&I UK Ltd* [2024] EWHC 398 (Ch); and *Re Project Lietzenburger Straße Holdco SarL* [2024] EWHC 563 (Ch) (*Re Aggregate*).

[22] See further insights set out in 'Schemes of arrangement and their international effectiveness' [2022] *Corporate Rescue & Insolvency* 124–26, by Tim Lees, Michelle McGreal and Ellen Choi. See also Chapter 10 on cross-border recognition where Reinhard Bork notes the importance in particular of the emphasis placed on the legal effects of recognition, rather than the form of process.

by mid-market companies.[23] The flexibility of the plan procedure – which can be used selectively, to promote a compromise or arrangement with some, but not all, creditors[24] – may produce some savings in appropriate cases, compared with more comprehensive procedures.[25] As was noted by a financial adviser in a recent Insolvency Lawyers' Association Annual Conference 2024,[26] the costs of a restructuring plan might be limited to 10 per cent of the level of costs usually necessary for a trading administration, a fully collective process in which control rights pass at least initially to an insolvency practitioner. Of course, the level of costs will be driven by the nature of the particular case, its complexities and whether the plan is opposed or not. Depending on the degree of complexity, the time-frame can be confined to a couple of months, or in contested cases the time-frame may span more than six months.[27]

(ii) Key Features of the Plan Procedure

There is very little by way of a statutory framework for a restructuring plan. It is contained in a very short section of the Companies Act 2006 (Part 26A) immediately following the separate Part 26 on schemes of arrangement, upon which Part 26A has been modelled. In addition to the statutory provisions the English Court has issued guidance on the approach required in preparing a restructuring plan for consideration by the court. This is set out in the 2020 'Practice Statement Companies: Schemes of Arrangement under Part 26 and Part 26A of the Companies Act 2006'. The Practice Statement is also noticeably short and provides only limited details on the procedure.

As with schemes of arrangement, restructuring plans allow a company to propose a 'compromise' or 'arrangement' with one or more of its creditors (or members) or classes thereof.[28] Unlike schemes, which have no threshold entry conditions and may be proposed by both solvent and insolvent companies, restructuring plans are available only to companies encountering, or likely to encounter, financial difficulties that will or may affect their ability to continue as a going concern.[29] The purpose of the restructuring plan must be to eliminate, reduce, prevent, or mitigate those financial difficulties.[30] A restructuring plan may be used for implementing a compromise or arrangement between a company and its creditors and/or members, and it may be an operational or financial restructuring or a combination of both (eg, writing off debt, facilitating a debt-to-equity swap; amending existing agreements).

[23] See below, text to n 26.

[24] Sarah Paterson and Adrian Walters, 'Selective Corporate Restructuring Strategy' (2023) 86(2) *Modern Law Review* 436.

[25] ibid.

[26] Insolvency Lawyers' Association Annual Conference 9 May: Mid-market restructuring plans presented by Matthew Weaver KC and Phil Reynolds (FRP Advisory).

[27] See for example *Re Project Lietzenburger Straße Holdco SarL* [2024] EWHC 468 (Ch) (*Re Aggregate*), the plan process was commenced in October 2023 and finally approved in March 2024.

[28] A compromise or arrangement for the purposes of section 901A Companies Act 2006 for restructuring plans is intended to be interpreted in the same way as in schemes of arrangement under Part 26 Companies Act 2006. See *Re Virgin Atlantic Airways Ltd* [2020] EWHC 2191 (Ch); *Gategroup Guarantee Limited* [2021] EWHC 775 (Ch); *Re Adler* [2024] EWCA Civ 24 and *Re Aggregate* [2024] EWHC 563 (Ch).

[29] Section 901A(2) Companies Act 2006.

[30] Section 901A(3)(b) Companies Act 2006.

As in schemes, creditors may need to be grouped into classes for the purpose of voting on a plan. A 'class' is not defined in the statute, but courts have developed the concept.[31] In plans, the basic voting requirement is for the plan to be supported by 75 per cent in value of creditors, or where creditors are divided into classes, 75 per cent in value of each class. However, the court is empowered to sanction a plan in the presence of a dissenting class where two conditions are met: (i) none of the members of the dissenting class are worse off than they would be in the relevant alternative (which is whatever the court considers would be most likely to occur in relation to the company if the compromise or arrangement were not sanctioned[32]); and (ii) the compromise or arrangement has been approved by the requisite majority in a class that would have a genuine economic interest in that relevant alternative.[33] This measure is commonly referred to as 'cross-class cram-down'. Where the court is satisfied that a class of creditors or members has no economic interest in the company, an order may be made to exclude them from voting on the plan.[34] However, the plan must still be capable of being characterised as a 'compromise' or 'arrangement'.

There are at least two hearings on a proposed restructuring plan: in the first (the 'convening hearing'), the court is invited to summon creditors to a meeting to vote on the plan; in the second (the 'sanctioning hearing') the court is invited to sanction the plan so as to render it binding. It has been suggested that for small/mid-sized entities the fact that the restructuring plan process involves two separate court hearings may mean that, from a costs perspective, it may not be a feasible option. However, there are a number of recent examples where such companies, including an entity already subject to an insolvent administration, have been able to make use of the process.[35] In such cases, it has been argued that it may be more appropriate and proportionate to simply have one hearing to decide whether to sanction a plan, but currently there is no legislative provision to facilitate that and it is unlikely that, absent a formal amendment in the legislation, English courts would be able to accommodate such a 'shortcut'. In some respects, the initial hearing may also be perceived as a necessary gateway and as protection against frivolous plans being pursued.

Prior to the first hearing, a proposal is devised and usually agreed in principle among key creditors, who may be party to a formal 'lock up' agreement where they have already agreed to support in principle the restructuring. The restructuring plan is then drafted. The plan will include the provisions relating to the terms of the compromise or arrangement, an Explanatory Statement (a statement explaining the effect of the compromise or arrangement, which will accompany notices of meetings to vote on the plan[36]), draft notices of creditors' meetings, voting forms and formal court documentation.

[31] Classes are confined to persons whose rights are not so dissimilar as to make it impossible for them to consult together with a view to their common interest, as articulated in *Re Hawk Insurance Co Ltd* [2001] EWCA Civ 241, citing *Sovereign Life Assurance Co v Dodd* [1892] 2 QB 573.

[32] Section 901G(4) Companies Act 2006.

[33] Section 901G Companies Act 2006.

[34] Section 901C Companies Act 2006 and *Re Smile Telecoms Holdings Ltd* [2022] EWHC 740 (Ch) and *Re Aggregate* [2024] EWHC 563 (Ch).

[35] eg *Re The Good Box Co Labs Limited* [2023] EWHC 274 (Ch) and *Re Amicus Finance Plc* [2021] EWHC 3036 (Ch).

[36] See s 901D.

A Practice Statement Letter is a formal letter sent to creditors, to provide them with sufficient notice and information to allow them to appear at the first court hearing to raise (i) any objections as to how the company has formulated the classes of creditors for the purposes of voting on the restructuring plan; (ii) any issues regarding the court's jurisdiction to consider the plan; and (iii) any roadblocks that would affect the court's ability to approve the plan. It is sent to affected creditors in good time (usually a minimum of 14 days before the date set for the first hearing), but the court has been flexible in certain cases[37] and has allowed a shorter notice period in circumstances where it is clear that the affected creditors had already been consulted in advance (if possible). The convening hearing itself will be subject to the court's availability, but ordinarily this will be 7 to 10 days after the filing of the application.

The *convening hearing* is designed to ensure that the creditors have been allocated into the correct classes by the debtor and that there are no fundamental jurisdictional hurdles to the court considering the plan. It also sets the timetable for the creditors' and/or shareholders' meetings and second (sanctioning) hearing. In particular, the court will consider any issues as to the constitution of meetings of members or creditors, or issues which otherwise affect the conduct of those meetings; any issues as to the existence of the court's jurisdiction to sanction the plan; any issues relevant to the conditions to be satisfied pursuant to section 901A of the 2006 Act as to the financial conditions; any issue relevant to an application made under section 901C(4) of the 2006 Act to exclude any creditors who do not have an economic interest in the company; and any other issue not going to the merits or fairness of the restructuring plan, but which might lead the court to refuse to sanction it. All persons affected by the restructuring plan are to be notified in good time to take appropriate advice and, if so advised, to attend the convening hearing.

The Explanatory Statement accompanying a notice summoning a meeting to vote on a plan should be in a form and style appropriate to the circumstances of the case, including the nature of the member and/or creditor constituency, and should be as concise as the circumstances permit.[38] The commercial impact of the restructuring plan must be explained, and members and/or creditors must be provided with such information as is reasonably necessary to enable them to make an informed decision as to whether the restructuring plan is in their interests, and on how to vote on the restructuring plan. The court will consider the adequacy of the Explanatory Statement at the convening hearing.[39] The court may refuse to make a convening order if it considers that the Explanatory Statement is not in an appropriate form. However, the court will not formally 'approve' the Explanatory Statement at the convening hearing, and it will

[37] The same approach to notice is adopted as applicable to schemes of arrangement. See *Indah Kiat International Finance Co BV* [2016] EWHC 246 (Ch); *Re Noble Group* [2018] EWHC 3092 (Ch) and *NN2 Newco Ltd, Re Politus BV* [2019] EWHC 1917 (Ch) and in the context of restructuring plan cases *Re Virgin Active Holdings Ltd and Others* [2021] EWHC 814 (Ch).

[38] *Re Virgin Active Holdings Ltd* [2021] EWHC 814 (Ch); *Re Amicus Finance plc* [2021] EWHC 2255 (Ch); *Re Nasmyth Group Ltd* [2023] EWHC 988 (Ch); and *Re C-Retail Limited* [2024] EWHC 1194 (Ch) and [2024] EWHC 1715 (Ch) (*Re Superdry*).

[39] See paragraph 6 of the Practice Statement (Companies: Schemes of Arrangement under Part 26 and Part 26A of the Companies Act 2006).

remain open to any person affected by the restructuring plan to raise issues as to its adequacy at the sanction hearing.[40]

After the convening hearing, the plan documentation will be posted or made available electronically to the affected creditors (and/or shareholders) and the meetings and date of the sanction hearing will be advertised. The creditors (and/or shareholders) meetings are usually held 10–20 days after the first hearing. Often the meetings take place on a virtual basis. There is often a gap between the meetings and the second hearing at court to approve the restructuring plan; this may be between 10 and 14 days but will be driven by the circumstances of the particular case; for example, it may be shorter where there is an impending debt maturity date.

The *sanctioning hearing* involves the court ensuring that the statutory formalities have been complied with, and takes place after the creditors' vote. Notwithstanding the affirmative votes of the (requisite majority of) creditors, the court retains its discretion in relation to whether it approves the plan, and must be satisfied that the plan is one that an intelligent and honest person acting in their own interest could reasonably approve.[41] In exercising that discretion, the court will usually be slow to differ from the views of the creditors where there is overwhelming creditor support (ie, each class of creditors has approved the plan in the requisite majority). In cases where the cross-class cram-down power is relied upon, the court will also need to ensure that the dissenting creditors are no worse off than in the relevant alternative and that the approving classes have a genuine economic interest. These are preconditions to the power being *available* pursuant to section 901G Companies Act 2006. The court must then decide whether to *exercise* the power. At this stage, the court's approach to considering whether the restructuring plan is fair will differ from its approach in scheme cases or where, in restructuring plan cases, the cross-class cram-down power is not relied upon, in that the court must be satisfied that creditors spanning across different classes are treated fairly under the plan, with no fairer plan likely to be produced.[42] If the court approves the plan, the plan does not become effective until it is filed with Companies House.

During the plan process, a party may apply for further disclosure of information relevant to consideration of the proposed compromise or arrangement. The documentation can be voluminous, and disclosure requirements may be quite onerous, especially where amendments are being made to complex financial documentation or where there are disputes in relation what the relevant alternative may be, and how the debtor's business/assets are to be valued and on what basis. The court process promotes timely, transparent, and full disclosure in relation to the restructuring plan application. In *Re Virgin Active Holdings Ltd*, for example, the landlords were successful in their application for further disclosure of information (subject to various confidentiality requirements) at the convening stage of the process, to enable them to consider the proposals.[43] At the same time, the case law cautions that the court will strive to ensure that the disclosure

[40] See the analysis of the procedure for restructuring plans in G McCormack, 'The UK Restructuring Plan in an age of uncertainty' [2024] JBL 483–61.

[41] See *Re National Bank Limited* [1966] 1 WLR 819.

[42] See *Re Adler* [2024] EWCA Civ 24.

[43] See *Re Virgin Active Holdings Ltd and Others* [2021] EWHC 1246 (Ch).

is proportionate, and that the disclosure requirements in the plan context should not become akin to those in full-blown litigation.[44]

As to the cost risk for those challenging a plan or an aspect of the plan process, the English court's position on costs is generally to allow creditors making a challenge to be awarded their costs as long as the position they take is reasonable and is framed in a way that the court considers to be helpful to its analysis in deciding whether to approve the plan.[45] One very recent development in relation to costs is an application made by a dissenting creditor challenging a plan, to require the company proposing the plan to provide security in respect of the challenger's costs. The court in an interim application was prepared to grant the creditor (a hospital trust) an order that the company provide security for 50 per cent of the creditor's expected costs, noting that the creditor could realistically expect some costs award to be made in its favour, even if the plan was ultimately sanctioned.[46] In doing so the court was careful not to stymie the pursuit of the plan, but at the same time to balance the creditor's risk in not be able to recover its costs. Challenges to restructuring plans inevitably affect the cost/time calculations for use of the procedure. If multiple interim applications are made, then the efficiencies in the timing and costs of the restructuring plan process are adversely affected. The risk of adverse costs should in theory encourage the plan company to deal in a transparent way with its stakeholders before it launches a plan, to avoid applications for disclosure and challenges more generally, but the threat of a challenge or requests for further information may also be used to gain leverage in the negotiations for restructuring.

(iii) Some Trends in Initial Use of the Plan Procedure

The UK restructuring plan had a 'head start' compared to the new restructuring frameworks in the EU and, as noted above, was used immediately after its introduction in the high-profile case of *Re Virgin Atlantic Airways*[47] to compromise significant debts with lenders and lessors. Since then, though, the plan has not been used as frequently as some of its European counterparts such as the Dutch WHOA. Since its introduction at the end of June 2020, the restructuring plan procedure has been successfully used (to obtain a sanctioned plan) in around 30 cases. One could attribute the lower-than-expected take up in the UK of the restructuring plan so far to the relatively benign economic climate and/or ability (and availability of options) to refinance. It is also true to say that the UK approach to restructuring has always been to promote consensual outcomes; so, while the number of restructuring plans is limited, the threat of the more powerful restructuring tool may have been a factor in any number of consensual restructurings. Of course, the evolution of the European restructuring market in the last three years will also be relevant, since there is now much more choice in relation to

[44] See for example *Re Superdry* [2024] EWHC 1194 where the court held that applications for disclosure in the context of restructuring plans should not be: burdensome; disproportionate; or; a distraction from the process itself.

[45] See *Re Virgin Active Holdings Ltd* [2021] EWHC 911 (Ch) and *Re Smile Telecoms Holdings Ltd* [2022] EWHC 740 (Ch).

[46] See Note issued by the Judge on 25 June 2024 in *Re Consort Healthcare (Tameside) plc* [2024] EWHC 1702 (Ch). Shortly after the security for costs order was made, the restructuring plan for the hospital trust appeared to be no longer being pursued.

[47] *Re Virgin Atlantic Airways Ltd* [2020] EWHC 2191 (Ch).

restructuring techniques (subject to the jurisdictional rules of the EU Recast Insolvency Regulation where it applies).

While the number of sanctioned restructuring plans remains low, the amount of debt restructured for some very significant international groups runs into several £ billions. The use of the plan outside of the purely domestic context is perhaps a key distinction when compared to its European cousins. The cross-class cram-down power has been used in some large and very complex cases, such as *Virgin Active* and most recently *Aggregate* and *McDermott International*,[48] the latter drawing on the guidance from the Court of Appeal in *Adler*. What was perhaps not so expected in the development of the restructuring plan is the fact that its use has also been proposed by some mid-size and smaller companies in the SME space, such as *Re Houst*[49] and *Re The Good Box Co*. The costs may, of course, be prohibitive for smaller businesses.[50] Access to the procedure by medium-sized businesses will depend on the continued willingness of the English courts to adopt a proportionate approach to the restructuring plan in terms of disclosure requirements.[51]

The plan has been used in a variety of different circumstances, including in relation to companies that have needed full operational as well as financial restructuring. This could be perceived as a key difference for the use of schemes of arrangement which were often used in a restructuring context to achieve financial restructurings, sometimes in conjunction with other procedures (such as administration or a company voluntary arrangement under the Insolvency Act 1986) to deal with the operational side of the business. The plan has, to date, been used to compromise lease arrangements, release guarantees, compromise secured, preferential, and unsecured creditors, convert debt to equity, and grant new security for new monies, and therefore can in theory (subject to some issues we raise below in relation to shareholders, moratoria and recognition) be used to provide a complete restructuring solution including operational aspects.[52] We have seen restructuring plans being use for domestically-focused businesses in the casual dining, retail and leisure sectors, where essentially the restructuring plan is being used to replace trading administrations and company voluntary arrangements.[53] Very recently, a restructuring plan has been issued to compromise liabilities under a construction contract in relation to a project company responsible for providing facilities and facilities management to an NHS trust.[54]

[48] *Re Virgin Active Holdings Ltd* [2021] EWHC 814 (Ch), *Re Aggregate* [2024] EWHC 468 (Ch); *Re McDermott International Ltd* [2024] EWHC 398 (Ch).

[49] *Re Houst Limited* [2022] EWHC 1941.

[50] See also Chapter 3 of this book (Kristin van Zwieten and Sjur Swensen Ellingsaeter).

[51] *Re Superdry* [2024] EWHC 1194 (Ch).

[52] Similar flexibility has been available in types of compromises available in the Netherlands, Germany and France (see by way of example, the cases referred to later in this chapter). However, there are certain exceptions in terms of Germany, for example in relation to the ability to conduct operational restructurings. For a more detailed analysis on rights *in rem* in restructurings and unexpired leases also see Chapters 5 (Edward Janger) and 6 (Sarah Paterson and Adrian Walters).

[53] The restructuring plan has also been used in a formal insolvency context in the case of *Re Amicus Finance plc* [2021] EWHC 3036 (Ch). In that case the secured creditors were crammed down by the administration expense creditors. Certain aspects of the approach in that case have been clarified by the Court of Appeal in *Re Adler*.

[54] *Re Consort Healthcare (Tameside) plc* [2024] EWHC 1702 (Ch), although we understand the plan is no longer being pursued.

In relation to leases of property, restructuring plans have been used to cram down landlords' claims even in cases where the shareholders remain in place.[55] This has caused significant upset in the property industry and has added some real negotiating power to corporates with large leasehold portfolios, such as retailers who are looking to reduce rents or relax covenants. The example of *Virgin Active* has been followed in a number of other recent cases in relation to landlords such as *Re Lifeways* and *Fitness First*.[56] More recently, restructuring plans have been launched and approved to deal with landlord claims and other property-related debts, for example in the case of the wholly-owned subsidiary of *Tasty plc* (operating the Wildwood restaurants) (unreported 4 June 2024) and a company in the *Superdry Group* (unreported 17 June 2024).[57]

There have been a number of unsuccessful cases. The most significant was *Re Adler* but the first was the *Re Hurricane Energy* case,[58] where the evidence indicated that the company had applied too early, there was no 'burning platform', and evidence on its value was heavily disputed, so the case which essentially sought to disenfranchise its shareholders when oil prices were low, was thrown out. Timing of course is not easy, as there have been a number of observations in some recent cases that debtors who propose restructuring plans too late have placed an unfair burden on the Court, and going forward it will be alive to the fact that procedurally (in terms of time and disclosure obligations) the Court will not take too kindly to being confronted with a limited time-frame to approve a restructuring plan, that in the absence of timely approval, will cause the company to face inevitable insolvency.[59]

Other unsuccessful restructuring cases share a common theme of trying to compromise preferential tax liabilities. Part 26A does not contain an absolute priority rule and it is in principle possible for the cross-class cram-down power to be exercised in relation to a dissenting preferential class, even when a more junior class will retain a stake. In one recent case, proposing a compromise of tax claims, the court has approved the plan (*Re Prezzo*);[60] in the earlier cases of *Re GAS* and *Re Nasmyth Group*, the court declined to sanction. Assuming the conditions for enlivening the cross-class cram-down power are satisfied, the critical question will be whether the plan is a fair one, and in particular whether it provides for a fair allocation of the restructuring surplus. *Adler* is now the leading authority on the fairness question. It takes as a starting point priority in the relevant alternative and asks whether departures from this have been justified. On the facts, the relevant alternative was an insolvent liquidation in which noteholders would have shared in a distribution *pari passu*, but this was not respected in a plan that retained

[55] *Re Virgin Active Holdings Ltd & Others* [2021] EWHC 1246 (Ch).

[56] *Re Listrac Midco Ltd* [2023] EWHC 460 (Ch) (*Re Lifeways Healthcare*); *Re Fitness First Club Limited* [2023] EWHC 1699 (Ch).

[57] For more detailed analysis on unexpired leases in a restructuring procedure, see Chapter 6 of this book (Sarah Paterson and Adrian Walters).

[58] *Re Hurricane Energy plc* [2021] EWHC 1759 (Ch), others include *Re Great Annual Savings Co Ltd* [2023] EWHC 1141 (Ch) (*Re GAS*) and *Re Nasmyth Group Ltd* [2023] EWHC 696 (Ch).

[59] See by way of example *Re Adler* [2024] EWCA Civ 24; *Re Aggregate* [2023] EWHC 2849 (Ch) and *Re McDermott International Ltd* [2024] EWHC 398 (Ch).

[60] *Re Prezzo Investco Ltd* [2023] EWHC 1679 (Ch).

maturity dates (so that longer maturity noteholders assumed more risk), for which there had not been given good justification.[61]

The Court of Appeal decision in *Re Adler*, while enhancing the understanding and operation of the restructuring plan procedure – in particular the parameters of fairness in the exercise of the cross-class cram-down power – has also made it plain that, like any court-driven process, a restructuring plan may be subject to an appeal process and the risks and attendant time and costs that go along with that. Following *Re Adler*, the first instance courts now appear to have adopted a practice whereby the sealing of the order for sanction is delayed pending expiry of the time period allowed for an appeal, so that if there is going to be an appeal, the practical effects of the restructuring plan can be stayed pending the outcome of any appeal. On the other hand, it may be considered that the *Re Adler* decision provides much greater certainty, and perhaps will result in fewer appeals in future cases. For example, *Re Adler* has informed subsequent decisions of the English courts, including *Re Aggregate* and *Re McDermott International Ltd*, which have relied upon cross-class cram-down in an effective manner, and factored in the considerations articulated in *Re Adler* in relation to the nature of a 'compromise' or 'arrangement', which we discuss below.

One further point of note from the cases to date relates to the question of who can promote a plan. In the *Re The Good Box Co* case, the plan was promoted by a creditor. This sounds much more dramatic than it in fact was, as the creditor in question had funded the company during a formal insolvency process and was also the founding member of the company. The English court was eager to ensure that this creditor had the company's consent, adopting the approach used for schemes of arrangement under Part 26 of the Companies Act 2006. It helped that the company had exhausted all other avenues, and the restructuring plan was the last chance to save something from the business.

Finally, the other fact that some may find surprising is the continued popularity of schemes of arrangement under Part 26 Companies Act 2006 for international restructurings.[62] Veon, Petropavlovsk and the case of *Vroon* (in conjunction with a Dutch WHOA) are a few examples of recent restructuring schemes. In certain cases, there was a single class of creditor and therefore no need to rely upon the cross-class cram-down power. In relation to Vroon, a combination of the scheme and Dutch proceedings were necessary. The English scheme was necessary due to the Rule in *Gibbs*,[63] as key agreements being compromised were governed by English law and only an English law process could be used to discharge those obligations. The Dutch WHOA in *Vroon* was required to implement the debt for equity swap and to protect the group against enforcement initiated by certain creditors. Unlike restructuring plans, there is no financial distress threshold for schemes, which can also make the process more appealing, especially when promoting business continuation.

[61] Permission to appeal against the Court of Appeal's decision in *Re Adler* was granted on 28 May 2024. In addition, on 5 June 2024, a second restructuring plan was issue by the Adler Group. This was then superseded by a successful consent solicitation process which was concluded in September 2024. This means that the second restructuring plan and the appeal of the first is unlikely to be pursued.

[62] *Re Veon Holdings BV* [2022] EWHC 3473 (Ch); *Re Petropavlovsk plc* [2023] EWHC 264 (Ch); *Re Lamo Holding BV* [2023] EWHC 1558 (Ch) (*Vroon*).

[63] *Anthony Gibbs & Sons v La Société Industrielle et Commerciale des Métaux* (1890) 25 QBD 399.

(iv) Some Issues

There are, of course, many aspects of the plan procedure that are yet to be fully resolved, and some ongoing issues and questions. We highlight below some issues relating to the position of shareholders and out-of-the-money creditor classes, the lack of a moratorium, and jurisdiction and recognition in cross-border cases.

(a) Shareholders and Out-of-the-money Creditor Classes

While there is no absolute priority rule as a matter of English law, the English court has already provided insights into how it will consider deviations from established priorities, including where shareholders may retain equity in circumstances where creditors are left without any allocation of value.[64] The retention of equity is usually justified on the basis that they are gifted the shares by creditors who do have an economic interest in the restructuring surplus in the relevant alternative, or in situations where the shareholders may have provided new money. Jurisdictions with absolute priority rules often have modifications or derogations.[65] It should also be noted that from a practical perspective, under the German StaRUG the treatment of shareholders is not necessarily straightforward or certain either, as discussed further below.

While section 901C of Part 26A Companies Act 2006 enables the court to find that a creditor or shareholder whose rights will be affected by the plan need not be permitted to participate in the meeting to vote on the plan, if it is satisfied that none of the members of the class have a genuine economic interest in the company, the plan still needs to constitute a 'compromise' or 'arrangement' with such classes. In this regard, obiter comments in the *Re Adler* appeal decision have caused some practitioners to take a cautious approach in terms of 'out-of-the-money' classes by providing for them to receive some modest compensation, so that the plan cannot be said to be a mere expropriation or confiscation (which would not constitute a compromise or arrangement as those concepts have been understood in the schemes jurisprudence). An example of this is the amendment of the plan in *Re Aggregate* (after creditors had voted) to provide a nominal amount to junior creditors despite them having no economic value in the plan.

[64] See *Re Virgin Atlantic Airways Ltd* (nn 20 and 28); *Re Houst Ltd* (n 49); *Re Virgin Active* (nn 17, 37, 45); *Re Prezzo Investco Ltd* (n 17); *Re Lifeways Healthcare* (n 56); *Re Hong Kong Airlines* [2022] EWHC 3210 (Ch); and *Re Adler* (n 17). For more analysis on the rules of priority in restructuring procedures, including in Germany, the Netherlands and Sweden, and under Part 26A, see Chapter 3 of this book (Kristin van Zwieten and Sjur Swensen Ellingsaeter).

[65] In the recitals to the EU Restructuring Directive at paragraphs 55–56, it is provided that Member States can protect a dissenting class of affected creditors by ensuring that such dissenting class is paid in full if a more junior class is to receive any distribution or keep any interest under the restructuring plan (the 'absolute priority rule'). But the Directive recognises that Member States should be able to derogate from the absolute priority rule, for example (as indicated in the recitals) where it is considered fair that equity holders keep certain interests under the plan despite a more senior class being obliged to accept a reduction of its claims. This appears to be the approach adopted in France, the Netherlands and Germany. The Directive also provides, at paragraph 57, that while shareholders' or other equity holders' legitimate interests should be protected, Member States should ensure that they cannot unreasonably prevent the adoption of restructuring plans that would bring the debtor back to viability.

(b) Moratorium

The absence of a moratorium within the statutory framework of a restructuring plan means that in some cases, the administration procedure in the Insolvency Act 1986, with its moratorium, has been used in conjunction with a restructuring plan. In the EU procedures that we consider in this chapter, this is not necessary, because the procedures benefit from an optional or automatic moratorium at least in the context of the public form of each procedure. In certain situations in the UK, a moratorium might be quite useful from the debtor's perspective. Indeed, the possibility of a restructuring plan with the benefit of a moratorium might change the whole negotiation dynamic. It could, in theory, make a restructuring plan a more feasible option, particularly where time is running short to find a solution due to upcoming maturity dates. In this regard it is noteworthy that in some of the recent cases where the UK restructuring plan has been used with parallel processes elsewhere, the parallel procedures have been ones that benefit from a stay eg the Dutch WHOA or Italian *Concordato*. There have also been more recent applications of parallel proceedings in cases such as *Re Atento*, *Re Cimolai*, and *Re McDermott International*.[66] In many cases, however, the absence of a moratorium in Part 26A is not an issue as parties are used to entering into standstill or lock up agreements prior to launching a scheme or restructuring plan process. These agreements can create the stability needed to implement the process without interference, and so in effect create a contractual moratorium by consensus.

(c) Jurisdiction and Recognition in Cross-border Cases

While the jurisdictional threshold for restructuring is not as expansive as, say, the US,[67] the English courts have been very receptive to assisting debtors with international interests in seeking to find compromises with their stakeholders. As noted above, schemes and restructuring plans can be used by debtors (or guarantors) as long as they can show a sufficient connection to the English jurisdiction. There is a long history of schemes being used by non-English entities. A sufficient connection could be established (for example) via having a new or existing English borrower or guarantor in the corporate structure, or due to English law-governed credit documents, or by the company moving its centre of main interests (COMI). In *Re Aggregate*, a Luxembourg incorporated company moved its COMI to England, just before launching a plan, which was later approved by the English court.

One technique used in the scheme context and now experimented with in the context of restructuring plans is to replace an existing issuer with an English newly-incorporated issuer which assumes the liabilities to creditors. This technique was used in *Re Gategroup Guarantee Ltd* and in *Re Adler*, the first restructuring plan case to be considered by the Court of Appeal. The case concerned a real estate business operating

[66] *Re Atento UK Ltd* [2023] EWHC 3076 (Ch) and *Re Cimolai SpA* [2023] EWHC 2193 (Ch). *Re McDermott International Ltd* (n 17).

[67] For the purposes of Chapter 11 of the US Bankruptcy Code, the s 109 definition of debtor includes a person that has a place of business or property in the US. Funds held by the debtor's attorney in a bank account in the US have sufficed for such purposes.

in Germany; the debtor structured its access to the English court's jurisdiction by forming an English special purpose vehicle to assume the liabilities of a German real estate company for the purposes of proposing a UK plan. It is understood that there was an attempt to implement a restructuring under the German Schuldverschreibungsgesetz (the Bond Act), but this failed. In the Court of Appeal, the Court focused on questions relevant to the exercise of the judge's discretion at first instance and did not consider the validity of the jurisdictional technique. However, the Court did signal that the question was an open one:

> The Appellants did not oppose the Plan before the Judge on the basis that the Issuer Substitution was an artificial device that could not justify the exercise of discretion to sanction the Plan. The point did not, therefore, arise for consideration on this appeal. For the avoidance of doubt, and without expressing a view one way or the other, I would wish to make it clear that the fact that this judgment does not deal with this issue should not be taken as an endorsement of the technique for future cases.[68]

As to recognition, there was a lot of concern post-Brexit as to how English proceedings would be received elsewhere. In that respect *Re Gategroup Guarantee Ltd*[69] may have actually assisted with recognition in certain jurisdictions, as its characterisation of the restructuring plan as an insolvency procedure means that recognition in certain jurisdictions may now be simpler.[70] In *Gategroup Guarantee Ltd*, part of the debt comprised Swiss bonds which were being compromised by the plan. They were subject to an exclusive Swiss jurisdiction clause, so there was a question as to whether that clause had the effect of excluding the English court's jurisdiction in relation to the restructuring plan. However, on the basis that the English court held that the restructuring plan was an insolvency proceeding for the purpose of the Lugano Convention[71] the English restructuring plan therefore fell outside of the Convention's scope (as it benefitted from the bankruptcy exception to the Convention) and therefore enabled the English court to consider and approve the restructuring plan, notwithstanding the Swiss exclusive jurisdiction clause in relation to the Swiss bonds.

There may be a range of reasons why parallel processes are required – whether to access a moratorium (as explored above), or to treat some other limitation in one process (or how it would be received elsewhere) by accessing another.[72] One key driver is to address the English law 'rule in *Gibbs*', which essentially provides that contractual obligations may only be discharged by the proper law governing the obligations (unless the creditor submits to a process in some other jurisdiction).[73] We have seen an English restructuring plan used in conjunction with a Hong Kong scheme for Hong Kong Airlines, and a restructuring plan used in combination with an Italian *concordato* in the *Cimolai* case. The Dutch WHOA has been used in conjunction with a UK scheme

[68] *Re Adler* [2024] EWCA Civ 24, [34].

[69] *Re Gategroup Guarantee Limited* [2021] EWHC 304 (Ch).

[70] See Chapter 10 of this book (Reinhard Bork) that considers cross-border recognition in more detail.

[71] The Convention on Jurisdiction and the Enforcement of Judgments in civil and commercial matters signed in Lugano on 30 October 2007. At the time the restructuring plan was applied for the Convention was applicable in the UK.

[72] See 'In sync across borders: embracing parallel processes for successful restructurings' – Tim Lees, Kasia Lorenc and Sarah Jane O'Leary (2023) 9 *Journal of International Banking and Financial Law* 620.

[73] *Anthony Gibbs Sons v La Société Industrielle et Commerciale des Métaux* (1890) 25 QBD 399.

of arrangement in the *Vroon* case, and in conjunction with a restructuring plan in the *McDermott* case. Where parallel procedures are used, especially when they are inter-conditional (that is, each expressed to be conditional on the other being sanctioned and becoming binding), the coordination of the procedures and timing of creditor and court approaches can become complex. It was apparent in both the *Vroon* and *Cimolai* cases that, despite the parties' best efforts, there were delays in achieving the approvals from the court. Inevitably there is also the added cost of having two separate procedures, and risks are increased when two court approvals are sought.

B. Dutch WHOA[74]

(i) Key Features

On 1 January 2021, the Act on the Confirmation of Private Restructuring Plans (Wet homologatie onderhands akkoord) (the WHOA) entered into force. The WHOA provides a cost-effective alternative to formal bankruptcy proceedings for viable enterprises to restructure their debt, while preventing the declaration of bankruptcy. Under the WHOA, both enterprises and creditors can request a compulsory agreement that determines the company's commitments for the restructuring of the debt. Creditors and shareholders can vote for the agreement but are divided into separate classes. The agreement will be approved by the Dutch court if the relevant class of creditors or shareholders has voted in favour of the agreement with a qualified majority of two-thirds. A cross-class cram-down is also possible, provided that at least one class which is in the money has voted in favour of it with a two-thirds majority. Once approved by the Dutch court, the agreement will also be binding upon dissenting creditors and shareholders.

The Dutch court must test various formal requirements in considering whether it can and should sanction the plan – even when the restructuring has overwhelming creditor support. This is because once sanctioned, a WHOA plan may not be appealed.[75] This is an important practical benefit of the WHOA, ensuring that legal certainty is achieved once the court has blessed it. The WHOA scheme has nevertheless also proven to be time-efficient. In one of the recent cases discussed below, *Biocity*, there was only four weeks between the start of the voting period and the sanction hearing, and within seven weeks a sanctioning judgment was rendered. Dutch courts have become familiar with complex restructuring matters in which international documentation is filed. Future restructurings may be even faster if expert evidence is no longer required on implementation steps, as has been required in some early cases. Finally, in relation to language, as has been the case with other restructuring processes in the Netherlands, sanctioning hearings are held in Dutch, through video-conference with real-time translation. However, all of the restructuring documentation may be in English in most cases. This offers a great advantage in terms of time and cost savings.

[74] This aspect of the chapter is based upon the expertise and input derived from materials and insights provided by Ilse van Gasteren and Evert Verwey.

[75] Amsterdam Court of Appeal, 19 February 2024 (*McDermott International Ltd*).

(ii) Trends in Use and Some Case Studies

Between 1 January 2021 and 1 July 2023,[76] there were 250 published public judgments rendered in respect of WHOA proceedings opened in the Netherlands. As the WHOA proceedings can either be public or non-public, the exact number of WHOA proceedings launched is unknown. In terms of the types of companies using the procedure, in 2021 and 2022, 99 per cent of the WHOA proceedings were in respect of small to medium-sized companies (although a recent evaluation report[77] suggests there may still be insufficient awareness of the procedure among SMEs, or that parties may be deterred by the high costs of preparing for the process and court and advisers' fees). Since 2023, the use of the WHOA by larger companies has also been noticeable, including in conjunction with parallel proceedings elsewhere, including in the UK and US. As noted above, one of the reasons for parallel proceedings stems from the fact that both public and non-public WHOA proceedings can involve a stay/moratorium, which is available for up to eight months.

Commentators have reported a noticeable shift to larger companies using the WHOA, with examples including *Fitness Centres*, the *Royal ICH Group*, *Vroon*, *Diebold Nixdorf*, *Steinhoff*, *Re McDermott International* and *BioCity*. We look at each in turn to draw out some key points.

(a) *Fitness Centres* (November and August 2021)[78]

Fitness Centres was noteworthy for several reasons. Secured lenders were crammed up by the preferential Dutch tax authority. The plan essentially affected the whole group's financing arrangements and included an extension of tax payment obligations, and under its senior facilities agreement a covenant holiday, amendments to financial covenants and amendment to the interest rate. The case showed the potential reach of the WHOA in relation to financial claims, and featured interim decisions that were sought to achieve certainty at an early stage, before putting the plan to a vote. The latter procedural point is potentially quite significant in terms of its impact on future cases. The WHOA scheme was deliberately designed to be 'light touch' in terms of the court's involvement, with a single court hearing. Frequent interim applications might run counter to this and undermine the efficiency of the Dutch WHOA. At the same time, in larger cases it may well be necessary to have more than one hearing, particularly while the case law is still quite nascent and there are questions about the interpretation likely to be adopted by the court.

For the Dutch market the biggest surprise in the *Fitness Centres* case was the 'cram up'. In this case, the cross-class cram-down power was used to force the senior lender into a covenant reset and a conversion of cash interest into a payment in kind. Such route requires the vote of an 'in-the-money creditor' and in this case the Dutch tax

[76] Evaluation 18 December 2023: https://repository.wodc.nl.
[77] Evaluation 18 December 2023: https://repository.wodc.nl.
[78] District Court of Amsterdam, 5 August 2021, ECLI:NL:RBAMS:2021:619.

authority was used for that. They have a (specific) prior ranking claim when it comes to certain pledged assets which are located on the debtor's premises. It is worth noting that the senior lenders in this case, based upon the evidence, were likely to be fully paid.

The WHOA also has an absolute priority rule, but the court can deviate from that if there are reasonable grounds and no prejudice to the non-consenting creditors. In this case the new monies provided a sufficient justification to deviate from the absolute priority rule. As a result, the shareholder in this case was allowed to keep all the equity by providing a relatively small amount of new liquidity (by way of commitment). This WHOA plan did create quite a bit of unrest in the Dutch market and may be the reason why initially there were limited large company cases, as secured creditors were perhaps concerned by the potential to be crammed down. Of course, this may also have provided an incentive for more junior creditors, in the context of negotiations, to drive a better bargain.

(b) *Royal IHC* (March 2023)[79]

This case concerned a supplier of maritime technology and expertise, and was the first WHOA plan to involve a syndicate of lenders. Following a number of earlier restructurings, the debtor sought a WHOA plan to sell part of its business and reduce its debt from €950m to €500m. Two out of nine lenders objected to the plan; the court approved the restructuring notwithstanding the objections of the two dissenting creditors. Certain aspects of the case are of wider interest, in particular the fact that the plan imposed an obligation on a dissenting lender to continue to make available an undrawn guarantee facility. This was allowed on the premise that it did not materially change the finance obligations or the creditor's rights. A similar approach has been taken in relation to restructuring plans and schemes of arrangement under English law, where the court has accepted that as long as no new obligations are imposed, the continuing access to an already committed facility is permissible ie it is not imposing any new obligations on the creditors.[80] A second interesting aspect was the fact that the WHOA altered the 'waterfall' (hierarchy of creditors) in the intercreditor agreement to facilitate debtor-in-possession (DIP) financing, despite restrictions in the WHOA plan on the ability to amend the ranking of rights *in rem* such as pledges and mortgages.[81] The Dutch Supreme Court has recently held (as expected) that the plan could not force the continued availability of the draw-down facility, but that it could affect any class of claim, including *in rem* claims, subject to compliance with the APR in a non-consensual case. This is very helpful from a Dutch restructuring perspective and it confirms that the WHOA is very flexible mechanism.

[79] District Court of Rotterdam, 9 March 2023, ECLI:NL:RBROT:2023:2800.

[80] This was an issue in *Re Apcoa Parking Holdings GmbH* [2014] EWHC 3849 (Ch), but not tested in that case.

[81] Art 384 WHOA sets out the absolute priority rule that states that distribution under the plan should follow ordinary rules on the ranking of claims.

(c) *Vroon* (May 2023 and June 2023)[82]

In *Vroon*, the complex capital and organisational structure of the group meant that a restructuring could not be achieved through a single compromise. In order to implement the restructuring, the group promoted interdependent processes: an English scheme and the Dutch WHOA plan. The English scheme allowed for certain debts which were governed by an English law framework agreement to be either written off or adjusted, and provided the holding company with the authority to enter into various restructuring documents to implement the restructuring. The Dutch WHOA plan provided for the moratorium and the transfer of shares in the holding company to a newly established Stichting Administratiekantoor (STAK), Vroon.

In the Dutch court, the main challenge was made by shareholders who contended that the restructuring did not allocate a fair amount of value to them, because the group had been incorrectly valued. It was argued that the debt value was too high and the value of the post-plan, reorganised business was too low. The Dutch court relied upon the valuation evidence provided by the management and the financial advisers, finding that it was adequately justified. Before the English court, the shareholders made similar arguments, challenging the basis of the management's characterisation of the relevant comparator to the scheme of arrangement, which, based upon the evidence, the English court held was likely to be an insolvent liquidation rather than a solvent wind down. The orderly sale argued for by the shareholders was not considered a realistic possibility in this case, not least based upon the fact that creditors had been unpaid for several years and enforcement action would be likely, as the Dutch stay would fall away if the scheme did not succeed. In these circumstances, the English court approved the scheme. One interesting aspect of this case is the fact that the English court allowed the shareholders to present their arguments even though the shareholders concerns related to the WHOA plan rather than the scheme. On the evidence in this case the shareholders were out of the money and not willing to provide any new monies. The shareholders were not a party to the scheme, but the English court exercised its discretion to allow their objection to be heard, considering their argument to be relevant to the court's consideration of what the appropriate alternative to the scheme was.

In terms of jurisdiction, the English court confirmed that there was sufficient connection based upon the English law-governed framework agreement which was used to rationalise and simplify the group's financial arrangements and formed the subject matter of the compromise. In addition, expert evidence was accepted that the scheme would have substantial effect in the Netherlands, Scotland and Singapore. Overall, the case demonstrates the usefulness of the English procedure alongside its EU counterparts. In this instance, both the English and the Dutch procedures were necessary to deliver the restructuring. The English scheme was needed to compromise English law-governed debt as a result of the rule in *Gibbs*[83] and the Dutch scheme facilitated a debt-for-equity swap. While the cost of running two procedures in tandem may be considerable, especially when they are subject to a challenge, there can be instances

[82] District Court of Zeeland – West Brabant, 26 May 2023 ECLI:NL:RBZWB:2023:5306.

[83] *Anthony Gibbs & Sons v La Société Industrielle et Commerciale des Métaux* (1890) 25 QBD 399.

where this can be justified and delivers value which produces a better outcome overall for stakeholders when compared with a formal insolvency process.

(d) *Diebold Nixdorf* (August 2023)[84]

This case related to the US-based group Diebold Nixdorf, which specialises in payment process services. It coupled the Dutch WHOA plan with a US Chapter 11 procedure to bring about a restructuring that involved the reduction of €2.1 billion debt through a debt-to-equity swap. In addition to the benefit of the stay in the US Chapter 11 and WHOA, the WHOA plan was also subject to a Chapter 15 recognition proceeding. The two parallel processes were necessary, as the complex group structure included Dutch and US holding companies and other companies incorporated in jurisdictions based in Europe. In particular, the combination was necessary to achieve the debt-for-equity swap and access a stay in relation to the different parts of the group. This was the first time a Dutch WHOA plan has been recognised in a different jurisdiction.

(e) *Steinhoff* (June 2023)[85]

A novel use of the WHOA was its application in the long running restructuring of the Steinhoff group, where it was employed to bring about a controlled wind-down, including delisting and liquidation. Arguably the most interesting aspect of this case was the fact that in order to facilitate recognition outside of the Netherlands, the debtor opted for a public version of the WHOA plan, which, by virtue of the EU Recast Insolvency Regulation, meant that the proceedings would be automatically recognised in the EU. In this case the holding company was a Dutch incorporated (listed) entity but most of its business operations were in South Africa and Germany, with little connection to the Netherlands. The court was, however, prepared to assume jurisdiction on the basis of Steinhoff's holding company having its COMI in the Netherlands. It has been suggested[86] that the case illustrates the suitability of the Netherlands for international groups, including for bond debt restructurings using Dutch finance entities as the issuer.

(f) *McDermott International Ltd* (February 2024)[87]

The case relied upon interdependent English restructuring plans and Dutch WHOA plans. WHOA plans were required to ensure the English restructuring plan was binding and effective on creditors of the two Dutch companies in the group, including the holding company, involving the provision of equity in the restructured business. The English restructuring was used to compromise the claims.

[84] District Court of Amsterdam, 2 August 2023, ECLI:NL:RBAMS:2023:6160.
[85] District Court of Amsterdam, 21 June 2023, ECLI:NL:RBAMS:2023:4152.
[86] Omar Salah and Joris Fliek (Norton Rose Fulbright), 'In a bright future for the Dutch restructuring practice', *Global Restructuring Review* 14 December 2023.
[87] District Court of Amsterdam, 10 October 2023 and Court of Appeal (Amsterdam), 19 February 2024.

McDermott International was a good example of the UK restructuring plan being tested to the limit in terms of disclosure, timing of the process and allocation of the restructuring 'surplus'. But it might also serve as a cautionary tale in terms of costs, as a result of the protracted proceedings. In terms of timing, the English case was pushed back by three months and listed for a five-day trial instead of one day. Costs amounted to approximately 20 per cent of new monies raised. Such delays, and a lengthier hearing for the court sanction stage, may in part be related to the fact that the unsecured creditor, who was owed US$1 billion from an arbitration award, sought to contest the plan. However, they may also have been in part due to the influence of the Court of Appeal decision in *Re Adler*, which may have encouraged parties seeking to challenge the fairness of plans; in particular it may have provided them with hope that while the debtor may present the plan as the only plan available, there may be some scope for seeking an alternative plan, especially where the debtor is looking to rely upon cross-class cram-down power.

In addition, the McDermott International plan put the Dutch WHOA plan firmly in the spotlight, because a restructuring expert in the Netherlands was appointed[88] to monitor issues arising in the context of the WHOA, including class composition and adherence to the absolute priority rule in a non-consensual case, to promote negotiations for a consensual deal, and subsequently to propose a (potentially amended) plan to the creditors and shareholders. This impartial appointment ultimately facilitated in that case the provision of an equity stake to the unsecured creditor who it had been proposed would be left out in the cold altogether. This was significant, and perhaps it is fair to say that it arose directly from the obiter comments in *Adler* regarding restructuring plans not expropriating claims for no value. While this created a lot of tension for the parties involved and saw negotiations play out in real time, it encouraged a plan that was ultimately acceptable to the debtor and the unsecured creditors. In addition, the case has also been helpful in clarifying how the Dutch process operates in practice and how two processes can in certain cases be usefully combined to achieve a restructuring.

(g) *Bio City Development Company* (BCDC)[89]

In May 2024, the District Court of Amsterdam sanctioned a WHOA plan in respect of bonds that were originally governed by English law.[90] The BCDC WHOA proceedings could be said to be the first judicial consideration in the Netherlands of restructuring techniques originally pioneered in the context of UK schemes of arrangement in the *Re Apcoa* case[91] and continued more recently in relation to restructuring plans. In this sense the WHOA plan may be perceived in some respect as a very successful transplant of the UK scheme/restructuring plan.[92]

[88] District Court of Amsterdam, 10 November 2023.

[89] For more insights into this case see Tim Lees, Ilse van Gasteren, Guido Bergervoet, Evert Verwey, Siert Klinkhamer, and Emma Buchanan, 'Expanding the restructuring toolkit: Change of governing law followed by Dutch scheme proceedings' (August 2024) 21(6) *International Corporate Rescue Journal*.

[90] District Court of Amsterdam 15 May 2024, ECLI:NL:RBAMS:2024:3441.

[91] *Re Apcoa Parking Holdings GmbH* [2014] EWHC 3849 (Ch).

[92] See further the analysis in Chapter 9 of this book (Winifred Tarinyeba Kiryabwire).

The BCDC case related to the issue of bonds governed by English law, the value of which exceeded BCDC's assets. The commercial terms of the restructuring included a sale of BCDC to one of the bondholders for cash, and a mandatory redemption of the bonds at a discount to par value to allow BCDC and its corporate group to operationally restructure on a solvent basis. The restructuring enjoyed overwhelming, but not quite universal, support from bondholders. In order to overcome a long-established rule of English law (the rule in *Gibbs*),[93] which provides that an *English law* debt can only be varied or compromised by *English law* unless the creditor submits to a foreign process, BCDC contractually amended the governing law of the bonds to Dutch law, which was achieved with a 50 per cent consent threshold. This enabled the debt to be effectively restructured pursuant to a WHOA plan that would bind the dissenting bondholders. To our knowledge, this is the first time a company has changed the governing law of its debt to Dutch law to support a WHOA restructuring. The District Court of Amsterdam found nothing objectionable in this.

The restructuring was implemented using powers of attorney granted under the restructuring plan. This is common in UK schemes/restructuring plans but had not yet explicitly been considered or approved by the Dutch courts. The Court found that the powers of attorney were a suitable instrument to implement the transaction and sanctioned the restructuring plan that included all transaction documents in draft. The Court also looked carefully at the implementation steps, which had been designed to avoid a tax disadvantage (albeit using a series of steps that were already 'tried and tested' in practice). In another 'first', the Dutch Court appointed an independent expert to provide a report confirming certain tax aspects of the restructuring. The expert confirmed there was nothing wrong in the structure, and the Court followed the expert's opinion. More broadly, the Court recognised that this was a more complex transaction than had been implemented previously using a WHOA plan on its own. Overall, the case points to growing experimentation with the WHOA proceedings, borrowing from or at least consistent with examples of similar experimentation in the UK.

C. The Accelerated Safeguard Procedure in France

(i) Key Features

The new accelerated safeguard procedure is designed to offer a streamlined rescue mechanism, allowing debtors to restructure within four months and without the unanimous consent of all creditors. The process is overseen by a court appointed judicial administrator (*administrateur judiciaire*) and also benefits from the court's approval. The legislation also allows for rescue finance to be provided, which then receives a super priority status. Accelerated safeguard proceedings are aimed at restructuring and reorganising the capital structures of distressed companies where it has not been possible to agree a deal consensually during the course of conciliation proceedings. Accelerated

[93] *Anthony Gibbs Sons v La Société Industrielle et Commerciale des Métaux* (1890) 25 QBD 399.

safeguard proceedings are available to companies regardless of their size. In accelerated safeguard proceedings, debtors remain in possession.

The restructuring plan is presented by the management to creditors or selected classes of creditors, ie financial creditors only or all affected creditors in different classes. No term out can be imposed by the court in case of a negative vote. Classes of affected parties, may include creditors and shareholders if their rights are affected by the restructuring plan, which would be the case, for instance, in the event of equitisation or, more broadly, any change in the shareholding. Such classes of affected parties are constituted by judicial administrators and are required to vote on the restructuring plan (to be presented by the *debtor only* in safeguard proceedings). Dissenting creditors may be crammed down. The approach to classification is similar to the approach in the UK, with only parties who are affected by the plan and have an economic interest in the company included in the classes; creditors sharing a sufficient community of interests will be in the same class and should benefit from equal treatment under the plan. Judicial administrators take into consideration (amongst other things) existing subordination agreements and security packages (eg there are likely to be separate classes for secured creditors, shareholders, preferential creditors and strategic suppliers) when constituting the classes, and certain claims, such as those arising from employment contracts or those secured by a French *fiducie* (similar to a trust), cannot be affected by a restructuring plan.

Following the constitution of classes of affected parties (which may be challenged by creditors), the restructuring plan is presented to the vote. To be adopted, the plan must be approved by a two-thirds majority vote within each class (*majorité des deux tiers des voix détenues par les membres ayant exprimé un vote*). After the plan has been adopted with a two-thirds majority vote, the plan must also be approved by the court. Before rendering its decision, the court verifies that the overall process has been conducted in accordance with applicable rules. The court also verifies (amongst other things) that individual dissenting creditors are no worse off than they would be in a judicial liquidation scenario (the best-interests-of-creditors test). The restructuring plan can be imposed by the court on dissenting creditors or creditor classes (cross-class cramdown) where the two-thirds majority has not been met, provided several conditions are met, namely: (a) the plan has been approved by a majority of the classes of affected parties, provided that (i) at least one of those classes is secured or senior to an ordinary unsecured creditor (*créanciers chirographaires*) or (ii) at least one of the classes of affected parties is 'in the money' other than a shareholders' class (upon a valuation of the company by an independent expert); and (b) the plan must comply with the absolute priority rule (ie dissenting senior creditors must be fully repaid before a junior ranking class is entitled to be paid or retains an interest).

France relies upon a two-stage restructuring model: the first stage involves the preparation of the restructuring plan following discussions with the affected parties during a confidential conciliation phase which may last up to five months. The second stage involves the opening of accelerated safeguard proceedings, which includes the possible cram down of creditors who are out of the money and equity holders. The second stage may last up to four months. The prevailing practice borrowed from the US now involves entering into lock-up agreements with stakeholders at the conciliation stage to satisfy the condition for initiating accelerated safeguard proceedings. This condition requires securing sufficient support from affected parties to make the adoption of the restructuring plan credible.

The procedure may be perceived as debtor-friendly because it is entirely driven by the debtor and, due to the prevailing culture under French law, especially as applied by commercial judges (who are not professional judges, but businessmen or artisans), tends to favour employees, often to the detriment of creditors. Protection for creditors is nevertheless provided at an individual creditor level with the 'best-interests-of-creditors' test[94] and on a collective level with the absolute priority rule, although the latter can be derogated from in certain circumstances.

The accelerated safeguard procedure has given rise to a number of issues in practice, including those arising from the fact that the safeguard plan can only be pursued by the debtor, and even if creditors suggest an alternative approach, the court is not obliged to consider it. Further, the debtor is in control of the valuation process, which hinges upon an independent expert report and is usually only provided to creditors after the first stage has concluded (ie after the confidential negotiations), leaving creditors with little time to consider their relative priorities and level of recovery before they are asked to vote on the safeguard plan. Another practical issue is the individual creditor's capacity to contribute to any new money requirements, which essentially favours banks, who are the only entities in France who are formally licensed to provide loans. These aspects of the procedure have not yet been tested before the French courts, and, anecdotally, creditors are increasingly seeking to avoid the possible effects of safeguard, in particular the potential to be crammed down. Instead, they may be seeking to enter into cooperation agreements, a concept borrowed from the US, where they collaborate and seek to formulate alternative proposals to those proposed by the debtor.

(ii) Data on Usage

There has been fairly limited experience in France of the new accelerated safeguard procedure (about 15 precedents) but it has been applied to high-profile/cross-border restructurings (*Pierre & Vacances*, *Orpea*, *Groupe Casino*) in addition to some mid-sized/small, capitalised companies (eg, *Arc Holdings*, *Electro Holding*, *Demain ES*).[95]

(iii) Some Significant Early Cases

There have been three significant cases to date: *Pierre et Vacances*, *Orpea* and *Groupe Casino*. The first was supported by the requisite majorities, but the two later cases included the application of cross-class cram-down power, and in the case of *Orpea* and *Groupe Casino* the shareholders' interest was diluted to almost zero as a result of the debt being equitised. The *Orpea* case, in particular, is a good illustration of how complexities that arise in a restructuring are not always anticipated in the enactment of the legislative framework. For example, it is not uncommon in a debt restructuring

[94] This test ensures that each dissenting creditor must receive at least as much under the plan as it would receive in a liquidation or sale. The administrator appoints independent valuers for these purposes.

[95] See Laïd Estelle Laurent, Jean Delapalme and Claire Blondel, 'Evaluating France's introduction of the classes of affected parties mechanism', *International Financial Law Review*, 9 July 2024.

that creditors who have an interest in the debt, at the level where value breaks, effectively may seek to take control of the company. However, the legislation does not provide clear guidance on how, if such tranche is held by multiple and different instruments with different profiles, they ought to be treated. The *Orpea* case serves as the first large-scale restructuring under the new regime, undertaken in a contentious environment. Numerous proceedings were initiated by creditors and shareholders in an attempt to oppose the restructuring, which included the equitisation of €3.8 billion in unsecured debt. The restructuring plan was ultimately imposed on dissenting parties using the cross-class cram-down power. This highly publicised case was particularly sensitive due to the nature of the company's operations, specialising in nursing homes.

The end of 2023 and the beginning of 2024 were notably marked by the restructuring of Groupe Casino. This high-profile case benefited from the lessons learned in the *Orpea* proceedings. This financial restructuring led to the equitisation of €3.5 billion in unsecured debt and of €1.3 billion in secured debt, and thereby the massive dilution of the founder's shareholding. Another notable feature is that the process was completed without litigation (attributable to the fact that a lock-up agreement had secured the parties' consent in advance) and within a record time-frame. Since the start of 2024, other major cases have emerged, including Atos SE. The Atos restructuring was implemented by way of an accelerated safeguard plan which was approved by the Nanterre Commercial Court in October 2024. It has set a landmark precedent by demonstrating the use of a French restructuring plan in a cross-border context, also taking place against a backdrop of significant political sensitivities (the group's activities include services relating to the provision of supercomputers used for nuclear test simulations). The plan provides for (i) the equitisation of €2.9 billion of financial debt, and (ii) the provision of €1.675 billion of new money and various share capital transactions. The financial restructuring is subject to regulatory approvals due to be completed by December 2024/January 2025.

D. Germany – The Rise of the StaRUG

(i) Key Features

The German 'Company Stabilisation and Restructuring Act' (Unternehmensstabilisierungs- und restrukturierungsgesetz – StaRUG), which implements the EU Restructuring Directive, entered into force on 1 January 2021. The StaRUG establishes a pre-insolvency restructuring procedure (the 'German Scheme'), which allows for the restructuring of a wide variety of claims (eg, financing agreements including intercreditor relationships and group collateral) by way of a restructuring plan. The German Scheme can be used by companies (in all industries other than the financial sector) for financial restructurings, reorganisations, the 'rightsizing' of debt, and sales transactions. The corresponding restructuring plan, when accepted and confirmed, has a binding effect on all stakeholders involved. In particular, it is possible to cram down dissenting creditor groups, if a majority of 75 per cent in value is reached within a class and across a majority of the other creditor groups (in addition to satisfying a limited absolute priority rule).

The debtor must be in a state of so-called 'impending illiquidity' in order to be able to use the German Scheme, which corresponds to the concept of financial distress. The initiation of the proceedings requires: (i) a notification of the debtor company to the restructuring court, including (ii) a restructuring concept; (iii) a confirmation that the company is threatened with impending illiquidity (but is not yet illiquid and/or over-indebted such as to constitute mandatory insolvency filing triggers); (iv) a description of the current state of negotiations with creditors, shareholders and third parties on the envisaged measures of the restructuring plan; (v) an overview of the precautions taken by the debtor to ensure its ability to fulfil its obligations under the StaRUG; (vi) a statement as to whether the rights of consumers, or medium, small or micro enterprises are affected, and (vii) a statement on whether opposition from a creditor group is to be expected.

The restructuring court shall in certain cases (including where the debtor applies for a moratorium) appoint a mandatory restructuring expert who will assist the debtor with the structure, negotiation and filing of the restructuring plan. The mandatory restructuring expert may also be granted supervisory duties and responsibility for monitoring cash management. In cases that do not require a mandatory restructuring expert and at the request of the debtor or a group of creditors holding at least 25 per cent of the voting rights in a group, the court shall appoint a facultative restructuring expert to assist in the preparation and negotiation of the restructuring concept and the plan based on it.

To facilitate negotiations over a restructuring plan, the court may order a moratorium of between three and eight months, which prevents creditors from enforcing their claims and security against the debtor and related group entities. Even though the moratorium covers foreclosure on immovables, the discontinuation of the foreclosure sale due to the moratorium must still be asserted separately before the foreclosure court (Zwangsversteigerungsgericht).

The restructuring court is also involved in the formation of creditor groups and the content of the restructuring plan as well as the ancillary documentation which accompanies the plan (for example liquidity forecasts, fair value and restructuring opinions). The restructuring plan will need to be sanctioned by the court in order to cram down dissenting stakeholder groups. The public announcement of all court decisions within a restructuring procedure can also be requested from the court in order to ensure automatic recognition of the court sanctioning within the European Union according to the EU Recast Insolvency Regulation.

There are still only a few cases heard under the German scheme procedure, known as the StaRUG and initially they were confined to small/medium sized entities. In recent years, however, the StaRUG has been used more and more frequently to restructure (listed) stock corporations – in particular, to impose a capital reduction on the shareholders. More recently, the first StaRUG cases have emerged in which partnerships and limited liability companies initiate a StaRUG procedure in order to transfer shares in the distressed company to a new investor without an approving shareholder resolution, in addition to a balance sheet restructuring.[96] The primary focus of the procedure is still to facilitate a financial restructuring, and the legislation does not really provide a framework to conduct operational restructurings as a result of its inability to affect

[96] OLG Stuttgart, order dated 21.08.2024–20 U 30/24 BeckRS 2024, 22200.

rights under operational contracts such as leases or employment contracts. Like the UK restructuring plan, the StaRUG offers a flexible mechanism to overcome holdout positions and can be directed at achieving a compromise with particular creditors or classes of creditor or with the entire creditor body. Also like the restructuring plan, it has a 75 per cent majority in value voting threshold and the ability to cram down classes across classes. It is very much driven by the debtor and includes (upon application) protection against creditors in the form of a moratorium against enforcement action (notably absent from the UK plan procedure). The moratorium is balanced, however, by an obligation for the management to safeguard the interests of the creditors (much like the so-called 'creditor duty' under English law when the company is bordering on insolvency)[97] and creditors also have the ability to influence the restructuring in terms of voting upon its terms.[98]

Looking more closely at the process itself, the StaRUG is a debtor-initiated process which is only available to debtors that are in a state of impending illiquidity, forecast to occur within 24 months. They cannot already be insolvent[99] (cash flow or balance sheet) and should there be a financial deterioration after the initiation of proceedings, the court can transfer the debtor to ordinary insolvency proceedings.[100] The scope of the restructuring plan encompasses all types of creditor claim except employee claims, tort claims and criminal fines.[101] Like a UK restructuring plan, the StaRUG can be used to compromise claims under loan agreements, including amending covenant terms, waiving termination rights, and extending maturity dates. The plan can affect secured creditors and shareholders, but not operational contracts such as leases or employment contracts.

The court is involved when the plan is first presented and then at the approval stage. In addition, unlike in UK restructuring plans, the German court is able to impose (it is not automatic, but available upon application) a general moratorium on creditor enforcement.[102] Another distinction from the UK approach is the fact that the StaRUG includes the option of a court appointed restructuring officer, which is mandatory in cases where the cross-class cram-down power is to be relied upon. The officer examines claims, reviews the debtor's financial position to ensure continuing compliance with the financial criteria for use, and monitors management and company funds. Voting on the plan closely follows the UK approach, in that it is left to the debtor to propose the categorisation of classes, and voting majorities are based on value with no separate numerosity or 'headcount' test. In terms of the exercise of cram-down, this follows what the EU Restructuring Directive refers to as the 'best-interests-of-creditors test'.[103] This is designed to ensure that creditors are no worse off within the plan when

[97] *BTI 2014 LLC v Sequana* [2022] UKSC 25.

[98] Section 270b Insolvency Code and section 24 StaRUG.

[99] Annex to section 5 of StaRUG sets out the necessary information required in the plan, including an assessment of the assets and liabilities at the time the plan is submitted. Section 14 of StaRUG requires a declaration of liability, balance sheet results and financial plan.

[100] Section 42 – ongoing obligations to notify insolvency and over indebtedness.

[101] Section 4 StaRUG including subordinated creditors included in section 39 Insolvency Code.

[102] Section 29(3) StaRUG.

[103] Article 2(6) of the EU Restructuring Directive defines the 'best-interest-of-creditors test' as a test that is satisfied if no dissenting creditor would be worse off under a restructuring plan than such a creditor would be if the normal ranking of liquidation priorities under national law were applied, either in the event of

compared to being without it. In addition, a majority of classes must approve cross-class cram-down.[104] StaRUG follows a traditional order of priority, which may, however, be deviated from in circumstances where, for example, a shareholder provides a material contribution, or the superior ranking creditor is not materially affected, for example in circumstances where there is a rescheduling of debt (no write-offs) for no more than 18 months.[105]

The main advantages of the StaRUG when compared to more formal insolvency proceedings available under German law are that it has limited court involvement, which means it can be cost-effective, and that it can take place on a confidential basis at the debtor's option. For confidential (non-public) German schemes, they are not considered to be an insolvency procedure for the purposes of the EU Recast Insolvency Regulation, and so are not subject to the Regulation's jurisdictional rules. The key advantage is that, as a confidential process, it does not have any stigma attached to its commencement. The English restructuring plan takes effect under the spotlight of the court process in a public setting and, as a procedural requirement, details must be filed at Companies House. Certain disadvantages may, however, stem from the fact that the German procedure is limited in regard to implementing an operational restructuring, which as discussed is limited because it cannot be used to compromise leases and employment claims.

In terms of jurisdiction to commence a StaRUG, the rule in confidential/non-public cases is that the restructuring court is competent if the company has its COMI in Germany. Public StaRUG proceedings must comply with the jurisdictional rules of the EU Recast Insolvency Regulation but benefit from recognition under it. In contrast, UK plans are public but do not benefit from any automatic recognition by the courts of Member States, but separate steps can be pursued if formal recognition is required in respect of them. We are not aware of any formal proceedings for recognition in Member States to date. Chapter 15 recognition is, however, often sought in the US to afford restructuring plans recognition and full effect.

(ii) Data on Usage

The StaRUG has now been in force since 2021, but there have been limited numbers of cases to date, and while the process was initially used for small cases, the more recent use cases have been in relation to large corporate restructurings. One example is the LEONI case.[106] LEONI is an automotive supplier, with operations in 24 countries, revenues of over €5 billion and debt in excess of €1 billion. In this case, a StaRUG was used in conjunction with a consensual deal at its Topco level. Its main shareholder received 100 per cent shares in Topco in exchange for €150 million of new money[107] and its debt was retranched into 'sustainable' and 'not sustainable' debts, with only the

liquidation – whether piecemeal or by sale as a going concern – or in the event of the next-best-alternative scenario if the restructuring plan were not confirmed.

[104] Section 26 StaRUG.

[105] See also below, Chapter 3 of this book (Kristin van Zwieten and Sjur Swensen Ellingsaeter).

[106] AG Nürnberg court order dated 21.06.2023 – RES 397/23.

[107] See section 12 of StaRUG New Financing.

'sustainable' left in place. Despite a challenge from retail investors that they had been unfairly left behind, the StaRUG was approved.

LEONI demonstrates that a StaRUG procedure is a serious option for large companies to implement a financial restructuring. Despite its size (as mentioned above, turnover of €5 billion and almost 100,000 employees), the StaRUG procedure in this case was completed within only about eight weeks. It included a cross-class cram-down, a delisting from the stock exchange and the capital being cut to zero with a capital increase for one investor. This illustrates the point that the StaRUG procedure is, if it is well prepared and the structure of the case fits, a very relevant tool for implementing a financial restructuring. Another recent example is Softline, in which the restructuring procedure was used to facilitate a squeeze out, using the 75 per cent majority needed under the StaRUG instead of the 95 per cent majority that would have been required under the German Stock Corporation Act, with a new money injection by the majority shareholder in exchange for a group restructuring, with the whole process completed in under six months. In another case, *Re Branicks*, the speed and efficiency of the StaRUG was much admired, as the plan was issued on 5 March and was approved on 26 March by the restructuring court.

(iii) Some Questions

In relation to access to the procedure, it remains unclear how (or if) access to the StaRUG is possible if a shareholder opposes use of the procedure. The legislation is silent on whether filings need to have shareholder approval. There are several court decisions which differ in their outcomes. In the only decision of a Higher Regional Court in Germany available, rendered by the Higher Regional Court (OLG) of Stuttgart, the competent court stated that a shareholder resolution is not required for the initiation of proceedings under the StaRUG if the restructuring proceedings are the only sufficiently promising alternative to insolvency proceedings.[108] The decision concerned a partnership and – for the first time – not a stock corporation. Furthermore, in *LEONI*,[109] the District Court in Nuremberg held that for joint stock companies in particular, no AGM approval was required. This was based upon the fact that in such corporations the board has unrestricted power to represent the corporation and, given the ability for StaRUG to cram down shareholders, it would run counter to the legislative scheme if they were able to veto the filing. In relation to limited liability companies, there is still uncertainty as to whether shareholder approval is required in order to file for StaRUG proceedings, but the decision of the Higher Regional Court in Stuttgart provides the first clear guideline for a nationwide judicial tier. However, the remaining uncertainty for other courts puts management in a difficult position where they may face opposition to the plan from a shareholder, but on the other hand owe a duty to act in the interest of creditors, which may necessitate a restructuring of the business.

In relation to the conduct of the procedure itself, other than in the *LEONI*[110] case, there has been little guidance in the court decisions to date relating to the exercise of the

[108] OLG Stuttgart, order 21.08.2024–20 U 30/24 BeckRS 2024, 22200.
[109] AG Nürnberg court order 21.06.2023 – RES 397/23 (*LEONI*).
[110] AG Nürnberg court order dated 21.6.2023 – RES 397/23.

cram-down mechanisms, including in relation to the interpretation of the 'no-worse-off' test and the assessment of the relevant alternative in this regard. It appears that from a procedural perspective, significant weight is place upon the explanations provided in the plan (prepared by the debtor) and the information provided in the typically comprehensive expert evidence. The experts are court appointed, and this seems to be a feature of European procedures, in contrast to those advisers appointed by the debtor in the context of UK restructuring plans.

While not yet widely used, the StaRUG, like the UK restructuring plan, may form part of a consensual deal, so that the legal framework influences outcomes although it is not formally applied. It will be interesting to see how the German procedure and other restructuring techniques available elsewhere in the EU are used to influence negotiations. (Of course, the ability to do this will also be subject to the jurisdictional rules of the EU Recast Insolvency Regulation where they apply). In relation to Germany in particular, it is noteworthy that the English scheme and restructuring plan are still considered as viable options to restructure German businesses and that, notwithstanding the availability of the StaRUG, these procedures continue to be used. A major reason for this is that the processes are 'tried and tested,' and certainty of outcome is an important consideration in the context of restructurings.[111]

IV. Preliminary Evaluation: The Same but Different?

The national restructuring measures implemented in the EU jurisdictions should essentially follow the common framework set out in the EU Restructuring Directive, but the Directive gives many options to Member States, giving rise to some variances.[112] Despite this, there are some preliminary observations that can be made about how the three procedures we have discussed compare with the UK restructuring plan.

The choice of restructuring procedure is deeply practical, being driven by issues such as certainty, cost, and time. Of course, as each of the procedures in France, Germany and the Netherlands becomes more embedded as part of the domestic corporate restructuring culture, there will be increased certainty and an opportunity to improve efficiencies as the techniques become more 'commoditised'. So, while the UK restructuring plan may have a head start in terms of being able to leverage the heritage of its sister procedure, the scheme of arrangement, in a cross-border context, we will no doubt continue to see other restructuring options develop as credible alternatives across Europe.

[111] See *Re Aggregate* and it is not insignificant that a second restructuring plan was launched in May 2024 in respect of the Adler Group. See further on *Re Adler*, Stefan Sax, Maria Berkner, and Joseph Saed: 'The Eagle Has Landed – Die Entscheidung des englischen Court of Appeal in Sachen Adler', NZI 2024, 357, 361 which notes that the appeal has not dampened the enthusiasm of German debtors to consider the English restructuring plan process.

[112] The European Commission (2022) Final Report 'study on the issue of abusive forum shopping in insolvency proceedings' recognises that a high level of diversity remains, which may incentivise continued forum shopping, included in the EU Restructuring Directive (Framework contract JUST/2020/PR/03/001 on legal analysis services, including compliance assessment of national transposing measures in the Justice and Consumers policy areas – Lot2.) https://commission.europa.eu/document/download/0664f511-6e09-4751-b7be-421fde651091_en?filename=Final%20Report%20-%20Abusive%20Forum%20Shopping_Febr%202022.pdf&prefLang=pl.

In terms of the story so far, it is noteworthy that while there are no size restrictions in the three EU jurisdictions as to application of the restructuring procedures, the Dutch WHOA procedure was initially used by a large number of small debtors. Likewise in Germany, the initial application of the StaRUG related to smaller debtors. Since 2023 there have been some examples in each jurisdiction of significant groups being restructured. In the UK, while the statistics relating to the use of the restructuring plan are limited in number to around 30, those cases have concerned a number of very large enterprises. One explanation for this initial difference in usage patterns may lie in the fact that in the UK there was already an established restructuring practice under the scheme of arrangement procedure, which Part 26A built upon. There may therefore have been less perceived risk (in terms of costs and certainty of outcome) in using the UK restructuring plan in high-value cases, compared with EU procedures that did not have an existing body of precedent to draw upon. In terms of use of foreign procedures by smaller debtors, these followed the removal of the pandemic protections and took place in a difficult economic climate. The fact that these procedures have relatively limited court involvement, compared with the alternatives under domestic law, could go some way to explain the numbers when compared to the UK restructuring plan. The UK restructuring plan does involve two court hearings and therefore may be less attractive to smaller entities that are already financially distressed; there are also alternative procedures available. Of course, there have been some uses of the plan in smaller cases, including for a company that was already in a formal insolvency procedure (*Re Amicus Finance*).

A second difference between the UK plan and its Dutch, Germany and French counterparts relates to the gateway for initiating each procedure. While all have a financial condition for entry which is designed to test the debtor's distress and requires, in certain jurisdictions, for them not to be in an existing state of actual insolvency, in the UK the threshold is slightly less onerous: the debtor simply needs to be in financial difficulties (which is not defined), which is arguably more flexible than the tests for the EU procedures. Whilst the procedures on both sides of the Channel are aimed at early intervention, the triggers for the EU procedures studied here are quite formal, as are the modes of initiation more generally. This may be a consequence of the fact that the EU procedures have a power to stay, and the UK restructuring plan does not, so that its initiation is a much more formal thing, with much more dramatic effects and more akin to formal insolvency proceedings with the necessary safeguards required.

A third difference to date has been in how the procedures have been used, and in particular in relation to what kinds of claims and stakeholder constituencies. Although the number of cases for restructuring plans in the UK have been much lower than for some of its European cousins, the variety of the type of debts that have been the subject of compromise is remarkable. It certainly appears from a practitioner's perspective that there has been a development in the English scheme technology which, by and large, seemed to be used primarily for financial restructurings. The plan is being used as a more comprehensive tool, including for businesses that need an operational restructure (*Re Virgin Active*, *Fitness First*, *Prezzo*, *Super Dry* are perhaps the most obvious examples of this). In the three EU jurisdictions, the focus in the larger cases has been on financial restructurings (for example *LEONI* and *Vroon*). Again, the use of the UK procedure may reflect that the procedure was not designed 'from scratch' but built on a well-established framework, with established patterns of use for financial restructurings, but filled some gaps in the existing framework (including the absence of a cross-class cram-down power) and then entrusted it back to the same courts – all of which would tend to invite more ambitious uses of Part 26A.

It may be argued that, in the restructuring plan cases to date in the UK, there has been less of a focus on the domestic market. This might be attributable to a number of factors: (i) the process is well suited to large, complex, capital and debt structures (especially those that include English law-governed debt); (ii) the more significant cases in terms of size tend to have a more international outlook and merit the cost of the procedure (which may be relatively low when compared to, say, US Chapter 11, but is not an insignificant factor); (iii) that there is a low jurisdictional threshold and test for substantial effect (in relevant jurisdictions abroad) is well established in the case law; (iv) the flexibility of the procedure in terms of compromises available is attractive (it can address different layers of debt and both financial and operational issues); (v) unlike some of the newer EU procedures, it can rely on jurisprudence from earlier schemes, which promotes predictability and certainty of outcome; and (vi) it is a relatively quick procedure to implement, compared to US Chapter 11.

Of course, the new EU procedures are now gaining ground and have some attractive features when compared to the UK restructuring plan. The option of a stay on claims, to allow a breathing space to restructure, is an attractive feature. In a couple of UK cases, these stays have been used by commencing an EU process to parallel a UK plan procedure. EU restructuring procedures also may be conducted as confidential procedures, which avoids the potential stigma associated with public proceedings; this may also help to explain the initial focus on small debtors that we observed in the Netherlands. And of course, the public version of these proceedings will benefit from automatic recognition under the EU Recast Insolvency Regulation; this may prove to be a major benefit in time.

Having looked at the UK restructuring plan in a European context, perhaps the only sensible conclusion is that it is too early to attempt to predict the ways in which these procedures will become important to restructuring practice. Certainly, the market continues to evolve, and on paper, debtors now have more options available to restructure than ever before, including in jurisdictions where previously there were very limited offerings. These procedures do have some common features, and as we have noted above, some practices are being borrowed across borders without losing anything in translation. Greater flexibility in the legal framework and the way it applies and evolves in practice is perhaps the most important common theme that permeates across each of the jurisdictions we have focused upon. What is of crucial importance to debtors and their stakeholders seeking to implement a restructuring is that the legal framework continues to operate in a manner that facilitates a predictable, timely and cost-effective solution, wherever that may be.

APPENDIX 1

Comparison Table: Rivals or Cousins?

	English Restructuring Plan	**French Accelerated Financial Safeguard**	**Dutch Scheme (WHOA)**	**German Restructuring Scheme (StaRUG)**
Precedent	Law in effect since 26 June 2020. Around 30 cases as at September 2024 (but draws on schemes of arrangement jurisprudence).	Law in effect since October 2021. About 15 cases as at September 2024.	Law in effect since 1 January 2021. Over 300 WHOA judgments as at September 2024. Since 2023 also used for large companies.	Law in effect since 1 January 2021. Mostly used for SMEs, but increasing number of cases including large and one recent significant case as at September 2024.
Creditor approval threshold	75% in value	$^2/_3$ in value	$^2/_3$ in value	75% in value
Availability of cross-class cram down	Yes, as long as 'one in the money' class approves and none of the members of the dissenting class are left worse off than they would be in the relevant alternative. Fairness test also needs to be satisfied.	Yes, if a majority of classes approve, with at least one secured or 'in the money' class, or at least one of the classes of affected parties is 'in the money'.	Yes, as long as 'one in the money' class approves and best interest test and (modified) absolute priority rule satisfied.	Yes, if majority of classes accept plan and best interest test and absolute priority rule satisfied.
Limits on what can be implemented in cases with a dissenting class	Fairness, which involves consideration of priority (*Adler*), and cannot leave dissenting classes worse off. Purpose must be to remedy financial difficulties.	Absolute priority rule. No worse off test.	Modified absolute priority rule. No worse off test.	Modified absolute priority rule. No worse off test.

(continued)

Appendix 1 *(Continued)*

	English Restructuring Plan	French Accelerated Financial Safeguard	Dutch Scheme (WHOA)	German Restructuring Scheme (StaRUG)
Cost	Depends on whether they are contested. Has been used for SME companies.	Depends on complexity and whether they are contested.	Depends on complexity and whether they are contested.	Depends upon the case and whether they are contested.
Ability for foreign debtors to access	Sufficient connection test successfully used in a number of cases for international groups.	COMI in France required – use in cross-border cases.	Public scheme requires COMI in Netherlands. Non-public scheme requires 'sufficient connection'	Public scheme requires COMI in Germany. Non-public scheme requires 'sufficient connection'
Financial condition for entry	Financial difficulties are required.	Debtor must not be cash insolvent, or filing must be within 45 days of cash 'insolvency'.	Requires a reasonable expectation of inability to pay debts.	Requires a state of impending illiquidity.
Ability to release guarantors	Yes	No	Yes, subject to certain jurisdictional requirements.	Yes, for 'upstream' guarantees.
Other notable features (in comparison with restructuring plans)	N/A	Stay on payments and action. DIP finance available. Enforcement protection available.	Moratorium possible for max eight months. Choice between a 'public scheme' which will benefit from recognition across EU under EU Recast Insolvency Regulation; or 'non-public scheme' which can remain confidential.	Choice between a 'public scheme' which will benefit from recognition across EU under EU Recast Insolvency Regulation; or 'non-public scheme' which can remain confidential. Enforcement protection available.

Appendix 2

Timeline: What's New in the European Context?

2009–10	UK consultations on restructuring moratoria
2011	EU parliamentary resolution for harmonisation of certain aspects of insolvency law
2014	European Commission Recommendation of 12 March 2014 on a new approach to business failure and insolvency (2014/135/EU)
2015	EU Recast Insolvency Regulation (2015/848)
2016	UK votes to leave the EU
2016–18	UK government consults on restructuring reforms
June 2019	EU Restructuring Directive approved
January 2020	Brexit, but transition period until 31 December 2020
April 2020	UK Government reforms announced which included the restructuring plan
June 2020	UK restructuring plan introduced by Corporate Insolvency and Governance Act 2020 as new Part 26A of the Companies Act 2006
January 2021	Dutch WHOA introduced
January 2021	German StaRUG introduced
October 2021	French Accelerated Safeguard introduced
July 2022	EU Restructuring Directive transposition deadline

3

Rules of Priority in Restructuring Procedures

KRISTIN VAN ZWIETEN AND SJUR SWENSEN ELLINGSÆTER*

I. Introduction

In state-supplied procedures for the coordinated realisation (conversion to cash) of a distressed debtor's estate, rules are provided to regulate the order in which the proceeds of sale are distributed to those with claims (rights) against the estate. In state-supplied restructuring procedures, rules of priority regulate not the distribution of cash but the distribution of *claims* – the order in which new claims are issued, in place of old ones, so that the debtor's distress can be addressed through a reorganisation of claims rather than a realisation of assets. Such rules are related to, but can fruitfully be distinguished from, rules that require a court – as a condition of confirming a reorganisation plan so as to render it binding on dissenters – to be satisfied that claimholders will not be left worse off under the plan than if it were not confirmed. The latter type of rule (often termed a 'best-interests-of-creditors' rule[1]) stipulates a baseline, or floor, for negotiations on a plan;[2] rules of priority are concerned with the distribution of value over and above that which claimholders can expect to receive in the 'non-plan world'. In other words, rules of priority address the question of *how much* better off claimholders expect to be under the plan, relative to each other. Since claimholders are, in principle, free to agree to a compromise of their rights against the debtor outside of the auspices of a state-supplied procedure, rules of priority constitute 'backstop', or default, rules that parties bargain in the shadow of.[3]

* The authors thank Joël Lozeman, Ilya Kokorin, Stephan Madaus, Vasile Rotaru and Michael Veder for input in relation to the comparative components of this chapter.

[1] Following US law terminology. As to the development of this requirement in US law, and its modern expression in § 1129 of the US Bankruptcy Code, see the overview in J Hicks, 'Foxes Guarding the Henhouse: The Modern Best Interests of Creditors Test in Chapter 11 Reorganizations' (2005) 5 *Nevada Law Journal* 820.

[2] Michael Veder in Christoph G Paulus and Reinhard Dammann (eds), *European Preventive Restructuring Directive (EU) 2019/1023: Article-by-Article Commentary* (CH Beck, 2021), Art 11, para 27. Of course, the choice of comparator will affect where the baseline is set, and correspondingly the size of the domain for a priority rule. See further below, p 80.

[3] I Ayres and R Gertner, 'Filling Gaps in Incomplete Contracts: An Economic Theory of Default Rules' (1989) 99 *Yale Law Journal* 87, 91.

The wider the power of the court to confirm a plan in the presence of dissenters, the more important these rules become. In particular, both types of rules become important when states go beyond simply empowering a court to confirm a plan that is supported by the requisite majority of members of every class of claimholder whose rights will be affected (so that dissenters within each class are bound), to empowering the court to confirm a plan in the presence of a dissenting *class*, so that members of dissenting as well as assenting classes can be bound. In Europe, this is 'cross-class cram-down'; in US law terminology, this is 'cram-down' in a 'non-consensual' case, with a plan supported by the requisite majority in each class being a 'consensual' one.[4]

In section II, we explain why this is so, taking as our starting point Clark's sketch of the early development of US reorganisation law.[5] We extend Clark's account by drawing on the work of others to chart the emergence of the absolute priority rule, now expressed in § 1129 of the US Code and applicable in (large)[6] non-consensual cases, and against this backdrop, explain why, in theory, it appears desirable for lawmakers to supply a clear rule of this kind to regulate the exercise of a cross-class cram-down power. We do not make a strong claim about the form that such a rule should take, except to say that when it comes to considering the position of non-adjusting creditors, we see benefits in supplying a rule of absolute priority of the kind contained in § 1129. That is to say, we see benefits in a rule that regulates conflicts between classes regarding the distribution of value over the baseline by requiring the court to approach the task of confirming the distribution of claims as if it were overseeing a distribution of cash in a realisation, such that it should decline to confirm a plan from which an unsecured class has dissented, and which would allow some more junior class to retain value, unless the claims that would be issued to the dissenting class amount (in expected value) to full satisfaction. This is what the US rule requires.

We then turn to the EU (section III), to explore recent experiments with the design of priority rules in three Member States. This experimentation has taken place as part of the transposition of the European Preventive Restructuring Directive,[7] so we begin with the Directive, which requires Member States to make provision (at least for larger companies) for class-based voting and cross-class cram-down, subject to inter alia baseline protection in the form of a 'best-interests-of-creditors' rule, and a priority rule, but with options in relation to the design of these rules, and of other related rules. On priority, Member States can choose from an 'absolute priority rule', similar to that in § 1129, or absolute priority with such derogations that Member States introduce where 'necessary in order to achieve the aims of the restructuring plan' ('absolute priority with exceptions'), or a *sui generis* alternative termed 'relative priority'. The latter is distinctive

[4] Harvey R Miller and Ronit J Berkovich, 'The Implications of the Third Circuit's Armstrong Decision on Creative Corporate Restructuring: Will Strict Construction of the Absolute Priority Rule Make Chapter 11 Consensus Less Likely?' (2006) 55(5) *American University Law Review* 1345. 'Cramdown' is shorthand for 'cramming down the throat of': *Collier on Bankruptcy*, 16th edn (LexisNexis, 2020), vol 7 § 1129.03.

[5] Robert C Clark, 'The Interdisciplinary Study of Legal Evolution' (1981) 90 *Yale Law Review* 1238.

[6] The rule is disapplied in a sub-chapter for small businesses: see below, text to n 78. Like Clark, we take as our paradigm case a large company restructuring.

[7] Directive (EU) 2019/1023 of the European Parliament and of the Council of 20 June 2019 on preventive restructuring frameworks, on discharge of debt and disqualifications, and on measures to increase the efficiency of procedures concerning restructuring, insolvency and discharge of debt OJ L 172, 26.6.2019, 18–55.

in that it does not take as its starting point that a dissenting class ought to be (expected to be) satisfied under the plan before a more junior class can retain value; instead, there is a vaguer requirement for the dissenting class to be treated 'more favourably' than junior ones. Our three Member States (Germany, the Netherlands, and Sweden) settled on a form of 'absolute priority rule with exceptions',[8] but with variation in the specificity of the exceptions, with some more open-ended than others. Our survey suggests that lawmakers confront a common set of questions in the design of priority rules, which can be sensibly answered in more than one way, and that the domain of these rules (which will determine the significance of the lawmaker's answers to these questions) will be contingent on a range of other design choices.

In section IV, we turn to the United Kingdom, where the legislature resolved to introduce a cross-class cram-down power without providing a rule of priority to regulate its exercise. Baseline protection is provided in the form of a rule that members of the dissenting class should not be expected to be left worse off under the plan than if it were not confirmed,[9] but, despite initial plans to include a form of 'absolute priority rule with exceptions', the statute is silent on the question of the relative entitlement of claimholders to value over and above the baseline. It has therefore been left to the courts to articulate the principles that ought to govern the exercise of the power. These courts are experienced at filling out sparse statutory frameworks through the supply of principles to guide the exercise of discretion, but in this case the task has been complicated by the legislative history,[10] and by the fact that the most analogous categories of case in the prior law had generated principles that were either vague, or clear but controversial, and which are not easily reconciled. The courts have worked at impressive speed to provide as much guidance as this kind of rule-making process[11] permits, and a form of priority principle is emerging, but – at least in its present form – it is vaguer in what it entitles the dissenting class to than even the vaguest of options in the Directive. Drawing on the analysis in section II, we suggest that this kind of approach is unlikely to be in the (long-run) interests of either professional investors or less sophisticated parties. We conclude, therefore, that this British experiment was a misstep.

II. Context and Theory

In 'The Interdisciplinary Study of Legal Evolution',[12] Robert C Clark suggested that, at least in the field of corporate and financial law, one way to generalise about the way in which the law had developed over time was by organising developments into phases of 'primary' and 'secondary' cost-reduction. In primary phases, lawmakers were responding to some external societal change that generated an opportunity for the law to reduce a cost. Where the lawmaker's response – the supply of some new legal principle or new 'institution defined and shaped by legal principles' – was successful, in the sense that it

[8] Albeit with some important differences in scope: below, text to n 181, and n 218.
[9] Companies Act 2006 s 901G(3), (4).
[10] See below, n 288.
[11] ie one in which the principle is revealed over time, through its instantiation in individual cases.
[12] Clark (n 5).

reduced the cost in ways superior to the 'identifiable alternatives', instances of it would 'proliferate'.[13] In secondary phases, attention turned inward, to reducing the costs of the principle or process itself. In these phases, which were characterised by 'cumulative doctrinal complexity',[14] the focus was on granular aspects of rule design, over which interested parties would do battle in a bid to secure the form of cost-reducing rule from which they would most expect to benefit.[15]

The development of US reorganisation law, Clark reasoned, could be explained at least in part as a response to the rise of large-scale enterprises. Some businesses were 'so large and complex' that there was unlikely to be a 'fair-sized pool of reasonably informed potential outside buyers' for their purchase in the event of default.[16] In these circumstances, creditors might be better off if the debtor's distress could be treated through a reorganisation, rather than a realisation (conversion to cash) and distribution. Achieving this would, however, require the parties to bargain over the surrender of existing claims and the issue of new ones in their place (or what Clark termed the issue of 'new tickets' against the debtor:[17] new claims, in place of the old ones, to the income expected to be generated by the debtor's assets). If creditors refused to consent to the debtor's liabilities being treated in this way, the distressed debtor would be forced back into a realisation (sale to a third party) process, even if this was only expected to yield a 'distress price' for the business.[18] Clearly, the more widely existing claims against the debtor are held, the more difficult it will be to procure consent to the 'new deal'.[19]

For Clark, key primary phases in the law's response included: first, the creative refashioning of existing procedures for the sale of assets to third parties so that they could be used to promote a reorganisation – so-called 'equity receivership reorganizations', in which an insolvent debtor's assets were transferred, in exercise of secured bondholders' foreclosure remedy,[20] to a new company in which claims would be issued to (some) stakeholders of the old company,[21] with judicially developed techniques for encouraging bondholders to participate[22] rather than insist on receiving (their portion of)

[13] ibid 1241.

[14] ibid 1247.

[15] ibid 1240–41, 1247. Clark emphasised that he was not attempting to offer a complete explanation for developments in the field of corporate and financial law, and that even where developments did appear to fit the suggested pattern, this did not mean that the result was necessarily the socially optimal one (1242).

[16] ibid 1254. For a contemporary account that similarly explains a debtor's inability to sell assets at full value by reference to information asymmetries, see Kenneth Ayotte and David A Skeel Jr, 'Bankruptcy Law as a Liquidity Provider' (2013) 80(4) *University of Chicago Law Review* 1557. Notice that in the case of distress linked to an industry shock, the most informed purchasers will also likely be liquidity constrained: A Shleifer and RW Vishny, 'Liquidation values and debt capacity: a market equilibrium approach' (1992) 47(4) *Journal of Finance* 1343.

[17] Clark (n 5) 1253.

[18] ibid 1251–52.

[19] Ayotte and Skeel (n 16) 1576.

[20] See David A Skeel Jr, *Debt's Dominion* (Princeton NJ, Princeton University Press, 2003) ch 2.

[21] See 'Address of Jerome N. Frank before the American Bar Association: Corporate Reorganizations and the Chandler Act' (July 25, 1938, Ohio), describing this a 'fictional foreclosure' (7); S Spring, 'Upset Prices in Corporate Reorganization' (1919) 32(5) *Harvard Law Review* 489, 493.

[22] By depositing their claims to enable a collective bid to be made for the assets for non-cash consideration (the surrender of the deposited claims). In practice, there were no outsiders competing in this bidding process. See Skeel (n 20) 59; Joseph L Weiner, 'Conflicting Functions of the Upset Price in a Corporate Reorganization' (1927) 27(2) *Columbia Law Review* 132, 137; Spring ibid 493, 499.

sale proceeds in cash,[23] and a device to enable suppliers to continue to be paid in the meantime;[24] secondly, the introduction of statutory procedures by which such a reorganisation could be achieved more directly, with a power for the court to bind dissentients to the will of a similarly situated majority.[25] But these innovations also necessitated the development of safeguards against the risk that the processes would be used by one stakeholder constituency to extract value from another, including valuation rules, without which 'there would be no way of telling where, down the contractually created ranks of creditors and preferred shareholders, it was fair to stop issuing shares and other claims in the newly organized entity owning the business'.[26]

The wider the power to bind dissentients to a reorganisation, the more complex this task of regulating the distribution of value in the reorganised debtor becomes. A lawmaker might do no more than supply a procedure through which the debtor may propose a plan for the restructuring of some or all stakeholder entitlements that, if endorsed by a majority in each of the classes into which affected stakeholders have been placed for the purposes of voting over the plan, and sanctioned by a court, will bind the minority in each class. (This is essentially the scheme of arrangement procedure provided in Part 26 of the Companies Act 2006 (UK)). If class composition is determined with reference to the rights that stakeholders have outside the plan (so that, for example, secured creditors are grouped separately from unsecured creditors to the extent of their security[27]), as well as those promised under it,[28] a plan that attracts the support of a majority in each class is presumptively one in which each class expects to do better under the plan than it would in the 'non-plan world'.[29] Provided that stakeholders were given 'the proper information by reference to which to vote',[30] and that there is nothing to suggest that any of the majority in one or more classes were influenced by collateral interests that mean their vote cannot be taken to be representative,[31] the court might be prepared to treat the question of how *much* better off each class will be, relative to the others, as settled by the parties – 'the affirmative vote in each class indicat[ing] that the different classes of creditors are all content with the allocation of the required compromises and anticipated benefits of the restructuring as between them'.[32]

[23] In particular, through the setting of the minimum bid or 'upset price', as to which see Skeel (n 20) 58–60, Weiner ibid, and Spring (n 21).

[24] The receivership certificate: see Skeel (n 20) 59–60.

[25] Clark (n 5) 1253, citing ss 77 and 77B of the Bankruptcy Act, introduced in 1933 and 1934, and Chapter X of the Chandler Act (1938).

[26] Clark (n 5) 1252.

[27] Assuming the priority of such security would be respected outside of the plan.

[28] So that a difference in treatment may warrant separation: *Re UDL Holdings Ltd* [2002] 1 HKC 172; below, text to n 226.

[29] *Re Stronghold Insurance Company Limited* [2018] EWHC 2909 (Ch), [2019] 2 BCLC 11, [49] per Hildyard J. The more relaxed the approach to class composition, the more likely that the court will need to verify this: see below, n 256.

[30] So as to make it appropriate for the court to treat them as 'the best judges of their commercial situation': *Re Algeco Scotsman PIK SA* [2017] EWHC 2236 (Ch), [2018] BCC 82, [38], also noted in Chris Howard, Presley Warner and Chris Beatty, *Restructuring Law and Practice*, 3rd edn (LexisNexis Butterworths, 2022) [7.518].

[31] *Re Noble Group* [2018] EWHC 2911 (Ch), [2019] BCC 349, [111].

[32] *In re AGPS Bondco Plc* [2024] EWCA Civ 24; [2024] Bus LR 745, [155] (*Re Adler*), per Snowden LJ and to similar effect, Robert T Swaine, 'Reorganization of Corporations: Certain Developments of the Last Decade' (1927) 27(8) *Columbia Law Review* 901, 920.

The obvious limitation of such a procedure is that it can only be used to treat classes of claim with the support of the majority in every class, however junior, and however valueless their claims might otherwise (in the non-plan world) be. One way of paralysing the veto power of such classes would be to combine the restructuring procedure with a procedure that enables the transfer of the debtor's assets to a new company, focusing the restructuring on the 'in the money' classes (asked to surrender their claims in exchange for claims against New Co), and leaving 'out of the money' classes behind in an empty shell,[33] except to the extent that those 'in the money' resolve that it is in their interests to issue new claims to the holders of more junior claims.[34] But this method for the treatment of those presently 'out of the money' requires a new company to be interposed, to which assets must be able to be transferred, free and clear of existing liabilities. (In English law, the administration procedure in Schedule B1 of the Insolvency Act 1986 can be used to execute such a transfer, a usage that courts have facilitated[35]). And such a hybrid process provides no means of resolving conflicts between 'in the money' classes over the distribution of value in New Co.

These challenges can be answered by introducing a 'cross-class cram-down' power: a power for the court to confirm a plan for the reorganisation of claims that has not been supported by the requisite majority in every class, provided there is assent from at least some classes that will see their rights altered.[36] Such a power provides a means of directly securing a 'new deal' with dispersed stakeholders in a large and complex business and reduces the ability of parties to 'hold up' the restructuring (that is, to threaten to obstruct the restructuring in order to extract value from other parties).[37] By removing such frictions, gains stand to be made. But the introduction of such a power also raises questions that do not arise – or do not arise to the same extent – in a simple (non-hybrid) procedure that is premised for its availability on support from the majority in each class. Since a majority in each class have *not* agreed, the plan cannot be received as one that presumptively leaves each class better off than they would be in the 'non-plan world'. To avoid the risk that the plan is nothing more than an attempt by assenting classes to expropriate value from dissenting classes, there needs to be some inquiry into the likely outcome for the dissenting classes if the plan is not confirmed,[38] and some process for verifying that the plan will likely produce an improvement on this. And then there is the question of how *much* better off each class will be, relative

[33] Because the consideration for the transfer is not cash, but claims.

[34] A choice must be made as to how to value the assets for the purpose of determining in which class 'value breaks'. Those 'below the line' are deprived of any option value their claim would otherwise have (Douglas G Baird, 'Present at the Creation: The SEC and the Origins of the Absolute Priority Rule' (2010) 18 *American Bankruptcy Institute Law Review* 591), while those above 'take all'. See Douglas G Baird and Thomas H Jackson, 'Bargaining After the Fall and the Contours of the Absolute Priority Rule' (1988) 55 *Chicago Law Review* 738; Sarah Paterson, 'Bargaining in Financial Restructuring: Market Norms, Legal Rights and Regulatory Standards' (2014) 14(2) *Journal of Corporate Law Studies* 333.

[35] Below, text to n 260.

[36] Without which there would be no reason to think that stakeholders will be better off under the plan than in the 'non-plan world' (n 29 above). This suggests that assent from a class that would be 'in the money' in the non-plan world is particularly important.

[37] Anthony J Casey, 'Chapter 11's Renegotiation Framework and the Purpose of Corporate Bankruptcy' (2020) 120 *Columbia Law Review* 1709, 1753–55.

[38] What English courts term the 'likely counterfactual comparator': *Virgin Active Holdings Limited* [2021] EWHC 1246 (Ch), [2022] 2 BCLC 62, [224] per Snowden J.

to the others. This is not a question that can be treated as settled by the parties: dissent means the court cannot treat all classes as 'content with the allocation of the required compromises and anticipated benefits of the restructuring as between them'.[39] But by what process, and by reference to which principles, should a court determine a complaint by a dissenting class that the plan is unfair because it distributes 'too much' value to an assenting class?

In the US, courts initially wrestled with this question in the context of equity receivership reorganisations, when asked to determine the conditions under which assets could be transferred free of liabilities to a new company in which senior creditors and at least some shareholders of the old company would share,[40] with junior creditors left behind. Rather than simply permit those 'in the money' on a present-day valuation to determine whether, and on what terms, 'out of the money' stakeholders would be entitled to share in New Co,[41] courts articulated a principle of priority to regulate the distribution of value in New Co. The principle, as articulated in the decision of the US Supreme Court in *Boyd*, was this: a transfer to a new company owned at least in part by shareholders of Old Co could only take place on a 'free and clear' basis if junior creditors had been made a 'fair offer' of a position in New Co that reflected their priority position in Old Co, and in particular the priority of debt claims over equity.[42] The principle was a 'fixed' one in the sense that its application did not depend on whether the aggrieved junior creditors were in or out of the money at the time of the transfer.[43] The principle did not 'require the impossible, and make it necessary to pay an unsecured creditor in cash as a condition of stockholders retaining an interest' – instead, the Court explained, the interest of the junior creditor could be preserved by the making of an offer 'on equitable terms' of a claim (the Court suggesting 'income bonds', ie contingent debt securities,[44] or preferred stock) in New Co.[45]

What exactly it was that *Boyd* required was contested.[46] One possibility was that the principle required claims to be distributed in the same way that cash would be distributed in a realisation (what Bonbright and Bergman termed 'absolute' or 'full' priority[47]), so that a junior class could not receive value unless the plan promised

[39] Above, text to n 32.

[40] Usually subject to the payment of a cash 'assessment', which entitled the subscriber to securities in New Co, but 'in practice … the contributions were structured so that the securities received were often worth more than the amount contributed to the reorganization': Bruce A Markell, 'Owners, Auctions and Absolute Priority in Bankruptcy Reorganizations' (1991) 44 *Stanford Law Review* 69, 76, and James C Bonbright and Milton M Bergman, 'Two Rival Theories of Priority Rights of Security Holders in a Corporate Reorganization' (1928) 28(2) *Columbia Law Review* 127. See also Paul D Cravath, 'The Reorganization of Corporations' in *Some Legal Phases of Corporate Financing, Reorganization, and Regulation* (Association of the Bar of the City of New York, 1923), 182.

[41] As was argued for in *Northern Pacific Railway Co v Boyd*, 228 US 482 (1913), 505–7.

[42] *Boyd* ibid 505, drawing on *Louiseville Trust Co v Louisville* 174 US 683 (see also Cravath (n 40) 191), and 508. As to the mechanism by which the refusal of such an offer would prevent a later challenge (waiver and estoppel), see *Boyd* ibid 508 and Markell (n 40) 81. *Boyd* was decided by a bare majority.

[43] *Boyd* (n 41) 507; Markell (n 40) 81.

[44] Markell (n 40) 80.

[45] *Boyd* (n 41) 508.

[46] Bonbright and Bergman (n 40) 155; John D Ayer, 'Rethinking absolute priority after *Ahlers*' (1989) 87 *Michigan Law Review* 963, 973.

[47] Bonbright and Bergman (n 40).

claims to a more senior class the value of which amounted to full satisfaction of principal and outstanding interest; this would have to somehow be reconciled with the need to raise new finance, which in receivership reorganisations was typically contributed by shareholders.[48] But valuing rights in the reorganised business would necessarily be a speculative exercise, and some therefore argued for a priority rule that would postpone any entitlement of a junior class to income to that of a more senior class (and in this sense preserve the relative position of classes), but not condition the ability of a junior claimholder to retain value on evidence that senior claimholders had been promised claims expected to amount to full satisfaction. The seminal paper on this is Bonbright and Bergman's,[49] though it must be said that this paper is somewhat vague in its specification of a relative alternative to absolute priority,[50] perhaps because the idea came not from theory, but from observations of practice, where senior bondholders appeared to emerge from reorganisations with claims that, whilst first-ranking in entitlement to income, did not in value come close to offering 'full compensation for … defaulted principal and interest',[51] while some junior claimholders received claims beyond that which could be explained as necessary to secure new finance.[52] Because an absolute priority rule would be costly to apply – necessitating a valuation exercise that was 'necessarily a guess' and which would invite litigation[53] – the authors were in favour of exploring the development of an alternative, provided it was sufficiently clear, but stopped short of doing so themselves.[54]

In time, however, the position hardened in favour of absolute priority. In the *Los Angeles Lumber*[55] decision, the Supreme Court held that a principle of full or absolute priority had been carried over into the new statutory reorganisation framework by its requirement that plans be 'fair and equitable'.[56] This would not prevent the issue of claims to shareholders for new finance, but only to the extent that claims were 'reasonably equivalent' to a 'fresh contribution' made 'in money or money's worth'[57] (the 'new value exception', or arguably more accurately, 'new value corollary'[58]). It has been argued that the Court's reading was a 'somewhat imaginative' one[59] that obscured the debate over *Boyd's* interpretation, and which can only really be understood by reference to the background of the judge that gave the opinion.[60] Mr Justice Douglas had previously led a review by the Securities and Exchange Commission (SEC) of reorganisation

[48] Markell (n 40) 76; Cravath (n 40) 182.

[49] Bonbright and Bergman (n 40), refining Swaine (n 32); see also Donald S Bernstein and Douglas G Baird's 'Absolute Priority, Valuation Uncertainty, and the Reorganization Bargain' (2005) 115 *Yale Law Journal* 1930.

[50] Also termed a 'rule of priority of income position' alternative to a 'rule of priority of principal'.

[51] Bonbright and Bergman (n 40) 141.

[52] ibid 144.

[53] ibid 161.

[54] ibid 164. Modern work by Baird offers a much clearer specification of a 'relative priority' alternative, similarly grounded in concerns about valuation costs: below, text to n 85.

[55] *Case v Los Angeles Lumber Products Co Ltd*, 308 US 106 (1939).

[56] ibid 116–20.

[57] ibid 121–22.

[58] See Markell (n 40), explaining why the 'exception' is better understood as exemplifying the rule's application; *Bank of America National Trust and Savings Association v 203 North LaSalle Street Partnership*, 526 US 434 (1999), 444.

[59] Skeel (n 20) 124; see also Ayer (n 46) 975, characterising the reasoning as 'poppycock'.

[60] Skeel (n 20) 119–27; Douglas G Baird and Robert K Rasmussen, 'Boyd's Legacy and Blackstone's Ghost' (1999) 8 *Supreme Court Review* 393.

practice from an investor protection standpoint, resulting in a scathing report[61] in which existing processes were characterised as little more than vehicles for insider managers and their bankers to wrestle for control[62] at the expense of ordinary outside investors.[63] In the *Lumber* case, an amicus brief submitted by the US Government – drafted to reflect the interests of the SEC and the Interstate Commerce Commission in securing an 'authoritative declaration' as to the interpretation of the 'fair and equitable' requirement – urged the Court to 'reaffirm the doctrine of absolute priority', with a new value corollary strictly limited to claims reasonably equivalent to a new contribution in money or money's worth, with a view to curtailing the ability of 'junior interests' to divert value away from outside investors.[64] This is, as Baird and Rasmussen argue, what Douglas J then did, in an opinion that 'tracks the brief'.[65]

Later, the reforms of 1978 produced a statutory expression of the rule in Chapter 11 of the Code, but importantly now confined – in line with the analysis above[66] – to cases in which the court was invited to confirm a plan in the presence of one or more affected or 'impaired'[67] dissenting classes (a non-consensual plan).[68] Classes who are set to receive nothing under the plan on account of their claims are deemed to dissent.[69] Whether the plan is consensual (supported by the requisite majority in each class) or non-consensual, § 1129(a) stipulates a 'best-interests-of-creditors' requirement that a dissenting member of any impaired class must be promised claims of a value not less than they would be expected to receive if the debtor were instead liquidated under Chapter 7 on the plan date. But in non-consensual cases, § 1129(b) adds to this baseline protection by requiring that, inter alia,[70] and with respect to each impaired dissenting class, the plan be 'fair and equitable', and providing that, for a dissenting class of unsecured claims, the condition that the plan be fair and equitable 'includes' a requirement that either class members are being promised value equal to the allowed amount of their claims, or that no holder of any more junior claim will receive any value on account of such claim.[71] As others emphasise, the rule is only one part of the 'fair and equitable' inquiry,[72] and it is accepted that the court must also be satisfied that creditors are not being promised value exceeding the allowed amount of their claims.[73]

[61] *Report on the Study and Investigation of the Work, Activities, Personnel and Functions of Protective and Reorganization Committees*, 1937.

[62] Aided by a small, elite reorganisation Bar 'charging all that the traffic will bear': ibid Part I, 866–68.

[63] See ibid vol 1, Section 11 ('Summary') and for further discussion and critical analysis, Skeel (n 20) ch 4.

[64] *Case v Los Angeles Lumber Products Co Ltd*, 1939 WL 48783 (US) (Appellate Brief) Supreme Court of the United States.

[65] Baird and Rasmussen (n 60), also exploring in this section the connection between Douglas J and Jerome Frank.

[66] As to the significance of this change, Markell (n 40) 88.

[67] See § 1129(a)(8), (b)(1)–(2) and § 1124; Miller and Berkovich (n 4) 1353.

[68] At least one impaired class must have accepted the plan, discounting any insider acceptances: § 1129(a)(10).

[69] § 1126(g), and Markell (n 40) fn 298.

[70] Other requirements include that the plan not 'discriminate unfairly'; see further Miller and Berkovich (n 4).

[71] § 1129(b)(1), and (2)(B). Separate provision is made as to the treatment of classes of secured claim in § 1129(b)(2)(A). We do not focus on this aspect of § 1129, but it is explored in detail by Ted Janger in Chapter 5 of this book.

[72] As emphasised by Anthony J Casey in 'Bankruptcy's Endowment Effect' (2016) 33 *Emory Bankruptcy Developments Journal* 142, 147.

[73] Markell (n 40) 72, citing, inter alia, *In re Evans Products Co*, 65 BR 870, 875 (SD Fla 1986), and Casey ibid.

The extent to which § 1129 accommodates or implies the continuation of the 'new value exception' (or, rather, 'corollary') has been much contested.[74] The application of both the absolute priority rule and the 'exception' was particularly controversial in small company cases, where it might not be meaningful to speak of the continuation of the business without the owner-manager entrepreneur, but in which the negotiation of a consensual plan might be foiled by creditor apathy,[75] the costs of the Chapter 11 process for a non-consensual plan (which include the costs of valuing the post-plan debtor for the purposes of applying the rule) might dwarf the estate,[76] and (assuming the exception's availability) the entrepreneur might be unable to offer reasonably equivalent value in 'money or money's worth', as that requirement has been understood by the courts,[77] for a continuing stake. This type of case has since been addressed by the introduction of a small business sub-chapter with a different process in which the rule does not apply;[78] otherwise, the status of the 'exception' remains an open question.[79]

A range of other questions of interpretation have also been litigated, including whether § 1129 would be infringed by a Chapter 11 plan that provides that, in the event an intermediate class dissents (so that the rule is engaged), an equal ranking or more senior class will waive some entitlement that it would have to value under the plan and distribute it to a more junior class ('gifting plans'),[80] and the extent to which the expression of absolute priority in § 1129 ought to affect the exercise of discretion to dismiss a Chapter 11 case on terms providing for a distribution of the estate to some senior and junior, but not intermediate, classes ('structured dismissals').[81] The extent to which pre-commencement claims can properly be paid as an expense of the process, so that they do not need to be treated by the plan (and therefore fall outside the rules governing plan confirmation, including, in non-consensual cases, the absolute priority rule), has also been controversial.[82] The testing of these kinds of questions can be

[74] See Michelle Craig, 'The new value exception: A plea for modification or elimination' (1995) 11 *Bankruptcy Developments Journal* 781, explaining the doctrinal debate in Part II; Ayer (n 46). In *Norwest Bank Worthington v Ahlers* 485 US 197 (1988), the Supreme Court declined to resolve the question but held that the 'labor, experience and expertise' being offered by farmers in exchange for a continuing stake in the farming enterprise could not constitute new value in 'money or money's worth'. In *LaSalle* (n 58), the Supreme Court again declined to resolve the question but held that market testing would be required to assess the adequacy of a proposed 'fresh contribution' by shareholders.

[75] Ted Janger, 'The U.S. Small Business Bankruptcy Amendments: A Global Model for Reform' (2020) (29) *International Insolvency Review* 254, 257.

[76] Jonathan M Seymour and Steven L Schwarcz, 'Corporate Restructuring under Relative and Absolute Priority Default Rules: A Comparative Assessment' (2021) *University of Illinois Law Review* 1, 31.

[77] See *Ahlers* (n 74) as discussed in Craig (n 74) 811–12.

[78] Sub-chapter V of Chapter 11, as to which see Janger (n 75), and Bruce Grohsgal, 'How absolute is the absolute priority rule in bankruptcy? The case for structured dismissals' (2017) 8 *William & Mary Business Law Review* 43, on historical precursors.

[79] *Collier on Bankruptcy* (n 4), § 1129.03[4](c).

[80] See Miller and Berkovich (n 4); Jonathan C Lipson, 'The secret life of priority: Corporate reorganization after *Jevic*' (2018) 93(2) *Washington Law Review* 631, 651–52, 700–07.

[81] See *Czyzewski v Jevic Holding Corp* 137 S Ct 973 (2017); Vincent Buccola, 'The Janus Faces of Reorganization Law' (2018) 44 *Journal of Corporation Law* 1, 8.

[82] See Buccola, ibid and Stephen J Lubben, 'The Overstated Absolute Priority Rule' (2016) XXI *Fordham Journal of Corporate & Financial Law* 581.

characterised, as Tung and Roe have argued, as a kind of 'jostling' over priority at the perimeters of the absolute priority rule.[83]

As to the rule itself, a large literature debates the desirability of the choice of an absolute priority rule for non-consensual plans, and the strictness with which the rule should be applied, having regard to the costs of its application, and its effects on investment incentives in prior periods.[84] In relation to the costs of its application, the requirement for the court to alight on a value for the post-confirmation, restructured debtor – without which the court cannot establish whether the claims being issued to a dissenting class are likely to amount to full satisfaction, such that there is value available to be distributed to some more junior class – has motivated work by Douglas Baird on the feasibility of a 'relative priority' alternative.[85] Taking as his paradigm case a restructuring of claims against a large company held by 'professional, sophisticated investors',[86] Baird takes as a given that it is desirable for new claims to be distributed in accordance with the priority that investor classes have constructed between themselves,[87] and explores how it might be possible to do so *without* requiring the value of these claims to be established at the time of confirmation. In particular, Baird explores the feasibility of postponing this question to some later period, when better information is available, with the option value of junior claims (represented in the 'possibility that the firm might increase in value enough to pay the senior investors in full'[88]) preserved in the interim. In Baird's words:

> Relative priority fully respects the right of senior creditors to be paid before junior creditors. It differs from absolute priority only in the way it identifies the time at which the rights of the players are assessed. Under existing Chapter 7 in the United States [the liquidation chapter of the Bankruptcy Code], the rights of stakeholders are assessed the moment that the bankruptcy petition is filed. Under existing Chapter 11, the rights are assessed only at the time that the plan is confirmed. A regime of relative priority postpones the moment of valuation further still.[89]

[83] Frederick Tung and Mark J Roe, 'Breaking Bankruptcy Priority: How Rent-Seeking Upends the Creditors' Bargain' (2013) 99 *Virginia Law Review* 1236.

[84] See Barry E Adler and George G Triantis, 'The Aftermath of North LaSalle Street' (2002) 70 *University of Cincinnati Law Review* 1225, and Stanley D Longhofer, 'A note on absolute priority rule, violations, credit rationing and efficiency' (1995 working paper), reviewing some of the literature; Anthony J Casey, 'The Creditors' Bargain and Option-Preservation Priority in Chapter 11' (2011) 78(3) *University of Chicago Law Review* 759, focusing on distortions produced by the rule in relation to the deployment decision within bankruptcy, and arguing that countervailing effects in the period prior to commencement are overstated.

[85] Douglas G Baird, 'Priority Matters: Absolute Priority, Relative Priority, and the Costs of Bankruptcy' (2017) 165 *University of Pennsylvania Law Review* 785, building on 'Present at the Creation' (n 34).

[86] 'Priority Matters' ibid, fn 40 and accompanying text.

[87] Outside of Baird's paradigm case (a restructuring of claims issued to professional investors on terms that clarify the entitlement of each, relative to the other) the presence of operational creditors will complicate this task. The terms for the payment of operational creditor claims (typically, that they will be paid as and when they fall due) will usually be unrelated to those governing the order in which investors are paid, save that the issue of security interests to the latter may limit the assets available for the former. (A point also made by Lubben (n 82) 605.) Baird assumes that operational creditors will be paid, and, focusing on the position as between investor classes, argues that respecting existing priority does not necessarily imply a commitment to absolute priority ((n 85) Part I; *cf* Barry Adler and George Triantis, 'Debt Priority and Options in Bankruptcy: A Policy Intervention' (2017) 91(3) *American Bankruptcy Law Journal* 563, section II). We are grateful to Tony Casey for discussion on this point.

[88] Douglas G Baird, 'Letter to Prof. dr. R.J. de Weijs', 7 March 2019; see also 'Priority matters' (n 85) 793.

[89] 'Letter' ibid.

Option value is not to be preserved because it is somehow unfair to deprive junior claimants of this (sophisticated investors can, Baird explains, 'adapt themselves to any priority regime',[90] such that it is not particularly meaningful to characterise the application of the prevailing rule to them as unfair). Instead, its preservation is simply an incident of postponing the 'day of reckoning' – the moment at which 'accounts are squared'[91] – to some later period, rather than (as in an absolute priority regime) requiring the court to function as though it were distributing cash in a realisation when confirming a plan for the distribution of claims, allocating value to claims down the priority waterfall.[92] Baird acknowledges that the challenges associated with implementing a relative priority rule[93] might be such that, in the end, an absolute priority rule is found superior 'simply because it is simplest to implement'.[94]

Whilst the choice of priority rule in § 1129 has been debated, nothing in the literature suggests that it would have been better if Congress had supplied the courts with power to confirm a plan in the presence of a dissenting class, but been silent on the question of when it would be fair to do so, and in particular as to the treatment of a complaint by a dissenting class that a plan is unfair because it distributes 'too much' value to an assenting class. To the contrary, the literature suggests that it was desirable to supply such a rule, for the reason that such rules can – provided that they are sufficiently clear in their specification of the entitlement of the dissenting class to value over and above the baseline – function to set the parameters for, or narrow the set of possible outcomes in, a non-consensual case, and in so doing facilitate the negotiation of consensual plans at lower cost.[95] This means that the fact that a priority rule may be (very) costly to apply – as with the rule in § 1129 – does not mean that it would be better not to supply any rule at all, and militates in favour of the supply of a clear rule (one that, as Baird puts it, 'defines entitlements of the players with precision')[96] over a vague fairness standard.[97]

[90] 'Priority matters' (n 85) 798.

[91] 'Priority matters' (n 85) 812, 791; see also Casey (n 84) 773.

[92] In contrast, in Casey's work on relative priority, the preservation of option value is itself the goal, in a bid to avoid the distortions in incentives to maximise value within the process that Casey expects absolute priority to produce (see above n 84).

[93] Even on simple facts involving only two classes of investor claim, one issued as equity and the other as debt, Baird identifies various challenges in implementing relative priority by giving the latter all equity and the former a call option on this, including in relation to the setting of the strike price, and the correction of distortions flowing from a mismatch between ownership and control rights prior to the exercise of the option: 'Priority Matters' (n 85) 815–19. We have also drawn attention to the complexities associated with the presence of operational creditors, unless it is simply assumed that they will be paid in full (n 87 above).

[94] 'Priority matters' (n 85) 819.

[95] See Lipson (n 80) 679; Seymour and Schwarcz (n 76); Baird, 'Letter' (n 88), comparing his conception of relative priority with vaguer European 'relative priority' (see below, section III) and suggesting that a loose standard expands rather than limits the 'range of possible bargains', provides 'no benchmarks' and 'does not create a sensible bargaining environment'; and *Jevic* (n 81) 987.

[96] Baird, 'Letter' (n 88).

[97] The precise effects of a clear priority rule on settlement dynamics will of course also depend on the rule's content. In Seymour and Schwarcz's analysis of the effects of the absolute priority rule in § 1129 (n 76), the rule is said to promote consensual resolution not only because it is clear, but because of what it is that the rule (clearly) requires: the threat of a costly valuation exercise with associated variance, combined with the threat for junior classes of being 'wiped out', is said to encourage junior insiders to reveal information relevant to value that in turn encourages senior classes to make concessions. Conversely, Paterson (n 34) has explored

To be sure, statutory frameworks that are initially unclear can become clearer over time, as players battle over their content. A cross-class cram-down power supplied without a priority rule, or which is expressed to be subject to a vague standard rather than a clear rule, will be tested, and this testing will generate guidance on the approach of the relevant courts to the resolution of priority conflicts (a process of secondary rule-production, to return to Clark's taxonomy). But it will be costly to test the framework in this way,[98] and this fact, combined with the effects of uncertainty on settlement dynamics, makes us suspect that it would be better for professional investors if the legislature simply specified the relative entitlement of the dissenting class to value (over and above the baseline) from the outset. There is, of course, one way in which such sophisticated players might benefit from vagueness in the long-run, and that is where it provides opportunities to 'jostle' for interpretations that enable value to be extracted from classes of less sophisticated player.[99] But this prospect simply adds to the case for the supply of a clear rule from the outset.

To what should the dissenting class be (clearly) entitled? We do not think this question admits of a single answer; everything must surely depend on the context. Priority rules do not operate in a vacuum, but rather as part of a complex system of legal rules and market norms.[100] Other features of the system might interact with a priority rule in such a way as to magnify its expected costs or mute its expected benefits. Literature on the absolute priority rule in § 1129 assesses the costs and benefits of this choice of rule *given other aspects of the legal framework* – given, for example, the automatic stay and exclusivity period (during which time the debtor alone can propose a plan) in Chapter 11,[101] or given the debtor's ability to grant security over all assets, including cash, and the treatment of these *in rem* rights by Chapter 11[102] – and assumes the capacity of courts to conduct the valuation exercise that the rule requires. Changing one or more of these background factors could be predicted to alter the analysis of the expected costs and benefits of introducing a rule modelled on § 1129, even before the lawmaker

how an approach to priority that does not (unlike § 1129) cap upside potential for senior creditor classes might disincentivise participation by those classes in settlement negotiations. We take this to mean that the supply of a clear priority rule may not be *sufficient* to create a 'sensible bargaining environment' (n 95 above), but not to mean that it is unnecessary to do so. See, to similar effect, *Jevic* (n 81), and, reaching the same conclusion, Lipson (n 80) 678–80.

[98] See the illuminating analysis in Tung and Roe (n 83) 1275–78.

[99] See ibid at 1274–75 on the inefficiencies that may flow from priority 'jumping' when those 'jumped' cannot adjust to that fact. See also Lipson (n 80) 647, and on the perception that experiments with a vague 'relative' alternative to absolute priority 'systematically disadvantaged small creditors and brought untoward benefits to insiders', Baird, 'Letter' (n 88) and above, text to n 63.

[100] A theme of Paterson (n 34) and of Paterson's later monograph *Corporate Reorganization Law and Forces of Change* (Oxford University Press, 2020), and of Skeel (n 20).

[101] Adler and Triantis (n 84) 1226.

[102] See Casey (n 84) on the effect of issuing a blanket lien on incentives to maximise value pre-and post-commencement, in a world in which absolute priority is stipulated; *cf* Melissa B Jacoby and Edward J Janger, 'Tracing Equity: Realizing and Allocating Value in Chapter 11' (2018) 96 *Texas Law Review* 673, taking a different view as to the entitlement of the secured lender under § 1129 having regard to other provisions of the Code. For a summary of the ways in which blanket security might be predicted to affect the debtor's bargaining power in Chapter 11 as analysed eg by Adler and Triantis (n 84), see Paterson *Corporate Reorganization Law and Forces of Change* (n 100) section 5.2.3.

considers firm-level factors that might affect the rule's suitability.[103] We do not therefore approach our survey of recent experiments with the design of priority rules in the EU (section III) and the UK (section IV) with some 'ideal' rule in mind, at least when it comes to the regulation of the kinds of conflicts that Baird focused on (between classes of professional investors, who can in principle adapt to any rule).

In relation to non-adjusting creditors – those who cannot adjust the terms of their relationship with the debtor to reflect their priority position or (in the case of involuntary creditors) do not consent to the relationship at all – we *do* see benefits in supplying a rule of absolute priority like that in § 1129.[104] Lawmakers routinely elevate the position of creditor constituencies thought to be non-adjusting, so that they rank above others in a realisation. If there are good reasons to write such a rule – and, at least in relation to involuntary creditors, we think that there are[105] – an absolute priority rule is attractive in requiring the realisation policy to be carried over, to the maximum extent possible, into the reorganisation framework. Take, for example, a rule elevating tort claims. Such a rule may be aimed not only at securing compensation for victims, but also at inducing debtors (through the threat of constraints on credit supply, as financial creditors adjust to possible demotion) to take greater precautions to avoid inflicting torts in the first place.[106] These incentive effects should be maximised by a priority rule that requires claims in the reorganisation to be distributed just as though they were cash in a realisation, so that a dissenting class must be likely to be *fully* satisfied under the plan before claims can be distributed (other than for new value) further down the priority waterfall. (In theory, the same result should follow from adopting Bairdian relative priority, which similarly seeks to strictly respect seniority but postpone valuation;[107] we do not pursue this further only because of our doubts about the feasibility of implementing such a rule).

III. Recent Experiments with the Design of Priority Rules in the EU

In 2019, the EU adopted the Preventive Restructuring Directive (PRD). The PRD requires Member States to have in place 'preventive restructuring frameworks' that

[103] See eg above text to nn 75 et seq on small companies; see also Adler and Triantis (n 84) on how arguments that absolute priority may introduce perverse incentives for managers in distress are most salient for closely-held firms (1234).

[104] This does not mean that we exclude the possibility of claims being issued for new value; we follow others in thinking of this as a corollary of, rather than an exception to, the rule (above, n 58).

[105] See also Adler and Triantis, 'Debt Priority and Options in Bankruptcy' (n 87) reporting 'little academic opposition' to proposals to give tort claimants priority over secured lenders (570).

[106] ibid; Christopher Painter, 'Tort Creditor Priority in the Secured Credit System: Asbestos Times, the Worst of Times' (1984) 36(4) *Stanford Law Review* 1045.

[107] Consistently with this, see Vasile Rotaru, 'The Restructuring Directive: A functional law and economics analysis from a French law perspective' (2019): https://droitetcroissance.fr/wp-content/uploads/2019/10/Vasile-Rotaru-The-Restructuring-Directive-a-functional-law-and-economics-analysis-from-a-French-law-perspective.pdf, [188], characterising Bairdian relative priority as 'in fact a rule of absolute priority with a delayed crystallisation'.

conform to the 'minimum standards' stipulated in the Directive.[108] As the instrument is a directive (rather than a regulation), it is left to Member States to determine how best to secure this result,[109] and, to the extent necessary, to transpose the Directive by reforming national restructuring laws, having regard to other features of the national context. Consistently with this, the Directive provides that a Member State's preventive restructuring framework may be contained in one or more procedures, so long as the overall framework coherently secures the rights and safeguards provided for in the Directive.[110] Matters are further complicated by the fact that, at almost every stage in the elaboration of its 'minimum standards', the Directive presents Member States with an option to derogate from, or add to, what is stipulated.[111] This optionality has been characterised as the product of 'difficult negotiations' on the text between 'stakeholders with profoundly divergent interests';[112] the result is an instrument that can perhaps at its highest be said to aim at securing 'a *degree of* harmonisation' among Member States.[113]

This optionality extends to the design of rules of priority and related 'best-interests-of-creditors' (baseline protection) rules. The Directive requires Member States to provide for class-based voting[114] and for cross-class cram-down. The exercise of the cross-class cram-down power shall be conditional on, inter alia, the plan being supported either by (a majority in) the majority of affected classes or by a specified number of 'in the money' affected classes (as Member States decide[115]), and on compliance with a 'best-interests-of-creditors' test,[116] a rule of priority,[117] and a requirement that 'no class of affected parties can, under the restructuring plan, receive or keep more than the full amount of its claims or interests'.[118] But options are provided in relation to the design of the baseline rule, and in relation to the design of the priority rule, which leaves room for Member States to diverge as to the entitlement of a dissenting class. Separate provision for Member States to render certain types of liabilities immune from treatment under restructuring frameworks creates further scope for divergence.[119]

We first set out the background to the PRD (subsection A), noting what was initially proposed in relation to rules of priority. We then examine the approach to priority in the final text of the instrument (subsection B), before turning in subsection C to the rules chosen by Germany, the Netherlands and Sweden.

[108] Directive (EU) 2019/1023 (n 7), Recitals 1 and 12.
[109] Article 288 TFEU.
[110] Directive (EU) 2019/1023 (n 7), Art 4(5); see also Recitals 16, and 96.
[111] According to one account, there are 70 options: see Reinhard Bork, 'Pre-insolvency frameworks: Developments in the European Union' (2024) 33 *International Insolvency Review* 6.
[112] Rotaru (n 107). The record of parliamentary debate on the Directive gives a clear sense of the challenge: see 'Verbatim report of proceedings of 27 March 2019', C/2024/03830, 123 et seq. See also Reinhard Dammann in Paulus and Dammann (eds) (n 2) 'Introduction'.
[113] Recital 8; see also JM Garrido et al, 'Restructuring and Insolvency in Europe: Policy Options in the Implementation of the EU Directive' IMF Working Papers (2021) No 152.
[114] Except in relation to SMEs: see below, text to n 138.
[115] Or where so provided, by at least one class of 'impaired' party: Art 11(1)(b), read with the proviso at the end of (1), and Recital 54; see also above, n 36.
[116] Arts 11(1)(a), 10(2)(d) and 2(1)(6), relevant whenever there are dissenting affected creditors.
[117] Arts 11(1)(c), read with (2).
[118] Art 11(1)(d).
[119] Art 1(5).

A. Background to the PRD

The PRD is the result of a legislative process initiated by the European Commission in 2016.[120] However, the Commission had already previously made efforts aimed at securing a greater convergence of national restructuring laws: the directive proposal of 2016 was preceded by a Commission Recommendation issued in 2014 which stipulated 'minimum standards' for 'preventive restructuring frameworks' to facilitate 'the efficient restructuring of viable enterprises in financial difficulty'.[121] One of the recommendations was to adopt class-based voting.[122] In relation to cross-class cram-down, the Recommendation provided that Member States should be able to introduce or maintain such a power for cases in which a plan was supported by a majority of classes.[123] No priority rule was specified, though the Recommendation did provide that Member States should specify such conditions for court confirmation as necessary to 'ensure the protection of the legitimate interests of creditors', and ensure that dissenting creditors' rights were not reduced below that which could reasonably be expected in the non-plan world.[124]

A review by the Commission published 18 months later concluded that the Recommendation had only had limited impact, and emphasised persisting differences in national legal frameworks ('Enterprises do not have the same opportunities to deal with their financial difficulties everywhere in the Union').[125] In the meantime, harmonisation of restructuring laws had, in 2015, been included in the Commission's Capital Markets Union plan, as part of work to remove 'national barriers to cross-border investment'. The CMU plan promised a 'legislative initiative on business insolvency' aimed at securing greater convergence in national insolvency and restructuring laws with a view to increasing 'legal certainty for cross-border investors' and encouraging timely restructuring.[126]

Accordingly, the Commission launched a proposal for what eventually became the PRD. In line with the Recommendation, the proposed directive would require Member

[120] 'Proposal for a Directive of the European Parliament and of the Council on preventive restructuring frameworks, second chance and measures to increase the efficiency of restructuring, insolvency and discharge procedures and amending Directive 2012/30/EU', COM(2016) 723 final.

[121] 'Commission recommendation of 12 March 2014 on a new approach to business failure and insolvency' [2014] OJ L 74, 65–70, Points 3 and 1. The backdrop to this work was a 2011 European Parliament Resolution recommending harmonisation of 'aspects of restructuring plans', with a view to securing a more 'level playing field' for the internal market: 'Report with recommendations to the Commission on insolvency proceedings in the context of EU company law' (2011/2006/INI) 17.10.2011; Horst Eidenmüller and Kristin van Zwieten, 'Restructuring the European Business Enterprise' (2016) 16 *EBOR* 625.

[122] Point 17.

[123] Point 18.

[124] Point 22(a), (c).

[125] 'Evaluation of the Implementation of the Commission Recommendation of 12.3.2014', 30 September 2015 section 2.1; see also Horst Eidenmüller, 'Contracting for a European Insolvency Regime' (2017) 18 *EBOR* 273, 275; *cf* Reinout Vriesendorp and Rick van Dommelen, 'The Netherlands: Normative Reports' in Bob Wessels and Stephan Madaus (eds), *Rescue of Business in Europe* (Oxford University Press 2020), noting the role of the Recommendation in kickstarting reform in the Netherlands.

[126] 'Communication from the Commission to the European Parliament, the Council, the European Economic and Social Committee and the Committee of the Regions: Action Plan on Building a Capital Markets Union' COM(2015) 468 final, section 6.2; Sjur Swensen Ellingsæter, 'Optionality and EU harmonization of restructuring and insolvency law: The case of the Preventive Restructuring Directive and priority rules' (2025) *EBOR* (forthcoming).

States to provide for class-based voting over restructuring plans, subject to a 'best-interests-of-creditors' test requiring that dissenters not be left worse off under the plan than they would be if the assets were instead realised,[127] and to empower courts to confirm a plan in the presence of one or more dissenting classes.[128] In contrast to the Recommendation, the exercise of the cross-class cram-down power would be conditional upon the plan complying with an 'absolute priority rule',[129] defined as follows: 'a dissenting class of creditors must be satisfied in full before a more junior class may receive any distribution or keep any interest under the restructuring plan'.[130] A recital would clarify that, '[a]s a corollary', no class of creditor would be permitted to receive or retain value exceeding the amount of those creditors' claims.[131] There are obvious similarities with the US position as we have described it.[132] As in the US case, such a rule would not necessarily prevent the issue of claims to juniors over the objection of a dissenting, more senior, class in exchange for new money. This would depend on the proper construction of the prohibition on receiving 'any distribution or keep(ing) any interest';[133] it is only if this were construed to encompass the issue of claims for new value that a 'new value exception' would be needed.

The absolute priority requirement proved controversial during the ensuing legislative process. A note from the Presidency to the Council reported – without further explanation – that 'a number' of national delegations had questioned its inclusion.[134] It was noted that cross-class cram-down would be a new concept for some Member States, and argued that some flexibility was needed to enable the concept to be fitted into national frameworks.[135] To accommodate the misgivings, the Council agreed upon an approach that would permit Member States to choose between different rules: absolute priority or a 'relative priority rule' alternative, which would introduce a 'different benchmark' for cross-class cram-down. Whereas absolute priority would entitle the dissenting class to be paid in full before a more junior class could retain value, relative priority would only entitle the dissenting class to be treated 'more favourably' than a junior class.[136]

Another area of compromise related to the position of SMEs, after some Member States expressed concern that the introduction of class-based voting could be 'burdensome, costly and, in many cases, unnecessary' for companies with a 'simple capital structure and limited number of creditors'.[137] The compromise was to permit Member

[127] 'Proposal for a Directive' (n 120), proposed Art 10, read with the definitions in Art 2.

[128] Provided at least one affected 'in the money' class assented. Proposed Arts 9(2) and 11.

[129] Proposed Art 11(1)(c).

[130] Proposed Art 2(10).

[131] Proposed Recital 28.

[132] Except that the US rule described in section II is that which regulates the position of a dissenting *unsecured* creditor class, with separate provision made in § 1129 for dissenting secured classes (n 71).

[133] See analogously on the construction of the (somewhat differently worded) § 1129 (n 74) above.

[134] 'Proposal for a Directive of the European Parliament and of the Council on preventive restructuring frameworks, second chance and measures to increase the efficiency of restructuring, insolvency and discharge procedures and amending Directive 2012/30/EU – Policy debate', 15201/17, Brussels 30 November 2017, 5.

[135] ibid.

[136] 'Proposal for a Directive of the European Parliament and of the Council on preventive restructuring frameworks, second chance and measures to increase the efficiency of restructuring, insolvency and discharge procedures and amending Directive 2012/30/EU – General approach' 12536/18, Brussels, 1 October 2018, 5–6.

[137] ibid 5.

States to exempt SMEs from class-based voting, which is reflected in the final text.[138] In such a case the PRD's requirements regarding rules of priority would not appear relevant, although the baseline 'best-interests-of-creditors' test would remain relevant, together with other stipulated safeguards.[139]

B. The PRD's Requirements Regarding Rules of Priority

Pursuant to Article 11(1)(c), the main rule is that cross-class cram-down shall be conditional upon the plan satisfying what has become known as the relative priority rule. This is the requirement that: 'dissenting voting classes of affected creditors are treated at least as favourably as any other class of the same rank and more favourably than any junior class'. This rule appears to bear little relation to what we have termed 'Bairdian relative priority', since the latter requires one class's entitlement to be satisfied ahead of another to be strictly preserved in the issue of new claims, and is designed only to avoid the costs of establishing whether the senior class is likely to be satisfied at the time of plan confirmation. In the Directive's version of relative priority, it is enough to establish that the plan promises a dissenting class 'more favourable' treatment than those junior to it. This entitlement is both vaguer and substantively weaker than the entitlement that a dissenting class would have under either Bairdian relative priority, or an absolute priority alternative.[140] The way in which such a rule is transposed might make it clearer (by putting 'flesh on the bones' of the concept of more favourable treatment), but the evident intention is to secure for the dissenting class something less than the expectation of full satisfaction before a more junior class can retain a claim.

The Directive's relative priority rule has no clear precedent. There is little in the extraneous materials to explain its introduction, but the rule's genesis is commonly ascribed to a report on 'best practices in European restructuring' authored by a research group led by Professor Lorenzo Stanghellini.[141] The Report was finalised against the backdrop of the Commission's directive proposal, and intended to influence negotiations on the final text. It argued for a 'relative priority rule' that would require that:

> (i) each dissenting class is to receive treatment at least as favourable as other classes within the same rank; (ii) no class of a lower rank is to be given equivalent or better treatment than it; and (iii) higher ranking classes must receive no more than the full present economic value of their claims.[142]

[138] PRD Arts 9(4) and 2(2)(c).

[139] See PRD Art 10(1)–(2).

[140] See Seymour and Schwarcz (n 76) 34–35 for discussion on what the Directive's relative priority rule requires as regards the treatment of a dissenting class of general unsecured creditors vis-à-vis equity holders.

[141] Matti Engelberg, 'A theory of relativity in restructuring developed with the Coase Theorem' (2023) 32 *International Insolvency Review* 212, 215; Axel Krohn, 'Rethinking priority: The dawn of the relative priority rule and the new "best interests of creditors" test in the European Union' (2021) 30 *International Insolvency Review* 75, 81; Michael Veder in Paulus and Dammann (eds) (n 2), Art 11, para 31.

[142] Lorenzo Stanghellini, Riz Mokal, Christoph G. Paulus, and Ignacio Tirado (eds), *Best Practices in European Restructuring: Contractualised Distress Resolution in the Shadow of the Law* (Wolters Kluwer Italia, 2018) 47 (Policy Recommendation #2.16).

The Report contains several arguments for this suggested rule, including: first, that an absolute priority rule gives parties incentives to reject a plan in expectation that other parties will bear the restructuring burden; and, secondly, that a relative priority rule permits shareholders to retain equity to a greater extent than an absolute priority rule would, which in turn provides shareholders with an incentive to initiate restructuring proceedings and to contribute their skills and knowledge to the debtor's business.[143] Both arguments have been criticised: the former on the basis that uncertain distributional entitlements can be expected to aggravate rather than ameliorate incentives to dissent;[144] the latter on the basis that such factors would at their highest point in favour of a different approach to the design of restructuring frameworks for SMEs.[145]

It is noteworthy that the European relative priority project does not appear to have been grounded in a desire to avoid the costs of the valuation exercise that the absolute priority rule requires;[146] indeed, the Report's version of relative priority would have required such an exercise, since the capping of the entitlement of senior classes in component (iii)[147] of the proposed rule would require the claims being issued to those classes to be valued. The position is even starker under the Directive, which both stipulates relative priority as the main priority rule, in a formulation that integrates components (i) and (ii) from the Report, and adds that, in addition to compliance with the rule of priority, Member States must ensure that 'no class of affected parties can, under the restructuring plan, receive or keep more than the full amount of its claims or interests'.[148] This of course mirrors the position under the 'fair and equitable' inquiry in § 1129 of the US Code,[149] but in that case the valuation exercise has already had to be conducted to ensure that a dissenting unsecured class will be satisfied in full, so as to permit the retention of value by some more junior class. In contrast, the Directive at once dispenses with absolute priority (and any benefits associated with stipulating the entitlement of the dissenting class in this way) and requires the costs of an absolute priority rule to be incurred.

The relative priority rule is, however, only one of several options that Member States may choose between. Article 11(2) provides that, by way of derogation from the relative

[143] ibid 46.

[144] Rolef de Weijs, Aart Jonkers, and Maryam Malakotipour, 'The Imminent Distortion of European Insolvency Law: How the European Union Erodes the Basic Fabric of Private Law by Allowing "Relative Priority" (RPR)' (2019) 125(4) *Tijdschrift voor Belgisch Handelsrecht* 477, section 6.3, citing some of the literature we cite in section II above on the effects of uncertainty; Baird, 'Letter' (n 88). *Cf* Sarah Paterson in Rodrigo Olivares-Caminal et al, *Debt Restructuring*, 3rd edn (Oxford University Press, 2022) [2.46].

[145] Seymour and Schwarcz (n 76).

[146] Also noted by de Weijs et al (n 144) section 5. The Directive does attempt to limit valuation costs, including by requiring the court's valuation exercise to be limited to cases in which the court is invited to conduct it (see Art 14).

[147] Somewhat surprisingly capped at the amount of the 'full present economic value of their claims'.

[148] Art 11(1)(d). Negotiations on the text of the Directive record the suggestion that: 'If Member States decide to not keep the absolute priority as a whole, it is suggested to keep the requirement that no party can receive more than what he is entitled to': 'Proposal for a Directive of the European Union and of the Council on preventive restructuring frameworks, second chance and measures to increase the efficiency of restructuring, insolvency and discharge procedures and amending Directive 2012/30/EU – Revised text proposal', 15708/17, 20 December 2017, fn 43.

[149] See above, text to n 73.

priority rule, Member States may instead provide that the claims of the dissenting class should be 'satisfied in full by the same or equivalent means' wherever 'a more junior class is to receive any payment or keep any interest under the restructuring plan'. In other words, the rule is that a cross-class cram-down is possible only if either (i) the claims of the creditors in the dissenting class are satisfied in full or (ii) more junior classes retain no value. As the recitals to the Directive put it:

> Alternatively, Member States could protect a dissenting class of affected creditors by ensuring that such dissenting class is paid in full if a more junior class receives any distribution or keeps any interest under the restructuring plan (the 'absolute priority rule').[150]

Again, as regards a class of dissenting unsecured creditors, this appears to us to be similar to what § 1129 requires,[151] although we note that the same recital goes on to say that:

> Member States should have discretion in implementing the concept of 'payment in full', including in relation to the timing of the payment, as long as the principal of the claim and, in the case of secured creditors, the value of the collateral are protected.[152]

This suggests that satisfaction 'in full' is not entirely an autonomous concept of EU law; instead, Member States have some leeway.

A third option for Member States is to adopt an absolute priority rule with exceptions. Member States may provide such exceptions where they are 'necessary in order to achieve the aims of the restructuring plan and where the restructuring plan does not unfairly prejudice the rights or interests of any affected parties'.[153] Recital 56 provides that 'for example' such instances might include where it is 'fair that equity holders keep certain interests under the plan despite a more senior class being obliged to accept a reduction of its claims' or where 'essential suppliers covered by the provision on the stay of individual enforcement actions are paid before more senior classes of creditors'. Although this option is often described as 'relaxed' absolute priority, it is an open question as to whether making the kind of 'exceptional' provision contemplated in Recital 56 would actually produce a departure from US law: we have already seen how the US rule may accommodate a new value 'exception', which may sweep up some of the first category of case,[154] and the second category may, at least to some extent, be accommodated within the US rules on the payment of expenses of the Chapter 11 process.[155] In short, the extent of any departure from the US position, properly understood, will turn on the precise way in which exceptions are formulated and applied at Member State level.

[150] Recital 55.

[151] Again, raising the same question as to the issue of claims for new value (above, text to n 133).

[152] Recital 55. As to the US law position in relation to the treatment of a dissenting class of secured creditor, which we have not considered in this chapter, see Chapter 5 in this book by Ted Janger.

[153] PRD Art 11(2) second subparagraph.

[154] (And in relation to SMEs, the Directive already makes broader provision for a different approach: above n 138).

[155] The Directive does touch on expenses rules at various points (see eg Art 6, Recitals 39 and 25; Art 18 on avoidance; Art 27 on practitioner supervision and remuneration; Art 10 on provision for new finance, broadly construed (see Garcimartin in Paulus and Dammann (eds) (n 2) Art 10 para 27)), but the intended relationship with rules of priority is unclear.

Some further scope for departure from the US position is opened by the fact that the Directive's priority rules regulate the treatment of the dissenting class vis-à-vis any '*junior class*', while § 1129 regulates the treatment of the dissenting (unsecured) class relative to 'the holder of any claim or interest that is junior to the claims of such class'.[156] It is not entirely clear what 'junior class' means here. One interpretation, which would align the Directive's absolute priority rule with that in § 1129, is that it refers to any creditor or shareholder whose priority position in a realisation would be junior to that of the dissenting class. A narrower construction would limit the term 'junior class' to those creditors and shareholders who have been placed in a class for the purposes of voting on the plan. The question matters because the Directive contemplates plans that affect some, but not all, stakeholders;[157] the former should generally vote on the plan (although here the Directive introduces further complexity by permitting Member States to exempt affected classes of equity and subordinated debt from voting[158]); the latter should not.[159]

The narrow construction is more consistent with how the Directive elsewhere uses the term 'class': the Directive elsewhere employs this term to refer to the groups into which the plan has placed creditors and equity-holders for voting.[160] A systematic interpretation therefore supports a narrow construction. However, a teleological interpretation supports the broader construction. If the Directive's rules of priority are understood to be confined to cases in which the junior class set to retain a claim over the objection of a more senior class is actually made party to a plan, the result is that the dissenting class is given the protection of the priority rule in a case in which the plan would alter the claims of the junior class, but not in a case in which the plan would leave the junior class whole. This undermines the protective function of the priority rule,[161] because it suggests that the more generously the junior class is treated relative to the dissenting class, the less likely it is that the dissenting class will be protected by the rule (eg the rule would be engaged where equity-holders are set to retain *some* equity in the presence of a dissenting creditor class, but not where they stand to retain *all* equity). The narrow construction also sits somewhat awkwardly with the Directive's examples in Recital 56 of permissible exceptions to absolute priority, which would not be necessary if the rule could be circumvented by simply leaving such claims outside the plan.[162]

[156] 11 USC § 1129(b)(2)(B). See also Hans Renman, 'Något om de nya planförhandlingsreglerna' (2022) 22 *Ny Juridik* 9.

[157] See Michael Veder in Paulus and Dammann (eds) (n 2), Art 8 section (II); Paterson (n 144) section 2(E).

[158] Art 9(3). The intention is to empower Member States to introduce mechanisms for readily 'wiping out' the most junior interests (Recital 57). This is, of course, precisely what a cross-class cram-down power would do. For analysis as to why the Directive offers so many options regarding equity classes, see Francisco Garcimartin in Paulus and Dammann (eds) (n 2) (Art 12); for present purposes it suffices to note that the exercise of this option should not affect the ability of a dissenting class of unsecured creditor to rely on a Member State's priority rule.

[159] Art 9(2); see also Art 15.

[160] Arts 8(1), 9.

[161] See Recital 55.

[162] We note, too, that the reference in this recital to 'equity holders' is a reference to shareholders generally, and not only those forming part of a voting class. Matti Engelberg et al similarly emphasise the Directive's provision for exceptions to absolute priority and argue for a broad construction of 'junior class', but note authority to the contrary in the Swedish context: Matti Engelberg, Sara Göthlin, Jan Bech and Kim Sommer Jensen, 'Statutory priorities in new Nordic restructuring laws: High-Level Report', 13 March 2024, 54–55. *Stockholm University, Faculty of Law Research Paper Series 134/2024*. Below, text to n 219.

For present purposes, it is enough for us to note that the way in which this question is resolved will determine the scope of a Member State's priority rule. But it does seem to us that, if such rules are given a narrow compass, Member States will need to provide controls elsewhere with a view to securing 'sufficient protection' for the dissenting class and avoiding 'unfair prejudice'– for this is what the Directive's rules of priority are directed to ensuring (Recital 55).

The significance of this question, and of a Member State's choice of priority rule more generally, will depend on other choices made in the transposition of the Directive, including in relation to class composition, the formulation of the 'best-interests-of-creditors' test, and the extent to which certain debts are made non-dischargeable. The approach to class composition will determine how likely it is that the cross-class cram-down power, and related priority rule, will be engaged (the more liberal the approach to class constitution, the less likely). The best-interests-of-creditors test will determine the size of the domain for a priority rule (since this test will set the baseline over and above which the priority rule will regulate the distribution of value). And deeming certain categories of debt to be non-dischargeable in a restructuring process (such that assets cannot remain in the hands of the debtor without payment of these claims in full) will mean that these claimholders no longer need the protection of a priority rule. On all three facets of framework design, the Directive leaves much to Member States to decide.

On class composition, the Directive stipulates only that classes should 'reflect sufficient commonality of interest based on verifiable criteria'; that 'at minimum' secured and unsecured creditors should be separated; and that Member States should 'put in place appropriate measures to ensure that class formation is done with a particular view to protecting vulnerable creditors such as small suppliers',[163] the intention being to signal the possibility of requiring vulnerable constituencies to be classed separately.[164] On baseline protection, the Directive stipulates that dissenters should not be left worse off than:

> if the normal ranking of liquidation priorities under national law were applied, either in the event of liquidation, whether piecemeal or by sale as a going concern, or in the event of the next-best-alternative scenario if the restructuring plan were not confirmed.[165]

The recitals indicate that Member States can decide which counterfactual should be used, but add that, in cross-class cram-down cases, a requirement that creditors not be left worse off than if the business were sold on a going concern basis should be designed so as to ensure that the business is valued 'in the longer term … based on the assumption that the business continues its activity with the minimum of disruption'.[166] This is not entirely easy to reconcile with the counterfactual nature of the test, and in theory could produce a rule that sets the baseline so high as to leave very little work for a priority rule to do. On non-dischargeability, the Directive provides that Member States

[163] Art 9(4).

[164] Recital 44.

[165] Art 2(1)(6). But this is only to be examined by the court where the plan is challenged on this ground: Art 10(2)(d) and proviso, Recital 50; see also Francisco Garcimartin in Paulus and Dammann (eds) (n 2), Art 10, para 28.

[166] Recital 49.

can choose to make, inter alia, tort claims entirely immune from treatment in restructuring frameworks.[167] This is an alternative way to respond to the policy concerns that we articulated in section II. On one level, it promises greater protection to tort victims than anything a priority rule can deliver (since even absolute priority does not command full satisfaction, but only insists that the dissenting class must be fully satisfied before a more junior class can retain value[168]); this may, however, come at the expense of achieving a restructuring even where doing so would be in the interests of the protected class.[169]

C. Choices Made when Transposing the PRD into National Law

This section turns to consider what priority rules Germany, the Netherlands and Sweden opted for when transposing the PRD, as well as related choices in relation to baseline protection, class composition and non-dischargeability. All three jurisdictions implemented a version of an absolute priority rule (APR), but with important differences. In selecting these for discussion, we do not mean to imply that no Member State has opted for relative priority; some have done so.[170] Our chosen jurisdictions are ones with which at least one of us is familiar, and together they provide some insights into the 'varieties of APR' that the Directive is engendering across the Union.

In German law, there was already a precedent for cross-class cram-down with an associated priority rule: the German Insolvency Act (the Insolvenzordnung, or InsO) has, since its entry into force in 1999, provided for the possibility of a company in insolvency proceedings having a plan sanctioned for the restructuring of its debts. To this end, creditors and shareholders are to be divided into classes. The statute provides that small creditors may (but need not) be placed into a separate class,[171] which reportedly inspired the Directive's provision to the same effect.[172] The Act then provides for the possibility of a cross-class cram-down in a statutory provision said to have been modelled on US law.[173] One condition is that members of the dissenting class are not likely to be worse off under the plan than they would be without the plan (the baseline protection or best-interests-of-creditors rule);[174] a second (which is the priority rule) is that the dissenting class receives a reasonable share of the value flowing from restructuring.[175] The latter requires, among other things, that no value is retained by

[167] Art 1(5)(c). Worker claims can also be excluded from the scope of restructuring frameworks: Art 1(5)(a).

[168] See also above, text to n 45, on the US Supreme Court in *Boyd* explaining that its priority principle would not require 'the impossible'.

[169] Since restructuring law's provision for majority action within a class can no longer be used.

[170] Among others, Austria, as discussed in Georg Wabl and Martin Trenker's chapter 'Austria' in Gert Jan Boon, Reinout Vriesendorp and Harold Koster (eds), *Implementation of the EU Preventive Restructuring Directive* (Eleven, 2024), and Romania (see Art 28, Law 216/2022).

[171] § 222(3) InsO.

[172] Above, text to n 164 and Reinhard Dammann in Paulus and Dammann (eds) (n 2) Art 9, para 52. For an explanation as to how this may facilitate the discharge of small claims in full in an InsO process, see Horst Eidenmüller, '§ 222' in Rolf Stürner, Horst Eidenmüller and Heinrich Schoppmeyer (eds), *Münchener Kommentar zur Insolvenzordnung*, 4th edn (CH Beck, 2020) para 134 with further references to Bundesregierung, 'Entwurf einer Insolvenzordnung (InsO)' (1992) 200.

[173] Horst Eidenmüller, 'What can restructuring laws do?' (2023) 24 *EBOR* 231.

[174] InsO § 245(1) no 1.

[175] InsO § 245(1) no 2.

creditors with lower-ranking claims or by shareholders, other than insofar as they make a commensurate contribution to the company's assets, and that no creditor is set to receive value under the plan in excess of their claim.

Germany chose to transpose the PRD by adopting a new Act: the Gesetz über den Stabilisierungs- und Restrukturierungsrahmen für Unternehmen (StaRUG), to sit alongside the insolvency plan procedure.[176] This Act sets out a restructuring framework involving class-based voting (but this time with a stipulation that small affected creditors form a separate class[177]) and the possibility of cross-class cram-down. Some claims are declared to be non-dischargeable, including claims arising from intentional wrongs.[178] As a main rule, cross-class cram-down is conditional upon the plan satisfying an absolute priority rule formulated in similar terms to that which applies for an insolvency plan, against the backdrop of the same baseline 'best-interests-of-creditors' rule.[179] The priority rule, which is set out in StaRUG § 27(1), has been translated by others as follows:

> (1) A class will be deemed to have received a fair share in the plan value if:
>
> …
>
> 2. neither an affected creditor who, without a plan, would have a subordinated claim to satisfaction compared to the creditors of that class in insolvency proceedings, nor the debtor or any person holding an equity interest in the debtor receives an economic value that is not fully compensated by a contribution to the debtor's assets …[180]

To return to our earlier discussion on when the PRD's rules of priority are activated, the reference to 'affected' creditors junior to the dissenting class appears to mean that the rule is not infringed by a plan that leaves some creditors wholly outside it, or unaffected,[181] whilst the rule as written would regulate any distribution of value to shareholders (who are referred to in more general terms).[182] The idea appears to be to facilitate a 'purely financial' restructuring – ie one which targets investor classes but leaves operational creditors untouched.[183] We note, though, that the legislation places

[176] Criticising this, see Eidenmüller (n 173). Others offer a more positive assessment, arguing that the StaRUG has some advantages relative to the InsO procedure, including in more readily facilitating plans that are selective (compromising some but not other claims): see Stephan Madaus and David C Ehmke, 'Germany' in Boon et al (n 170).

[177] See § 9(2) StaRUG, and § 8 no 2, indicating that it may be appropriate for the plan to provide for a class comprising small affected creditors to be paid in full (consistently with n 172 above). The stipulation to form a separate class likely reflects the difference in voting rules between InsO and StaRUG, the former requiring a majority in both value and number (InsO § 244), whereas StaRUG's requirement only concerns value (StaRUG § 25): see Bundesregierung, 'Entwurf eines Gesetzes zur Fortentwicklung des Sanierungs- und Insolvenzrechts (Sanierungs- und Insolvenzrechtsfortentwicklungsgesetz – SanInsFoG)' (November 2020) 119.

[178] § 4 no 2 StaRUG; see also text to n 167. A similar provision appears in that part of InsO relating to individual debtors: § 302 InsO.

[179] That members of the dissenting class are not expected to be left worse off than they would be without a plan: § 26(1)1.

[180] Per an unofficial translation published by Allen Overy. See Allen & Overy, 'The German StaRUG-Scheme: Act on the Stabilisation and Restructuring Framework for Businesses' (23 December 2020).

[181] Baseline protection must still be provided (above n 179). Additionally, the selection of the creditors whose rights are to be affected must follow appropriate criteria (*sachgerechte Kriterien*), see § 8 StaRUG.

[182] Consistently with this, the StaRUG provision restraining creditors from recovering value in excess of their claims is also confined to 'affected' creditors (§ 27(1)1), unlike the equivalent provision in InsO (§ 245(2)1).

[183] See § 8 StaRUG.

some limits on the selection of those to be 'affected',[184] and that the cross-class cram-down power is not available unless a majority of classes support the plan.[185] And in any case, the rule in § 27(1) will clearly regulate any complaint by a dissenting creditor class about the distribution of value to shareholders. In this regard, it is important to emphasise that this rule does not prevent the issue of claims in exchange for a fresh contribution, provided that the new value given amounts to 'full compensation'. Hence, there is no absolute prohibition on shareholders retaining equity.

Additionally, StaRUG § 28 contains exceptions to the priority rule in § 27. First, a shareholder may retain shares if her contribution to realising the value of the plan is indispensable due to personal circumstances and she gives a legally binding undertaking to make such a contribution.[186] This would appear most salient in the SME context, which in the US, as we have seen, was eventually addressed through the introduction of a sub-chapter in which the absolute priority rule does not apply, against the backdrop of concern that the kinds of fresh contributions that could be made by owner-manager entrepreneurs would not necessarily amount to 'money or money's worth' for the purpose of the so-called 'new value exception'.[187] Secondly, in an apparent departure from the US position and from that in InsO, the rule in § 27 is not infringed by a plan that permits equity retention, against the objection of a creditor class, if the dissenting class is subject to only minor alterations of their rights. The statute gives an example of such an alteration: a maturity extension of not more than 18 months.[188]

To summarise, the main rule under the German transposition of the PRD is absolute priority, with the caveat that the scope of the rule as between creditor classes appears limited to those 'affected' by the plan. As between creditors and shareholders, there are several avenues through which shareholders may retain shares despite the dissent of a creditor class: first, if the shareholder provides new money (and here the German position is clearer than the US position, where the availability of the new value exception remains contested[189]); secondly, if the shareholder commits to making personal efforts that are indispensable for the restructuring; thirdly, if the impairment of the claims of the members of the dissenting class is only minor. The latter requires courts to determine when an alteration is sufficiently trivial to attract the exception, but they must do so in such a way as to give effect to the Directive's overall goal of protecting dissenting classes through the supply of a priority rule.[190]

We now turn to the priority rules chosen when the PRD was transposed in the Netherlands and Sweden. The transposition processes in Dutch and Swedish law share similarities. First, unlike in Germany, there was no legislative precedent for class-based voting and cross-class cram-down. Maintaining or refining the status quo was thus not an option. Secondly, these jurisdictions settled on a similar approach to the design of their priority rules, with the same baseline best-interests-of-creditors test.

[184] ibid, and n 181.
[185] § 26(1)3.
[186] § 28(2)1.
[187] Above, text to n 77.
[188] § 28(2)2. See also Madaus and Ehmke (n 176), explaining this as an incentive for early initiation (5).
[189] Above, text to n 79.
[190] Above, text to n 161 et seq.

The Dutch transposition of the PRD is set out in a new section of the Dutch bankruptcy code. This is commonly referred to as WHOA, the acronym of the reform legislation that introduced it.[191] Under the WHOA framework, the best-interests-of-creditors rule and priority rule are engaged when a dissenting creditor or shareholder (or, in the case of the priority rule, a dissenting creditor or shareholder in a dissenting class) asks the court to apply these rules. The explanatory memorandum accompanying the introduction to the legislation explains that these rules were modelled on US law.[192] The former rule sets the baseline at what the relevant stakeholders would have been entitled to in a liquidation in bankruptcy (or what we might think of as a coordinated realisation).[193] The latter is an absolute priority rule, expressed in terms that very much capture the essence of the US rule as discussed in section II above: the Dutch rule targets distributions of value that deviate from the way in which value would be distributed in a liquidation in bankruptcy, to the detriment of the dissenting class.[194] A plan that proposes a distribution of value to a junior class over the objection of a more senior class would engage the rule, unless the senior class is expected to be fully satisfied (such that the proposed distribution is not to its detriment).[195] It appears implicit in the requirement that the distribution of value follows ordinary priorities that no class should be promised value in excess of its claims.[196]

The priority provision goes on, however, to stipulate an exception to the rule: deviations from the ordinary system of priority are permissible where 'there are reasonable grounds for such deviation and the creditors or shareholders concerned are not harmed in their interests as a result'.[197] This is an open-ended exception that will derive its content from the case-by-case development of the law. A great deal of thought was put into the design of the system of case allocation, and judicial training, with a view to facilitating the development of WHOA specialisation,[198] and a rich body of decisions has rapidly emerged.[199] Early cases suggest that the issue of claims to a junior class for new value, over the objection of a dissenting class, will be treated as a matter for the

[191] The new legislation being termed the 'Wet homologatie onderhands akkoord'. An account of the background to the Act, for which planning began in 2012, is helpfully set out in the Explanatory Memorandum to the bill as initially introduced (see the unofficial English translation prepared by De Brauw Blackstone Westbroek, available at https://www.debrauw.com/articles/new-dutch-scheme-the-act-on-court-confirmation-of-extrajudicial-restructuring-plans).

[192] ibid section 3.4.

[193] § 384(3); see also § 378(1)(e), and Gert Jan Boon, Reinout Vriesendorp and Harold Koster, 'Netherlands' in Boon et al (n 170) 7, explaining that this may be assessed on the basis of a piecemeal or a going concern sale, depending on the facts.

[194] § 384(4)(b), see also § 378(1)(f).

[195] Consistently with this, ECLI:NL:RBAMS:2021:6522 (Amsterdam District Court) 3 November 2021, [9.17] *et seq.*

[196] As confirmed in a decision by the Lower Court of Amsterdam of 21 June 2023, ECLI:NL:RBAMS:2023:4152 (*Steinhoff International Holdings NV*), para 12.13.

[197] § 384(4)(b) as per an unofficial translation published by De Brauw Blackstone Westbroek, above (n 191).

[198] See Nicolaes Tollenaar, 'Het Wetsvoorstel Homologatie Onderhands Akkoord onder de Loep Genomen' [2019] (32) *Tijdschrift voor Insolventierecht* 217.

[199] Decisions cannot be appealed (see Chapter 2 in this book by Gabrielle Ruiz and Philip Hertz), but questions may be referred to the Supreme Court by the Supreme Court's advocate general with a view to obtaining guidance for future cases, as in the *Royal IHC* case, ECLI:NL:PHR:2024:346. The Supreme Court ruled in that case in ECLI:NL:HR:2024:1533 (25 October 2024). In addition, it is also possible for lower courts to ask preliminary questions of the Supreme Court (see eg the Supreme Court's decision of 25 February 2022, ECLI:NL:HR:2022:328).

application of the exception (the courts developing criteria for evaluating the adequacy of new value that bear obvious similarities to the criteria developed by US courts),[200] and that the exception may also be available to permit a shareholder to retain value where their continued involvement is instrumental for the success of the business,[201] in line with the German position. The case law also suggests that the kind of fact pattern that we note above may fall outside of the scope of the German absolute priority rule (where a class of creditor is 'unaffected' because the intention is that they be paid in full) would fall within the scope of the Dutch rule, but potentially be permissible by way of application of the exception.[202] But for two other facets of the Dutch framework, one might therefore have speculated that the regimes could, in the end, substantially converge.

There are, however, two facets of the Dutch regime that make it quite distinct. One is that the legislation provides that creditors who are SMEs (as defined) with claims for payment for the supply of goods and services or arising in tort are not only to be placed in a separate class, but that members of this class are presumptively entitled to at least 20 per cent of their claims;[203] this may only be departed from for 'compelling reasons'.[204] The other is that ordinary unsecured creditors are to be assured of a 'cash-out' alternative to plan participation, at the value they would be expected to receive in a bankruptcy.[205] Both rules could, we suggest, be conceptualised as offering some protection to less sophisticated players from the risk that a priority rule with an uncertain exception could be exploited by more sophisticated players at their expense. But this protection may be very costly: it has been argued, for example, that the cash-out rule incentivises hold-outs,[206] and that the 20 per cent rule risks distorting the reorganisation decision.[207]

The Swedish transposition of the PRD is set out in the 2022 Business Restructuring Act (lag om företagsrekonstruktion). Baseline protection is provided for dissenting creditors in the form of a rule that the court should refuse to sanction the plan on the

[200] See the closely reasoned decision of the Court of Midden-Nederland in ECLI:NL:RBMNE:2022:1329 (31 March 2022), [4.45]–[4.47]. The Court notes that the inclusion of a statutory provision on new value was considered but dropped during the legislative process.

[201] Decision of the Court of Midden-Nederland of 12 April 2023, ECLI:NL:RBMNE:2023:1773 para 5.42.

[202] As was held on the facts in ECLI:NL:RBMNE:2022:1329 (n 200): see [4.50] et seq; see also (reaching the opposite conclusion but reasoning in the same way) ECLI:NL:RBLIM:2022:4990. Both decisions are cited in fn 638 of Boon et al (n 170). Appearing to take the same view, R van den Sigtenhorst *Tekst & Commentaar Insolventierecht* (Wolters Kluwer, 2024), commentaar op art. 384 Fw, lid 4 onder b (we thank Ilya Kokorin for discussion and a machine translation). Parliament clearly contemplated the use of the WHOA to implement 'purely financial' restructurings (Explanatory Memorandum (n 191) section 3.5), as in the German case (above, text to n 183).

[203] § 374(2).

[204] § 384(4)(a). This provision was introduced during the passage of the Bill, and explained as one securing 'minimum protection' through a 'hard and fast rule' (Chamber file 35 249 Nr 10). See ECLI:NL:RBLIM:2021:8857 as cited in *Tekst & Commentaar Insolventierecht* (n 202).

[205] § 384(4)(c). See also the advocate general of the Supreme Court's cassation claim in ECLI:NL:PHR:2024:346, [3.8]–[3.9] discussing the legislative history. A provision was added to exclude professional lenders with security from the 'cash-out option' (§ 384(4)(d)); the scope of this is contested: *Tekst & Commentaar Insolventierecht* (n 202), section 10.

[206] See Frederik De Leo, 'Herstructureringsprocedures in België, Nederland en de richtlijn', Tvl 2020/40.

[207] See Hidde Volderba, 'Crises, Creditors and Cramdowns: An evaluation of the protection of minority creditors under the WHOA in light of Directive (EU) 2019/1023' (2021) 17(3) *Utrecht Law Review* 65.

objection of an affected party if they are expected to be left worse off under the plan than they would be in the event of a liquidation in bankruptcy (as in the Dutch WHOA procedure).[208] A priority rule is then supplied to regulate the exercise of the power to sanction a plan in the presence of a dissenting class. The rule is one of absolute priority, expressed in terms that closely follow the text of Article 11 of the Directive. If a class of creditors rejects the plan, sanctioning is as a main rule conditional upon the court determining that the dissenting class will have their claims fully satisfied, or that no class which in an insolvent liquidation would have a more junior priority is set to receive a payment or retain a right under the plan.[209] A separate provision prevents parties from retaining or receiving more than the full value of their claims.[210]

As in the Dutch case, the Swedish absolute priority rule is, however, expressed to be subject to an exception of uncertain scope. Deviations from absolute priority are permissible when justified by 'special reasons'.[211] The preparatory works to the provision state that the choice of the term 'special reasons' is meant to signal that courts are to be restrictive in permitting exceptions to absolute priority.[212] They go on to state that plans permitting shareholders to retain shares should only be crammed down upon dissenting creditor classes in cases where this is the only possibility for having a plan sanctioned.[213] This may be the kind of case which, in the German regime, is covered by a specific exception to the APR (where the personal contribution of the shareholder is necessary to enable the restructuring to be achieved),[214] and, in the Dutch regime, is understood to be eligible to fall within the more open-ended exception.[215] The literature also suggests that the Swedish provision is – like the Dutch provision – understood to permit the issue of claims for new value by way of the application of the exception.[216] What is permissible under the Dutch regime by way of a deviation from the main priority rule may well therefore be equally permissible under the Swedish regime.

The extent to which the Swedish regime goes beyond this will depend on various factors. One is the way in which the courts develop the concept of 'special reasons', and here it is noteworthy that the Swedish regime does not feature the rules that were inserted into the WHOA framework to shore up the position of certain unsecured creditors in restructuring negotiations (the 20 per cent rule, and the cash-out rule).[217] A second factor relates to the scope of the priority rule. We have seen how the Dutch APR is general, applying to regulate any distribution to a more junior class over the objection of a more senior one, not simply an 'affected' junior class. A proposal to leave

[208] chapter 4, § 24.

[209] chapter 4, § 25(4); see also Engelberg et al (n 162) 5.2.3.

[210] chapter 4, § 25(5).

[211] chapter 4, § 26.

[212] Prop 2021/22:215, 396; Marie Karlsson-Tuula, *Lagen (2022:964) om företagsrekonstruktion: En kommentar* (Norstedts Juridik, 2022) 153.

[213] ibid.

[214] Above, text to n 186.

[215] Above, text to n 201.

[216] Engelberg et al (n 162) fn 75. The same is true in the German regime, but there the question is addressed in the design of the rule itself, which only regulates the issue of a claim to a junior class over the objection of a more senior class where the junior claimholder has not given full compensation, see above, text to n 180.

[217] Above, text to nn 203–205.

one class whole is, therefore, a matter for the application of the exception. The Swedish legislation provides that the absolute priority rule applies in cases where a class (*grupp*) with lower priority under the plan stands to receive a payment or retain rights.[218] The Court of Appeal for Western Sweden has recently upheld a lower court's decision that was, among other things, based on the interpretation that *grupp* refers only to junior creditors/shareholders that are part of a class voting on the plan, rather than *any* junior creditor or shareholder.[219] This position has been strongly criticised,[220] but if it persists, the Swedish rule would have a much narrower scope than the Dutch one, and even the German rule – which we have seen is narrow only in relation to creditor classes, and not in relation to the retention of value by equity-holders.

To summarise: all three jurisdictions have opted for a form of absolute priority rule, but with variation in the approach to permitting exceptions. In this respect, the German regime is relatively more certain than the Dutch and Swedish regimes; the latter defer the resolution of hard questions about the extent to which deviations ought to be permissible, and task the courts with answering them, while the German regime prescribes a closed set of exceptions up front. The Dutch and Swedish strategy – main rule now, but with exceptions yet to be fully elucidated – may reflect the fact that, in both jurisdictions, the introduction of a cross-class cram-down power was a novelty. In such a context, a potential benefit of deferring some hard choices to later periods is that this allows the lawmaker's approach to questions of priority to be refined in the light of experience with the new framework, having regard to those other facets of the legal framework that affect the scope and functioning of the priority rule. Against this must be weighed the costs of uncertainty, both to the sophisticated players who will jostle over the exceptions, and to those less well-positioned to do so. In the Dutch and Swedish cases, however, this uncertainty should not be overstated: the main rule is one of absolute priority, and courts will have to interpret the exception in such a way as to ensure it does not swallow the rule, given the rule's protective function. In contrast, the UK position is considerably more uncertain.

IV. Experiments with Priority Rules in the United Kingdom

Prior to 2020, UK law made provision for class-based voting in the context of scheme of arrangement proceedings, but not for cross-class cram-down. Successive versions of the Companies Acts made provision for a company – initially one in liquidation,[221] but from 1907,[222] companies more generally – to propose a compromise or arrangement

[218] See Engelberg et al (n 162) 5.2.3, citing Schytzer (2023), Renman (2022) pp 29–44, Ehrenpil (2023) p 266 f.

[219] Judgment in case number Ä 1828-24.

[220] Including on the basis that there are insufficient controls elsewhere to ensure an adequate level of protection for a dissenting class aggrieved by a proposal to leave another whole: Engelberg et al (n 162).

[221] Joint Stock Companies Arrangement Act of 1870 (33 & 34 Vict c 104) 'An Act to facilitate compromises and arrangements between creditors and shareholders of Joint Stock and other Companies in Liquidation'.

[222] Companies Act 1907 (7 Edw 7 c 50) s 38; Christian Pilkington, *Schemes of Arrangement in Corporate Restructuring* (Sweet and Maxwell, 2016) section 2.1.2.2.

with its creditors (and, from 1900, its shareholders[223]), or a class thereof, which, if supported by the requisite majority at a meeting summoned by the court, and then sanctioned by an order of the court, would bind all such creditors (or shareholders) or classes. It was held early on that the scheme procedure could be used to bind secured, as well as unsecured, creditors,[224] but the courts also held that the concept of a 'class' was to be interpreted in such a way as to prevent the procedure from being used to work a 'confiscation and injustice', and confined to 'those persons whose rights are not so dissimilar as to make it impossible for them to consult together with a view to their common interest'.[225] In determining whether those being made party to a proposed scheme can vote together, or whether meetings of separate classes are required, the court will look both at the rights that the scheme would vary (the parties' existing rights) and the rights that the scheme would confer; differential treatment might warrant the separation of those who would otherwise, in terms of existing rights, be sufficiently similarly situated to vote together.[226] To the extent that separate meetings are required, each can block the scheme.

Outside of the Companies Acts, provision was also made in the Insolvency Acts of 1985–86 for a company and its creditors to enter into a 'voluntary arrangement'. In the company voluntary arrangement (CVA) procedure, directors make a proposal to the company and its creditors for a composition in satisfaction of the company's debts or a scheme of arrangement of its affairs.[227] If supported by an insolvency practitioner,[228] the proposal is put to the company and to the creditors for approval.[229] The decision of the company is made by its shareholders, acting by a simple majority,[230] but if this majority is not obtained, the agreement may still become binding, if supported by the requisite majority (in value) of creditors. If the proposal is approved in decisions of the shareholders and the creditors, or at least in the creditors' decision,[231] the arrangement takes effect as if it were made by the company at the date of the creditors' decision, and binds all those creditors entitled to vote at the meeting as if they were a party to it,[232] subject to a right of ex post challenge before the court on grounds of unfair prejudice or material irregularity.[233]

The statutory framework governing CVAs does not make provision for class-based voting: 'a CVA is determined by a single vote of all creditors'.[234] This suggests the possibility of the procedure being used to bind dissenting creditors who could not be bound

[223] Companies Act 1900 (63 & 64 Vict c 48) s 24; see also Edward Manson, *A practical guide to company law as amended by the Companies Act, 1900* (London, 1900) 170.

[224] *In re Alabama, New Orleans, Texas and Pacific Junction Railway Company* [1891] 1 Ch 213.

[225] *Sovereign Life Assurance Co (in liquidation) v Dodd* [1892] 2 QB 573, 583 per Bowen LJ.

[226] *Re Hawk Insurance Co Ltd* [2001] EWCA Civ 241, [2002] BCC 300, [30] and [51] per Chadwick LJ; see also Jennifer Payne, *Schemes of arrangement: theory, structure and operation* (CUP, 2021) 58, 62.

[227] Insolvency Act 1986 s 1(1). As to historical antecedents for individuals, see *Lazari Properties 2 Ltd and others v New Look Retailers Ltd* [2021] EWHC 1209 (Ch), [2021] Bus LR 915, [68] et seq.

[228] As to the role of the IP nominee, see ss 1(2), 2 of the Insolvency Act 1986 and Kristin van Zwieten (ed), *Goode on Principles of Corporate Insolvency*, 5th edn (Sweet & Maxwell, 2018), [12-39].

[229] Insolvency Act 1986 ss 3, 4.

[230] In value: Insolvency Rules 1986 rr 2.36, 2.35.

[231] Insolvency Act 1986 s 4A(2), subject to the right of a member to apply to the court: s 4A(3), (6).

[232] And those who would have been entitled had they had notice: Insolvency Act 1986 s 5(2).

[233] Insolvency Act 1986 s 6.

[234] *SISU Capital Fund Ltd v Tucker* [2005] EWHC 2170 (Ch), [2006] BCC 463, [134] per Warren J.

in scheme proceedings, because their existing rights are such that they would be classed separately, requiring a separate meeting at which the scheme might be rejected. There are, however, other features of the statutory framework that significantly limit the extent to which the procedure could be used to achieve such a de facto cross-class cram-down. Most obviously, the statute provides that neither the company nor the creditors can approve a proposal which would affect the right of a secured creditor to enforce its security, or under which a preferential debt is to be paid otherwise than in priority to non-preferential creditors, without the consent of the rights-holder.[235] The procedure is therefore not a vehicle for junior creditors to impose a compromise on more senior ones. Conversely, the capacity of the latter to impose a compromise on the former is also limited, because the statutory framework provides that, although those with security may vote on the proposal, to the extent that their claims are secured, these votes have nil value for the purposes of determining whether the requisite majority of creditors have approved the proposal.[236] (Surprisingly, preferential creditors cannot have their priority altered but can contribute to obtaining the requisite majority; until recently, however, the categories of preferential debt were quite limited[237]).

Taken together, these features suggest that the CVA is most accurately characterised as a procedure for the treatment of unsecured debt by agreement between the company and the requisite majority (in value) of its unsecured creditors,[238] albeit with the qualification that this majority may be derived from the support of preferential creditors (even though their priority cannot be affected), and/or subordinated creditors. The qualification is less surprising when one looks at the context in which the CVA emerged. The procedure was introduced on the recommendation of the Cork Committee in a report that also recommended the reduction or elimination of most categories of preferential debt[239] and assumed that subordination agreements were not enforceable in bankruptcy.[240] The Committee saw a need for a fast, out-of-court procedure for achieving 'simple moratoria or compositions' with the general body of unsecured creditors[241] – for example, 'a straightforward moratorium on the payment of debts to unsecured creditors for a limited period, or such a moratorium coupled with a composition, say the reduction of all debts by 25%'[242] – and expected that the primary beneficiary of the CVA procedure would be small companies.[243]

In practice, however, the CVA procedure has been used by some medium and large-sized companies to propose arrangements that are highly selective, targeting very limited categories of unsecured claim whilst leaving others unaffected.[244] This is

[235] Insolvency Act 1986 s 4(3), (4).

[236] Insolvency Rules r 15.31(4), (5); *Goode* (n 228) [12.42].

[237] As noted by Paterson (n 144) [3.298]; see also *New Look* (n 227) [120].

[238] Which 'gives rise to a species of statutory contract between the creditors bound by the arrangement on the one hand and the debtor on the other': *Re Brelec Installations Ltd* [2001] BCC 421, 423 per Blackburne J.

[239] *Insolvency law and Practice: Report of the Review Committee* (1982) Cmnd 8558, ch 32.

[240] ibid [1448], though the Committee advocated for change on this point ([1449]).

[241] ibid [420], [430].

[242] ibid [408]. At the same time, the Committee recognised (in its chapter on individual voluntary arrangements) that there would need to be flexibility to adjust the relative position of the parties under some circumstances, eg to facilitate new finance: ibid [364], as noted in *New Look* (n 227) [184].

[243] ibid [430].

[244] But nevertheless invited to vote on the arrangement. See further Chapter 6 in this book by Paterson and Walters.

the kind of case which might, if proposed as a scheme rather than a CVA, only be achievable with a statutory cross-class cram-down power (since, as we have seen, differential treatment of the otherwise similarly situated may warrant division into separate classes, each of which may block the scheme[245]). Consistently with this, challenges to these arrangements on the ground that they are 'unfairly prejudicial' have provided the setting for the judicial refinement of two 'techniques'[246] for identifying unfairness – the 'vertical comparison' and 'horizontal comparison'[247] – which, in substance, are a form of best-interests-of-creditors rule (providing baseline protection) and priority rule (regulating the distribution of value over and above the baseline), although the latter is vaguer than the former. The vertical technique involves comparison of the 'projected outcome of the CVA with the projected outcome of a realistically available alternative process'; the realistic alternative 'sets a "lower bound" below which a CVA cannot go'.[248] But the mere fact that those targeted by a selective CVA are not expected to be left worse off than in the realistically available alternative process does not mean there is no 'unfair prejudice', because the court should then turn to compare the position of creditors under the terms of the arrangement (the horizontal technique) with a view to identifying any unfair 'imbalance',[249] or, as Mr Justice Zacaroli put it in *New Look*, with a view to determining whether there is a 'fair allocation of the assets available within the CVA between the compromised creditors and other sub-groups of creditors'.[250]

The fact that an arrangement will prejudice some, but not others, does not necessarily make it 'unfairly' prejudicial,[251] but differential treatment across the creditor body calls for justification.[252] The starting point for this inquiry appears to be the priority that creditors would have in the relevant alternative – that is, the court will look to see whether the distribution of value under the arrangement reflects the priority with which creditors would be entitled to look to the assets outside the arrangement – but the court may be satisfied that the elevation of some claims ahead of others of equal or more senior ranking is justified, for example because the satisfaction of those claims is necessary for the business to be able to continue to trade.[253] An 'objective justification' is needed, but the presence of such justification will not necessarily preclude a finding of unfair prejudice: in *New Look*,[254] Zacaroli J held that where majority approval for a selective CVA is obtained through the affirmative vote of uncompromised creditors (a de facto cross-class cram-down), the court should also consider whether a different (fairer) allocation of assets, consistent with that justification, was possible.

[245] Above, text to n 226.

[246] *Mourant & Co Trustees Ltd v Sixty UK Ltd (in admin)* [2010] EWHC 1890 (Ch), [2010] BCC 882, [67].

[247] *Prudential Assurance Co Ltd v PRG Powerhouse Ltd* [2007] EWHC 1002 (Ch), [2007] Bus LR 1771, [74] et seq; *Mourant & Co Trustees Ltd v Sixty UK Ltd* ibid; *Discovery (Northampton) Ltd v Debenhams Retail Ltd* [2019] EWHC 2441 (Ch), [2020] BCC 9, [12]–[13]; *New Look* (n 227) [107] et seq.

[248] *Debenhams* ibid [12]; see also *New Look* (n 227) [108].

[249] *Doorbar v Alltime Securities Ltd (No 2)* [1995] BCC 728 (an individual voluntary arrangement case), at 731 per Knox J, cited in *Powerhouse* (n 247) [87].

[250] See above (n 227) [193].

[251] *Powerhouse* (n 247) [88], drawing on the individual voluntary arrangement decision in *In re a Debtor (No 101 of 1999) (No 1)* [2001] 1 BCLC 54; *New Look* (n 227) [156], [170].

[252] *Sixty UK Ltd* (n 246) [67]; *Debenhams* (n 247) [12]; *New Look* (n 227) [111].

[253] *New Look* (n 227) [113], [175]; *Powerhouse* (n 247) [90].

[254] *New Look* (n 227), see particularly [192] et seq.

As between the two procedures, only the scheme procedure can be used to propose an adjustment of rights at every level of a large company's capital structure, but this use is premised on the support of the requisite majority in each class. It is true that, as Professor Payne has rightly emphasised,[255] courts have developed the concept of a class in such a way as to minimise, rather than maximise, the number of classes required. Perhaps most remarkably, courts have held that, in determining whether differences in existing rights warrant separation into classes for the purposes of voting on a compromise or arrangement, courts should have regard to the present 'quality' of these rights – that is, the quality of these rights outside the restructuring – so that, if the realistic alternative to a scheme is an insolvency procedure in which differences in rights would no longer be important (whether because of the formal effect of commencement on those rights, or because of the expected value of the assets in that procedure and the priority position of the rightsholders), the rightsholders may properly be grouped together.[256] In this way, junior classes can be compressed, but the rights of these claimholders cannot be varied without the consent of the majority in the (amalgamated) class.

There is, however, understood to be a workaround, albeit one that is only available where the debtor's assets can be transferred, and the costs of doing so (including having regard to any tax implications)[257] are not prohibitive. In such a case, it is possible to achieve something functionally equivalent to a cram-down of a junior class by combining the scheme procedure with a procedure for the transfer of assets to a new company in which senior claimholders will share, with junior claimholders left behind in an 'empty shell'. It is for the company to identify with whom it wishes to enter into a compromise or arrangement,[258] and in these cases the scheme is focused on those senior claimholders who are asked to give up their claims in exchange for rights in the transferee company; junior claims are formally unaffected and simply left outside the scheme. As to the transfer, the most obvious mechanism for achieving this is the administration procedure in the Insolvency Act 1986, in which the administrator has a power of sale[259] that can (the courts have held)[260] be exercised without prior consultation with unsecured creditors ('pre-packaged' administration), subject always to the administrator's duties.

In considering the scheme component of such hybrid arrangements, it has been held that those with no 'real economic interest' in the company need not be consulted in the proposal of the scheme, and that whether a junior claimholder has such an interest should be assessed by reference to their position if the restructuring does not proceed. If the only alternative to a consensual restructuring of the kind proposed in

[255] Payne (n 226) section 2.3.2.

[256] *Re Apcoa Parking Holdings GmbH* [2014] EWHC 3849 (Ch), [2015] Bus LR 374 [107] et seq; *Re Stronghold Insurance Company Limited* [2018] EWHC 2909 (Ch), [2019] 2 BCLC 11, [48] et seq; see also the illuminating analysis in Howard et al (n 30) [7.375] et seq. This helps to explain why it has been said that, even where a scheme is supported by all classes, the court will still check that claimholders are likely to do better under the scheme than in the relevant alternative: see *Virgin Active* (n 38) [224], drawing on *Telewest Communications No 2* [2005] BCC 36.

[257] Payne (n 226) 238.

[258] *Re Mytravel Group Plc* [2005] 2 BCLC 123, [10] (CA).

[259] Insolvency Act 1986 Sch 1, para 2.

[260] *Re Tranbus International Ltd (in liquidation)* [2004] EWHC 932 (Ch), [2004] 1 WLR 2654.

the scheme is an insolvency proceeding in which the junior claimholder would receive nothing, they have no such interest.[261] It has further been held that, although a junior claimholder would have standing to object to the eventual sanctioning of the scheme on the ground that the overall arrangement is unfair to them, where the only alternative to a scheme is an insolvency procedure in which the claimholder is set to receive nothing, it is not unfair to permit those who would be 'in the money' in this counterfactual to decide how to 'divide up any value or potential future benefits which use of such business and assets might generate following the restructuring', even if this involves deciding, for commercial reasons, to gift some claims to existing shareholders and managers.[262]

This is of course precisely the kind of argument that was rejected by the US courts (albeit in a different context[263]) when they articulated a 'fixed' principle to regulate the conditions under which assets could be transferred to a new company owned by (some) stakeholders of the old company: recall that the principle was fixed in the sense that its application did not depend on whether the aggrieved junior creditors were in or out of the money at the time of the transfer.[264] It has been argued that the English courts' focus on the counterfactual obscures the issue that the US courts sought to address directly through the supply of a priority principle – the distribution of value sought to be preserved by restructuring[265] – and that the deployment of the 'in / out of the money' heuristic may deter, rather than promote, consensual settlement, because those found to

[261] *Re Mytravel Group Plc* [2004] EWHC 2741 (Ch), [2005] BCC 457, particularly [55]–[58]. On appeal, the Court of Appeal (above, n 258) found that Mann J had not needed to address this and set aside that part of his order containing the economic interest finding, but the judge's *obiter* discussion has been treated as a statement of the principle. Mann J relied on *Re Tea Corporation* [1904] 1 Ch 12, in which the relevant claimholders (ordinary shareholders) had in fact been invited to vote on a scheme (which would see the assets of a company in liquidation transferred to a new company in which stakeholders would share) and rejected it. But at first instance Buckley J used a counterfactual analysis (relying on a concession that, if the assets were realised, the ordinary shareholders would get nothing) to conclude that he could sanction the plan as one between the company and the senior classes. On appeal, the decision of Buckley J was affirmed. The law had only recently been changed to provide that the scheme procedure applied to compromises or arrangements with shareholders as well as with creditors (see above, n 223), and the Court of Appeal was clearly anxious to ensure that this development would not give shareholders the ability to veto a restructuring of an insolvent company in liquidation by way of a transfer scheme, which parties experimented with from very early on: see eg *Re the Dominion of Canada Freehold Estate and Timber Company Limited* (1886) 55 LT 347.

[262] *Re Noble Group* [2018] EWHC 3092 (Ch), [2019] BCC 349, [79]–[89] per Snowden J (the judge noting that the reasons for issuing claims to shareholders and managers were 'credible': [88]); *Re Virgin Active Holdings* (n 38) [240]–[242]. These cases drew on *Re Bluebrook Ltd* [2009] EWHC 2114 (Ch), [2010] BCC 209, in which Mann J considered an objection to sanction by a class that would be left behind, the members of which argued that they were not 'out of the money' and value was therefore being unfairly lost to them ([10]). The valuations provided by the company focused on what a third-party purchaser would presently pay. The judge expressed some anxiety about whether this was the correct approach ([49]) but held that the evidence did not raise a 'sufficient possibility of there being some unrealisable value … of which the senior lenders will be the unfair beneficiaries if the restructuring goes ahead' ([52]). But it seems clear from the later cases that courts will approach the question of who is 'in the money' through the counterfactual: *Re Swissport Fuelling Limited* [2020] EWHC 3413 (Ch), [45]–[50].

[263] Against the backdrop of concerns that reorganisation law was serving ordinary outside investors poorly: above, text to nn 60–65.

[264] Above, text to n 43.

[265] Which, by definition, is not captured by a counterfactual analysis, as argued in Riz Mokal and Michael Crystal, 'The Valuation of Distressed Companies – A Conceptual Framework' (2006) 3(3) *International Corporate Rescue* 126.

be presently 'in' the money appear capable of 'taking all'.[266] The contrast with a restructuring procedure that requires the court to focus directly on the value of new claims being issued, and to ensure that senior claimholders are not issued with rights the value of which is expected to exceed their existing claims,[267] is stark.

It may be objected that these cases were concerned with the scheme component of the restructuring, not the transfer, and that where the transfer took place through administration, junior claimholders would also have been protected by the administrator's duties. But it seems questionable that these duties would carry junior claimholders much further. An administrator is entitled to abandon pursuit of the statutory objective of rescuing the company itself where it is not reasonably practicable to achieve this, as would be argued to be the case where there is no effective means (in the absence of a formal cross-class cram-down power) of adjusting rights across the company's capital structure with a view to restoring it to solvency.[268] In exercising their power of sale in pursuit of the remaining statutory objectives, the administrator must take reasonable care to achieve the best price reasonably obtainable in the circumstances.[269] This suggests that the administrator would need to be satisfied that the price for the transfer (those liabilities that the new company will assume) exceeds the price that the administrator expects would be obtained if the assets were instead sold to a third party,[270] which provides a measure of baseline protection for those left behind. But it seems doubtful that this duty could be argued to require administrators to go further and attempt to quantify the expected value of the claims that senior classes will hold in New Co, and to insist that this be translated back into the terms of the scheme, and still more doubtful that the administrator could be said to be required to somehow regulate the decision of the purchasers to gift some value to others.

We have laboured somewhat the historical position, but it is impossible to understand the case law on the approach to questions of priority in the restructuring plan procedure introduced by the Corporate Insolvency and Governance Act 2020 without this background. In 2018, having consulted on the matter, the Government announced its intention to introduce a new restructuring procedure, modelled on the scheme procedure ('so that jurisprudence on class formation that has been built up over many years can be used to guide courts in their examination'),[271] but with statutory provision for cross-class cram-down, so that all classes of claimholder – including the

[266] See Paterson (n 34) particularly section C, also noted above n 97.

[267] Above, text to n 73 (US law) and n 148 (EU Preventive Restructuring Directive).

[268] Insolvency Act 1986, Sch B1, para 3. The administrator must perform their functions with the objective of rescuing the company as a going concern unless they 'think' it is not reasonably practicable to achieve this objective, or that the next specified objective (achieving a better result for the creditors as a whole than would be likely if the company were wound up) would achieve a better result for the creditors as a whole: para 3(3), read with (1). This decision will only be open to challenge if made in bad faith, or clearly perverse: *Davey v Money* [2018] EWHC 766 (Ch), [2018] Bus LR 1903, [255].

[269] *Re Charnley Davies Ltd (No 2)* [1990] BCLC 760, 775. It is true that the administrator must also take care in relation to the timing of any sale (*Davey v Money*, ibid, [392]), but a reasonable administrator would have to weigh the costs of delay against the likelihood that merely threatening to delay the transfer will produce an offer on substantially different terms.

[270] See, consistently with this analysis, Howard et al (n 30) 393–94, noting the additional requirements in relation to marketing and the disclosure of valuation evidence in pre-packs.

[271] Department for Business, Energy & Industrial Strategy, 'Insolvency and Corporate Governance: Government Response' (August 2018), [5.151].

most junior – could be effectively treated in a plan. The exercise of the class cram-down power would be conditional on, inter alia, compliance with a 'no worse off' test[272] and a rule of priority. On priority, the Government observed 'Where a cross-class cram down is to be applied, a requirement is needed to safeguard creditor interests that respects and applies the ordinary order of priority in liquidation and administration'[273] and promised a flexible absolute priority rule. The legislation would provide that 'a dissenting class of creditors must be satisfied in full before a more junior class may receive any distribution or keep any interest under the restructuring plan', but the court would be given power to confirm a plan deviating from the rule where 'necessary to achieve the aims of the restructuring' and 'just and equitable in the circumstances'.[274] The parallels with the Dutch and Swedish rules described in section III.C above are obvious.

In the event, by the time that the legislation was introduced and then passed in a fast-track legislative process three months into the COVID-19 pandemic,[275] the new procedure did not contain an absolute – or indeed any form of – priority rule. As envisaged, the new plan procedure in Part 26A of the Companies Act 2006 is modelled closely on the scheme procedure in Part 26, but has some notable differences, including most obviously that the statute enables the court to 'exercise its discretion … to sanction a restructuring plan, notwithstanding that there is a dissenting class or classes of plan creditors'.[276] This power is only available where the court is satisfied as to two conditions, both of which reference the 'relevant alternative', defined to mean 'whatever the court considers would be most likely to occur in relation to the company if the compromise or arrangement were not sanctioned'.[277] One is that the plan has been supported by the requisite majority in at least one class that would receive a payment 'or have a genuine economic interest in the company' in the event of the relevant alternative. The other is that the court is satisfied that none of the members of the dissenting class will be worse off under the plan than they would be in the event of the relevant alternative.[278] On the question of the entitlement of the dissenting class to value over and above this baseline, the legislation is silent. It has therefore been left to the courts to articulate the approach to be taken in a case in which a dissenting class objects to the exercise of the power on the basis that the plan distributes 'too much' value to some other class, or as Lord Justice Snowden put it in *Adler*, to develop 'appropriate principles' to guide the exercise of the discretion.[279]

Unsurprisingly, in the early non-consensual Part 26A cases, the courts looked to the approach taken in those limited categories of case where a de facto cross-class cram-down could already be achieved (certain forms of CVA, and transfer schemes)

[272] The 'next best alternative' to the plan: ibid, [5.174]–[5.175].
[273] ibid, [5.163].
[274] ibid, [5.163] and [5.164]. The original proposal had included a vaguer priority rule: see Kristin van Zwieten, 'Mid-crisis restructuring law reform in the United Kingdom' (2023) 24 *European Business Organization Law Review* 287, text to n 96.
[275] See further van Zwieten ibid.
[276] *Adler* (n 32) [105].
[277] Section 901G(4).
[278] Conditions B and A in s 901G.
[279] *Adler* (n 32) [106].

to develop the principles that would guide the exercise of the new statutory power. In the first case in which the power was exercised, it was held that, in the same way that a court hearing a challenge to a CVA would interrogate whether differences in the treatment of creditors under the arrangement were justified (through the 'horizontal comparison' technique), with a view to evaluating the fairness of the proposed allocation as between those who would be compromised and those who would not be,[280] justice might require the judge invited to exercise the power in Part 26A to 'see whether a restructuring plan provides for differences in treatment of creditors inter se, and if so whether those differences are justified' with a view to ascertaining 'whether there has been a fair distribution of the benefits of the restructuring (what some commentators have called the "restructuring surplus") between those classes who have agreed the restructuring plan and those who have not'.[281] On the facts, an obvious difference in treatment between secured and unsecured creditors was justified by the secured nature of the former's claims (in other words, by their existing priority).[282] At the same time, the early cases (this time drawing on the schemes of arrangement case law) also suggested that a complaint as to the distribution of the restructuring surplus by a stakeholder who would be 'out of the money' in the relevant alternative should be given little weight.[283] Both ideas were well-grounded in analogous case law, but they sit uncomfortably together: the horizontal inquiry is concerned with the distribution of value that is expected to be unavailable (to the parties) in the non-plan world, so it is far from obvious why its application should be limited by reference to a heuristic that assumes away – by focusing on the counterfactual[284] – the existence of this value.

Subsequent cases have confirmed the centrality of the horizontal comparison to the exercise of the discretion. As Snowden LJ put it in what is now the leading case (*Adler*):

> [A] key issue for the court in exercising its discretion to impose a plan upon a dissenting class is to identify whether the plan provides for differences in treatment of the different classes of creditors *inter se* and, if so, whether those differences can be justified …
>
> … As a matter of principle, when the court exercises its discretion to impose a plan upon a dissenting class, it subjects that class to an enforced compromise or arrangement of their rights in order to achieve a result which the assenting classes of creditors consider to be to their commercial advantage. In my judgment, that exercise of a judicial discretion to alter the rights of a dissenting class for the perceived benefit of the assenting classes necessarily requires the court to inquire how the value sought to be preserved or generated by the restructuring plan, over and above the relevant alternative, is to be allocated between those different creditor groups.

[280] Above, text to n 250.

[281] *Re DeepOcean 1 UK Ltd* [2021] EWHC 138 (Ch), [2021] BCC 483, [63].

[282] ibid [64].

[283] ibid [64], subsequently put more forcefully in *Virgin Active* (n 38) [226]–[266], with the caveat that the judge thought the court might well decline to sanction a plan that 'discriminated arbitrarily or capriciously' between out-of-the-money stakeholders ([265], having noted his finding in *Noble* (above n 262) that there were 'credible' commercial reasons for conferring benefits on out-of-the-money shareholders).

[284] As cogently argued by Mokal and Crystal in relation to the schemes case law (above, n 265). An important recent working paper by Sarah Paterson argues that the '"out of the money" approach' should not be maintained in Part 26A: 'The conceptual foundation of cross-class cramdown' (October 2024 working paper).

> It is this concept that has been encapsulated in the expression 'the fair distribution of the benefits of the restructuring' … To similar effect … Professor Sarah Paterson [has] … suggested that the essential question for the court is whether any class of creditor is getting 'too good a deal (too much unfair value)'.[285]

The starting point for evaluating the 'relative treatment of creditors' under the plan[286] is their position in the 'non-plan world', ie in the relevant alternative. As Zacaroli J put it in *Re Houst*, the court will 'look to see whether the priority, as among different creditor groups, applicable in the relevant alternative is reflected in the distributions under the plan'.[287] By this the courts do not mean that, where in the non-plan world, the dissenting class would be entitled to be satisfied before a more junior class could look to the debtor's assets, the judge should first establish whether the dissenting class is likely to be satisfied under the plan and then, if not, whether the retention of value by the junior class is nevertheless justified. That would be to supply a principle of absolute priority – albeit one with an open-ended exception (wherever the retention of value by the junior class is 'justified') – and the courts have been clear that such a principle cannot be supplied, given the legislative background.[288] Instead, the idea appears to be to make existing seniority relevant to the resolution of conflicts over the distribution of value, without making the ability of a junior class to retain value conditional on evidence that a more senior dissenting class will be satisfied, much as Bonbright and Bergman aimed to do when mooting a relative alternative to absolute priority.[289] The way that this is achieved is by asking the court to remind itself of the position of the dissenting class vis-à-vis others in the relevant alternative (which it must already have established to confirm that the dissenting class will not be worse off), and then to ask whether there is good reason (justification) for permitting a more junior class to retain value over the objection of the dissenting class.

At the same time, the courts have maintained the position that the views of those 'out of the money' as to the fairness of the proposed allocation of the benefits of the restructuring are to be given little weight.[290] The relationship between this principle and the principle that differential treatment falls to be justified is presently unclear, but the early case law suggests that where the dissenting class is 'out of the money' in the relevant alternative, and aggrieved by the fact that the plan would distribute value to some equal or more junior-ranking class, it may suffice to establish that those 'in the money' had some 'credible' commercial reason for departing from the order of priority that

[285] *Adler* (n 32) [159]–[161].

[286] *DeepOcean* (n 281) [62].

[287] *Re Houst* [2022] EWHC 1941 (Ch), [2022] BCC 1143, [30], endorsed in *Adler* (n 32) at [159] (see also [165]); see also *Re Great Annual Savings* [2023] EWHC 1141 (Ch), [2023] Bus LR 1163, [105]; *Re Fitness First Clubs Ltd* [2023] EWHC 1699 (Ch), [73].

[288] That is, given that the Government considered but apparently decided against the inclusion of an absolute priority rule: above text to n 274, and *Virgin Active* (n 38) [289], *Houst* (n 287) [30]. It is not clear how much weight should be placed on this, however, given the emergency context in which the legislation was enacted: see van Zwieten (n 274).

[289] Above, text to n 49.

[290] *In re Great Annual Savings Co Ltd* (n 287) [110]; *Re Fitness First Clubs Ltd* (n 287) [107]; *In re Prezzo Investco Ltd* [2023] EWHC 1679 (Ch), [2024] Bus LR 848, [76]; and see *Adler* (n 32) [252] reprising *Virgin Active* (see n 283 above), albeit in analysing a different question (on the facts in *Adler*, the dissenting class was 'in the money'). See later *Re Project Lietzenburger Straße Holdco SÀRL* [2024] EWHC 468 (Ch), [209]–[215], and the decisions of Miles J cited immediately below.

would attain in the relevant alternative.[291] In contrast, by analogy with the CVA case law, where the complaint is from a dissenting class that would be 'in the money' in the relevant alternative, the court will probe whether there is a 'sufficiently good reason'[292] for the particular departures from priority in the relevant alternative that the plan would produce, which will import consideration of whether a different ('fairer') plan, consistent with the stated commercial objectives, was possible.[293]

The early cases suggest that 'good reasons', or justifications, for departure from the priority position that would attain in the relevant alternative include where the elevation of a junior claim is necessary to enable business continuity;[294] where claims are issued to junior claimholders for new value (*Adler* indicating that the courts will develop guidance similar to that developed by US courts to test the sufficiency of a fresh contribution[295]); and where the issue of claims to an existing shareholder is thought necessary to secure their continued involvement in the business.[296] These are of course the kinds of cases that, in the jurisdictions we have surveyed in section III, either fall outside the scope of the absolute priority rule, or within exceptions to it. Does this mean that the English position could in principle (depending on the development of the categories of justification, which are not closed) converge with that in jurisdictions with an absolute priority rule? We do not think so. The fundamental difference is that the UK position does not specify that, as a starting point, the dissenting class is entitled to be satisfied before a more junior class can retain value. Instead, there is a vaguer commitment to reflecting existing seniority, vaguer even than the relative priority rule in the PRD.

This significantly widens the set of permissible outcomes in a non-consensual case, even before one allows for the possibility that the courts might apply only the lightest standard of review to cases in which the dissenting class would be 'out-of-the-money' in the non-plan world. The overall result appears to us to be an invitation to parties to jostle not only over the boundaries of a priority rule, but over the core itself. For the reasons given in section II, we are highly doubtful that it is in the interests of sophisticated players to battle – as they have been doing – to establish the benchmark, and then to test the legal position on a set of basic and predictable questions (such as the approach to new value; payments in the ordinary course of business to maintain continuity; contributions by shareholders other than in money or money's worth)

[291] We say this because in *Adler* (n 32) the Court of Appeal emphasised that in *Virgin Active* (n 38), a case involving a dissenting out-of-the-money creditor class, there were 'rational commercial reasons' for the decision to confer benefits on some shareholders over the objection of a creditor class, and referred to these as 'justifications' for departure from priority in the relevant alternative. *Cf*, however, the more recent first instance decision in *UK Commercial Property Finance Holdings v Cine-UK Limited* [2024] EWHC 2475 (Ch), where Miles J appears to confine the horizontal comparison technique to treating complaints about the distribution of value by 'in the money' classes ([68]), and his later decision in *Re Chaptre Finance Plc* [2024] EWHC 2908 (Ch). Two other recent decisions, however, run in the opposition direction, and suggest considerable uncertainty as to the relationship between the principles: *Re Revolution Bars Limited* [2024] EWHC 2949 (Ch), and *Re Ambatovy Minerals Societe Anonyme* [2025] EWHC 279 (Ch).

[292] *Re Great Annual Savings* (n 287) [128].

[293] *Adler* (n 32) [173]–[181], endorsing the CVA analysis in *New Look* as discussed above (text to n 227) (Zacaroli J having held in *DeepOcean* that an analogous inquiry was warranted in Part 26A (above, text to n 281)), and the reasoning in *Great Annual Savings* (n 287).

[294] *Re Houst* (n 287) [35]; *Adler* (n 32) [170].

[295] *Adler* (n 32) [168]–[169], and above, text to n 57.

[296] *In the Matter of Cimolai SPA* [2023] EWHC 2193 (Ch), [53].

that can (as our survey in section III demonstrates) be answered by statute. Making such statutory provision will not end the process of rule production (the focus will then shift to questions of interpretation, over which sophisticated players will still 'jostle'[297]), but it will narrow the set of conceivable outcomes and in this way provide a starting point for players seeking to adjust to the new regime.

As for less sophisticated players, their position appears precarious. They will be less well-positioned to influence the way in which the priority principle is developed by the courts, and perhaps more likely to fall under the 'light-touch' approach to the treatment of complaints by 'out of the money' classes, given English law's permissive approach to security interests. The contrast with the jurisdictions that we surveyed in section III, which specify that, as a main rule, a dissenting unsecured class ought to be paid in full before a more junior class can retain value, and which offer various forms of additional protection to non-investor creditor classes, is striking. At present, the only potential constraint we see on these tendencies is that the courts have also signalled that the 'relevant alternative' to a plan might be a plan on different terms.[298] It is possible that by this route (by analogy with our analysis of the position under the PRD[299]), baseline protection will be raised beyond the level applicable in the CVA and transfer scheme cases,[300] making the approach to questions of priority less significant.

V. Conclusion

The analysis of priority rules turns out to be rather complicated, once attention is paid to their interaction with other components of a restructuring procedure that determine their domain, including rules on expenses, on baseline protection (the form of 'best-interests-of-creditors' test), and on non-dischargeability. But this complexity, and the fact that the enactment of any new rule will inevitably be followed by debate over its proper interpretation ('cumulative doctrinal complexity' being, as Clark explained, the hallmark of secondary phases of rule production[301]), should not be permitted to obscure the basic function of priority rules, which is to narrow the set of outcomes in non-consensual cases, with a view to supporting what Baird calls a 'sensible bargaining environment'.[302] This militates in favour of supplying a rule that precisely specifies the entitlement of the dissenting class to value over the baseline. Professional investors can adjust to any version of a priority rule other than a vague one. We have argued that precision is better for less sophisticated players too, but that for at least some of these players, and under certain conditions, there may be particular benefits in precisely specifying that the entitlement of the dissenting class is to absolute, or full, priority.

[297] Above, text to n 99.
[298] *Adler* (n 32) [163].
[299] Above, text to n 166.
[300] Where the comparison is with an alternative process, not the same process on different terms (above, text to n 248, and n 261).
[301] Above, text to n 14.
[302] See above n 95.

4

The Cramdown: A Conceptual Framework

RIZ MOKAL, STEPHAN MADAUS,
IRIT MEVORACH, AND IGNACIO TIRADO*

I. Introduction

Amongst all the innovations to UK insolvency law introduced by the Corporate Insolvency and Governance Act 2020 ('CIGA'), perhaps the most striking is the cross-class cramdown mechanism in the new restructuring plan process.[1] The court now has power to sanction a plan even if it has not attracted the requisite statutory majority in one or more classes, so long as each of two conditions is met.

The first, 'Condition A', requires the court to be satisfied that no member of the (or any) dissenting class would be worse off under the plan than they would be in the event of the 'relevant alternative', which is whatever the court considers would be most likely to occur in relation to the debtor company if the plan were not sanctioned.[2] The second, 'Condition B', requires the plan to have been approved by at least one claimant class whose members would, in the relevant alternative, receive a payment, or have a genuine economic interest in the company.[3]

If both Conditions A and B are met, the cramdown power is available, which is to say that the court has power to sanction the plan. However, the court is not bound to exercise the cramdown power, and there is no presumption that it should do so. Instead, the judge has a discretion whether or not to exercise the power 'in light of all the relevant factors and circumstances'.[4] The question is how the court should go about deciding whether to exercise this power in relation to a particular proposed plan. The statute does not provide any guidance as to this question.

In this chapter, we construct a framework for the analysis of the contexts in which the cramdown power arises and whether, when, and how it should be exercised. We will refer

* We are grateful to Dermot Costello, Johan Jol, Jennifer Payne, Hilary Stonefrost, Robert van Moorsel, Kristin van Zwieten, and Glenn Zahn for helpful comments and suggestions. The views expressed here and any mistakes are the authors' alone.

[1] See Companies Act 2006, Part 26A, inserted into the Act by the Corporate Insolvency and Governance Act 2020 (CIGA). In this chapter, we will refer to the restructuring plan process as 'the RP' and to any individual real or hypothetical plan as 'plan'.

[2] Companies Act 2006, s 901G(3)–(4).

[3] ibid, s 901G(5).

[4] *In re AGPS Bondco plc* [2024] Bus LR 745 (CA), [153]–[154] (Snowden LJ).

to this framework as the 'fair allocation of the restructuring surplus' (FaiRS) approach. The FaiRS approach draws on an understanding of the rationale for and nature of restructuring. It is also rooted in the fundamentals of theories of normative defensibility and of bargaining, each of which has applications far beyond restructuring. Having developed the framework, we then assess the current state of the cramdown case law by reference to it.

The chapter is structured as follows. Section II introduces the notion of normative defensibility, which goes under labels such as 'fairness' or 'justice'. It sets out the primary bases for such defensibility, and notes how these bases relate to restructuring and to cramdown. Section III introduces the concept of *rationality* and the very basics of bargaining theory. Both are relevant to understanding the restructuring process as a process of bargaining amongst stakeholders, which in turn is relevant to understanding the role of cramdown. Section IV explains the distinctive role of restructuring in relation to a distressed debtor. This section does much heavy lifting. It introduces and explains the concepts of fundamental value, market price, transaction price, and primary and downstream markets. Using these concepts, it explains how prices are established in healthy and in pathological markets and in circumstances where one or more parties is distressed. Section V discusses the nature of valuation by reference to primary and downstream markets and explains how to estimate fundamental value. Section VI examines the RP as a normatively constrained bargaining game. Section VII introduces the Relative Priority Rule as a key guide to the exercise of the cramdown power, while Section VIII explains the circumstances in which that Rule may be departed from. Section IX analyses the incentives created within the RP process if the FaiRS approach is followed. Section X draws on the FaiRS approach and the pre-history of the cramdown represented by the English court's decision in *MyTravel*[5] and *Bluebrook*[6] to highlight key points in the current state of the case law. Section XI concludes.

This chapter draws on and develops arguments and analyses that several of its co-authors have published over many years.[7] We have also benefited from the insightful literature on the RP and the cramdown.[8]

[5] *In re MyTravel Group plc* [2005] 2 BCLC 123.

[6] *Re Bluebrook Ltd* [2010] BCC 209.

[7] We refer to key parts of this literature here though, needless to say, none of us necessarily agrees with absolutely everything that even we ourselves have written in the past, let alone with what may have been written by one or more of the others. See in particular Ronald B Davis, Stephan Madaus, Alberto Mazzoni, Irit Mevorach, Rizwaan Jameel Mokal, Barbara Romaine, Janis Sarra, and Ignacio Tirado, *The Insolvency of Micro, Small, and Medium Enterprises – A Modular Approach* (Oxford, Oxford University Press, 2018); Stephan Madaus, 'Leaving the Shadows of US Bankruptcy Law: A Proposal to Divide the Realms of Insolvency and Restructuring Law' (2018) 19 *EBOR* 615–47; Lorenzo Stanghellini, Riz Mokal, Christoph Paulus, and Ignacio Tirado, *Best Practices in European Restructuring – Contractualised Distress Resolution in the Shadow of the Law* (Florence, Wolters Kluwer, 2018); Riz Mokal and Ignacio Tirado, 'Has Newton had his Day? Relativity and Realism in European Restructuring' (2019) 34(4) *Butterworths Journal of International Banking and Financial Law* 233–35; Riz Mokal, 'The Difficulties with "Financial Difficulties"' (2020) 35(10) *Butterworths Journal of International Banking and Financial Law* 662; Stephan Madaus, 'Corporate Reorganisation Law and the Shaping Powers of Market Realities and Doctrinal Concepts' (2022) 42(1) *Oxford Journal of Legal Studies* 1195; Stephan Madaus, 'Insolvency law through the lens of a contract theory of restructuring' in Emilie Ghio, John Wood and Jennifer Gant (eds), *Re-Examining Insolvency Law and Theory: Perspectives for the 21st Century* (Cheltenham, Elgar, 2023); Riz Mokal, 'Third-Party Releases in English Restructuring Law: Pragmatism and Propriety' in Lindsey Simon, Ralph Brubaker, Riz Mokal, Sid Pepels, and Ruud Hermans, *Third Party Releases by Means of Bankruptcy Law Guarantees and (Mass) Tort* (The Hague, Eleven, 2024).

[8] See in particular Jennifer Payne, *Schemes of Arrangement: Theory, Structure and Operation*, 2nd edn (Cambridge, Cambridge University Press, 2021), at paras 5.8 (restructuring plans) and 5.4.3 (valuation in the context of schemes of arrangement); and Sandra Frisby, 'Of Rights and Rescue: A Curious Confluence?'

II. Normative Defensibility – A Thumbnail Primer

The traditional labels for normative defensibility are 'fairness', 'equity', 'justice', their cognates, or some combination thereof.[9] Whatever the label, the essential point is that the distribution of a resource can be shown to be adequately supported by appropriate reasons and that it is not marred by inappropriate reasons.[10]

In previous work we, together with others, have constructed detailed frameworks within which to assess, justify, and critique various dimensions of insolvency[11] and resolution[12] laws by reference to appropriate reasons. In that work, we have conceptualised each of those domains of law essentially as a scheme of fair and efficient cooperation amongst all relevant stakeholders. For a deeper understanding of the normative framework for the analysis in this chapter, the reader is referred to that previous work, which we will not repeat here. The FaiRS approach similarly conceptualises restructuring law in general and the RP cramdown power in particular as key parts of a fair and efficient scheme of cooperation amongst all relevant stakeholders. For the purposes of this chapter, the following thumbnail sketch will have to do.

There are four core categories of appropriate reasons: prior entitlement, consent, desert, and need. The normative appeal of each category is readily salient and is best introduced subject to the *ceteris paribus* ('all else being equal') condition.

First, a valid prior entitlement to the resource that is the subject of a distribution is, by definition, a normatively defensible basis for a distribution in right of that entitlement. Prior entitlements, most obviously those enshrined in the rights of creditors and

(2020) 20(1) *Journal of Corporate Law Studies* 39; Jennifer Payne, 'Debt Restructuring in Transition' (2023) 139 *Law Quarterly Review* 101; Gerard McCormack, 'The UK Restructuring Plan (RP) in an Age of Uncertainty' [2024] *Journal of Business Law* 438; Rodrigo Olivares-Caminal and Nino Goglidze, 'The Collective Will in Corporate Debt Restructuring' [2024] *Journal of Business Law* 351; John Wood, 'Creative Destruction and the Post COVID-19 Economy: A Critique of the (Un)Creative Rescue Value contained within the Permanent CIGA 2020 Reforms' [2023] *Journal of Business Law* 197. See also two important papers by Sarah Paterson, 'Judicial Discretion in Part 26A Restructuring Plan Procedures' (24 January 2024), available at SSRN: https://ssrn.com/abstract=4016519; and 'The Conceptual Foundation of Cross-Class Cramdown' (18 September 2024), available at SSRN: https://papers.ssrn.com/sol3/papers.cfm?abstract_id=4959732. For a comprehensive critique of those two papers, see Mokal, 'Cram Dos, Don'ts, and Darn Its: The "Too Much Unfair Value" Approach to the UK Cramdown', *The Barrister*, 3 February 2025, available at: https://barrister-magazine.com/cram-dos-donts-and-darn-its-the-too-much-unfair-value-approach-to-the-uk-cramdown/; working paper available at SSRN: https://ssrn.com/abstract=4993883.

[9] For two excellent introductions to the current state of a literature stretching over millennia, see David Miller, 'Justice' in Edward N Zalta and Uri Nodelman (eds), *The Stanford Encyclopedia of Philosophy* (Fall 2023 Edition): https://plato.stanford.edu/archives/fall2023/entries/justice/, and Julian Lamont and Christi Favor, 'Distributive Justice' in Edward N Zalta (ed), *The Stanford Encyclopedia of Philosophy* (Winter 2017 Edition): https://plato.stanford.edu/archives/win2017/entries/justice-distributive/.

[10] In addition to resource distributions, issues of normative defensibility arise in relation to the standing of persons natural and legal, of other living beings, and of the natural world, as well as in relation to the character, inclinations, and intentions of persons, of traditions, cultural norms, tax regimes, welfare systems, and other human institutions, of war and peace, and of other states of affairs. This chapter will fail conspicuously to resolve all these issues.

[11] See in particular R Mokal, *Corporate Insolvency Law – Theory and Application* (Oxford, OUP, 2005), chapters 1–3; and Ronald B Davis, Stephan Madaus, Alberto Mazzoni, Irit Mevorach, Rizwaan Jameel Mokal, Barbara Romaine, Janis Sarra, and Ignacio Tirado, *The Insolvency of Micro, Small, and Medium Enterprises – A Modular Approach* (Oxford, Oxford University Press, 2018), 32–46.

[12] See in particular Ronald B Davis, Stephan Madaus, Monica Marcucci, Irit Mevorach, Riz Mokal, Barbara Romaine, Janis Sarra, and Ignacio Tirado, *Financial Institutions in Distress: Recovery, Resolution, and Recognition* (Oxford, Oxford University Press, 2023), 276–92.

shareholders against the debtor and/or certain of its assets, are always in play in any legitimate restructuring. Such entitlements cannot be decisive in this context, however, since it is the present or anticipated fact that they cannot all be met in full (or, at least, that they cannot be met optimally), from the assets available to meet them, that provides the raison d'être for the restructuring.

Next as to consent, the fact that all those with a stake in a distribution have freely and knowledgeably consented to that distribution is a powerful reason for considering that distribution to be normatively defensible. Being treated as bound by that to which one has freely and knowledgeably consented is to be treated with the respect due to an equal and autonomous member of the relevant community. The same reasoning can be extended to democratic decision-making in which a due majority of the members of a community binds the minority, so long as the decision-making process treats all members as equal and autonomous in the relevant senses.[13] The relevance to restructuring is obvious.

Turning to desert, a distribution may and often should favour one who has (relevantly) made a greater contribution to the creation of the resource that is the subject of the distribution. This is for both deontological and consequentialist reasons: other things being equal, there is no better claim than mine to the value that I have created, and recognising my claim to such value likely incentivises me to create more. Contribution, including in particular by way of modification of prior entitlements, is crucial to the FaiRS approach. We explain this below.

Finally, as to need, the distribution of any resource amongst members of a community should favour the member in greatest need of that resource. In any insolvency,[14] including any restructuring, the primary resource whose distribution is at issue is the right to benefit from the debtor's assets.[15] However, need cannot provide defensibility since *ceteris* is not *paribus*: as noted, different stakeholders hold different prior entitlements against the debtor and/or certain of its assets, and all assets at play in a restructuring are likely to be subject to such prior entitlements. Therefore, a party's need for the debtor's assets, considered by itself, is generally irrelevant. That does not mean that need itself is irrelevant, however. Another profound resource at issue in any legal proceeding is the protection of the law, and much of the law, including restructuring law, can be conceptualised as responding to need, by seeking to protect those of the law's subjects who are not readily able to protect themselves. An example is the court's assessment of the financial sophistication of the stakeholders to whom a restructuring proposal is put, and the more protective stance it takes towards less sophisticated such stakeholders.[16]

Two inappropriate reasons for a distribution are nepotism, which in this context means the allocation is distorted in favour of those with relations to the debtor and/or

[13] For a development of these ideas in the context of English insolvency law, see Mokal, *Corporate Insolvency Law* (n 11), particularly chapters 1 to 3.

[14] Understood properly as a 'scalar', 'continuous', and 'vague' characteristic of certain obligors: see Riz Mokal, 'What is an Insolvency Proceeding? *Gategroup* lands in a Gated Community' (2022) 31(3) *International Insolvency Review* 418, 421–32.

[15] See Mokal, *Corporate Insolvency Law* (n 11), 78–79.

[16] For an excellent example, see Miles J's judgment in *Re ALL Scheme Limited* [2021] EWHC 1401 (Ch), [101], [102(viii) and (x)], [104]–[105], [132]–[133], [138].

to another stakeholder constituency with influence in the restructuring, and prejudice, which here means discrimination on improper grounds, such as the nationality of the claimants in a particular class.[17]

III. Bargaining Theory – A Thumbnail Primer

Turning to bargaining theory, we start by introducing two useful concepts.

The first is rationality. The most common approach to rationality treats it as applying to the selection of means in circumstances where the ends are treated as given. In the context of English insolvency law, the concept has been explained thus:[18]

> Let us take a person who has the ability to select and pursue his own aims and interests. 'The rational applies to how these ends and interests are adopted and affirmed, as well as to how they are given priority.' In selecting the means with which to attain those objectives, rationality implies the ability to be guided by such principles as: 'to adopt the most effective means to ends'. Rational persons can also weigh up how the final ends they are choosing contribute towards furthering their conception of the good, and how they cohere with each other.

In this chapter, we will use rationality in this means-to-ends sense. In relation to the distribution of a resource, we will assume that each rational person or group of persons seeks to maximise their share of the resource.

The second concept is that of a game. This term derives from game theory, which studies strategic interaction; that is, interaction in which each party makes choices that seek, amongst other things, to anticipate and respond to the choices of the other parties to the interaction.[19]

Turning to bargaining theory, law and economics scholars Robert Cooter and Michael Gilbert provide a convenient recent treatment.[20] In the terminology they use (much of which is not unique to them), any interaction which may yield an agreement is a 'bargaining game'. In a 'noncooperative solution' to such a game, the parties cannot come to an agreement. In this event, each participant in the bargaining game walks away with their 'non-cooperative payoff'. For each player, their non-cooperative payoff is their 'threat value': the player can make a highly credible threat to walk away from the bargaining unless they receive through the bargain something in excess of

[17] 'The rights and liabilities of claimants against the assets are the same regardless of their nationality or place of residence. *A distinction between foreign and English claimants would respond to no principle known to the law*', as Lord Sumption (writing with Lord Toulson) put it with characteristic tautness in *Stichting Shell Pensioenfonds v Krys* [2015] AC 616 (PC), [34] (emphasis added). English insolvency law's '*Gibbs* principle' is an aberrant and disreputable example of prejudice whose consideration is left to another day. (See Irit Mevorach and Riz Mokal, 'X Marks the Cross-Border Restructuring Spot? The *Gibbs* Past and the Model Laws Future', presentation at Insolvency Service Annual Conference, 10 November 2023: https://sites.google.com/view/forward-thinking-2023/home, considering the rule associated with *Antony Gibbs Sons v La Société Industrielle et Commerciale des Métaux* (1890) 25 QBD 399 (CA)).

[18] Mokal, *Corporate Insolvency Law* (n 11), 72 (footnotes omitted), citing and quoting from John Rawls, *A Theory of Justice* (Cambridge MA, Harvard University Press, 1971), 47–48.

[19] David Gauthier, *Morals by Agreement* (Oxford, Clarendon Press, 1986), 21.

[20] Robert Cooter and Michael Gilbert, *Public Law and Economics* (New York, Oxford University Press, 2022).

their non-cooperative payoff. The sum of the threat values of all the players is the 'non-cooperative value of the game'.[21]

If a bargain is reached, the game ends in a 'cooperative solution', each player receives a 'cooperative payoff', and the sum of all these co-operative payoffs is the 'cooperative value of the game'. A bargain worth making creates what Cooter and Gilbert call the 'cooperative surplus', which they define as 'the amount by which the game's cooperative value exceeds its noncooperative value'.[22] Putting these elements together, Cooter and Gilbert explain that:[23]

> Bargaining has three elements: establish threat values, determine the cooperative surplus, and distribute the surplus. The threat value and cooperative surplus depend on rationality alone. Distribution of the surplus depends on psychology and other factors.

While the 'other factors' on which the distribution of the cooperative surplus *should* depend are the normative factors discussed above, the factors on which the distribution of the cooperative surplus would in fact depend include the players' respective bargaining power.

The bargaining power of each party to a bargaining game may be understood as a function of four factors.[24] The first is that party's outside option, which is what the party expects to receive in the event that the bargaining fails. In other words, the outside option is identical to the party's threat value. The more attractive that outside option, the higher that party's bargaining power. The second factor is the party's inside option, which is the party's position and resources while the bargaining is ongoing. Again, the greater the party's inside option, the greater its bargaining power. The third is the party's time preference, which reflects how impatient that party is to reach a cooperative outcome. The greater that impatience, the lower the party's bargaining power. And the fourth is risk aversion: the greater the party's desire to avoid a non-cooperative outcome, the lower its bargaining power.

IV. Why Restructure, Ever?

When a corporate obligor is in financial difficulties, it or its insolvency officeholder (referred to hereafter jointly or, if appropriate, severally, as 'debtor') can always raise money by selling its business in whole or part as a going concern or, in what often amounts to the same thing, by selling their claims to the value of that business. If the corporate owner of the business trades publicly, it is easy enough to sell its shares. If a buyer for the going concern cannot be found, the debtor may sell piecemeal some or all of the assets constituting that business. Why, then, ever go to the trouble to restructure the debtor's liabilities and affairs?

The answer to this rhetorical question is foundational but it is not always obvious. It has been missed in the *MyTravel* decision,[25] to lasting unhelpful effect. The answer is therefore worth spelling out.

[21] ibid, 14–15.
[22] ibid, 15.
[23] ibid, 16.
[24] Jon Elster, *The Cement of Society* (New York, Cambridge University Press, 1989), 74–94.
[25] *In re MyTravel Group plc* [2005] 2 BCLC 123, discussed below.

It is in the interests of the stakeholders as a group of any distressed debtor (including the debtor itself) to preserve and realise for their own benefit, to the greatest extent practicable, the 'fundamental value' of the debtor's estate. A sale, even of the entire going concern (or of its value), may not do the trick. Accordingly, stakeholders as a group rationally engage in a restructuring rather than a sale when a restructuring, net of its costs, would preserve and realise fundamental value for the benefit of stakeholders as a group to a greater extent than would a sale, net of its costs.

A. Fundamental Value

The fundamental value of an asset or a business is the present value of the expected future payoffs from that asset or business.[26] In the context of English restructuring law, this proposition was characterised as a 'truism' back in 2006 and explained as follows:[27]

> It is important to note what to most readers may be a statement of the obvious, that the *present* value of any asset is a function not only of its present but also of *all future* streams of income generated by it. This is simply another way of saying that what a rational and well-informed buyer would be willing to pay for an asset depends not just on what use can be made of the asset today but also [on] what uses can be derived from it the next day, the next year, and so on. The *present* value of a ten-year lease of land is higher than that of a one-year lease of that same piece of land, even though what the lessee can do with the land *today* is identical for most practical purposes in both scenarios, precisely because the ten-year lease continues to generate a stream of 'income' (i.e. use) long past the point in time at which the one-year lease ceases to do so.

The importance of fundamental value has long been recognised. In some European jurisdictions, it went under the concept of goodwill or *avviamento*.[28] In the Anglophone literature, its importance was described by Irving Fisher in 1907.[29] The subsequent year, the celebrated Mr Justice Oliver Wendel Holmes stated in the US Supreme Court that 'the commercial value of property consists in the expectation of income from it'.[30] In 1930, Irving Fisher explained as follows:[31]

> Capital, in the sense of capital value, is simply future income discounted or, in other words, capitalized. *The value of any property, or rights to wealth, is its value as a source of income and is found by discounting that expected income* (emphasis added).

[26] Riz Mokal, 'Liquidity, Systemic Risk, and the Bankruptcy Treatment of Financial Contracts' (2015) 10(1) *Brooklyn Journal of Corporate, Financial & Commercial Law* 15, 25.

[27] Michael Crystal and Rizwaan Jameel Mokal, 'The Valuation of Distressed Companies: A Conceptual Framework – Part I' (2006) 3(2) *International Corporate Rescue* 63, 65 fn 14.

[28] Goodwill remains relevant to the assessment of fundamental value. For example, one of the two methods for assessing fundamental value noted by Sylvain Marsat and Benjamin Williams, 'Does Price Influence Assessment of Fundamental Value? Experimental Evidence' (2013) 14(4) *Journal of Behavioral Finance* 268, 268 is 'the actual net book value plus a goodwill that assesses intangible assets, since they are a potential profit'.

[29] Irving Fisher, *The Rate of Interest: Its Nature, Determination and Relation to Economic Phenomenon* (New York, Macmillan, 1907), 49–50.

[30] *Galveston, Harrisburg & San Antonio Railway Co v Texas* (1908) 210 US 217, 226. Holmes J was in the minority in that case but this dictum was approved by a unanimous Supreme Court in *Consolidated Rock Products Company v Du Bois* (1941) 312 US 510, 526.

[31] Irving Fisher, *The Theory of Interest – As Determined by Impatience to Spend Income and Opportunity to Invest It* (New York, Macmillan, 1930), 12.

The concept of fundamental value is indispensable because the phenomenon to which the concept refers is ubiquitous, important, and important to understand. An understanding of fundamental value also helps us to notice the peculiarities and limitations of market price, which we may consider the price that would be attained in an arm's length market sale between reasonably knowledgeable solvent parties.[32]

B. Primary Markets and Downstream Markets

An intuitive way of understanding the distinction between fundamental value and market price is to note the distinction between what we will call a 'primary' market and the market 'downstream' of it. A market is downstream of a primary market in the sense that the product sold in the primary market is used in the creation of the product sold in the downstream market.

Consider the markets for widgets (the widget market) and for widget-making foundries (the foundry market). The widget market is downstream of the foundry market and the sellers in the former are the buyers in the latter. The price of foundries is set in the foundry market. However, the value to a potential buyer of a new foundry is determined in the widget market, since a newly-acquired foundry would be put to use making a product that sells in that market and it is the expectation of earning the revenues from such sales that has motivated the purchase in the first place.

In a well-functioning economy, the primary and downstream markets will tend to remain in harmony in the relevant sense that there is a predictable relation between the price of widgets and the price of foundries. More specifically, the market price of a foundry will tend towards the payoffs that can be earnt by using it, that is, towards the foundry's fundamental value. For a potential buyer, the 'mere comparison between price and estimated [fundamental] value enables the [potential buyer] to ascertain whether an asset is cheap or dear'.[33] This shows that prices in the primary market are set by buyers and sellers estimating (amongst other things) the payoffs the product of the primary market would create in the secondary market. (That is, the buyers and sellers of foundries agree prices with a keen eye to widget prices.)

In a hypothetical world in which markets function well and buyers and sellers are solvent and trade knowledgeably and at arm's length, the prices in the primary market may communicate meaningful information about the fundamental value of the product trading in that market.[34] (That is, the market price of a foundry may be used in

[32] A particularly brilliant early analysis of fundamental value and its difference from market price is Gabriel Preinreich, 'Annual Survey of Economic Theory: The Theory of Depreciation' (1938) 6(3) *Econometrica* 219. Preinreich's remark, at 239, that 'Theory is an insidious affliction … which is difficult to shake off' had several of your present interlocutors nodding in recognition. Another observation that hit home, ibid, was: 'the solution of any economic problem ultimately resolves itself into the task of solving all other problems at the same time. In the circumstances, the last-comer is always in a strategic position. No matter how many simultaneous equations his predecessors may have set up, he can always prove their naïveté by pointing to another equation, which they ought not to have overlooked'.

[33] Marsat and Williams (n 28), 268.

[34] In fact, it is a general maxim of valuation (not restricted to restructuring) that 'whatever the valuation method used, price [determined in the primary market] should *not* be relevant in estimating fundamental

seeking to estimate the fundamental value of that foundry.) That hypothetical world is not, however, always a good approximation of the real world. We consider next some of the most important reasons why market prices may not adequately communicate information about fundamental values.

C. Prices in Pathological Markets

Markets may suffer pathologies in which market prices consistently exceed or fall short of fundamental values. Using the examples (amongst others) of the 'Dutch Tulip Mania' and the 'South Sea Bubble', the finance economist Robert Jarrow defines an asset price bubble, in the standard way,[35] as the state in which 'the market price exceeds the asset's fundamental value'.[36] Building on the notion of the present value of all future payoffs from the asset, Jarrow explains the fundamental value of an asset as 'the price a trader would pay if after purchase, they had to hold the asset in their portfolio forever'.[37] In the other direction, a severely illiquid market is one in which the asset's market price may significantly undershoot its fundamental value.[38]

D. Market Price versus Transaction Price

Further still and importantly, the sale of many types of commercial assets and virtually all businesses does not take place at a pre-existing market price. There are a number of reasons for this, of which the simplest to state is that assets are often not, and businesses are hardly ever, fungible, that is, perfectly substitutable one with others.[39] If a sale of such an asset or business is to occur, therefore, a *transaction price* has to be established through bargaining between the seller and potential buyers.[40] The transaction price is highly sensitive to the peculiarities of the parties as well as to the context in which it is established. We discuss next the establishment of transaction prices when the seller and/or the primary market are distressed.

value': Marsat and Williams (n 28), 268 (emphasis added). Marsat and Williams show experimentally that, in fact, the price of an asset affects subjective estimates of the asset's fundamental value.

[35] Compare, for example, R Mokal, 'Liquidity, Systemic Risk, and the Bankruptcy Treatment of Financial Contracts' (n 26) 25.

[36] Robert Jarrow, 'Asset Price Bubbles' (2015) 7 *Annual Review of Financial Economics* 201, 202.

[37] ibid, 204.

[38] See for example Markus Brunnermeier and Lasse Pedersen, 'Market Liquidity and Funding Liquidity' (2009) 22(6) *Review of Financial Studies* 2201, 2202, defining 'market liquidity' as 'the difference between the transaction price and the fundamental value', and Mokal, 'Liquidity, Systemic Risk, and the Bankruptcy Treatment of Financial Contracts' (n 26) 31, defining a liquid market as one 'which enable[s] assets to change hands *at or close to* their fundamental value'.

[39] This is true for companies whose shares do not trade publicly and therefore do not have a market price. It is also true of a publicly-traded company whose distress has resulted in a collapse of its market capitalisation, leaving the question of the ascertainment of fundamental value acute.

[40] This process is a paradigm of a bargaining game; see for example Abhinay Muthoo, *Bargaining Theory with Applications* (Cambridge, Cambridge University Press, 1999), 1.

E. Forced Sales and Fire Sales

A distressed or forced sale (hereafter, a forced sale) of an asset occurs when the seller cannot meet its own obligations without selling that asset.[41] A forced sale is very relevant to the present discussion since such a sale of some or all of the debtor's estate may be the alternative to a distressed restructuring. And there is a significant empirical literature which documents that forced sales – for example, in the markets for commercial aircraft,[42] publicly-traded equity,[43] housing,[44] and corporate securities[45] – occur at transaction prices representing significant discounts even on market prices (to say nothing of fundamental values). A recent survey of the literature (which also covers 'fire sales' as described below) shows that the discounts can reach and even exceed 50 per cent of the market price.[46]

The reasons that forced sales enable buyers to appropriate more of the asset's fundamental value, to the disadvantage of sellers, can be readily understood by considering the distressed seller's bargaining power by reference to the four criteria set out above. The seller's likely outside option might well be insolvency, which would make it highly risk averse, and its inside option might rapidly diminish as it ran out of operating cash and as ever more liabilities fell due which it was unable to pay, with the result that it would have a high time preference. This would severely drain its bargaining power, which is to say that it would be left desperate to sell and willing to accept a price well below fundamental value and often even below any market prices. The rational response for potential buyers would be to make 'lowball' bids, that is, offers pitched low to capitalise on the seller's desperation. Unsurprisingly in these circumstances, the transaction price would likely significantly undershoot fundamental value.

All these reasons hold a fortiori when the distressed debtor must sell not an asset piecemeal but some or all of its business as a going concern. Additionally, in selling a business, there may be a 'stigma of distress', whereby potential buyers extrapolate from the business's current difficulties excessively to discount its future prospects and therefore underestimate its fundamental value. This may be because of the 'adverse selection effect', which in this context kicks in when potential buyers assume that a business with more promising prospects – that is, a higher fundamental value – would have been retained by the debtor and its stakeholders, notably, through a restructuring. In these circumstances, that the business was on the market at all would be taken as a signal that the seller and its stakeholders consider the market price to exceed the business's

[41] Andrei Shleifer and Robert Vishny, 'Fire Sales in Finance and Macroeconomics' (2011) 25(1) *Journal of Economic Perspectives* 29, 30.

[42] Todd Pulvino, 'Do Asset Fire Sales Exist? An Empirical Investigation of Commercial Aircraft Transactions' (1998) 53(3) *Journal of Finance* 939; Todd Pulvino, 'Effects of Bankruptcy Court Protection on Asset Sales' (1999) 52(2) *Journal of Financial Economics* 151.

[43] Joshua Coval and Erik Stafford, 'Asset Fire Sales (and Purchases) in Equity Markets' (2007) 86(2) *Journal of Financial Economics* 479.

[44] John Campbell, Stefano Giglio, and Parag Pathak, 'Forced Sales and House Prices' (2011) 101(5) *American Economic Review* 2108.

[45] Mark Mitchell and Todd Pulvino, 'Arbitrage Crashes and the Speed of Capital' (2012) 104(3) *Journal of Financial Economics* 469.

[46] Claudia Curi and Maurizio Murgia, *Asset Sales: Their Role in Restructuring and Financing Firms* (Cham, Springer, 2020), chapter 5.

fundamental value. The rational response for potential buyers would be to make lower bids. Finally, and in any case, it may be difficult simply to assemble a group of new investors with the financial wherewithal to purchase the going concern. This depresses demand and therefore also price.[47] Again, the transaction price would fail to capture a significant proportion of the fundamental value.

To make matters worse, consider the not uncommon scenario in which a debtor is distressed because it operates in an industry and/or an economy which itself is distressed. A recent example is passenger airline distress during the periods of the COVID-19 pandemic and resulting lockdowns, in which air travel was legally restricted across much of the world. Airline operators came under severe stress as, massive government assistance notwithstanding, revenues evaporated and liabilities accumulated. In this sort of scenario, consider Air A, which seeks to respond to its difficulties by selling certain of the aeroplanes in its fleet. However, B Airlines, a potential buyer, is itself in dire straits and, far from expanding its capacity, is seeking to sell certain aircraft of its own. This reduces the demand for and therefore the price of A's planes. And as A and B, and other similarly troubled operators C, D, and E, put aircraft on the market, the supply goes up, pushing down the price faced by X Air, a small specialist operator which thinks it sees an opportunity, and which may well be persuaded to buy an additional plane. This is the phenomenon of the *fire* sale, which is a forced sale in a distressed market. Fire sales are likely to occur when those like A to E who are able to derive best value from that asset type are more likely to be selling rather than buying, with the result that there is a significant proportion of inexpert buyers of the asset type, like X, who anticipate (amongst other things) making less than best use of those assets and who therefore make lower bids.[48] The corrosive effect on transaction prices is obvious.

F. Restructuring of Economically Distressed Businesses

Finally in this part of the discussion, it should be remembered that the fundamental value of an 'economically distressed' business would characteristically be realised by breaking up the assets constituting that business and selling those assets piecemeal. Here, the fundamental value is the sum of the proceeds of the sale of those assets. This is another way of saying that economically distressed businesses lack a 'going concern surplus'; that is, there is not a positive difference in the present value of the future payoffs of the going concern on the one hand and the business's constitutive assets considered piecemeal on the other.[49]

Note that it would be rational to restructure an economically distressed business if an immediate liquidation would destroy its fundamental value, for example, where a restructuring would obviate the need for forced or even fire sales of the assets constituting the business.

[47] See Crystal and Mokal (n 27), 64–65 and the sources cited therein.

[48] Andrei Shleifer and Robert Vishny, 'Fire Sales in Finance and Macroeconomics' (2011) 25(1) *Journal of Economic Perspectives* 29, 30.

[49] See Crystal and Mokal (n 27), 63–64.

G. Rationale for Restructuring

Putting all this together, we reiterate that it is rational for the stakeholders, as a group, of a debtor in present or anticipated financial difficulties to seek to restructure the debtor rather than sell some or all of its business, when restructuring rather than a sale would be likely better to preserve that business's fundamental value and realise that value for the stakeholders.

V. Valuation

As noted, the restructuring process often requires determination of the *present* value of a business, which is the value to be preserved and distributed through the restructuring. The foregoing discussion shows, crucially, the irrationality of seeking to derive that value from the price that *that* business would attain in a market sale at *that* time.

A. Hypothetical Sale: Primary Market versus Downstream Market

That is not to say that valuation by reference to a notional sale can play no role. To the contrary, the price estimated by conceptualising a hypothetical sale may be a useful heuristic in certain cases, so long as it is understood that (using the terminology introduced above) the market by reference to which that price is determined is the downstream one rather than the primary one. Let us explain.

Consider Fundries Ltd, a manufacturer of widget-making foundries, which traded successfully for over a century under the banner 'Find the Fun in F[o]UN-dries' but is now distressed. Fundries has recently sought to shift from selling foundries making widgets for use in the fossil fuel extraction industries to those producing widgets crucial to carbon alternatives. The stakeholders, all highly sophisticated players in the energy generation markets, are unanimous in their belief that the business's fortunes are renewable. If given breathing space and a second chance to navigate the winds of change, they consider that it would ride the waves to a sunny future. Over 75 per cent of the stakeholders do, however, feel that the banner needs rethinking.

The Fundries business has been marketed to other foundry manufacturers (that is, in the primary market) with a view to applying the proceeds of sale towards discharging Fundries' liabilities to the maximal extent. The offers have, however, left the current stakeholder disappointed. There is much stress amongst foundry manufacturers. Fundries is not alone in grappling with the anticipated decline in the fossil fuel extraction industries, and many competitors are seeking to sell up. This stress amongst potential buyers of the Fundries business and the glut of foundry manufacturing plant are depressing prices. The Fundries stakeholders consider that potential buyers do not adequately understand the distinctive structure of its business, the innovative way it proposes to reposition itself, or the high quality of its top management. Information as to these matters has been gleaned by the stakeholders over extended periods of interaction with Fundries but cannot cost-effectively be established to the satisfaction of potential buyers.[50] Further, the market is all too aware of Fundries' distress and of the peril besetting it unless it achieves a rapid resolution. The stakeholders consider that this weakening of Fundries' bargaining position is attracting lowball bids.

Against this background, Fundries' stakeholders embark on a restructuring of its liabilities and assets. For this purpose, they have to determine the present value of its business. How should that business be valued?

It should be obvious that this valuation cannot rationally be undertaken by assuming a sale on the foundry manufacturing market, that is, the primary market. It is *precisely and only* because the debtor and/or some of its stakeholders consider that a price determined in that market would not adequately capture the business's fundamental value that they have embarked on a restructuring in the first place. Otherwise, they would sell.

For similar reasons, market testing (on the primary market) for the purposes of restructuring is of ambiguous utility. Bids significantly below the stakeholders' estimates of fundamental value may underline for the stakeholders the value-destructiveness of a sale and the wisdom of restructuring. Bids approaching the stakeholders' estimates of fundamental value may be taken as indicating that a restructuring may not be necessary after all (since a sale would adequately preserve and realise the value in the business). Alternatively, suppose the stakeholders consider that they have good reasons for thinking that primary market prices are depressed (because, say, many similar businesses are distressed and seeking to sell) and/or that the distress of their business is so well known as to be bound to attract lowball offers. In that event, bids approaching their estimates of fundamental value may give them reason to consider such estimates unduly pessimistic and to proceed with a restructuring on the basis that it would preserve and realise more value than they had previously anticipated and therefore more value than would a sale.

Against this background, the valuation of a distressed business should focus on the downstream market (in case of Fundries, on the market for the right type of foundries). The restructuring is to be undertaken in order best to preserve the business's fundamental value for its stakeholders' benefit. That value is the present value of the business's future payoffs, which will arise from sales of foundries. The payoffs in the foundry market are therefore a key determinant of the payoffs in the foundry manufacturing market. Therefore, if the valuation is to occur by reference to a notional sale, it should envisage a buyer deciding what to bid by reference to the expected sales of foundries.

Note that we have not yet mentioned inalienable assets, such as non-transferrable licences,[51] which would be lost upon an actual sale of the business but which may be

[50] Economists are familiar with the idea of information which is '*observable*' by X but which is not cost-effectively '*verifiable*' to the satisfaction of Y or Z. This is particularly true of information about income streams and individual skills, where such '*private information*' is particularly '*persistent*', that is, difficult to communicate to others to their satisfaction over an extended period of time. See for example Noah Williams, 'Persistent Private Information' (2011) 79(4) *Econometrica* 1233, 1233. Another important type of observable but unverifiable information relevant to insolvency law arises when an agent 'misbehaves' in certain ways, that is, does not act in the principal's interests. See Mokal, *Corporate Insolvency Law* (n 11), 173.

[51] Of the sort at issue in *In re MyTravel Group plc* [2005] 2 BCLC 123 (Ch).

preserved in a restructuring. A similar example is of an asset that determines upon its holder's entry into a formal insolvency proceeding[52] but which may be preserved in a restructuring. In fact, such assets represent a special case of the general phenomenon with which we are concerned. Such assets are part of the fundamental value of a business that is preserved only if the business is priced by reference to the value of its product in the downstream market but which value is lost if the business is priced by reference to a sale in the primary market.

B. Estimating Fundamental Value

There are three established methods for estimating fundamental value.[53] The discounted cashflow approach most directly seeks to capitalise future income of the business to be restructured and is one that any rational buyer focusing on that business's value in the downstream market would utilise in deciding what to bid. The market comparison approach attempts to estimate fundamental value by identifying relevantly comparable but healthy businesses and extrapolating from their financial performance metrics. The key assumption here is that those metrics adequately reflect the present value of the future payoffs from the relevantly similar businesses and therefore serve as a basis for estimating the present value of the future payoffs from the business that is the subject of the restructuring. And the comparable transaction approach seeks to pin down fundamental value by identifying sales of relevantly comparable businesses. This method is farthest removed from the downstream market, since it does not itself seek to take account of the present value of future payoffs but instead seeks to free-ride on the parties to comparator transactions having adequately done so in agreeing the prices in those comparators. This explains why this method should not be used on a standalone basis but instead 'is best utilised to corroborate valuations obtained by other methods'.[54]

In relation to these methods, it has been noted that:[55]

> Not all of these methods would be equally appropriate in each case, and there might be additional methods suitable on the facts which might be used in combination with some or all of the above. It is important to note that the practice in the US courts is to use several methods in any given case, with each method acting as a check on the others. In particular, the comparable companies and comparable transactions methods rely on data from companies other than the one then in question, and so should be combined together with the [discounted cashflow] method, which yields a valuation derived from the performance of the relevant company itself.

[52] Of the sort at issue in *Money Markets International Stockbrokers Ltd v London Stock Exchange Ltd* [2002] 1 WLR 1150 (Neuberger J).

[53] See Crystal and Mokal (n 27), 67–68, quoting Kerry O'Rourke, 'Valuation Uncertainty in Chapter 11 Reorganizations' [2005] 2 *Columbia Business Law Review* 403, 420–21.

[54] *MFS/Sun Life Trust-High Yield Series v Van Dusen Airport Services Co* 910 F Supp 913, 942 (SDNY 1995).

[55] Crystal and Mokal (n 27), 68 (footnotes omitted).

C. Valuation Uncertainty and Disputes

Finally, valuation (including by each of the three methods set out above) is at least as much art as science. It is a process of estimation based not just on hard data (such as the prices of the business's product) but also on numerous assumptions requiring judgement. Uncertainties are ineliminable and arise from both 'strategic' and 'structural' factors.[56] Therefore, different, equally competent, good faith valuers working with the same information may nevertheless arrive at different conclusions. This is the nature of the beast.

In restructuring, different stakeholder classes may place different values on the business. This phenomenon is no different in principle from any settlement negotiation in which parties disagree because, for example, they attach different probabilities to various possible outcomes.

The view is sometimes expressed that English restructuring law should not involve valuation disputes. This point has been made about the RP process by reference to the supposed desire to this effect of the government of the day.[57] In our view, the notion that valuation disputes should always be avoided is magical thinking, and invitations for judicial decision-making to take account of the desires of government officials should be treated with the greatest caution.

It is, of course, perfectly reasonable for the government, and indeed for all those with a stake in the restructuring regime, to hope that most cases would not involve excessive valuation battles. The facts, however, are that valuation is complex and uncertain, that a lot often rides on its outcome, and that parties with the incentives and means to dispute a valuation will seek to do so. The court should (and does) case manage as best it can. However, and subject to proper case management concerns, it would not, in our respectful view, be right for a court to preclude parties from adducing competing valuations and/or challenging valuation evidence from another party, if such parties consider this worth their while in the circumstances of that case.

Further and critically, the court's role when construing a statutory provision 'involves an objective assessment of the meaning which a reasonable legislature as a body would be seeking to convey in using the statutory words which are being considered'.[58] Explanatory notes to statutes 'may cast light on the meaning of particular statutory provisions', and other 'external aids to interpretation' such as Law Commission reports and Government White Papers 'may disclose the background to a statute and assist the court to identify not only the mischief which it addresses but also the purpose of the legislation, thereby assisting a purposive interpretation of a particular statutory provision'.[59] Subject only to these considerations (if and insofar as relevant), it is not the court's role to interpret legislation, or to exercise discretionary powers, with a view to giving effect to the hopes, beliefs, or assumptions of a government or of government officials. Judges at the highest levels have repeatedly emphasised that 'The beliefs and

[56] Explained in Crystal and Mokal, (n 27), 66–67.

[57] S Paterson, 'Judicial Discretion in Part 26A Restructuring Plan Procedures' (24 January 2022), 14–15.

[58] *R (O) v Secretary of State for the Home Department* [2023] AC 255, [31] (Lord Hodge, with whom the other members of the Court agreed).

[59] ibid, [30] (Lord Hodge).

assumptions of those who frame Acts of Parliament cannot make the law'.[60] The position is a fortiori as to the hopes, wishes, and expectations of those in the executive with responsibility for consulting on future legislation and for drafting the text of statutory bills.

VI. The Restructuring Plan as a Normatively Constrained Bargaining Game

Plainly, restructuring is a bargaining game, and the RP process seeks to provide a set of normatively defensible rules by which this game is to be played.

The FaiRS approach conceptualises a restructuring plan as essentially seeking, first, to preserve and perhaps create value in the debtor enterprise, and second, to distribute this value in a normatively defensible manner. This conceptualisation yields the notion of a 'restructuring surplus' – the cooperative surplus at issue in the restructuring – which is 'the value sought to be preserved and perhaps created by the implementation of the plan itself'.[61] In the terms introduced above, the restructuring surplus is that part of the fundamental value of the relevant estate which would be lost to the stakeholders in the relevant alternative and which is sought to be preserved for their benefit by the plan.

Equally plainly, Condition A sets the minimum threat value for each member of each dissenting class.[62] It thereby ensures that the plan is not expropriative, that is, that the plan does not take value which would be available to members of a dissenting class in the relevant alternative and reallocate such value to another. Instead, by virtue of Condition A, 'only the restructuring surplus is in play in relation to members of dissenting classes'.[63]

Condition B is best understood as intended to establish that, in relation to the proposed plan, the parties have got as close as practicable to a cooperative solution. It does so by showing that some sufficient constituency of the relevant stakeholders whose rights are to be affected by the plan considers the plan to be in their interests.[64]

In relation to any restructuring, and in relation to the RP process in particular, the court plays two key roles as to the distribution of the restructuring surplus. On the facts of that particular restructuring, the court satisfies itself that the restructuring allocates

[60] *Inland Revenue Commissioners v Dowdall O'Mahoney & Co* [1952] AC 401 (HL), 426 (Lord Radcliffe); endorsed in, for example, *Kirkness (Inspector of Taxes) v John Hudson & Co Ltd* [1955] AC 696 (HL), 714 (Viscount Simonds); *Re Attorney General of Northern Ireland's Reference (No 1 of 1975)* [1977] AC 105 (HL), 143 (Viscount Dilhorne); and *Bettison v Langton* [2002] 1 AC 27 (HL), 44 (Lord Scott).

[61] R Mokal, 'The Two Conditions for the Part 26A Cram Down' (2020) 35(11) *Butterworths Journal of International Banking and Financial Law* 730, 730.

[62] English restructuring law has long accepted the importance of setting a threat value for dissentients by reference to the relevant alternative. For an early example, see the judgment of David Richards J in *In re T & N Ltd* [2005] Pensions LR 1, [2004] EWHC 2361 (Ch), [82], citing *In re English, Scottish and Australian Chartered Bank* [1893] 3 Ch 385.

[63] ibid, 730. See also *In re AGPS Bondco plc* [2024] Bus LR 745 (CA), [150]–[152].

[64] For discussion of the inadequacies of Condition B, see Mokal, 'The Two Conditions for the Part 26A Cram Down' (n 61), 731–32.

the restructuring surplus in a normatively defensible manner. And in doing so, the court seeks to set up salutary incentives for parties to future restructurings, including incentives to reach a cooperative solution so as to minimise the need for resort to a cramdown at all.

In any given case, the checks on the composition of voting classes and, at the sanction stage, on intra-class fairness, are intended, in part, to minimise nepotism (as defined above). In properly constituted classes, if the intra-class information provision and assessment conditions are duly met, the court may be reasonably confident that, in relation to the plan about which information has been duly provided, members of each class are good enough judges of their own interest. And if the intra-class fairness conditions are also met, the court may be reasonably confident that each class constitutes a meaningful common interest-based constituency not unduly tainted by nepotism that is able to bind itself and its members through a broadly democratic decision-making process. In such circumstances, if the requisite super-majorities in each affected class have voted for a plan, the restructuring game can be regarded as practically having attained a cooperative solution. In this event, the court may be reasonably confident that the plan allocates the restructuring surplus in a normatively defensible manner, that is, in a manner acceptable to autonomous stakeholders making a reasonably well-informed and considered decision. In summary, in relation to the assenting class, the proposed allocation is justified by consent.

If, however, one or more stakeholder classes does not vote for the plan, this consent-based justification is not available in relation to its members. Instead, the normative defensibility of the proposed allocation must be tested by reference to some other appropriate metric. The FaiRS approach considers contribution (in the sense introduced above) as the appropriate metric: the defensibility of the proposed allocation to the dissenting classes should be assessed by reference to their contribution to the creation of the surplus.

Claimants affected by the plan contribute to the surplus *qua* claimants (that is, as holders of extant legal rights at stake in the restructuring, as opposed to, say, as contributors of new value):[65]

> through variations in or releases of existing rights against the debtor and occasionally against a third party such as an insurer or guarantor. Such amendments may take the form of debt repayment holidays, maturity extensions, interest write-offs, principal write-downs, releases or amendments of security, guarantee, or insurance arrangements, debt for equity swaps, and so on.

Such modifications of the parties' rights and obligations are intended to provide the debtor with a chance of trading out of such difficulties as beset it, or (in some cases) to enable a value-preserving wind-down of its business, each in the interests of such of its stakeholders as retain a genuine economic stake in it or (in some cases) who may realistically gain such a stake in the event that the plan proves efficacious. Where the plan *does* prove efficacious and stakeholders receive returns pursuant to the plan in excess of those they would have received in the relevant alternative, such surplus returns are

[65] Mokal, 'The Two Conditions for the Part 26A Cram Down' (n 61), 730.

conceptualised as the payoff for these stakeholders' contributions to the creation of the restructuring surplus.[66]

VII. The Relative Priority Rule as Default

In relation to the restructuring surplus, the FaiRS approach advocates starting with the 'Relative Priority Rule' (RPR),[67] which, at its most abstract, requires the plan presumptively to treat each dissenting class at least as favourably as any other class of the same rank and more favourably than any junior class.[68] More specifically, the RPR entails comparing the estimated returns, in the relevant alternative, of each dissenting class with the estimated returns of any class ranking below or on par with that dissenting class which is to receive or retain value pursuant to the plan. The plan proposes to permit the debtor to continue to benefit from the value of these returns. The ratio of these returns is a function of both the quantum and the priority of the claims held by members of the classes being compared. That ratio, therefore, 'provides a default approximation of the relative contribution to the restructuring surplus made by members of the two classes', and that is the presumptively appropriate allocation of their respective shares of the surplus.[69] For example, if the dissenting mezzanine class would receive 40 pence on the pound in the relevant alternative while the junior class would receive 20 pence on the pound, the default position is that the plan should be approved only if it provides at least twice as much per pound to the mezzanine holders as to the juniors.

In short, it is normatively defensible – that is, fair – that the (relevant part of the) restructuring surplus is distributed amongst dissenting and any equal ranking and/or junior classes in proportion to their respective contributions to the creation of such surplus. This contribution is proxied by the relative returns to the relevant classes in the relevant alternative.

Importantly, the debtor (or other party) proposing the plan should not be able to bring about a violation of the RPR by the 'simple expedient of leaving the junior class outwith the plan' and thereby 'left with uncompromised claims (or claims subjected only to minimal cosmetic modifications) and the prospect of (in effect) full and timely repayment if the plan were to be sanctioned'.[70] In this respect, the FaiRS approach argues for the rejection of the relatively laissez-faire attitude traditionally taken by the courts to the question of which claimants should be made subject to the restructuring.[71]

[66] ibid, 730.

[67] Introduced in Lorenzo Stanghellini, Riz Mokal, Christoph Paulus, and Ignacio Tirado, *Best Practices in European Restructuring – Contractualised Distress Resolution in the Shadow of the Law* (Florence, Wolters Kluwer, 2018), 45–47, and developed in Riz Mokal, 'The Court's Discretion in relation to the Part 26A Cram Down' (2021) 36(1) *Butterworths Journal of International Banking and Financial Law* 12, 15–16. The RPR is also the default cramdown rule in Directive (EU) 2019/1023 of the European Parliament and of the Council of 20 June 2019 on Preventive Restructuring Frameworks; see Articles 11(1)(c) and 11(2).

[68] Mokal and Tirado, 'Has Newton had his Day?' (n 7), 235.

[69] Mokal, 'The Court's Discretion in relation to the Part 26A Cram Down' (n 67), 15.

[70] ibid, 16.

[71] The high point of that traditional approach is Peter Gibson LJ's statement in *Sea Assets Limited v Penerbangan Garuda Indonesia* [2001] EWCA Civ 1696, [51], that 'the proposer of a scheme is free to select the creditors to whom a scheme of arrangement should be put'.

It recommends instead that, 'provided that the court is presented with adequate evidence, it should be astute to forestall this form of abuse of the plan proponent's … freedom to choose to whom to propose the plan'.[72]

VIII. Departing from the Default Rule

Further and critically, respect for relative priority in the distribution of the restructuring surplus is only the starting point. The RPR focuses on the contributions to the restructuring surplus made through the variation of existing rights, but that is not the only way in which to contribute to that surplus and thereby become a legitimate recipient of some part of that surplus. Accordingly, the FaiRS approach considers that departure from the RPR may be appropriate if normatively defensible by reference to:[73]

> whatever restructuring-relevant considerations the court was persuaded were in play in the given restructuring … In essence, these would be commercial considerations that facilitated the restructuring and which, characteristically, left even the dissentients better off than would be the case if the plan were to adhere to the relative priorities of dissentients and value recipients junior to them.

An important example is the provision of new value, whether through new funding or the continuation of supplies or services. In relation to new money, the court must guard against an excessive allocation of the surplus in return to the provider. The inquiry, in particular, is how much of the surplus is being allocated in right of each £1 of new value, and how such allocation compares with the cost of funding each £1 from alternative sources. And in relation to future services by the debtor's existing decision-makers, the court should be particularly mindful that existing creditors acting through statutory majorities are generally much better placed than the court to assess the expected value of such services and that a cramdown would disapply this critical safeguard.[74]

It is worth noting that a comparison of monetary values is primary to the exercise envisaged by the FaiRS approach. Given that money is the primary unit of account and the primary mode of exchange, this is unsurprising. Further, it would also be surprising in the heavily commercial contexts in which cramdown becomes an issue if it were impossible serviceably to value in money or money's worth the differences the plan proposes to make to the relationships between the debtor and members of the relevant stakeholder groups.[75] That said, however, there is nothing in the FaiRS approach to *restrict* comparisons to such values, and, in particular, the 'restructuring-relevant considerations' that the court may take into account need not be cashed out in monetary terms. What matters is that the court is able to make a sensible comparison

[72] Mokal, 'The Court's Discretion in relation to the Part 26A Cram Down' (n 67), 16.
[73] ibid, 15.
[74] ibid, 15–16.
[75] For an interesting example, see *In re Sino-Ocean Group Holding Limited* [2025] EWHC 205 (Ch), [120]–[128] (Thompsell J), where the court received, tested, and accepted evidence of the value, in money or money's worth, of the benefits of the continued involvement of Chinese state-owned shareholders in the debtor's post-restructuring business.

between, on the one hand, stakeholders who, the plan proposers assert, are to be given more under the plan than their ostensible peers in return for contributions over and above those of such peers, and on the other hand, those ostensible peers. It is also worth emphasising that no credible approach to the exercise of the court's cramdown discretion can avoid such comparisons altogether.

IX. The Parties' Incentives

We should say a word about the ex ante incentives created by the FaiRS approach. Since litigation burns up resources both private (particularly the parties' attention, money, and time) and public (particularly the scarce and precious resource that is the court's time and attention), the court's cramdown power should be used in such a way that it incentivises parties in future restructurings to bargain together productively toward a cooperative solution so as to minimise the need for an exercise of the cramdown power in the first place.

The legal regime creates incentives by setting the key rules of the bargaining game. The basic such rules concern the three elements of the bargaining situation identified by Cooter and Gilbert: establishing threat values, determining the restructuring surplus, and determining how to distribute that surplus. Given the structure of the bargaining game that is restructuring, the second of these elements provides the starting point.

Starting, then, with the determination of the restructuring surplus, the party proposing the plan must establish that such a surplus exists; that is, that there is a positive difference between the value of the restructuring estate in the event that the plan is efficacious, and in the relevant alternative. As a practical matter, the very fact that a restructuring plan has been proposed in good faith shows that the proposer considers that such a surplus exists.[76] Nevertheless, this must be established to the satisfaction initially of the stakeholders who are to be invited to vote on the plan and who, as a group, would presumably likely vote for it only if convinced, relevantly, of an affirmative answer. Further and if a cramdown is required, the existence and indeed quantum of the surplus would characteristically have to be established to the satisfaction of the court. RP practice has responded to the resulting incentives. It is characteristic for the explanatory statement sent to stakeholders pursuant to statute[77] to explain the analysis underlying the plan proposer's identification of the relevant alternative, and to be accompanied by a 'Relevant Alternative Report' prepared by a financial advisory firm which includes the estimated values of the restructuring estate in both the plan scenario and the relevant alternative.

Second, we have noted above that Condition A sets the *minimum* threat value of each member of each dissenting class. This means that the bargaining may focus, as sharply as practicable, on the distribution of the restructuring surplus.

[76] Michael Crystal and Riz Mokal, 'The Valuation of Distressed Companies: A Conceptual Framework – Part II' (2006) 3(3) *International Corporate Rescue* 123, 125.

[77] Companies Act 2006, s 901D.

These incentives are not unique to the FaiRS approach but instead arise from the legislation itself.

It is at the third stage – the distribution of the restructuring surplus – that the court's adoption of the FaiRS approach can create *distinctive* positive incentives. It does so by anchoring the parties' bargaining to what, in principle, is a common default point, viz the RPR. In practice, the push for a restructuring is led by a coalition of stakeholders (usually including the debtor and often certain of its senior lenders) constructed prior to the commencement of the formal restructuring proceeding. In particular, parties are incentivised to seek to ascertain – and, if necessary, dispute – the relative returns in the relevant alternative for the members of each class to whom the plan is to be or has been proposed and for the members of any equal-ranking or more junior class that are to receive or retain value pursuant to the plan.

The FaiRS approach thereby provides structure for this stage of the bargaining (as well as a rationale for that structure; see above). This stage of the bargaining then has two core objectives. First, the parties seek to agree on their relative returns in the relevant alternative, which each properly advised party may treat as its *practical* threat value, that is, what it can treat as its entitlement, were it to end up in a dissenting class. This also adjusts the parties' relative bargaining power so as more closely to reflect the parties' expected relative contributions to the creation of the restructuring surplus. Second, the parties can bargain on whether certain stakeholders should receive a higher payoff compared to their ostensible peers because of their additional contributions to that surplus.[78]

The value of the anchoring provided by the FaiRS approach can be understood by comparing it with the 'Absolute Priority Rule' (APR) familiar in US bankruptcy practice. The APR provides, in short, that the members of a dissenting class are to receive the full face value of their outstanding claim before those of any junior class receive or retain anything under the plan.[79] At best, the APR fails to provide any anchoring for the parties at the third stage of bargaining, that is, about the distribution of the restructuring surplus. Instead, it leaves parties exactly where they would be in the absence of the APR, since the only value anchoring their bargaining is the full face value of their outstanding claims. Worse than failing to create positive incentives, the APR may create perverse incentives for parties to hold out for full payment in the expectation of freeriding on the sacrifice of sufficient others who might be willing to take a cut. It is for these sorts of reasons that the legal scholar Stephen Lubben has observed:[80]

> there is no absolute priority rule of the kind described in the literature under current law. It is not clear that there ever has been such a rule. And even if there were, adopting such a rule would be inconsistent with Chapter 11 [of the US Bankruptcy Code], or any other sensible

[78] The importance of incentivising parties more accurately to identify their outside options is explained in Mokal, 'The Court's Discretion in relation to the Part 26A Cram Down' (n 67) 14–15.

[79] We focus here on the APR itself and ignore, for the purposes of this chapter, jurisdictions in which the APR is the default rule and the court is permitted to depart from it in appropriate circumstances. That is the position in several EU States which have implemented this model as permitted by the European Preventive Restructuring Framework Directive; see Mokal, 'The Court's Discretion in relation to the Part 26A Cram Down' (n 67), 15.

[80] Stephen J Lubben, 'The Overstated Absolute Priority Rule' (2016) 21 *Fordham Journal of Corporate and Financial Law* 581, 584 (footnote omitted).

system of reorganization. That is, Chapter 11 will not work under the kind of rigid absolute priority rule many academic commentators promote, and thus the rule would be certainly flouted.

We conclude this section by noting the obvious. At each of these three stages, the incentives identified above are *pro tanto* rather than all-things-considered. They weight stakeholders' decision-making rather than binding it. And they certainly do not abolish disagreement; no practicable legal arrangement can. The question is how the FaiRS approach does in this regard as against the available alternatives. For the reasons we have explained, our answer is that it does well.

X. The Restructuring Plan Jurisprudence

There is now a rich and increasingly sophisticated jurisprudence on the court's approach to its cramdown discretion, which, at the time of writing, is to be read in the light of the Court of Appeal's *AGPS* decision.[81] In this section, we analyse critical issues in this jurisprudence using the framework set out above. We will also draw on two decisions, predating the introduction of the restructuring plan, both made by Mann J in scheme of arrangement cases, each of which effectively sought to bring about a cramdown: *MyTravel*[82] and *Bluebrook*.[83] These cases and *MyTravel* in particular raised a host of issues which remain highly relevant to making sense of the restructuring plan.

The debtor in *MyTravel* (MyTravel) was the holding company in a group whose members leased a fleet of aircraft, owned hotels, and sold holiday and travel services. Amongst the group's assets were licences issued by the UK Civil Aviation Authority. The group became insolvent. Having attempted but failed to restructure voluntarily, the group proposed a scheme of arrangement[84] pursuant to which its assets would be transferred to a new company (Newco). All but one category (bondholders) of MyTravel's creditors were to be given rights in Newco while shareholders would receive four per cent of Newco's equity. The only exception was the bondholders, whose claims were subordinated in the event that MyTravel went into liquidation, and who, pursuant to the scheme, were to be left with their claims against MyTravel's empty shell, although Newco was to offer to buy them out in return for two per cent of its equity. The envisaged effect of the proposed scheme was thus to bring about a cramdown of the bondholders.

In *Bluebrook*, three schemes of arrangement were proposed as an intended prelude to the transfer of the debtor group's business to new companies, which were to assume certain of the debtors' liabilities. However, the mezzanine lenders (the Mezz) were not made party to any scheme and were to be left with formally unamended claims against

[81] *In re AGPS Bondco plc* [2024] Bus LR 745 (CA), [118] *et seq.*

[82] *In re MyTravel Group plc* [2005] 2 BCLC 123 (Ch); set aside by the Court of Appeal as unnecessary for deciding the case: ibid.

[83] *Re Bluebrook Ltd* [2010] BCC 209 (Ch).

[84] Pursuant to what is now Part 26 of the Companies Act 2006.

the emptied husks of the debtors. This was the effective cramdown in relation to them envisaged by that restructuring.

In both cases, Mann J rejected the arguments of the objecting creditors – the bondholders in *MyTravel* and the Mezz in *Bluebrook* – and sanctioned the schemes.

A. Basis on which Business to be Valued

First, on what hypothesis should the restructuring estate be valued? There are two obvious possibilities. The first is to value the business in its present state, that is, with whatever part of the fundamental value the restructuring is intended to preserve. Put simply, the business is valued so as to *include* the restructuring surplus. The second is to value it in the state in which it would be in the relevant alternative, that is, on the basis that the restructuring surplus has been lost. For the reasons we have explained, the first approach is, in our view, correct and the second is untenable.

MyTravel provides a useful illustration of the point. In relation to a very extensive business that was plainly a going concern, the court was asked to assess whether the bondholders had an economic interest in the company on a liquidation basis, that is, valuation on the basis that the business was being wound up, the operating licences of its aircraft fleet had been revoked, the business thereby brought to a crashing halt, the going concern extinguished, and the assets subjected to forced sales.

In our view, this was an unreal scenario, and a valuation assuming this scenario was the antithesis of the purpose for which that valuation had been proffered. That scenario and that valuation flew in the face of the established facts, namely, that all stakeholders wished to preserve the going concern, including in particular the operating licences for the air fleet, and that they all wished to avoid a sale. In short, it could not have been clearer that the very well-resourced and well-advised stakeholders, acting with reasons of self-interest for getting this right, considered a sale to be destructive of the business's fundamental value, which they all considered would be best preserved through a restructuring. Regrettably, however, Mann J accepted that the business should be valued on that liquidation basis.[85]

The *MyTravel* decision was the subject of extended academic criticism, which also highlighted the indispensability of a proper going-concern valuation based on the discounted cashflow, market comparison, and/or comparable transactions approaches, amongst others.[86]

By the time that Mann J sat to hear *Bluebrook* some years later, no party appearing before him contended that the business being restructured should be valued on a liquidation basis. Instead, the debtors presented valuations of the going concern based on the discounted cashflow and market comparison methods, amongst others.[87]

[85] *In re MyTravel Group plc* [2005] 2 BCLC 123 (Ch), particularly [55]–[60], holding that since the bondholders' claims could realistically only be enforced in a winding-up, it was the debtor's value in a winding-up that mattered.

[86] See Crystal and Mokal, 'The Valuation of Distressed Companies – Part I' (n 27), and Crystal and Mokal, 'The Valuation of Distressed Companies – Part II' (n 76). It is important to acknowledge at this point that Michael Crystal QC was leading counsel to the bondholders' committee (whose arguments the court rejected).

[87] *Re Bluebrook Ltd* [2010] BCC 209 (Ch), [13], [40].

The critique of this aspect of *MyTravel* and the different approach taken in *Bluebrook* seems to have had a salutary effect on the reception of the RP, with the result that the court has not been asked to value a restructuring estate on a counterfactual premise. Regrettably, however, another aspect of the *MyTravel* approach appears to have made inroads into restructuring plan jurisprudence. We consider this next.

B. Determination of Whether a Class Retains an Economic Interest

Second, for the purposes of determining whether or not to permit members of a class to participate in a meeting to consider a restructuring plan even though the plan would affect their rights, on what hypothesis should the court determine whether 'members of that class [have] a genuine economic interest in the [debtor] company'?[88] Again, should the question be addressed by assuming the value of the business in its present state, that is, as including whatever part of the fundamental value of the business the restructuring is intended to preserve? Or should it be answered by assuming the value of the business in the state in which it would be in the relevant alternative, where the restructuring surplus has been lost? For reasons parallel to those we have given above, the first approach is, in our view, correct and the second is untenable.

Here, the case law appears, with respect, to be on the verge of taking a wrong turn. The view gaining strength would appear to be that this question is to be answered on the assumption that the debtor is in the relevant alternative.[89]

In our respectful view, this would be a mistake. The question whether the class has a real economic interest in the debtor has to be answered *for the purposes of the restructuring*. In particular, it is to be answered for the purpose of deciding whether that class has an interest that entitles it to a voice in the restructuring. And, as we have explained, restructuring makes sense only on the basis that the stakeholders consider there to be fundamental value of which a part would be lost to them in the relevant alternative. It is the existence of this restructuring surplus that forms the very basic premise of any restructuring. Given this premise, it is not easy to understand why the question whether a class has an economic interest in the debtor now, for the purposes of determining whether it has a stake and should therefore be given a voice in the restructuring, should be answered on the hypothesis that that restructuring has failed and the relevant alternative has materialised.

This point is not new. In *MyTravel*, a key part of the restructuring surplus consisted of the going-concern surplus. However, Mann J was persuaded that the question whether a class had an economic interest in the debtor company had to be answered

[88] Section 901C(4) read with section 901C(3) of the Act.

[89] *Re CB&I Ltd* [2024] BCC 551 (Ch), [117] (Michael Green J), citing *In re Virgin Active Holdings Ltd* [2022] 1 All ER (Comm) 1023, [247]–[249] for this point with obvious reluctance. See also *In re Houst Ltd* [2022] BCC 1143 (Ch), [27].

by reference to (what we would now call) the relevant alternative.[90] This aspect of his decision was criticised as follows:[91]

> in order to determine which of the company's current investors retain a real economic interest in the company as things currently stand, the value to be determined is the existing going concern value of the company's business, which, after all, is the value the proposed scheme is intended to both preserve and apportion. Assuming that the alternative to the proposed reorganisation would be a liquidation, it is difficult to see the rationale of determining the rights of any of the parties by assuming the very outcome that the scheme of arrangement is intended to avoid, namely, a liquidation of the business and resulting dissipation of the going concern surplus.

This point holds equally in relation to a plan. In our view, it is plainly borne out by the statutory text, which pointedly omits reference to the relevant alternative.[92]

It is worth noting that a useful but certainly not decisive way of responding to a junior class's complaint that the debtor's business is being undervalued and that, on a proper valuation, that junior class retains an economic interest in the debtor, is by giving that class the opportunity to buy out (some of) those ranking above it in the debtor's capital structure.

The *Bluebrook* case provides a good example. In that case, the Mezz objected on fairness grounds and, relevantly, on the basis that the debtor group's business was being undervalued for the purposes of the restructuring. However, the intercreditor agreement gave the Mezz the right 'to compel a sale to them of the rights and obligations of the senior lenders for the amount of the outstanding senior debt' ('buy-out option').[93] Analytically, the effect of the buy-out option was that the Mezz could effectively trump the debtors' valuation of the business if each of two conditions was met. The first condition was that the Mezz considered in good faith (and not merely as a matter of bargaining and forensic positioning) that, properly valued, the business had enough in it to pay off the senior debt in full yet leave something for them. The second condition was that the Mezz could raise sufficient funds on that basis, for example, by persuading third-party lenders of their valuation of the business. In *Bluebrook*, the Mezz conspicuously failed to exercise the buy-out option, and in our respectful view, Mann J was entirely right in placing some weight on this fact in rejecting their valuation challenge.[94]

The key reasons why it is not decisive that a junior dissenting class held (or was granted), yet failed to exercise, a buy-out option arise from the second of the two conditions mentioned above and are amongst the reasons that motivate stakeholders to go down the restructuring (rather than the sale) route in the first place. First, the junior class may, by dint of extended experience with the business, be able to *observe* its expected future cashflows without being able to verify such cashflows to the satisfaction

[90] *In re MyTravel Group plc* [2005] 2 BCLC 123 (Ch), [45], [48], [55]–[58].

[91] Crystal and Mokal, 'The Valuation of Distressed Companies – Part II' (n 76), 126.

[92] See Companies Act 2006, s 901C(4) of the Act; compare the final seven words of Companies Act 2006, s 901G(5).

[93] *Re Bluebrook Ltd* [2010] BCC 209 (Ch), [4(iv)] (Mann J).

[94] ibid, [77(vii)] and [78].

of outside investors. Second, the relevant markets may be distressed, leaving an investment in them at that point an undesirable prospect. And third, the funds required may be extensive, no single investor may be willing to take on the requisite risk, and/or it may be excessively costly to construct a coalition to do so.

C. Selection of Stakeholders to Participate in Restructuring

Third, the court has retreated from the permissive attitude to stakeholder selection, whose wisdom we have questioned. A more searching approach appears to have been heralded by Snowden J in the scheme case of *Co-Operative Bank*, who said that 'leaving people who have the same or sufficiently similar rights against the company out of the scheme cannot be an entirely arbitrary decision' but ought instead 'to have a rational commercial justification'.[95] And in deriving guidance from the Court of Appeal's *AGPS* decision, Mr Justice Miles stated perspicaciously in the *Cine-UK* sanction judgment that:[96]

> the exclusion of a creditor or class of creditors from a plan without a proper justification may well render the plan unfair to those creditors [who are] included within it who would be in a similar position in the relevant alternative.
>
> … I am unable to accept … at least in unqualified form, that the exclusion or inclusion of creditors from a restructuring plan is a simple or unqualified choice for the company … Putting it another way, questions of fairness in restructuring plans are not concerned with the relationship between the company and individual creditors: fairness in this context is primarily a matter of relative treatment of the creditors as between themselves (with like to be treated as like as the default position).

For the reasons we have explained above, we respectfully agree.

D. 'Compromise or Arrangement'

Fourth, the plan must constitute a 'compromise or arrangement', which has the same meaning in relation to restructuring plans as to schemes of arrangement. This has been given a broad interpretation. All that is required is some element of give and take, as opposed to mere surrender or forfeiture.[97] This point was recently reiterated, albeit *obiter* and provisionally, by Snowden LJ in *AGPS*.[98] We respectfully agree.[99]

[95] *In re the Co-Operative Bank plc* [2017] EWHC 2269 (Ch), [38].

[96] *In re Cine-UK Limited* [2024] Bus LR 1944 (Ch), [112], [126] (Miles J).

[97] See *Re Savoy Hotel Ltd* [1981] Ch. 351, per 359D–F (Nourse J at 359D–F;); *Re Lehman Brothers International (Europe) (in admin)* [2018] EWHC 1980 (Ch), [64] per Hildyard J. For a comprehensive discussion, see *In re T & N Ltd (No 4)* [2007] Bus LR 1411 (Ch), [43]–[55] (David Richards J).

[98] *In re AGPS Bondco plc* [2024] Bus LR 745 (CA), particularly at [258]–[278], citing (amongst others) Jennifer Payne, *Schemes of Arrangement*, 2nd edn (Cambridge, Cambridge University Press, 2021), at 319.

[99] The point was previously made in R Mokal, 'The Two Conditions for the Part 26A Cram Down' (n 61), 731.

E. Meeting of Conditions Leaves Discretion at Large

Fifth, the mere fact that Conditions A and B are met does not give rise to any presumption that the court will exercise its discretion in favour of a cramdown.[100] We think this must be correct, since the satisfaction of the two Conditions does not mean that the allocation of the restructuring surplus is normatively defensible. It may not be so if, for example, the dissenting class will do better under the plan than in the relevant alternative but where its returns under the plan are grossly inadequate in comparison with its contribution to the creation of the restructuring surplus.

F. Intra-Class Rationality is Irrelevant

Sixth, the intra-class rationality test developed in the scheme jurisprudence does not apply to the exercise of the court's cramdown power.[101] The premise of that test is that the assenting majority in a class has sufficient in common with the dissentients and that it is not acting out of interests adverse to those which define the class. Therefore, it is fair for the court to proceed on the assumption that the scheme is also in the interests of the dissentients. That premise does not hold where the question is not whether the scheme advances the interests of members of the same one class but whether it is fair to impose the plan on one or more dissenting classes. We respectfully agree. Starting from first principles, rationality, as developed in the scheme jurisprudence, is the means/ends, self-interest-directed rationality we have deployed in this chapter. That notion of rationality has nothing to say about questions of distribution.[102]

G. Different Plan as Relevant Alternative

Seventh, the court will accept, where appropriate, that the relevant alternative is a different plan.[103] We respectfully endorse this position. In our view, the court should consider the plausibility of the relevant alternative posited by the plan proposers by

[100] *In re Virgin Active Holdings Ltd* [2022] 1 All ER (Comm) 1023, [224] (Snowden J); *In re AGPS Bondco plc* [2024] Bus LR 745 (CA), [153]–[154] (Snowden LJ).

[101] *In re Great Annual Savings Co Ltd* [2023] Bus LR 1163 (Ch), [99]–[100] and [102]–[103] (but not [101]) (Adam Johnson J); *In re AGPS Bondco plc* [2024] Bus LR 745 (CA), [121]–[148] (Snowden LJ), though note the apparent qualification at [131].

[102] For a development of this point concerning rationality in the scheme jurisprudence, see Mokal, 'Cram Dos, Don'ts, and Darn Its' (n 8).

[103] *In re Houst Ltd* [2022] BCC 1143 (Ch), [38] (Zacaroli J); *In re Great Annual Savings Co Ltd* [2023] Bus LR 1163 (Ch), [106] (Adam Johnson J); *In re AGPS Bondco plc* [2024] Bus LR 745 (CA), [173]–[182] (Snowden LJ). Thompsell J's dicta in *In re Sino-Ocean Group Holding Limited* [2025] EWHC 205 (Ch), [22(i) and (ii)] should not be read as demanding greater specificity in the identification of an alternative plan than is strictly necessary to satisfy the court that Condition A has been met. In some circumstances, indeed, the plan put before the court may be sufficiently unbalanced as to suggest to the court that any of a range of practicable alternative plans may constitute the relevant alternative. In this regard, we respectfully endorse Richards J's duly cautious but more open approach in *In re Revolution Bars Limited* [2024] EWHC 2949 (Ch), [40]–[42].

taking into account factors such as (and without limitation) the nature of the business and of its stakeholders and the likely size of the restructuring surplus.

In *MyTravel*, Mann J accepted the scheme proposers' position that the only alternative to the scheme before him was for MyTravel to be wound up and for the group's business to be liquidated.[104] With respect, this was entirely implausible and *MyTravel* provides a case study of the sort of facts which strongly indicate that the relevant alternative to the proposed restructuring is a restructuring on alternative terms. Given the nature of the business and the seriousness with which its stakeholders sought to preserve it, it was plain that there was a very significant restructuring surplus which, equally plainly, would be lost in the event that the group was liquidated. For this reason, the well advised and highly rational stakeholders were very unlikely to permit the loss of that surplus by permitting liquidation. In bargaining terms, the outside options of the stakeholders across the board were devastating compared to their plan returns.

This point was made thus in criticism of Mann J's judgment on this issue:[105]

> it is highly doubtful whether, on the facts, insolvent liquidation was [the relevant] alternative. Judging by the conviction with which the commercially astute parties best informed about its affairs (its directors, its bank lenders, and the latter's financial advisers PricewaterhouseCoopers) pursued its restructuring, MyTravel clearly had a significant going concern surplus (i.e. there was a large positive difference between the enterprise and liquidation values of its business).
>
> To the extent to which this was true, neither MyTravel's bondholders nor its Converting Creditors [the other, favoured creditors] would have wished the company to end up in insolvent liquidation, since to do so would have resulted in the loss of the going concern surplus, a loss suffered by all of them as a group. The real dispute, therefore, was about the distribution of the surplus (as represented by the equity in Newco) as between the Converting Creditors on the one hand and the bondholders on the other. In the negotiations preceding the promulgation of the original scheme, the former had been willing to offer 8% of that equity to the latter. This was accompanied by an attempt to pressurise the bondholders into acceptance: the offer came with the threat that it would be halved if not accepted by a stipulated date. Keeping these facts in mind, we can see that the most plausible alternative to the proposed scheme was not a liquidation but instead a higher offer of equity (i.e. more than 8%) by the Converting Creditors to the bondholders. Both sets of parties would have had an incentive to come to an agreement in something like these terms.
>
> Instead, by persuading the court that the rights of the parties were to be valued by reference to their position in a non-existent and highly unlikely liquidation which represented the antithesis of the purpose in aid of which the valuation was to be carried out, the Converting Creditors were able to strong-arm the bondholders into accepting their initial offer.

We consider this analysis equally relevant in the plan context and envisage similar attempts to postulate implausible scenarios said to constitute the relevant alternative. In many such cases, the court would wish carefully to consider whether the real relevant alternative was an alternative plan.

[104] *In re MyTravel Group plc* [2005] 2 BCLC 123 (Ch), [57].
[105] Crystal and Mokal (n 76), 128 (footnotes omitted).

H. Key to Cramdown is Fair Distribution of Restructuring Surplus

Eighth and fundamentally, the court regards the question whether to exercise its cramdown power as one of a fair distribution of the benefits of the restructuring, that is, of the 'restructuring surplus',[106] which, as Snowden LJ confirmed, is 'the value sought to be preserved or generated by the restructuring plan, over and above the relevant alternative'.[107]

I. Relative Priority Rule

Ninth, in considering the fairness of the proposed distribution amongst different classes, the RPR is an important consideration. As Zacaroli J explained[108] (in a dictum approved by Snowden LJ[109]):

> a relevant reference point is the treatment of the creditors in the relevant alternative. The court will look to see whether the priority, as among different creditor groups, applicable in the relevant alternative is reflected in the distributions under the plan.

Crucially, where the relevant alternative to the plan is an insolvency proceeding in which distributions may be made from the estate equally to certain creditors, it has been said that the restructuring surplus should be distributed *pari passu*.[110] We broadly agree, though would caution against widespread confusion as to the nature of the *pari passu* principle.[111]

The Sino-Ocean Group restructuring plan provides an important example of the application of the RPR with due sensitivity to the proper, limited role of the *pari passu* principle. In sanctioning the plan, Thompsell J stated:[112]

> As between the different creditor groups in the case before me, it seems to me that the Plan Company has done its best to allocate fairly the value preserved or generated by the Plan over and above the relevant alternative. Whilst this has led to different groups of creditors who have (except for Class D) *pari passu* rights against the Plan Company receiving different values of Plan Consideration, this is explained by the fact that *in the relevant alternative, the different classes would have different rights against other companies in the Plan Company's Group and so would be anticipated to receive different recoveries. The Plan Company has tried to ensure that each class of creditor obtains a similar multiple of those recoveries as the value that it receives by way of Plan Consideration.* As between the creditors of the different classes, I consider

[106] *In re Houst Ltd* [2022] BCC 1143 (Ch), [29] (Zacaroli J); *In re AGPS Bondco plc* [2024] Bus LR 745 (CA), [161] (Snowden LJ).

[107] *In re AGPS Bondco plc* [2024] Bus LR 745 (CA), [160] (Snowden LJ).

[108] *In re Houst Ltd* [2022] BCC 1143 (Ch), [30] (Zacaroli J).

[109] *In re AGPS Bondco plc* [2024] Bus LR 745 (CA), [159] (Snowden LJ); see also *In re Prezzo Investco Ltd* [2024] Bus LR 848 (KBD), [68(iv)] (Richard Smith J).

[110] *In re AGPS Bondco plc* [2024] Bus LR 745 (CA), [165] (Snowden LJ); *In re Cine-UK Limited* [2024] Bus LR 1944 (Ch), [115] (Miles J).

[111] See Riz Mokal, 'The Mysterious *Pari Passu* Principle' (2024) 39(7) *Butterworths Journal of International Banking and Financial Law* 443.

[112] *In re Sino-Ocean Group Holding Limited* [2025] EWHC 205 (Ch), [112].

therefore that this departure is justified in that it produces what is sometimes referred to as a fair distribution of the benefits of the restructuring (emphasis added).

J. Departures from Relative Priority

Tenth, a departure from the RPR is not fatal to the success of the plan,[113] so long as such departure can be justified as being for good reason or on a proper basis.[114] Noting the inadvisability of prescribing an exhaustive list of such proper bases, Snowden LJ gave the example of 'some additional benefit or accommodation to assist the achievement of the purposes of the restructuring in the interests of creditors as a whole', which, he said would justify the providers being accorded 'some priority or a proportionately enhanced share of the benefits'.[115] For the reasons we have explained, we respectfully agree.

Closely relatedly, in assessing the fairness of the proposed distribution of the restructuring surplus, 'it may be relevant to take account of the source of the benefits to be received under the restructuring'.[116] This is where the court takes account of ways, other than through modification of existing rights against the debtor, of contributing to the creation of the restructuring surplus. The continuation of supplies critical to the survival of the business through and beyond the restructuring is an important example.[117] Another is new money, in relation to which Snowden LJ astutely observed that the court should scrutinise whether:[118]

> the new money was provided on more expensive terms than the company could have obtained in the market from third parties; or if the extent to which the existing debt was elevated was disproportionate to the extra benefits provided by the new money.

Sino-Ocean provides an interesting example of the court's approach and one with which we respectfully agree. The plan proposed to permit shareholders to retain a very substantial proportion of equity even though they would receive nothing in the relevant alternative, such that it was 'clear' to the court that the plan allocated them 'disproportionate value'.[119] However, the two largest shareholders were Chinese state-owned enterprises (SOEs), and Thompsell J said it was 'common sense that operating within a jurisdiction like the PRC [People's Republic of China] there would be advantages in being perceived as being a company in which the PRC had a significant interest'.[120] The court accepted expert evidence that excessive dilution of the SOEs' equity stake in the business would materially reduce the net present value of the business's cash flow.[121] This justified (what would otherwise be) the disproportionate allocation of value to shareholders.

[113] *In re Houst Ltd* [2022] BCC 1143 (Ch), [30] (Zacaroli J); *In re Prezzo Investco Ltd* [2024] Bus LR 848 (KBD), [68(iv)] (Richard Smith J).
[114] *In re AGPS Bondco plc* [2024] Bus LR 745 (CA), [159], [166] (Snowden LJ).
[115] ibid, [167].
[116] *In re Houst Ltd* [2022] BCC 1143 (Ch), [31] (Zacaroli J).
[117] *In re AGPS Bondco plc* [2024] Bus LR 745 (CA), [170].
[118] ibid, [169].
[119] *In re Sino-Ocean Group Holding Limited* [2025] EWHC 205 (Ch), [113].
[120] ibid, [125].
[121] ibid, [120]–[128].

K. Class-Skipping and Gifting

Eleventh and finally, at least some courts appear rather relaxed in permitting gifting.[122] We respectfully suggest greater caution.

The Court of Appeal's decision in *Tea Corporation*[123] appears to provide the first mention of a gift in English restructuring law. A distressed company (Tea Corp) and its liquidator proposed a scheme pursuant to which Tea Corp's assets would be transferred to a new company (Newco) which would address all of Tea Corp's liabilities. At first instance, Buckley J found as a fact that Tea Corp's assets might realise enough to discharge all of its liabilities and still leave a surplus. Tea Corp had issued preference and ordinary shares, and Buckley J held that value broke in the preference shareholder class and that the ordinary shareholders 'had no interest in the matter'.[124] The scheme nevertheless proposed to permit (in particular) the ordinary shareholders to acquire a proportion of Newco's equity. Buckley J sanctioned the scheme on this basis. The Court of Appeal unanimously rejected the appeal brought by an ordinary shareholder. Romer LJ explained that the offer of some of Newco's equity to ordinary shareholders:[125]

> must be regarded as rather in the nature of a gift by the creditors and the preference shareholders to the ordinary shareholders, and not as shewing that [ordinary shareholders] had an interest in the assets which they were surrendering. Certainly the ordinary shareholders cannot be heard to complain of a gift being made to them when they had no right to it but for the scheme, and there is no appeal on behalf of the creditors or the preference shareholders from this provision of the scheme.

The facts of *MyTravel* involved not merely a 'gift' but also class-skipping. That is, the scheme sought to skip over the bondholders, who would be left with claims against the denuded MyTravel, in order to give MyTravel shareholders equity in Newco.

For any court, any suggestion of a gift (whether or not so called), particularly a class-skipping one, should set alarm bells ringing. A gift is an expression of love, concern, or admiration in which something of one's own is given without expectation of return; and gifts, properly so called, are rarely (if ever) given in commercial contexts. Instead, when confronted with a plan that proposes a gift and in particular a class-skipping one, the court should, in our respectful view, bear in mind seven considerations.

First, the court should presume unless satisfied to the contrary that there is a quid pro quo in which something *of material value and belonging to the restructuring estate* – in *MyTravel*, that four per cent of Newco's equity, in circumstances in which Newco's value was to derive from the assets transferred to it by MyTravel – is being given away. This calls for particular care in the valuation of both sides of the bargain, that is, of that which is being given away from the estate and that (if anything) which the estate and therefore all its stakeholders as a group are to receive in return.

[122] See for example *In re Virgin Active Holdings Ltd* [2022] 1 All ER (Comm) 1023, [266]. For a different and in our respectful view preferable approach, see *In re Great Annual Savings Co Ltd* [2023] Bus LR 1163 (Ch), [111] et seq (Adam Johnson J).

[123] *Re Tea Corporation Limited* [1904] 1 Ch 12 (CA).

[124] ibid, 18.

[125] ibid, 24.

Second, the court should satisfy itself that the valuation methodology is suitable on the facts for capturing all of the fundamental value which the restructuring is intended to preserve and maximise.

Third, it should satisfy itself that any skipped class really is out of the money, assessed by reference to the present, restructuring surplus-containing value of the estate.

Fourth, it should consider the credibility of the proposed relevant alternative, bearing in mind the possibility that the actual relevant alternative may be an alternative plan.

The relevance of the second to fourth points has been explained above.

Fifth, the court should ask whether the classes purporting to give the gift are gifting a part of their share of the restructuring surplus. In this respect, it should require evidence of the returns pursuant to the plan in both the scenario in which the gift is given, and that in which it is not given. It should also consider the relation between the quantum of any diminution in the returns of the classes giving the gift and the quantum of the gift itself. Plainly, it is one thing for such classes to be generous with an appropriate portion of their returns, and another to purport to gift value which, on their evidence, does not exist. The latter case, in particular, should raise the question whether the purported gift consists of value that would have gone to another stakeholder class.

Sixth and relatedly, the court should assess the inherent probabilities of the key assumptions underlying the plan (in addition to the inherent probabilities of the existence of a restructuring surplus and of the postulated relevant alternative). *MyTravel* provides other examples, such as that the highly sophisticated Converting Creditors would be unlikely to agree to give up debt against MyTravel in return for equity in Newco unless they thought that a good bargain, in circumstances where any value in Newco derived from MyTravel's assets. In *MyTravel*, Mann J dismissed this point as follows:[126]

> Obviously the creditors think that the company as it stands has some value to them in that they are likely to receive some, but not all, of their debts if there is a winding up. They also obviously think that a restructuring is potentially a better way of recovering more of their debt at some point in the future. However, to go on to say that this proves that the present company presently has a value which exceeds the amount of the unsubordinated debt is an enormous leap. Where is that value said to come from? All the evidence that I have seen demonstrates that it does not exist. *The hopes of the other creditors as to the future prospects for another company (Newco) do not generate extra value in the present company* (emphasis added).

The reference to 'all the evidence I have seen' should be read keeping in mind that the evidence provided to the court did not include a valuation of the going concern, and, as we have seen, the court agreed that the appropriate basis for valuation was liquidation. But this leads to the final point.

Seventh is the issue arising from the emphasised sentence in the excerpt above. The court should bear in mind that any future value in the restructured debtor (or in another entity in the position of Newco) can only come from the synergies between the factors of production – land, labour, capital, and entrepreneurship – that constitute the debtor's going concern, together with some or other measure of serendipity. The questions that

[126] *In re MyTravel Group plc* [2005] 2 BCLC 123 (Ch), [70].

may usefully structure the court's thinking, even though they would almost always be impossible to answer with any precision, are to what extent any future value would likely be a product of (i) the existing going concern, (ii) the contributions to it made by modifying the existing rights of stakeholders, (iii) other contributions, such as new value by way of funding, supplies, or services, and (iv) luck.

Several of these seven points are implicit in Miles J's dictum in *Re ALL Scheme Limited* in relation to an insolvent debtor whose shareholders are to retain a stake in the restructured entity:[127]

> In a scheme or restructuring in which the existing shareholders, who would, by definition, receive nothing in a formal insolvency, are being permitted to retain a material stake in the restructured company, it is likely to be essential for the scheme company to provide a detailed statement of the underlying assumptions and valuation methodology that are said to justify such an outcome so that creditors can reasonably assess, objectively, whether the allocation of losses and the division of benefits among stakeholders is appropriate and fair.

We respectfully agree and suggest that the same level of scrutiny should be directed at any supposed gift, particularly if it is a class-skipping one.

XI. Conclusion

We have sought in this chapter to provide a conceptual framework, the FaiRS approach, for the analysis of the cramdown. The framework is animated by theories of both normative defensibility and of bargaining. We situate the cramdown power in its proper context as a key part of a sophisticated restructuring regime, and we explain how this regime should deal with issues of valuation, maximisation, and distribution. Finally, we analyse the case law, commenting on aspects in which it coheres with the FaiRS approach and also on those respects in which that approach would counsel reform.

[127] *Re ALL Scheme Limited* [2021] EWHC 1401 (Ch), [102(xi)].

5

Floating Charge Envy

EDWARD J JANGER

I. Introduction

Two countervailing Transatlantic currents motivate this chapter: cross-class cramdown has floated East, while in the US secured lenders and law and economics scholars envy the UK's 'floating charge'. Once just a controversial feature of the US Bankruptcy Code (Chapter 11 or 11 USC), cross-class cramdown has 'gone global'. Meanwhile, secured lenders and law and economics scholars in the US have fantasised about an enterprise lien akin to the floating charge for decades; they suffer from floating charge envy.

With the recent introduction of Part 26A to the UK Companies Act 2006, along with the EU Directive on Preventive Restructuring Frameworks, cross-class cramdown has crossed the pond.[1] This migration requires courts in the UK to sanction plans over creditor objection, and therefore to quantify their cramdown entitlements. As with Chapter 11 in the US, now, under a Part 26A plan, a UK debtor may seek to confirm a restructuring[2] and continue to operate the business over the objection of a creditor class; but it can only do so if (1) the objecting class's treatment is 'no worse than' the treatment it would receive in the 'relevant alternative' and (2) the plan is supported by at least one class who would receive a payment or have a genuine economic interest in the event of the relevant alternative.[3] Courts interpreting section 901G have further imposed a requirement of horizontal equity. Where creditors would have received similar treatment in the relevant alternative, deviations from similar treatment must be justified.[4]

[1] Directive (EU) 2019/1023 of the European Parliament and of the Council of 20 June 2019 on preventive restructuring frameworks, on discharge of debt and disqualifications, and on measures to increase the efficiency of procedures concerning restructuring, insolvency and discharge of debt, and amending Directive (EU) 2017/1132. See further Chapters 2 and 3 in this book.

[2] Where the debtor is in financial difficulties and the purpose of the proposed compromise or arrangement is to eliminate, reduce or prevent, or mitigate the effect of these difficulties: s 901A.

[3] Companies Act 2006, s 901G.

[4] The *Adler* case, *Re AGPS Bondco PLC* [2024] EWCA Civ 24, explaining why the 'rationality test' applicable to schemes (which require the support of each class) is insufficient.

It is now, therefore, necessary to calculate an objecting class's hypothetical recovery in the relevant alternative to determine whether a plan of reorganisation can be confirmed. To put it another way, if a class does not accept the plan, the court must price the debtor's call-option on the dissenting class's claim; that is, the cost of continuation. Courts will have to do the maths. This chapter explores what will happen when they do the calculations, and then considers the fate of the floating charge as an enterprise lien, and consequently, of floating charge envy.

Some signposts are emerging. The recent *Adler* case considered the rights of unsecured bondholders to insist on both 'no worse than' treatment and explored possible bases for discrimination between creditors of similar priority.[5] And, at least one court has sanctioned a plan under Part 26A over the objection of a senior secured creditor, after concluding that the treatment of the objecting creditor was 'no worse than' in the relevant alternative.[6] These cases suggest two comparisons between US and UK law: (1) how is the 'floating charge' in the UK different from an asserted blanket 'floating lien' in the US; and (2) how do the cramdown standards differ in practice between the two countries?

Under UK law, it is generally understood that a floating charge holder can take a lien on the debtor's entire undertaking. A lien on the assets of the firm is treated as a lien on the value of the firm itself – an enterprise lien.[7] Subject to the rights of certain preferential creditors, the floating charge holder is said to sit atop the distributional hierarchy with regard to the value of the enterprise; they can claim priority in the present value of the income stream generated by operating the business.

Under Chapter 11, by contrast, even secured creditors who claim a blanket lien on all the firm's assets are only entitled to the value of their collateral in cramdown.[8] In the US, the value of the collateral and its relationship to the value of the firm is frequently the subject of dispute. Dissenting junior creditors may argue that a senior creditor is claiming value beyond the value of its collateral, leaving them worse off. Or in a so-called 'cram-up', the junior creditors may accept the plan, while paying an objecting secured creditor the value of its collateral.

With the advent of cross-class cramdown in the UK, such a cram-up is theoretically possible. However, the formulation is different. In the US, the secured creditor is entitled to insist on receiving at least the 'value of their collateral'. In the UK, the floating charge holder's baseline priority entitlement is determined by what it would receive in the 'relevant alternative'. In liquidation, these are likely to be the same, but where the enterprise continues, *and* would continue in the relevant alternative, the calculation is not simple.[9]

The central puzzle considered by this chapter is whether now, in either country, a secured creditor's priority entitlement extends to the entire undertaking (the business

[5] *Re AGPS Bondco PLC* [2023] EWHC 916 (Ch), and in the Court of Appeal, [2024] EWCA Civ 24 (*Re Adler*).

[6] *Re Amicus Finance plc (in administration)* [2021] EWHC 3036 (Ch).

[7] See nn 57 and 58 below and the discussion that follows.

[8] 11 USC § 1129(b)(2)(A).

[9] Christopher Akinrele, Matthew Thorn, Jade Porter, and Matthew Roderick, 'UK restructuring plan: cramming up a super-senior creditor class in a unitranche structure', *International Restructuring Newswire Q2* (Norton Rose Fulbright, 2024) at 24.

enterprise) or only the value of its assets. Can a creditor in the US or the UK take security over the going concern surplus of an insolvent enterprise, and therefore include it as part of its cramdown entitlement?

Melissa Jacoby and I have explained that in the US, when a business enterprise recapitalises in the face of financial distress, the going concern increment is allocated to the estate by both Article 9 of the Uniform Commercial Code (UCC) and the Bankruptcy Code.[10] This chapter first describes our efforts to correct a common misnomer. The term 'absolute priority' does not apply to secured creditors. It is sometimes used, rhetorically, to pretend that the US has a floating charge – placing the secured creditor atop a hierarchical distributional 'waterfall'. But that assumption rests on both a misunderstanding of property law – the State law of secured credit – and a misreading of the Bankruptcy Code. Instead, the secured creditor's asset-based priority is limited to the otherwise realisable value of its collateral.[11] Our analysis focuses on the question of whether, in rescue, rights against the firm's property (rights *in rem*) are coextensive with rights against the firm (rights *in personam*). We contend that under US law, they are not. While this distinction is sometimes ignored in practice,[12] it is also generally conceded as a legal and conceptual matter.[13] We further argue that this is the correct answer as a normative matter.[14]

The chapter next seeks to identify, as a doctrinal matter, the source of this difference between the law in the US and in the UK, where, as noted above, the value of a floating charge holder's collateral is understood to extend to the going concern value of the enterprise. It considers three possible sources: (1) the scope of security – realisable priority; (2) the treatment of circulating assets upon the opening of a proceeding – equitable realisation; and (3) the ability to place a lien on future assets. Finding each of these possibilities unconvincing, it considers, somewhat impertinently, whether the UK's common understanding of the floating charge holder's right to the going concern value of the firm may rest on a false assumption about the equivalence between piecemeal liquidation and sale of the enterprise as a going concern. The chapter concludes that, even if one assumes an enterprise lien, the adoption of Part 26A causes the two systems to converge somewhat, but a difference may remain, where the 'relevant alternative' would involve a continuation of the going concern. However, it is not obvious that even this difference is justified.

[10] Melissa B Jacoby and Edward J Janger, 'Tracing Equity: Realizing and Allocating Value in Chapter 11' (2018) 96 *Texas Law Review* 673.

[11] ibid at 694. See also, Edward J Janger, 'The Logic and Limits of Liens' (2015) *University of Illinois Law Review* 589, 602. Indeed, Stephan Madaus and I have suggested that in the US, the UK, and Europe the right way to approach this question is through the concept of realisable priority. What could the secured creditor realise in the absence of the proposed plan of reorganisation. In the US the secured creditors' cramdown entitlement is the 'value' of the collateral on the 'effective date' of the plan. Under the EU Directive and Part 26A, value is measured by the 'relevant alternative'.

[12] See the discussion of the *Tribune* case, at n 31.

[13] Christopher W Frost, 'Secured Credit and Effective Entity Priority' (2019) 51 *Connecticut Law Review* 575, 579 (https://opencommons.uconn.edu/law_review/420). See also, Anthony J Casey and Andrew Verstein, 'Deconstructing the Senior Creditor' in Adam Badawi (ed), *Encyclopedia of Law and Economics, Corporate Law and Economics*, available at SSRN: https://ssrn.com/abstract=4708447.

[14] Jacoby and Janger, 'Tracing Equity (n 10).

The road map is as follows. First, the chapter introduces cross-class cramdown in the US and UK. Second, it identifies and explains the implications of two distinctions under US law: (1) the distinction between security and recourse – rights *in rem* and rights *in personam*; and (2) the distinction between realisation of firm value through piecemeal liquidation of property and realisation of value through the capitalised earnings of continued operations. The takeaway is that, unlike in the UK, the priority of secured creditors in the US does not extend to the going concern surplus. The next sections seek to identify the source of this distinction. Section IV asks whether the distinction lies in what a secured creditor can own as a matter of property law? The answer is no. Section V continues the comparison, considering whether the difference lies in how the property interest is translated from a property interest into a distribution in bankruptcy, when a debtor restructures its debts (through recapitalisation *or* sale) and continues as a going concern? It develops the principle of equitable realisation that operates in US law, with examples, and finds that principle missing in the UK. This is a difference that matters. Mathematical examples are offered, both under the Bankruptcy Code and Part 26A. With the advent of cross-class cramdown, the floating charge holder can no longer claim a legal entitlement to the full value of the enterprise, but only the value in the 'relevant alternative'. This narrows the distinction between the US and UK, but unlike in the US, the relevant alternative might be a going concern sale or other outcome that continues the business as a going concern. So, the entitlement is not limited to asset value. Finally, section VI even questions this residual difference, tentatively suggesting that giving priority to an unattached and inchoate interest in property that doesn't yet, and may never, exist does not satisfy the requirements for an asset-based distributional priority.

In conclusion, the chapter offers the following takeaway:

1. If one accepts that in the US, the secured creditor's lien is on assets, while in the UK, the lien extends to the value of the enterprise, then cross-class cramdown in the UK will narrow the difference between the US and the UK, but it will still allow the floating charge holder to capture the going concern value, up to what would be recovered in the relevant alternative. By contrast, in the US, the entitlement will be limited to the value that is traceable to assets owned on the petition date.
2. However, an exploration of the source of the perceived difference between the floating charge and the Article 9 security interest raises questions about whether the characterisation of the floating charge as a lien or charge on circulating assets is sufficient to create a priority in the value of the enterprise as a going concern.

II. Cross-Class Cramdown in the UK and the US

This book has been occasioned by the new Part 26A restructuring plan or 'superscheme' that was added by the Corporate Insolvency and Governance Act 2020 (UK) (CIGA) – in particular, the advent of cross-class cramdown. Unlike a traditional scheme of arrangement, the 'superscheme' may be confirmed over the objection of a dissenting class of creditors if it can meet certain requirements. This will require UK courts to answer questions that are familiar to courts in the US, but which have not yet been addressed in the UK.

In the US, (cross-class) cramdown requires that the plan be 'fair and equitable', while in the UK, a Part 26A plan of reorganisation must offer the objecting creditor a distribution that is 'no worse than' what they would receive in the 'relevant alternative'. The focus of this section is to flesh out the meaning of 'fair and equitable' for secured creditors in the US, and to consider whether the US approach has implications for the UK. This exercise is further worthwhile because European jurisdictions are in the process of implementing the EU Directive on Preventive Restructuring Frameworks, which as other chapters of this book explore, similarly provides for cross-class cramdown.[15]

A. The Introduction of Cross-class Cramdown by CIGA: UK

Schemes of arrangement are not new in the UK. Under the Companies Act 2006, they have long been used to restructure financial debt for both solvent and insolvent companies. Pursuant to a scheme, a class of creditors can bind other members of the same class to a restructuring by a vote of 75 per cent of the affected class (and a headcount test). Dissenting creditors *within* a class could be bound, so long as the requisite majority was willing to sign off. There was no statutory provision for binding an entire dissenting class. CIGA, however, included new section 901G, which provides for 'cross-class cramdown' to bind a class of creditors even when its members have not voted to accept the plan.[16] Cross-class cramdown of a dissenting class of creditors is available when two conditions are met: (1) 'none of the members of the dissenting class would be any worse off than they would be in the event of the relevant alternative'; and (2) a class that is in the money in the relevant alternative and is impaired under the scheme has voted to accept the arrangement.[17] The requirements of 'no worse than' treatment, as well as the need to identify an accepting class that is 'in the money', require the court to value the firm *and* its assets in order to calculate anticipated distributions for both secured and unsecured creditors. The distribution in the 'relevant alternative' establishes an entitlement floor.

The difficulties associated with quantifying this entitlement floor were revealed in the Court of Appeal's recent ruling, declining to sanction the *Adler* restructuring plan.[18] The court was required to compare the value of the firm under both the plan and the 'relevant alternative', to consider (1) whether the plan was supported by a class that was 'in the money', (2) the 'no worse than floor', and (3) to evaluate the value of the proposed distributions to the accepting and rejecting classes. While *Adler* considered the entitlements of non-consenting *pari passu* creditors, the time is coming when it

[15] Directive (EU) 2019/1023 of the European Parliament and of the Council of 20 June 2019 on preventive restructuring frameworks, on discharge of debt and disqualifications, and on measures to increase the efficiency of procedures concerning restructuring, insolvency and discharge of debt, and amending Directive (EU) 2017/1132. See Chapter 2 by Ruiz and Hertz, and Chapter 3 by van Zwieten and Ellingsaeter.

[16] Cross-class cramdown under § 901G in England is similar to what is referred to as 'cramdown' in the US under 11 USC 1129(b).

[17] Companies Act 2006, c 46, Part 26A. The 'relevant alternative' is defined in section 901G(4) as 'whatever the court considers would be most likely to occur in relation to the company if the compromise or arrangement were not sanctioned under section 901F'.

[18] *Re AGPS Bondco PLC* [2023] EWHC 916 (Ch) (*Re Adler*).

will be necessary to quantify the *in rem* entitlement of fixed and floating charge holders in relation to each other and to junior creditors. Junior claimants may argue that the seniors are receiving more than the value of their collateral – claiming so much of the value of the firm that the juniors are left worse off than in the 'relevant alternative'. Or the juniors may accept the plan, and bind an objecting senior creditor, by paying them the value of their collateral. This is sometimes called a 'cram-up'.[19] Crucially, one cannot quantify the distribution in the 'relevant alternative' without determining the 'legal' status of the class members (or priority position) and their likely distributional entitlement alternative under the alternative scenario.[20]

This question has arisen in the US, and, as noted above, the terminology in the US is somewhat different from that in the UK. The standard is whether the plan is 'fair and equitable'.[21] That term has been frequently misunderstood as establishing a hierarchy of claims against the firm. Terms like 'absolute', 'relative', and 'absolute with exceptions' are bandied about in comparative discussions. However, treating the matter as one of hierarchy alone misses an important distinction between claims against and interests in the firm, and claims against the assets of the firm. It is, therefore, worth taking a moment to define these terms carefully as they are used in the US, before mapping them onto the UK concepts.

B. Consensual Confirmation and Cramdown: The US Template

Under Chapter 11, a plan of reorganisation can be confirmed if the required statutory majorities of a class vote in favour of a plan.[22] Dissenting creditors in an accepting class are bound ('"consensual" confirmation' or, alternatively, 'within class cramdown'). A plan can also be crammed down on a dissenting class (cross-class cramdown), but only if the plan is deemed 'fair and equitable', and it does not 'discriminate unfairly'.[23] The term 'fair and equitable' is sometimes treated as the equivalent of the 'absolute priority' rule. That rule requires that a (dissenting) senior class must be paid in full before any value flows through to a junior class of claims or interests. In its simplest form, it means that if creditors are not paid in full, then equity is wiped out. While the term 'absolute priority' does not appear anywhere in the Bankruptcy Code, it is applied colloquially to any situation where value distribution follows a hierarchical priority 'waterfall'. Once one actually reads § 1129(b), however, one sees that such a priority waterfall applies only to unsecured claims (*in personam* claims) and equity interests (ownership), but not to secured creditors (rights *in rem*).

[19] See Akinrele et al, 'Cramming up a Super Senior', n 9.

[20] In *Re Virgin Active Holdings Ltd* [2021] EWHC 1246 (Ch), Mr Justice Snowden (as he then was) articulated a three-part test for satisfying the 'no worse off' than in the 'relevant alternative' requirement. First, what would be the most likely outcome if the plan were not sanctioned. Second, what would be the consequences of that outcome for the dissenting creditors. Thirdly, those consequences should then be compared to the outcome and consequences for the dissenting creditors under the proposed restructuring plan.

[21] 11 USC § 1129(b).

[22] 11 USC §§ 1129(a) (confirmation when all classes accept), 1126 (solicitation and voting).

[23] 11 USC § 1129(b) (fair and equitable standard).

(i) Fair and Equitable for Unsecured Claims and Interests: The 'Absolute Priority Rule'

For unsecured creditors with contractual debt claims against or equity interests in the debtor, the fair and equitable standard is treated as a true question of priority. Section 1129(b)(2)(B) provides:

> (2) … the condition that a plan be fair and equitable with respect to a class includes the following requirements:
>
> …
>
> (B) With respect to a class of unsecured claims—
>
> (i) the plan provides that each holder of a claim of such class receive or retain on account of such claim *property of a value*, as of the effective date of the plan, *equal to the allowed amount of such claim*; or
>
> (ii) the *holder of any claim or interest that is junior* to the claims of such class *will not receive or retain under the plan on account of such junior claim or interest any property* … (emphasis added).

Under this formulation, no junior class of creditors or interests may receive a distribution on account of its junior rights, unless the senior class has been paid in full. This is what is generally referred to as the 'absolute priority rule',[24] under which claims are ranked in a distributional waterfall. But, as will be explained below, § 1129(b)(2)(B) only applies to *in personam* claims against the firm. A similar 'waterfall' rule applies to ownership interests in the firm pursuant to § 1129(b)(2)(C), should they be in the money. Absolute priority does not apply, however, to claims of priority against the firm's assets – security or rights *in rem*. Those are governed by § 1129(b)(2)(A), discussed below, which uses a different formulation.

In practice, even the absolute priority rule is not as absolute as it is sometimes portrayed. Under what is sometimes referred to as the 'new value corollary' or '*Case v Los Angeles Lumber* exception', a junior creditor may purchase an interest in the reorganising debtor by lending the reorganising debtor money or contributing new capital. Where this is the case, the court must assess the distribution in light of the new value contribution – that the price is fair, and not a sweetheart deal.[25] Sometimes this is characterised as an exception to the absolute priority rule. However, it is more accurately considered to be a corollary. If old equity is receiving a distribution in a cramdown plan, the court must ascertain that the distribution is only repayment for the 'new value', and not 'on account of' the old junior interest.[26]

[24] 11 USC §§ 1129(b)(2)(B) (classes of unsecured creditors), 1129(b)(2)(C)(equity interests). The statutory language is drawn from *Boyd v Northern Pacific Railway Co*, 228 US 482, 57 L Ed 931 (1913) a pre-Code case that established the 'absolute priority' of debt over equity.

[25] The new value corollary to the absolute priority rule as first stated in *Case v Los Angeles Lumber Products Co*, 308 US 106, 84 L Ed 110 (1939). The US Supreme Court has been coy about whether the *Case* rule was carried forward into the Bankruptcy Code when it was adopted in 1978. But it has stated that any new investment by old equity must be exposed to the market. *Bank of America National Trust & Savings Association v 203 North LaSalle Street Partnership*, 526 US 434, 143 L Ed 2d 607 (1999). Since the *LaSalle* case, lower courts have generally been willing to assume that the *Case* rule has survived. More recently, it was expressly written into the Code for small businesses by the Small Business Reorganization Act of 2019. 11 USC § 1191.

[26] This ability to preserve a relationship with the old owners is particularly important for small businesses, where the owner and the business may be one and the same. For this reason, in 2019, Congress passed the Small Business Reorganization Act, that allows the debtor owner of a small business to count 'sweat equity' as

(ii) *Fair and Equitable for Secured Creditors*

For secured creditors, the fair and equitable standard does not entitle the claimant to a hierarchical priority in the value of the firm. Instead, it entitles the creditor to retain a lien on its collateral, but only at the 'stripped down' (marked to market) value of that collateral, and to payments with a present value of at least the present value of its collateral as of the effective date of the plan:

> (2) [T]he condition that a plan be fair and equitable with respect to a class includes the following requirements:
>
> (A) With respect to a class of secured claims, the plan provides—
>
> (i)
>
> (I) that the holders of such claims *retain the liens securing such claims*, whether the property subject to such liens is retained by the debtor or transferred to another entity, *to the extent of the allowed amount* of such claims; and
>
> (II) that each holder of a claim of such class *receive* on account of such claim deferred *cash payments totaling at least the allowed amount* of such claim, *of a value, as of the effective date of the plan, of at least the value of such holder's interest in the estate's interest in such property* (emphasis added).[27]

This is not 'absolute priority'. Instead, it is an entitlement to a realisation on the value of the collateral as of the 'effective date' of the plan. This is reflected both in the required payment amount, and in the adjustment of the value of the lien. Both are tied to the amount 'allowed' under § 506(a) – the value of the collateral.[28] It does not entitle the secured creditor to payment in full ahead of junior classes, only to payment in full of the value of its security. If there are unencumbered assets, or if the value of the firm as a going concern exceeds the value of the collateral, that is not reflected in the cramdown entitlement. As such, value may flow through to the unsecured creditors even when the secured creditor has not been paid in full, so long as the allowed secured claim is satisfied. Indeed, as will be discussed in the next subsection, when the debtor continues to operate, value will flow through even if the secured creditor has a lien on substantially all the property of the debtor.

(iii) *Unfair Discrimination*

Unfair discrimination considers when and why it might be permissible to offer different distributions to creditors with similar legal rights. What constitutes a legitimate justification? This is the issue addressed by Lord Justice Snowden in *Adler*. There the court held that distinguishing between bond issues solely based on the date of their maturity

its new value contribution. Small Business Reorganization Act, PL 116-54, 133 Stat 1079, codified at 11 USC §§ 1181–1195.

[27] 11 USC § 1129(b)(2)(A).

[28] 11 USC § 506(a) sets the allowed secured claim as the 'value of the creditor's interest in the debtor's interest in the collateral'. This can be changed if the creditor makes the so-called, § 1111(b)(2) election of 'non-strip down treatment'. Even then, however, the present value of the distribution need not exceed the value of the collateral on the effective date of the plan.

was not a sufficient basis for different treatment.[29] In the US, courts have struggled to articulate a consistent test for discrimination. Some courts apply what is referred to as the *Aztec* test, that focuses on the reason for the distinction:

> (1) whether the discrimination is supported by a reasonable basis; (2) whether the debtor can confirm and consummate a plan without the discrimination; (3) whether the discrimination is proposed in good faith; and (4) the treatment of the classes discriminated against.[30]

The Third Circuit took a different approach in *In re Tribune*, focusing instead on the magnitude of the difference between distributions:

> A rebuttable presumption of unfair discrimination exists when there is (1) a dissenting class; (2) another class of the same priority; and (3) a difference in the plan's treatment of the two classes that results in either (a) a materially lower percentage recovery for the dissenting class (measured in terms of the net present value of all payments), or (b) regardless of percentage recovery, an allocation under the plan of materially greater risk to the dissenting class in connection with its proposed distribution.[31]

As can be seen, some courts focus on the reason for the discrimination, others on the extent and nature of the discrimination.

So, the 'fair and equitable' standard considers the priority of claims based on their pre-bankruptcy entitlements. For asset-based claims this turns on the value of the collateral, while for other claims and interests one looks at the value of the firm itself. That standard establishes a distributional floor. Second, one must separately consider 'discrimination' and assess the horizontal equity between similarly situated creditors once the distributional floor has been established.

III. Security v Recourse: Assets v Earnings and Liquidation v Continuation

The 'fair and equitable standard' as articulated in the Bankruptcy Code, thus, maintains a distinction between priority that derives from a claim to the debtor's property (security) and priority amongst *in personam* claims against the debtor (recourse), and ownership interests in the debtor (equity). However, this distinction is muddied when a secured creditor claims a floating lien on substantially all of the debtor's assets (a 'blanket lien') and the debtor continues to operate, either because the debtor recapitalises in Chapter 11, or the business enterprise is sold as a going concern. Even in the US, distributions are often calculated using a working assumption that all value should flow first to the secured creditor, then in succession to claims and interests in order of priority.

[29] *In re Adler Group* (n 4) at 42–44 (paras 148–172).

[30] *In re Aztec Co*, 107 BR 585 (Bankr MD Tenn 1989). *Aztec* has been followed in the Fourth and Ninth Circuits. *Liberty National Enterprises v Ambanc La Mesa Ltd Partnership (In re Ambanc La Mesa Ltd Partnership)*, 115 F 3d 650, 656 (9th Cir 1997), cert denied, 522 US 1110, 140 L Ed 2d 105 (1998). See generally *In re Bryson Properties, XVIII*, 961 F 2d 496, 502 (4th Cir), cert denied, 506 US 866, 121 L Ed 2d 134 (1992). See also, 7 *Collier on Bankruptcy* P 1129.03, 16th edn (LexisNexis 'Practical Guidance' online 2024).

[31] *In re Tribune Co*, 972 F 3d 228, 241 and fn 16 (3d Cir 2020).

'Absolute priority' is often assumed to apply to the secured creditor.[32] Therefore, if the secured creditor, holding a blanket lien, is not being paid in full, then 'absolute priority' in the US should mean that the unsecured creditors will be left out of the money and have no right to object. It is a commonplace at the beginning of many bankruptcy cases for the secured party to assert that: 'All of the assets are liened, that the secured creditors are undersecured, and that therefore, there will be no distribution to the "junior" creditors'. In such cases, the unsecured creditors can be crammed down, even with a zero distribution, because no class junior to them is receiving anything. The 'unsecureds' receive no benefit from the reorganisation. This rationale has been used to justify going concern sales that distribute all of the value of the debtor to the secured creditors, or that allow the secured creditor to credit bid[33] at a going concern sale.[34] The analysis above demonstrates, however, that this assertion will frequently be wrong, at least in cases where the debtor continues to operate.

A. Cognitive Dissonance – Assuming an Enterprise Lien

As a normative matter, law and economics scholars long for a system that *would* allow for a truly hierarchical capital structure. Doing so would facilitate quick bankruptcy auctions by eliminating the need for bankruptcy processes that seek to protect the interests of disparate creditor constituencies.[35] But wishing does not make it so.

[32] One example can be found in an op-ed involving the Chrysler bankruptcy, where Professor Todd Zywicki expresses outrage that the 'absolute priority rule' was not followed when secured creditors were not paid in full, yet a distribution was made to unsecured employees and labour unions. Todd J Zywicki, 'Chrysler and the Rule of Law: The Founders put the contracts clause in the Constitution for a reason', *Wall Street Journal* (May 13, 2009): https://www.wsj.com/articles/SB124217356836613091.

[33] Under the Bankruptcy Code, a secured creditor has the right to use its secured claim as currency in an auction of the collateral asset(s) in the debtor's § 363 sale. The creditor can offset up to the full face value of its claim against the collateral purchase price, allowing it to acquire assets of the debtor on which it holds a lien in exchange for full or partial cancellation of the debt. See also text accompanying nn 45–47.

[34] See, eg, Ralph Brubaker, 'The Post-RadLAX Ghosts of Pacific Lumber and Philly News (Part II): Limiting Credit Bidding', 34(7) *Bankruptcy Law Letter*, July 2014, 1–13, at 4, referring to ('Two monumental developments in Chapter 11 practice that the Code drafters likely did not anticipate, though, have skewed negotiations over allocation of reorganization surplus decisively in favor of senior secured creditors, in a manner that the Code drafters also likely did not anticipate. The first is the ascendancy of secured credit in Chapter 11 debtors' capital structures, such that it is now common that a dominant secured lender has blanket liens on substantially all of the debtor's assets securing debts vastly exceeding the value of the debtor's business and assets … The second, related phenomenon is the rise of "relatively expeditious going-concern sales of the debtor's business and assets to a third-party purchaser" as a prominent means of realizing the debtor's going-concern value in Chapter 11'.) (citations omitted).

[35] Douglas G Baird and Thomas H Jackson, 'Corporate Reorganizations and the Treatment of Diverse Ownership Interests: A Comment on Adequate Protection of Secured Creditors in Bankruptcy' (1984) 51 *University of Chicago Law Review* 97, 106–8 and fn 40 ('Bankruptcy is, in short, a mechanism to make disparate owners act as one owner would act, and thereby to reduce the costs such dispersion would otherwise bring'.); ibid at fn 52 ('Secured credit is to unsecured credit what unsecured credit is to equity interests'.); Alan Schwartz, 'A Theory of Loan Priorities' (1989)18 *Journal of Legal Studies* 209, 211 ('[T]he optimal priority contract … would rank the initial financer first'); cf Alan Schwartz, 'The Fairness of Tender Offer Prices in Utilitarian Theory' (1988) 17 *Journal of Legal Studies* 165, 167–68 (noting that the single-owner standard is widely accepted by courts and legal commentators). In Douglas G Baird, 'The Rights of Secured Creditors after ResCap' (2015) *University of Illinois Law Review* 849, Baird recognises the asset-based nature of the secured claim but continues to assume the possibility of a blanket lien on going concern value. Ibid at 860 (The debate over '[w]hether one looks at a secured creditor as holding the discrete parts worth less than the going

The positive law is in tension with the normative views of those academics. As Christopher Frost has put it,

> [a] significant question … is whether a secured creditor can legitimately claim priority in all of the value of the business as a going concern (the 'enterprise value'). This position is an operating assumption of most, if not all, of the theoretical analysts, but one that is challenged by those writing in the doctrinal branch.[36]

Frost, who shared the normative preference for simplicity, took up the challenge and sought to craft a doctrinal argument for entity priority under US law, built on asset-based security. He succeeded, but only up to a point. He concluded, forthrightly, that an enterprise lien can be created, but only where the enterprise is a closed system, and where all of the value created is the proceeds of liened collateral. Indeed, this exception appears to prove the rule. Frost concedes that such an arrangement is fragile at best, with many opportunities for leakage.[37] This point has also been emphasised in recent work by Sarah Paterson when comparing the Article 9 blanket lien to the floating charge.[38] Frost is not particularly happy about this conclusion and suggests that an enterprise lien might be desirable.

Floating charge envy has had consequences, both in the literature and also in actual cases. It has generated cognitive dissonance in both the US case law, and scholarly literature. For example, in his important and influential article, 'The Creditors' Bargain and Option-Preservation Priority in Chapter 11', Tony Casey concludes his introduction with the following:

> Respecting nonbankruptcy contract rights creates the following priority at the time of a sale: (1) the senior creditor's nonbankruptcy liquidation value of the collateral; (2) the junior creditor's option value; and (3) *the senior creditor's right to the residual value – after the junior option has been paid out – up to the face value of the senior debt.* Implementation of this priority is accomplished by requiring a senior creditor to buy out the contractually bargained-for option rights of junior creditors – even those who are out of the money – before it can take control of or sell the debtor's assets in Chapter 11 (emphasis added).[39]

Casey's article is unabashedly normative. However, the paragraph reads as a description of doctrine. Casey assumes the existence of a single distributional hierarchy. Nonetheless, in a later article, Casey, writing with Andrew Verstein, acknowledges that as a doctrinal description it may be wrong, and laments that the US does not have the same rule as the UK:

> In other jurisdictions, like the United Kingdom, an even broader type of payment priority against the debtor is possible. This is achieved through a floating charge in the United Kingdom, but this approach is not practicable in the United States. (Jacoby and Janger 201[8]).

concern or whether it enjoys a right to the first cashflows of the firm … will undoubtedly continue … Both sides cling to their views as if they were articles of religious faith'.).

[36] Christopher W Frost, 'Secured Credit and Effective Entity Priority' (2019) 51 *Connecticut Law Review* 575, 579 (https://opencommons.uconn.edu/law_review/420).

[37] ibid at 589, 617–22.

[38] Sarah Paterson, 'Finding our way: secured transactions and corporate bankruptcy law and policy in America and England' (2018) 18 *Journal of Corporate Law Studies* 247.

[39] Anthony J Casey, 'The Creditors' Bargain and Option-Preservation Priority in Chapter 11' (2011) 78 *University of Chicago Law Review* 759, 765.

> Under the floating charge, a lender has payment priority as to the value of all of the debtor's assets at the time of enforcement, but not with respect to particular assets that the debtor has sold. This structure can allow assets to come in and out of a broad pool. Something akin to the floating charge over some pools might be constructed in the United States through the use of legal entities but doing so brings major costs with it. (Casey 2015).[40]

Thus, in the US, distributional Anglophilia can lead to doctrinal confusion. It is often simultaneously assumed that the secured creditor has first priority in the value of the firm, while recognising that this priority only extends to assets.

This cognitive dissonance – assuming an enterprise lien, notwithstanding the scope of Article 9 and the text of the Bankruptcy Code – has reached practitioners as well. The ABI Commission Report on the Reform of Chapter 11, a document drafted by the leading insolvency academics and practitioners seeks to have it both ways. For the most part the Commission Report treats secured creditor entitlements as turning on the value of the collateral. Examples include its proposed treatment of adequate protection claims,[41] as well as the proposed approach to valuation of collateral for the purposes of determining the allowed secured claim.[42] Yet the same report devotes an entire chapter to the concept of option value preservation priority, as proposed by Casey. In that chapter, it correctly suggests that a secured creditor cannot be said to own the option value of the firm – namely, the likelihood that the fortunes of the firm will improve after a plan becomes effective. Accordingly, they propose the creation of an 'option value preservation priority'.

While the concept of 'option value preservation priority' limits the scope of the secured creditor's lien to the *current* value of the firm (exclusive of potential upside), and sets an upper limit on absolute priority, it still assumes that the secured creditor can capture the full present value of the going concern. The Commission assumes that the strike price of the option is payment in full of the secured creditor's debt, rather than the value of its collateral. In so doing, the Commission, like Casey, simply assumes that the existence of a blanket lien over the firm's assets confers a priority claim on the enterprise value.[43] The point here is not to criticise the concept of option preservation value (it is an important contribution), but to highlight that the assumption of a lien on enterprise value turns on the conflation of the ability to place a lien on all or almost all of a business's assets under State law with the ability to place a lien on the going concern value of the operating business enterprise. Practitioners at the highest level, as well as many scholars, have failed to appreciate the difference between the value of the firm and the value of its assets.

[40] Anthony J Casey and Andrew Verstein, 'Deconstructing the Senior Creditor' in Adam Badawi (ed), *Encyclopedia of Law and Economics, Corporate Law and Economics*, available at SSRN: https://ssrn.com/abstract=4708447, 1–28, at 17, citing Jacoby and Janger, 'Tracing Equity' (n 10).

[41] ABI Commission to Study the Reform of Chapter 11 (American Bankruptcy Institute, 2014) at 67–73 (IV.B. Financing the Case: 1. Adequate Protection): available at: https://abiworld.app.box.com/s/vvircv5xv83aavl4dp4h.

[42] ibid at 180–83 (V.F. General Valuation Standards) (considering whether liens should be valued at the realisable value of the collateral, or based on their value to the reorganisation).

[43] ibid at 207–24 (VI.C Value Determinations, Allocation and Distributions: 1. Creditors' Rights to Reorganization Value and Redemption Option Value).

The case law is confused as well. This can be seen by reading between the lines in the US Supreme Court's decision involving the right to credit bid when the debtor is sold as a going concern. In *RadLAX Gateway Hotel, LLC v Amalgamated Bank*,[44] the Supreme Court held that a plan of reorganisation could not be crammed down over a secured creditor's objection unless the secured party was given the opportunity to credit bid.[45] On the one hand, this holding seems unexceptional, as that right is provided for in § 363(k) of the Bankruptcy Code. The curious thing about that case, and the lower court decisions that preceded it, was that the case involved a going concern sale of the company. In other words, the secured creditor was being allowed to credit bid its secured claim, based on a purported blanket lien, to buy the operating entity, not just its assets. Credit bidding in a bankruptcy sale of the going concern allows the bidder to purchase the enterprise value of the firm.[46] However, the value of the firm as a going concern is measured by the capitalised value of future earnings. These earnings are not entirely attributable to disposition of the secured creditor's collateral.

Ralph Brubaker has pointed out that credit bidding rights must be limited if the going concern value of the firm is not part of the secured creditor's collateral.[47] At least one court has done so. In *In re The Free Lance-Star Publishing Co*, an investor purchased the secured creditor's claim at a discount and then sought to credit bid the full amount of the debt when the debtor was sold out of bankruptcy. Noting the discounted purchase price and further noting that there were questions about whether the creditor's liens on all of the assets were perfected, the court limited the creditor's credit bid to the amount it had paid for the claim.[48]

B. Distinguishing Security from Recourse – Rights *in Personam* v Rights *in Rem*

Melissa Jacoby and I join Brubaker in his scepticism about a lien on goodwill, and extend his point by suggesting that this cognitive dissonance may actually rest on the failure to recognise *two* distinctions: (1) the distinction between rights against a firm itself (recourse); and rights against the firm's assets (security); and (2) the distinction between bankruptcy proceedings where value is realised through a sale of assets (liquidation) and those where value is realised through the capitalised earnings of the going concern (through a recapitalisation or going concern sale).[49] Under US law, the first distinction

[44] *RadLAX Gateway Hotel, LLC v Amalgamated Bank*, 566 US 639, 132 S Ct 2065, 2073 (2012).

[45] ibid.

[46] See n 33 above. For examples, see *In re Pacific Lumber Co*, 584 F 3d 229, 236–37 (5th Cir 2009); *In re Philadelphia Newspapers, LLC*, 599 F 3d 298, 298, 301 (3d Cir 2010).

[47] Ralph Brubaker, 'Credit Bidding and the Secured Creditor's Baseline Distributional Entitlement in Chapter 11', 32(7) *Bankruptcy Law Letter*, July 2012, at 11–12.

[48] 11 USC § 363(k) permits limiting credit bidding rights for cause, and at least two courts have done so where the value of the secured creditor's collateral was at issue. *In re The Free Lance-Star Publishing Co of Fredericksburg*, 512 BR 798, 806–7 (Bankr ED Va 2014) (secured creditor had not demonstrated that its lien covered the entire enterprise). *cf In re Fisker Automotive Holdings, Inc*, 510 BR 55, 59 (Bankr D Del 2014) (credit bid limited where a secured creditor purchased secured claims at a substantial discount and sought to credit bid at the going concern sale).

[49] Jacoby and Janger, 'Tracing Equity', n 10.

inheres in the nature of security under US law, and the second is built into the fabric of Chapter 11. Where the value of the firm is being realised through capitalised earnings it is not obvious that all that value is encumbered.[50] The difference is illustrated by the following mathematical examples.

(i) US: Security Rights in Liquidation – Single Asset

The difference between security and priority can be seen in the following example. Imagine, for example, a debtor that is liquidating. It has assets worth $100,000. These consist of inventory, accounts receivable, equipment and real estate. Further imagine that one creditor has a security interest in the debtor's inventory. The inventory is worth $50,000, while the creditor holding a security interest in that inventory is owed $500,000. Five other unsecured creditors are each owed $100,000, so claims total $1,000,000.

If the secured creditor was entitled to 'absolute priority', the secured creditor's priority would be coextensive with the value of the firm ($100,000). It would have a right to be paid in full before junior unsecured creditors received anything. The distributions would look like this: Secured Creditor receives 20 per cent ($100,000/ $500,000), while the other creditors would receive $0.

Of course, that's not the right answer on these facts. The secured creditor's lien only encumbers *some* of the debtor's assets. The bankruptcy would proceed in two steps. First the inventory would be sold, yielding $50,000. The proceeds of that sale would go to the secured creditor, for a distribution on the secured claim of 10 per cent. Since the inventory was worth less than the full amount of the debt, this would leave an unsecured deficiency claim of $450,000. Second, the remaining $50,000 in unencumbered assets would be sold, and the proceeds would be distributed to the unsecured creditors (including the secured creditor's deficiency). Those claims total $950,000, so the distribution would be: 50,000/ $950,000 or 5.263 per cent. The secured creditor would thus receive an additional $23,683 (5.263 per cent of $450,000) – $73,683 in total. The remaining creditors would split $26,317 five ways, with each receiving $5263.40 (5.263 per cent of their $100,000 claims).

This illustrates the difference between security and recourse. The secured creditor has recourse against the debtor for $500,000, but it only has a secured claim, entitled to a distributional priority to the extent of its collateral. The secured creditor still realises their priority, but the distribution is only 14.74 per cent per cent instead of 20 per cent. This is because its priority is tied to the value of its collateral, not the value of the firm, and its deficiency is a non-priority recourse claim entitled only to a pro rata distribution on equal footing with the other unsecured creditors. Here, the answer seems obvious because the secured creditor did not have a lien on all of the assets of the firm.

[50] Anthony Casey and Andrew Verstein, 'Deconstructing the Senior Creditor' in Adam Badawi (ed), *Encyclopedia of Law and Economics, Corporate Law and Economics*, available at SSRN: https://ssrn.com/abstract=4708447.

(ii) US: Floating Liens in Liquidation – Blanket Lien

But what if the secured creditor has managed to perfect its liens on substantially all of the debtor's property, real and personal? In liquidation, if the secured creditor has actually managed to perfect its interest in all the assets of the firm under the relevant property regime, the secured creditor *would* receive all of the debtor's property, while the other creditors will receive nothing. This is, however, a special case, difficult to obtain, even in liquidation, and as Frost points out, almost impossible where the debtor continues to operate. Issues may arise under each of the various property regimes as to whether the secured creditors' rights are comprehensive. Article 9 security interests must be recorded in the proper State filing system. Real estate mortgages must be recorded in the proper county. While some types of assets (aircraft, copyright) must be recorded in a federal system. Government licences may not be property, and franchise agreements or other licences may not be transferrable under non-bankruptcy law. Only if the creditor has jumped through all the hoops, and the property is amenable to sale, will the secured creditor have secured a lien on all of the debtor's value.[51] Even then, as the next section demonstrates, the maths only works if the debtor liquidates.

(iii) US: Security in Going Concern Sales and Recapitalisation

The asset-based priority of a secured creditor who has placed a lien on substantially all of the debtor's property is only coextensive with entity value if the debtor liquidates and ceases operations. The genius of Chapter 11 is that it allows the creditors to realise the value of the firm as a going concern, either through a recapitalisation or going concern sale, if this is the best way to maximise creditor recovery.

But when a debtor enterprise continues in operation under Chapter 11, the maths changes because the manner of realising the value of the firm has changed. The goal of Chapter 11 (and, for that matter, Part 26A) is to avoid the necessity of winding up the business enterprise when preserving the going concern increment will produce greater value than liquidation. Chapter 11 offers the creditors the option to realise the value of the firm from the continued earnings from operation. In this situation, the firm's assets are not sold, and the value of the collateral is not established. Instead, the assets remain as a component of the value of the going concern. The recourse claimants against the firm, in effect, must redeem those assets from the secured creditors, who, otherwise, would have had a right to foreclose. The question, therefore, is 'at what price?'.

Again, a numerical example might be useful. Assume, as before, that the debtor had assets that could be liquidated for $100,000, all subject to a lien held by a secured creditor holding a claim of $500,000. Similarly, five other trade creditors each hold unsecured claims of $100,000. But this time, assume that the debtor is generating an operating profit, and the market value of its capitalised earnings would be $200,000.

[51] Some assets may not be alienable (or lienable) at all, such as gaming licences, liquor licences and/or taxi-cab medallions.

The goal of a rescue regime is to preserve the value of that going concern increment (the extra $100,000) by allowing the debtor to continue its business. But who gets the extra $100,000 when the value of the firm is realised through continued operations rather than sale of assets? Broadly speaking, there are two options.

- If the secured creditor's priority is measured by the value of the assets, then the maths would work this way: The secured creditor would have an entitlement to the value of its collateral of $100,000. It would have a deficiency claim of $400,000. Unsecured claims would total $900,000, so unsecured creditors would receive $100,000/ $900,000 or 11.1 per cent. The secured creditor would be entitled to a total distribution of $144,444 or 28.88 per cent.
- If the secured creditor's priority were instead treated as a claim against the firm itself, then the secured creditor would have a first priority claim to all of the value of the firm – $200,000 or 40 per cent. The other creditors would receive nothing.

As explained below, the US, as a matter of property law and bankruptcy law, follows the first approach and the UK is understood to follow the second, though whether this is a product of property law, bankruptcy law, or corporate law is a difficult question.

(iv) The 'Allowed Secured Claim'

In the US the secured creditor's entitlement is determined through a combination of State law and federal bankruptcy law. In reorganisation cases, secured creditors' State law security entitlements are translated into distributional entitlement in bankruptcy through the concept of the 'allowed secured claim'.

Under § 506(a), a claim is a 'secured claim to the extent of the value of such creditor's interest in the estate's interest in such property'.[52] In other words, the secured claim is determined by the value of the collateral – the property securing the debt. What that property is, and the priority of claims against it, is left to non-bankruptcy law, with real property governed by the law of mortgages and personal property security governed by Article 9. Crucially, the scope of Article 9 is limited to 'personal property',[53] and a security interest does not attach until a secured creditor has 'rights in the collateral' to convey.[54] In liquidation, this entitlement is determined by the sale price of the collateral. The secured creditor receives the proceeds less the cost of sale.

When the debtor reorganises, however, the collateral is not sold, so the allowed secured claim must be either agreed to by the parties or determined by the court in cramdown. The cramdown entitlement is established by § 1129(b)(2)(A). Under that section, the secured creditor's lien is stripped down to the allowed secured claim – the value of the collateral as determined under § 506(a), and the present value of payments is established by the value of that collateral. In other words, a secured creditor which objects to its treatment under the plan can be 'crammed down' by being paid the 'value' of the property securing its claim. Or to put it another way, the baseline cramdown

[52] 11 USC § 506.
[53] UCC § 9-109.
[54] 11 USC § 9-203.

entitlement of a secured creditor must be traced to collateral, and more particularly, collateral owned on the petition date.

(v) The Going Concern Increment

But if a firm reorganises or is sold as a going concern, and continues to operate, the value of the firm will be realised through earnings from operation, rather than sale of assets, and its value will be determined by the capitalised value of those earnings, not by the value of the collateral (which will not be sold). Value is realised over time, and the sale price includes two components – ownership of the assets and a right to the income stream from operations, net of expenses. The value of a going concern is not measured by the value of its property, but by the anticipated value of the future earnings stream.[55] Those earnings are produced by using property, disposing of property, and labour by (often at-will[56]) employees. Some of that property has intrinsic value, but some may have value that is entirely firm-specific, and that can be realised only by that particular firm, and only if the firm continues to operate. Some of the earnings will not be traceable to property at all.[57]

Treating a going concern sale as a liquidation is, therefore, a false equivalence. And this false equivalence makes a difference. Even when all of the firm's assets are encumbered, this does not necessarily mean that the creditors with claims against those assets are entitled to the additional increment of going concern value. This is the source of the cognitive dissonance described above. The view that a lien on property captures the going concern increment proceeds from two related mistakes: (1) the failure to distinguish between security from recourse – claims of priority based on ownership of assets (rights *in rem*) from claims against the firm itself (rights *in personam*); and (2) the failure to distinguish piecemeal liquidation of the firm in bankruptcy from reorganisation through a recapitalisation or going concern sale.

C. Security v Recourse in the UK: The Puzzle of the Floating Charge

Unlike in the US, the UK does not appear to suffer from any disagreement or confusion. The combination of fixed and floating charge, together, is understood to give a secured creditor a lien on the value of the entire undertaking – the enterprise.[58] The sections that follow consider the implications of this difference in cramdown, and

[55] Jacoby and Janger, 'Tracing Equity' (n 10). It bears noting that the value of the income stream to creditors is capped at the full amount of the debt. Therefore, the sale price also includes the value of equity's option to buy out the debt claims at par.

[56] In US labour law, at-will employment is an employer's ability to dismiss an employee for any lawful reason, without having to establish 'just cause' for termination, and without warning. Similarly, the employee has the right to quit, for any reason, or no reason at all.

[57] ibid.

[58] For a careful analysis of the differences between US and UK secured credit, see Sarah Paterson, 'Finding our way: secured transactions and corporate bankruptcy law and policy in America and England' (2018) 18 *Journal of Corporate Law Studies* 247.

further consider whether the lack of disagreement in the UK is because the floating charge is actually different from the floating lien, or is a product of failure to recognise the false equivalence between piecemeal liquidation and a going concern sale. They seek to pinpoint the source of the difference between US and UK law with regard to an enterprise lien, considering whether it derives from: (1) the scope of security; (2) the consequences of opening a bankruptcy proceeding; or (3) the approach to future assets. They conclude that none of these is fully sufficient to create the 'enterprise lien' that is generally understood to exist in the UK, and query, therefore, whether cross-class cramdown's migration East may reveal that cognitive dissonance is a transatlantic phenomenon.

IV. The Scope of Rights *in Rem*: US v UK

The difference between US and UK security is often explained as a difference in the scope of security. The conventional understanding is that in the US, security is focused on the assets, but in the UK, because of a floating charge on circulating assets, it is possible to take a lien on the enterprise itself – a lien on the entire undertaking.[59] Sarah Paterson takes this approach in her thoughtful article, 'Finding our way: secured transactions and corporate bankruptcy law and policy in America and England'. As she puts it, 'by the end of the nineteenth century the ability of a lender to take security over all or substantially all of the assets of an English company with comparative ease was well-established in law'.[60] This sentence reveals two important insights. First, like security in the US, the floating charge is a lien on property, and second, the difference between the two systems is thought to lie in the availability of a catch-all security device. As Paterson explains it, in the US, an Article 9 security interest lets the secured lender get almost everything, but because of the multiplicity of property regimes, and limits on the scope of Article 9, either because of the nature of property, or because of statutory exclusions, there may be gaps.[61] By contrast, the floating charge, as a lien against the 'undertaking', is thought to fill in the gaps left by the fixed charge holder, with nothing left over.

This explanation is unsatisfying for two reasons: (1) first, as a practical matter, the difference between a floating charge and the lien obtainable by US secured creditors (at least sophisticated ones) is not all that great; but more importantly, (2) a lien on assets must be realised through some form of disposition of the collateral. Selling a firm's property does not automatically convert a lien on property into a lien on the capitalised earnings of the firm. The earning stream produced by operating the company

[59] As Paterson describes it, 'In 1870 the English Court of Appeal determined that where a company charged its "undertaking and all sums of money arising therefrom" the word "undertaking" captured all present and future property of the company'. Ibid at 249 (citing *Re Panama New Zealand and Australian Royal Mail Co* (1869–70) LR 5 Ch App 318).

[60] ibid. See also, John Armour, 'The Chequered History of the Floating Charge' (2004) 13 *Griffith Law Review* 25, 27; Gabriel Moss, 'Fictions and Floating Charges: Some Reflections on the House of Lords' Decision in Spectrum', and Roy Goode, 'The Case for the Abolition of the Floating Charge' both in Joshua Getzler and Jennifer Payne (eds), *Company Charges: Spectrum and Beyond* (Oxford, OUP, 2006).

[61] UCC § 9-109(a), (d).

may not all derive from the disposition of property. It might be produced by the labour of the owners, the work of at-will employees, the synergy of firm-specific assets and labour, etc. Indeed, preserving that going-concern surplus is the *sine qua non* of a rescue regime.[62] This section considers the question of the scope of security from the perspective of lien law. It concludes that control over the firm's assets may give the secured creditor the power to prevent the business from generating a going concern surplus, but that is not the same thing as owning the business or that surplus. The next section (section V) compares the allocation, in insolvency, of the going concern increment.

A. US: What does the Secured Creditor Own?

So, what is the difference between a so-called, 'blanket lien' under US law and a 'floating charge' under UK law? In the US, transactional lawyers often talk about a financing as secured by a 'blanket lien'. As a matter of transactional intention, the debtor may wish to give a secured creditor a lien on the value of the firm, and a hierarchical payment priority ahead of all other creditors. However, as a legal matter, there is no such thing. Instead, what they are describing is a financing secured by a perfected Article 9 security interest in the debtor's personal property, and a mortgage on all the debtor's real estate. By doing so, it is possible to create a lien on substantially all of a firm's property. But this confers only the right to foreclose on that property and sell it (a right *in rem*). It does not confer a senior right against the firm itself (*in personam*), or the power to operate the firm. A debtor can promise to pay a particular creditor ahead of others. But that promise to grant priority is not enforceable in bankruptcy. The problem is that the agreement regarding priority would not be binding on the bankruptcy trustee.[63] This is because the trustee's status as a perfected lien creditor is enforceable against third parties while a contract right is only binding on the debtor. As Jay Westbrook has pointed out, the only way to make such an agreement effective is through a lien on the debtor's property.[64] But, Westbrook too is careful to point out, a lien on *property* is not a lien on the value of the firm, nor does it grant control over the firm. It merely allows the creditor to capture the value of the firm through the exercise of control over assets.[65] Riz Mokal has made a similar point specifically about the floating charge.[66]

[62] The House Report for the US Bankruptcy Code of 1978 puts it this way: 'The purpose of a business reorganization case, unlike a liquidation case, is to restructure a business's finances so that it may continue to operate, provide its employees with jobs, pay its creditors, and produce a return for its stockholders. The premise of a business reorganization is that assets that are used for production in the industry for which they are designed are more valuable than those same assets sold for scrap. Often, the return on assets that a business can produce is inadequate to compensate those who have invested in the business. Cash flow problems may develop, and require creditors of the business, both trade creditors and long-term lenders, to wait for payment of their claims. If the business can extend or reduce its debts, it often can be returned to a viable state. It is more economically efficient to reorganize than to liquidate, because it preserves jobs and assets'. HR Rep No 95-595, at 220 (1977) (citations omitted).

[63] Jay Laurence Westbrook, 'The Control of Wealth in Bankruptcy' (2004) 84 *Texas Law Review* 795.

[64] ibid at 810.

[65] ibid.

[66] Riz Mokal, 'The Floating Charge – an Elegy' in Sarah Worthington (ed), *Commercial Law and Commercial Practice* (Oxford, Hart Publishing, 2003).

Precisely because property rights are binding on third parties, property law imposes limits both on the alienability of certain property rights, and on the process by which property rights can be transferred. Property law does not work like contract law. The procedures for creating effective property rights and their scope are legally defined. This is certainly true where non-possessory liens on property are involved.[67] For real property, it is necessary to comply with a State's recording procedures to make a mortgage binding on third parties. For personal property, it is necessary to comply with the notice requirements of Article 9 of the Uniform Commercial Code.[68] More importantly, Article 9 only applies to property that is within its scope. Under § 9-109(a) the statute applies to security interests 'in personal property'. Even there, there are exclusions: for example, property subject to liens created by federal law,[69] and even within the category of personal property, some types of property are excluded.[70]

While it may not be possible to obtain a lien on all of the value of a firm under Article 9, it is, nonetheless, possible for a secured creditor to hold a lien on almost all the valuable assets of a debtor. Real estate mortgages require local recording, but Article 9 gives the creditor the power to get almost everything else by simply obtaining a security agreement and filing a proper financing statement where the debtor is located. While in the US, there is no floating charge, there is a 'floating lien'[71] that allows the security agreement to extend to 'after-acquired property'. Conceptually, at least, both allow the secured party to perfect a lien on circulating assets (as the debtor acquires them). Indeed, the floating lien is, in many ways, more powerful than the floating charge, because it is not subject to preferential claims and carve-outs. In sum, while there is no such thing as a 'blanket lien' per se, a functional lien on substantially all of the debtor's property can be created with a combination of real estate mortgages, common law pledges, and an Article 9 security interest.

But a floating lien on circulating assets is not the equivalent of a lien on the going concern value of a firm. Under UCC § 9-204, a security agreement can cover 'after-acquired' property: 'a security agreement may create or provide for a security interest in after-acquired collateral'. But a security interest that covers property as it is acquired does not necessarily cover property that has not yet been acquired. Indeed, the language of Article 9 is quite clear with regard to the fact that it does not. For a security interest to attach, three requirements must be met under UCC § 9-203: (1) there must be an agreement that grants security – a 'security agreement'; (2) the creditor must have given 'value' – consideration; and (3) the debtor must have 'rights in the collateral' that it has the power to convey. A security interest does not 'attach' until all three of these requirements are met. There is, therefore, no enforceable security interest in property that the debtor has not yet acquired. In such a case, the debtor will not have 'rights in the collateral'.

To the extent that an Article 9 security interest *might* capture going concern value, the argument has been made that 'goodwill' counts as property to which a security

[67] *Twyne's Case* 3 Co Rep 80b, 76 ER 809 (1601).
[68] UCC, § 9-310.
[69] UCC, § 9-109(c).
[70] UCC, § 9-109(d).
[71] 11 USC § 9-204.

interest can attach, and that goodwill captures the increment of value between present assets and future assets. Article 9 allows a creditor to take security by identifying its collateral by type. The residual category is 'general intangibles'. General intangibles are defined, in effect, as personal property that does not fit into any of the other categories:

> 'General intangible' means any personal property, including things in action, other than accounts, chattel paper, commercial tort claims, deposit accounts, documents, goods, instruments, investment property, letter-of-credit rights, letters of credit, money, and oil, gas, or other minerals before extraction. The term includes payment intangibles and software.[72]

Even if 'general intangible' reaches all remaining forms of personal property, whether 'goodwill' counts as property is an open question in the case law.[73] Jacoby and I have argued that goodwill is merely an accounting entry, not an entitlement. It is inserted onto the balance sheet when a company is sold and the sale price exceeds the book value of the assets. Goodwill is another name for the going concern increment. But giving it a name on the balance sheet does not make it property. And, even if one *can* place a lien on a firm's present goodwill, as Casey has pointed out, one cannot obtain a lien on the firm's 'option value'.[74]

Thus, while it is a possible, if costly, exercise for a creditor to cobble together a lien on substantially all of the debtor's assets at any given moment in time, it is hard to argue that the secured creditor has the ability to take a security interest in the value of the capitalised future earnings of the going concern. This would require translating a lien on the assets of a firm into a lien on the value of the enterprise; to do so would require the security to 'attach' to income and rights that do not yet exist. While, as noted, many commentators have tried to wish such a power into being,[75] they largely concede that it is not possible to do so, even if the debtor purports to grant a 'blanket lien'.

B. UK: The Nature and Scope of the Floating Charge?

While US law makes possible for a creditor to take security in substantially all the property owned by the debtor at any given moment, including circulating assets, it is not clear that this turns the asset-based lien on property into a lien on the value of capitalised future earnings. It is also clear that both the floating lien and the floating charge are considered a form of asset-based priority. So, the question remains, why is it generally understood that the floating charge captures the going concern increment, while the security interest does not? Does it lie in the nature of the floating charge or its scope?

[72] UCC § 9-102(42).

[73] Ralph Brubaker, 'Credit Bidding and the Secured Creditor's Baseline Distributional Entitlement in Chapter 11' (2012) 32(7) *Bankruptcy Law Letter*, July 2012, 1 at 11–12.

[74] Anthony Casey, 'Option Preservation Value Priority', n 39 at 774.

[75] Alan Schwartz, 'A Theory of Loan Priorities' (1989) 18 *Journal of Legal Studies* 209, 216–18, 240–41; Douglas G Baird, 'Security Interests Reconsidered' (1994) 80 *Virginia Law Review* 2249; Paul M Shupack, 'Preferred Capital Structures and the Question of Filing' (1995) 87 *Minnesota Law Review* 787 (https://scholarship.law.umn.edu/mlr/2064).

As a historical matter, the US floating lien and the UK floating charge arise from the same practical conundrum. How can a business enterprise use circulating assets as collateral, while continuing to operate the business? In the US this problem arose when factors in the garment industry sought to take a security interest in a textile maker's book accounts while allowing the debtor to continue to collect those accounts receivable on its own. In *Benedict v Ratner*, the Supreme Court (per Justice Brandeis) held that the failure of the creditor to exercise 'dominion or control' over the accounts meant that no property interest was created.[76] Accounts receivable financing developed, nonetheless, as inventory and receivables lenders developed formal devices for demonstrating control. By the time Article 9 was drafted a quarter century later, the focus shifted from dominion to notice, and the rule in *Benedict v Ratner* was expressly overruled by § 9-204. So, in the US, a lien on circulating assets could be created by agreement and perfected by filing.

By contrast, while English law made it relatively easy for a secured creditor to take a lien on all of the present and future value of a business enterprise by taking a lien on the undertaking, 'dominion' was a problem there too.[77] When a creditor took a 'fixed charge' of the firm's assets – 'the chargee's consent was required for any disposal' of collateral.[78] This was not practical for a firm that sought to operate in the ordinary course of business. The solution was to create a floating charge, that allowed the debtor to continue to use the assets in the ordinary course until there was a default or liquidation of the business.[79] The mechanism was slightly different, however.

Instead of the lien on 'after-acquired property' attaching when the debtor obtains rights in the collateral, the floating charge remains an inchoate charge over the firm until the occurrence of a contractually defined event (perhaps default) which causes the charge to crystallise. At that point the floating charge attaches and becomes a fixed charge, while terminating the right of the debtor to use the assets in the ordinary course of business.[80] A question remains, however, whether the inchoate floating charge over a non-specific mass of assets takes priority over ordinary contract claims. The answer under UK law is certainly yes, but the basis for this priority is a bit unclear. Some characterise the floating charge as creating an interest in an open-ended fund,[81] while Professor Worthington characterises it as a defeasible fixed charge,[82] while

[76] *Benedict v Ratner*, 268 US 353, 361–62 (1925) (Brandeis, J) ('But it would seem clear that whether the collateral consist of chattels or of accounts, reservation of dominion inconsistent with the effective disposition of title must render the transaction void.'). See Edward J Janger, 'Brandeis, Progressivism, and Commercial Law: Rethinking *Benedict v. Ratner*' (1998–1999) 37 *Brandeis Law Journal* 63.

[77] *Re Panama New Zealand and Australian Royal Mail Co* (1869–70) LR 5 Ch App 318.

[78] For this analysis, I am thankful to Louise Gullifer (ed), *Goode and Gullifer on Legal Problems of Credit and Security*, 7th edn (London, Sweet & Maxwell, 2023), § 4.1. (https://uk.westlaw.com/Browse/Home/Books/GoodeGullifer). See also Paterson, 'Finding our way' (n 38), at 250.

[79] John Armour, 'The Chequered History of the Floating Charge' (2004) 13 *Griffith Law Review* 25, 27; Gabriel Moss, 'Fictions and Floating Charges: Some Reflections on the House of Lords' Decision in Spectrum' in Joshua Getzler and Jennifer Payne (eds), *Company Charges: Spectrum and Beyond* (Oxford, OUP, 2006) ch 2.

[80] *Evans v Rival Granite Quarries Ltd* [1910] 2 KB 979, 999.

[81] *Re Spectrum Plus* [2005] UKHL 41; [2005] 2 AC 680 at [139].

[82] Sarah Worthington, *Proprietary Interests in Commercial Transactions* (Oxford, Clarendon Press, 1996), 74–77.

others characterise it as a power to obtain a fixed charge.[83] Regardless of its conceptual nature, there is general agreement that the combination of fixed and floating charges allows a secured creditor to obtain a lien that covers all of the assets and future income of the firm, and that it takes priority over all but statutorily designated preferential creditors.[84]

Notwithstanding agreement as to its effect, the desirability of an enterprise lien is not uncontroversial in the UK. As in the US, concerns have been raised that insufficient assets might be left over for unsecured and other operating creditors in the event of insolvency. Parliament has treated this as a problem of priority, by creating classes of preferential creditors whose interests take priority over the floating charge holder.[85] Sir Roy Goode called attention to the policy implications associated with the floating charge when the Cork Committee was considering a revision to English insolvency law in 1982. As a result, the Cork Committee proposed a 10 per cent carve-out from the floating charge holder's collateral to pay unsecured creditors.[86] The Enterprise Act of 2002 implemented a much smaller version of the proposed carve-out, known as the 'prescribed part'.[87] Also, and significantly, the costs of administration of the proceedings can be deducted from the floating charge, sometimes exceeding its value.

None of this detracts from the fact that the floating charge is treated as a lien on the value of the firm, not just its assets. And, paradoxically, the difference appears to lie in the fact that the floating charge does not 'attach' until it has 'crystallised', but that it nonetheless grants priority. Crystallisation does not occur until the creditor withdraws the ability of the debtor to use collateral in the ordinary course of business. So, the difference, if it exists, would appear to lie not in the charge's scope, but in its very inchoateness: under US law, the inchoateness of the floating charge would defeat its priority. In the US, priority requires attachment and perfection. Attachment and perfection occur on a continuing basis as rights in the collateral are acquired, while priority relates back to the date the financing statement was filed. In the UK, priority does not require attachment, but attachment will generally terminate the debtor's ability to continue the business, as a practical matter.[88]

C. So, Scope is not the Difference …

So, in comparing the purported 'blanket lien' to the 'floating charge', the mechanism for turning a lien on property into a lien on earnings does not turn on the ability to obtain a lien on all present assets. That can be done under both systems. Neither does it turn on the ability of a lien or charge to attach to after-acquired property. That can be done

[83] Robert Stevens, 'Contractual Aspects of Debt Financing' in D Prentice and A Reisberg (eds), *Corporate Finance Law in the UK and the EU* (Oxford, OUP, 2011), 220.

[84] Louise Gullifer, *Goode and Gullifer on Legal Problems of Credit and Security*, 7th edn (London, Sweet & Maxwell, 2023), para 4-03.

[85] The Companies Act, 1883 (46 & 47 Vict c 28), s 4.

[86] Hon Roy Goode, 'The Case for the Abolition of the Floating Charge', at fn 7 in Getzler and Payne (n 60); Report of the Review Committee on Insolvency Law and Practice (Cmnd 8558, 1982), 1538–49.

[87] Insolvency Act 1986, s 176A(3)(a) and the Insolvency Act 1986 (Prescribed Part) Order 2003.

[88] For a discussion of 'future assets' as collateral, see section V below.

under both systems as well. Indeed, the floating lien may be even more powerful than the floating charge in this regard, given the statutory carve-outs from the priority of the floating charge.[89] The issue, it seems, is whether that lien or charge on assets can somehow be converted to a lien on the value of the enterprise as a going concern because of its ability to reach future assets prior to attachment/crystallisation.

One is led to wonder whether, in the absence of cross-class cramdown, this question has been fully examined. Where all classes agree to a scheme, the question does not come up. Where assets are sold piecemeal in administration, it does not come up either. The place where a difference might arise is in the case of a going concern sale, but here it seems, the priority of the floating charge holder over the value of the firm has simply been assumed, as the going concern sale is treated as a sale of the assets.

V. Insolvency Treatment of Liens: US v UK

So, both the US and UK systems of secured credit allow the creditor to obtain a lien on substantially all of a debtor's property at any given time. In the US, this is accomplished through an Article 9 security interest on present assets and a floating lien (also an Article 9 security interest) on after-acquired property, which attaches as the debtor acquires rights in the collateral.[90] In the UK, it is accomplished through the combination of a fixed and floating charge, with the latter postponing attachment. The question remains, how does the UK convert a lien on existing assets into a lien on the present value of the future earnings from operations of the business as a going concern? The importance of the question can be seen if one imagines two different types of businesses. On the one hand, a firm might be largely a collection of property. For example, a real estate investment trust does little but own a collection of income-producing property. There, the value of the business is likely to approximate the sum of the value of the various properties. But imagine instead, a magazine, where the assets consist of workstations, an above-market lease, and an IP back-catalogue of yesterday's news. Virtually all of the business's value is in the synergies of the talented group of reporters, whose employment contracts are 'at will'. The same might be said of a restaurant, with a celebrated chef, or a bar with a celebrity bartender. The encumbered assets produce relatively little of the business's value. The value lies in the going concern. In a going concern sale, that increment of value is allocated to the floating charge holder. This is the source of 'floating charge envy'. But what is the legal mechanism that accomplishes this magic?

This section considers whether the source is a difference between the allocation of enterprise value in bankruptcy proceedings in the US under Chapter 11, and in the UK, and then whether the difference survives under Part 26A. It suggests that, at least in part, the historic difference between the systems' respective approaches to

[89] Adrian J Walters, 'Statutory Erosion Of Secured Creditors' Rights: Some Insights From The United Kingdom' (2015) *University of Illinois Law Review* 543, 548–58.

[90] Under UCC § 9-204, a security agreement may extend to after-acquired property. But under UCC §9-203, attachment requires (1) a security agreement, (2) an extension of value, and (3) that the debtor has rights in the collateral. So, the security interest does not attach until the debtor acquires the property.

value allocation in rescue lies in a feature of US bankruptcy law that is missing in the UK – 'equitable realisation'. The opening of a bankruptcy proceeding in the US freezes the relative positions of creditors in place, until assets can be distributed, or a plan confirmed. The claims of unsecured creditors are fixed on the petition date,[91] as is the pool of assets subject to the secured creditors' liens.[92] In the UK this does not happen when a floating charge crystallises, when a scheme is proposed, or when an administration is opened. This provides a possible basis for distinction, but as a normative matter, it is deeply inequitable, as it allows the secured party to capture reorganisation surplus based solely on its power to veto continuation.[93] This section then considers whether the difference survived the advent of cross-class cramdown. It concludes that it did, but only in part.

A. Equitable Realisation in Rescue

A significant difference between the US and the UK is the effect of the opening of a bankruptcy proceeding. As Melissa Jacoby and I have explained, the opening of a bankruptcy proceeding in the US is a partial realisation. The filing of a bankruptcy petition stays the individual collection efforts of creditors, but also freezes the relative positions of creditors, pending the realisation of the value of the firm, either by liquidation, going concern sale or recapitalisation. Interest stops accruing on unsecured claims and floating liens stop floating.[94] This freezes the proportional entitlements of unsecured creditors and establishes the pool of assets available for distribution to the secured creditors. We call the combined effect of these rules 'equitable realisation'. It freezes the creditors in place while they determine the best way to realise the value of the firm.

Equitable realisation limits the secured creditor's secured claim to the assets owned on the petition date. This is because, upon bankruptcy in the US, floating liens stop floating, so liens on after-acquired property do not cover property acquired after a proceeding is opened.[95] By contrast, in the UK, the floating charge continues to float over the enterprise, even once restructuring has commenced, and even after crystallisation. What is the effect of this difference? Does it convert an interest in property into an interest in capitalised earnings?

(i) Assets v. Earnings in the US

The choice between liquidation and rescue involves a choice about how to realise value for creditors: will value be realised from the sale of assets, or by continuing the business and realising the value of the firm? In both systems, outside of bankruptcy, secured and unsecured creditors have a practical veto over continuation. To continue the firm, a deal must be struck between the claimants with rights against the firm (recourse), and

[91] 11 USC § 502.
[92] 11 USC § 552.
[93] Westbrook, 'The Control of Wealth in Bankruptcy' (n 63); Mokal, 'The Floating Charge – an Elegy' (n 66).
[94] 11 USC §§ 362, 502, 552.
[95] 11 USC § 552.

claimants with rights against assets (security). If recourse claimants want to continue the firm, they need a deal with the secured claimants over the use of the assets. If the secured claimants want to benefit from the fact that operating the business is more valuable than the assets, they must reach an agreement with recourse claimants.

In the US, the deal is struck in Chapter 11, either through a consensual plan of reorganisation (all classes accept), or through cross-class cramdown (where secured creditors get the full value of their collateral, and/or out-of-the-money classes are wiped out).

(ii) Continuation and the Problem of Time in the US

Liquidation contemplates ending the enterprise and realising its value in a single moment of time – when the case is opened and the assets liquidated. The firm is worth only as much as its assets. Rescue seeks to avoid the inefficiencies of forced realisation. Rescue introduces the problem of time, and it does so along two axes: (1) choosing between liquidation and rescue requires time, and (2) valuing the entitlements requires a prediction about the future of the firm and how it relates to the value of the assets. The value of the assets may change over time. The value of the firm may change over time. The relative allocation between assets and earnings may also change, and working out this allocation must be done under conditions of uncertainty.

Chapter 11 allows the debtor to buy time with the automatic stay and giving the debtor-in-possession the power to operate the business. It also limits the power of hold-outs through class voting, and cramdown. The puzzle in rescue is how to deal with the fact that those values may change 'while the patient is on the table'.

B. Equitable Realisation in the United States

Chapter 11 contains an ingenious mechanism for addressing the fact that, in rescue, the value of the firm is not realised immediately – a process that Melissa Jacoby and I call 'equitable realization'. To facilitate an effective decision about how to realise the value of the firm, the relative positions of creditors are frozen at the moment the proceeding is opened. Interest stops running on unsecured claims,[96] and floating liens on after-acquired property stop floating.[97] As a result the unsecured creditor's pro rata share against the firm is fixed as of the petition date, and the secured creditor's pool of collateral is fixed as well. Unperfected security interests are avoided,[98] and, to the extent that collateral is sold after the petition date, the value of that collateral is realised, the secured claim attributable to that collateral is fixed, and the lien attaches to the proceeds.[99] Crucially, new property that is acquired by the debtor after the opening of the proceeding is not covered by pre-petition liens unless it constitutes identifiable proceeds of property owned on the petition date.

[96] 11 USC 502(b).
[97] 11 USC 552(a).
[98] 11 USC 544.
[99] 11 USC 552(b).

This section explains the plan process in the US and suggests that the absence of 'equitable realisation' in the UK explains much of the reason for floating charge envy. It also suggests that the way the floating charge gobbles up value is deeply inequitable. To understand the US approach to *in rem* rights, it is necessary to understand five statutory terms: (1) the allowed secured claim; (2) strong arm – the avoidance of unperfected liens; (3) adequate protection; (4) treatment of floating liens; and (5) fair and equitable.

(i) Confirmation in a Nutshell

Chapter 11 seeks to facilitate the continuation of a business enterprise when to do so will benefit all of the creditors. To achieve this, the drafters of Chapter 11 had to facilitate the continuation of the business (which, again, takes time), while preserving the relative positions of lienholders, unsecured creditors and equity. The mechanism chosen was negotiation in the shadow of judicially determined entitlement and junior creditor objection.

To understand how Chapter 11 implements this approach, imagine a debtor with a combination of both encumbered and unencumbered assets. Under Chapter 11, a debtor has two paths to confirm a plan: (1) through acceptance by statutory majorities of all impaired classes; or (2) through cross-class cramdown. Under the first approach, all impaired classes must vote by at least ½ in number and ⅔ in debt amount to support the plan. Dissenting class members can then be bound. Alternatively, if an impaired class does not accept the plan, the plan can be confirmed over its objection so long as the non-accepting class is shown to be receiving its statutory entitlement: secured creditors are entitled to the value of their collateral – their allowed secured claim as determined by the court;[100] unsecured creditors are entitled to absolute priority. Any class that is not paid in full is entitled to its pro rata share of the residual value of the firm. Junior classes (ie equity) are wiped out.

(ii) Equitable Realisation and Floating Liens in the US

But what is the secured creditor's entitlement? That is determined by reference to the 'allowed amount' of the 'secured claim' under § 506. The 'allowed amount' is calculated by determining the value of the 'creditors' interest in the estate's interest in such property'. It is the value to the creditor of the collateral. So, the first question that must be answered is 'what is the secured creditor's collateral?'

(a) The Allowed Secured Claim

As in the UK, the scope of a secured creditor's collateral is determined by agreement – the security agreement specifies what is covered and creates the security interest through a voluntary transfer of a property interest.[101] However, the next question that must be

[100] 11 USC §§ 506(a), 1129(b)(2)(A).
[101] UCC §§ 9-102(74), 9-203.

answered is whether that property interest is enforceable against third parties, and in what order of priority. These questions are not answered by the Bankruptcy Code; they are answered by property law, in this case Article 9. To have an allowed secured claim, the security interest must have attached pursuant to an enforceable security agreement, and it must have been perfected, usually by filing a UCC-1 financing statement in the appropriate registry.[102] For attachment to occur, there must be a security agreement, and the creditor must give value, but most importantly, the debtor must have rights in the collateral to convey. A security interest can attach to property acquired after the agreement was signed, pursuant to an after-acquired property clause, but not until the debtor acquires an interest in the property.

(b) Strong Arm

This is crucial, because security interests that are unperfected as of the date of the bankruptcy petition can be avoided pursuant to the trustee's strong-arm power, contained in § 544 of the Bankruptcy Code. So, the allowed secured claim is determined based on the value of the collateral at the relevant moment. For the purposes of this discussion, the relevant moments are (1) the petition date, for the purposes of determining adequate protection; (2) the date of sale if the collateral is sold; or (3) the effective date of the plan, for the purposes of plan confirmation.[103]

Section 506 then, rather cryptically, goes on to say that the 'value shall be determined in light of the purpose of the valuation and of the proposed disposition or use of such property'. I have argued elsewhere that the value should be determined by reference to the 'realizable value' of the collateral – the amount the creditor would realise if the collateral were sold.[104] That said, the case law makes a distinction between situations where the debtor is retaining the collateral and situations where the collateral is being sold. This led the ABI Commission on the Reform of Chapter 11 to recommend that the valuation standard for adequate protection should focus on the realisable sale value of the collateral, while in cases where the debtor is reorganising the focus should be on the replacement value or value to the debtor.[105] In both cases, however, the focus is on the value of the property, not the value of the firm.

(c) Adequate Protection

A key aspect of treating creditors equitably in bankruptcy is assuring that the value of their asset-based claim does not decline during the case, while the debtor's fate is being determined. Since creditors with asset-based priority would have been able to foreclose on their collateral, in the absence of the automatic stay, the risk they face is that the value of their collateral may decline. Therefore, a secured creditor may seek to have

[102] UCC §§ 9-203, 310.
[103] 11 USC §§ 361, 362(d), 1129(b).
[104] Jacoby and Janger, Tracing Equity, n 10. Edward J Janger and Stephan Madaus, 'Value Tracing and Priority in Cross-Border Group Bankruptcies: Solving the Nortel Problem from the Bottom up' (2019) 27 *University of Miami International & Comparative Law Review* 334.
[105] ABI Commission Report (n 41) at 67–73 (IV.B. Financing the Case: 1. Adequate protection).

the stay lifted if the value of its collateral is not given 'adequate protection'. Adequate protection can be provided by making periodic payments to curtail the principal as the collateral value declines, providing a replacement lien on new collateral, or through an equity cushion, if the creditor is oversecured.[106]

(d) Floating Liens v Proceeds

When considering the allowed secured claim and the consequence of adequate protection, one must consider how these terms interact with the State law regarding floating lien on circulating assets. A lien that covers after-acquired property continually changes value during the case. Further, a floating lien on after-acquired property also attaches to the proceeds of the sale of that collateral. So, over time, as the business continues to operate, a floating lien and its proceeds may expand to cover all of the property owned by the debtor, even if at the time of the bankruptcy filing, there was considerable unencumbered property. The result is that the longer the case goes on, the fewer unencumbered assets will be available to pay junior creditors.

To address this problem of collateral expansion, 11 USC § 552 does two things. First, at the moment of bankruptcy, security agreements that cover after-acquired property do not extend to new property acquired by the estate, except, second, to the extent that the new property is proceeds arising from the disposition of property owned on the petition date. Thus, in addition to fixing the relative positions of unsecured creditors by stopping the accrual of interest, § 552 fixes the pool of collateral available to the secured creditors as of the petition date. This is the key aspect of equitable realisation: assets unencumbered on the petition date remain unencumbered; and firm value that cannot be traced to the disposition of encumbered assets remains unencumbered as well.

(e) Fair and Equitable Treatment of Floating Liens

Because of § 552, a floating lien claimant's allowed secured claim does not include assets or property that the debtor did not own on the petition date or the proceeds thereof. So, for a secured creditor secured by a lien on the debtor's inventory, if a piece of inventory is sold for $10, the allowed secured claim attributable to that inventory is $10, the amount realised upon sale. The claim is now secured by the sale proceeds. If the $10 in proceeds is used to buy more inventory, that new inventory is also proceeds. And, if it sells for $15, the $15 is proceeds. However, those proceeds secure an allowed secured claim of only $10. The value of the collateral was realised on the first sale, thus fixing the allowed secured claim.

Under this analysis, the value of a blanket lien remains tied to the value, as of the effective date of the plan, of the assets of the firm owned on the petition date. If the value of that collateral increases before realisation, the secured creditor captures that increase. However, to the extent that the value of the firm increases as a result of continuing to operate, and the present value of the projected earnings of the firm exceeds the value

[106] 11 USC § 361. The statute provides a fourth method, such other relief as will result in the 'realization of the indubitable equivalent of such entity's interest in the property'.

as assessed on the petition date, that excess is allocated to the estate. An undersecured creditor may capture a piece of that excess value through its deficiency claim, but it is not part of the allowed secured claim entitled to priority.

(iii) Credit Bidding and Reorganisation Surplus – An Illustration

The difference between a secured creditor's rights *in rem* (security) and an *in personam* claim against the value of the firm as a going concern (recourse) can be illustrated using a credit bid example. In cases like *Radlax* and *Philadelphia Newspapers*, discussed above, a secured creditor asserted the right to credit bid at a going concern sale of the firm as a whole. In *Radlax* the Supreme Court affirmed the right of the secured party to credit bid, under § 1129(b)(2)(A)(ii), without considering whether the firm itself was collateral for the loan. The problem with this conclusion, and its link to the asset-based nature of secured credit, can be illustrated with the following example.

Imagine that a debtor has three lenders, one secured by the firm's inventory, accounts, and general intangibles, one secured by the firm's real estate, and a third secured by the firm's equipment. Further assume that each lender is owed $2,000,000, and that the real estate, the circulating assets, and the equipment could each be sold for $400,000. Finally, assume that the discounted cash flow value of the firm as a going concern is $1,800,000. The sale date arrives, and each of the three creditors shows up. Each one seeks to credit bid its secured debt in the full amount. The real estate lender breaks the tie by bidding by credit bidding $2,000,000 and offering an additional $1 from its pocket, winning the bid. The example is absurd, of course, because the real estate exchanged for the full firm was only worth $400,000. The reason it is absurd is that, although the firm was being sold as a going concern, the firm was not the real estate lender's collateral; only the real estate was.

This example squarely raises the question of whether the going concern increment constitutes a secured creditor's collateral in an asset-based system of secured lending. It is hard to argue that money that has not yet been earned by the firm is property subject to the secured creditor's lien. While a going concern sale of the firm *does* involve a sale of the firm's assets, and hence of the secured creditor's collateral, this does not mean that the value of the collateral and the value of the firm are the same. When the firm operates, some value will be produced by using the hard assets; some value will be produced by the know-how of the at-will employees; and some value will be a product of the synergy of all of the above.

(iv) Implications

The striking implication of the numerical example above is that even if one assumes that a secured creditor has obtained a lien on all of the property of the firm as of the petition date (even if one includes goodwill), this does not mean the secured creditor will own all of the value of the firm when the firm exits bankruptcy through recapitalisation or sale. For example, when one piece of inventory is sold, the secured creditor's interest in that item is realised. The money received is proceeds, and subject to the lien. When that money is used to purchase two more pieces of inventory, those new pieces of inventory are also proceeds. But the claim secured by those proceeds is fixed by the amount realised upon sale of the item owned on the petition date.[107] So as the amount of proceeds grows, the secured creditor's collateral increases, providing adequate protection; the allowed secured claim does not. The excess value of the inventory is property of the estate available for distribution to creditors with claims against the firm.

C. Equitable Realisation and the Floating Charge under Part 26A

It is here that the rights of the secured creditor in the US and the UK diverge in a way that matters. In the UK the commencement of insolvency proceedings and even the crystallisation of a floating charge do not stop the charge from continuing to float over newly acquired property. In other words, in any scheme or administration where the enterprise continues to operate, the floating charge will continue to capture the accumulated earnings of the enterprise.

(i) No 'Equitable Realisation'

In most respects the floating charge operates in a manner similar to the 'floating lien' on 'after-acquired property' in the US. The security agreement (contract) grants a lien on property that has not yet been acquired, and when it is acquired, the contract (charging agreement) grants a lien, which attaches and perfects.[108] The most important difference, bigger than the scope of the lien, is that there is no English law equivalent to § 552 of the Bankruptcy Code. Floating charges keep floating, even after a proceeding has been opened. This means that the charge will continue to gobble up collateral, even after the case has commenced.[109] This is true, even after crystallisation.[110] As *Goode and Gullifer* explains it, the effect of crystallisation is to, 'end … the authority conferred on the debtor company to manage the assets comprising the security'.[111] But termination of the power to manage assets does not stop the floating charge from fastening onto after-acquired property. It continues, 'In consequence [of crystallisation], the charge becomes converted into a fixed charge, fastening on all assets in which the company then has or subsequently acquires an interest'.[112] Neither does crystallisation terminate the power of the debtor to operate the business, so long as it is done with the charge holder's consent.[113] Indeed, this is treated as a natural implication of the fact that even a fixed charge can cover future assets.[114]

[107] 11 USC § 506(a).

[108] *Holroyd v Marshall* (1862) 10 HLC 191, 11 ER 999.

[109] *NW Robbie & Co Ltd v Witney Warehouse Co Ltd* [1963] 1 WLR 1324, CA; *Ferrier v Bottomer* (1972) 126 CLR 597 at 603, 607; *Leichardt Emporium Pty Ltd v AGC (Household Finance) Ltd* [1979] 1 NSWLR 701.

[110] *Re JD Brian Ltd* [2011] IEHC 113; [2011] 3 IR 244.

[111] *Goode and Gullifer on Legal Problems of Credit and Security*, n 84 at para 4-31.

[112] ibid.

[113] ibid.

[114] *Holroyd v Marshall* (1862) 10 HLC 191, 11 ER 999.

On this view, there is no 'equitable realisation'. Unlike § 552(a), which stops the floating lien from floating upon the opening of a proceeding, the floating charge continues to float. Unlike under § 1129(b)(1)(A), upon confirmation, the lien is not stripped down to the value of the collateral. Therefore, if the continued operations allow the value of the entity to increase, or if the value of earnings exceeds the value of assets, that value remains subject to the floating charge, apparently, whether the entity recapitalises pursuant to a scheme, or is sold as a going concern. Because the fixed and floating charge holder can claim priority in all assets, present and future, the assumption is made that the secured creditor also has a priority in the value of the firm, even if value is realised through the earnings rather than from the sale of assets.

There may be reasons why an English lawyer might challenge this continuing assumption. For example, the cases upon which these assumptions are made predate the Enterprise Act of 2002 that shifted insolvency law from an equity receivership to an administration for the benefit of creditors. This shift brings into question who gets credit for the going concern increment: the secured creditor or the administrator. To the extent that the increase in value of the firm was achieved through the labour of the administrator, there is authority that it should be allocated to the estate. In *In re Collins*,[115] a liquidation case, the debtor held certain 'uncompleted' contracts. The debtor's 'fees were still unearned'.[116] According to the court, 'the trustee rightly contend[ed] that these debts, arising from his completion of these various contracts, were not debts owing to the bankruptcy which could be mortgaged'.[117] As the court noted, 'The trustee in bankruptcy in such a case may, if he thinks it for the benefit of the estate, carry on the business and the contract; but he is not obliged to do so'.[118] The court in *In re Collins* seems to be making a distinction between property of the estate when the case is opened, and property earned by continuing the business, post-opening. If that property is allocated to the trustee in administration, then the idea that a floating charge captures earnings from continued operations of the business rests on shakier ground.

If one puts the *In re Collins* caveat to one side and assumes that the floating charge accomplishes an enterprise lien, and that it does so because of the absence of equitable realisation, the result is profoundly inequitable. This is because the effect is to continue to operate the business at the expense of junior creditors. Indeed, an example of this can be seen in one of the cases frequently cited for the proposition that the floating charge continues to float after crystallisation. In *Robbie v Witney Warehouse*, cited above, the debtor continued to operate after crystallisation. With the secured party's permission, it sold a new piece of inventory on credit to an existing trade creditor. When the creditor sought to set off its new credit against its old debt, the court said that the new inventory was owned by the charge holder, and that the debtor had no interest in it. Therefore, there was no right of setoff. The continued operations increased the charge holder's recovery, while increasing the trade creditor's exposure.[119]

[115] *In re Collins* [1925] Ch 556.
[116] ibid at 558.
[117] ibid at 561.
[118] ibid at 563.
[119] *Robbie v Witney Warehouse*, n 109.

As a matter of positive law, however, it appears difficult to contend that there is anything equivalent to 'equitable realisation' in English law if a debtor's entry into administration does not crystallise a floating charge or prevent further assets from coming within the scope of the charge.

(ii) Implications pre-Part 26A

The absence of equitable realisation – the fact that floating charges do not stop floating – can be used to explain the difference between the cramdown entitlement of the secured creditor in the United States and the secured creditor's entitlement in the UK. The US secured creditor is treated as having a claim against asset value, while the UK creditor has a claim against the value of the firm. In the US, § 552(a) stops the lien from floating on the petition date, and in cramdown, the secured party's liens are stripped down to the value of their collateral on the effective date. In the UK, neither of these things happens, so that the secured creditor ends up with a true hierarchical claim against the value of the firm (or so it is assumed). Up until now, however, the comparison has been between secured creditors in the US, who are subject to equitable realisation and cramdown, and secured creditors in the UK, where it is impossible to cramdown the floating charge holder, so the claim of all asset value, and of a veto over continuation, join together to create an apparent priority over enterprise value. US secured creditors justifiably envy this combination of lack of realisation and control. The effect, however, is that secured creditors who could not capture the going concern by foreclosing on assets, capture that value through a going concern sale.

(iii) Implications of Part 26A

The advent of cross-class cramdown would appear to have changed all of this. The floating charge holder can now be bound to a plan so long as it pays more than the relevant alternative. This may be a piecemeal liquidation, a going concern sale, or a competing scheme, but the question remains: how do the differences between the floating lien and the floating charge, coupled with the difference between § 1129(b)(1)(A) and section 901G affect the results? Does floating charge envy (and its attendant inequity) survive? As it turns out, the differences are reduced but they remain. What follows are some simple examples.

Returning to the numerical example from above: assume that the debtor had assets that could be liquidated for $100,000, all of which were subject to a lien by a secured creditor holding a claim of $500,000. Similarly, five other trade creditors each hold unsecured claims of $100,000. Again, assume that the debtor in operation is generating an operating profit, and the market value of its capitalised earnings would be $200,000. The goal of a rescue regime is to preserve the value of that going concern increment (the extra $100,000) by allowing the debtor to continue in operation. The question is how the extra $100,000 should be distributed when the value of the firm is realised through continued operations rather than sale of assets.

Under § 506(a), in the US, the secured creditor would have an allowed secured claim of $100,000 and a deficiency of $400,000. Under § 1129(b)(2)(A), it would receive a distribution on the secured claim with a value of $100,000. The deficiency would join the other $500,000 in claims, and receive a distribution of $100,000/ $900,000, or 11.1 per cent. Under § 1129(b)(2)(A), if one were to apply it to a floating charge as currently understood, it would yield a different result. The verbal formulation is that the creditor is entitled to 'deferred cash … of a value, as of the effective date of the plan, of at least the value of such holder's interest in the estate's interest in such property'. So, if the value of the collateral is the value of the firm, then the floating charge holder would be entitled to the full $200,000 value of the firm. This may be one reason why the drafters of section 901G of the UK Companies Act 2006 used a different formulation. Instead, the floor was set as the value of the 'relevant alternative'. If the relevant alternative is liquidation, as in this example, the difference between the US and the UK disappears.

However, floating charge envy is not completely dead. Mr Justice Snowden (as he then was) articulated a three-part test for determining if the treatment in the proposed plan would be 'no worse than' the treatment in the 'relevant alternative'. First, what would be the most likely outcome if the plan were not sanctioned? Second, what would be the consequences of that outcome for the dissenting creditors? Thirdly, those consequences should then be compared to the outcome and consequences for the dissenting creditors under the proposed restructuring plan.[120] If the relevant alternative is not liquidation, but a going concern sale to a different buyer, perhaps in an administration, then the secured creditor in the UK still has a chance to benefit from the somewhat smaller going concern increment. Under the same example, if there were another bidder who was willing to pay $150,000 for the debtor as a going concern, then that would be the relevant alternative. The floating charge holder could capture that additional $50,000 increment, and the distribution to unsecured creditors would be reduced by that amount. So, at the end of the day, the advent of cross-class cramdown under Part 26A has had the effect of allocating the going concern increment to the unsecured creditors, unless, and only unless there is a competing going concern sale option that can be used as the relevant alternative.

VI. Unattached Liens on Future Assets: Are (Should) they (Be) Security?

The preceding subsection accepted the proposition that the floating charge, combined with a fixed charge *could* capture all of the assets of an enterprise and, because those liens did not stop floating after the opening of a proceeding or crystallisation of the lien, the lien on assets could actually morph into a lien on capitalised earnings, but argued that the result is inequitable. This section questions that proposition, and suggests that the idea of an enterprise lien built upon a lien or charge on assets may not survive the reflection required by cross-class cramdown.

[120] *In re Virgin Active Holdings Ltd* [2021] EWHC 1246 (Ch).

A. The Problem of Future Assets

The fundamental question posed above is: what is the mechanism that converts a lien on assets into a lien on the capitalised earnings of the firm as a going concern? At bottom, both a lien and a charge constitute a right to foreclose on, and sell, the debtor's property. This sale of property presupposes a winding up of the business. In the US, Chapter 11 makes it possible to continue the operations of the business and either recapitalise or sell the business as a going concern. In the UK, continuation is made possible by either a scheme of arrangement (or now a restructuring plan) or a going concern sale in administration. In both systems the question is posed, does a lien on the assets translate into a lien on earnings from operation – the value of the firm? The question is posed squarely by the aforementioned example of a highly valuable magazine or newsletter, with hard assets that consist of a computer and an office chair; the value is in the owner, and the journalistic skills of its staff. Does a lien on the office furniture, the money in the bank accounts, and the receivables attributable to the sales and advertising revenue of this month's issue translate into a lien on the value of the firm as it continues to operate? At any given moment, the foreclosure will only yield the value of the present assets. Does it also cover the future income stream?

B. US – Attachment and the Problem of Future Assets

Under US law, this question is answered in bankruptcy through § 552. But outside of bankruptcy, the answer is the same. The problem of circulating assets is solved through the floating lien. As the firm operates, the lien attaches to assets as they are acquired. This means that, at any given moment, the lien holder has a right to foreclose on the assets owned by the debtor at that time. It does not include a right to foreclose on future assets.

This is true as a matter of State law, not just bankruptcy law. For a security interest to attach, § 203 provides that there must be a security agreement, the creditor has to give value, and the debtor has to have rights in the collateral. The floating lien (the security interest) does not attach until the debtor acquires an interest in the collateral. A security interest does not attach to earnings that have not yet been earned. So, when measured at any given moment, the value of the lien is the value of the assets it captures at that moment.

C. UK – The Floating Charge and the Puzzle of Future Assets

So, how does this insight translate to the UK floating charge? Even a lien on everything that continues to float does not capture property that doesn't exist yet. One possible response is that the floating charge works precisely because it does not 'attach', and therefore there is no requirement for property to exist for it to be subject to a lien. But it is not clear that such an inchoate lien should be sufficient to form the basis for priority. While the notion of a lien is that it creates a property interest, a number of scholars have questioned whether that is the true source of the floating charge's power. Jay Westbrook cites the following bankers' refrain: 'The fixed charge for priority; the floating charge for control'.[121] The suggestion is that the power of the floating charge to capture the value of the firm lies in the fact that it operates as a veto on the continuation of the business. Control of property gives the charge holder the power to extract value. Riz Mokal has gone further. He has argued that the very inchoate nature of the floating charge, and the fact that it is subordinate to administrative expenses and preferential claims make it relatively worthless as either a real property interest or priority. Instead, it is a governance device that places control in the hands of the charge holder and allows it to capture the firm's value through the power to obstruct. He argues that for these reasons, the floating charge is unjustified, as based on extortion, and should be abandoned.[122] If there is no property underlying the charge, the 'value' of the floating charge lies in this practical power, rather than the value of the collateral. This may not justify treating it as a property interest.

At some point in the not-too-distant future, a court in the UK will be asked to cramdown a floating charge holder, where the relevant alternative is a going concern sale. When the time comes, the court will be forced to answer the difficult question: Can a lien cover property or value that does not yet exist?

D. Valuing a Floating Charge in the Relevant Alternative – The Problem of Recursivity

The section above demonstrated that if the relevant alternative was liquidation, the difference between the floating charge and the floating lien evaporated. But it conceded that if the relevant alternative was a different going concern sale, the floating charge holder would still be able to capture the smaller going concern increment. This rested on the assumption that there was some articulable basis for treating a floating charge as a lien on the future earnings of the firm. If, as in the US, the charge is only an interest in present assets, or if, as suggested by Mokal and Westbrook, the mechanism by which it captures future value is a veto right rather than a property interest, one must ask whether it survives cross-class cramdown. Part 26A deprives the floating charge holder of its absolute veto, and forces consideration of the entitlement in the relevant alternative.

The question thus remains, what is the floating charge holder's entitlement if the relevant alternative is continuation, perhaps through a going concern sale in administration? How much of the value in the relevant alternative can be traced to the value of the 'property' being sold, and how much rests in the former veto right? Is the floating charge holder's priority in the value of the firm, or in the value of the assets of the firm? Even in an administration, where the firm was sold as a going concern, the entitlement might be limited to the value of present assets. Obviously, this question has not been presented to the UK courts, but answering it will require them to give thought to the underlying nature of the floating charge.

[121] Westbrook, 'The Control of Wealth in Bankruptcy' (n 63).

[122] Riz Mokal, 'The Floating Charge – An Elegy' (n 66).

VII. Conclusion

In conclusion, US secured creditors and law and economics scholars often assume, and when they don't assume they wish, that they could obtain a lien on all of the value of a firm. This gives rise to floating charge envy – they wish that the US could be more like the UK. This essay considers two questions: (1) does the assumed difference between US and UK law survive the adoption of cross-class cramdown under Part 26A? and (2) does the UK's floating charge suffer from the same cognitive dissonance as exists in the US? With regard to the first question, the answer is that, even if one assumes that the floating charge creates a lien on the present value of a going concern, the difference between the UK and the US has narrowed. In cases where the relevant alternative is liquidation, US law and UK law converge. But in cases where the relevant alternative is continuation, the floating charge holder can capture a portion of the going concern increment.

With regard to the second question, the idea of placing a lien on all of the value of a firm grew up in an era of liquidation, and assumes the equivalence of liquidations and going concern sales. It has been argued that this assumption is invalid. Imposing a lien on all present assets at any given moment in time may not be sufficient to convert a lien on property into a lien on the capitalised earnings of a going concern. Instead, the floating charge would appear to rely on control rather than entitlement to capture the going concern increment. The advent of cross-class cramdown deprives the floating charge holder of that all-important control over the case. It no longer has an absolute veto. With that element of control gone, so may be the ability to capture the going concern increment – and with it, any reason for floating charge envy.

6

Developing Restructuring Law in Silos: Part 26A and Unexpired Leases

SARAH PATERSON AND ADRIAN WALTERS

I. Introduction

In her 2015 book, *The Silo Effect*, the financial journalist Gillian Tett set out to investigate how silos arise in organisations and what, if anything, 'we can do to master our silos, before these silos master us'.[1] Tett describes what she calls 'the silo effect' as the fragmentation of modern life in terms of how people organise themselves, interact with each other, and even imagine the world.[2] We can observe the silo effect at work in the way in which law is developed, practised, taught, and judged in England and Wales. Civil service departments and their executive agencies are increasingly specialist, as are lawyers working in large law firms. Academics increasingly teach and research in narrower and narrower fields. And the judiciary responds to this specialisation by becoming increasingly specialist itself. Nowhere is this more visible than in corporate restructuring law, where large corporate restructuring cases are channelled to judges with relevant experience; most major law firms have an identifiable corporate restructuring law team (and barristers specialise in the field); a relatively small group of academics work on corporate restructuring law, who know each other well; and the Insolvency Service, an Executive Agency of the Department for Business and Trade, takes the lead on corporate restructuring law matters. As a result, corporate restructuring law frequently develops in what we might call a domain-specific silo.

Furthermore, corporate restructuring law develops in something of a geographical silo. For sure, lawyers, policy-makers, academics, and judges working in the law of England and Wales (henceforth 'English law') pay more attention to approaches in other jurisdictions when developing corporate restructuring law than they once did. The business of large law firms in London is increasingly international and US law firms with offices in London have become significant players in the London market. The Insolvency

[1] Gillian Tett, *The Silo Effect: Why Every Organisation Needs to Disrupt Itself to Survive* (Abacus 2015) xi.
[2] ibid, x.

Service demonstrates real interest in comparative analysis, and UK judges and academics frequently meet colleagues from other jurisdictions at international colloquia and the like. Nonetheless, it can be difficult for any of these actors in the domestic system to understand fully the approach in another, so that while the broad strokes of other systems may inspire change, the detail of English corporate restructuring law frequently develops in its own geographical silo. This is, of course, precisely what accounts of institutional path dependency might predict.

There are huge benefits that come with this siloed approach in increasingly complex modern markets. There are, however, dangers too. First, we know that we must pay some regard to the impact that the things we do in formal restructuring procedures have on the world outside them. How much regard we should have to this is a matter of debate.[3] Scholars viewing corporate restructuring law through an economic lens typically consider that formal rules to facilitate restructuring should be developed with careful attention to the incentive effects they create for healthy companies. So-called progressive scholars are typically less concerned with this issue and countenance a more expansive role for corporate restructuring law, directed at achieving wider social goals.[4] We regard it as incontestable that all corporate restructuring law scholars and policymakers should pay *some* regard to corporate restructuring law's effects on corporate behaviour outside the relevant legal procedures and – of particular salience to this chapter – corporate restructuring law's impact on the decisions of debtors to opt for a formal corporate restructuring procedure rather than to address their financial troubles without recourse to one. Secondly, there are challenges with drawing inspiration from other jurisdictions in developing corporate restructuring law without considering the detail of the specific issues that arise.

An important aspect of corporate restructuring law in which we argue that both the domain-specific and geographical silo effects have become acute is the treatment of unexpired leases. A bundle of unexpired leases of serial sites from which a struggling debtor-tenant trades may present the debtor-tenant with an existential threat, so that renegotiating or surrendering unprofitable leases is essential to the survival of the debtor-tenant's entire business enterprise. The difficulties faced by many large retailers, casual dining operators, and hospitality businesses in meeting the terms of their existing leases in recent years are a case in point. Retailers have struggled with the size of their leasehold estate and the cost of their rental bill as customers have switched from the high street and the shopping centre to online shopping.[5] Casual dining and other bricks-and-mortar businesses have seen their margins squeezed by increasing competition.[6] The COVID-19 pandemic has only served to intensify these challenges with the consequence that, for many debtor-tenants, renegotiating their leases and

[3] For a particularly good discussion see Douglas G Baird, 'Bankruptcy's Uncontested Axioms' (1998) 108 *Yale Law Journal* 573, 578.

[4] ibid (noting that Baird uses the label 'traditionalist' to describe these scholars). For further discussion see Sarah Paterson, *Corporate Reorganisation Law and Forces of Change* (Oxford, OUP, 2020) 2–6.

[5] Carina Kaiser and Julia Freybote, 'Is E-commerce an Investment Risk Priced by Retail Real Estate Investors? An Investigation' (2022) 39(3) *Journal of Property Research* 197.

[6] Oliver Barnes, 'Jamie Oliver to steer clear of challenging mid-market in London return' *Financial Times* (London, 16 August 2023): https://www.ft.com/content/7723babe-a93b-43d1-bf8c-e1f369022c78 (accessed 3 April 2024).

reducing the size of their leasehold estates has become central to their survival strategy.[7] Moreover, the debtor-tenants we have in mind need *collective* resolution. As a result of changes in market conditions, their difficulties arise from a bundle of leases with multiple landlords rather than being confined to a single lease with an individual landlord. Against this backdrop, the debtor-tenant must seek to renegotiate those leases that have become unaffordable on sites that still have the potential to be profitable if the rent can be adjusted downwards. Furthermore, they must repudiate leases for sites that are no longer profitable, and that are unlikely to be profitable on any commercial terms as to the rent that could be negotiated.

English corporate restructuring law has developed on a trajectory in which scant attention has been paid to the increasingly dramatic differences between the way leases are treated inside and outside the procedures it offers, and with very little regard to the way in which unexpired leases are handled in other jurisdictions. These differences occur across four crucial dimensions: the right to surrender; bargaining power; cost; and information asymmetry. We are concerned about these specific issues for several reasons. First, we are concerned that debtor-tenants will be forced to resort to a formal corporate restructuring procedure exclusively or largely to deal with an overrented (priced above market-rate) lease portfolio, imposing both cost and risk on the business. There is a question as to whether, if law reform efforts focused on making changes to property law instead, the leases could be more efficiently renegotiated outside such a procedure. Secondly, we are concerned that the treatment of unexpired leases in the formal corporate restructuring procedure will have unintended consequences for the rental market outside it, driving the market rather than reflecting it, so that the tail ends up wagging the dog. And finally, we are concerned that the treatment of unexpired leases in formal corporate restructuring procedures raises foundational questions about the nature of a lease that are not being addressed by, and indeed may not even be visible to, those best able to tackle them – namely lawyers, academics, and policy-makers who specialise in real property. These are far from niche concerns and the principal contribution that we hope to make in this chapter is to bust the treatment of unexpired leases in English corporate restructuring law out of the corporate restructuring law silo.[8]

English corporate restructuring law tools to address unexpired leases have been developed comparatively recently by practitioners and courts exploiting open-ended legislative frameworks in the Insolvency Act 1986 and the Companies Act 2006.[9] These developments have been noted, digested, and commented on as technical developments *within* corporate restructuring law[10] but, to our knowledge, they have not been

[7] Andrew Edgecliffe-Johnson, 'WeWork to renegotiate most of its leases amid viability concerns' *Financial Times* (New York, 6 September 2024): https://www.ft.com/content/5b1e9325-86be-4faf-8f2f-3f142a8f472a#post-9a219486-fd32-4f0e-afb4-9cebde8349ec (accessed 3 April 2024).

[8] Tett uses the term 'silo-busting' to describe the process by which barriers between silos are broken down. See Tett (n 1) 304.

[9] There are, of course, officeholder powers to disclaim onerous property including leaseholds in the Insolvency Act 1986, ss 178–182 and 315–321 that are of considerable vintage. But these are confined to corporate liquidation and individual bankruptcy. Our focus here is on corporate restructuring law tools that address unprofitable leases as part of a business enterprise continuation strategy.

[10] Sarah Paterson, 'A Fine Balance: Insolvency Practitioners and the Leveraging of Intermediary Power' in Paul S Davies and Tan Cheng-Han SC (eds), *Intermediaries in Commercial Law* (Oxford, Hart Publishing, 2022); Rodrigo Olivares-Caminal, Randall Guynn, Alan W Kornberg, Eric McLaughlin, Sarah Paterson, and Dalvinder Singh, *Debt Restructuring* (Oxford, OUP, 2022) 199–208; 267–73.

systematically analysed or theorised by academics across the pre and post-bankruptcy divide. In the US, section 365 of the Bankruptcy Code equips bankruptcy trustees – which include Chapter 11 debtors-in-possession – with explicit powers to reject or assume executory contracts and unexpired leases.[11] These powers represent some of the most invasive interventions in the private, non-bankruptcy rights of creditors found anywhere in US corporate restructuring law. As they have been on the statute book since 1978, we might expect them to have been subjected to intense scholarly focus. In fact, the scholarly treatment of the issue is remarkably thin, given the enormous literature on Chapter 11 more generally. George Triantis has noted some difficulties of statutory interpretation.[12] Kenneth Ayotte has reviewed the specific decisions debtors make within the options provided by Chapter 11 for unprofitable executory contracts and unexpired leases and the timing of those decisions.[13] Thomas Jackson has expressed the view that 'the ability to reject should depend on nonbankruptcy attributes'; has expressed some concern that this may not be the case; but has stopped short of any systematic analysis of the problem and what to do about it.[14] Indeed, there appears to be virtually no comprehensive review of the regime in the scholarship, especially as it pertains to the rejection or renegotiation of unexpired leases. We attribute this gap in the literature to four scholarly tendencies: first, a tendency for scholars to focus on the restructuring of loan and bond debt;[15] secondly, a tendency for scholars to apply their insights to other uses of US bankruptcy law besides the renegotiation or repudiation of executory contracts or unexpired leases;[16] thirdly, even when scholars do consider the powers in section 365, a tendency to dwell more on the assumption and assignment of executory contracts or unexpired leases rather than on their renegotiation or repudiation;[17] and finally, and significantly for us, a tendency for bankruptcy scholars to co-author with other bankruptcy scholars, or perhaps law and finance scholars, but not with other specialists such as real property scholars. We suspect that this gap may also explain why the US statutory regime for handling unexpired leases in bankruptcy was not considered in any detail in recent developments of English corporate restructuring legislation, notwithstanding that the reform decision was undoubtedly partly inspired more broadly by US Chapter 11. A second contribution that the chapter makes

[11] 11 USC § 365.

[12] George G Triantis, 'Termination Rights in Bankruptcy (The Story of Stephen Perlman v Catapult Entertainment, Inc)' in Robert K Rasmussen (ed), *Bankruptcy Law Stories* (New York, Foundation Press, 2007), 58.

[13] Kenneth Ayotte, 'Leases and Executory Contracts in Chapter 11' (12 August 2014) available at SSRN: https://ssrn.com/abstract=2462892 accessed 10 April 2024.

[14] Thomas Jackson, *The Logic and Limits of Bankruptcy Law* (Cambridge MA, Harvard University Press, 1986) 109–21.

[15] Kenneth Ayotte and David A Skeel, Jr, 'Bankruptcy Law as a Liquidity Provider' (2013) 80(4) *University of Chicago Law Review* 1557, 1589 whose purpose is specifically to focus on the problem of debt overhang and adverse selection problems and the related concern that addressing underinvestment by solving for these issues may result in overinvestment; Vincent SJ Buccola, 'Bankruptcy's Cathedral: Property Rules, Liability Rules, and Distress' (2019) 114(3) *Northwestern University Law Review* 705 who focuses on methods of addressing excessive leverage.

[16] Buccola (n 15) focuses on prepackaged plans in which he assumes that nonfinancial creditors will 'ride through' the case (at 727); concluding a going concern sale; and taking advantage of the automatic stay.

[17] Buccola (n 15) 710. Among notable exceptions are Michael T Andrew, 'Executory Contracts in Bankruptcy: Understanding "Rejection"' (1988) 59 *University of Colorado Law Review* 845 and Jesse M Fried, 'Executory Contracts and Performance Decisions in Bankruptcy' (1996) 46 *Duke Law Journal* 517.

is to analyse and evaluate the differences between the treatment of unexpired leases in both regimes.

We start by comparing the treatment of unexpired leases inside English corporate restructuring law procedures with the position outside it. This enables us to draw out several crucial differences that illuminate the extent to which this treatment of unexpired leases has developed in its own domain-specific silo. First, we consider how it is possible for debtor-tenants to achieve something close to the functional equivalent of surrender inside the new Part 26A restructuring plan procedure (Part 26A) where it could not do so outside these procedures, and how this result developed from the Company Voluntary Arrangement (CVA). Secondly, we consider how Part 26A affects the distribution of bargaining power between the debtor-tenant and the landlord that exists outside a formal corporate restructuring procedure. Thirdly, we consider the debtor-tenant's cost of what we call functional surrender, and of modification, of unexpired leases inside Part 26A. Finally, we consider how information asymmetry is addressed outside Part 26A and the impact of Part 26A on information asymmetry. At each stage, we also compare the position with the position in US Chapter 11 to highlight that, notwithstanding the inspiration that Chapter 11 provided for the development of Part 26A generally, the treatment of unexpired leases has developed in a geographical as well as a domain-specific silo.

The differences we observe across the four dimensions of surrender; bargaining power; cost; and information asymmetry map onto the concerns we articulated above: that debtor-tenants will opt for Part 26A exclusively to address unprofitable leases; that Part 26A ends up driving the rental market for healthy firms; and, at a foundational level, that Part 26A brings about what amounts to an ex post re-characterisation of the nature of a lease without any apparent reference to property law. We also seek to show why these concerns are more acute in Part 26A than they are in Chapter 11. Our account provides a broader overview of the problem of unprofitable leases and enables us to reach some preliminary conclusions on the areas that real property lawyers, on the one hand, and bankruptcy lawyers, on the other, should be discussing across their respective domain-specific silos to inform law reform debate in each and to avoid them being, as Tett puts it, 'excessively rigid' or 'dangerously entrenched'.[18] We hope that our analysis also demonstrates the value of studying specific issues in corporate restructuring law across geographical silos.

II. The Different Treatment of Leases Inside and Outside of Formal Corporate Restructuring Procedures

A. Outside Corporate Restructuring Law Procedures

Outside formal corporate restructuring procedures, we do not always hold contract counterparties to their bargain. In many circumstances, a party to a contract that has concluded that it does not wish to be bound by its bargain may seek to repudiate the

[18] Tett (n 1) 306.

contract, or to use the threat of repudiation to motivate renegotiation.[19] In that event, if the parties to the contract cannot settle the matter among themselves, namely, one party seeks to repudiate the contract and the other party does not accept the repudiation, the non-assenting party has the right to apply to the court to seek compensation for the breach. It is possible that the counterparty may be successful in seeking an order for specific performance (to oblige the other party to perform the contract) or an injunction (to prevent the other party from repudiating the contract). Yet these are extraordinary equitable remedies, and a high hurdle must be cleared for the court to grant them.[20] The more usual remedy will be an award of monetary damages.[21]

Contract theorists interpret contract law's willingness to permit contractual breach, and the remedies which follow, in various ways. One such theoretical approach is the theory of efficient breach.[22] There is a vast literature on the theory of efficient breach, which falls outside the scope of this chapter. For present purposes, it will suffice to focus on the argument that it is sometimes efficient to breach a contract: for example, because the value of performance has fallen, or the cost of performance has risen.[23] Contract law then provides the appropriate remedies to facilitate non-performance in these cases.[24]

Leases are, however, a rather curious beast. In English law, outside Part 26A, the parties will ordinarily enter a contract for the grant of a lease. But the lease is not solely a creature of contract law. A lease also creates a tenancy: one party, the landlord, grants to the other party, the tenant, 'exclusive possession of identifiable premises for a definite period while retaining a reversion'.[25] As Garner and Frith put it, '[A] tenancy is an estate in land. The tenancy may be created by a contract, but once created it possesses qualities that run beyond the purely contractual'.[26] The implication is that leases are subject to property law rules as well as contract law rules. This is borne out by features of English property law that are designed to protect the landlord's reversionary interest such as the running of certain covenants with the land[27] and the landlord's ability to restrict alienability.[28] It also follows that, as a property law matter, the abandonment of the tenancy by the tenant of itself has no effect on the tenant's property rights or the corresponding duty of the tenant to pay rent.[29] A formal surrender is required to convey the tenant's estate to the landlord as owner of the reversionary interest. As a further consequence, the landlord has two options when their tenant abandons the tenancy and

[19] Jack Beatson, Andrew Burrows, and John Cartwright, *Anson's Law of Contract*, 31st edn (Oxford, OUP, 2020) 503.
[20] ibid, 578.
[21] ibid, 578–79.
[22] Stephen A Smith, *Contract Theory* (Oxford, OUP, 2004) 115; Gregory Klass, 'Efficient Breach' in Gregory Klass et al (eds), *Philosophical Foundations of Contract Law* (Oxford, OUP, 2015) 362–87.
[23] Smith (n 22) 117.
[24] ibid, 116.
[25] Simon Garner and Alexandra Frith, *A Practical Approach to Landlord and Tenant*, 8th edn (Oxford, OUP, 2017) 33. For the US, see Robert H Kelley, 'Any Reports of the Death of the Property Law Paradigm for Leases Have Been Greatly Exaggerated' (1995) 41 *Wayne Law Review* 1563.
[26] Garner and Frith (n 25) 36.
[27] ibid, 138–39.
[28] ibid, 79–80, discussing some developments. For a discussion of similar developments in the US, see Alex M Johnson, Jr, 'Correctly Interpreting Long-Term Leases Pursuant to Modern Contract Law: Toward a Theory of Relational Leases' (1988) 74 *Virginia Law Review* 751, 751–52.
[29] Garner and Frith (n 25) 495. For the US, subject to the discussion that follows, see Kelley (n 25) 1582.

stops paying rent. First, the landlord can accept the surrender of the lease by re-entering the premises, terminating both the lease and the tenant's duty to pay rent. Secondly, the landlord can do nothing and continue to pursue the tenant for the rent for the remainder of the lease.

It is immediately apparent that as a matter of English law, outside a formal restructuring procedure, the tenant cannot compel the landlord to accept surrender without a continuing liability for the full amount of the rent for the remainder of the lease. Thus, surrender will only be effective to release the tenant from the lease if the landlord agrees.[30] Multiple rationales have been offered to explain this legal position under which the landlord holds most of the cards, but it is immediately clear that it does not sit comfortably with efficient breach theories in contract law. By contrast, some US States have imposed a duty on the landlord to mitigate damages, in line with the contract law concept of mitigation.[31] This more modern, contract-based approach is only available in some US States[32] and even where it does apply, if the market has deteriorated to such an extent that the premises cannot be re-let or can only be re-let at an exceptionally low rent, the distressed debtor-tenant is largely held to its bargain.[33] Nonetheless, as we will develop further below, the difference between the treatment of unexpired leases inside a formal restructuring procedure and outside it is undeniably starker in England than the difference between the treatment of unexpired leases inside the US's corporate restructuring procedure, Chapter 11, and outside it in those US States that have moved towards a more contract-orientated approach to lease surrender.

B. Inside Corporate Law Restructuring Procedures

English corporate restructuring law has no explicit statutory regime permitting the repudiation of unexpired leases but has arrived at approximate functional equivalence through ingenious lawyering and judicial acquiescence. The story of this development

[30] Garner and Frith (n 25) 495. The effect outside bankruptcy is illustrated by the efforts in 2023 of Meta to break a 20-year lease on two buildings in a London development. The lease had no break clause and Meta reportedly had to pay the equivalent of around seven years of rent to surrender it. See Helen Thomas, 'The London office market is becoming harder work' *Financial Times* (London, 4 October 2023). Thomas's article points out that inflexible, long-term commercial leases are 'starting to feel like a relic from another era'. Nonetheless, as this kind of lease was common in the UK's pre-pandemic commercial real estate market, there are still plenty of leases on such terms in existence.

[31] *Schneiker v Gordon* 843 P 2d 1378 (Colo 1993) cited in Dawn R Barker, 'Commercial Landlords' Duty Upon Tenants' Abandonment – To Mitigate' (1995) 20 *Journal of Corporate Law* 627, 635; Ian Davis, 'Better Late Than Never: Texas Landlords Owe A Duty to Mitigate Damages When A Tenant Abandons Leased Property' (1997) 28 *Texas Tech Law Review* 1281, 1283–85.

[32] In New York and Pennsylvania, for example, a commercial real estate tenant has no unilateral right outside of bankruptcy to terminate the lease in the absence of a break clause, and the landlord has no duty to mitigate damages by seeking to re-let after repudiation – see David Crump, 'Should The Commercial Landlord Have A Duty to Mitigate Damages After The Tenant Abandons? A Legal and Economic Analysis' (2014) 49 *Wake Forest Law Review* 187; *Holy Properties Limited, LP v Kenneth Cole Productions, Inc* 661 NE 2d 694 (NY 1995); *Stonehedge Square Limited Partnership v Movie Merchants, Inc* 715 A 2d 1082 (Pa 1998).

[33] Moreover, in some of the 'landlord-mitigation' states the duty to mitigate can be expressly waived in the lease – see Jacqueline Sandler, 'Waiving the Duty to Mitigate in Commercial Leases' (2014) 5 *William & Mary Business Law Review* 647.

starts with the CVA.[34] The contours of the CVA are set out in some rather skinny provisions in the Insolvency Act 1986,[35] somewhat fleshed out by the Insolvency Rules.[36] The CVA is available for a company to make a proposal to its shareholders and its creditors for a composition in satisfaction of its debts or a scheme of arrangement of its affairs.[37] All creditors receive notice of, and are entitled to vote on, the CVA proposal,[38] although secured creditors only vote for the unsecured portion of their debt.[39] There is no provision in the statute for creditors to vote in classes or in separate meetings. The Insolvency Rules provide simply that if a majority of 75 per cent of creditors (present and voting) support the CVA, of whom at least 50 per cent are unconnected creditors, the CVA is approved.[40] The court is not involved in reviewing the terms of the CVA unless there is a challenge. The CVA can be challenged on two grounds: that the proposal unfairly prejudices the interests of a creditor or member, or that there was a material irregularity in the way approval of the CVA was obtained.[41]

Starting with the case of *Powerhouse* in 2007, enterprising corporate restructuring professionals developed a method of mobilising the CVA to address their client's problem of an overrented leasehold estate.[42] In the early cases, leases that the debtor wished to surrender were simply terminated pursuant to the terms of the CVA. However, in the *Instant Cash Loans* case Zacaroli J decided that it was not possible for a tenant to compel a landlord to accept a surrender in an English law scheme of arrangement, because surrender relates to a property right and the scheme of arrangement jurisdiction only extends to contractual matters between the debtor and its creditors.[43] This reasoning would also apply to CVAs because a CVA, like a scheme, involves a compromise or arrangement between the company and its creditors or members.[44] However, rent is not strictly a requirement of a lease.[45] And the obligation to pay rent is generally regarded as a contractual matter.[46] Thus, Zacaroli J decided in *Instant Cash Loans* that it was possible to write the rent sum down to zero in the arrangement. This creates something that is very close to a functional surrender, notwithstanding that it would not have been possible for the tenant to surrender the lease unilaterally outside of a formal proceeding, because a landlord is unlikely to wish to leave the unoccupied premises with the tenant while receiving no rent.[47]

[34] Insolvency Act 1986, ss 1–7B.
[35] ibid.
[36] The Insolvency (England and Wales) Rules 2016 (2016 No 1024).
[37] Insolvency Act 1986, s 1.
[38] Insolvency Rules (n 36), r 15.28(5).
[39] ibid, r 15.31(4) and (5).
[40] ibid, r 15.34.
[41] Insolvency Act 1986, s 6.
[42] *Prudential Assurance Co Ltd v PRG Powerhouse Limited* [2007] BCC 500.
[43] *Re Instant Cash Loans Limited* [2019] EWHC 2795 (Ch).
[44] Compare the Companies Act 2006, s 895 and Insolvency Act 1986, s 1.
[45] Garner and Frith (n 25) para 1.26, 14.
[46] ibid, para 6.14, 66.
[47] The landlord may do so for a time in order to avoid paying rates on unoccupied premises to the relevant local authority – see https://www.gov.uk/apply-for-business-rate-relief/empty-property-relief. However, landlords will worry about the risk of squatters and illegal use of the premises, the premises falling into disrepair, and the risk of lapsed insurance, and so are likely to prefer to take the empty premises back in most cases.

A crucial feature of many of these CVAs is that only landlords were compromised. Typically, leases were divided into several 'buckets': leases that the debtor-tenant wished to keep; leases in respect of which it wished to get as close to surrender as possible; and leases in the middle that it preferred to retain but only if it could renegotiate terms.[48] In most cases all other unsecured creditors were paid in full. And equally crucially, the CVA compromised future rent as well as any outstanding but unpaid rental instalments. Thus, the success of these CVAs turned on three legal issues. First, the CVA jurisdiction had to be broad enough to compromise future rental payments. Secondly, the CVA jurisdiction had to permit differential treatment of creditors. And finally, the CVA proposal had to be able to withstand a challenge on the grounds of unfair prejudice or material irregularity.

The first of these issues had been tested as early as 1995 in debtors' favour. In *Cancol*, Knox J held that a CVA could compromise future rent.[49] There was a bit of a hiccup in 2006 when Neuberger LJ seemed to suggest, *obiter*, that it would be unfairly prejudicial to pay a landlord a reduced rent for the period after the CVA had been approved,[50] but when the position was finally reviewed after a slew of unchallenged CVAs compromising landlords in the 2000s, Norris J followed *Cancol*.[51] And when Zacaroli J was invited to overrule *Cancol* on the point in *New Look* he declined to do so.[52] It now appears settled that a CVA can compromise future rent, absent intervention from a higher court.

The second issue was also decided by a series of cases in the debtor's favour. Indeed, the cases now firmly establish that a CVA will not be automatically unfairly prejudicial because creditors are treated differently in the proposal.[53] In *Powerhouse*, Etherton J set out a two-stage approach to the question of whether a differential proposal was unfairly prejudicial to a complaining creditor or group of creditors. The first stage was what he called a 'vertical' comparison: a comparison of what the complaining creditor or creditors receive under the CVA proposal with what they would receive in the event of a winding up.[54] Over time, judges have moved the vertical comparison away from a comparison with liquidation and towards a comparison with whatever the court considers would be most likely to happen if the CVA were not approved.[55] Assuming that this is an insolvent sale of the business and assets or assets, and the landlord cannot show that a purchaser of the business and assets or assets would want to assume the relevant lease, this is unlikely to provide a ground for complaint for a landlord whose lease is being written down to zero in the CVA. The second stage is what Etherton J called a 'horizontal' comparison, in which the treatment of the complaining creditor or class of creditor is compared with the treatment of other creditors who would rank equally with

[48] See, for example, the categorisation of leases in *Discovery (Northampton) Ltd v Debenhams Retail Ltd* [2019] EWHC 2441 (Ch), [16]–[19].

[49] *Re Cancol Ltd* [1995] BCC 1133.

[50] *Thomas v Ken Thomas Ltd* [2006] EWCA Civ 1504, [39].

[51] *Debenhams* (n 48) [23]–[61].

[52] *Lazari Properties 2 Limited v New Look Retailers Limited* [2021] EWHC 1209 (Ch), [212] (*New Look*).

[53] *Powerhouse* (n 42) 88; *Inland Revenue Commissioners v Wimbledon Football Club* [2004] EWCA Civ 655 at [18]; *New Look* (n 52) [155]–[159].

[54] *Powerhouse* (n 42) [71].

[55] Known as the 'relevant alternative' in Part 26A restructuring plans – see Companies Act 2006, s 901G(4).

the complainant in the counterfactual.[56] However, and as noted above, uneven treatment has not necessarily been found to be prejudicial. Indeed, judges have found that differential treatment may be necessary to ensure fairness;[57] or that it may be necessary to treat trade creditors more favourably in order to secure their continued support of the business for the purpose of the CVA;[58] or that the risks of sorting out creditors who can be compromised without risking the stability of the company from those that cannot outweigh the benefits.[59]

So far so good for a debtor wishing to mobilise the CVA to achieve something functionally similar to a surrender of a lease that could not be surrendered outside it. There is, however, a further fly in the ointment. We can assume that a landlord whose lease is to be written down to zero or whose lease is to be very heavily modified is highly unlikely to support the CVA. At this point, recall that for the CVA to be approved the proposal must be supported by the vote of 75 per cent by value of creditors present and voting. These so-called 'landlord CVAs' have relied on two sleights of hand to secure the majority vote, notwithstanding landlord opposition. The first move is to dilute the landlords' vote in determining the denominator for the 75 per cent calculation. This move relies on the fact that under the Insolvency Rules a debt of an unliquidated or unascertained amount is valued at £1 unless the chairman puts a higher value on it.[60] Debtors have not been so bold as to suggest that landlords' claim for future rent, which is unliquidated because the lease might be terminated early, should be admitted for £1. Instead, they have initially discounted the future rental stream to produce a net present value using a formula developed in a different context in *Re Park Air Services*,[61] and then applied a further, somewhat arbitrary, discount of 75 per cent to that discounted claim.[62] The second move is to admit all other unsecured creditors with outstanding claims to vote on the CVA, notwithstanding that if the CVA is approved these claims will be paid in full. These creditors can expect to vote for the CVA proposal, given that they are unaffected by it. And assuming they have a relatively large aggregate claim and the landlords' claims have been sufficiently discounted, they may be able to 'swamp' the landlords' claims and force the CVA through.

As CVAs became more frequently challenged, however, both techniques came under fire. The discount applied to the landlords' claims steadily decreased as debtors began to worry about the risk of a successful challenge. Thus, by the time the *New Look* case was heard in 2021 a straightforward discount of a mere 25 per cent was applied to the landlords' claims.[63] And even more crucially, while Zacaroli J found on the facts of *New Look* that it was not a case in which the statutory majority had been secured by the votes of unaffected creditors, in an important passage he stated:

> [I]f assets that would, in the relevant alternative, have been available for all unsecured creditors are allocated in a greater proportion to other creditors (e.g. where critical creditors are

[56] ibid.
[57] *Sea Voyager Maritime Inc v Bielecki* [1999] 1 BCLC 133, 149; *Wimbledon Football Club* (n 53) [18].
[58] *Wimbledon Football Club* (n 53) [18].
[59] *Debenhams* (n 48) [107].
[60] Insolvency Rules (n 36) r 15.31(3).
[61] *Re Park Air Services Plc* (also known as *Christopher Moran Holdings Ltd v Bairstow*) [2000] 2 AC 172.
[62] Inga West, 'The Evolution of Landlord CVAs: at a Tipping Point?' Presentation at the Annual Insolvency Lawyers' Association Conference, 23 April 2021, on file with the author.
[63] *New Look* (n 52) [287]–[298].

> paid in full), then the fact that the requisite majority was reached by reason of the votes of those creditors may point towards the CVA being unfairly prejudicial, even if there was an objective justification for their payment in full.[64]

These *obiter* remarks strongly suggest that the practice of 'vote swamping' in CVAs may not pass the unfair prejudice test in a future challenge. And challenges to landlord CVAs have become more frequent now that the British Property Federation is taking a leadership role in guiding landlords on what to look out for.[65] Overall, there is a question mark about whether the legal analysis crucial to the success of landlord CVAs will stand up to scrutiny going forwards.

Debtor-tenants may, therefore, increasingly turn to the new Part 26A restructuring plan procedure as the principal tool for cherry-picking among their unexpired leases. Part 26A was introduced into the Insolvency Act 1986 by the Corporate Insolvency and Governance Act 2020. It is adapted from the existing scheme of arrangement process, in which creditors vote in classes determined by their rights going into the scheme and the rights that they are granted under it. However, crucially, and unlike schemes of arrangement, the court has the power to impose the plan over the objection of an entire dissenting class (a so-called 'cross-class cram-down power').[66] This means that landlords whose leases are being written down to zero can be placed in a separate class and if, as we would expect, they vote against the plan, the debtor can ask the court to impose it on them against their wishes. Indeed, debtor-tenants have taken some of the technology developed in the CVA context and adapted it for use with Part 26A, now that vote swamping in CVAs is questionable.

Importantly, for our purposes, there was no explicit discussion of how to address unexpired leases in the two Insolvency Service consultations that preceded the introduction of Part 26A. Specifically, there was no comparison of the approach that was developing in CVAs with the position outside them. And while the introduction of a new scheme-like procedure with a cross-class cram-down power was heavily influenced by US Chapter 11, there was no explicit comparison of how unexpired leases were treated in the US regime with the incrementally developing position in England and Wales. Instead, Part 26A has been developed to address unexpired leases in a domain-specific, geographical silo.

This is significant because US federal corporate restructuring law deals *explicitly* with unexpired leases. Section 365 of the US Bankruptcy Code permits a Chapter 11 debtor-in-possession[67] to 'assume', 'assign' or 'reject' unexpired leases. If the debtor-in-possession assumes the lease, then all outstanding defaults must be cured, adequate assurance that the debtor will continue to perform must be forthcoming, and ongoing liabilities are payable with administrative priority. The power to assign raises some difficult issues where there is a non-bankruptcy law prohibition on assignment,[68] but otherwise enables the debtor to assign the unexpired lease to a third party. Rejection is treated as a breach of the lease immediately preceding the commencement of the

[64] ibid [195].
[65] https://bpf.org.uk/media/company-voluntary-arrangements-cvas/.
[66] Companies Act 2006, s 901G.
[67] On filing a voluntary Chapter 11 case, the debtor becomes a debtor-in-possession: see 11 USC §§ 1101(1), 1107(a).
[68] Ayotte and Skeel (n 15) 1609 fn 124.

Chapter 11 case:[69] the counterparty has a general unsecured claim for damages, the face value of which is capped in the case of a real estate lease.[70] Crucially for our purposes, in all cases the capped damages claim can be further compromised in the reorganisation plan. This is subject only to an administrative expense claim for certain benefits which the estate received under the unexpired lease after commencement of the case and before rejection.[71] The express powers in section 365 apply to unexpired leases in broadly the same way as they do to executory contracts. In other words, the default approach under US federal law is to equate unexpired leases with contracts.

In contrast, and as we have already noted, Part 26A contains no express provisions addressing unexpired leases at all. Moreover, Part 26A is customarily brief on what the court must consider in deciding whether to impose, or 'cram down', the plan on the dissenting class. It provides merely that the court must be satisfied that, if the compromise or arrangement were to be sanctioned, none of the members of the dissenting class would be any worse off than they would be in the event of the relevant alternative.[72] We have already met this requirement in a CVA context, and the comments made above about the position of the landlord apply equally here. The second condition is that the statutory majority has been achieved in at least one class 'who would receive a payment, or have a genuine economic interest in the company, in the event of the relevant alternative'.[73] This second requirement may be relatively easily navigated if, for example, there is a class of leases which is being modified, rather than written down to zero, with amendments that are acceptable to a majority of landlords in that class.

This is not, however, the end of the matter. This is because the legislation is expressed in permissive and not mandatory terms, providing that if the two conditions are met the fact that the dissenting class has not agreed to the compromise or arrangement does not *prevent* the court from sanctioning it.[74] Furthermore, section 901F provides that if the statutory majority agrees the compromise or arrangement, the court 'may' sanction it. Thus, the legislation leaves a discretion for the judge in deciding whether to sanction the plan or not, even if the statutory conditions are met. Perhaps unsurprisingly, given the total absence of guidance in the legislation, the courts have been struggling to put in place a structured decision-making framework for the exercise of this discretion. This raises questions far beyond the scope of this chapter. For the moment, two points are made. First, the courts have shown themselves willing to impose a Part 26A restructuring plan on an entire class of dissenting landlords whose leases are being written down to zero, provided they are satisfied that those landlords are no worse off than they would be in the relevant alternative.[75] Secondly, although courts have paid some attention to whether proposed plans unfairly transfer value from the affected landlords to those that

[69] 11 USC § 365(g) ('[T]he rejection of an executory contract or unexpired lease of the debtor constitutes a breach …').

[70] 11 USC § 502(b)(6).

[71] 11 USC § 365(d)(3). See further American Bankruptcy Institute, 'Commission to Study the Reform of Chapter 11 2012-2014: Final Report and Recommendations', 117.

[72] Insolvency Act 1986, s 901G(3).

[73] ibid, s 901G(5).

[74] ibid, s 901G(2).

[75] *Re Virgin Active Holdings Limited* [2021] EWHC 1246 (Ch).

will end up owning the equity in the firm, where they conclude that the landlords would not recover anything in the relevant alternative, such concerns have been given little weight.[76] We return to the issue of allocative fairness below. For now, we observe that the cross-class cram-down power in Part 26A may become the primary mechanism in UK law for targeting unprofitable leases if vote swamping, as we anticipate, does become more difficult in CVAs. We now turn to draw out the important differences that arise compared to the position in English law outside Part 26A and compared to US Chapter 11.

C. Dimensions of Difference: Right to Surrender; Bargaining Power; Cost; Information Asymmetry

(i) Right to Surrender

The first crucial difference between the treatment of leases inside and outside Part 26A is that outside Part 26A the debtor-tenant may have no ability to surrender the lease, while inside Part 26A it may be able to achieve something functionally close to surrender. As we have seen, the technology to achieve this arises in part from Part 26A itself and in part as an incremental development from innovation in CVAs. Nonetheless, the differential treatment inside and outside Part 26A is rather stark and it seems remarkable, with the benefit of hindsight, that there was little to no consideration of it when Part 26A was introduced. Moreover, while the cross-class cram-down provision in Chapter 11 was explicitly examined when Part 26A was developed, there was no explicit comparison between the impact of Part 26A on unexpired leases and the US section 365 regime. Overall, the ability functionally to surrender an unexpired lease in Part 26A has developed in a domain-specific, geographical silo.

(ii) Bargaining Power

In Part 26A, the debtor-tenant can bundle together the leases it wishes to modify in a specific way; put the proposal to the landlords as a group; and ask the court to impose the modification via the cross-class cram-down power if the statutory majority of landlords do not agree. Of course, the debtor will have to convince the court that the landlords as a class will be no worse off than they would be in the event of the relevant alternative. And at least one impaired class must have supported the plan. Furthermore, the courts have made it very clear that they expect the landlord to have a right to terminate the lease if they do object to the terms.[77] Thus, Part 26A enables the debtor-tenant to change the bargaining structure, from a series of individual bargains struck with individual landlords to a collective offer available for acceptance. And Part 26A requires the landlord to force the debtor-tenant to put its threat of rejection into action if the landlord holds firm. Once again, it seems remarkable that no explicit consideration was given to

[76] ibid.

[77] *Virgin Active* (n 75) at [64].

this dramatic shift in relative bargaining power inside and outside Part 26A when the new statutory regime was introduced. Moreover, the English law regime shifts bargaining power in ways that are different from, and arguably more dramatic than, the shift in bargaining power in Chapter 11.

Under the US Bankruptcy Code, the debtor-tenant does have more bargaining power in bankruptcy, by virtue of its power to assume and assign or reject the unexpired lease, than it does outside bankruptcy in those States that have no unilateral right of surrender. Moreover, the Chapter 11 regime consolidates the bargaining process and changes the bargaining dynamics. Where the debtor is seeking to renegotiate a bundle of leases outside bankruptcy, if terms cannot be agreed with individual landlords, each landlord may start its own legal action, and each of these legal actions may be in a different State. Under section 365, if terms cannot be agreed with any landlord, the landlord has a claim for damages in common with all other landlords in the same position, and any challenges are addressed together by the federal bankruptcy court within strict boundaries established by the Bankruptcy Code. In this way, the Chapter 11 regime reduces the hold-out problem. While there is no statutory right to modify an unexpired lease without the landlord's consent, debtor-tenants can use the threat of rejection to motivate bargaining.[78] In other words, section 365 provides the credible threat that the debtor-tenant needs to get the landlord to the table. This also addresses the free rider problem. If the landlord refuses to renegotiate, it may find that other landlords agree terms with the debtor so that the debtor-tenant becomes confident it can live without the lease in question. Thus, the landlord who sits tight and refuses to negotiate risks having its lease rejected and being left with an unsecured claim for damages paid at cents in the dollar.

Nonetheless, it is considerably more difficult for the debtor to bundle leases that it wishes to modify (as opposed to reject) in an omnibus motion in US Chapter 11 because modification requires landlord consent and cannot be addressed through mobilisation of the cross-class cram-down power. Moreover, in the US context it is the debtor that must ultimately make the assume/reject decision if modifications cannot be agreed while, in the English law context, it is ultimately the landlord who must make that decision. It is very interesting that notwithstanding the significant influence Chapter 11 had on the decision to implement Part 26A, and the careful attention that was paid to some of its provisions in developing the new procedure, no explicit regard was had to section 365.

(iii) Cost

The third significant difference in the treatment of unexpired leases inside and outside of a formal corporate restructuring procedure relates to the debtor-tenant's cost of surrender or modification. CVAs can be a relatively low-cost procedure, particularly

[78] Josiah M Daniel III, 'Lawyering on Behalf of the Non-Debtor Party in Anticipation, and During the Course, of an Executory Contract Counterparty's Chapter 11 Bankruptcy Case' (2014) 14 *Houston Business & Tax Law Journal* 230, 251.

as court involvement is kept to a minimum and only seriously engaged in the event of a challenge. And the courts have held that the normal 'loser pays' principle applies to challenges to CVAs, so that there is a serious risk of an adverse costs order for an unsuccessful claimant and thus a serious disincentive to raising a challenge.[79] However, as we have seen, doubts around the technology that practitioners have used to promote landlord CVAs may mean that they fall out of favour. Part 26A restructuring plans are more expensive, not least because the court is more involved. Moreover, it is considerably more likely that a dissenting creditor could raise a challenge to a Part 26A restructuring plan without suffering an adverse costs order and may even have their costs covered by the company. This is because the court may take the view that the dissent served a purpose in ventilating the issues before the court and, hence, in helping the court to decide whether to sanction the plan or not.[80] There is, therefore, considerable risk of an expensive challenge to a Part 26A restructuring plan.

As we have already explained, in those US States that do permit surrender outside Chapter 11 the landlord has a duty to mitigate damages.[81] As we have also seen, however, while the counterparty has a general unsecured claim for damages for breach of the unexpired lease under Chapter 11, that damages claim is capped in the case of a commercial real estate lease: section 502 provides that damages are capped at the greater of one year's rent or the rent for 15 per cent – not to exceed three years of the remaining term – of the lease.[82] Indeed, the position is even more favourable because the debtor can compromise the damages claim at the dividend rate in the Chapter 11 plan. This recently led the *Financial Times* to comment that WeWork's Chapter 11 filing would allow the company, 'at least in the US, to rationalise its portfolio by terminating scores of leases with little financial penalty'.[83] This means that it may also be considerably cheaper to address an overrented leasehold estate in Chapter 11 than outside it. Nonetheless, Chapter 11 is a considerably more expensive procedure than Part 26A. This means that on a cost-benefit analysis, the benefit of addressing unexpired leases within Part 26A may be considerably greater than the benefit of addressing them in Chapter 11.

(iv) Information Asymmetry

Finally, no account of the differences in the treatment of unexpired leases inside and outside formal corporate restructuring procedures would be complete without an examination of the renegotiation mechanism itself. Outside corporate restructuring a tenant

[79] *Discovery (Northampton) Limited and others v Debenhams Retail Ltd* [2020] EWHC 1430 (Ch), [13].

[80] *Virgin Active Holdings Limited* [2021] EWHC 911 (Ch), [29].

[81] See n 31 and accompanying text.

[82] 11 USC § 502(b)(6). 11 USC § 365 already federally pre-empts any right the landlord has under State law to refuse to accept the tenant's surrender of a commercial real estate lease. 11 USC § 502 represents a further erosion of landlords' rights outside bankruptcy especially in those States that adhere to the traditional common law rules on tenant abandonment and surrender. For a short account of the history and rationale of 11 USC § 502 see Blake Rohrbacher, 'More Equal Than Others: Defending Property-Contract Parity in Bankruptcy' (2005) 114 *Yale Law Journal* 1099, 1121–23.

[83] Stephen Gandel and Joshua Franklin, 'Overdue Commercial Property Loans hit 10-year High at US Banks' *Financial Times* (New York, 9 November 2023).

can, of course, attempt to reach a negotiated settlement with its landlord. As Szumilo and Wiegelmann identify, the bargaining dynamics may vary because different types of property investor may have different incentives.[84] Thus, a pension fund that relies on income will be incentivised to prefer partial rent to no rent, whereas an investment fund that periodically reports the value of assets and income return may prefer a rent deferment.[85] Szumilo and Wiegelmann also note the possibility of an income-sharing arrangement, where rent is a percentage of the debtor-tenant's revenue. But, overall, outside a formal corporate restructuring procedure, the negotiating process reduces information asymmetry. The tenant learns what is motivating the landlord and where the landlord's red lines are. At the same time, the landlord is likely to demand significant information from the tenant about the debtor-tenant's financial position, to ensure that it obtains what it can accept as a fair deal in the renegotiation.[86]

The dynamics are fundamentally different in Part 26A because the debtor-tenant can ultimately functionally surrender the lease at a low financial cost without having to engage extensively with the landlords – or even at all. At the sanction hearing for the Part 26A restructuring plan for the UK gym group Fitness First, the judge noted:

> Even though the Company had clearly decided by January 2023 and, indeed, Teneo had been instructed by May 2022 to prepare for a restructuring, there was no engagement with Landlord Creditors until the Practice Statement Letter … was sent to all creditors on 17th April 2023.[87]

This seems remarkable when we consider the information that a tenant would need to share with a landlord to reach a consensual renegotiation outside Part 26A. In any commercial negotiation, the landlord is likely to demand sufficient financial information about the debtor's underlying operating performance to be able to consider other demands to compensate it for the benefit that other creditors may receive through the renegotiation. For example, where the debtor-tenant leases more than one property from the landlord, the landlord may be able to strike a better bargain on some of the better properties. This may not even require a cash payment – the landlord might extend the lease of some of the better properties to give it greater confidence in the long-term value of its overall portfolio with the debtor-tenant. Similarly, the landlord may be able to alter covenants in these leases to reduce risk. More dramatic options are also available: taking equity in the debtor-tenant; sharing intellectual property rights; or even entering a partnership arrangement.[88] And, crucially, if there is to be any type of deferred rent or income-sharing arrangement, the landlord will be in possession of the financial information to strike a deal. The risk is that, by contrast, in Part 26A the landlord is not in possession of any, or at least not enough, of the relevant information.

[84] Nikodem Szumilo and Thomas Wiegelmann, 'How Struggling Businesses Can Renegotiate Rent' *Harvard Business Review* (5 May 2020): https://hbr.org/2020/05/how-struggling-businesses-can-renegotiate-rent (accessed 10 April 2024).

[85] ibid.

[86] ibid.

[87] *Fitness First Clubs Ltd* [2023] EWHC 1699 (Ch), [27].

[88] Szumilo and Wiegelmann (n 84).

Levels of engagement were at the centre of the *Virgin Active* dispute,[89] and landlords continue to press the information asymmetry issue. In the recent Part 26A restructuring plan for the retailer Superdry, one of the landlords, Prudential, sought additional disclosure after the plan had been launched.[90] However, while Prudential was successful in obtaining sight of further financial information, it failed in some of its disclosure requests. Notably, it was denied sight of cash-flow forecasts for individual group companies and financial detail that had been used to construct the target post-reorganisation operating model for the group.[91] The question remains as to whether the level of disclosure that the landlord is able to demand in a Part 26A restructuring plan is equivalent to the disclosure it would demand in order to achieve a consensual plan outside it.

The British Property Federation has complained bitterly about information asymmetry between debtor-tenants and landlords, and many of their best practice guidelines relate to levels of engagement.[92] The risk of information asymmetry is considerably heightened in the UK compared to the US because leases can be bundled together into different baskets and a collective deal put to the landlords as part of the cross-class cram-down request. This ability to bundle leases together into different categories with different treatment and to impose the plan centrally is a powerful tool in the Part 26A toolbox. It enables the debtor to negotiate with enough creditors to secure support but potentially to shut out others. It is clear that the courts are increasingly alive to this risk – as the judgments referred to above and in *Sunbird* show.[93] Nonetheless, we would suggest that there is a greater risk that the debtor-tenant will exploit information asymmetry in Part 26A than in US Chapter 11.

III. Does it Matter?

Thus far, we have identified four explicit dimensions to the differences between the treatment of unexpired leases inside and outside Part 26A: the right of surrender; bargaining power; cost; and information asymmetry. We have suggested that none of these received extensive consideration in the consultations that preceded Part 26A, which was largely developed in a corporate restructuring law silo. And we have suggested that each of them is more significant in Part 26A than it is in Chapter 11, so that the UK would have benefitted from explicitly considering Chapter 11's approach rather than developing this aspect of Part 26A in a geographical silo. In this section, we put a bit more flesh on the bones of why this analysis matters. We have already explained why the CVA may be seen as a less attractive proceeding for compromising unexpired leases in the immediate future and so, in this section, we will focus on Part 26A restructuring plans.

[89] *Virgin Active* (n 75).
[90] *In the matter of C-Retail Limited* [2024] EWHC 1194 (Ch).
[91] ibid, [11] and [14]–[17].
[92] British Property Federation, 'Insolvency Engagement Document' available at: https://bpf.org.uk/media/2448/bpf-cva-engagement-document-v3-2407.pdf (accessed 1 December 2023).
[93] A scheme case but applicable on this point – *Re Sunbird Business Services Ltd* [2020] EWHC 2493 (Ch).

A. Entering Part 26A to Deal with Unexpired Leases

Thomas Jackson most famously offered a justification for, 'the time-honored proposition that non-bankruptcy entitlements … should be recognized in bankruptcy'.[94] Jackson does spend some time considering the specific example of unexpired leases, although his focus is not on surrender or modification. His general concern is that if specific consequences follow from filing for a formal corporate restructuring procedure that do not apply outside of it under ordinary private law, incentives will become distorted to such an extent that formal corporate restructuring procedures are instigated even when this is not in the creditors' collective interest.[95] Jackson is focused on decision-making by creditors, but we can apply his analysis equally to debtors. The risk is that if a loss-making lease can be surrendered in a formal corporate restructuring procedure but not outside it, or if a lease can be more readily heavily modified in a corporate restructuring procedure than outside it, the debtor-tenant may be incentivised to resort to bankruptcy too easily, with all the direct and indirect costs that that entails but more crucially with all the uncertainties it entails about the robustness of the business to survive the formal process.

Our first concern, then, is that a debtor-tenant who is in only moderate financial difficulty may resort to Part 26A too readily because of the advantages it offers in addressing unexpired leases. Part 26A restructuring plans are distinctive in two important ways. First, it is not necessary to compromise all liabilities: trade creditors can relatively easily ride through the case unaffected. Secondly, the debtor-tenant can impose lease modifications through the plan, provided that the landlord retains the right to terminate the lease if it does not accept the modifications. These additional features potentially render the Part 26A restructuring plan a very attractive proposition for terminating or modifying unexpired leases and bring into stark relief our concern that debtors will resort to the procedure too readily. Judges have several levers they can pull to ensure that this is not the result and, given the relative ease with which debtor-tenants can deploy Part 26A to surrender or modify leases, they should be willing to use them.

If a class of landlords whose leases are either functionally surrendered or significantly modified in the Part 26A restructuring plan rejects the plan, recall that for the court to be willing to impose the plan over the landlords' dissent, the landlords must be no worse off under it than they would be in the relevant alternative. The first lever the court has is to put the debtors' feet to the fire over their analysis of the relevant alternative and the treatment of landlords within it. In considering whether the landlord is worse off than it would be in the relevant alternative, in our view courts should consider not just the distribution that the landlord would receive as an unsecured creditor but also – where the relevant alternative is a sale of all or part of the business as a going concern – the possibility that the landlord would receive better, modified terms from the purchaser.[96] The core issue here is that the premises may be worth

[94] Thomas H Jackson, 'Bankruptcy, Non-Bankruptcy Entitlements, and the Creditors' Bargain' (1982) 91(5) *Yale Law Journal* 857, 858.

[95] ibid, 890.

[96] Sarah Paterson, 'Judicial Discretion in Part 26A Restructuring Plan Procedures': https://ssrn.com/abstract=4016519 (accessed 10 April 2024).

more to a purchaser in a specific sector than they would be worth on the open market. For example, if the premises are adapted for a specific use, such as a gym, and have an established clientele of gym members, the premises may be worth considerably more for a purchaser who wishes to buy the chain of gyms than they would be worth as a single lot on the open market. This becomes much more obvious when we break out of the corporate restructuring silo and consider how leases are treated under ordinary private law.

Secondly, the court must be alive to the question of whether unaffected creditors are getting too good a deal. A holistic review is essential: the court must demand that the debtor provides evidence for why trade creditors have been excluded and why this does not make a material difference to the landlords. It seems to us that it will rarely be justifiable to compromise leases but not unsecured debt. And the court must also be alive to the question of whether the plan results in an 'unfair' transfer of value to other creditors and to those who will retain equity in the group after the restructuring. To unpack this, we must start with the financial treatment of a lease. In his fabulous new book, *The Financial Restructuring Tool Set*, Mike Harmon identifies the ambiguity over whether an operating lease in a lease-heavy business, such as a retailer or a casual dining operator, ought to be treated as debt or as an operating expense on the firm's balance sheet.[97] Harmon prefers to treat the leases as debt in a lease-heavy business because 'a lease is just a different way of financing productive long-term assets used in the business'.[98] This leads Harmon to view an improvement in EBITDAR (earnings for the business before not only interest, tax, depreciation and amortisation (EBITDA) but also rent) as a signal that the total enterprise value of the firm has increased. If EBITDAR increases after rejection of leases in a Chapter 11 case, then Harmon identifies that there may have been a transfer of value from the landlords to other stakeholders. He admits that his treatment is not universally accepted. Indeed, when we asked him, Harmon pointed out that the financial services company Lazard had valued clothing retailer J Crew on an EBITDA, rather than EBITDAR, basis when it ran both a multiples valuation and a discounted cash-flow valuation of the business. Nonetheless, we find Harmon's approach extremely useful for our analysis.

This is because, by focusing on changes in EBITDAR, Harmon draws out whether lease rejection has improved the fundamental operating performance of the debtor. If a debtor-tenant's EBITDAR goes up when a lease is effectively rejected in a Part 26A plan, then value is transferred from the landlord to those that will end up owning the firm. We should be very concerned if the issues with surrender; bargaining power; cost; and information asymmetry make it possible for other stakeholders to capture value from landlords by seeking to reshape leasehold estates inside Part 26A rather than outside it. If this were to become a widespread feature of Part 26A plans, then there would undoubtedly be a strong incentive to use it to achieve a restructuring of an over-rented leasehold estate rather than making any attempt to negotiate consensually.

[97] Mike Harmon, *The Financial Restructuring Tool Set* (New York, Columbia University Press, 2025) 148 fn j.

[98] ibid.

We consider that our analysis acquires even more force when we bust Part 26A not only out of its corporate restructuring law silo but also out of its geographical silo. This is because the risk that debtors will be tempted to resort to a formal corporate restructuring tool solely to address unexpired leases may be somewhat moderated in a US context because of an issue that we have addressed in earlier work. The issue is that there are challenges with selecting specific liabilities to compromise in Chapter 11.[99] A specific issue arises in so-called non-consensual plans, in which the court is asked to impose a plan of reorganisation over the wishes of a dissenting class. This is because two rules, known informally as the cram-down rules, are engaged: a rule that states that a non-consensual plan must not discriminate unfairly with respect to non-accepting impaired classes,[100] and the absolute priority rule, which provides that no junior class shall recover until a more senior class has recovered in full.[101] The overall result of these rules is that it may prove especially difficult to confirm a plan over the objections of dissenting landlords in which a substantial number of unsecured trade creditors ride through the plan unscathed.

In our earlier work, we exposed (and criticised) a technique developed in the Mattress Firm bed store bankruptcy for rejecting leases while leaving a substantial number of other creditors unimpaired. We called this technique 'target claim unimpairment' because it relies on an interpretation of unimpaired claims adopted by the Courts of Appeal in the Second, Third and Fifth Circuits. This interpretation is that a claim is unimpaired if the debtor proposes to pay the full amount of an allowed claim in bankruptcy even if that allowed claim is less than the amount the creditor would have been entitled to under non-bankruptcy law. And recall that the landlord's claim for damages on rejection is capped at the greater of one year, or 15 per cent not to exceed three years, of rent for the remaining term of the lease. However, this technique is not for the faint-hearted debtor-tenant. While in the face of mounting problems in meeting the terms of leases negotiated in an entirely different market, and the serious obstacles to surrender outside bankruptcy, tenants may have little choice but to resort to this type of expensive, uncertain, aggressive use of the US Bankruptcy Code, it is undoubtedly a narrow and rocky path to navigate. Overall, Chapter 11 probably remains more of a last resort for addressing an overrented estate than Part 26A.

B. Market Implications

Our second concern is that the compromise of leases within Part 26A will lead the commercial real property market rather than reflect it. To put this another way, we see less objection to the use of Part 26A to reduce a landlord's hold-out power to realign the lease terms with the current market so that the debtor can survive, than with the use of Part 26A to force terms on landlords that other, perfectly healthy leaseholders

[99] Sarah Paterson and Adrian Walters, 'Chapter 11's Inclusivity Problem' (2023) 55 *Arizona State Law Journal* 1227.
[100] 11 USC § 1129(b)(1).
[101] ibid.

subsequently demand. To unpack this concern, it is helpful to set out reasonably extensively some observations of Norris J relating to the Debenhams CVA:

> Normally, it would seem wrong in principle that a tenant should be able to trade under a CVA for the benefit of past creditors at the present and future expense of its landlord. But suppose that past creditors consisted of suppliers who provided goods under 'one-off' contracts of 'short-term supply' deals that would naturally reflect the current market price for such supplies; and suppose the landlord could under the lease charge a rent fixed at an historic high or which automatically escalated by a fixed percentage unrelated to the value of money … Would it not be 'unfair' for the suppliers to be unable to receive the market price for their goods in order that the landlord should receive a 100% premium over the market price for his supply? What would be 'unfair' about a scheme the object of which was to ensure that everybody got the market price for what they supplied? As a matter of *principle* I would not have thought it 'unfair' that a landlord might receive less than his contracted-for rent in such circumstances.[102]

Norris J is referring here to the long-term, upward-only rent review commercial leases that were very common in the UK but that are rapidly becoming a thing of the past. In today's highly challenging environment, tenants are increasingly able to negotiate for either-way rent reviews (where the rent can go up, down, or stay the same); turnover rent reviews (linked to trading success) or stepped rents (fixed increases at defined points in time). The objective is for the rent to reflect the market value of the premises or the tenant's trading success.[103] Yet a problem arises if that market value is artificially impacted by the dramatically reduced rents that debtor-tenants can impose on landlords in a Part 26A restructuring plan. Healthy tenants who are suffering no financial difficulty at all may push for 'most-favoured tenant' clauses that promise the tenant they will receive terms at least as favourable as the landlord's other tenants. If those other tenants have imposed dramatically low rents through a Part 26A restructuring plan, the results may be drastic for the landlord.

We have seen that in the US context the landlord's damages claim for rejection is capped in Chapter 11. This was originally intended to prevent short-term 'claim swamping' by long-term claims but was presumably sized as a proxy for the damage that the landlord would suffer based on the assumption that the landlord would be able to re-let the premises in question within the time-frame envisaged.[104] Thus, the cap was designed to prevent landlords from swamping the vote of other unsecured creditors[105] (the very reverse of the vote swamping issue we explored in a UK context) while representing a realistic assessment of their economic loss. But this may be very far from the truth today in the highly challenging retail environment.[106] And, as we have seen, in the target unimpairment cases the landlord is denied any vote, so that no cap is

[102] *Debenhams* (n 48) [66].

[103] DMH Stallard, 'Is the end in sight for upward-only rent reviews?' 20 September 2021: https://www.dmhstallard.com/news-insights/blog/is-the-end-in-sight-for-upward-only-rent-reviews-1 accessed 10 April 2024.

[104] John T Baxter, 'Bankruptcy 101: Lease Assumption, Assignment, and Rejection' (2023) XIII (335) *The National Law Review.*

[105] ibid.

[106] Ethan Rothstein, 'Even Developers Agree the US has Way too Much Retail Space' (*Forbes*, 5 April 2017): https://www.forbes.com/sites/bisnow/2017/04/05/even-developers-agree-the-u-s-has-way-too-much-retail-space/ (accessed 10 April 2024).

needed for the purposes of ensuring that the landlord's vote does not disproportionately determine the vote of an unsecured class. Similarly, the stipulation that the debtor must decide whether to reject a non-residential lease within 120 days of petition (extended to 210 days under the CARES Act[107]), unless it manages to extend the period for an additional 90 days, was developed in a very different era when commercial landlords considered it unfair for debtors to have the time to determine what they would like to do – assume, assign or reject the lease – while the landlord could re-let with relative ease. Nonetheless, all the other limitations with the Chapter 11 regime that we have highlighted also apply to the extent to which the regime impacts on the ordinary rental market.

C. Foundational Questions

Our final concern is that the sophisticated and complex treatment of unexpired leases in Part 26A raises foundational questions about the nature and treatment of leases more generally that have not been asked, still less answered. For us, there are two relevant issues: the first is the implications of the no surrender rule outside Part 26A for the ability to reject or compromise an unexpired lease within it; the second is the question of whether a lease is properly treated as a financial liability or an operating expense.

As we have seen, Zacaroli J has held that a debtor-tenant cannot impose a surrender in Part 26A but can write the rent down to zero.[108] The rationale is that surrender implicates a property right while the obligation to pay rent is merely contractual. Yet we cannot help but feel that this issue merits further consideration. The question of the relationship between property law and contract strikes right at the heart of landlord and tenant law. For example, the lease will contain multiple covenants, besides the covenant to pay rent. However, a covenant in a lease does not necessarily just bind the parties to it: it can 'run with the land'. In other words, it is more than a mere contractual term. In our view, the partially contractual approach that Zacaroli J adopts would merit more consideration by property lawyers.

Similarly, we have drawn on Mike Harmon's analysis of the lease as a financial liability rather than an operating expense. This has important implications for how we think about potential transfers of value between landlords and those who would own the business after the restructuring. We suggest that this issue would also benefit from discussion between finance professionals specialising in real estate finance and those working in financial restructuring.

Once again, we consider that our analysis is strengthened when we reach outside our geographical silo. US landlord and tenant law already appears to be moving in the direction of a contractual approach to lease surrender, making the foundational question considerably less pressing. Indeed, peering over the edge of the geographical silo suggests that England should also, perhaps, be revisiting the common law rules on surrender.

[107] Coronavirus Aid, Relief, and Economic Security Act (2020).
[108] *Instant Cash Loans* (n 43).

IV. Silo-Busting

All of this leads us to suggest that it is time to bust leases out of the corporate restructuring and English law silos in considering how we hope to address holistically the dislocations that have been caused by the changing shape of the high street. In June 2021 Sarah Olney MP introduced a Private Members' Bill in the UK Parliament that sought not only to prohibit the use of upward-only rent review clauses in future commercial leases, but also to extinguish existing upward-only clauses.[109] This Bill appears to have ground to a halt with very little comment, but indicates that it is perhaps time to consider reform of leasehold renegotiation outside Part 26A, while being informed by it.

Crucially, we wonder if the experience of lease modification and rejection in restructuring indicates that the time has come to reconsider whether contract doctrines such as repudiation and mitigation should have a place in landlord and tenant law in the UK and in those US States that have not already moved in this direction. In our view, developments within Part 26A and in Chapter 11 undermine the 'property' aspect of the lease, adopting what Jason Brock and Jim Phillips call (in a different context) a 'partial contractualization' of the commercial lease.[110] It seems to us profoundly unsatisfactory to have, drawing on Brock and Phillips again, 'an inconsistent patchwork of approaches'.[111] Brock and Phillips' work is part of a body of literature suggesting that the time has come to abandon commercial landlord and tenant law as part of property law and to fully assimilate it within contract law. We suggest that the analysis in this chapter provides more grist for that mill and, at the very least, suggests that the time has come to re-evaluate the common law of surrender.

More radical options outside corporate restructuring law might also fruitfully be considered. In the UK, the Commercial Rent (Coronavirus) Act 2022 introduced an arbitration process to resolve disputes regarding Covid rent arrears. The deadline for making reference to the arbitration process was 23 September 2022 and it was not subsequently extended. The arbitration process introduced considerable uncertainty for both landlord and tenant and, therefore, shifted bargaining power quite dramatically. The arbitration process was accompanied by a code of practice issued by the Government to help parties in the process of negotiation,[112] and anecdotal reports suggest that many parties decided to avoid the scheme and reach commercial settlements.[113] Yet there has been very little analysis of the lessons learnt from this process for the ongoing efforts to move rents onto a sustainable footing in a very different environment.

[109] Commercial Rent (Prohibition of Upward-Only Reviews) Bill, Private Members' Bill (2021-22) 54.

[110] Jason Brock and Jim Phillips, 'The Commercial Lease: Property or Contract' (2000–2001) 38 *Alberta Law Review* 989, 991.

[111] ibid.

[112] *Commercial Rent Code of Practice following the COVID-19 Pandemic*, 7 April 2022: https://www.gov.uk/government/publications/commercial-rent-code-of-practice (accessed 31 March 2025).

[113] Clyde & Co, 'Covid rent arrears arbitration service closes: What now?': https://www.clydeco.com/en/insights/2022/09/covid-rent-arrears-arbitration-service-closes-what (accessed 31 March 2025).

Silo busting is not, however, unidirectional. Just as we consider the time has come to analyse the implications of the treatment of leases within Part 26A for landlord and tenant law, so too we think the time has come to reconsider what landlord and tenant law has to say about the treatment of leases within Part 26A. Moreover, just as we consider that English lawyers should bust out of their geographical silo in considering the treatment of unexpired leases in Part 26A, so we believe that US lawyers would benefit from understanding how they are treated in Part 26A. Specifically, we consider that the treatment of a capped damages claim by a landlord under Chapter 11 as an unimpaired claim requires some interrogation. We are also of the view that the cap of the damages claim in Chapter 11 needs a fresh look in the new market environment. And we consider that the possibility of a transfer of value from one group of unsecured financial creditors, the landlords, to the shareholders via the rejection process requires serious consideration. Similarly, in our opinion, the English courts must take into account all payments that a landlord may receive in the event of the relevant alternative; should be cautious about treating a termination right as an end to the landlord's concerns; and should take very seriously indeed the risk of a transfer of value from the landlords to those owning the firm after the restructuring. In both jurisdictions we are concerned about transparency. In our view, a debtor should always be required to show that it has attempted to bargain with the landlord, and shared relevant information with them, before resorting to a cram-down technique.

Finally, we advocate for a more radical approach to busting the geographical silo. We hope that our unpacking of the Anglo-American position already provides some useful insights. We suspect, however, that much more could be learned by understanding the process of lease negotiation in other jurisdictions. For example, in the *Virgin Active* litigation the court heard that the company's clubs outside the UK had generally been able to reach consensual agreements with landlords. Experience of renegotiation in Italy, Thailand, Singapore, and Australia had been more positive than in the UK.[114] It would be very interesting to understand what was different about the negotiating dynamics in those jurisdictions and what lessons the UK and the US could learn.

V. Conclusion

Part 26A and real property law are misaligned. There is not the room here for us to work out fully how they could be better aligned. Rather, our purpose has been to demonstrate that corporate restructuring law's more contract-based approach has developed in the corporate restructuring law silo with apparent disregard for debates in property law about the nature of the lease and the relative rights of landlord and tenant outside a formal corporate restructuring procedure. By the same token, property lawyers are also seemingly often oblivious to the misalignment. As corporate restructuring lawyers, we doubt that this state of affairs is healthy. Moreover, in our view, a proper understanding

[114] *Virgin Active* (n 75) [8].

of the stakes outside formal corporate restructuring procedures, and the impact of corporate restructuring law on landlords' rights, is essential to the resolution of questions of allocative fairness between landlords and other stakeholders in the corporate restructuring law process. And finally, we consider that lawyers, policy-makers, scholars and judges would all do well to look beyond their geographical silo in addressing the detail of how corporate restructuring law interferes in the important area of long-term leases.

7

Commencing Corporate Insolvency Proceedings at the Right Time: Directorial Responsibility in Financial Distress

FELIX STEFFEK

I. Context

A. Economic Problem

This chapter investigates when corporate restructuring and liquidation proceedings should be commenced as well as whether and, if so, how this should be regulated by way of public ordering. Restructuring and liquidation proceedings are understood as formal proceedings that are regulated in company or insolvency law as opposed to transactions governed by contract law.[1] The focus of this chapter is exclusively on companies in financial distress. For this purpose, financial distress is defined as being (or about to be) in breach of a financial debt obligation.[2] As regards the corporate form, this chapter reflects core economic and legal principles. It does not engage with the differences between private and public companies and similar differentiations. As will become apparent, such differentiations can be dealt with within the analytical and normative framework proposed. Similarly, this chapter does not differentiate between the different

[1] Examples are restructuring plans under the Companies Act 2006 (CA 2006), Pt 26A, creditors' voluntary winding ups under the Insolvency Act 1986 (IA 1986), ss 97 ff and administrations under the IA 1986, Sch B1.

[2] Economic theory uses various kinds of definitions for financial distress. For the definition used here, see DR Brown, CM James and RM Mooradian, 'The Information Content of Distressed Restructurings Involving Public and Private Debt Claims' (1992) 33 *Journal of Financial Economics* 93, 102; for other definitions, *cf* SA Davydenko, IA Strebulaev and X Zhao, 'A Market-based Study of the Cost of Default' (2012) 25 *Review of Financial Studies* 2959 (illiquidity); A Schwartz, 'A Normative Theory of Business Bankruptcy' (2005) 91 *Virginia Law Review* 1199, 1200 (if a business had positive earnings were it not required to service its debt); RB Whitaker, 'The Early Stages of Financial Distress' (1999) 23 *Journal of Economics and Finance* 123, 124 (cash flow less than current maturities of long-term debt); G Andrade and SN Kaplan, 'How Costly Is Financial (Not Economic) Distress? Evidence from Highly Leveraged Transactions That Became Distressed' (1998) 53 *Journal of Finance* 1443, 1450 (EBITDA less than interest expense, attempt to restructure debt or default).

types of restructuring proceedings. Again, such differentiations can be reflected by fleshing out further details of the framework developed.

What is the economic problem at hand? In financial distress, those in control of the company, and consequently, of the business, are exposed to harmful incentives. These incentives are the result of limited liability in combination with the rules and principles of corporate attribution. In the large majority of jurisdictions, the liability of shareholders is limited by statute.[3] The liability of directors is usually not limited by statute, but as a result of the statutory rules and legal principles of attributing their acts to the company.[4] If a director acts for the company and within their authority, the company and not the director is liable. In many jurisdictions such as England and Wales, this generally applies not only to contract but also to tort.[5]

As a result, neither shareholders nor directors are liable for the debts of the company in financial distress. However, both keep their upside potential. Should the company return to solvency, then the shareholders will benefit from an increased share value while the directors will have the prospect of keeping their position and the associated benefits such as directorial pay. Importantly, the shareholders' upside potential is unlimited. The more profit the company generates, the higher will be their financial claims against the company. The combination of downside protection and upside potential incentivises shareholders and directors to act against the interests of other stakeholders in financial distress, in particular the company's creditors. The value-destructive decisions may be a result of either rational or irrational choice.[6] In any case, such decisions can, overall, destroy more value than they create, in which case they are socially undesirable.

To give just some examples of the harmful incentives that can arise: directors may linger for resurrection, ie, they may delay the commencement of a restructuring or liquidation of the business even though there is no good reason to do so – with the result that creditors sustain unjustified value losses. Or directors might take excessive risks, gambling for resurrection, knowing that directors and shareholders will benefit from the upside while it will only be the creditors who suffer from the downside.[7] A further undesirable action by directors is the channelling of assets away, distributing them to preferred recipients such as family members or expected partners in a future business

[3] For English law, this is the case in CA 2006, s 3(1) in combination with IA 1986, s 74(2)(d) and (3); for German law, see § 13(2) Gesetz betreffend die Gesellschaften mit beschränkter Haftung (Private Companies Act) and § 1(1) Aktiengesetz (Public Companies Act).

[4] On this generally, PL Davies, S Worthington and C Hare, *Principles of Modern Company Law*, 11th edn (London, Sweet & Maxwell, 2021) ch 8.

[5] See, eg, *Williams v Natural Life Health Foods Ltd* [1998] UKHL 17; for German law, see the '*Baustoff*' judgment of the German Supreme Court (Bundesgerichtshof) in *Entscheidungen des Bundesgerichtshofes in Zivilsachen (BGHZ)* 109, 297.

[6] Examples of irrational choice are overoptimism (ND Weinstein, 'Unrealistic Optimism About Future Life Events' (1980) 39 *Journal of Personality and Social Psychology* 806), illusion of control (DC Langevoort, 'Organized Illusions: A Behavioral Theory of Why Corporations Mislead Stock Market Investors (and Cause Other Social Harms)' in CR Sunstein (ed), *Behavioral Law and Economics* (Cambridge, Cambridge University Press, 2000) 144, 149 f) and selective perception (L Festinger, *A Theory of Cognitive Dissonance* (Stanford CA, Stanford University Press, 1957)).

[7] J Armour, G Hertig and H Kanda, 'Transactions with Creditors' in R Kraakman et al (eds), *The Anatomy of Corporate Law: A Comparative and Functional Approach*, 3rd edn (Oxford, Oxford University Press, 2017) 111.

to be founded.[8] The common characteristic of such actions is that a manager taking decisions in the interests of creditors would not have made such choices. Some of these decisions by directors are made in coalition with the shareholders against the creditors. Some actions might be taken in coalition with new investors, such as expected debt or equity investors, against old investors, namely old creditors and old shareholders.[9] From a social perspective, such actions are undesirable if they, overall, destroy more value than they create.

B. Policy Goals

What are the policy goals concerning the harmful incentives just described from a welfare-oriented perspective that aims at maximising the sum of benefits and costs for all stakeholders combined?[10] A key goal is to amend the governance of the business at the right point in time in order to maximise the expected value of the assets (or, put differently, of the business). This chapter focuses particularly on this policy goal. It can be achieved by shifting the governance structure in place for the solvent state of the business to a governance structure geared towards restructuring or liquidation. Restructuring is understood as making changes to the business and its finance structure while maintaining the business's (as opposed to the company's) existence. Liquidation, instead, describes a procedure that results in the winding-up of the business.

A further policy goal is the prevention of actions that, by undermining a collective approach to managing the company's financial distress, reduce the overall value of the business.[11] In other words, managerial decisions in the interest of one or some, but not all, creditors shall be avoided if their impact on the value of the business is suboptimal. While this policy goal is important, this contribution focuses on the effect of changing a shareholder-oriented governance architecture to a creditor-oriented one. A secondary policy goal is to undo or compensate for the costs caused if undesirable actions as just described occur.

C. Legal Strategies

Thus far, the description of the economic problem and the associated policy goals has taken an economic, or functional, perspective.[12] Against this background, what are the

[8] RC Clark, 'The Duties of the Corporate Debtor to Its Creditors' (1977) 90 *Harvard Law Review* 505.

[9] S Paterson, 'The Paradox of Alignment: Agency Problems and Debt Restructuring' (2016) 17 *European Business Organization Law Review* 497.

[10] For more details on the normative goal of maximising the welfare of all affected by a company's activities, see J Armour, H Hansmann, R Kraakman and M Pargendler, 'What is Corporate Law' in R Kraakman et al (eds), *The Anatomy of Corporate Law: A Comparative and Functional Approach*, 3rd edn (Oxford, Oxford University Press, 2017) 22–24.

[11] On collectivity as a response to corporate financial distress, see TH Jackson, *The Logic and Limits of Bankruptcy Law* (Cambridge MA, Beard Books, 1986).

[12] On the functional method, see R Michaels, 'The Functional Method of Comparative Law' in M Reimann and R Zimmermann (eds), *Oxford Handbook of Comparative Law*, 2nd edn (Oxford, Oxford University Press, 2019) ch 13.

legal strategies or legal mechanisms employed to solve the economic problem identified and achieve the set policy goals? As a starting point, legal strategies can take the form of private or public ordering. Private ordering happens when private actors use their legal autonomy by way of, for example, contract, articles of association or unilateral legal decision-making.[13] Public ordering takes the form of, for instance, primary and secondary legislation, as well as case law.[14] In financial distress, both private and public legal ordering can strengthen the position of company outsiders (creditors) against the insiders (directors and shareholders).

In the context of this contribution, private and public ordering take the following five forms:

1) Decision rights to commence restructuring and liquidation proceedings;[15]
2) Incentives to act in the creditors' interests;[16]
3) Constraints to minimise the costs of debtor control;[17]
4) Avoidance of transactions undermining the collective management of financial distress;[18] and
5) Information rights and duties.[19]

This chapter focuses on the first legal strategy, ie, the right to open formal restructuring and liquidation proceedings. The other strategies are referred to in context. Conceptually, the first strategy takes the form of a decision strategy in combination with a delegation strategy. The decision element concerns the choice whether or not to commence proceedings. The delegation element reflects the fact that such choice is made by one or some stakeholders with effect for many or all stakeholders. In other words, the legal order delegates the opening decision to one, or a specific group of, stakeholders.

Every commencement strategy needs to determine three issues, namely (i) who has the right to open; (ii) what kind of proceeding; and (iii) the necessary financial state of the company.

In terms of the first issue, ie, who has the right to open proceedings, three regulatory models are on offer:

1) Creditor control: provides creditors with the right to open proceedings as outsiders;
2) Debtor control: allows the company insiders, namely directors and shareholders, to commence proceedings; and

[13] See, eg, OE Williamson, 'The Lens of Contract: Private Ordering' (2002) 92 *American Economic Review* 438.

[14] See, eg, JR Macey, 'Public and Private Ordering and the Production of Legitimate and Illegitimate Legal Rules' (1997) 82 *Cornell Law Review* 1123.

[15] For example, a creditor's right to apply for an administration order under IA 1986, Sch B1 para 12(1)(c).

[16] For example, allowing directors to remain in post after the opening of a scheme of arrangement under CA 2006, Pt 26.

[17] For example, directors' liability for wrongful trading under IA 1986, s 214.

[18] For example, the right to avoid transactions at an undervalue and preferences under IA 1986, ss 238 f.

[19] For example, information rights and duties between borrower company and lender agreed in the loan documentation.

3) Third party control: assigns commencement rights beyond the immediate stakeholders, in particular to state agencies.

English law uses all three regulatory models in combination. This can, for example, be seen in IA 1986, sections 124 and 124a, which provide the directors and shareholders[20] as insiders, the creditors as outsiders and the Secretary of State as a third party with the right to petition for the opening of a winding up.

D. Imperfect Contracts

The economic problem identified above could, and should, be left to private ordering, in particular by way of contract or provisions in the articles of association, if such private coordination was efficient. However, this is not the case. Instead, private ordering is suboptimal. Creditors negotiating with directors and, possibly, shareholders fail in a significant number of instances to solve the governance problem identified above through contracting. Consistent with the focus of this contribution, this failure particularly applies to the commencement of restructuring and liquidation proceedings at the right time. The failure of private ordering is due to at least three obstacles.

First, uncertainty as to the future state of the company and the best type of proceeding to be chosen at the relevant time stands in the way of efficient contracts. At the time of contracting, eg, when providing the company with credit, it is difficult to foresee how exactly the business of the company will develop, what the finance side of the balance sheet will look like, how the supply and customer markets will present themselves, which persons will be managing the company etc, when the decision is to be made whether to commence a formal procedure and, if so, which one.[21] As a result, the resulting contracts risk being either incomplete[22] or overly restrictive.[23]

Second, creditors face severe collective action problems when trying to solve the triggering of restructuring and liquidation proceedings by way of contract.[24] The large number of creditors that need coordination is only the starting point. In addition, there are different creditor groups with different interests. Secured creditors may prefer not to trigger formal proceedings which will limit the enforcement of their security, while unsecured creditors may prefer early commencement of proceedings that are governed by their interests. More recently, the rise of private lending, credit insurance and credit default instruments have further complicated the landscape of creditor preferences.[25] Further, creditors enter and exit the credit relationship with the company at different

[20] Under certain conditions laid down in IA 1986, s 124(2).

[21] A Schwartz, 'A Contract Theory Approach to Business Bankruptcy' (1998) 107 *Yale Law Journal* 1807, 1839.

[22] O Hart and J Moore, 'Foundations of Incomplete Contracts' (1999) 66 *Review of Economic Studies* 115.

[23] For empirical research on overly restrictive loan contracts, see N Gârleanu and J Zwiebel, 'Design and Renegotiation of Debt Covenants' (2009) 22 *Review of Financial Studies* 749.

[24] See generally Jackson, *The Logic and Limits of Bankruptcy Law* (n 11); D Baird and RK Rasmussen, 'Antibankruptcy' (2010) 119 *Yale Law Journal* 648; EJ Janger, 'Privacy Property, Information Costs, and the Anticommons' (2003) 54 *Hastings Law Journal* 899, 925 ff.

[25] See generally N Lalafaryan, 'Private Credit: A Renaissance in Corporate Finance' (2024) 24 *Journal of Corporate Law Studies* 41.

points in time. This fluidity in the body of creditors adds to the collective action problems hindering a private solution.

Third, different groups of creditors have different capacities and possibilities to adjust their credit relationships with the company to their interests.[26] While some lenders, such as banks, are in a position to perfectly adjust their loan contracts to their interests and, in particular, the opening of restructuring and liquidation proceedings, other creditors fail to do so. Suppliers, for example, are usually thought to apply their standard terms irrespective of whether they fit the specific counterparty's characteristics. Finally, creditor groups such as consumers and tort creditors do not negotiate credit terms at all. The former lack the negotiating power and interest in negotiating (rational apathy),[27] since the costs of negotiation usually exceed the expected benefits. The latter are, practically, not in a position to negotiate, as the tortious event usually predates the credit relationship.

As a result, we empirically witness only *some* private ordering of the triggering of insolvency proceedings. A good example are clauses in intercreditor agreements[28] regulating the decision-making among the parties towards the opening of insolvency proceedings. Another example is the agreement between lenders and companies on the financial state of the company which causes a floating charge to crystallise.[29] This event is then the basis for the commencement of an administration proceeding under IA 1986, schedule B1, paragraph 14 by the holder of a qualifying floating charge. On the other side, suppliers, employees and consumers practically never negotiate clauses which directly determine their own influence on the opening of insolvency proceedings.

Against this background and the economic problem identified above, there is a strong case for the public ordering of the commencement of restructuring and liquidation proceedings. Empirically, this is confirmed by all advanced insolvency law systems opting for public regulation – at least concerning some aspects. For England, the examples of IA 1986, sections 124 and 124a have already been given.[30] While there is consensus in positive law that state rules on directorial involvement in the opening of insolvency proceedings are desirable, the question when and under what conditions such rules shall trigger restructuring and liquidation proceedings is an open one. Comparing insolvency laws, this shows in many aspects. A well-known example is the difference between jurisdictions *requiring* directors to open insolvency proceedings when insolvency grounds are met and other jurisdictions that *do not require* directors to take such action. An example of the former is German law, which mandates directors – under the threat of both civil and criminal liability – to initiate insolvency proceedings

[26] E Warren and JL Westbrook, 'Contracting out of Bankruptcy: An Empirical Intervention' (2005) 118 *Harvard Law Review* 1197, 1213 ff.

[27] ibid, 1219 ff.

[28] *cf* the Intercreditor Agreement templates offered by the Loan Market Association: https://www.lma.eu.com/documents-guidelines/documents.

[29] E Ferran, E Howell and F Steffek, *Principles of Corporate Finance Law* (Oxford, Oxford University Press, 2023) 399.

[30] Above under section I.C.

when the company is either balance sheet or cash flow insolvent.[31] An example of the latter is US law, which does not impose a duty on directors to file for bankruptcy proceedings.[32]

II. Normative Framework for Commencing Insolvency Proceedings

A. Residual Claimant Principle

Having established a strong case for the public ordering of the commencement of restructuring and liquidation proceedings while realising that the optimal point in time is an open question, an attempt is now made to establish some basic principles in response. A particular focus is on the distribution of governance rights and the responsibility of directors in this process.

A good starting point for designing the governance of opening insolvency proceedings is the residual claimant principle.[33] In the context of finance, the residual claimant is the investor who has the last claim on the company's assets but still receives some payment. Put differently, the residual claimant has the right to the net cash flow.[34] As the residual claimant is the last to claim, their payout varies and depends on the value of the assets. The position of the residual claimant is fluid.[35] In the solvent company, the shareholders are the residual claimants.[36] In a company, where the debts exceed the value of the assets, the creditors are the residual claimants.[37] In a company with layers of debt of different ranks, the residual claimant is the lowest-ranking group of creditors still to receive payment. For example, in a debt structure with secured, preferential unsecured and unsecured debt, the preferential unsecured creditors are the residual claimant if the unsecured creditors receive no payment while the preferential unsecured creditors are paid half of the nominal value of their claims.[38]

In the interest of clarity of argument, this chapter is based on a version of the residual claimant principle, which respects ex ante priority rights and values the assets at the

[31] § 15a Insolvenzordnung (German Insolvency Act) in combination with § 823(2) Bürgerliches Gesetzbuch (German Civil Code) for civil liability.

[32] D Scarlino, 'Zone of Insolvency, Directors' Duties and Creditors' Protection in US' (2018) 29 *European Business Law Review* 1.

[33] For the history of the residual claimant principle, see SE Kim, 'Tracing the Diverse History of Corporate Residual Claimants' (2021) 95 *Southern California Law Review Postscript* 43.

[34] EF Fama and MC Jensen, 'Separation of Ownership and Control' (1983) 26 *Journal of Law and Economics* 301, 302.

[35] Kim, 'Tracing the Diverse History of Corporate Residual Claimants' (n 33) 46.

[36] O Hart, *Firms, Contracts, and Financial Structure* (Oxford, Oxford University Press, 1995) 63 ff; FH Easterbrook and DR Fischel, *The Economic Structure of Corporate Law* (Cambridge MA, Harvard University Press, 1991) 38, 69.

[37] Ferran, Howell and Steffek, *Principles of Corporate Finance Law* (n 29) 370; P Aghion and P Bolton, 'An Incomplete Contracts Approach to Financial Contracting' (1992) 59 *Review of Economic Studies* 473, 475.

[38] For further examples, see LA Bebchuk, 'Using Options to Divide Value in Corporate Bankruptcy' (2000) 44 *European Economic Review* 829, 834 f.

point in time at which the residual claimant is determined. This is worth mentioning for two reasons. First, other versions of the definition of residual claimant, in particular those based on option theory, have been developed.[39] A definition of the residual claimant based on option theory has the consequence that equity and debt investors can be residual claimants at the same time. Second, the value of the business at the time of commencing a formal proceeding and at the time of the conclusion of the proceeding can, and often will, differ.[40] The definition of the residual claimant employed in this chapter does not equate to a rejection of attempts to define the residual claimant(s) based on option theory or of endeavours to design restructuring and liquidation procedures using option theory. Instead, the issue focused on here, ie, the commencement of insolvency proceedings at the right time, can be discussed at a fundamental level without exploring the impact of option theory. Option theory might well be useful to further refine the arguments developed in this chapter.[41] However, for the claims developed in this chapter, it is not necessary to do so. It should be noted, however, that valuing the assets at the point in time when the residual claimant is determined will reflect possible future scenarios and the income expected under these scenarios.

According to the residual claimant principle, the governance of the company should follow the residual claimant.[42] The residual claimant has the strongest incentive to exercise control and decision rights effectively, since it is the residual claimant that has the most to gain from such decisions. Good decisions will increase the payout that the residual claimant can expect, while bad decisions will decrease expected gains and may even wipe out all claims. Hence, according to the residual claimant principle, the residual claimant should have the ultimate control, while those managing the company should be responsible to the residual claimant. The principle has two aspects, the attribution of rights (to the residual claimant) and the imposition of duties (on the manager).

Advanced company and insolvency laws generally follow the residual claimant principle as regards both rights and duties.[43] In the solvent company, the shareholders are the residual claimants and decision rights are in their hands. The shareholders can amend the corporate constitution,[44] appoint and remove directors[45] and a shareholders' resolution is required to liquidate the company.[46] Mirroring this as regards duties, in the solvent company, directors are required to exercise their duties in the interests

[39] See, eg, BS Black, 'Corporate Law and Residual Claimants' (2001), *Stanford Law and Economics Olin Working Paper No 217*, available at: https://ssrn.com/abstract=1528437, at 14ff.

[40] As illustrated by CD Boone and AJ Casey, 'A Primer on Option Valuation in Restructuring' (2024), *ECGI Finance Working Paper No 766/2024*, available at: https://ssrn.com/abstract=1528437, at 4 f.

[41] See, eg, the text at n 58.

[42] AA Alchian and H Demsetz, 'Production, Information Costs, and Economic Organization' (1972) 72 *American Economic Review* 777, 782; JF Zender, 'Optimal Financial Instruments' (1991) 46 *Journal of Finance* 1645, 1655.

[43] AR Keay, 'Shareholder Primacy in Corporate Law: Can it Survive? Should it Survive?' (2010) 7 *European Company and Financial Law Review* 369, 377 ff; M Schillig, 'The Transition from Corporate Governance to Bankruptcy Governance – Convergence of German and US Law?' (2010) 7 *European Company and Financial Law Review* 116, 118 ff.

[44] CA 2006, ss 21(1), 283.

[45] CA 2006, s 168(1) as regards removal and, for example, Model Articles for Private Companies, art 17(a) as regards appointment.

[46] In English law under IA 1986, s 84(1)(b).

of the shareholders.[47] In the solvent company, creditors cannot initiate an insolvency proceeding.

In the insolvent company, the creditors are provided with the right to trigger an insolvency proceeding,[48] independently of the shareholders' consent. The creditors can commence insolvency proceedings that are managed in their interest.[49] This applies to both restructuring and liquidation proceedings, even though their specific governance varies.[50] The creditors now hold the ultimate governance rights, replacing the shareholders. Again, mirroring this as regards duties, insolvency practitioners are required to act in the interests of the creditors. Case law has extended this for the company that is insolvent but not yet the subject of an insolvency proceeding. Here, directors are required to consider the interests of creditors as part of their directorial duties.[51]

B. Deviation from a Strict Application of the Residual Claimant Principle

Strikingly, company and insolvency laws do not strictly follow the residual claimant principle in terms of the moment in time, or, to be more precise, the financial state of the company, which triggers the creditor-oriented governance. This applies in particular to the role of directors in ensuring the switch between shareholder- and creditor-oriented governance regimes. A strict application of the residual claimant principle would require the switch to happen exactly at the point in time at which the assets of the company are no longer sufficient to satisfy all debts. In this moment, the shareholders cease to be the residual claimants, and the creditors move into this role. This financial state can be described as economic (as opposed to legal) balance sheet insolvency. Economic balance sheet insolvency arises if the claims against the company exceed the value of the assets, ie, the value of the business.[52] This is the case if the present value of all future income is lower than the present value of all liabilities owed. In the case of economic balance sheet insolvency, the shareholders do not have any claim to the net cash flow, which now, instead, goes exclusively to the creditors.

Directors have an important role to play in effectuating the switch to a creditor-oriented governance. Economic balance sheet insolvency is not empirically perceivable by company outsiders.[53] This is different for cash flow insolvency, which usually causes events perceivable by outsiders, such as a creditor's payment request that is not

[47] CA 2006, s 172(1) ('for the benefit of its members as a whole').

[48] For example, in the case of an administration under IA 1986, Sch B1 para 12(1)(c).

[49] Such as a compulsory winding-up of an insolvent company, an administration or a company voluntary arrangement.

[50] Some proceedings such as a scheme of arrangement may only concern specific classes of creditors (CA 2006, s 895(1)(a)).

[51] See *West Mercia Safetywear Ltd v Dodd* [1988] BCLC 250; *BTI 2014 LLC v Sequana SA* [2022] UKSC 25.

[52] Jackson, *The Logic and Limits of Bankruptcy Law* (n 11) 13; see also DG Baird, 'Bankruptcy's Uncontested Axioms' (1998) 108 *Yale Law Journal* 573, 581.

[53] F Steffek, 'Insolvency (Corporate)' in J Basedow, KJ Hopt, R Zimmermann and A Stier (eds), *The Max Planck Encyclopaedia of European Private Law* (Oxford, Oxford University Press, 2012) 900, 903.

complied with. However, in a functioning credit market, cash flow insolvency occurs after balance sheet insolvency since the debtor can borrow against its unencumbered assets. Hence, it is economic balance sheet insolvency that marks the transfer of the financial residual claimant position from shareholders to creditors. The directors are the stakeholders who are best placed to detect and act upon this financial state as they have access to the relevant liquidity and accounting data as insiders in charge.

However, English law does not require directors to commence insolvency proceedings at the onset of balance sheet insolvency. This applies to both balance sheet insolvency in its economic and its legal form as laid down in the Insolvency Act 1986.[54] Instead, directors may remain in place and manage the company until the point of no return has been reached, described in IA 1986, section 214(2)(b), as the point in time when 'there was no reasonable prospect that the company would avoid going into insolvent liquidation or entering insolvent administration'. In the practice of the application of the rule in the courts, this usually requires the presence of both balance sheet and cash flow insolvency.[55] Even if this state is reached, there is no strict mandate for directors to apply for the opening of an insolvency proceeding. Instead, the director is required to take 'every step with a view to minimising the potential loss to the company's creditors'.[56] Under certain conditions, this allows continued trading, in particular if the continued trading reduces the net deficiency and minimises the risk of loss to individual creditors.[57] Often, however, this will mean applying for the commencement of an insolvency proceeding.

Why do advanced insolvency laws such as the UK's opt for this deviation from the residual claimant principle? Since in the financial state when the company is balance sheet insolvent (economic or legal) the expected asset value under the control of directors and shareholders is higher than it would be under the control of the creditors. Why is this the case even though the creditors are now the residual claimants and, following a strict application of the residual claimant principle, should have better incentives than shareholders to increase the value of the company's assets? The answer lies in the fact that the creditors' upside is limited while the shareholders' upside is unlimited.

The creditors' upside is limited as they do not benefit from the company's success beyond the satisfaction of their fixed claims. Even in the best of cases, creditors are paid the nominal value of their claims. They do not receive more if the company has more assets. This is different for the shareholders. As residual claimants *they* enjoy unlimited access to the company's net value. The more profits the company makes, the more the shareholders receive. As a result, creditors and shareholders have different incentives

[54] IA 1986, s 123(2).

[55] In the following cases the court held that the moment of truth had only arrived after both balance and cash flow insolvency were present: *Roberts v Frohlich* [2011] EWHC 257 (Ch); *Singla v Hedman* [2010] EWHC 902 (Ch); *Re Bangla Television Ltd* [2010] BCC 143 (Ch); *Re The Rod Gunner Organisation Ltd* [2004] 2 BCLC 110 (Ch); *Re Brian D Pierson (Contractors) Ltd* [2001] 1 BCLC 275 (Ch); *Re Produce Marketing Consortium Ltd (No 2)* [1989] BCLC 520 (Ch); in the following cases the court rejected the moment of truth while there was balance but no cash flow insolvency present: *Bezant v Rausing* [2007] EWHC 1118 (QB); *Re Cubelock Ltd* [2001] BCC 523 (Ch); *Re Continental Assurance Company of London plc* [2001] BPIR 733 (Ch); *Re Sherborne Associates Ltd* [1995] BCC 40.

[56] IA 1986, s 214(3).

[57] *Grant v Ralls* [2016] EWHC 243, 245; for a critical discussion, see K van Zwieten, 'Disciplining the Directors of Insolvent Companies' (2020) 33 *Insolvency Intelligence* 2.

when assuming the role of residual claimant. The creditors, as a group, are content to just lift the value of the assets above the aggregate sum of debts. This occurs right at the moment when economic balance sheet insolvency ends. The creditors will not benefit from higher profits and are, as a result, not interested in achieving them. In fact, if such profits require the taking of higher risks, the creditors are incentivised not to aim for them. The shareholders, on the other side, have an incentive to increase the asset value far beyond the sum of liabilities.[58] This explains why the shareholders, when the asset value drops below the sum of liabilities, usually have the incentive to maximise the value of the business, while the creditors are only interested in pushing the asset value back to cover the liabilities. Put differently, the expected business value under debtor control is higher than the expected business value under creditor control.

This distribution of incentives changes, however, as the financial state of the company worsens, ie, as the assets cover less and less of the liabilities. At some point, the shareholders (represented by the directors) have no realistic option left to bring the company back into solvency. This is invariably the case[59] when the business cannot generate enough income to cover its costs (excluding the cost of finance).[60] At this point, shareholders and directors suffer from the value-destructive incentives described above. They may start to gamble for resurrection, linger for resurrection or even engage in 'tunnelling' assets out of the company. At this point, the creditors' incentives are more productive since the creditors are interested in preserving, and if possible, increasing the asset value in order to maximise the satisfaction of their claims. In other words, at this point in time, the expected value of the business under debtor control is smaller than the expected value of the business under creditor control.

As set out above, there is no comparative consensus when this point in time, or, put differently, financial state, is reached. As mentioned, English law identifies it in IA 1986, section 214(2)(b) as the point in time when 'there was no reasonable prospect that the company would avoid going into insolvent liquidation or entering insolvent administration'. German law chooses an earlier point in time (or, to be more precise, financial state) and requires directors to apply for insolvency proceedings, at the latest, six weeks after balance sheet insolvency has set in.[61] However, the legal definition of balance sheet insolvency in German law defines a financial state that is generally much worse than economic balance sheet insolvency.[62] For example, balance sheet insolvency under German law requires not only that the company's liabilities exceed its assets; in addition, it must be more probable than not that the business cannot be continued beyond the next 12 months, which is understood as a liquidity issue.[63] US law sits on the other side of the spectrum and does not impose any hard duty on directors to apply for the commencement of insolvency proceedings.

[58] For an explanation from the perspective of option theory, see Boone and Casey, 'A Primer on Option Valuation in Restructuring' (n 40).

[59] Absent the investment of fresh outside capital.

[60] Schwartz, 'A Normative Theory of Business Bankruptcy' (n 2) 1200.

[61] § 15a(1) Insolvenzordnung (German Insolvency Act).

[62] F Steffek, '§19 Überschuldung' in H Prütting, R Bork and F Jacoby (eds), *KBP Kommentar zur Insolvenzordnung* (Köln, RWS Verlag, 2023) no 26.

[63] § 19(2) Insolvenzordnung (German Insolvency Act).

C. Differentiating between Restructuring and Liquidation Proceedings

The deviation from the residual claimant principle due to the different upside potential of shareholders and creditors and the resulting governance incentives is the first step in developing a normative framework. The second step requires differentiating between restructuring and liquidation proceedings. The reason for this distinction is the difference in the expected business values. In the case of a restructuring, it is the expected restructuring value that matters while in the case of a liquidation it is the expected liquidation value. These values are differently impacted upon by false positives and false negatives. A false positive refers to a situation where the decision-maker is of the opinion that the time for commencement has come but, in reality, this is not (yet) the case. A false positive, in other words, means opening the proceeding too early. This can apply to both restructuring and liquidation proceedings. A false negative, on the other hand, describes a situation where the decision-maker concludes that it is not (yet) time to start the proceeding but, in fact, the time has arrived. A false negative, hence, denotes commencing a proceeding too late. Again, this applies to both restructuring and liquidation proceedings.

In the following, the costs of opening restructuring and liquidation proceedings too early or too late will be investigated in turn. This will be done under the assumption that these types of proceedings achieve what they are supposed to achieve.[64] Hence, it will be assumed that a restructuring proceeding achieves a cost-effective restructuring of the financial structure of the company and, if necessary, a readjustment of the business. Likewise, it is presumed that a liquidation proceeding winds down the business and distributes the resulting funds in a cost-effective way to the creditors according to their rank in insolvency. Applying the residual claimant principle, it is further assumed that both restructuring and liquidation proceedings generally have a creditor-centric governance.

Against this background, what are the costs of opening restructuring proceedings too early? This will trigger direct procedural costs such as court fees and advisory fees for the company and the affected stakeholders. It may also cause indirect insolvency costs due to a potentially negative signal to the market as regards the solvency of the company. However, given that the proceeding will likely end quickly and without much effect due to its too early commencement, these costs will generally be lower. What are the costs of opening restructuring proceedings too late? This course of action risks losing restructuring value. This loss will be particularly high if the late opening makes the restructuring unfeasible and, ultimately, leads to liquidation. This may be due to the market of suppliers and customers having lost trust in the business or the economic substance of the business having eroded due to the lack of finance.[65] In comparison,

[64] For an approach using option theory to design claims and decision rights in insolvency proceedings, see Boone and Casey, 'A Primer on Option Valuation in Restructuring' (n 40) 7 ff.

[65] ie, financial distress has led to economic distress; on this, see Baird, 'Bankruptcy's Uncontested Axioms' (n 52) 580 ff.

the cost of opening a restructuring too late will generally be higher than starting a restructuring too early. Put differently, a false negative is more costly than a false positive in the case of opening restructuring proceedings. It follows that, if in doubt, restructuring proceedings should be opened too early. The term 'in doubt' refers to the uncertainty in determining the expected business value in the restructuring. Such uncertainty can also take the form of differing valuations by different relevant stakeholders.[66]

Turning to liquidation, what are the costs of opening such proceedings too early? This means that the business is wound up, ie, liquidated in the sense of selling the assets and turning them into liquid cash. If this happens too early, then an efficient, ie, socially optimal, chance of restructuring the business was present and has been lost. Given the generally wide spread between the restructuring value of a business and its liquidation value, this loss of opportunity comes at a high cost. Commencing a liquidation too late, on the other hand, only means that instead of being liquidated at the right time the business is liquidated too late. Given the typically low payouts in liquidations,[67] such losses are generally smaller than the loss of the restructuring value in cases of opening liquidation too early. Hence, for liquidation the false positive is more costly than the false negative. Normatively, this means that, if in doubt, liquidation proceedings should be opened too late.[68]

Reconstructing existing insolvency laws along these lines confirms the normative pattern developed. Taking English law as an example, the opening of restructuring proceedings is facilitated at an early point in time, favouring the risk of early over late commencement. Restructuring plans under CA 2006, Part 26A, require 'that the company has encountered, or is likely to encounter, financial difficulties that are affecting, or will or may affect, its ability to carry on business as a going concern'.[69] A scheme of arrangement under CA 2006, Part 26 does not require any financial condition for its commencement according to the statutory rules in Part 26. Instead, it is left to the creditors voting on the scheme and the court approving it to consider whether the financial state of the company justifies a scheme of arrangement. Quite the opposite applies for liquidation proceedings under English law. As explained, directors are not required to apply for a winding-up at the onset of balance sheet insolvency (neither in its economic nor its legislated form,[70] which occurs later) under English law. Instead, only at the very late point of 'no reasonable prospect that the company would avoid going into insolvent liquidation or entering insolvent administration' are directors put under pressure to act, and even then, such action does not necessarily mean applying for liquidation.[71]

[66] On this see, eg, K Ayotte, 'Disagreement and Capital Structure Complexity' (2020) 49 *Journal of Legal Studies* 1.

[67] See F Steffek, *Gläubigerschutz in der Kapitalgesellschaft* (Tübingen, Mohr Siebeck, 2011) 235 f, reporting payout rates for unsecured creditors of private companies in England and Germany in liquidation between 2% and 7% in the period 1995 to 2007.

[68] Again, the term 'in doubt' refers to the uncertainty in determining the expected business value.

[69] CA 2006, s 901A(2).

[70] In IA 1986, s 123(2).

[71] K van Zwieten, *Goode on Principles of Corporate Insolvency Law*, 5th edn (London, Sweet & Maxwell, 2018) 14–47.

D. Classes of Creditors

Some, but not all companies have complex debt structures with different classes of creditors. Using proprietary and contractual means, the creditors and the company (and perhaps the group it is a part of) can create layers of creditor classes with different priorities as regards their claims on the assets.[72] First and second lien, mezzanine debt and subordinated debt as well as intercreditor agreements are just some of the means used to assign different ranks in insolvency. Distinguishing different ranks of creditors allows a more fine-grained determination of the residual claimant.[73] A secured creditor whose security covers the entirety of their claim is not a residual claimant, even if the company's liabilities exceed the value of the assets.[74] Insofar as the value of the security does not cover the secured creditor's claim they are, however, an unsecured creditor.

Some priorities between creditors are created by statute, for example the elevation of preferential unsecured creditors above the company's general unsecured creditors.[75] If the preferential creditors are all paid while the general unsecured creditors only receive a fraction of their nominal claims, then the preferential creditors are not residual claimants while the general unsecured creditors are. Some of the preferential unsecured creditor classes are privileged by legislation since the relevant creditors do not have the information or capacity to negotiate for their own, socially desirable protection. This applies, for example, to the preferential status of employee claims.

Against the background of the possibility of complex debt structures where only specific classes of creditors are the residual claimants, the question arises whether and, if so, how this should be reflected in the governance of opening insolvency proceedings. An argument for such reflection is the residual claimant class's incentive for opening the proceedings at the right time. However, there are a number of relevant arguments against distinguishing different classes of creditors in the framework of public ordering. As explained for the employees' claims as preferential unsecured claims under English law, different classes of creditors have different capacities and incentives to monitor the company and to open proceedings. Assigning exclusive commencement powers to a class with weak monitoring capacity and incentives risks late commencement, which is especially harmful for restructurings. A legislative challenge would be that the same class of creditors may be in a good position to apply for proceedings in one company and in a weak position in another company. This is an argument for public ordering to only provide a basic framework for the opening of insolvency proceedings, avoiding the exclusion of those creditor classes that are strong monitors. Also, if it is correct, as argued above,[76] that restructuring proceedings should, if in doubt, be opened too early, then it might be the better option to draw the circle of creditor classes with the power to

[72] Ferran, Howell and Steffek, *Principles of Corporate Finance Law* (n 29) 341 f; Ayotte, 'Disagreement and Capital Structure Complexity' (n 66).

[73] On the definition of residual claimant employed in this chapter, see above under II.A.

[74] J Armour, A Hsu and A Walters, *The Impact of the Enterprise Act 2002 on Realisations and Costs in Corporate Rescue Proceedings: A Report Prepared for the Insolvency Service* (December 2006) 5.

[75] See the categories of preferential debts in IA 1986, s 386.

[76] Under section II.C.

open restructurings too widely rather than too narrowly. Further, at the point of opening proceedings, it is often uncertain in which class of creditors exactly the value breaks, ie, which class is the residual claimant at the relevant time.

This background may explain why most insolvency systems solve the issue of the role of classes of creditors in the commencement of proceedings not on the side of the creditors' standing to apply but on the side of their position and voting power within the proceedings. A scheme of arrangement, for example, may be applied for by the company, any creditor or member of the company and, if applicable, the liquidator or administrator,[77] but then requires different meetings and votes of different classes of creditors (and the members, if affected).[78] The general approach of legislatures and courts – in particular for restructuring proceedings – to require a better result for the creditors in the specific proceeding than in the next best alternative proceeding, in addition creates a disciplining effect at the point of applying for the opening of the proceeding.

While there may be scope for a more differentiating public ordering approach as regards different classes of creditors, given the space limitations of this chapter this is not explored further. Such investigation would also need to consider, whether there is a case for efficient private ordering, possibly supported by public ordering, given the elaborate clauses concerning the opening of insolvency proceedings found in some intercreditor agreements.[79]

E. Summary

The residual claimant principle provides a useful starting point for designing the governance of the solvent and the insolvent company. In particular, it supports the distribution of the rights and duties as regards the opening of insolvency proceedings in the form of restructuring and liquidation proceedings. However, due to the differing upside potential of shareholders (unlimited) and creditors (limited), a deviation from strict application of the residual claimant principle is recommended in that a shareholder-centric governance should remain in place for some time after the onset of balance sheet insolvency. Only when the expected business value under creditor control exceeds the value under debtor control has the right time arrived to switch to a creditor-centric governance. Differentiating further, the differences in costs generally caused by opening a restructuring or a liquidation too early or too late suggest that restructurings, if in doubt, should be opened too early while liquidations, if in doubt, should be opened too late. The term 'in doubt' refers to the uncertainty in determining the expected business value. While there might be scope to further differentiate between different classes of creditors in the public ordering of the opening of proceedings, possibly facilitating private ordering, there are good reasons why many jurisdictions draw the circle of potential applicants wider rather than narrower.

[77] CA 2006, s 901C(2).

[78] CA 2006, ss 896(1), 899(1); *Re Hawk Insurance Co Ltd* [2001] EWCA Civ 241; *Sovereign Life Assurance Company v Dodd* [1892] 2 QB 573 (CA); *Re Telewest Communications plc* [2004] EWHC 924 (Ch).

[79] *cf* the Intercreditor Agreement templates offered by the Loan Market Association.

III. Normative Framework for Directorial Responsibility

A. Policy Aims

What follows from the general normative framework for the opening of insolvency proceedings developed above for the optimal design of directorial responsibility in financial distress? Since directors, as corporate insiders, are in the best position as regards information and decision-making, they should play a key role in ensuring that insolvency proceedings are commenced at the right time. The policy aim is for directors to contribute to starting restructuring proceedings when the expected restructuring value under debtor control is lower than the expected restructuring value under creditor control. If in doubt, such commencement should happen too early. Liquidation proceedings should be opened when the expected liquidation value under debtor control is lower than the expected liquidation value under creditor control. Unlike restructuring proceedings, directors should contribute to this, if in doubt, too late.

Policy-making concerning the responsibility of directors also needs to address the harmful incentives created by deviation from the residual claimant principle. While it is conceptually desirable to leave a debtor-centric – ie, shareholder-centric – governance in place after the onset of balance sheet insolvency until the expected business value under debtor control is lower than under creditor control, both shareholders and directors are exposed to increasing value-destructive incentives in this phase. Some essential incentives have already been introduced.[80] Directors may linger for resurrection, gamble for resurrection or give value away, without a legitimate reason, to preferred recipients. The common characteristic identified for such undesirable actions is that a manager taking decisions in the interests of creditors would not have made such choices. Another way to formulate this policy goal is to avoid value losses due to deviation from a collective solution of financial distress.[81] A more recent article has shown that such governance costs can have two essential sources: conflict of interests and lack of competence.[82]

B. Commencing Restructuring Proceedings

What is the current framework to ensure that restructuring proceedings commence when the expected restructuring value under creditor control is higher than the expected restructuring value under debtor control? Starting with private ordering, directors have the incentive to commence restructuring proceedings at the right time if they come with the promise of allowing the director to remain in place such that they can continue to

[80] Above under section I.A.

[81] A theme present in the seminal book on *The Logic and Limits of Bankruptcy Law* by TH Jackson (n 11).

[82] Z Goshen and R Squire, 'Principal Costs: A New Theory for Corporate Law and Governance' (2017) 117 *Columbia Law Review* 767 (the article addresses the solvent business, but the insights are equally applicable to the insolvent business).

enjoy the private benefits of their position. English law facilitates this by offering formal restructuring proceedings in addition to private workouts that do not require replacing the directors with an insolvency practitioner. This applies for restructuring plans under CA 2006, Part 26A, schemes of arrangement under CA 2006, Part 26 and company voluntary arrangements under IA 1986, Part 1. In addition, restructuring proceedings often come with the expectation of profits for equity investors, which indirectly encourages directors to maximise such profits.

Creditors can play an important role in commencing such proceedings if they have the necessary information and incentives to play an active part in monitoring the company and, if necessary, commencing restructuring proceedings. The latter can happen either by the creditors acting within their own procedural rights,[83] or by the creditors collaborating with, or even pressuring, the directors where they are not equipped with the right to trigger a proceeding in law.[84] Creditor-led commencement faces two significant barriers. It will not happen if the creditors, as company outsiders, do not succeed in acquiring the necessary information. It will also fail if the gain expected in actively engaging in gathering information and starting the restructuring proceeding is lower than the expected cost of doing so. Usually only institutional creditors, such as professional providers of credit in the form of bank or private credit,[85] take an active role in opening restructuring proceedings.

In summary, the initiative of directors and creditors to open restructuring proceedings fails when directors are not moved by the incentive to remain in post or maximise the shareholders' profits and creditors do not engage due to a lack of information or lack of expected benefit. There are manifold scenarios which are characterised by this description. To name just one, such a setting occurs when directors do not have the required competence and there is no controlling creditor in place. With private regulation leading to suboptimal outcomes in a relevant number of cases, there is, hence, a case to explore public intervention.

Insolvency law policy-making and scholarship has for a long time struggled with the public regulation of such scenarios. More recently, the EU Directive on Restructuring and Insolvency[86] requires that debtors have access to early warning tools, which can detect circumstances that could give rise to a likelihood of insolvency and can signal the need to act. The idea is that such early warning tools might include (i) alert mechanisms when the debtor has not made certain payments, (ii) advisory services by public or private organisations, and (iii) incentives for third parties with relevant information about the debtor, such as accountants, tax and social security authorities, to flag to the debtor a negative development.[87]

[83] This applies to restructuring plans, CA 2006, s 901C(2)(b), and schemes of arrangement, CA 2006, s 896(2)(b).

[84] Such as in the case of company voluntary arrangements, IA 1986, s 1(1).

[85] For an overview of the providers of debt finance, see Ferran, Howell and Steffek, *Principles of Corporate Finance Law* (n 29) 335.

[86] Directive (EU) 2019/1023 of the European Parliament and of the Council of 20 June 2019 on preventive restructuring frameworks, on discharge of debt and disqualifications, and on measures to increase the efficiency of procedures concerning restructuring, insolvency and discharge of debt, and amending Directive (EU) 2017/1132 (Directive on Restructuring and Insolvency) [2019] OJ L172/18.

[87] Directive on Restructuring and Insolvency, art 3(2).

Such access to early warning tools, while to be supported, is, however, not sufficient to solve the failure of private ordering identified. The warning tools envisaged by the Directive are not specific to the value of the business at hand. They do not require the directors to meaningfully engage with the specific factors that are relevant for the liquidity and success of their particular company. Also, the warning tools do not provide an impulse for specific action. They will, therefore, not lead to meaningful action where directors are not competent enough or too conflicted to act.

Against this background, the following three directorial duties are suggested for introduction to English law by way of statutory reform: express duties (i) to identify and document the operational and financial factors relevant for insolvency before financial distress sets in, (ii) to establish a company-specific early warning system based on these factors, and (iii) to comply when an early alert is triggered (by initiating restructuring activity) or explain. Since these duties concern directors who would otherwise fail to commence restructuring proceedings at the right time, they should be laid down expressly in the law as opposed to being read into the existing directors' duties by way of interpretation. Express regulation leads to more visibility and enforcement.

The duty to identify and document the operational and financial factors for insolvency before financial distress sets in ensures that directors engage with the specific risks of their individual company. The requirement to document these risks guarantees that directors think these risks through in a meaningful way. The duty to establish early warning systems based on these factors is inspired by the EU Directive but improves on the warning system by connecting it to the specific risk factors at play. The third element, finally, the duty when an early alert is triggered to comply (by initiating restructuring activity) or explain provides a significant impulse to directors to not only register the alert but to take the next step and take appropriate action (or explain why no action is taken). This includes engaging with contractual workouts and the different types of formal proceedings available. While these three duties tighten public regulation of directors' duties in financial distress, they do not go beyond the best practice that should anyway be followed by the board. They do not, therefore, create inefficient costs.

C. Commencing Liquidation Proceedings

Liquidation proceedings should be commenced when the expected liquidation value under creditor control exceeds the expected business value under debtor control. If in doubt, this should happen later rather than earlier. The corporate insiders, shareholders and directors, have little intrinsic incentive to commence liquidation proceedings at the right time. First, such proceedings have the effect that the creditors and the insolvency practitioner take over the governance of the company and in many cases oust the directors. This holds true in English law independently of whether the proceeding is an administration,[88]

[88] IA 1986, Sch B1, para 61. Under this provision, the administrator may leave a director of the company in place, but the director can be removed by the administrator, and the administrator has superior powers of administration.

a creditors' voluntary winding up[89] or a compulsory winding up.[90] Second, a liquidation usually does not promise any payouts to the shareholders.

Public ordering traditionally reacts to this by providing the creditors and possibly other third parties with the right to apply for liquidation proceedings in addition to the powers of the corporate insiders to open them. As mentioned above, IA 1986, sections 124 and 124a provide not only the directors and shareholders[91] but also the creditors and the Secretary of State with the right to petition for the opening of a winding up. Such or similar powers for outsiders, in particular creditors, to trigger liquidation proceedings on the condition that certain insolvency grounds are present can be found in all advanced insolvency laws.[92] They suffer, however, from the fundamental weakness of relying on company outsiders who do not have access to meaningful financial information, unless negotiated for and complied with, and who, in addition, often suffer from rational apathy to act upon it.

In response to this weakness, some jurisdictions, as mentioned above,[93] impose duties on directors to apply for liquidation proceedings when a certain financial state (insolvency ground) is met. English law does not mandate directors to open liquidation proceedings expressly. However, it exerts indirect pressure to do so via rules and legal principles holding directors to account for their actions in the context of the company's financial distress. Under IA, section 214, directors are held liable for the creditors' losses if they do not take 'every step with a view to minimising the potential loss to the company's creditors' when there is 'no reasonable prospect that the company would avoid going into insolvent liquidation or entering insolvent administration'. This leaves open the possibility of other action, but it might come to the point when applying for liquidation is the only or one of a few alternatives that avoids liability.[94]

Other statutory rules and principles exert further pressure on directors towards commencing liquidation proceedings. The Company Directors Disqualification Act (CDDA) 1986 sanctions wrongful trading[95] and insolvent trading[96] by way of disqualification and civil liability.[97] The line of case law following *West Mercia Safetywear*,[98] more recently fundamentally considered by the UK Supreme Court in *Sequana*,[99] requires directors to consider the interests of creditors as part of their directorial duties. Neither the CDDA 1986 nor case law expressly requires directors to apply for the opening of

[89] IA 1986, ss 100 ff.
[90] IA 1986, ss 135 ff; *Measures Bros Ltd v Measures* [1910] 2 Ch 248.
[91] Under certain conditions laid down in IA 1986, s 124(2).
[92] For a comparative overview, see Steffek, 'Insolvency (Corporate)' (n 53).
[93] Under section I.D.
[94] *Re Welfab Engineers Ltd* [1990] BCLC 833, 837; PL Davies, 'Directors' Creditor-Regarding Duties in Respect of Trading Decisions Taken the Vicinity of Insolvency' (2006) 7 *European Business Organization Law Review* 301, 314; AR Keay, 'What Future for Liquidation in Light of the Enterprise Act Reforms?' [2005] *Journal of Business Law* 143, 156; S Griffin, *Personal Liability and Disqualification of Company Directors* (Oxford/Portland OR, Hart Publishing, 1999) 75 f.
[95] CDDA 1986, s 10.
[96] Under the general provisions concerning unfitness in CDDA 1986, ss 6, 7.
[97] CDDA 1986, 15A.
[98] *West Mercia Safetywear Ltd v Dodd* [1988] BCLC 250.
[99] *BTI 2014 LLC v Sequana SA* [2022] UKSC 25.

liquidation proceedings. However, the worse the financial state of the company the fewer alternative actions to an application may be available, such that, in practice, the commencement of liquidation may be the only alternative left to avoid liability at some point.

In essence, no further public ordering (in addition to wrongful trading under IA 1986, section 214, the *West Mercia* line of cases, the CDDA 1986 and other functionally similar rules and principles[100]) is required for English law in order to motivate directors to commence liquidation proceedings. However, the law should be streamlined and the regulatory messages to directors could be clarified. To give an example, the *West Mercia* line of cases has seen a development both in doctrine and practical relevance that was not envisaged when wrongful trading under the Insolvency Act 1986 was legislated for. Liability under the *West Mercia* principle starts much earlier than that under IA 1986, section 214.[101] A further example concerns the question whether the damage caused by directors shall be paid to the company (as required under *West Mercia* and IA 1986, section 214) or whether it can also be paid to specific creditors (as possible under CDDA 1986, section 15B).[102]

In summary, the rules and principles concerning directors' duties in the context of company financial distress are not well coordinated. In the context of this investigation, it is recommended to clarify in the express language of the law when the commencement of insolvency proceedings is mandated and what the consequences are if this is omitted. In particular, directors of micro and small companies, who do not benefit from comprehensive accounting and legal advice, need clear legal guidance. The current formulation in IA 1986, section 214 to take 'every step with a view to minimising the potential loss to the company's creditors' is useful as it identifies the goal. It would, however, be better to complement it with a provision clarifying that an insolvency proceeding should be commenced if that will maximise the expected value of the insolvent business.

D. Avoiding Value Losses and Deviation from Collectivity

Finally, solutions need to be found to avoid undesirable value losses due to deviation from the residual claimant principle, namely, when leaving a shareholder-centric governance in place for some time – led by the directors – even though the creditors have become the residual financial claimants. From a comparative perspective, most jurisdictions use a combination of legal strategies that can be described as constraints and information strategies.

In English law, constraints on directors come in the form of laws aiming to prevent directors from wrongful trading,[103] to make directors consider the interests

[100] Such as the liability for fraudulent trading in IA 1986, s 213, or the liability for misrepresentation and deceit in the context of a corporation's financial distress.

[101] See, eg, the discussion of the differing points in time in *BTI 2014 LLC v Sequana SA* [2022] UKSC 25, 94 (Lord Reed) and at 174 (Lord Briggs); also see the discussion in *Re BHS Group Ltd, Wright v Chappell* [2024] EWHC 1417 (Ch), [470] ff.

[102] For a detailed debate, see van Zwieten, 'Disciplining the Directors of Insolvent Companies' (n 57) 8 f.

[103] IA 1986, s 214.

of creditors,[104] to prevent unfit directors from managing companies[105] and to undo transactions that unfairly prefer some creditors over others or transfer value out of the company.[106]

Information is acquired through contractual clauses, in particular in loan contracts.[107] In addition, case law provides some basic protection in the form of liability for misrepresentation[108] and deceit.[109]

In overview, English law has the relevant elements in place to discipline directors while a debtor-centric governance is in place during financial distress. As with triggering liquidation proceedings, however, there is scope for improving coherence and clarity. That is beyond the scope of this contribution.

IV. Conclusion

This contribution has explained why the large majority of, if not all, insolvency laws deviate from a strict application of the residual claimant principle. A strict application of the residual claimant principle would require the commencement of insolvency proceedings with a creditor-centric governance immediately after the value of the company's assets falls below the sum of liabilities. This would conform with the principle that the governance focus should follow the residual claimant, as it is the residual claimant who has the strongest incentive to exercise governance rights efficiently. The reason for the deviation is the upside limitation of the creditors and the unlimited upside of the shareholders. The resulting incentives mean that there is a state of financial distress after the onset of economic balance sheet insolvency, in which the value of the business under shareholder control is still higher than the value under creditor control.

This contribution distinguishes the commencement of restructuring proceedings from the commencement of liquidation proceedings. It investigates the difference in costs – in the sense of value loss – in cases where restructurings and liquidations are commenced too early or too late. Since the costs of opening restructurings too late usually exceed the costs of opening them too early, it concludes that if in doubt such proceedings should be opened too early. For liquidation, the costs of commencing too late or too early present themselves vice versa. As a result, liquidation proceedings should be opened too late, if in doubt. 'In doubt', in both cases, is a short form for the uncertainty of determining the expected value of the business in a restructuring or liquidation at the time of opening. Such uncertainty can also take the form of differing valuations by different stakeholders. This chapter has also discussed whether the

[104] *BTI 2014 LLC v Sequana SA* [2022] UKSC 25; *Roberts v Frohlich* [2011] EWHC 257 (Ch); *West Mercia Safetywear Ltd v Dodd* [1988] BCLC 250.

[105] CDDA 1986.

[106] IA 1986, ss 239 ff.

[107] L Gullifer and J Payne, *Corporate Finance Law: Principles and Policy*, 3rd edn (Oxford, Hart Publishing, 2020) 215 ff.

[108] *Hedley Byrne & Co Ltd v Heller & Partners Ltd* [1964] AC 465; *Williams v Natural Life Health Foods Ltd* [1998] 1 WLR 830; *Lochgelly Iron and Coal Co v M'Mullan* [1934] AC 1.

[109] *Pasley v Freeman* (1789) 3 Term Rep 51, 100 ER 450 (KB); *Derry v Peek* (1899) 14 App Cas 337; *Lindsay v O'Loughnane* [2010] EWHC 529 (QB), [86]; *GE Commercial Finance Ltd v Gee* [2005] EWHC 2056 (QB), [96].

existence of different classes of creditors is relevant for the commencement of proceedings. While there are instances of private ordering addressing different creditor ranks, the initial case of public intervention based on different classes of creditors seems less strong. In particular, given the diversity of business and finance structures, there is a strong case for only more fundamental public ordering while leaving further differentiations to private ordering.[110]

As a consequence of deviating from the residual claimant principle in designing the commencement of insolvency proceedings, legal systems need to solve the problem of value-destroying incentives to directors and shareholders of companies in financial distress while they are still in charge of decision-making. The commonality of such rules and principles is the avoidance of value losses and of deviations from the collectivity of solving corporate financial distress.

Judging English law against this yardstick, this contribution argues for the introduction of three express directors' duties to support the commencement of restructuring proceedings at the right time, ie, duties (i) to identify and document the operational and financial factors relevant for insolvency before financial distress sets in, (ii) to establish a company-specific early warning system based on these factors, and (iii) to comply or explain when an early alert is triggered. A case is also made to improve the coherence and clarity of the rules and principles governing the commencement of liquidation and the protection against illegitimate and inefficient value losses under debtor control in financial distress.

[110] If necessary, supported by the public framework.

8

Freestanding Moratorium: Successes and Failures

NATALIE MROCKOVA

I. Introduction

The Corporate Insolvency and Governance Act 2020 (CIGA 2020) introduced many changes – some temporary, others permanent – to the English restructuring landscape. This chapter focuses on the new freestanding moratorium that was introduced in June 2020 with the intention of providing a breathing space in which distressed companies could consider options for corporate rescue without the need to give up control or enter costly formal proceedings. Section II considers the steps that led to the introduction of the freestanding moratorium. Section III then looks at how the new moratorium works and compares the law with the original proposals and similar rules elsewhere.[1] Section IV identifies and critically examines the limitations of the moratorium in practice. Section V concludes by considering how well the moratorium fulfils its goals. The analysis considers the formal law, the legislative history, and empirical evidence of the law's reception in practice, and compares the new procedure with English administration (a pre-existing domestic alternative), US Chapter 11 (the inspiration for many aspects of the new moratorium) and Chinese Reorganisation (a hybrid that combines many aspects of the above). Where appropriate, a comparison is also drawn with the European Preventive Restructuring Directive 2019/1023, which influenced the final version of the English freestanding moratorium in CIGA 2020.

This chapter considers three aspects of the moratorium debate: it explains the rules against the background of several rounds of consultation with stakeholders (sections II and III); it compares the English freestanding moratorium with other relevant procedures internationally (section III); and it identifies factors that limit its utility in practice (sections IV and V). These discussions help us better evaluate the successes and failures of the new moratorium, and reveal ways in which the law can be improved.

[1] The comparison is complicated by the fact that the other procedures – English administration, US Chapter 11, and Chinese Reorganisation – are all rescue proceedings rather than just standalone moratoria. Nevertheless, the Insolvency Service and the UK Government were influenced by these and other foreign procedures, and so it is still useful to consider them.

II. The Process Leading Up to the Freestanding Moratorium

The idea of introducing a new moratorium had been contemplated for many years. There were many discussions and several consultation rounds that eventually resulted in the freestanding moratorium introduced in CIGA 2020. Its introduction was accelerated – and perhaps rushed[2] – in response to the COVID-19 pandemic, in order to give debtors a chance to consider their options and thereby enable earlier, less complicated, and less costly corporate restructuring. English insolvency law already recognised and permitted moratoria under other procedures in the Insolvency Act 1986: interim and main moratoria in administration (in or out of court),[3] and a limited moratorium for small companies in company voluntary arrangements (CVAs).[4] However, research showed that the latter was a dead letter[5] (and so was repealed and replaced by the freestanding moratorium)[6] and the former (main moratorium in administration) is usually only available in larger cases due to its cost and complexity. Read together, the consultation documents present the new moratorium as ultimately aiming to provide a low-cost breathing space from creditors and other stakeholders for any company, in principle irrespective of its size,[7] that is struggling to repay its debts while it explores its options for moving forward. As we will see, this is very much consistent with recent corporate restructuring reform initiatives in other jurisdictions.

We, therefore, begin by looking at the process that led to the introduction of the freestanding moratorium in England – the motivation, its permutations, its changing aims, and the resolution of competing interests – in order to understand what had been considered and how we ended up with the current rules. This is a necessary first step that will enable us to critique the law in the later part of this chapter. This section considers the reform process in general. Section III then considers particular proposals in detail in the context of the competing views, comparisons, and the law as eventually codified.

The recognition of the importance of a rescue-oriented corporate insolvency regime dates back to 1982, when the influential Cork Report highlighted the perceived advantages of encouraging corporate rescue.[8] The Cork Review Committee were inspired by the recently enacted Chapter 11 of the US Bankruptcy Code 1978

[2] See sections IV and V for further discussion.

[3] Insolvency Act 1986 (IA 1986), Sch B1 paras 42–44.

[4] IA 1986, s 1A and Sch A1. This moratorium was available where at least two of the three conditions in s 382(3) of the Companies Act 2006 were satisfied, namely (i) a turnover of no more than £10.2 million; (ii) a balance sheet total not exceeding £5.1 million; and (iii) a maximum of 50 employees.

[5] Sandra Frisby and Adrian Walters, *Preliminary Report to the Insolvency Service into Outcomes of Company Voluntary Arrangements* (23 March 2011): https://papers.ssrn.com/sol3/papers.cfm?abstract_id=1792402.

[6] CIGA 2020, Sch 3 para 30. *Insolvency and Corporate Governance: Government Response* (BEIS, 26 August 2018) (Government Responses 2018): https://assets.publishing.service.gov.uk/media/5b8514ac40f0b67f45d1f233/ICG_-_Government_response_doc_-_24_Aug_clean_version__with_Minister_s_photo_and_signature__AC_final.pdf, at para 5.14.

[7] But see below about the limitations arising where debt market arrangements reach or exceed £10 million.

[8] *Report of the Review Committee on Insolvency Law and Practice* (1982) Cmnd 8558 (led by Sir Kenneth Cork) at para 193.

(Chapter 11) and rescue tools more broadly. The US mechanism could be initiated with or without the court's involvement and allowed the debtor to remain in control – an arrangement known as a debtor in possession (DIP). Although the Committee saw the advantages of allowing debtors to stay in charge of distressed companies, the DIP regime was not seen as appropriate for the UK in light of the scandals and corruption among liquidators and receivers in the 1960s and 70s that were the cause for the reform process in the first place.[9] In the end, the UK Insolvency Act 1986 adopted some aspects of the US regime, but a freestanding DIP collective mechanism with an effective stay on enforcement was not seriously considered in the UK until much later. This remained the case despite a wave of reforms introduced by the Enterprise Act 2002. Market players, therefore, started calling for even more profound changes that would bring the English regime closer to the US Chapter 11.[10]

The intention to introduce a freestanding moratorium that could enable a more efficient rescue regime was first announced in July 2010 when the Insolvency Service launched a consultation[11] about the existing restructuring regime and proposed a new moratorium to supplement England's restructuring tools for struggling (but not necessarily insolvent) companies. The report recognised that for many distressed companies, effective resolution and rescue are impossible because negotiations may fail or are complicated due to stakeholders holding out (often where the distressed debt was acquired for a quick return), lack of information about the identity of some of the creditors, termination clauses, and landlord repossessions of business premises.[12] These and other difficulties led the Insolvency Service to propose the introduction of a restructuring moratorium.[13] It would be based on the DIP (as in the US Chapter 11) with a supervisor, in order to provide a breathing space to enable the debtor company to negotiate with stakeholders and to reduce the tactical advantage of holdouts. The breathing space could also be used to reach a contractual compromise with creditors. It was hoped that the proposed mechanism would reduce the costs of administration and other more complex mechanisms by reducing the involvement of the court and insolvency practitioners (IPs), and by removing the multitude of steps and safeguards of the existing procedures.[14] It was hoped that by allowing debtors to remain in possession,

[9] For an excellent overview see Paul Omar and Jennifer Gant, 'Corporate Rescue in the United Kingdom: Past, Present and Future Reforms' (2016) 24 *Australian Insolvency Law Journal* 40.

[10] eg The European High Yield Association (EHYA), a trade association for the leveraged finance industry, wrote to the Treasury in April 2007 (and again several times after) calling for changes including the introduction of a moratorium that would allow for a DIP, a stay on financial creditors and cross-class cramdown: 'Rescue Culture and Chapter 11: The Path to Insolvency Reform?' (14 November 2008, accessed on 1 September 2009) at: http://www.internationallawoffice.com/newsletters/detail.aspx?g=1a783d5c-95b2-497a-a673-371cc8de7d08; and a letter from EHYA to the Treasury on 22 February 2008, which includes specific proposals for allowing the use of the proposed moratorium in CVAs.

[11] *Proposals for a Restructuring Moratorium – A Consultation* (July 2010) (IS Proposals 2010). The document is no longer available online. A summary is available at: https://www.wired-gov.net/wg/wg-news-1.nsf/0/C8C3097CBDBE1B608025776C003CA412?OpenDocument.

[12] ibid, at para 2.10 of the report.

[13] ibid.

[14] These safeguards primarily protect creditors by giving them (and the court) oversight and voting rights. Their removal is problematic, but in the end the government decided that it was important to balance creditor protection with desirability to enable early and cheaper corporate rescue. For more, see discussion in sections III.A, E, F, H and I.

directors might be incentivised to act early.[15] The proposed moratorium would last for three months and could be extended by a further three months. Similarly to the US Chapter 11, it would need to be sanctioned by a court to ensure that the business was viable. The scope of the proposed moratorium would be very similar to the existing small company moratorium in CVAs.

The 2010 proposal stirred a lot of discussion among IPs and stakeholders.[16] At the same time, consultations, working groups and reform committees started being set up across Europe and beyond.[17] Their work considered a new 'modular' approach to small companies,[18] ways of enabling rescue for companies with limited financial means,[19] and wide-ranging proposals by UNCITRAL and the World Bank.[20] The European Commission published its *Recommendation on a new approach to business failure and insolvency* (2014/135/EU) in March 2014[21] and the Commission then set up an Experts' Group on Restructuring and Insolvency in January 2016. These efforts eventually led to the adoption of the EU Preventive Restructuring Directive (2019/1023) (PRD 2019).[22] The Insolvency Service published its updated proposals in May 2016 (IS Proposals 2016),[23] in which it suggested the introduction of a broadly-worded moratorium and invited stakeholders to consider a number of updates to its original proposal in 2010. First, the moratorium would be obtained by filing the documents in court (not by court order) and any objections could still be made within 28 days. Second, it proposed that a debtor would be able to designate certain contracts as essential. Third, the onus would be put on the debtor to 'satisfactorily demonstrate that although it is experiencing financial difficulties, at the outset there is a reasonable prospect that a compromise or arrangement can be agreed with its creditors'.[24] Finally, directors' duties would remain the same, but directors would be protected from liability for wrongful trading during the proposed moratorium.

[15] In line with academic literature which predicts that allowing DIPs would encourage earlier intervention. See eg Andrew Campbell and Paula Moffatt, 'Early Intervention' in Matthias Haentjens and Bob Wessels (eds), *Research Handbook on Cross-Border Bank Resolution* (Cheltenham, Elgar Publishing, 2019).

[16] See eg the Insolvency Practitioners' Association responses and discussion papers between 2010 and 2018 at: https://insolvency-practitioners.org.uk/press-publications/corporate-insolvency/.

[17] For a useful summary, see: https://economy-finance.ec.europa.eu/system/files/2023-02/dp182_en_0.pdf.

[18] Ronald Davis, Stephan Madaus, Alberto Mazzoni, Irit Mevorach, Rizwaan Mokal, Barbara Romaine, Janis Sarra, and Ignacio Tirado, *Micro, Small, and Medium Enterprise Insolvency: A Modular Approach* (Oxford, Oxford University Press, 2018).

[19] eg the impetus for introducing the Small Business Reorganization Act of 2019 as Subchapter V of Chapter 11 USC.

[20] Both noted by the UK Government in its 2018 Response at para 5.3: World Bank's *Doing Business*; UNCITRAL Legislative Guide on Insolvency Law at: http://www.uncitral.org/uncitral/en/uncitral_texts/insolvency.html.

[21] Full text at: https://eur-lex.europa.eu/legal-content/EN/TXT/?uri=CELEX%3A32014H0135&qid=1719394767681 (European Recommmendation).

[22] Full text at: https://eur-lex.europa.eu/eli/dir/2019/1023/oj.

[23] *A Review of the Corporate Insolvency Framework*. All the documents are available at: https://www.gov.uk/government/consultations/a-review-of-the-corporate-insolvency-framework.

[24] *A Review of the Corporate Insolvency Framework: A Consultation for Options for Reform* (Insolvency Service, May 2016) (IS Proposals 2016): https://assets.publishing.service.gov.uk/media/5a816394ed915d74e33fdef9/A_Review_of_the_Corporate_Insolvency_Framework.pdf, at para 7.23.

The consultation ran from May to July 2016 and attracted 71 written submissions and two broadly representative roundtable discussions in June 2016. The *Summary of Responses: A Review of the Corporate Insolvency Framework* was published in September 2016 (IS Responses 2016).[25] It stated that

> [t]wo thirds of respondents who commented on this proposal agreed in principle that the introduction of a pre-insolvency temporary moratorium would facilitate business rescue. Stakeholders provided helpful feedback on the proposed length of the moratorium period, its supervision, and on suggested safeguards.[26]

The respondents called for stronger safeguards for creditors and clarification of key concepts and requirements, disputed the proposed length of the moratorium, and questioned the role of the court and secured creditors in the process.

The government published its official response in August 2018 (Government Responses 2018).[27] It promised to introduce a new moratorium that would 'give those financially distressed companies which are ultimately viable, a period of time when creditors (including secured creditors) cannot take action against the company, allowing it to make preparations to restructure or seek new investment'.[28] The new moratorium would encourage earlier intervention and would reduce the cost of obtaining protection[29] – in other words, it was intended to address the primary criticism levelled against the existing moratoria under pre-CIGA administration and CVAs. Many of the proposals had broad support, but several were strongly contested by respondents. Importantly, the government agreed that the moratorium should commence by the filing of documents in court; it rejected the idea that debtors could designate certain contracts as essential; and it proposed a different approach both to the relevant financial condition of the debtor for the use of the moratorium, and to the purpose of the proposed moratorium.[30]

In the end, the government fast-tracked the legislative process to deal with the COVID-19 pandemic and its consequences, and introduced the proposed changes through CIGA 2020. This did not allow sufficient time to think through the necessary compromises and consequences of the many exclusions and carve-outs that were inserted into the law. As we will see below, several solutions proposed in the Government Responses 2018 did not make it into CIGA or were altered at the last minute. Moreover, as we will discuss in sections IV and V, some compromises have clearly gone too far and reduced the value and utility of the new moratorium.

[25] Insolvency Service, *Summary of Responses: A Review of the Corporate Insolvency Framework* (September 2016), available at: https://assets.publishing.service.gov.uk/media/5a80d29940f0b62305b8d57f/Summary_of_responses_26-10-16_Redacted.pdf.

[26] ibid, at para 1.6.

[27] Government Responses 2018 (n 6).

[28] ibid, at 9.

[29] ibid, at paras 5.6 and 5.13.

[30] For a discussion see section III, below.

III. How does the Freestanding Moratorium Work?

In order to achieve its goal of providing a low-cost[31] breathing space with appropriate safeguards to all stakeholders, Parliament had to make a number of concessions and compromises. This section looks at the key features of the new freestanding moratorium and their evolution throughout the 2010, 2016 and 2018 consultations. It also compares these features with similar tools in other jurisdictions.

A. Control

One of the most revolutionary innovations of the freestanding moratorium is that it allows the debtor to remain in control of the company during the process, with the limited oversight of a 'monitor.' A DIP mechanism was viewed favourably by the Cork Committee in 1982, and stakeholders have been calling for a DIP mechanism similar to the US Chapter 11 ever since. Allowing the debtor company's directors to remain in charge (with some supervision as a safeguard) was envisaged throughout the consultation period and was generally welcomed by stakeholders.[32] The consultation respondents and the legislator all agreed that the DIP mechanism would be crucial in encouraging early intervention (as it would minimise or avoid the negative signalling and associated reputational risk to the directors) which was seen as key to a successful rescue.[33]

Nevertheless, it was also recognised that a DIP regime can be abused. Directors' incentive is to stay in control and continue to be paid, while shareholders' incentives are for the company to do well and for the creditors to be repaid in full. This can lead to a conflict of interests which, in the context of insolvency or financial distress, may encourage the directors to use the DIP regime to hold onto power as a delaying tactic where liquidation is inevitable; or they may refuse to acknowledge any problems until it is too late (where outside supervision may have enabled timely intervention and rescue of the company or its business). Consequently, it was accepted that further safeguards were necessary. The exact details of the DIP and supervision model were, however, developed over time in response to the numerous objections and suggestions from the respondents. In order to balance the interests of the debtor company and its rescue efforts on the one hand and the legitimate interests and expectations of the creditors and other stakeholders on the other hand, the directors and monitors were given certain rights and duties that would create a system of checks and balances while enabling the debtor to remain in charge.

It was agreed that directors would retain their normal powers and responsibilities[34] but with the added obligation of providing certain information to the monitor. This was enshrined in the law as a legal duty to provide information, and non-compliance

[31] In the end, it was decided that parties have to contractually negotiate the monitor's fees, following Government Responses 2018, at para 5.73.

[32] IS Proposals 2016, at para 7.40; Government Responses 2018, at paras 5.8, 5.59, 5.65–5.69, and 5.71–5.72.

[33] IS Proposals 2016, at para 7.6; Government Responses 2018, at para 5.6.

[34] IS Proposals 2016, at para 7.31.

would result in sanctions and potential termination of the moratorium.[35] A further safeguard took the form of imposing a duty on the debtor to seek consent from the monitor for numerous activities, including when directors obtain credit, grant security, and enter into other specified transactions.[36] Restrictions were also imposed on directors when making certain payments, and in the disposal and hire-purchase of property.[37] Moreover, the debtor must notify the monitor before filing a winding-up application or administration application, or appointing an administrator.[38]

The government also agreed to introduce an additional safeguard – besides the requirement on debtors to report to and seek consent from the monitor – by imposing new sanctions that were aimed at deterring abuse by dishonest or reckless directors, and sanctions for asset disposal outside the normal course of business without the monitor's consent.[39] The law, as implemented, imposes new sanctions for fraudulent behaviour occurring during or up to 12 months prior to the moratorium and for false representation in obtaining the moratorium.[40]

The initial proposals envisaged that – in order to incentivise directors to use the moratorium – directors would not be subject to the wrongful trading provisions under section 214 of the Insolvency Act 1986 so long as they continued to satisfy the eligibility criteria.[41] Respondents in the 2016 consultation process had mixed views about this and the consultation respondents in 2018 largely rejected this proposal as being unnecessary and unhelpful.[42] They argued that if the director could show they were genuinely trying to rescue the company, they could not be liable for wrongful trading anyway. This argument was accepted and CIGA 2020 does not contain such an exclusion.

The need for supervision of the debtor was also accepted from the beginning, but finalising the details was complicated. It was agreed that the supervisor would be called 'a monitor' in order to avoid confusion with other procedures. It was also agreed that the monitor would be an officer of the court,[43] which would empower them to deal with the stakeholders (as any wrongful interference with their work would constitute contempt of court) and also impose on them a duty to act honourably and fairly and be subject to the oversight and direction of the court.[44] This was seen as an important safeguard for suppliers and creditors.[45] Originally, it was thought that any IP, solicitor or accountant who met certain basic qualifying criteria could act as a monitor,[46] but the majority of respondents in the 2016 and 2018 consultation processes felt that only a qualified IP could act as a monitor, in order to encourage creditor confidence and

[35] Government Responses 2018, at para 5.66; IA 1986, ss A36 and A38.
[36] IA 1986, ss A25, A26 and A27, respectively.
[37] ibid, ss A28, A29 and A30, respectively.
[38] ibid, s A24(1).
[39] Government Responses 2018, at paras 5.44, 5.65 and 5.69.
[40] IA 1986, ss A38, A46 and A47.
[41] IS Proposals 2016, at paras 7.7 and 7.34.
[42] IS Responses 2016, at para 2.9; Government Responses, at paras 5.41–5.43.
[43] IA 1986, s A34 IA.
[44] Government Responses 2018, at para 5.72.
[45] ibid.
[46] IS Proposals 2016, at para 7.41.

ensure sufficient protection of all stakeholders.[47] As a result, only IPs are, at present, allowed to act as monitors in the moratorium,[48] although the government expressed its willingness to explore widening the scope of qualified persons 'as other professionals may develop a regulatory framework to address the fears of respondents'.[49]

The monitor has three main jobs: they have to (i) check that the application complies with the eligibility criteria, (ii) monitor the continued eligibility of the debtor company to use the moratorium, and (iii) consider the debtor's requests for certain activities such as obtaining credit, granting security, and applying for administration or winding up.[50] The exact details and evolution of the eligibility[51] criteria are discussed in section III.D, below, but in short, the monitor must provide an initial statement that the company is eligible (most importantly that it is, or is likely to become, unable to pay its debts)[52] and they are of the view that it is likely that the moratorium will result in the rescue of the company as a going concern.[53] Once the moratorium commences, the monitor is subject to an ongoing duty to monitor the debtor company's affairs to ensure that 'it remains likely that the moratorium will result in the rescue of the company as a going concern'.[54] In recognition of the need to keep the supervision light – and low-cost – the monitor is able to request and rely on information provided by the debtor company.[55] As mentioned earlier, directors must provide such information or else face liability and potential termination of the moratorium. If in doubt, the monitor can also apply to the court for directions.[56] The debtor is, therefore, subject to extensive supervision by the monitor; nevertheless, the monitor's actions can be challenged in court.[57]

Importantly, the monitor has a right and in some cases a duty to bring the moratorium to an end by filing a notice in court.[58] The notice to terminate the moratorium must be made where the monitor concludes that it is no longer likely to result in the rescue of the company as a going concern, that the objective of rescuing the company as a going concern has been achieved, that directors' failure to provide information makes him unable to properly act as monitor, or that the company is unable to pay the necessary defined debts.[59] This was seen as a crucial safeguard and one of the most important aspects of the role of a monitor during the consultation process.[60] In response to the fears that this would expose the monitor to litigation and potential liability (given the intended limited scope of their day-to-day involvement), the government concluded that they should get immunity from liability for erroneous termination so long as they

[47] IS Responses 2016, at para 2.17; Government Responses 2018, at para 5.60.
[48] IA 1986, s A54(1).
[49] Government Responses 2018, at para 5.60.
[50] This follows the recommendations in Government Responses 2018, at paras 5.31–5.34 and 5.65.
[51] Eligibility and qualifying conditions are dealt with together in this chapter. In CIGA 2020, the term 'eligibility' only refers to the company falling within a defined category listed in IA 1986, Sch ZA1.
[52] IA 1986, s A6(1)(c).
[53] ibid, s A6(1)(e).
[54] ibid, s A35.
[55] IS Proposals 2016, at para 7.42; Government Responses 2018, at para 5.65.
[56] IA 1986, s A37.
[57] ibid, ss A42 and A43.
[58] ibid, s A38(1). For more on termination of the moratorium, see section III.E, below.
[59] For details, see section III.F, below.
[60] Government Responses 2018, at para 5.67.

acted in good faith.[61] In the end, CIGA 2020 used slightly different wording, stating that the monitor's actions can be challenged in court by anyone 'unfairly harmed' by the moratorium[62] and that the court can confirm, reverse or modify the monitor's actions or make any such orders as it thinks fit,[63] but in doing so it must consider 'the need to safeguard the interests of persons who have dealt with the company in good faith and for value'.[64] Although the wording of the statute is quite convoluted here, the High Court provided guidance in 2022 in *Minor Hotel Group MEA DMCC v Dymant*[65] and basically affirmed the government's guidance in its 2018 consultation document. In short, it stated that the monitor has wide discretion to decide whether the conditions for termination are satisfied. Their decision would only be questioned if it was taken in bad faith or if no reasonable monitor could have reached the same conclusion.[66] This is a good approach that appropriately balances the need for court suspension with the desirability of certainty for IPS (and, in turn, low cost for the users of the moratorium).

The freestanding moratorium has some common features with 'light touch' administration where the administrators can permit directors to continue to exercise management powers under Schedule B1 paragraph 64(1) of the Insolvency Act 1986, as in the case of *Re Debenhams*.[67] Consequently, one might argue that an effective DIP regime already operates under English law. However, unlike in the new moratorium, the first step in the 'light touch' administration is still for an administrator to take over, before considering whether they have sufficient confidence in the existing management and handing some powers back to them. Moreover, the administrator is much more heavily involved in at least some aspects of the day-to-day management than is the case with monitors.

The freestanding moratorium was originally inspired by the US Chapter 11, but the supervision frameworks of the two differ in many aspects. Most importantly, Chapter 11 is subject to heavy supervision by the court – which leads to greater cost (and often also longer duration). A supervisor ('a trustee') can be appointed by the court where the latter finds that 'cause' exists in affecting the rights of relevant stakeholders; such a trustee then supervises the debtor more closely.[68] However, the new moratorium is similar to the recently implemented Subchapter V of US Chapter 11, which is aimed at small business reorganisations.[69] In that procedure, the process is controlled by a supervising trustee throughout.

Halfway between, with aspects of both English administration and US Chapter 11, lies the Chinese Reorganisation regime under the Enterprise Bankruptcy Law 2006 (EBL). It allows for a DIP process, but the debtor remains under the extensive control of the administrator and the court. The details relating to power-sharing, the DIP regime,

[61] ibid, at para 5.68.
[62] IA 1986, s A42.
[63] ibid, s A42(4).
[64] ibid, s A42(7).
[65] *Minor Hotel Group MEA DMCC v Dymant* [2022] EWHC 340 (Ch). For a detailed discussion see section III.E, below.
[66] ibid at [22], relying on the interpretation of the word 'thinks' under IA 1986, Sch B1.
[67] *Re Debenhams Retail Ltd (in administration)* [2020] EWHC 921 (Ch).
[68] 11 USC § 1104(a)(1), (2).
[69] 11 USC § 1183; Edward Janger, 'The US small business bankruptcy amendments: A global model for reform?' (2020) *International Insolvency Review* 254 at 257, 263.

and administrator supervision are unclear, but in practice, the court is actively involved, which increases the cost (and duration) of the process.[70]

Ultimately, the purposes of US Chapter 11, UK administration and Chinese reorganisation restructuring, on the one hand, and of the freestanding moratorium, on the other hand also differ: each of the former is intended as a restructuring process which leads to the resolution of the financial distress. The freestanding moratorium, on the other hand, can be used merely as a temporary breathing space in which the company considers its options and there is no need to reach any particular conclusion or, indeed, propose or agree a restructuring plan.[71] Moreover, the control arrangements in the moratorium are broadly in line with the PRD 2019, which envisaged a DIP regime as an integral part of the preventive restructuring framework,[72] with explicit support for 'limiting the involvement of a judicial or administrative authority in a preventive restructuring framework to where it is necessary and proportionate'.[73] Given the focus on low cost and high speed, the comparatively more light-touch supervision and less involved role of the monitor seem justified.

B. Commencement Options

Initially, it was thought that the moratorium would need to be sanctioned by a court.[74] However, given the desire of the debtor company to reduce the cost and enable early intervention, it was concluded in later consultations and reflected in CIGA 2020 that the court would play a minimal role and most procedural steps would be left to the directors and the monitor.[75] As a result, the consultation papers and the legislation state that, in most cases, the freestanding moratorium will be triggered when the directors file the relevant documents at court – similarly to the out-of-court appointment of administrators, but without the need to provide prior notice to floating charge holders.[76] For companies that are incorporated under the Companies Act 2006[77] and not subject to an outstanding winding-up petition, the moratorium begins as soon as all the relevant documents are filed.[78]

However, respondents found it hard to agree on two further issues: creditors' right to challenge the moratorium, and the impact of a winding-up petition. There were many different views about how to deal with creditors' ability to challenge the moratorium, as is discussed in section III.I, below. In short, the Insolvency Service and the

[70] Arts 13, 73–74 and 89 of the Enterprise Bankruptcy Law 2006 (EBL). In China, stigma still plays an important role, which means that, in practice, the DIP process is not trusted even with the safeguards in place: Natalie Mrockova, *Corporate Bankruptcy Law in China* (Oxford, Hart Publishing, 2021) at section 4.3.2.6.

[71] *cf* the original proposals, which saw the moratorium as necessarily leading to an agreement or arrangement of some kind, and which were subsequently abandoned: see section III.D, below.

[72] PRD 2019, Art 5.

[73] ibid, Art 4(6).

[74] IS Proposals 2010. Cf IS Proposals 2016, at paras 7.13–7.15.

[75] IS Proposals 2016, at paras 7.13–7.15; IS Responses 2016, at para 2.4; Government Responses 2018, at paras 5.19–5.20.

[76] IA 1986, ss A3 and A7(1)(a).

[77] Overseas companies are dealt with separately: ibid, ss A5, A7(1)(c).

[78] ibid, ss A3, A6–A7.

legislator concluded that creditors could not question the moratorium itself – in order to ensure certainty and enable the directors and the monitor to get on with trying to find a solution to the debtor's financial distress. Nevertheless, several safeguards (discussed in detail in later sections) were included. First, the monitor would have to be satisfied that the company is likely to be rescued (which would be difficult without the agreement of key financial creditors). Second, certain debts (including, importantly, financial creditors' debts) would not be stayed. Third, creditors could question directors' and the monitor's actions during the moratorium, in court, in order to provide some accountability and oversight for creditors. Finally, the law would introduce new sanctions to punish directors' fraudulent behaviour and false representations concerning the moratorium.

Another disputed issue was the impact of an outstanding winding-up petition against the debtor company. The original proposal excluded cases where there was a pending winding-up petition, but many respondents thought that such an exclusion was unjustified and unnecessary, that its existence would not necessarily preclude successful rescue, and it could be abused as an indirect way of preventing a debtor company from making use of the new moratorium.[79] Therefore, it was agreed by the government that it should be possible to allow companies with pending winding-up petitions to have access to the new moratorium but only subject to certain safeguards that would prevent abuse and ensure the integrity of the process.[80] The consultation reports contain little detail, but, in the end, the legislative regime within the Insolvency Act 1986 seems to have found a good balance: if the debtor is subject to a pending winding-up petition, the debtor can only commence the moratorium if the court approves the application. The court will only allow the moratorium 'if it is satisfied that a moratorium would achieve a better result for the company's creditors as a whole than would be likely if the company were wound up (without first being subject to a moratorium)'.[81]

The High Court shed some light on this requirement in 2023 in *Re Grove Independent School Ltd*.[82] The Court was asked to approve a moratorium where the company was subject to a pending winding-up petition filed by HM Revenue & Customs (a creditor), on the basis that that the moratorium would enable the company to seek refinancing. Insolvency and Companies Court Judge Greenwood agreed that the Court has a discretion under section A4(4) of the Insolvency Act 1986 to allow the moratorium, and that the discretion was narrowed by the requirement in section A4(5). In order to determine whether a moratorium would achieve a better result for the company's creditors as a whole than would be likely if the company were wound up, he said it was necessary for the Court to first consider the likely outcome for creditors as a whole (1) where the moratorium was granted, and (2) where the moratorium was not granted. He went on to say that the relevant standard is one of it being 'likely', which is a higher bar than 'reasonably likely' in administration applications. In this context, the judge held, 'likely' means on the balance of probabilities and not simply a real prospect of success. On the facts, the company's

[79] See submissions reproduced in IS Responses 2016, at 288, 302, 379, 461, 480, 555, 623, and 630; and Government Responses 2018, at paras 5.21–5.22.

[80] Government Responses 2018, at paras 5.22–5.25.

[81] IA 1986, ss A4, A7(1)(b).

[82] *Re Grove Independent School Ltd* [2023] EWHC 2546 (Ch).

secured creditor, Lloyds Bank, confirmed its support for the application and said it would continue to provide financing facilities to the company during the moratorium. This appears to have been crucial in leading the judge to agree to grant the moratorium.

Once the monitor is satisfied that the qualifying conditions are met, they notify the registrar of companies and every creditor of the moratorium.[83]

In the context of commencement and creditor challenge, the freestanding moratorium is quite different from its counterparts. Other English procedures and those in the US and China all allow creditors to challenge the commencement of the moratorium in court. For example, in administration, creditors have a grace period when they can challenge the application prior to the granting of the main moratorium.[84] Moreover, creditors can also apply to the court to lift the moratorium.[85] In China, this is done by challenging the restructuring process itself since the moratorium is linked to the restructuring process.[86] Similarly, creditors can challenge in court Chapter 11 proceedings and thereby the moratorium (see below). Crucially, however, the alternatives are all full procedures where stakeholders' interests and entitlements are compromised. The freestanding moratorium, on the other hand, cannot do this. The different approach to creditors' ability to challenge the moratorium is, therefore, justified.

The commencement options are similar in out-of-court administration and Chapter 11, but different otherwise. English out-of-court administration served as the basis of the government's proposal for the freestanding moratorium in 2018, requiring the supervisor to file their consent to act and confirm that the company satisfies the eligibility test and qualifying conditions.[87] However, in-court administration still requires court approval as well. Administration has two types of moratoria: the interim moratorium commences when the company files a formal notice of its intention to appoint an administrator (having 10 days to appoint); the main moratorium then starts when the administrator is appointed. In the US Chapter 11, the procedure and the automatic moratorium commence concurrently, when the relevant documents are filed in court.[88] Similarly, in China the restructuring process and moratorium are tied together, but the procedure only begins once approved by the court.[89] Interestingly, in the US and China, the court may refuse the petition at the outset for cause, or convert it into liquidation straight away – a power that is absent in the English procedures.[90] These variations make little difference in practice where the moratorium is uncontested. However, where creditors or other stakeholders wish to challenge and terminate the moratorium, the highlighted differences make it comparatively more or less difficult, allow the stay to be lifted more or less quickly, and require different types of evidence. The freestanding moratorium is triggered automatically once the debtor files the documents in court – unless subject to a winding-up petition and subject to the monitor's confirmation that the qualifying conditions have been met – and lasts for the initial 20 days unless it is terminated or extended, as discussed in section III.E, below.

[83] IA 1986, s A8(2).
[84] ibid, Sch B1 para 44.
[85] ibid, Sch B1 para 43.
[86] See Mrockova (n 70) chapter 4, section 4.2.
[87] IA 1986, Sch B1 para 22; Government Responses 2018, at para 5.19.
[88] 11 USC § 362(a).
[89] EBL, Arts 19–20.
[90] 11 USC § 1112(b); EBL, Art 70.

C. Documents Required when Filing

It is clear from the discussion above that there was widespread support for the introduction of the freestanding moratorium but also fear of its abuse. Both in the 2016 and the 2018 consultations, stakeholders called for more safeguards to protect the interests of various stakeholders in the process. One of the ways that the government responded was by tightening the requirements of what the parties would have to provide in order to be able to gain access to the moratorium in the first place. The Insolvency Act 1986 requires two sets of documents: one from the directors and one from the monitor. Directors have to provide two statements: one saying that they wish to obtain a moratorium (similar to the statement in out-of-court administration that the company wishes to appoint an administrator and so begin administration), and another confirming that they are of the view that the company is, or is likely to become, unable to pay its debts.[91] The second set of documents must be issued by the (proposed) monitor. They have to confirm that they are qualified and consent to act as a monitor; that the company is eligible;[92] and that in the monitor's view it is likely that the moratorium may result in the rescue of the company as a going concern.[93] As we will see in the next section, it is the last two requirements that provide strong safeguards by making the monitor – an officer of the court – the gatekeeper for access to the freestanding moratorium.

The requirement that the rescue of the company as a going concern should be likely was inspired by the English administration, where the administrator is required to confirm that a purpose of the administration is *reasonably* likely to be achieved. One such purpose is saving the company as a going concern. However, the role of this purpose (saving the company as a going concern) is one of the main areas where the freestanding moratorium and administration differ: the former focuses only on companies that can likely be saved as a going concern, while the latter posits saving the company as a going concern as *only one* of the statutory purposes, but also allows for other outcomes. Indeed, the approach of the US and Chinese rescue procedures is similar to that of English administration. More about that – and eligibility criteria more broadly – in sections III.D and IV.

D. Eligibility[94]

There was a lot of discussion about which companies should be eligible to use the freestanding moratorium. In the end, the Insolvency Act 1986 limits access to the procedure through four key criteria. First, the company must be incorporated under the Companies Act 2006 or, if unregistered, it must at least be capable of being wound up under the Insolvency Act 1986 (the latter category includes some overseas companies)[95] and this fact has to be confirmed by the monitor.[96] As we already

[91] IA 1986, s A6(1)(a) and (d).
[92] See section III.D, below.
[93] IA 1986, s A6(1)(b), (c) and (e).
[94] Eligibility and qualifying conditions are dealt with together in this chapter. See n 51 above.
[95] IA 1986, ss A3 and A54(1).
[96] ibid, s A6(1)(c).

discussed in section III.B, which type of company it is and whether it is subject to a pending winding-up petition will determine the correct commencement procedure that needs to be followed (in or out of court). The remaining three criteria have been discussed extensively in the 2016 and the 2018 consultations and some of the legislative choices have been identified as limiting the utility of the new moratorium in practice.[97] We will now look at each of them in turn.

The second criterion relates to the financial state of the company's affairs. It requires that the directors confirm that the company 'is, or is likely to become, unable to pay its debts'.[98] The correct entry level was widely debated by the Insolvency Service, the government and the stakeholders who responded to the consultations. Both proposals in 2016 and 2018 envisaged as a threshold that the debtor 'is already or imminently will be in financial difficulty, or is insolvent'.[99] And each time, the respondents expressed a range of views, with no clear majority for or against the proposal. Several respondents thought that the moratorium should 'adopt' the test used in administration – 'is or is likely to become unable to pay its debts'[100] – while others thought that the proposed test would fail to encourage the directors to act early enough to enable the rescue of the company[101] which is the purpose of this moratorium (see below) and of the preventive rescue regime more broadly.[102] Some respondents also feared that the proposed wording 'could be mis-used by directors to delay an inevitable insolvency, increasing creditor losses in the process'.[103] There was also a discussion of the proper role of the moratorium in the context of existing procedures in the English restructuring landscape. The government recognised that analysing 'legislative frameworks in other countries reveals that there is no consensus position on the financial state in order to qualify for restructuring processes, including those jurisdictions with provision for a moratorium'.[104] In the end, the government was persuaded by those fearing misuse and by the need to encourage early intervention, and decided to exclude companies that were already insolvent.[105] Instead, the test would be 'one of prospective insolvency, that is, based upon the requirement that a company will become insolvent if action is not taken'.[106] As such, it was hoped the requirement would prevent abuse of the stay by healthy companies with relatively small or short-term issues (ie no prospective insolvency and merely in financial distress) but also encourage directors to act before actual insolvency arises (ie the goal of early intervention).

The law as implemented has moved away from the government's proposal in two important ways: first, it *does* allow insolvent companies to use the moratorium

[97] For a detailed discussion see section IV, below.
[98] IA 1986, s A6(1)(d).
[99] IS Proposals 2016, at para 7.18.
[100] IA 1986, Sch B1 para 11; IS Responses 2016, at para 2.6; Government Responses 2018, at para 5.26.
[101] Indeed, value may be maximised through sale of the business rather than restructuring in such cases.
[102] As embodied in eg the PRD.
[103] Government Responses 2018, at para 5.28.
[104] ibid, at para 5.27.
[105] ibid, at para 5.28.
[106] ibid, at para 5.29.

(through the wording of 'is … unable to pay its debts'[107]) and, second, it adopts the test used in administration, which focuses on actual or imminent inability to pay debts but does not consider the debtor's 'financial difficulties'. This is an interesting legislative choice given the discussion above and the fact that the 2018 proposal was much more closely aligned with Article 4(1) of the PRD 2019, which suggested that preventive restructuring frameworks should only be available to companies that are likely to become insolvent but not those already insolvent. Nevertheless, if we look at the purpose of the two sets of rules, the different approach makes more sense: Articles 1(1)(a) and 4(1) of the PRD 2019 state that preventive restructuring frameworks should aim to *prevent* insolvency while, arguably, the purpose of the freestanding moratorium in England is broader and is aimed at addressing not only prevention of insolvency but also restructuring of companies in financial difficulties more broadly. This reading is supported by the other changes brought about by CIGA 2020 (eg the repealing of the CVA moratorium) and by the particular (during the COVID-19 pandemic) and general difficulty with drawing the line between advanced prospective insolvency and early actual insolvency. This problem can be nicely illustrated by the Chinese Reorganisation procedure: on paper, it requires that the debtor applying to restructure shows that the company is 'obviously likely to become insolvent'[108] (ie prospective insolvency) but in practice courts usually take a broader view and generally allow insolvent companies to use the reorganisation procedure too.[109]

A completely different approach was taken in US Chapter 11, which does not even have a requirement relating to the applicant's financial status; instead, it requires that the application be made in good faith.[110] Such an approach found little support in the English reform process and so was not adopted.

In the end, given the purpose and the intended role of the freestanding moratorium as both a standalone and add-on breathing space for struggling companies that can still be rescued, the departure from the early proposals and the clear divergence from the PRD and other jurisdictions make sense and can be justified.

The third eligibility criterion concerns the long-term viability of the debtor company. Such a requirement was envisaged as an optional feature of preventive restructuring frameworks in Article 4(3) of the PRD 2019. The Insolvency Service and government proposals in 2016 and 2018 envisaged that the onus would be put on the debtor to 'satisfactorily demonstrate that although it is experiencing financial difficulties, at the outset there is a reasonable prospect that a compromise or arrangement can be agreed with its creditors'.[111] This raised several issues. Firstly, there was a discussion about how easy it should be to satisfy this requirement, and the consensus was that the bar should be set high. As a result, the government proposed that the test should change from one of a 'reasonable prospect' of rescue to 'more likely than not'.[112] There was also a heated debate

[107] The term 'unable to pay its debts' has the same meaning as s 123 IA 1986 (s A54(1) IA 1986), but in administration the test is inability to pay the debts *as they fall due* – the latter part is missing in the new freestanding moratorium. See also discussion of this issue in *Minor Hotel Group* (n 65), discussed in section III.E.

[108] Art 2(2) EBL.

[109] Mrockova (n 70) at 123, 143.

[110] 11 USC § 1112(b)(1).

[111] IS Proposals 2016, at para 7.23.

[112] Government Response 2018, at para 5.31.

about whether creditors (or certain types of creditors) should have a say in the granting of the moratorium. The government overrode the calls for such creditor involvement on the basis of added cost and complexity and the fact that key financial creditors will need to be on board in any case in order for rescue to be 'likely'. Furthermore, the original proposal was for the debtor to show that the company satisfied the test, but the government in the end decided that the assessment would be made by the monitor, in order to safeguard creditors' interests.[113] Finally, the 2016 proposal suggested that the company would need to agree a compromise or make an arrangement with its creditors by the end of the moratorium period.[114] This condition makes sense when read alongside the original length of the moratorium. In the 2016 proposal, the moratorium would last for three months (plus a possible extension of three more months), which would give the debtor enough time to agree a compromise or make an arrangement with its creditors. However, when the 2018 proposal reduced the length of the moratorium to 20 days and clarified the role of the new moratorium as being a standalone breathing space to consider options rather than a procedure with a particular goal at the end, the requirement that the debtor would need to reach an agreement of any sort by the end of the moratorium was sensibly dropped as well.[115] The moratorium, as enacted, reflected these conclusions: the monitor must be 'of the view that it is likely a moratorium would result in the rescue of the company as a going concern'.[116]

Nevertheless, there remain many difficulties with this requirement. It is unclear how much work needs to be undertaken by the monitor when reaching this view. This is problematic, as it makes the extent of the role – and so the appropriate fees and likely exposure to liability – unclear. Some clarification was provided by the High Court in 2022 in *Minor Hotel Group MEA DMCC v Dymant*[117] in the context of termination of the moratorium (the case is discussed in detail in section III.E, below). In short, the monitor has a wide discretion and their conclusion will only attract liability if they acted in bad faith or no reasonable monitor could have ever reached the same conclusion. Moreover, the meaning of 'likely' is also unclear: is it the same, similar, or completely different from 'reasonably practicable' used in administration? This is an important question because the goal of rescuing the company as a going concern is a concept borrowed from Schedule B1 paragraph 3(1)(a) of the Insolvency Act 1986, which cites it as the primary objective of administration. It then goes on to say that the administrator may focus on the other, lower objectives if it is 'not reasonably practicable to achieve' the rescue of the company as a going concern.[118] As such, the concept of reasonably practicable has a standard meaning in English insolvency law, but the concept of likelihood – apart from understanding that it is a higher standard than reasonable practicability – does not. Moreover, it is also not entirely clear why there is so much focus on rescuing the company rather than the company or the business. While the rescue of the company may be an ideal outcome, excluding the rescue of the business makes the law

[113] ibid, at para 5.32.
[114] IS Proposals 2016, at para 7.13.
[115] Government Responses 2018, at para 5.16.
[116] IA 1986, s A6(1)(e).
[117] *Minor Hotel Group MEA DMCC v Dymant* (n 65).
[118] IA 1986, Sch B1 para 3(3)(a).

unnecessarily narrow. By contrast, there is no viability requirement in the US Chapter 11 or Chinese Reorganisation. We return to this point (with a suggestion that the scope should be widened) at the end of section IV.

Finally, the fourth criterion of eligibility is that the company is not excluded from the scope of the law under Schedule ZA1 of the Insolvency Act 1986. The moratorium, as enacted, excludes two broad groups of companies. Firstly, it excludes a company if 'at any time during the period of 12 months ending with the filing date' a moratorium was in force or the company was subject to an insolvency procedure,[119] unless a court orders that the previous moratorium should be disregarded.[120] This exclusion is broadly in line with the 2016 and 2018 proposals and has proved largely uncontroversial.[121]

The second set of exclusions is a list of certain types of companies for which the moratorium is inappropriate as a restructuring mechanism. They are, inter alia, insurance companies, banks, electronic money institutions, investment banks and firms, parties to capital market arrangements in an amount of over £10 million, payment institutions, recognised investment exchanges and clearing houses, and securitisation companies.[122] These exclusions were envisaged (and not questioned) throughout the consultation period[123] and are not uncommon in other jurisdictions. Indeed, the PRD 2019 envisaged and recommended that some of the companies on the list should be excluded.[124] Nevertheless, as discussed in section IV, some of these exclusions unnecessarily limit the availability – and so effectiveness – of the new moratorium and so should be reviewed.

E. Length, Extension, Continuation, and Termination

There was a lot of discussion about the appropriate length (and possible extensions) of the new freestanding moratorium. Initially, it was envisaged that the moratorium would last for three months, with the possibility of a further three-month extension.[125] This would have been in line with the PRD 2019 proposal that the stay should be up to four months and extensions should be allowed, but that the total length should generally not exceed 12 months.[126] However, the majority of respondents in 2016 and 2018 disagreed with the proposal, citing the need to lower the risk of abuse, ensure access to finance, and safeguard creditors' interests.[127] The respondents in 2016 made various suggestions, ranging from 21 days, or variable length depending on the size of the company, to more than three months if the moratorium was to be connected with a

[119] IA 1986, Sch ZA1 paras 2(1)(b) and 2(2)(b).
[120] ibid, Sch ZA1 para 2(1)(b) and s A42(6).
[121] IS Proposals 2016, at para 7.20; Government Responses 2018, at para 5.21. Note that the original proposals included a winding-up petition which has now been removed: see section III.B, above.
[122] IA 1986, Sch ZA1 paras 3–13.
[123] See eg IS Proposals 2016, at para 7.19, Government Responses 2018, at para 5.35.
[124] PRD 2019, recital 19.
[125] IS Proposals 2010; IS Proposals 2016, at para 7.35.
[126] PRD 2019, Art 6(6) and (8).
[127] IS Responses 2016, at para 2.13; Government Responses 2018, at para 5.8.

scheme of arrangement.[128] The government suggested that the ideal length would be 28 days.[129] In the end, the law adjusted the period further, to 20 *business* days,[130] but with the possibility to extend.[131]

The question of whether, how, and for how long an extension should be available also attracted a wide range of opinions. Initially, it was suggested that the moratorium could only be extended with the support of all secured creditors and more than half of all voting unsecured creditors by value.[132] The respondents, however, felt that this would give creditors too big a role to play. 58 per cent of respondents to the 2018 consultation process felt that the support of secured creditors should not be necessary; alternative views suggested that the majority of secured creditors (rather than all of them) should agree or that secured creditors could be crammed down by the court.[133] The majority of respondents in 2018 said that secured creditors should not have any control over an initial extension, and the government agreed, saying that the debtor should be able to extend the initial moratorium period by a further 28 days so long as the monitor confirms that the qualifying conditions continue to be met.[134] Any further extensions should then only be possible for larger, more complex debt structures and only with the approval of creditors (secured and unsecured, each by a majority by value)[135] or with court approval where seeking consent for an extension from creditors is impracticable.[136] The PRD 2019 also envisaged that it should be possible to extend the moratorium (in 'well-defined circumstances') and that this could be controlled or requested by 'judicial or administrative authorities, debtor, creditor or supervising practitioner'.[137]

In the end, the law incorporated much of the feedback and guidance above and created a detailed system for extending the moratorium. Initially, the directors can extend the moratorium by a further 20 business days (note the reduction from 28 to 20 days) without anyone's approval so long as they confirm to the court that they have paid all the relevant debts due and that, in their view, the company is, or is likely to become, unable to pay its pre-moratorium debts. This has to be accompanied by a statement from the monitor that, in their view, it is likely that the moratorium will result in the rescue of the company as a going concern.[138]

If the directors seek to extend the initial 20-day period by more than the permitted 20 days, they need authorisation from the creditors or the court. Where the directors seek permission from the creditors, they follow the same procedure as above but also have to include a statement that creditors' consent has been obtained and the revised end date for which that consent was obtained.[139] The relevant creditors that need to be

[128] IS Responses 2016, at para 2.14.
[129] Government Responses 2018, at paras 5.46–5.50.
[130] IA 1986, s A9(2).
[131] ibid, ss A10–A15.
[132] IS Proposals 2016, at para 7.36.
[133] IS Responses 2016, at para 2.15.
[134] Government Responses 2018, at paras 5.51–5.53.
[135] ibid, at paras 5.54–5.55.
[136] ibid, at para 5.55.
[137] PRD 2019, Art 6(7).
[138] IA 1986, s A10.
[139] ibid, s A11.

consulted are the pre-moratorium creditors whose debts are stayed and have not yet been paid in full.[140] Agreeing by a majority in value, they can extend the moratorium more than once so long as, in total, it does not exceed 12 months.[141]

Directors can also apply to the court to extend the moratorium. In that case, the directors have to confirm that they have continued to pay all the relevant (non-stayed) debts as they have fallen due, that the company is, or is likely to become, unable to pay its pre-moratorium debts, and whether pre-moratorium creditors have been consulted (and explain if not). The application also has to be supported by the monitor, who needs to confirm whether, in their view, it is likely that the moratorium will result in the rescue of the company as a going concern.[142] The court can grant the extension (focusing on the interests of pre-moratorium creditors and likely rescue of the company) or can make any other order that it thinks appropriate.[143] The court can extend the moratorium more than once and there is no maximum total period.

Given that the freestanding moratorium is not attached to any actual procedure and there is no particular expected outcome, the structure and length of the moratorium under Part A1 of the Insolvency Act 1986 is very different from other mechanisms. Under the English administration regime, there is an interim moratorium where the application has been made but the administration has not yet started, and a main moratorium from when an administrator is appointed until the end of the procedure (ie 12 months in the first instance, but extendable).[144] Similarly, in China there is an interim moratorium until an administrator is appointed and a main moratorium for the duration of the Reorganisation (ie six months, with a possible extension of three more months).[145] In US Chapter 11, an automatic stay is imposed from the filing of the petition until a restructuring plan is confirmed: the debtor has 120 days to make such a plan, and after 180 days creditors can propose theirs. Either period can be (and often is) extended by a court. The moratorium is in place throughout.[146] Consequently, the freestanding moratorium is the shortest moratorium amongst these mechanisms. This can be partly explained by the fact that the English freestanding moratorium has no defined outcome that the parties have to achieve. Nevertheless, it may be a bit too short.[147]

The law imposes a duty on the monitor to observe the debtor company and bring the moratorium to an end by filing a notice with the court[148] in four circumstances.[149] The first such situation arises where the company has been rescued. Second is where the monitor is unable to carry out their functions due to the directors' failure to provide necessary information.[150] The third is where the monitor thinks that

[140] ibid, s A12.
[141] ibid, s A12(3), in line with the PRD 2019 proposal.
[142] ibid, s A13(1)–(2).
[143] ibid, s A13(4)–(5).
[144] ibid, Sch B1 paras 42–44.
[145] EBL, Arts 20 and 75.
[146] 11 USC § 362(a).
[147] See sections IV and V for further discussion.
[148] The filing of this notice brings the moratorium to an end: IA 1986, s A38(3).
[149] ibid, s A38(1).
[150] ibid, s A36.

the moratorium is no longer likely to result in the rescue of the company as a going concern.[151] The fourth is where the monitor thinks that the company is unable to pay the debts that are not covered by the stay (ie moratorium debts or pre-moratorium debts without payment holiday[152]) and that have already fallen due.[153]

The duty to terminate was considered by the High Court in *Minor Hotel Group MEA DMCC v Dymant*.[154] The judge in this case was asked to provide more clarity about the degree of care and potential liability faced by monitors. It gives rise to some important issues in practice, since monitors are supposed to act as gatekeepers (by eg confirming the debtor's eligibility) and de facto supervisors (eg the debtor's continued compliance with certain requirements) whilst keeping their presence and services 'light-touch' – and relatively cheap. This creates uncertainty about what the monitors need to do to discharge their duties, which needed to be clarified. Sir Alastair Norris held that monitors have a lot of discretion when deciding whether the conditions for termination are satisfied, and that the only situations in which a judge would question the exercise of that discretion is where there is evidence that the decision was taken in bad faith or it was clearly perverse (in the sense that no reasonable monitor could have reached the same decision).[155] This is in line with the Government's 2018 proposal that monitors should get immunity from erroneous decisions relating to termination so long as they have acted in good faith.[156] When considering the duty to terminate where the company is unable to pay the relevant debts, the judge held that the court should *not* apply the same test as in administration under section 123 IA 1986 (the cash-flow insolvency test) because that test focuses on the debts as they fall due which 'introduces an element of futurity'.[157] Instead, the monitor needs to focus on present-day debts. That can be done by asking whether the debtor company 'has the immediate prospect of receiving third party funds or owns assets capable of immediate realisation'.[158] 'Immediate' was to be judged by the monitor using their 'commercial judgment … (as to which the monitor is allowed considerable latitude)'.[159] Finally, the judge also confirmed that the court has the discretion to intervene in the monitor's actions and make any provision it thinks fit under section A45(2) of the Insolvency Act 1986 (where the court is asked by any person affected by the moratorium to intervene) but that the discretion will be exercised subject to the 'balance of harm' consideration.[160] Given that in *Minor Hotel Group* no harm actually arose due to the non-termination of the moratorium, the Court refused to sanction the monitor or terminate the moratorium on the facts.

[151] ibid, ss A35 and 38(1)(a).
[152] See section III.F, below.
[153] IA 1986, s A38(1)(d).
[154] *Minor Hotel Group MEA DMCC v Dymant* (n 65).
[155] ibid, at [22], relying on the interpretation of the word 'thinks' under Sch B1 IA 1986.
[156] Government Responses 2018, at para 5.68.
[157] *Minor Hotel Group MEA DMCC v Dymant* (n 65) at [30].
[158] ibid at [33].
[159] ibid.
[160] ibid at [38]–[40].

Besides termination by the monitor under section A38, the restructuring moratorium will also be terminated upon entry by the debtor company into an insolvency procedure,[161] or by decision of the court.[162]

It is common in other jurisdictions for moratoria (and the restructuring processes to which they attach) to be terminable as well. In China, the administrator must ask the court to terminate the Reorganisation and the attached moratorium where the financial situation of the debtor company has worsened, which has made the rescue unlikely; where the debtor has acted fraudulently or otherwise wrongfully; or where the debtor's acts have made it impossible for the administrator to carry out their duty.[163] The court can also convert the restructuring into a liquidation (and so prevent the main moratorium from being triggered) at the initial hearing,[164] or if the debtor fails to submit a reorganisation plan within the relevant time frame.[165] This regime is, therefore, very similar to the English freestanding moratorium, except so far as the underlying processes differ (moratorium only vs moratorium coupled with restructuring).

The US Chapter 11 (and the attached moratorium) can also be terminated by the court in two situations. First, the debtor (when in control) can ask the court to terminate the procedure.[166] Or, second, 'any party in interest' can apply to the court to terminate the restructuring or convert it into Chapter 7 liquidation 'for cause'. The transfer into Chapter 7 can take place eg where there is a substantial or continuing loss to the estate and no reasonable likelihood of rehabilitation; gross mismanagement of the estate; unauthorised use of cash collateral that is substantially harmful to a creditor; failure to comply with filing and reporting duties; or failure to provide information.[167]

The PRD 2019 also highlights the importance of being able to terminate the moratorium.[168] The Directive says that the stay should be lifted (a) where it 'no longer fulfils the objective of supporting the negotiations on the restructuring plan', (b) at the request of the debtor or supervising practitioner, (c) where relevant creditors would be unfairly prejudiced, or (d) where it would lead to the insolvency of a creditor.[169]

Interestingly, the US and EU regimes give the power to apply for termination to creditors and other interested parties, while the English freestanding moratorium puts the monitor at the centre of the process. CIGA 2020 states that the monitor should apply for termination where the purpose has been achieved or become unlikely to be achieved, if the due payments have not been made, or if the debtor has failed to provide necessary information – ie a much more narrow set of circumstances than in the other procedures. This further reinforces the fact that the freestanding moratorium is there to provide a short-term breathing space in which the debtor, with some assistance from the monitor, should come up with a strategy for what to do next in order to save the

[161] IA 1986, s A16.
[162] ibid, ss A42, A44.
[163] EBL, Art 78.
[164] ibid, Art 70(1).
[165] ibid, Art 79(3).
[166] 11 USC § 1112(a).
[167] 11 USC § 1112(b).
[168] PRD 2019, Art 6(9).
[169] ibid, paras (a)–(d).

company, rather than actually start implementing any particular plan. If that is correct, then giving creditors and other interested parties only a very limited role in the process is more justifiable.

F. Scope

A moratorium can stay enforcement actions ('enforcement holiday') and debt repayment ('repayment holiday'). It is common practice for moratoria to impose both or some degree of both holidays. Indeed, the PRD 2019 states that certain claims may be excluded from the scope of the stay 'in well-defined circumstances, where such an exclusion is duly justified' and where (a) the enforcement is not likely to jeopardise the restructuring or (b) it would unfairly prejudice the creditors of those claims.[170] Although there was general agreement about the extent of the enforcement holiday in the consultation process that led to the implementation of CIGA 2020, there was a long debate about which creditors' claims should be stayed under the new moratorium, with a lot of pressure from certain stakeholders to be excluded from the stay.

The freestanding moratorium imposes a wide *enforcement holiday*. It prevents creditors from submitting a winding-up petition (only by directors), commencing of administration (only by directors) and appointing an administrative receiver.[171] Similarly, the moratorium prevents forfeiture of leases, repossession of goods under hire-purchase agreements and those under retention of title clauses, except where the court says otherwise.[172] Notably, the monitor has no such power. During the moratorium, the holder of an uncrystallised floating charge on the property of the company is prohibited from giving notice which would have the effect of either (i) causing the floating charge to crystallise or (ii) restricting the disposal of the property of the company.[173]

The scope of enforcement holiday under the freestanding moratorium is similar to other rescue tools in England and elsewhere. The moratorium attached to the English administration stays the enforcement of security and disallows the repossession of goods under a hire-purchase agreement and forfeiture except where permitted by the administrator of the court.[174] The US Chapter 11 provides a wide stay on enforcement of all judgments, collection activities, foreclosures and forfeitures, and repossessions.[175] The court may lift the stay to permit enforcement of security where, for example, the debtor has no equity in the property and the property is not necessary for effective restructuring.[176] China modelled its provisions on the US Chapter 11, and so its stay is also very wide. The court will only permit enforcement of security where the secured asset is at risk of being destroyed or its value is at risk of being reduced dramatically to the extent of impairing the rights of secured creditors.[177]

[170] ibid, Art 6(4).
[171] IA 1986, s A20.
[172] ibid, ss A21–A22.
[173] ibid, s A22.
[174] ibid, Sch B1 para 43.
[175] 11 USC § 362(b).
[176] 11 USC § 362(d).
[177] EBL, Arts 19 and 75.

The new moratorium also imposes a limited *repayment holiday*. There was a long debate about which debts should be excluded from the scope of the stay. It was understood from the beginning that the debtor would have to continue paying 'ongoing trading costs and debt obligations' during the moratorium.[178] The remainder of this section looks at the scope of the repayment holiday. The role of essential suppliers and financial contracts will then be dealt with in more detail in sections III.G and III.H below.

CIGA 2020 separated debts into three categories. The first category contains pre-moratorium debts without a payment holiday.[179] These are the debts that arose *before* the moratorium came into force or that arose from an obligation incurred before the moratorium came into force but which fall due during the moratorium *and* are of the type listed in CIGA 2020.[180] This includes the monitor's expenses and remuneration, goods and services supplied during the moratorium, wages or salary arising under a contract of employment, redundancy payments, rent, and debts or other liabilities arising under 'a contract or other instrument involving financial services'.[181] The last type of debt includes loan agreements, securities contracts, and financial leases, and is explored in detail in section III.G below. These are generally accepted as falling outside the scope of the freestanding moratorium. All other pre-moratorium debts fall into the second category and are stayed.[182] The third category consists of moratorium debts, which are debts arising *during* the moratorium, or after the moratorium but due to an obligation that was incurred during the moratorium.[183] The debtor must continue to pay pre-moratorium debts without holidays (first category) and moratorium debts (third category) throughout the freestanding moratorium.

These significant restrictions on the scope of the stay stand in contrast with moratoria elsewhere and make the English freestanding moratorium very unusual. The government planned to exclude financial contracts in another context – namely, when considering banning *ipso facto* clauses, which used to allow suppliers of goods and services to terminate their contract where the debtor entered formal insolvency[184] – but such an exclusion was never discussed in the context of the freestanding moratorium. As we will discuss in section IV, the extensive carve-outs are one of the main limitations on the practical utility of the new moratorium, because they limit the extent of the breathing space significantly and may mean that the debtors that would otherwise be willing to use the freestanding moratorium do not do so. And even in cases where debtors do use the moratorium, its assistance is only of limited use because the debtor has to continue to repay numerous creditors (ie it is a limited pay holiday) – which partly defeats the purpose of a moratorium in the first place.

[178] IS Proposals 2016, at para 7.11.
[179] IA 1986, s A18(3).
[180] ibid, ss A18(3) and A53(1).
[181] See ibid, Sch ZA2.
[182] ibid, s 18(3).
[183] ibid, s A53(2).
[184] Government Responses 2018, at para 5.102; now IA 1986, s 233B. For an in-depth discussion, see Kristin van Zwieten, 'Mid-Crisis Restructuring Law Reform in the United Kingdom' (2023) 24(2) *European Business Organization Law Review* 287.

G. Essential Contracts

There was a long and heated discussion throughout the consultation process about the special treatment and definition of the 'essential contracts' that could be locked in for the duration of the moratorium. This proposal was based on empirical evidence from 2013 which found that key trade suppliers withdrew their services during formal insolvency procedures in 41 per cent of cases, and 49 per cent of suppliers demanded 'ransom' payments to continue.[185] In recognition of this issue, the Insolvency Act 1986 was amended in October 2015 to ensure the continuity of supply of utilities and IT goods and services to insolvent businesses.[186] The 2016 Insolvency Service proposal expressed the government's view that, in order to enable effective rescue, the scope of protected contracts should be widened further, and proposed allowing debtors to designate some contracts as 'essential contracts'.[187] Such contracts, subject to safeguards, could not then 'be terminated or varied during a moratorium or subsequent CVA or administration'[188] and the supplier would have to continue the supply of goods or services so long as the debtor paid them on time and in full throughout the moratorium.[189] The decision about which contracts should be designated as essential would be made by the debtor when applying for the moratorium. It was recognised that such a designation would interfere with the freedom of contract, and so it should only be permitted where 'absolutely necessary'.[190] As a safeguard, the suppliers would be able to challenge such a designation in court.[191]

The 2016 consultation demonstrated a lot of disagreement about whether, how and who should be able to designate contracts as essential. The concerns were largely about the potential abuse of this power by the debtors (as such designation would become binding at the time of the filing, subject to any pending challenge), and that allowing contractors to challenge such designation was an insufficient and costly safeguard, and could overburden the courts.[192] A similar level of concern was expressed in the 2018 consultation. The respondents recognised that termination of key supplies (often through *ipso facto* clauses) is problematic, but this was overridden by their concern about the unfettered rights of directors to designate contracts as essential without any – court's or monitor's – oversight.[193] The government considered all the arguments and responded in its 2018 official communication by abandoning this proposal and instead moved to prohibit the enforcement of termination clauses for the supply of goods and services[194]

[185] IS Proposals 2016, at 8.1–8.2 expressly cited this study: R3 and ComRes: *Association of Business Recovery Professionals Membership Survey*, August 2013, Termination Clauses: https://www.r3.org.uk/media/documents/policy/research_reports/R3_Membership_Survey_Termination_Clauses_09_August_2013.pdf.

[186] IA 1986, ss 233–233A.

[187] IS Proposals 2016, at para 8.6.

[188] ibid, section 8 'Key Points'.

[189] ibid, at para 7.29.

[190] ibid, at para 8.10.

[191] ibid, at para 7.30.

[192] IS Reponses 2016, at paras 3.1–3.7.

[193] Government Responses 2018, at paras 5.90–5.94.

[194] ibid, at para 5.104: it was suggested that this would cover contractual licences for use of software and patents.

when entering a formal insolvency process (which exists in many other jurisdictions)[195] or freestanding moratorium or restructuring plan.[196]

The government's position was reflected in CIGA 2020, which does not mention essential contracts but instead specifies that payments for goods and services supplied during the moratorium must continue to be made during the moratorium[197] and that the Insolvency Rules can further specify what is (not) covered.[198] Nevertheless, in recognition of the problems with termination clauses, section 14 of CIGA 2020 amended the provisions for the protection of supplies of goods and services to effectuate the ban on termination clauses, as discussed above.[199] As a result, so long as the suppliers of goods and services continue to be paid on time, they cannot enforce their termination clause.[200] This has brought the English restructuring regime largely into line with the international best practice and the World Bank and UNCITRAL principles.[201] Although problematic, this arrangement is likely to enable corporate rescue in more cases, as it addresses the negative impact of the early termination-of-supply practices identified in the 2013 survey, mentioned above. Time will show how effective it is and whether the market finds ways around it.

H. Financial Contracts

Despite the original desire to give debtors legal protection from (all) creditors while they explore their options, the position of financial creditors under the freestanding moratorium has changed significantly over the period that the moratorium proposals have been debated. Initially, they were to be treated like any other creditor and were, in theory, also within the scope of contracts that could be designated as 'essential contracts'.[202] The 2016 Insolvency Service proposals did not see this as problematic because, in practice,

> it would be unusual for a company not to consult, as a minimum, its largest secured creditors before making an application for a moratorium, to ensure that there was support for the principle of restructuring. If that support was not forthcoming it would be questionable whether there was a realistic prospect of rescue, as required by the qualifying conditions.[203]

[195] ibid, at paras 5.88–5.97. See also para 7.23 in 'Post Implementation Review of the Corporate Insolvency and Governance Act', 21 February 2023: https://www.legislation.gov.uk/ukia/2023/69/pdfs/ukia_20230069_en.pdf.

[196] Government Responses 2018, at para 5.98.

[197] IA 1986, s A18(3)(b).

[198] ibid, s A18(4).

[199] Now ibid, s 233B.

[200] Here, IA 1986, ss A18 and 233B interact: s A18(3)(b) confirms that goods and services supplied to the debtor must be paid in full (ie the payment holiday does not cover these payments) while s 233B ensures that the suppliers cannot easily terminate the supply of such goods and services when the debtor commences the moratorium.

[201] For a fuller discussion see 'Post Implementation Review of the Corporate Insolvency and Governance Act' (21 February 2023) at 7.15–7.17 at: https://www.legislation.gov.uk/ukia/2023/69/pdfs/ukia_20230069_en.pdf.

[202] See section III.G.

[203] IS Proposals 2016 at para 7.27.

However, many respondents to the 2016 and 2018 consultations felt that financial creditors should be excluded from the proposals.[204] It was feared that including finance providers 'would lead to them withdrawing their products and services much earlier, perhaps at the first sign of financial difficulties'[205] and long before directors were even considering the use of the moratorium, which could *cause* financial difficulties for the debtor rather than *resolve* them. The government accepted these concerns in the context of the proposed ban on *ipso facto* clauses (now section 233B of the Insolvency Act 1986),[206] but such exclusion was never discussed in the context of the freestanding moratorium. Nevertheless, the Insolvency Act 1986 provides that payment for debts or other liabilities arising under a contract or other instrument involving financial services must continue to be made during the moratorium.[207] The result is a moratorium with an unusual scope.

The exclusion of financial creditors from the scope of the moratorium is not common in other procedures and jurisdictions. The new moratorium, therefore, stands in contrast to the moratorium attached to English administration,[208] to the US Chapter 11,[209] and to the Chinese EBL.[210] As mentioned earlier, the PRD 2019 permits the exclusion of certain types of creditors from the scope of the stay so long as they are well-defined and duly justified and where such an exclusion would be unlikely to jeopardise the restructuring or unfairly prejudice those creditors.[211] Here, there is no satisfactory definition of 'financial creditors' in the law, which causes uncertainty in practice.[212] Moreover, there is no justification or even discussion of this exclusion in the consultation documents or in any publicly accessible documents. Finally, it is arguable, and there is some data to suggest, that this exclusion also has a negative impact on the likelihood of rescue.[213] Taken together, therefore, the exclusion of financial creditors is problematic and should be reconsidered by the government.

Although it is true that, in practice, debtors would always seek to communicate and get approval from their large financial creditors (and, arguably, such approval is impliedly necessary in order to be able to show that 'rescue of the company as a going concern [is] likely', one of the eligibility criteria), that is not the same as saying that no financial creditors' claims are to be stayed at all. As we will see in section IV, arguably, this exclusion is one of the main reasons why the moratorium has been so rarely used in practice, as it limits the scope and the utility of the moratorium too much.

[204] IS Responses 2016 at para 3.3.
[205] Government Responses 2018, at para 5.102.
[206] ibid. See also n 184 above.
[207] IA 1986, s A18(3)(f).
[208] ibid, Sch B1 para 23.
[209] 11 USC § 362.
[210] EBL, Art 19.
[211] PRD 2019, Art 6(4).
[212] Insolvency Service, *Post Implementation Review of the Corporate Insolvency and Governance Act* (PIR 2023) published on 21 February 2023; available at: https://www.legislation.gov.uk/ukia/2023/69/pdfs/ukia_20230069_en.pdf, at para 11.4. See also text to n 230 below.
[213] And at least in the case of smaller companies, there is some support that it does have such an impact: PIR 2023, at para 3.8. See also section IV for a normative discussion of this issue.

I. Creditors

One of the most controversial topics when finalising the details of the freestanding moratorium in the CIGA 2020 consultation process was the appropriate level of protection for creditors. The discussion focused primarily on the role that they should play, what powers and rights they should have, and how their rights and interests should be balanced against the interests of other stakeholders and the ultimate aim of enabling a low-cost, quick rescue of the debtor company. In the end, creditors' day-to-day oversight and rights were limited, while some creditors were completely excluded from the scope of the new moratorium (and so protected from the resulting stay on enforcement).

In restructuring mechanisms around the world, creditors often have significant control and monitoring rights. It was initially discussed whether similar rights should be given to creditors under the new moratorium. As we saw earlier, the 2016 and the 2018 consultations considered whether creditors should be given the right to be consulted and to control the commencement of the moratorium through a vote (for all or some of the creditors, by majority vote), but in the end, both notions were rejected by the government[214] and it was decided that the moratorium would commence when the debtor filed all the relevant documents. However, the government noted that 'it is likely in practice that the company or the proposed monitor will have to undertake some level of consultation with key stakeholders in the restructuring process'.[215] In the eyes of the government, that was sufficient. Indeed, such an arrangement will, in most cases, suffice, as key stakeholders – main lenders and security holders – will at least be consulted in order to determine whether the rescue of the company is likely. However, it is unclear whether relying on market arrangements provides an appropriate level of protection to all deserving creditors in all cases.

In response, many creditors called for a right to challenge the moratorium application in court. In the end, the government permitted a general right to challenge the directors' and monitor's actions during the moratorium,[216] but refused to grant a specific right to challenge the moratorium application itself.[217] Despite the cost, it was believed by creditors – and accepted by the government – that permitting recourse to a court was necessary to ensure robust creditor safeguards, which would, in turn, inspire confidence in the restructuring moratorium itself.[218] It was also deemed appropriate to give creditors the right to agree further extensions of the moratorium in some cases.[219]

Creditors also asked for a right to request information from the debtor or the monitor throughout the moratorium period. The Insolvency Service, in the 2016 and the 2018 proposals, resisted such requests due to a fear that it could overburden the process, lead to vexatious requests, endanger commercially sensitive information,

[214] Government Responses 2018, at para 5.31.
[215] ibid. A similar sentiment appears in IS Proposals 2016, at para 7.27.
[216] IA 1986, ss A44 and A42.
[217] See section III.B for more details.
[218] Government Responses 2018, at para 5.20.
[219] IA 1986, s A11. See also section III.E.

and lead to unnecessary delays and an increase in cost. Nevertheless, the government recognised that these concerns needed to be balanced against the view of most of the consultation respondents who called for creditors' right to request information.[220] The government promised it would 'seek to develop a solution that provides creditors with information in a timely manner, whilst minimising the burden on the monitor and the debtor company'.[221] In the end, the moratorium was enacted without giving creditors the right to request information ad hoc; instead, it states that the monitor must provide updates in specified circumstances – for example, when the moratorium commences,[222] when it is extended or terminated,[223] and when the monitor is being replaced.[224] This seems like a reasonable compromise.

Finally, certain creditors are altogether shielded from the impact of the moratorium. This is achieved by excluding them from the scope of the moratorium in the first place. As discussed in sections III.G and III.H above, financial creditors and certain other pre-moratorium and moratorium debts continue to be payable throughout the moratorium. This is yet another provision aimed at protecting creditors' rights.

When viewed as a package, respondents in the consultation process were divided in their opinions on whether these safeguards were sufficient to protect creditors' rights in the new moratorium.[225] Throughout the consultation period, creditors were considered as a group, but in the end, CIGA 2020 excluded certain creditors (financial creditors and some others – see section III.F) from the payment holiday. As a result, creditors' protection in the freestanding moratorium is very varied: those who were excluded from the scope of the stay continue to hold all their pre-existing rights, while those covered by the freestanding moratorium have comparatively more limited protection than is the case in the moratorium attached to administration, the Chapter 11 moratorium, or the Chinese Reorganisation moratorium. These regimes afford creditors significant control and monitoring rights. This is especially so for secured and preferential creditors, but there is also a right to vote and be consulted for unsecured creditors, which is completely missing in the freestanding moratorium.

Moreover, one must be careful with drawing comparisons between the freestanding moratorium, on the one hand, and full restructuring processes, on the other. In the former, the debtor is supposed to consider its options over a relatively short period of time (20 days with easy extension of further 20 days); in the latter it is supposed to propose or make changes to stakeholders' entitlements with long-term far-reaching impact. This in itself can justify why there is a greater need to give rights and protections to creditors in restructuring processes – since their long-term position is likely going to be affected by the decisions taken throughout the procedure – compared with the relatively limited rights and protections to creditors in the freestanding moratorium – where the debtor, under supervision, considers its options but usually does not make any long-term changes.

[220] IS Responses 2016, at paras 2.19–2.20; Government Responses 2018, at para 5.84.
[221] Government Responses 2018, at para 5.87.
[222] IA 1986, s A8(2)(b).
[223] ibid, s A17(2) and (4).
[224] ibid, s A39(8)(b).
[225] IS Responses 2016, at para 2.8; Government Responses 2018, at para 5.36.

IV. Limitations of the Freestanding Moratorium in Practice

There was a lot of excitement leading up to the implementation of the new moratorium. In the 2016 and 2018 consultations, respondents welcomed the introduction of a standalone breathing space for companies looking to examine their restructuring options. R3, the UK trade association for insolvency and restructuring professionals, said that about 22 per cent of the companies with whom its members worked in 2015 could have used the mechanism.[226] Similarly, the government predicted a 'best estimate' of 1,250 cases per annum.[227] Unfortunately, the actual use of the new moratorium has fallen short of these expectations and has been disappointingly low. Between 26 June 2020 and 31 October 2024, the moratorium was only used in 57 cases,[228] ie just over one per month since the law came into force, and there have been only two court cases in that time, despite the many remaining uncertainties (*Minor Hotel Group* in 2022 and *Re Grove Independent School* in 2023[229]).

The government committed to review the permanent CIGA 2020 measures – including the new moratorium – within three years of their implementation. This review was based on an independent empirical assessment (carried out by Professor Peter Walton and Dr Lézelle Jacobs from the University of Wolverhampton), and the results were published in early 2023. The report agreed that the use of the new moratorium was 'considerably lower than expected',[230] but it suggested that there are three reasons that have contributed to the limited use. First, the volume of insolvency and restructuring procedures, in general, has been considerably lower during and since the COVID-19 pandemic, due to the enhanced financial support and other supportive measures available from the government (indeed, there were only 96 schemes of arrangement between 2020 and 2022, while the normal pre-COVID level was around 220 cases per annum).[231] Second, it always takes time for the industry to adopt new measures – indeed, the initial volume of administration and CVA cases was also comparatively low.[232] Finally, the estimates on the predicted use of the moratorium (and the CIGA 2020 restructuring plans) were unrealistic.[233]

There are several issues that have been identified as contributing to the limited use of the new moratorium. Here we look at five of the most common criticisms of the new moratorium, in descending order of severity. Section V then considers these issues

[226] IS Responses 2016 – R3 submission.

[227] Insolvency Service, *Impact Assessment in respect of the Corporate Insolvency and Governance Bill* (April 2020), at para 6.11.

[228] Company Insolvency Statistics October 2024: https://www.gov.uk/government/statistics/company-insolvencies-october-2024/commentary-company-insolvency-statistics-october-2024.

[229] See section III for details.

[230] Insolvency Service, *Post Implementation Review of the Corporate Insolvency and Governance Act* (PIR 2023) (n 212). The conclusions are supported by 55 semi-structured interviews, two case studies, and a survey of 91 insolvency practitioners.

[231] ibid, at para 3.3.

[232] ibid, at para 3.4.

[233] ibid, at para 3.6.

against the stated purposes of the new moratorium, before concluding whether the new moratorium provides a useful and successful tool for corporate rescue.

First, it is commonly accepted that the *scope of the moratorium is too narrow*. This is true in two respects: the debts that are covered and the companies that are eligible. Despite the initial plan to postpone debt enforcement by all creditors, the legislative provisions exclude all *financial creditors* from the scope of the pre-moratorium debts that have a payment holiday.[234] This exclusion should be removed in order to enable more companies – and especially SMEs – to use the new moratorium. The moratorium contains sufficient checks and balances to apply to all creditors: it is very short; the commencement of the moratorium depends on the monitor certifying that the company satisfies certain entry criteria; the debtor is continuously supervised by an expert; and there are extensive safeguards for creditors' rights. As such, it is not justifiable to continue treating financial creditors in the new moratorium so much more favourably than in any other restructuring procedure in England or elsewhere. There are three arguments to support this conclusion. First, there is vetting by the monitor before the moratorium can commence. Second, the stay is only for a short period of time. And, third, in practice, the debtor company will generally need the support of its main lender(s) in order to be able to show that rescue of the company is likely, and so, impliedly, interests of (main) financial creditors will be taken into account by the debtor and the monitor (when making the initial statement of eligibility and through the continuous monitoring of compliance). Taken together, this provides sufficient safeguards for financial creditors and so their claims should be included in the scope of the stay.[235]

Moreover, Schedule ZA1 of the Insolvency Act 1986 explicitly *excludes companies which are party to a capital markets arrangement in an amount of over £10 million*. This excludes many medium-sized and large companies from being eligible to use the moratorium. This exclusion was criticised by commentators[236] and by the 2023 Post-implementation Review, which suggested that the government should 'consider amending eligibility criteria to allow large, mid-market and larger SME companies to use the procedure'.[237] Such exclusion is unnecessary and unjustified and should, indeed, be removed in order for the moratorium to become available to a wider range of deserving debtors.

Second, Insolvency Practitioners are often *reluctant to act as monitors*. The government foresaw this problem in 2018 when some respondents warned that 'insolvency practitioners would be uninterested in a monitor role if it was limited in scope, as fees for such work would be relatively modest'.[238] The government dismissed this concern, saying that it would not be an issue as 'there will be no prohibition on insolvency practitioners providing additional services to a company in a moratorium, such as

[234] See section III.F.

[235] This conclusion is supported by other commentators (eg Jennifer Payne, 'An Assessment of the UK Restructuring Moratorium' [2021] *Lloyd's Maritime and Commercial Law Quarterly* 454) and is one of the proposals of the post-implementation review in 2023 (PIR 2023, at para 6.3).

[236] See eg Sarah Paterson, 'Restructuring moratoriums through an information-processing lens' (2023) 23(1) *Journal of Corporate Law Studies* 37.

[237] PIR 2023, at para 6.3.

[238] Government Responses 2018, at para 5.70.

restructuring advice or consultancy services'.[239] Reluctance to act is further exacerbated by the perceived lack of clarity about the monitor's 'level of engagement with the operation of the business and possible rescue plan' and their potential liability for decisions.[240] Moreover, empirical evidence suggests that there is also a 'perceived reputational risk of acting as a monitor in cases where a company rescue is not achieved', with 85 per cent of Insolvency Practitioners indicating that this was at least a slight deterrent and 36 per cent indicating that it was a significant deterrent to using the new moratorium.[241] As a result, Insolvency Practitioners often recommend using (more expensive) administration rather than the new moratorium.[242] The way to deal with these issues is to further clarify the rules and liability exposure of monitors and to allow the market to familiarise itself with the new tool, as interviews with Insolvency Practitioners who had actually used the new moratorium confirm that they found it fairly straightforward and the burden not too onerous.[243] It is also clear that allowing other relevant professionals to act as monitors – as envisaged throughout the consultation – 'may lead to reduced costs and be more consistent with company rescue'.[244]

Third, the moratorium may be *too short* to provide the necessary breathing space to find a way forward, especially in larger cases.[245] We saw that the PRD 2019 suggested a period of up to four months, and the original proposal envisaged three months (with a further three months as an extension). The moratorium, as enacted, gives 20 business days (plus an extra 20 days as an extension). The length of the moratorium must balance the need for proper consideration of all options (pro-debtor) and the danger of abuse and destruction of value by existing management (pro-creditor). Arguably, up to 40 days may not be enough to review all relevant options and reach a sufficient level of consensus with key stakeholders, which limits the utility of the new moratorium – especially in larger, more complex cases. Consequently, this perception will likely filter out some cases that would and should benefit from the freestanding moratorium because the length of the stay is thought to be insufficient.

Fourth, *allowing debtors to remain in control* has the undisputed advantages of removing procedural delays of handing over the management and overcoming the reputational and personal disincentive present in other types of control arrangements. Nevertheless, there is some evidence that debtor companies are averse to being monitored and having to obtain consent for some actions (such as getting credit, dealing with company property in certain ways, etc[246]).[247] Moreover, the extensive freedom for the debtor causes concern and fear of abuse for the creditors.[248] It is likely that, as

[239] ibid.
[240] PIR 2023, at paras 4.10 and 6.5.
[241] ibid, at paras 5 and 4.10.
[242] ibid, at paras 4.10 and 6.5.
[243] ibid, at para 6.2.
[244] ibid, at para 6.4.
[245] See eg Wai Yee Wan, *Court-supervised Restructuring of Large Distressed Companies in Asia: Law and Policy* (Oxford, Hart Publishing, 2022) at section 7.2.1.
[246] See section III.A above.
[247] See assessment at: https://viewpoints.stevens-bolton.com/post/102i7xg/whats-wrong-with-the-ciga-moratorium.
[248] See section III.A above for discussion.

the market becomes more familiar with the new moratorium, these limitations will be minimised.

And finally, the new moratorium states that the stay is only available where the monitor believes that it is likely to result in the *rescue of the company as a going concern*. The 2016 proposal used the term 'rescue of the business'. The respondents to the 2016 consultation envisaged 'rescue of the business', 'rescue of the company or business', and 'rescue of the whole or part of a business' as all being worthwhile aims. Without any explanation or justification, the terminology was changed in the 2018 consultation where the government only used the term rescue of the company. This approach was then adopted by CIGA 2020, and so all the provisions in Part A1 of the Insolvency Act 1986 now focus on the rescue of the company as a going concern. The wording is likely borrowed from administration, where the administrator's first objective is saving the company as a going concern. However, in administration, there are two further objectives that enable broader use of that procedure. There is no such fall-back provision here. Moreover, it may also be that the focus on saving the company is there to encourage earlier intervention. However, that in itself is not a good enough reason to exclude cases where saving the business is still likely. Such an overly narrow eligibility criterion is potentially problematic, as it excludes worthy cases where it is likely that the business may be saved but the monitor would not have enough evidence or time to be able to form the view that the company can be saved as well. It may also be that rescuing the company is simply not possible, but rescuing its core business *is*, which should still be seen as a worthwhile venture that should be encouraged and enabled by tools such as the freestanding moratorium. Given the lack of any explanation or justification and the resulting narrowing down of the scope of potential users of the moratorium, it is recommended that the wording of the statute should also be changed.

V. Concluding Thoughts: Success or Failure?

It is hard to describe the freestanding moratorium as either a success or a failure. In some aspects, it has done very well; in others, it has failed miserably. And then there are some features that could potentially work well once there is more understanding in the market of how to use them. As the 2023 Post-implementation Review put it: 'the evidence is ambiguous'.[249] This section will, therefore, evaluate the new moratorium against its own goals.[250] We will look at seven key goals that were identified during the consultation period and see whether and to what extent they have been fulfilled.

First, one of the generally accepted core purposes was to create a *low-cost* restructuring tool.[251] In this regard, the new moratorium has undoubtedly succeeded. This

[249] PIR 2023, at 3.

[250] For a full analysis of the reform goals, see Natalie Mrockova, 'The Freestanding Moratorium and its Policy Goals: A Partial Success' *Lloyd's Maritime and Commercial Law Quarterly*, forthcoming (2025).

[251] IS Proposals 2016, at para 7.6: 'The Government is keen to reduce the costs … of restructuring'; Government Responses 2018, at para 5.10: 'A key objective of the Government's proposals is to reduce the costs … of restructuring'.

was achieved by clearly defining and streamlining the entry process, reducing procedural steps, limiting or removing some safeguards (most importantly creditor voting), streamlining the provision of information to stakeholders, and reducing court involvement.[252] There are three main sources of cost in the new moratorium. First are the costs of preparing the report on eligibility and preparing and filing the relevant legal materials by the monitor and the debtor company, which were estimated by the government to amount to £17,000 per case. The data shows that, on average, the cost has actually been even lower: £13,700 per case.[253] The second cost arises out of ongoing monitoring. The government estimated £1,000–£3,000 per day and with the duration of 20 days that cost is approximately £6,400 per case (one third of the cases were extended, and so the cost would go up accordingly). However, the data suggests that the monitoring costs may be significantly higher than predicted (also due to the uncertainty regarding the necessary level of involvement of the monitor, as discussed above).[254] The third cost is an optional one that arises from creditor challenges. This only accrues to the particular creditor(s) and depends on the nature and complexity of the claim.[255] We have to be careful – given the low level of claims to date – with drawing general conclusions from these numbers and seeing them as representative of the cost of the moratorium. But so far, the costs have been comparatively very low.

Second, another goal often mentioned in the consultation period was the aim of *enabling and encouraging early intervention*.[256] This was the main reason for allowing debtors to remain in control and for allowing pre-insolvency use of the moratorium. However, it has been questioned by Professor Paterson whether moratoria are capable of incentivising such early intervention (especially in large companies) due to their signalling implications.[257] She has argued that the 'moratorium is of value when the benefits it brings outweigh the signalling disadvantages which are associated with it for large corporates in distress',[258] which is why many large companies may prefer to use pre-packaged administration or (previously) the London Approach (and recently also schemes of development) where it is only the key stakeholders who know about the financial distress and a deal is only made public once the core agreement has been reached.[259] That is a valid concern, at least until the market becomes more familiar with the new moratorium and until the scope of its application (including the intended pre-insolvency focus and the importance of being able to save the company as a whole) is fully internalised by market players. Thereafter the signalling implications may not be as severe as feared.

Ultimately, there is insufficient evidence to determine whether the goal of encouraging early intervention has been met. On the one hand, more than three quarters of

[252] As envisaged in Government Reponses 2018, at para 5.13.
[253] PIR 2023, at paras 5.13–5.21.
[254] ibid.
[255] ibid.
[256] IS Proposals 2016, at para 7.6: 'the importance of encouraging directors whose company may be facing financial distress to act early to address their company's problems'; Government Responses 2018, at paras 5.6 and 5.17.
[257] Paterson (n 236).
[258] ibid at 39.
[259] ibid, at 42–46.

all cases that used the freestanding moratorium have so far led to a successful rescue of the company or at least (a part of) its business.[260] Of the cases that used the moratorium, therefore, it appears that they used the procedure early enough. However, it is impossible to quantify whether the law enables early intervention more broadly. The low number of cases may indicate that the law, as written, is insufficient to incentivise early intervention in most cases. But because it is not clear why the debtors and Insolvency Practitioners have not been using the new moratorium more, the low volume cannot, by itself, support or deny this claim.

Third, the new moratorium also aimed to '*provide enough time* [to enable the debtor company] to consider options' (emphasis added).[261] As we saw in section III.E, there was a lot of disagreement at the consultation stage as to what was the appropriate length of the new moratorium. The initial proposal saw it as three months (plus the possibility to extend by three more), while most respondents thought this would be too long. The PRD 2019 envisaged European restructuring moratoria to be for up to four months. The views were similarly mixed at the Post-implementation Review stage.[262] In practice, among the debtor companies that used the new moratorium, only a third needed an extension.[263] Interviews with Insolvency Practitioners who used the moratorium suggest that companies found it easy to extend where needed.[264] Based on this experience, we may conclude that – although shorter than originally proposed and shorter than moratoria elsewhere – the length of the moratorium is appropriate and *does* give debtor companies enough time to consider their options.

However, this may not be the whole story, as the data does not account for self-deselection, ie cases that could have benefited from the moratorium but chose not to due to the fear that it was too short. This hypothesis finds some support in the interviews carried out as a part of the Post-implementation Review where 57 per cent of the Insolvency Practitioners thought that the moratorium was too short (34 per cent said it was 'a little too short', while 23 per cent thought it was 'far too short'), and only 21 per cent thought that the length was 'about right'.[265] Therefore, it is clear that in some cases (the successful cases that have used the moratorium) the length of time was sufficient and this goal wa satisfied; but there are likely at least some deserving cases for whom the duration is too short. For the latter category, it is important to see whether more understanding of how the extensions work would encourage more market participants to use the moratorium, or whether it will be necessary to lengthen the initial period to encourage greater use of the moratorium in practice. In the end, a combination of the two may be necessary.

Fourth, a goal connected to the one above is that the moratorium should provide 'a period of protection so [debtors] can *seek advice, negotiate with creditors, and*

[260] PIR 2023, at para 3.10. See also goal six, below.

[261] This was also identified as one of the core goals of the new moratorium in PIR at para 1.7. This goal was also echoed in IS Proposals 2016, at paras 7.6 and 7.9, and Government Responses 2018, at para 5.9.

[262] PIR 2023, at para 3.11.

[263] Companies House data at ibid.

[264] PIR 2023, at para 3.11.

[265] ibid.

agree plans for their rescue as going concern' (emphasis added).[266] Indeed, initially the Insolvency Service thought that the purpose of the moratorium should be reaching a compromise with creditors.[267] As the length was reduced from three months to 28 days (in the 2018 consultation), the government said that there would be no required outcome but that it expected that the moratorium would lead to an agreement of some sort with the creditors, or the moratorium would be used as a conduit to another insolvency or restructuring procedure.[268] Overall, the data here is also ambiguous. On the one hand, 54 per cent of Insolvency Practitioners in the Post-implementation Review considered the new moratorium 'not effective' in the context of this goal.[269] But we cannot say that the new moratorium was entirely unsuccessful either, because it has clearly been used successfully in practice. Many Insolvency Practitioners have used it successfully in concluded cases, as nicely illustrated in the Post-implementation Review case study in Bespoke Managed Space, where the moratorium held off aggressive creditors while the debtor worked toward the approval of a CVA.[270] The Post-implementation Review concludes that this is 'the least successful … of all objectives relating to [the moratorium]',[271] but the evidence shows that the goal hasn't failed entirely either.

Fifth, another connected goal is that the moratorium should *prevent strategic holdouts by creditors* (and so enable the debtor to consider its options without being harassed or pressurised). The negative impact of creditor pressure and strategic threats on the likelihood of a successful rescue was noted throughout the consultation period. The 2016 consultation noted that one of the benefits of the proposed moratorium would be 'reducing [creditors'] incentive to adopt tactical approaches aimed at exploiting the threat of delay or disruption for financial gain'.[272] This would create a 'protected grace period' for exploring options and possible arrangements.[273] There have been cases where the CIGA 2020 measures managed to successfully hold off aggressive creditors.[274] However, because financial creditors are largely excluded from the scope of the moratorium, this exclusion makes this goal largely unachievable.

Sixth, the ultimate goal of the new moratorium is to provide greater opportunities for *company survival*.[275] As mentioned in section II, the very creation of the new moratorium was driven by the global trend to enable greater opportunities for corporate rescue and provide more debtor-friendly tools (with safeguards) to this end. The European Recommendation in 2014, the Insolvency Service's Proposals in 2016 and the Government Responses in 2018 all repeated this goal as the focus of their efforts.[276] Throughout the process, it was understood that for such rescue to be feasible, the

[266] This was identified as the first goal of the new moratorium in PIR 2023, at para 1.7.
[267] IS Proposals 2016, at para 7.6.
[268] Government Responses 2018, at paras 5.16–5.17 and 5.50.
[269] PIR 2023, at para 3.8.
[270] ibid, at para 3.9.
[271] ibid, at para 3.8.
[272] IS Proposals 2016, at para 7.9.
[273] ibid, at para 7.10.
[274] PIR 2023, at paras 1.7 and 3.9.
[275] ibid, at paras 1.7 and 3.10.
[276] See eg IS Proposals 2016, at para 7.6; Government Responses 2018, at para 5.13.

moratorium would have to be low-cost, encourage early intervention, provide enough time to consider options and possibly reach some form of an agreement, and prevent harassment by creditors (ie the goals discussed above). Commentators have been sceptical about the moratorium's ability to enable the rescue of the company. Professor Payne suggests that the excessive protection of financial creditors along with other legislative choices have tipped the legislative provisions implementing the freestanding moratorium out of balance and have reduced its utility as a restructuring tool.[277] It is true that the final version of the new moratorium protects financial creditors too much and does so at the expense of the debtor and the goal of corporate rescue. This should be remedied in order to enable the mechanism to be used as intended and to enable this goal to be achieved more broadly.

Nevertheless, the data provides some hope. Although the interviewed Insolvency Practitioners were ambivalent about the ability of the new moratorium to enable corporate rescue, the moratorium was used successfully in many cases.[278] The Post-implementation Review found that over 50 per cent of cases led to a successful rescue of the company as a going concern, and over 25 per cent of cases resulted in the company going into a CVA. That is a comparatively very high proportion of successful rescues (although we must consider that less eligible debtors may have decided not to use the moratorium in the first place, which could have affected the statistics). For comparison, data between 2016 and 2022 shows that less than two per cent of administration cases led to the rescue of the company or entry into the CVA.[279]

Moreover, it is not possible to measure accurately the indirect impact of the new moratorium (and associated measures) on legal practice. It was suggested by one respondent (a turnaround practitioner) in 2016 that 'the very existence of a moratorium may encourage earlier intervention and consensual commercially negotiated solutions without even having to resort to a formal moratorium'.[280] This is an important point in the context of the goal of corporate rescue. This, together with the Post-implementation Review data on the successful outcomes of the existing cases, may indicate that this goal has been at least partly fulfilled by the new moratorium. A more definite view can, however, only be taken once we have more data. It is true that further reform and guidance, as highlighted in section IV, would likely make the law more useful and successful in allowing more companies to benefit from this measure. However, even in its current form, the moratorium has served a useful purpose.

The seventh and final goal that has been identified as driving the introduction of the new moratorium concerns the ability of *all companies* to use it. This was an important feature throughout the consultation process,[281] but the data on this point is mixed. In theory, there are almost no limits on the size of the company that can use the new moratorium, and so this goal appears to be fulfilled. However, upon closer inspection, it is clear that there are significant headwinds for large and small companies. Large companies face two main hurdles. First, companies with capital market debts in excess

[277] Payne (n 235).
[278] PIR 2023, at para 3.10.
[279] ibid.
[280] IS Responses 2016, at para 2.2.
[281] IS Proposals 2016, at 7; Government Responses 2018, at para 5.5.

of £10 million are excluded,[282] which was identified as a major restriction on access which prevents many medium and large companies from being eligible to use the law at all.[283] This is, arguably, a consequence unintended by the drafters and should be reconsidered[284] in light of its impact on the scope of eligible companies and its conflict with this goal.

The second problem for large companies is the short duration of the moratorium.[285] Arguably, the initial period of 20 days (and even the extended total period of 40 days) is far too short for more complex, larger cases. This was also the conclusion of the PRD 2019, the consultation proposals, and of respondents who envisaged that large complex cases should be able to use this tool and would be likely to need a longer period of time.

For small companies, the moratorium may simply not provide the necessary breathing space that they need given that claims by their main creditor – the bank – are not stayed and so it can prevent their rescue efforts at any stage.[286] Although the new moratorium is mostly used by smaller companies,[287] it is conceivable that if financial creditors' claims were stayed, the tool would be available to a greater number of viable companies. Even if the financial creditors' claims were to be stayed, these companies would still need to keep the main lender on side, as discussed above, which would provide sufficient safeguards to those creditors. However, making the payment holiday provisions of the moratorium applicable to them would change the starting point and would likely create a healthier environment for their negotiations.

In conclusion, the introduction of the freestanding moratorium, along with the other changes made by CIGA, concludes a long process of reorienting the English insolvency law away from liquidation and towards rescue: a journey that began in 1982 with the Cork Report. However, as argued in this chapter, the reality of the moratorium is far from perfect. The volume of use, the remaining issues in the design of its provisions, and the mixed assessment as to whether this design fulfils its own goals all lead to the conclusion that the new moratorium has been a useful tool for some companies in practice, but that its potential far exceeds its current use and utility. Further changes and more guidance are clearly needed.[288]

[282] IA 1986, Sch ZA1.

[283] See eg PIR 2023 at paras 4.12 and 5.69, Paterson (n 236) at 50–51.

[284] The responses from Insolvency Practitioners were mixed when asked about removing the £10 million limitation: 26 per cent said it should remain, 36 per cent said it should be removed, and 37 per cent didn't know: PIR 2023, at para 4.12.

[285] See also the discussion of the length of the moratorium above.

[286] PIR 2023, at para 3.8.

[287] PIR 2023, at para 5.69.

[288] For a further discussion, see Mrockova (n 250).

9

Restructuring Reforms in Africa and the Problem of 'Misfitted' Transplants

WINIFRED TARINYEBA KIRYABWIRE

I. Introduction

Restructuring law reforms have been on the policy agendas of various jurisdictions in Africa for nearly three decades. The reforms were and continue to be driven by the need to have efficient mechanisms for resolving financial distress. This was initially considered a critical component of economic growth initiatives. Latterly, crises, including the Covid-19 crisis and resultant period of economic uncertainty, have prompted a renewed focus on restructuring laws as a mechanism for the treatment of financial distress – not only in cyclical downturns or isolated instances of sectoral distress, such as those which can be observed in the construction or housing sectors, but also in the context of broader economic shocks.

As was the case historically in relation to the introduction of liquidation and other insolvency procedures across the continent, restructuring reforms have been transplanted from developed economies, particularly those with colonial ties such as the United Kingdom (which has influenced common law jurisdictions in Africa) and France (in the case of the Central Africa OHADA region[1]). The Cork Committee reforms in the United Kingdom[2] have been a major point of reference as well as specific aspects of the US Chapter 11 process.

The restructuring measures include proceedings that can only be commenced prior to the insolvency of the debtor, such as the conciliation and preventive settlement procedures in the OHADA region (see section III.A), the business rescue procedure in South Africa and the corporate rescue procedure in Zimbabwe (see section III.B). In addition, some countries such as Uganda, Kenya and Nigeria have adopted the UK style administration procedure. A similar procedure exists in Malawi but is referred to as a reorganisation procedure. A debt restructuring procedure – the company voluntary

[1] OHADA is the acronym for the French Organisation pour l'harmonisation en Afrique du droit des affaires (Organisation for the Harmonisation of Corporate Law in Africa).

[2] Report of the Insolvency Law Review Committee on Insolvency Law & Practice (Cork Report 1982) Cmnd 8558.

arrangement (CVA) – that is modelled on the UK CVA (as it existed prior to the 2020 reforms) has been adopted in Kenya and Nigeria. In section III, I provide an analysis of each of the measures and their suitability for resolving financial distress in the transplanting jurisdictions. It is important to point out at the outset that, in this chapter, the term 'business rescue procedure' is used in relation to the business rescue procedure as provided for in the Companies Act of South Africa, and the term 'corporate rescue procedure' in used in relation to the corporate rescue procedure as provided for in the Insolvency Act of Zimbabwe. The corporate rescue procedure of Zimbabwe is a replica of the business rescue procedure of South Africa, and it is evident that it was transplanted from South Africa. These terms are not, therefore, used to denote the distinction between business and corporate rescue outcomes used in other jurisdictions (ie as a reference to a sale of a business of a distressed entity (business rescue), or to a business reorganisation (corporate rescue)).

The restructuring measures draw heavily (substantively and procedurally) from the jurisdictions of origin. Such provisions relate, for example, to the pre-insolvency restructuring measures, the criteria for determining financial distress, the procedural rules for commencing proceedings, the nature and scope of the moratoria, procedural requirements for approving restructuring plans, the role of third parties, who may or may not be insolvency practitioners, and involvement of the courts (to either provide oversight or sanction the restructuring plan). While these processes and tools are considered crucial for restructuring, they are largely designed to facilitate creditor coordination, which is not necessarily an issue of concern in the resolution of financial distress in concentrated debt markets. Their appropriateness for jurisdictions where the capital structure, level of development of the insolvency profession and functioning of courts, are different to those of the jurisdictions of origin, is questionable.

The question which this chapter seeks to address is whether these restructuring measures, that have been largely transplanted from advanced economies, are the appropriate tools or policy choices for resolving financial distress in the transplanting African jurisdictions. This chapter is organised as follows: section II presents literature on legal transplants and a brief history of insolvency law in Africa, section III covers restructuring reforms in selected jurisdictions in Africa, and section IV concludes.

II. Legal Transplants and Insolvency Law in Africa

A. Legal Transplantation

Legal transplantation has been the subject of academic debate in various contexts. The debates largely relate to the nature[3] and effects of transplantation.[4] At the heart of these

[3] Some legal theorists argue that legal transplants are not wholesale but subject to conceptual and contextual adaptation. See P Legrand, 'The Impossibility of "Legal Transplants"' (1997) 4(2) *Maastricht Journal of European & Comparative Law* 111.

[4] Berkowitz et al classify legal reforms into receptive and unreceptive transplants based on the underlying process of adopting the reforms, and argue that process is critical to successful transplantation. See Daniel Berkowitz, Katharina Pistor and Jean-Francois Richard, 'The Transplant Effect' (2003) 51 *American Journal of Comparative Law* 163.

debates is the realisation that although the law is an experienced and eager traveller,[5] its nature and character changes along the journey. In Africa, colonialism was the single most significant driver of legal transplantation. Other factors include globalisation and economic integration agendas that advocated for harmonisation of legal frameworks to facilitate trade and commerce, as well as reforms driven by international financial institutions such as the World Bank and International Monetary Fund.

Legal transplantation has taken place in public and private law. Constitutional and human rights law reforms are replete with various aspects of legal transplantation, some of which receive wide acceptance, while others are the subject of controversy. Insolvency law is in the category of private law. Countries borrow liberally from each other in reforming their insolvency laws, and in this sense, stories of legal transplantation can be told across developed,[6] emerging and developing jurisdictions. The often-cited Cork Committee reforms of the UK have inspired reforms in various countries across the world including in Africa.[7] In Asia, India and Singapore have looked to both the US and the UK in the development of their restructuring laws.[8] The latter two jurisdictions do appear to be the main 'exporters' of restructuring procedures. The South African business rescue procedure (with elements transplanted from both the United States and the UK) has also been exported to various Southern African jurisdictions as indicated in section III below. The US has featured more prominently in relation to specific aspects of modern-day restructuring reforms, as well as inspiring broader policy shifts away from a penal system of insolvency law and towards a more rescue-oriented approach. In both the US and UK, measures for resolving financial distress have evolved in tandem with the socio-economic history of those jurisdictions;[9] a critical question in relation to transplants from such jurisdictions is therefore whether they are likely to be a good 'fit' for jurisdictions with different institutional features and histories.

B. A Brief History of Insolvency Law in Africa

Initial insolvency frameworks in Africa could very easily be mapped against the colonial history of the continent. A journey across common law Africa, from Nigeria and Ghana in West Africa, to Kenya and Uganda in East Africa, not only reveals similarities

[5] Inga Markovits, 'Exporting Law Reform – But will it Travel?' (2004) 37 *Cornell International Law Journal* 95.

[6] Jennifer Payne, 'Debt Restructuring in English Law: Lessons from the United States and the Need for Reform' (2014) 130 *Law Quarterly Review* 282–305.

[7] The Cork Committee report is widely referenced in insolvency reforms in various jurisdictions in Africa. Some jurisdictions, such as South Africa and Nigeria or Kenya, have restructuring procedures that adopted some of the post-1986 UK reforms, particularly reforms introduced in the UK by the Enterprise Reform Act of 2002.

[8] Gerard McCormack and Wai Yee Wan, 'Transplanting Chapter 11 of the US Bankruptcy Code into Singapore's Restructuring and Insolvency Laws: Opportunities and Challenges' (2019) 19 *Journal of Corporate Law Studies* 69; Sumant Batra, *Corporate Insolvency Law and Practice*, 1st edn (Delhi, Eastern Book Company, 2017).

[9] See Fiona Tolmie, *Corporate and Personal Insolvency Law*, 2nd edn (London, Routledge-Cavendish, 2003), chapter 1; Harvey R Miller and Shai Y Waisman, 'Is Chapter 11 Bankrupt' (2005) 47(1) *Boston College Law Review* 129; Nathalie Martin, 'The Role of History and Culture in Developing Bankruptcy and Insolvency Systems: The Perils of Legal Transplantation (2005) 28(2) *Boston College International and Comparative Law Review* 1.

in the legislative texts and approaches to insolvency, but also points to England as the source of the various laws including company law and insolvency law (both individual and corporate). Similarly, Francophone Africa's frameworks were based on the French civil code[10] and so were those of Egypt[11] and Mozambique.[12] Insolvency frameworks in the southern part of the continent were either based on common law (such as Zimbabwe and Malawi) or in the case of South Africa, on Roman-Dutch law.

Irrespective of the origin, there are some common aspects. Firstly, most jurisdictions had frameworks for resolving financial distress for both individuals and corporate entities in various pieces of legislation and the approach was fairly consistent across jurisdictions: a public formal process that largely left debtors humiliated and ostracised, and in the case of corporate entities, with minimal chance of recovery. Secondly, the tools in insolvency law were very formal and court driven, irrespective of the fact that in Africa, the majority of economic actors operate outside the formal system.[13] In relation to insolvency, it is acknowledged that very few firms resolve financial distress using insolvency frameworks.[14] Thirdly, the frameworks largely focused on providing for an orderly mechanism, albeit inefficiently, for collecting and realising the assets of an insolvent debtor for the benefit of the general body of creditors, supported by a stay of individual enforcement action by creditors. To this end, the insolvency frameworks were consistent with the historical philosophical foundations of insolvency law in the jurisdictions of origin, as articulated by Baird et al:

> When a debtor has many creditors, the actions of each creditor often run counter to what is in the interest of creditors as a group … many creditors are likely to pursue the debtor's assets at the same time. Assets are sold off piecemeal, destroying whatever synergy existed between them. Moreover, each creditor must spend increasing resources to beat other creditors to the assets. Bankruptcy law … responds to this collective action problem … forces diverse creditors to work together and stops the destructive race to assets.[15]

In the modern period, there has been a policy shift from liquidation as the primary tool for resolving financial distress, to rescue-oriented measures. This approach is consistent

[10] D Ngaunde Leno, 'National Report for Cameroon' in D Faber et al (eds), *Commencement of Insolvency Proceedings* (New York, Oxford International and Comparative Law Series online edition 2012): https://doi.org/10.1093/oso/9780199644223.003.0004 (accessed 20 December 2023).

[11] ESM Ahmed, 'Restructurings in Egypt: A New Tool to Eliminate the Bankruptcy Stigma' in INSOL International, *INSOL World: The Quarterly Journal of INSOL International*, 4th Quarter 2023, p 16–18.

[12] HM Kida, A Rocha, and FAO Rezende, 'A Brief Historical Evolution of the Insolvency Regime in Mozambique', in INSOL International, *INSOL World: The Quarterly Journal of INSOL International*, 4th Quarter 2023, p 14.

[13] This problem is not unique to Africa and has been acknowledged in other jurisdictions. *See* Meghanna Ayyagari, Thorsten Beck, Asli Demirguc-Kunt, 'Small and Medium Enterprises Across the Globe' (2007) 29 *Small Business Economics* 415–34, at 417–19 for a comparison of the size of SMEs and the informal sector in various jurisdictions including advanced, emerging and developing countries. It is also possible that insolvency law is one of the areas where the problem is systemic. See R Dave, 'Legal Culture, Path Dependence and Dysfunctional Layering in Belgian Corporate Insolvency Law' (2018) 27 *International Insolvency Review* 374–79.

[14] Boughanmi and Nigam attribute this to various factors such as cost and complexity. See Afef Boughanmi and Nirjhar Nigam, 'A Survey of Corporate Bankruptcy Reforms: Lessons to be Learned for Worldwide Good Practices' (2017) 3 *European Journal of Interdisciplinary Studies* 7–21 at 19.

[15] Douglas G Baird, Thomas H Jackson and Barry E Adler, *Bankruptcy: Cases, Problems, and Materials*, Revised 3rd edn (New York, New York Foundation Press, 2001), 2, 20.

with broader economic growth policies, such as initiatives to promote entrepreneurship (a rescue-oriented as opposed to penal system of dealing with financial distress is considered a key enabler) and more recently, policies to mitigate risks associated with the post Covid-19 economic uncertainties resulting from, among other things, high interest rates and low productivity, leading to increased financial distress. In this phase, the restructuring reforms have largely been transplanted from developed economies. This was a deliberate policy choice that is attributed to various factors including historical ties, a strong perception of successful reforms in advanced economies, and legal harmonisation initiatives largely driven by institutions such as the World Bank and IMF. The need for efficient resolution of financial distress has been widely expressed by many stakeholders, including the World Bank, a key influencer of insolvency reforms in Africa:

> by clarifying the expectations of creditors and debtors about the outcome of insolvency proceedings, well-functioning insolvency systems can facilitate access to finance, save more viable businesses and sustainably grow the economy.[16]

Policy discussions on restructuring reforms in most jurisdictions in Africa started in the 1980s and early 1990s as part of wider economic reforms. The objectives of the reforms varied but there were some common aspects, such as the desire to make existing frameworks for resolving financial distress more efficient, consolidating frameworks for resolving financial distress, and enhancing creditor confidence through transparent and efficient processes for collection and realisation of assets. The reforms also looked beyond the existing tools for a coordinated realisation and distribution, primarily liquidation procedures, to alternatives for resolving financial distress, with the objective of rescuing viable but financially distressed businesses.

Following the Asian financial crisis, various policy interventions were designed to build resilience and promote financial stability, including principles for effective insolvency and debtor-creditor systems.[17] The principles were developed in 2001 and provided a basis for country assessments and recommendations for reform in four broad areas; that is debtor creditor rights, risk management and corporate workouts, legal frameworks for insolvency, and institutional and regulatory frameworks. Subsequently, the World Bank's *Doing Business* assessments played a key role in shaping policy discussions.[18] These assessments covered various business environment parameters, including insolvency. For each parameter, the assessment used a standard

[16] World Bank Group, 'Ease of Doing Business in Uganda 2016: Measuring Regulatory Quality and Efficiency, Uganda Economy Profile' 90: https://openknowledge.worldbank.org/entities/publication/436a15c6-0c42-518f-a403-f975359ad56b (accessed 16 April 2024).

[17] See The World Bank Group, *Principles for Effective Insolvency and Creditor/Debtor Regimes* https://documents1.worldbank.org/curated/en/391341619072648570/pdf/Principles-for-Effective-Insolvency-and-Creditor-and-Debtor-Regimes.pdf (accessed 20 September 2024).

[18] See Timothy Besley, 'Law Regulation and the Business Climate: The Nature and Influence of the World Bank Doing Business Project' (2015) 29 *Journal of Economic Perspectives* 99–120; Rush Doshi, Judith G Kelley, and Beth A Simons, 'The Power of Ranking: The Ease of Doing Business Indicator and Global Regulatory Behaviour' (2019) 73 *International Organisation* 611–43; IEG/World Bank Group, 'Doing Business and Country Reforms: An Independent Evaluation Group Issues Paper' No 166167 (29 June 2021): https://documents1.worldbank.org/curated/en/585591647361683445/pdf/Doing-Business-and-Country-Reforms-An-Independent-Evaluation-Group-Issues-Paper.pdf (accessed 21 September 2024).

template for advanced, emerging and developing countries. The assumption was that the mechanisms used to resolve financial distress should be easily replicated across jurisdictions. The scope for the assessment of insolvency measures included the recovery rate for secured creditors through reorganisation, liquidation or receivership, taking into account time, cost and the outcome of the proceedings.[19] The reports provided individual country rankings in comparison to all the countries that participated in the process, as well as regional comparatives such as high-income OECD countries[20] and Sub-Saharan Africa. The best practices identified included clear rules for commencing insolvency proceedings, streamlining insolvency proceedings, effective reorganisation proceedings, creditor participation procedures, avoidance provisions, post-commencement financing and regulation of the insolvency profession.[21] The policy direction signalled by this best practice guidance was a formal process for resolving financial distress through reorganisation. It is not, therefore, surprising that procedures such as UK-style administration, irrespective of its shortcomings, have been widely adopted in Africa. A publication by the International Finance Corporation attributed improvements in recovery rates and improved ease of resolving insolvency country rankings to the introduction of reorganisation proceedings.[22]

Four categories of procedure, all of which can in theory be used to achieve a restructuring, will be explored below. A few key points emerge from this analysis. Firstly, in some cases there has been a failure to consider key differences between the jurisdictions of origin and the transplanting economies. Secondly, there has been a failure to understand the nature of financial markets and financing patterns in the transplanting economies, to determine the appropriate tools for resolution of financial distress. Thirdly, the restructuring procedures have been transplanted into an environment where key enablers are lacking, such as a well-developed insolvency profession, an efficient judiciary, and strong rule of law. These difficulties have also been observed in emerging economies and contribute to inefficiencies in the resolution of financial distress.[23]

A further important observation should be added to these. Across Africa, there were early and later adopters in the modern wave of restructuring reforms. Strikingly, there is little to suggest that policy-makers in later adopters took note of the experience of earlier adopters. It is not clear why policy-makers did not take into consideration the outcomes of the restructuring reforms in early adopter jurisdictions, where it would have been evident that transplantation had been an exercise in futility, and perhaps prompted a difference in approach. For example, the wholesale transplantation of the

[19] https://subnational.doingbusiness.org/en/data/exploretopics/resolving-insolvency/what-measured (accessed 10 December 2023).

[20] The Organisation for Economic Co-operation and Development has 37 European members, plus the United States.

[21] ibid.

[22] Valentina Saltane, Rong Chen and Nuria Moya Guzman, 'Measurable Results! Doing Business Project Encourages Economies to Reform Insolvency Frameworks' (January 2013), *IFC Smart Lessons Publication* no 75249: https://openknowledge.worldbank.org/entities/publication/f8fc70e3-d06b-524e-9333-572e80d79e9f.

[23] See Aurelio Gurrea-Martinez, *Reinventing Insolvency Law in Emerging Economies* (Cambridge, Cambridge University Press, 2024).

business rescue procedure (a South African procedure that was inspired by both the US Chapter 11 and UK administration procedures) from South Africa to Zimbabwe 10 years after its adoption in South Africa, and 13 years later in Rwanda, did not consider the unique circumstances of South Africa that might not be replicated in Zimbabwe and Rwanda. Neither did the reform processes of the adopting countries consider any post-enactment developments in South Africa. The same applies to the adoption of UK-style CVA and administration procedures in Nigeria, five years after they had been adopted in Kenya. Both Nigeria and Kenya also appear to have overlooked the fact that the administration procedure in early adopter jurisdictions such as Uganda (2011) was lying idle on the statute books.

III. Restructuring Reforms in Selected Jurisdictions in Africa

This section analyses restructuring measures adopted in five jurisdictions in Africa, namely South Africa, Zimbabwe, Kenya, Uganda, and Nigeria. I have classified the restructuring reforms into four categories. In the first category, are the conciliation and preventive settlement procedures in the OHADA region (comprising 17 countries in Central Africa) pursuant to the Uniform Act of Bankruptcy of 2015 (OHADA UBA). In the second category are the business rescue procedure in the Companies Act of South Africa of 2007 (CASA) and the corporate rescue procedure in the Insolvency Act of Zimbabwe of 2018 (Insol Act-Zim). The first and second categories are pre-insolvency measures; that is, they can only be triggered when a company is in financial distress, but not yet insolvent.

In the third category is the administration procedure in the Insolvency laws of Uganda and Kenya, as well as the Companies and Allied Matters Act of Nigeria (CAMA). In these jurisdictions, the administration procedure is modelled on the UK administration procedure. Some jurisdictions, such as Uganda, adopted UK-style administration as originally provided for in the Insolvency Act 1986 (ie without reference to the Enterprise Act 2002 reforms or subsequent UK reforms). The administration procedure in Kenya and Nigeria is closely aligned with the position in the UK following the 2002 Enterprise Act reforms, but not the current position after the Corporate Insolvency and Governance Act (CIGA) reforms. In Malawi, the Insolvency Act provides for a reorganisation procedure that is similar to administration. Therefore, section III.C analyses the administration procedure together with the reorganisation procedure. In the fourth category is a debt restructuring procedure, namely, the company voluntary arrangement in Kenya and Nigeria. This is modelled on the CVA in the UK.

Except for in the fourth category (the CVA procedure), the trigger for commencing the procedures is financial distress as defined in the laws of each jurisdiction. The proceedings are largely formal, time-bound and require a restructuring plan that must be approved by creditors in accordance with the criteria specified in the law and sanctioned by the courts. Some of the measures are consensual, such as the conciliation procedure in the OHADA region, while others require approval by a majority of the creditors and have mechanisms for imposing the plan on dissenting creditors. All the proceedings provide for a moratorium on creditor enforcement but preserve the rights of secured creditors.

A key policy consideration in restructuring reforms is whether the process is controlled by the debtor or the creditor. Across the world, jurisdictions have different approaches and, in some jurisdictions, some restructuring procedures may be debtor-in-possession or creditor-in-possession procedures. For example, the UK-style administration procedure is controlled by an administrator and the board of directors acts under the direction and oversight of the administrator. The Chapter 11 process in the United States is a debtor-in-possession procedure but also considered attractive to both secured and unsecured creditors.[24] In fact there are concerns that Chapter 11 is heavily skewed towards controlling creditors and that it has not achieved the right balance between creditor and other interests.[25] The OHADA UBA conciliation and preventive settlement procedures both involve third parties, but their role and nature of involvement is consistent with the debtor-in-possession model, while the business/corporate rescue procedure in South Africa and Zimbabwe involves the appointment of an expert whose role is similar to the insolvency practitioner in the administration procedure.

A. Resolving Financial Distress – Conciliation and Preventive Settlement

The OHADA UBA provides for two pre-insolvency restructuring procedures, both inspired by French law. The first is a confidential and consensual conciliation procedure that is primarily a debt restructuring procedure that is only binding on the parties to the proceedings. This conciliation procedure in the OHADA UBA is facilitated by a conciliator appointed by the court,[26] whose primary responsibility is to facilitate an amicable agreement between the debtor and creditors.[27] To this end, the law requires the conciliator to be independent,[28] have access to relevant information[29] and submit regular reports to the court.[30] The OHADA UBA does not expressly require the conciliator to be an insolvency practitioner, although he or she is required to prove his professional qualifications.[31] The second procedure is the preventive settlement procedure, which is also a debtor-in-possession debt restructuring procedure that has some

[24] Aurelio Gurrea-Martinez, 'Building a Restructuring Hub: Lessons from Singapore' (2021) *Singapore Management University Yong Pung How School of Law Research Paper* no 16/2021, 24–28: file:///C:/Users/wtari/Downloads/SSRN-id3940512.pdf (accessed 16 May 2024).

[25] Harvey R Miller and Shai Y Waisman, 'Is Chapter 11 Bankrupt' (2005) 47(1) *Boston College Review* 129, 170.

[26] OHADA UBA, article 5-4 para 1.

[27] OHADA UBA, article 5-5 para 2.

[28] OHADA UBA, article 5-2 para 2.

[29] OHADA UBA, article 5-5 para 2.

[30] OHADA UBA, article 5-6 para 1.

[31] OHADA UBA, article 5-4 para 2.

elements of confidentiality, and is structured as a consensual procedure (the procedure involves appointing an expert, whose primary role is to facilitate creditor agreement to a restructuring plan). The preventive settlement procedure also leaves the debtor in possession but requires the involvement of an expert appointed by the court. The expert is required to be registered as a judicial administrator.[32] The roles of the expert include assessing the financial situation of the debtor,[33] evaluating the debtor's viability/prospects of recovery,[34] creditor engagements/meetings,[35] drafting the preventive settlement agreement[36] and filing it in court.[37]

The trigger for commencement of proceedings is financial distress. However, the debtor must not yet be insolvent.[38] The OHADA UBA defines *insolvency* as inability to pay due debts out of available assets.[39] The OHADA UBA does not define *financial distress* and neither does it provide for a period or window of distress prior to insolvency, although it is envisaged that insolvency is on the horizon. For the conciliation procedure, article 5-1 states in part '... experiencing difficulties which are proved or predictable but [who] have not yet reached insolvency'. Similarly, in relation to the preventive settlement procedure, article 6 provides that 'it shall be open to a debtor who, without being insolvent, shall confirm financial or serious economic problems'.

There are two key challenges with the trigger criteria in OHADA UBA measures. The law does not have a precise definition of financial distress. The definition is subjective and leaves room for judgement, which means the measures could be commenced either too early or too late. The second challenge relates to the use of the balance sheet test of insolvency in the OHADA UBA law. This requires the debtor to provide reliable and credible information that the business is solvent. Hence the need for up-to-date and reliable financial statements, including a credible basis for valuing the assets of the debtor. In an environment where there are gaps in application and enforcement of financial reporting, and valuation standards and asset prices cannot be accurately determined, the determination of the solvency of the debtor may be difficult but also the subject of prolonged disputes.

Two other factors are also worth considering in relation to the valuation of assets for purposes of balance sheet insolvency. The first relates to how creditors, and particularly lenders, treat assets of debtors in secured lending transactions, particularly bank finance. Secured creditors know ex ante that both the determination of the value of assets and realisation of the assets in the event of default are fraught with challenges. Therefore, as a matter of practice, asset values are always discounted. Bank regulators also often provide guidance on loan-to-value thresholds as a risk management measure, to limit exposures in the event of unpredictable movements in asset prices. Secondly, it is also widely acknowledged that in most African jurisdictions, SMEs either lack, or do

[32] OHADA UBA, articles 4-1 and 4-2.

[33] OHADA UBA, article 12 para 1.

[34] OHADA UBA, article 7 para 2.

[35] The expert in a preventive restructuring under OHADA UBA is not required to organise formal and structured creditor meetings but to 'hear them and facilitate negotiations to reach an agreement'.

[36] OHADA UBA, article 13 para 1.

[37] OHADA UBA, article 13 para 4.

[38] OHADA UBA, articles 5-1 para 1 and 6 para 1.

[39] OHADA UBA, article 1-3.

not have sufficient assets to use as collateral to obtain credit, while others may depend on the assets of the business owners to obtain credit. Gaps in legal and institutional frameworks for registration and verification of asset ownership further complicate the determination of business assets and liabilities.

(i) Commencement of Conciliation and Preventive Settlement Proceedings

The conciliation and preventive settlement proceedings may be commenced by either the debtor or any one or more creditors, or jointly by both debtors and creditors.[40] The law does not prescribe a value threshold for creditors to commence proceedings, nor does it distinguish between financial and non-financial creditors. Therefore, any creditor can commence conciliation or preventive settlement proceedings. The OHADA UBA law requires the party commencing proceedings to provide wide-ranging information, including basic and readily available information such as a certificate of incorporation, business activities of the debtor, employees and particulars of creditors.[41] Some information may require professional/expert input, such as financial statements, the cash position, and the maturity profile of the debtors' debts. It is important that credible and reliable information is made available to all parties. The OHADA law, though prescriptive and requiring information that may necessitate expert/professional input, provides exceptions for information that may not be available or is incomplete.[42]

Permitting both debtors and creditors, and in some cases, other stakeholders to commence restructuring proceedings is consistent with restructuring procedures in advanced and some emerging economies. However, in the absence of a precise definition of financial distress as well as the challenge of information asymmetry among creditors, there is a risk that the determination of financial distress by the debtor will be subjective and not based on objective criteria, which presents uncertainties for creditors.

(ii) Moratoria

The moratorium for conciliation proceedings is granted at the request of the debtor and after the court has received an opinion from the conciliator, and is limited in scope; that is, the court may defer the payment of sums already due to creditors and order a stay of creditors' proceedings.[43] The moratorium for the preventive settlement procedure is wider in scope, comes into effect when the decision to commence proceedings is made, remains in effect for up to three months, and may be extended for a further month.[44] The moratorium extends to pre-commencement claims, individual lawsuits, enforcement proceedings, liens, precautionary measures and extra-judicial executions – except for claims for wages, and actions for recognition of disputed claims or against signatories

[40] OHADA UBA, articles 5-2 and 6 para 2.
[41] OHADA UBA, articles 5-2 and 6-2.
[42] OHADA UBA, article 5-2 para 3.
[43] OHADA UBA, article 5-7.
[44] OHADA UBA, article 9 para 1.

of bills of exchange.[45] Although a moratorium is critical to the restructuring process, it may not always achieve the intended objective. In relation to the conciliation procedure, the debtor has a period or window when they may be exposed to creditor enforcement or collection action prior to being granted a moratorium by the court. The moratorium in the preventive settlement and business/corporate rescue procedures gives better protection to the debtor. However, it only provides relief in relation to financial creditors and existing claims of non-financial creditors. This is because in the absence of restrictions on recourse to *ipso facto* clauses in executory contracts, non-financial creditors such as suppliers, insurers and landlords may take action that significantly impairs business continuity.

(iii) Determination of Prospects of Recovery

There is no requirement to assess the prospects of recovery under the conciliation procedure. This is appropriate because the procedure is a mechanism that simply allows the parties to restructure repayments and the outcome does not impact on non-participating creditors. The preventive settlement procedure requires the debtor to provide information about both the financial/economic difficulties and the prospects of recovery and settlement of liabilities.[46] In preventive settlement proceedings, an assessment of prospects of recovery is critical to the proceedings because, although the proceedings may be commenced by one or a few creditors, a restructuring plan approved by the majority of creditors is binding on all creditors.

(iv) The Treatment of Secured and Dissenting Creditors

Secured creditors who are not party to conciliation proceedings are not bound by the proceedings but also cannot take enforcement action during the period of the proceedings.[47] The preventive settlement procedure is a consensual procedure where creditor support is required prior to confirmation by the court. One of the roles of the expert appointed by court is to facilitate negotiations between creditors and the debtor in order to arrive at an agreement.[48] There are no thresholds for creditor approval. Upon confirmation, the plan is binding on all prior creditors[49] and the secured creditors retain their interests in the collateral of the debtor.[50] The court is also mandated to seek creditor consensus,[51] and if that fails, to cram down dissenting creditors, subject to hearing and determination by the court that it is in the interests of the company's creditors to do so (in the sense they will not be left worse off under the plan than the alternative), so that the plan can become binding on dissenting creditors.[52]

[45] OHADA UBA, article 9.
[46] OHADA UBA, article 6 para 3.
[47] OHADA UBA, articles 5-7 and 5-12.
[48] OHADA UBA article 12 para 3.
[49] OHADA UBA article 18 para 1.
[50] OHADA UBA article 18 para 2.
[51] OHADA UBA article 15.2 para 4.
[52] OHADA UBA article 15.2 para 4.

The conciliation procedure is a simple confidential procedure that need not involve all creditors, which, on one hand, may be considered ideal for the resolution of financial distress in MSMEs (micro, small and medium enterprises). However, considering the predominant use of bank finance among MSMEs and their simple capital structure arrangements, it is possible that the conciliation procedure is best suited to the resolution of obligations owed to non-financial creditors, such as suppliers and landlords, but not necessarily financial creditors. This is because contract and banking frameworks already allow for informal workouts and restructuring such that it is not necessary for insolvency law to provide an additional tool. The preventive settlement procedure is an attempt to provide a simplified collective pre-insolvency financial distress resolution tool. The confidential elements may have the potential to address the problem of stigma and encourage early resolution. However, the lack of a clear definition of financial distress and use of the balance sheet test of insolvency are limiting factors.

B. Resolving Financial Distress – Business/Corporate Rescue

Like the OHADA UBA measures in III.A above, the business/corporate rescue procedures are pre-insolvency measures. However, a key distinguishing feature is that the approach of the OHADA UBA measures (conciliation and preventive settlement) is largely consensual, with minimal court involvement, while the business/corporate rescue measures are court-driven processes. The corporate rescue procedure of Zimbabwe is a replica of the South African business rescue procedure, so the two procedures will be analysed together.

The Companies Act of South Africa defines business rescue as proceedings to facilitate the rehabilitation of a company by providing for temporary supervision and management of the affairs of the company, a temporary moratorium and the development and implementation of a rescue plan.[53] The Insolvency Act of Zimbabwe provides a similar definition for corporate rescue proceedings.[54] The definition of business/corporate rescue in both jurisdictions state, in part,

> to rescue the company by restructuring its affairs, business, property, debt and other liabilities, and equity in a manner that maximises the likelihood of the company continuing in existence on a solvent basis or, if it is not possible for the company to continue in existence, results in a better return for the company's creditors or shareholders than would result from the immediate liquidation of the company.[55]

This implies that reorganisation is the preeminent objective of the business/corporate rescue proceedings. Available literature indicates that the conceptualisation of the South African business rescue procedure as a reorganisation procedure was inspired by the US Chapter 11 procedure.[56] Where reorganisation is not viable, the fallback position has similarities to one of the objectives of the UK administration procedure, that is seeking

[53] CASA, s 128(1)(b)(iii).
[54] Insol Act-Zim, s 121.
[55] CASA, s 128(1)(b)(iii); Insol Act-Zim, s 121(1)(b)(iii).
[56] Andre Boraine 'Insolvency Law Reform – An Update' (1999) 371 *De Rebus* 66–68: https://journals.co.za/doi/abs/10.10520/AJA02500329_8368 (accessed 12 December 2023).

a better return for all creditors than would be achieved through liquidation. Therefore, the business/corporate rescue procedure combines elements of the US Chapter 11 and UK administration procedure.[57] The South African business rescue procedure has been adopted by other countries within the region, such as Zimbabwe (corporate rescue procedure),[58] Zambia,[59] Namibia,[60] and Lesotho,[61] as well as some countries outside Southern Africa, such as Rwanda.[62]

In both South Africa and Zimbabwe, a business is considered to be financially distressed if it appears reasonably unlikely that it will be able to pay all of its debts as they fall due within the immediately ensuing six months or if it will likely be insolvent within the same period.[63] Therefore, the test for financial distress is imminent cash flow or balance sheet insolvency. In South Africa, a company is considered to meet the solvency and liquidity test if the assets of the company exceed liabilities and if it will be able to pay its debts as and when they become due in the course of business within 12 months from the date of assessment or from the date of making a distribution.[64] Therefore, in South Africa, the distinction between pre-insolvency financial distress and actual insolvency is the six-month window period prior to actual insolvency. This may be easy to determine in cases of cash flow insolvency but not balance sheet insolvency. In Zimbabwe, the financial distress period/window must occur before a debtor is deemed unable to pay their debts, which is the trigger for commencing insolvency proceedings such as reorganisation or liquidation. The Insolvency Act of Zimbabwe provides that a debtor is deemed unable to pay their debts when there is evidence that they are unable to pay their debts when they are due and payable or that their liabilities exceed the value of their debts.[65] Therefore, in both South Africa and Zimbabwe, a debtor in financial distress is on the brink of insolvency. Although some scholars, such as van Zwieten, point to the need for a careful balance between director responsibilities and early resolution of distress,[66] triggers that are close to insolvency may create incentives for parties to commence restructuring when it is too late. Early intervention is considered a key success factor and near insolvency or actual insolvency increases the likelihood of liquidation as the only realistic option.[67] In jurisdictions with less developed financial markets and where the majority of businesses are MSMEs that primarily rely on bank finance, it is important to consider the risks of attempting to resolve distress closer in time to insolvency.

[57] Farouk Cassim et al (eds), *Contemporary Company Law*, 2nd edn (Cape Town, JUTA, 2015) 861–64.

[58] The corporate rescue procedure in the Insolvency Act of Zimbabwe of 2018 (Insol Act-Zim).

[59] The business rescue procedure in the Corporate Insolvency Act of Zambia of 2017.

[60] Namibia does not yet have a business rescue law but business rescue was considered among the measures to address economic challenges and to this end, the President appointed a business rescue team in July 2021: https://nasia.org.na/wp-content/uploads/2023/07/tst-02-july-2021-p-12.pdf (accessed 13 June 2024).

[61] The Insolvency Act of 2022 of Lesotho provides for the Corporate Rescue Procedure.

[62] The Law Relating to Insolvency of 2021 of Rwanda provides for various restructuring measures including a procedure called reorganisation that is substantively and procedurally similar to the business rescue procedure.

[63] CASA, s 128(1)(f) and Insol Act-Zim, s 121(1)(f).

[64] CASA, s 4.

[65] Insol Act-Zim, s 3.

[66] Kristin van Zwieten, 'Mid-Crisis Restructuring Law Reform in the United Kingdom (2023) 24 *European Business Organization Law Review* 287–315.

[67] Payne, 'Debt Restructuring in English Law' (n 6) at 285.

(i) Commencement of Business/Corporate Rescue Proceedings

The business/corporate rescue proceedings are commenced by a resolution of the directors indicating that the company is in financial distress and that there is a reasonable prospect of rescuing it. The laws also permit affected persons (shareholders or creditors, employees or trade unions) to commence rescue proceedings for various reasons, including financial distress, failure to meet employment, contractual or other obligations, or for just and equitable grounds.[68] The procedural and information requirements for commencement of proceedings differ depending on the party commencing proceedings. A board resolution and sworn statement of the affairs of the company are required for proceedings commenced by the company.[69] Affected persons must obtain a court order to commence rescue proceedings.[70] While a debtor will be in better position to determine financial distress and therefore commence proceedings within the 'six-month distress window', debtors can creatively cause or avoid a financial distress situation. For example, they can structure or re-negotiate contractual obligations with one or a few creditors to avoid a cash flow distress scenario.

Any creditor can commence business/corporate rescue proceedings and there is no threshold on the claims for creditors. However, all creditors are required to be notified in order to allow them to participate in creditor meetings to approve the plan. Creditors face greater challenges in determining financial distress compared to debtors. But it is also possible that certain categories of creditors, such as financial creditors, may be better positioned to predict or determine financial distress than others, eg trade creditors, landlords and utility providers, among others. Therefore, although in theory, any creditor can commence proceedings, non-financial creditors will usually be disadvantaged by lack of information. In addition, there is a risk of 'nuisance' proceedings brought by creditors with low-value claims or whose claims have not been paid due to factors that are not necessarily related to financial distress. However, this risk is mitigated by court scrutiny prior to granting an order to commence proceedings.

Commencement of the business/corporate rescue proceedings triggers a moratorium, which remains in place for the period of the proceedings and which extends to legal proceedings and enforcement action against the company or property belonging to or in possession of the company.[71]

(ii) Determination of Prospects of Business/Corporate Rescue

South Africa and Zimbabwe require a two-pronged test for commencing the business/corporate rescue proceedings, that is financial distress – defined by imminent cash flow or balance sheet insolvency – and the existence of a reasonable prospect of rescuing the company.[72] This is critical because it prevents abuse and potential destruction of value when debtors commence restructuring proceedings simply to hold off creditor

[68] See CASA, ss 129 and 131; Insol Act-Zim, ss 122 and 124.
[69] CASA, s 129(3)(a) and Insol Act-Zim, s 122(3)(a).
[70] CASA, s 131; Insol Act-Zim, s 124.
[71] CASA, s 133 and Insol Act-Zim, s 126.
[72] CASA, s 129(1)(a) and (b) and Insol Act-Zim, s 122(1)(a) and (b).

enforcement. However, where the creditors of the debtor in distress include a bank(s) and the parties were unable to resolve distress using the consensual restructuring tools available in banking frameworks, it is unlikely that parallel or subsequent attempts to resolve distress, using any of the pre-insolvency restructuring frameworks involving multiple creditors, will lead to a different outcome. In addition, in cases where existing lenders are unwilling to provide further funding (due to various factors including banking framework constraints, or absence of post-commencement or debtor-in-possession financing frameworks) or where they hold security interests in a significant portion of the borrower's assets, thus constraining the borrower's ability to obtain further credit, it will be difficult to demonstrate viability of a rescue or restructuring plan. In the South African case of *Anthonie Welman v Marcelle Props 193 CC and Investec Bank Ltd*,[73] when considering an application to commence business rescue proceedings in respect of a company that had no prospects of paying all its due debts in the next six months, Tsoka J dismissed the application on grounds that 'business rescue proceedings are not for the terminally ill … nor are they for the chronically ill. They are for ailing corporations, which, given time, will be rescued and become solvent'. In *Commissioner, South African Revenue Service v Louis Pasteur Investments (Pty) Ltd (in provisional liquidation) and Others*,[74] Millar J stated:

> Business rescue provides a shield for a business that, absent the delivery of the proverbial mortal blow by an unsympathetic creditor, can be rescued. It does not and nor was it ever intended to provide a sword to be used by the directors and/business rescue practitioners to keep the creditors at bay, irrespective of the payment of a better dividend and saving of the business.

The South African courts have demonstrated that in the absence of information demonstrating credible prospects of recovery or rescue, an application to commence rescue proceedings will be dismissed.[75] Cash flows and post-commencement financing are important to the determination of recovery/rescue prospects. Therefore, in bank-dominated economies, resolution of bank debt is critical to the restructuring plan. This may be by restructuring existing debt or releasing security for additional financing. This further points to the importance of early resolution of bank debt. However, pre-insolvency measures are independent of bank debt restructuring frameworks and, therefore, if commenced in parallel to or following failure to resolve bank debt, effective resolution of distress may be significantly limited.

(iii) The Treatment of Secured and Dissenting Creditors

Under the business/corporate rescue proceedings secured and unsecured creditors have voting interests equal to the value of what is owed to them.[76] Approval of a plan requires 75 per cent approval by creditors, of whom at least 50 per cent must be

[73] *Anthonie Welman v Marcelle Props 193 CC and Investec Bank Ltd* [2012] ZAGPJHC 32 (Case no 33958/2011).

[74] *Commissioner, South African Revenue Service v Louis Pasteur Investments (Pty) Ltd (in provisional liquidation) and Others*, [2022] ZAGPPHC 230 (Case no 12194/2017), [84].

[75] See the *Welman v Marcelle Props* (n 73) and *South Africa Revenue Service* (n 74) cases.

[76] CASA, s 145(4)(a); Insol Act-Zim, s 138(4)(a).

independent.[77] An approved plan is binding on all creditors.[78] It is important to note that in bank-dominated economies, a significant portion of the claims against the debtor will be claims by financial creditors such as banks. Therefore, the support of financial creditors is critical to securing approval for the plan.

C. Administration/Reorganisation

The UK-style administration procedure is one of the most widely adopted insolvency reforms in Africa. Although it has some similarities to some of the pre-insolvency measures above, particularly the business/corporate rescue measures discussed in III.B., a key distinguishing feature is that the administration procedure is an insolvency procedure. This section presents an analysis of the administration procedure, as provided for in the laws of Kenya, Uganda and Nigeria, and the reorganisation procedure in Malawi. The Insolvency Act of Malawi, in force from 2016, defines a company in reorganisation as one where an administrator has been appointed.[79] Therefore, the reorganisation procedure in Malawi is similar to the administration procedure. In some jurisdictions such as Uganda, administration is a stand-alone procedure. In Kenya and Nigeria, the procedure may be used concurrently with the Company Voluntary Arrangement (CVA). However, the common practice in Kenya is to use it as a stand-alone procedure. In Nigeria, the procedure was introduced in 2020 and, so far, it is used as a stand-alone procedure. Although some jurisdictions provide for out-of-court appointments, the procedure is widely conceptualised as a formal court-driven procedure. Therefore, hybrid procedures such as pre-packs are not used.

In all the four jurisdictions, the trigger for commencing administration/reorganisation is actual or imminent cash flow insolvency.[80] Administration/reorganisation may be commenced by the company, directors, holders of a qualifying floating charge or a liquidator. Commencement of administration/reorganisation triggers a moratorium on creditor enforcement. The process involves the appointment of an administrator, who must be an insolvency practitioner, and places control of the business in the hands of the administrator. The administrator is an officer of the court, with prescribed responsibilities that include investigating the affairs of the company and presenting a plan that is required to be approved by a majority in value of the creditors present and voting.[81] Once approved, the administration plan/deed is binding on all creditors. Therefore, conceptually, the administration/reorganisation procedure is a restructuring tool.

The significance of the administration/reorganisation procedure is that in some countries, such as Uganda, it signalled the desire among policy-makers for frameworks to rescue businesses in financial distress. Prior to reforms that introduced administration,

[77] CASA, s 152(2)(a) and (b); Insol Act-Zim, s 144(2)(a) and (b).
[78] CASA, s 152(4); Insol Act-Zim, s 144(4).
[79] Insolvency Act of Malawi (Insol Act-M), s 13(1).
[80] See Insolvency Act Uganda (Insol Act-Ug), ss 3 and 139(2); Insolvency Act of Kenya (Insol Act-K), ss 531(a), 443, 541, and 557; Insol Act-M, s 17(a); Companies and Allied Matters Act of Nigeria (CAMA), ss 449(a), 472(2)(a).
[81] Insol Act-M, s 15(1)(a).

apart from the remedies in laws such as contract and mortgage laws, the only available tools for resolving financial distress were receivership (a process that serves the interests of a secured creditor with security interests in substantially all of the debtor's assets) and liquidation. The benefits of administration are thus best analysed in comparison to receivership and liquidation. In comparison to the latter Roy Goode states:

> The primary objective of administration is not to bury the company forthwith but to restore it to profitable trading where possible and, in the event that liquidation becomes unavoidable (as is usually the case), to deal with the business or assets in such a way as to produce better dividends for creditors than if the company had gone into winding up from the outset.[82]

The extant literature on insolvency reforms in various jurisdictions in Africa consistently points to the United Kingdom as the source of inspiration for this procedure. In Uganda, the insolvency law reform report cited the administration procedure in the Insolvency Act 1986 of the UK as the source of inspiration, and recommended that Uganda should borrow and adopt the procedure, albeit with a caution that it should suit local circumstances.[83] One of the key considerations that was overlooked in the introduction of this reform relates to the capital structure of businesses in Africa. Companies in Africa have a narrow range of options for raising capital, and the majority primarily rely on short-term, often secured, debt finance provided by banks. Therefore, in order to obtain support for the plan, an administration/reorganisation procedure should either be commenced by or supported by the financial creditor.

The administration/reorganisation procedure has often been introduced simultaneously with other insolvency reforms including measures to regulate the insolvency profession. However, across the continent, this is at varying levels of development. In an environment where the administrators are insolvency practitioners with varying levels of skill and professional regulation/oversight, new to the company, and perhaps operating in an environment where business records are poorly kept and business transactions intertwined with those of the entrepreneur, as is usually the case with family-owned SMEs, achieving the objectives of administration/reorganisation may be fraught with challenges. In jurisdictions such as Kenya, the administration procedure has suffered several setbacks such as high costs, protracted litigation, inability to raise post-commencement finance, and failure to resolve financial distress within the time frame envisaged in the law.

There are jurisdictional differences in some conceptual and procedural aspects of the procedure that are a result of both local adaptation and post-1986 reforms to the procedure in the jurisdiction of origin, that were adopted in some of the jurisdictions such as Kenya and Nigeria. Subsections III.C.(i) and (ii). below present the similarities and differences in objectives and procedures for appointment of an administrator across the legal frameworks in Uganda, Kenya, Malawi and Nigeria, while subsections (iii) to (iv) discuss some key issues that policy-makers arguably ought to have considered prior to adopting the reform.

[82] Roy Goode, *Principles of Corporate Insolvency Law*, 3rd edn (London, Sweet & Maxwell, 2011) 406.

[83] Uganda Law Reform Commission (ULRC), 'A Study Report on Insolvency Law', Law Comm Pub no 13 of 2004, 50–51.

(i) The Objectives of Administration/Reorganisation

The objectives of administration/reorganisation as provided in the statutes of the four jurisdictions signal a policy shift from liquidation to either rescuing the company (or some aspects of the business) or resolving the financial distress in a manner that produces better outcomes for all creditors. The former has broader societal benefits, including preserving jobs and economic activities related to the value chain of the business, while the latter is a better outcome in comparison to processes such as receivership, which serve the interests of a single creditor.

A review of the objectives of administration/reorganisation in the four jurisdictions indicates on one hand, similarities and differences to the UK (the objectives of administration as originally stated in section 8 of the Insolvency Act 1986 (UK) and the current objectives as provided for in Schedule B1 of the Act), as well as differences among the four countries. The differences are both in form and substance. Some jurisdictions, such as Kenya, follow the UK approach by expressly providing for objectives of administration, while Nigeria provides for the purpose of administration and Uganda focuses on the outcomes of the process. In Malawi, the law provides for objectives of reorganisation. As shown below, some jurisdictions adopted only some of the objectives of administration, as originally provided for in the UK Insolvency Act 1986, while others either adopted the current UK objectives or modified/enhanced them.

The similarities in the objectives relate to rescue and achieving a more advantageous realisation of the company's assets than would occur on a winding up.[84] Therefore, to the extent that administration/reorganisation provides an alternative to piecemeal and perhaps premature 'fire sales' of the debtors assets by secured creditors, through receivership and liquidation of economically viable businesses that are in financial difficulty, there is alignment between the UK and the transplanted reforms in Africa in terms of policy direction and expectation.

The Insolvency Act of UK provides for *rescuing the company as a going concern*, as the first objective (albeit that the commitment to pursuing this objective is a qualified one).[85] This is different to the original objective under the Insolvency Act 1986 prior to the reforms that were introduced by the Enterprise Act 2002.[86] It has been stated that following the 2002 reforms, the UK adopted a single-purpose approach to administration, whereby the revised objectives are presented in a hierarchical manner, with the going concern objective as the pre-eminent or priority objective.[87] The laws in Kenya, Nigeria, Malawi and Uganda provide for the rescue objective. However, its nature and scope vary, with some countries adopting a similar approach to the current UK law, while others have adopted the objective as originally stated in the 1986 UK Act. Malawi

[84] See Insolvency Act 1986 UK (Insol Act-UK) s 8(3)(a) and (d); Insol Act-Ug, s 140(1)(b)(i) and (iii); Insol Act-K, s 522(1)(a) and (b); Insol Act-M, s 14(1)(a) and (b); CAMA, s 444(1)(a) and (b).

[85] Insol Act-UK Sch B1 para 3(1)(a).

[86] Section 8(3) of Insol Act-UK originally provided for the 'survival of the company, and the whole or any part of its undertaking, as a going concern', as one of the four statutory purposes of administration.

[87] Goode, *Principles of Corporate Insolvency Law* (n 82), 401. Note that Insol Act-UK Sch B1 para 3 only provides for a qualified commitment to the first of the objectives, because the administrator should move to objective (b) if they think that (a) is not reasonably practicable or that (b) would achieve a better result for the company's creditors.

and Nigeria have a ranking of the objectives similarly to the UK law and therefore, in those jurisdictions, going concern rescue of the company itself is the preeminent objective. Section 522 of the Insolvency Act of Kenya simply lists the three objectives, while section 140(1) of the Insolvency Act of Uganda provides for the going concern objective as one of the outcomes that may be achieved and the administrator has discretion to choose the most suitable option.

The Insolvency Act of Kenya provides for the first objective of administration as 'to maintain the company as a going concern'.[88] The Insolvency Act of Malawi provides for a more expansive objective that includes rescuing the company as a going concern, restoring solvency and restoring the company and its business operations as a going concern.[89] Nigeria and Uganda provide options to either rescue the company in whole or in part.[90] Therefore, the laws provide for different outcomes of the administration procedure. In Kenya and Malawi, the administration procedure is designed to achieve corporate rescue, while the laws of Nigeria and Uganda provide options for either corporate or business rescue. It is arguable that rescuing the company may be a more favourable objective, considering the socio-economic nature of African enterprises, particularly family-owned businesses. On the other hand, an approach that allows the administrator more leeway to determine an appropriate outcome, depending on the circumstances of each company, may be more desirable. The latter may be more aligned with the UK approach as well as supporting a rescue culture that allows a good business idea to be rescued from the shackles of poor management which may have led to the existing problems.

The objective of achieving a better outcome for the company's creditors as a whole (the second in the UK list of objectives) is provided for as a possible outcome or objective in the laws of Nigeria, Kenya and Malawi.[91] In Uganda, the objective is worded slightly differently and aims for achieving a more advantageous realisation of the company's assets than would be effected in a liquidation.[92] The literature appears to suggest that even in jurisdictions such as the United Kingdom, this was a more realistic outcome of administration than the rescue of the company itself as a going concern objective.[93] In Africa, if policy-makers had given careful consideration to this objective, it would have been presented as the preeminent objective, as the first step towards building a culture of collective approaches to resolving financial distress. Achieving a better outcome for the general body of creditors has the potential to encourage collective and cooperative approaches to resolution of financial distress rather than

[88] The first objective of administration in s 522(1)(a) of Insol Act-K is to maintain the company as a going concern.

[89] Insol Act-M, s 14(1)(a).

[90] Section 140(1)(b)(i) of Insol Act-Ug provides for the survival of the company and the whole or any part of its undertaking as a going concern, while s 444(1)(a) of CAMA provides for rescuing the company, the whole or any part of its undertaking, as a going concern.

[91] See Insol Act-K, s 522(1)(b); CAMA, s 444(1)(b) and Insol Act-M, s 14(1)(b).

[92] Insol Act-Ug, s 140(b)(1)(iii).

[93] See Bolanle Adebola, 'An Invitation to Encourage Due Consideration of the Survivability of Rescued Businesses in the Business Rescue System of England and Wales' (2017) 26(2) *International Insolvency Review* 129; Paul J Omer and Jennifer Ghant, 'Corporate Rescue in the United Kingdom: Past, Present and Future Reforms' (2016) 132 *South African Law Journal* 39.

value-destroying fire sales using unilateral creditor collection tools such as receivership, which are primarily for the benefit of a single secured creditor.

The third objective of UK administration is to realise the property in order to make a distribution to one more secured or preferential creditors (but in pursuing this, the UK administrator must not cause unnecessary harm to the interests of the creditors of the company as a whole).[94] The laws of Nigeria, Kenya and Malawi have a similar objective.[95] The Insolvency Act of Uganda does not have this objective.

The objectives of administration/reorganisation in the four African jurisdictions examined here (Kenya, Uganda, Nigeria and Malawi) largely reflect the position in the UK from 1986 to the period following the 2002 reforms but not the post-2020 reforms (so that there is no statutory control on *ipso facto* clauses). The primary goal of introducing the procedure was to provide a tool that facilitates the rescue of financially distressed but viable business. However, apart from the broader issue of whether administration/reorganisation was the appropriate tool, the determination of the objectives of administration required an assessment as to what could be reasonably achieved, taking into account the peculiar circumstances of each jurisdiction.

(ii) Appointment of an Administrator

Under the UK Insolvency Act 1986, there are three ways an administrator may be appointed, that is, (i) by the court[96] following an application made individually or jointly by the company, directors of the company, one or more creditors of the company, or the justices chief executive of a magistrates court;[97] (ii) at the request of the holder of a qualifying floating charge;[98] or (iii) by the company or its directors, out of court.[99] Similarly in Kenya[100] and Nigeria,[101] the laws permit a company, its directors, the holder of a qualifying floating charge and the court to appoint an administrator. In Malawi, the appointment of an administrator requires an application to court individually or jointly by the company, its directors, one or more creditors of the company or by the

[94] Insol Act-UK, Sch B1 para 3(1)(a).

[95] Insol Act-K, s 522(1)(c); Insol Act-M, s 14(1)(c); CAMA, s 444(1)(c).

[96] Insol Act-UK, Sch B1 paras 10–13 provide that the court may make an administration order in respect of a company if satisfied that the company is or I likely to become unable to pay its debts and that the administration order is reasonable likely to achieve the purpose of administration.

[97] ibid, para 12.

[98] Appointment of an administrator by the holder of a qualifying floating charge does not require an application to court but must comply with the requirements of the Insol Act-UK, Sch B1 paras 14–21 which include powers to appoint an administrator by a floating charge instrument relating to a debenture secured by the whole or substantially the whole of the company's assets, notice to and consent of the holders of prior floating charges, and filing in court a notice of appointment together with a statutory declaration.

[99] Appointment of an administrator by the company or its directors does not require an application to court but must comply with the requirements of the Insol Act-UK, Sch B1 paras 22–34 including giving at least 5 business days' notice to persons entitled to appoint an administrative receiver or administrator, and filing the notice together with a statutory declaration in court.

[100] See Insol Act-UK, ss 530–532 (appointment by court following an application by any of the persons mentioned in s 532), 534–540 (appointment by holder of a qualifying floating charge), 541–543 (appointment by the company or its directors).

[101] See Insol Act-UK, ss 448–451 (appointment by court following an application by any of the persons mentioned in ss 450(1)), 452–458 (appointment by holder of a qualifying floating charge, following an application to court under s.450), ss 459–471 (appointment of an administrator out of court by the company or its directors).

holder of a qualifying security interest.[102] In Uganda, the law provides for a two-step process starting with provisional administration, a time-bound process of not more than 30 days,[103] that involves all the processes prior to the confirmation of an administration deed. These processes start with the company passing a special resolution to the effect that it needs to make a settlement with its creditors,[104] and filing a petition for an interim order.[105] The board is also required to appoint a provisional administrator by a special resolution and, following grant of an interim protective order, to issue a notice of appointment of a provisional administrator. The second step is the actual administration, which commences on the execution of the administration deed and appointment of an administrator.[106] The deed is binding on the company, directors, shareholders, administrator and all creditors as at the date of the deed for up to 21 days or such further period as the court may prescribe.[107]

The differences in procedural aspects such as the process for appointing an administrator indicate that the transplantation of the administration procedure across Africa has not been consistent with how the process has evolved in the UK. In some jurisdictions, such as Uganda, the UK administration was conceptualised as a court-driven process, hence the recommendation of the Uganda Law Reform Commission for Uganda to adopt a similar approach. The administration procedures in Kenya, Malawi and Nigeria reflect the position in the UK as of 2002. In this respect, the transplanted reforms have evolved at a slower pace than the reforms in the jurisdictions of origin. The procedural aspects need not have replicated the UK process. Local circumstances such as the level of development of the insolvency profession and the functioning of the judicial system are critical to determining the most suitable approach for each jurisdiction.

(iii) Requirements for the Commencement of Administration

Although the laws permit various parties to commence administration proceedings, each of the parties faces limitations or constraints similar to those highlighted in III.A and III.B. in relation to the pre-insolvency measures – that is, information asymmetry among creditors, stigma (see also III.B.(iv). below), and debt covenant restrictions. In all the four jurisdictions, the insolvency laws permit unilateral enforcement action by a creditor through the receivership process, which was commonly used by creditors, particularly financial creditors such as banks. Although there is evidence that in jurisdictions such as Kenya, banks have placed some companies into administration, in situations where administrations often fail to achieve the intended objective, there is a risk that creditors will be more attracted to unilateral processes such as receivership. Alternatively, creditors may use their privileged position (such as where a bank is able to detect financial distress early due to their monitoring capabilities) to take action that may exacerbate the debtor's financial situation. Such actions may include tighter control

[102] See Insol Act-M, ss 15–33.
[103] Insol Act-Ug, s 145(1)(a).
[104] Insol Act-Ug, s 139(3).
[105] Insol Act-Ug, s 139(4).
[106] ibid, s 162.
[107] ibid, s 150(2).

of the debtor's cash flows, which may impact working capital. If the debtor has other creditors such as suppliers and trade creditors, unpaid employment obligations and unpaid taxes, the ability of these types of creditors to monitor and commence administration in a timely manner is limited, at least before the company is defaulting on debts as and when they fall due.

(iv) Administration and Control of the Debtor

The appointment of an administrator leads to loss of managerial control. In jurisdictions where managerial control is exercised by the entrepreneur/shareholder and the majority of businesses are family-owned Small and Medium Enterprises (SMEs), the stigma associated with a public process and loss of control resulting from appointment of an administrator will force an entrepreneur to seek alternatives to resolve financial distress. Even if administration was the only viable solution, stigma and loss of control will inhibit timely commencement, which is critical for the achievement of the objectives of administration.

In addition to the problem of loss of control, there are challenges related to the capacity and competence of administrators. In most jurisdictions, the administration procedure was introduced simultaneously with other insolvency reforms, including the regulation of insolvency practitioners.[108] Some jurisdictions also have initiatives to develop the insolvency profession. In most jurisdictions in Africa that have the administration/reorganisation procedure, both the regulation and insolvency professional development initiatives are in nascent stages, and this has impact on the outcomes of administration.

The allure of the UK-style administration procedure appears illusory. In Uganda, the procedure was adopted in 2011 and for the period it has been in existence, only six companies have been placed in administration. Therefore, in Uganda, the procedure is a 'dead letter.' In Kenya, about 50 companies have been placed in administration from 2020–23.[109] There is no data on the outcomes, but some high-profile cases have lasted several years and ultimately ended up in liquidation, with creditors receiving much less than they would have received if the companies had been liquidated at the time administration proceedings were commenced. Recent adopters, such as Nigeria, continued the transplanting tradition with no consideration of the experiences of early adopters. Considering the manner in which administration has evolved in the UK, it appears that is it more valuable as a tool used in combination with other procedures, such as a CVA or in pre- packs.

[108] The World Bank provides four pillars for building insolvency regimes. Competence and integrity of the insolvency profession is one of the elements of the institutional and regulatory frameworks pillar. See The World Bank, 'Principles for Effective Insolvency and Creditor/Debtor Regimes' (2021 edn): https://documents1.worldbank.org/curated/en/391341619072648570/pdf/Principles-for-Effective-Insolvency-and-Creditor-and-Debtor-Regimes.pdf (accessed September 2024). Gurrea-Matinez also argues that qualified industry professionals are critical to the design of insolvency frameworks. Aurelio Gurrea-Matinez, 'Insolvency Law in Emerging Markets' (2021) *Iber-American Law and Finance Working Paper* 3/2023, p 15: https://papers.ssrn.com/sol3/papers.cfm?abstract_id=3606395 (accessed 16 September 2024).

[109] See https://brs.go.ke/office-of-the-official-receiver/ (accessed 26 September 2024).

D. Company Voluntary Arrangements

A Company Voluntary Arrangement (CVA) is a debt restructuring procedure whereby a company enters into a composition with its creditors in satisfaction of its debt or a scheme of arrangement of the affairs of the company. A form of scheme of arrangement procedure existed in the Companies Act of the UK and company laws of most common law jurisdictions in Africa. The Cork Committee reforms introduced a simplified CVA into the insolvency framework of the UK,[110] and this approach has been adopted in some African jurisdictions such as Kenya and Nigeria. The key features of the CVA relate to commencement, development, approval and sanctioning of a debt restructuring plan. The CVA, as provided for under English law and the laws of Kenya and Nigeria, may be proposed by the directors of the company (the company need not be insolvent)[111] or during insolvency, by an administrator or liquidator.[112] The process requires the appointment of a third party to oversee the development and implementation of the plan,[113] company and creditor approval of and court sanctioning of the plan.[114]

Under UK insolvency law, the CVA is a simplified debt restructuring procedure and although it may be used by both small and large companies, empirical evidence shows that over 90 per cent of companies entering a CVA in the UK were small and micro companies.[115] This may suggest that it might be appropriate for African jurisdictions, where the majority of businesses are MSMEs. However, the CVA has not delivered on its promise in the UK. This is attributed to availability in the UK of more efficient tools, such as the pre-pack, and to key crucial limiting factors. Initially under the Insolvency Act 1986, the CVA did not have a moratorium. This undermined its effectiveness as a stand-alone pre-insolvency restructuring procedure. In 2000, a small company moratorium was introduced. However, the procedural requirements for obtaining it were onerous and data indicates that only a very small proportion of small companies applied for it.[116] The UK small company moratorium was subsequently removed in 2020.[117] The inability of a CVA to bind preferential and secured creditors (both limitations are explained further below) may explain why the procedure is largely used by small companies in the UK. This weakness is a factor that

[110] Part 1, Insol Act-UK.

[111] Insol Act-UK, Part 1 s 1(1); Insol Act-K, s 625(1) and CAMA, s 434(1).

[112] Insol Act-UK, Part 1 s 1(3); Insol Act-K, s 625(4) and CAMA s 434(3).

[113] A nominee (UK and Nigeria) or supervisor (Kenya). All jurisdictions require the appointed person to be an insolvency practitioner.

[114] Insol Act-UK, Part 1 s 1(3) and (4); Insol Act-K, s 625(1) and CAMA, s 437.

[115] Peter Walton, Chris Umfreville and Lézelle Jacobs, 'Company Voluntary Arrangements: Evaluating Success and Failure' (R3 and Institute of Chartered Accountants for England & Wales publication, May 2018), 3: https://publications.aston.ac.uk/id/eprint/37094/1/R3_ICAEW_CVA_Report_May_2018.pdf (accessed 21 January 2025). See also Adrian Walters and Sandra Frisby, 'Preliminary Report to the UK Insolvency Service into Outcomes in Company Voluntary Arrangements: Evaluating Success and Failure', 9: https://papers.ssrn.com/sol3/papers.cfm?abstract_id=1792402 (accessed 5 April 2024).

[116] See Walton, Umfreville and Jacobs, 'Company Voluntary Arrangements: Evaluating Success and Failure' (n 115) 3; Payne, 'Debt Restructuring in English Law' (n 6) at 288–89.

[117] Kristin van Zwieten, 'Mid-Crisis Restructuring Law Reform in the United Kingdom' (2023) *European Business Organization Law Review* 287–315.

policy-makers in African jurisdictions should have considered in view of the extensive use of secured debt finance. CVAs in the UK are beleaguered by high costs, primarily associated with the nominee appointed to oversee the plan and low-level payouts/dividends to creditors.[118] Also, only a small fraction of CVAs in the UK (18.5 per cent) achieve their objective.[119] These factors should have been considered by policy-makers in the jurisdictions in Africa that transplanted this procedure from the UK. Sections III.C.(i)–(iv) below present an analysis of key features of the CVA as provided for in laws of Kenya and Nigeria.

(i) Commencement of a CVA

A CVA may be commenced prior to or during insolvency. Only company directors have the right to commence a CVA prior to insolvency.[120] Similarly to the UK, the laws of Kenya and Nigeria provide that the directors of a company may make a proposal for a CVA where the debtor wishes to enter into a composition in satisfaction of its debts or a scheme for arranging its financial affairs.[121] By not requiring the debtor to be in financial distress, the CVA presents potential for early resolution of financial distress. In this respect, Payne states that a CVA can be used as a debt restructuring and early rescue tool.[122] In addition, although the CVA requires the involvement of a nominee/supervisor, management remains in place, and therefore it is a debtor-in-possession procedure.[123] Despite these potential advantages, there are significant limitations associated with the process.

The CVA is commenced by the directors or the administrator or liquidator of a company presenting a debt restructuring proposal. A proposal made by the directors must be presented to the nominee/supervisor, who is required to assess and report to court on the viability of the plan and also present it to the members and creditors of the company for approval. By adopting a similar approach to the UK, the laws in Kenya and Nigeria ignored key contextual considerations. The first relates to the financing of businesses. It is not clear why it was felt necessary to introduce an early financial distress resolution tool in Insolvency law (in Kenya) and Company law (in Nigeria) that exists in parallel to bank debt resolution tools including informal workouts. As indicated earlier, a CVA is not binding on secured creditors and yet secured bank debt is the most widely used form of formal credit. Secondly, a prevalent dynamic in SMEs in Africa is that ownership, management and to some degree, financing, are often intertwined. In situations where the directors are also the owners, and where the company is financed largely by shareholders and external credit secured by both company and personal assets of owners as well as by personal guarantees of the owners, it is unlikely that they will seek

[118] Walton, Umfreville and Jacobs, 'Company Voluntary Arrangements: Evaluating Success and Failure' (n 115) 46–48.

[119] Walton, Umfreville and Jacobs, 'Company Voluntary Arrangements: Evaluating Success and Failure' (n 115) 3.

[120] Insol Act-K, s 625(1) and CAMA, s 434(1).

[121] ibid.

[122] Payne, 'Debt Restructuring in English Law' (n 6) at 287–88.

[123] ibid at 288; Goode, *Principles of Corporate Insolvency Law* (n 82) at 494.

early resolution due to the problem of stigma, even when the process leaves them largely in control. This is because financial distress is perceived as failure.

The supervisor/nominee is required to report to the court within 28 days (in the case of Nigeria) or 30 days (in the case of Kenya). This requires the supervisor to assess the viability of the plan. The time frame assumes that the supervisor/nominee has the capacity to do so and that the information availed by the debtor will allow for timely and credible assessment. In Africa, both these cannot be assumed because the regulation and development of the insolvency profession started with insolvency reforms, and is thus still nascent in most jurisdictions. The record-keeping, governance and financial reporting practices of SMEs in Africa are well documented. Therefore, the ability of the supervisor/nominee to assess the viability of the plan may be limited by his or her own competencies and lack of credible/reliable information. In situations where ownership and management are fused, the relevance of member/shareholder approval is questionable.

(ii) The Moratorium for a CVA

The CVA, as originally provided for in the Insolvency Act 1986 (UK), did not provide for a moratorium, and this was considered a key weakness of the procedure and perhaps one of the reasons why a CVA is used together with other insolvency processes such as administration. The law in Nigeria does not provide for a moratorium for a CVA. Therefore, similarly to the UK, it would be practical to use a CVA concurrently with administration.

The Insolvency Act of Kenya does not permit a moratorium for companies with debt that is in excess of Kenyan Shillings 1 billion (approximately USD 7.8 million) or for insurance companies, banks, certain project companies, companies in liquidation, and companies that either are or have been in administration or in a CVA in the last 12 months.[124] A moratorium is only permitted for eligible companies whose debt is below the equivalent of USD 7.8 million. The directors of an eligible company proposing a CVA are permitted to apply for a moratorium, which commences on the day the application is made and ends on the day of creditor meetings are held.[125] The moratorium extends to cover resolutions or applications to place the company into administration or liquidation, company meetings, actions by landlords and actions to enforce any security over the company's property or to possess goods in the company's possession, or property that is the subject of an uncrystallised floating charge.[126] It appears that, in attempting to approach the issue of the moratorium in this manner, Kenya was following the pre-2020 UK approach of a small company moratorium.

The moratorium, although potentially useful to eligible companies, has features that may be limiting factors. Although in theory the limited scope moratorium permits SMEs to use the CVA with the benefit of the moratorium, in practical terms it may not be helpful where the debt is secured, as is usually the case with bank debt. The time lag

[124] Insol Act-K, ss 639–642.
[125] Insol Act-K, ss 643–645.
[126] Insol Act-K, ss 649–650.

between the time of proposing the CVA and making the application for a moratorium exposes the debtor to the risk of creditor enforcement action. Some eligible companies might find it difficult to meet the requirements for the moratorium, particularly the requirement that the application be supported by a statement from the supervisor indicating that the proposal has a reasonable prospect of being approved and implemented and that the company is likely to have sufficient funds to carry on business during the proposed period of the moratorium.[127] These requirements are similar to the small company moratorium requirements in the UK, prior to the 2020 reforms. A 2018 study in the UK showed that although there was a higher likelihood of positive outcomes in CVAs where small companies used the moratorium, very few small companies actually did use the moratorium.[128] This was attributed to the onerous requirement that an application for a moratorium should be supported by the supervisor's opinion on the likelihood of success of the CVA.

For companies in Kenya that are ineligible for the moratorium, the absence of a moratorium is one of the shortcomings of the CVA[129] because, although the company may not yet be insolvent, there is no mechanism for preventing unilateral creditor enforcement action. It is important to note that the most recent amendments to the UK insolvency law abolished the small company provision and introduced a more general moratorium.[130]

(iii) The Treatment of Secured and Preferential Creditors

Another limitation of the CVA is that it is not binding on secured and preferential creditors.[131] This is an important consideration in jurisdictions where financial markets are not developed and therefore bank credit (particularly secured credit) is the most widely used finance, and where the insolvency laws have wide-ranging preferential creditors including tax authorities and employees.[132] Therefore, the CVA would not help resolve financial distress of a debtor whose principal creditors include secured creditors (such as a bank which has security interests over a significant portion of the debtor's assets) and creditors who have preferential status, such as unpaid employee and tax obligations. In situations where the major creditor is a bank, it is possible that the directors would only consider a CVA after exhausting the options available for resolving distress within the banking frameworks; if these have failed, it is likely that the debtor may be approaching the zone of insolvency, relations with the bank may be strained and therefore the bank, as secured creditor is unlikely to consent to a CVA. Empirical data in the UK suggests that there are low levels of secured debt among CVAs, therefore suggesting that CVAs are not suited to secured debt restructuring.[133]

[127] Insol Act-K, s 643(5).

[128] Walton, Umfreville and Jacobs (n 115) 3–7. See also Walters and Frisby (n 115) 10.

[129] Payne, 'Debt Restructuring in English Law' (n 6) at 288–89.

[130] For important differences between the small company moratorium and the new freestanding moratorium, see Kristin van Zwieten, 'Mid-Crisis Restructuring Law Reform in the United Kingdom (2023) *European Business Organization Law Review* 287–315.

[131] Payne, 'Debt Restructuring in English Law' (n 6) at 288–89. See CAMA, s 437(4)(a) and (b).

[132] See Insol Act-K, second Sch and CAMA, s 657.

[133] Walters and Frisby, 'Outcomes in Company Voluntary Arrangements' (n 115), 10.

(iv) A CVA During Administration/Liquidation

Similarly to the UK, the Insolvency laws of Kenya and Nigeria permit an administrator or liquidator to propose a CVA.[134] In this respect, the combined administration/CVA or liquidation/CVA may produce better outcomes for creditors. Goode, for example, states that the CVA is not suitable for preserving the business but may be useful where it is necessary for the business to continue trading, or to facilitate a more favourable disposal of assets than in a liquidation.[135] Payne also states that in jurisdictions such as the UK, the CVA is valuable when used in combination with processes such administration. As indicated in section III.B. above, although widely adopted across Africa, administration is largely a white elephant on the restructuring landscape. Kenya has only registered one CVA since 2015 when it was introduced onto the restructuring landscape of Kenya. Therefore, twinning a CVA with administration will not necessarily lead to better outcomes, particularly for so long as there remains an underdeveloped insolvency profession, and inadequate tools for the restructuring of secured debt. A CVA combined with liquidation is not likely to resolve the inefficiencies of the process, given the signal sent by the commencement of such proceedings and the limited ability to continue to trade in liquidation.

IV. Conclusion

This chapter has shown that although the restructuring reforms in Africa signal a policy shift from relying on liquidation as the primary tool for resolving financial distress, the reforms have followed the pattern of insolvency frameworks, that is, largely transplanted from advanced economies. Among the common law jurisdictions, the reforms are largely inspired by reforms in the United Kingdom and some aspects of the US Chapter 11 process. The restructuring measures in the Francophone OHADA region draw heavily on the French system. The South African business rescue procedure, although 'home grown', uses approaches that draw heavily on the US Chapter 11 and the UK administration procedure, such as director displacement and substantial court involvement.

Apart from in relation to the CVA, the transplanted measures use approaches and tools suited to intra-creditor resolution of financial distress in large companies with complex financing structures, yet capital structures and financing arrangements differ from advanced economies. The CVA suffers from its own limitations, ones which might also have inhibited UK restructuring practice were it not for the presence of alternatives in the UK. In addition, there are procedural and substantive differences in the design of transplanted procedures, which produce inconsistencies across similar procedures in different jurisdictions. Inconsistencies are not, of course, per se problematic. But those identified above seem to be a product of factors such as the timing of adoption of the reforms (looking to original rather than revised legislation in the exporting

[134] Insol Act-K, s 625 and CAMA, s 434.

[135] Goode, *Principles of Corporate Insolvency Law* (n 82) at 494–95. See also Walters and Frisby, 'Outcomes in Company Voluntary Arrangements' (n 115) at 31.

jurisdiction), and a piecemeal approach transplantation that does not produce a good 'fit' with the overall insolvency framework and broader context.

Transplantation dilemmas also exist among advanced economies and some scholars have not only warned against a simplistic transplantation of restructuring processes such as the US Chapter 11,[136] but also questioned its relevance in the current economic environment. Baird and Rasmussen argue that the US Chapter 11, which, in its historical form, was developed in the context of equity receivership of railroads – which was considered ideal because the assets were dedicated to a particular economic activity and needed to be kept together in a firm – is not suited to the current economic environment where assets are not dedicated to a particular firm.[137] This is not the case with the majority of businesses in Africa, particularly MSMEs, most of which operate in sectors such as trade, agriculture and construction, which do not require asset-specific investments. The transplanted measures often have limitations that the transplanting jurisdictions either ignore or are oblivious to. Miller and Waisman, for example, argue that despite the weakness of the reorganisation procedure under Chapter 11 of the US Bankruptcy Code – such as concerns relating to cost, excessive creditor control, relevance of Chapter 11 to a post-Industrial Revolution economy, and diminished debtor protection resulting from subsequent legislative changes – it remains an important neutral forum for resolution of multi-party competing interests.[138] Jennifer Payne's analysis of restructuring measures in the UK prior to the most recent (CIGA 2020) reforms, indicates that each of the measures – that is, informal workouts, CVAs, schemes of arrangement, and administration – has significant flaws.[139] For example, informal workouts lack a moratorium to prevent creditor enforcement; CVAs are expensive, lack (or in some cases have a limited scope) moratorium, and are not binding on secured and preferential creditors; schemes of arrangement do not have a mechanism for cross-class cram down; and administration can only be triggered during insolvency and is also expensive. These shortcomings are sometimes not easily resolved by reform processes in the jurisdictions of origin, as evidenced by the identified challenges in the most recent reforms in the UK,[140] and these complexities are often replicated in the transplanted reforms.

The allure of restructuring reforms in advanced economies puts developing and emerging economies in a double bind as they seek to align their frameworks with advanced economies but in doing so neither address the need for local solutions nor present a coherent approach.

[136] Payne, 'Debt Restructuring in English Law' (n 6) at 302.
[137] Douglas G Baird and Robert K Rasmussen, 'The End of Bankruptcy' (2002) 55 *Stanford Law Review* 751.
[138] Harvey R Miller and Shai Y Waisman, 'Is Chapter 11 Bankrupt' (2005) 47(1) *Boston College Law Review* 129, 170, 180, 181.
[139] Payne, 'Debt Restructuring in English Law' (n 6) at 298.
[140] See van Zwieten, 'Mid-Crisis Restructuring Law Reform' (n 66).

10

Recognition in Cross-border Restructurings

REINHARD BORK

I. Introduction

Nowadays, restructurings have more and more cross-border implications. Debtors have assets abroad, are obligated to foreign creditors, have debts governed by foreign law, are engaged in contractual relationships with counterparties in other jurisdictions, or have other cross-border affairs, eg offices, branches, or subsidiaries in a different country. Where such debtor companies are reorganised, this will inevitably implicate more than one jurisdiction and more than one set of laws. This raises the question as to whether the cross-border effects of a restructuring being undertaken in state A, under the laws of state A, are recognisable in state B.[1] Let me illustrate this with two examples, both of which are modelled on cases from court practice concerning English restructurings.

My first example is derived from the *Equitable Life* decision of the German Bundesgerichtshof (Federal Court of Justice).[2] A scheme of arrangement, sanctioned by the High Court in London, provided for a waiver of all claims against an insurance company in exchange for a new contractual relationship with the debtor company. A German creditor, who had unsuccessfully opposed the scheme in the English proceedings, sued the company for payment in Germany. The Bundesgerichtshof did not consider the scheme to be recognisable under the European Insolvency Regulation (EIR)[3] or national cross-border insolvency regime.[4] The court regarded the scheme as a solvent scheme and therefore held that the scheme proceedings could not be 'insolvency proceedings' for the purpose of recognition under section 343 InsO (and equally under

[1] A general introduction to recognition in insolvencies is given in Reinhard Bork, *Cross-Border Insolvency Law* (Cheltenham, Edward Elgar, 2023) ch 4.

[2] BGH, 15.02.2012 – IV ZR 194/09, NJW 2012, 2113 at [21] et seq; see on this decision, Reinhard Bork, *Zeitschrift für Europäisches Privatrecht 2013*, 132–46.

[3] Regulation (EU) 2015/848 of the European Parliament and of the Council of 20 May 2015 on insolvency proceedings (recast) OJ of 5 June 2015, L 141/19.

[4] §§ 335–358 Insolvenzordnung (InsO, German Insolvency Regulation) English text available at: https://www.gesetze-im-internet.de/englisch_inso/ (accessed 13 June 2024). (InsO).

the EIR). It also refused recognition under the Brussels I-Regulation[5] (as it then was), albeit only because the English court lacked jurisdiction under mandatory rules regarding insurance companies.

The second example stems from the *Hydrodec* decision of the Supreme Court of New South Wales (Australia).[6] In this case, a company incorporated and with its registered office in the United Kingdom (but with subsidiaries in a range of jurisdictions, including Australia) tried to prevent Australian creditors from filing for insolvency proceedings in Australia by invoking the English stand-alone moratorium under Part A1 of the Insolvency Act 1986 (IA 1986), a moratorium designed to facilitate restructuring.[7] Subsequently, winding-up proceedings were applied for in Australia and the company applied for recognition of the moratorium as a main proceeding under the Model Law with a view to obtaining a stay of the Australian insolvency process.[8] The Supreme Court of New South Wales treated the moratorium as 'insolvency proceedings' for the purposes of recognition under the Australian Cross-Border Insolvency Act 2008, the Australian version of the UNCITRAL Model Law on Cross-Border Insolvency.[9] However, the Court did not recognise the moratorium as main insolvency proceedings, because the debtor did not have its centre of main interest (COMI) in England, but in the United States. Winding-up proceedings were then opened in Australia.

Both decisions deal with recognition of English restructuring measures and in both cases recognition was denied, albeit for very diverging reasons. These examples raise three questions that I will address below. First, what is the object of recognition? Second, what is the legal framework for recognition? Third, what are the main issues in this context?

II. The Object of Recognition

To begin with the object of recognition, recognition is primarily about the legal *effects* of the restructuring process[10] and only secondarily about the restructuring proceedings

[5] Council Regulation (EC) No 44/2001 of 22 December 2000 on jurisdiction and the recognition and enforcement of judgments in civil and commercial matters, OJ of 16 January 2001, L 12/1. In English terminology often labelled as 'Judgments Regulation'. I will stick here to the name typically used in the European Union.

[6] *Re Hydrodec Group Plc* [2021] NSWSC 755; on this case (albeit concentrating on the COMI issue); Paul Apáthy and Angus Dick, 'Recognition of UK Part A1 Moratorium process rejected by NSW Supreme Court', 21 July 2021, available at: https://hsfnotes.com/apac-rti/2021/07/21/recognition-of-uk-part-a1-moratorium-process-rejected-by-nsw-supreme-court/ (accessed 2 January 2024); Scott Atkins and Kai Luck, '*Re Hydrodec Group* [2021] NSWSC 755' (2021) 30 *International Insolvency Review* 460–68; Graham Roberts and Ben Williams, 'Australian court winds up UK company and dismisses recognition application by UK monitors' [2021] *Corporate Rescue & Insolvency (CRI)* 118–20.

[7] As regards the moratorium, see further Natalie Mrockova, Chapter 8 in this book.

[8] Or to stay proceedings in exercise of the power to give relief under s 521(2)(a) of the Corporations Act 2001, which the Court also declined.

[9] United Nations Commission on International Trade Law, UNCITRAL Model Law on Cross-Border Insolvency with Guide to Enactment and Interpretation (New York, UN Publications, 2014) (ML): https://digitallibrary.un.org/record/1487896?v=pdf.

[10] See for this focus Stephan Madaus, 'The Cross-border Effects of Restructurings' in Katharina de la Durantaye, David Paulus, Ignacio Tirado, Jay Westbrook and Wolfgang Zenker (eds), *Verbindungslinien im Recht: Festschrift für Christoph Paulus zum 70. Geburtstag* (Munich, CH Beck, 2022), 471–87 at 475.

as such or the court decision that brought about these effects. For example, where a shareholder to whom shares have been assigned in a restructuring plan asserts rights in connection with these shares, we would ask whether the claimant can be recognised as a legitimate shareholder of the company. Of course, this depends on whether the court order that sanctioned the restructuring plan is recognisable, but this is a preliminary question to the actual topic. Similarly, where a creditor whose claims have been compromised by an English scheme of arrangement demands payment of the full (uncompromised) amount, the main question concerns the substantive position of the claimant as a creditor of the company (and in particular the extent of the company's obligation to them), and the eligibility of the scheme decision for recognition is only a prerequisite for determining this. The same holds true where a company claims that insolvency proceedings should not be commenced due to a foreign moratorium, as in the *Hydrodec* example above. Such an application is primarily about the recognition of the enforcement ban as a legal consequence of the moratorium, and only secondarily about the recognition of the moratorium order as such.

This distinction between a decision and its effects is not some mere quibble, but an important point to understand. In principle, recognition of a foreign court decision means two things: first, that a foreign decision is not ignored but treated as existent and valid; secondly, that the effects attributed to the decision by the foreign law are extended to the domestic territory.[11] Both must be kept apart. It may very well be that the foreign court decision is recognised as such, meaning that the recognising courts treat the decision as existing and valid without further review, but that not all of its legal effects are recognisable (for example, because one of them violates public policy). Conversely, it is also possible that the court decision is not recognised (for example, because the prerequisites for recognition under national insolvency or procedural law are not met) but its legal effects are, for example on the basis of the prevailing rules of substantive private international law.

The distinction between recognition of a decision opening insolvency proceedings and the extension of its effects is nicely mirrored in Article 19(1) EIR (recognition of the decision to open main proceedings) and Article 20 EIR (extension of its effects). It also finds its expression in the rules on the recognition of decisions concerning the course and closure of the proceedings, including the approval of compositions (Article 32 EIR). I will come back to this aspect later on.[12]

III. The Legal Framework for Recognition

Before dealing with the details, the legal framework should be sketched out.[13] It follows from what has been said so far that recognition of the legal effects of restructurings can

[11] *cf* M Veder, 'Article 19 – Principle' in R Bork and K van Zwieten, *Commentary on the European Insolvency Regulation*, 2nd edn (Oxford, OUP, 2022), para [19.02].

[12] Below at section VI.

[13] Extensive elaborations on recognition of restructurings are given by Chris Howard, Presley Warner and Chris Beatty, *Restructuring Law & Practice*, 3rd edn (London, LexisNexis, 2022) at [15.169] et seq; Geoff O'Dea, *Restructuring Plans, Creditor Schemes, and Other Restructuring Tools* (Oxford, OUP, 2022) at [2.70]

be based on cross-border insolvency law, cross-border civil procedure law, and private international law. This taxonomy follows the framework of EU law, which provides for rules on cross-border insolvency law in the EIR, on cross-border civil procedure law (Brussels I^{bis} Regulation), and on the private international law for substantive legal relationships (Rome I–III Regulations).[14]

As regards cross-border insolvency law, Articles 19, 32 of the EIR are no longer available in the 'recognition toolbox' when it comes to recognition within the EU of English restructuring proceedings,[15] because these provisions concern recognition and enforcement of decisions by a court of an EU Member State in connection with the opening, course and closure of proceedings (and approval of compositions) falling within the scope of the EIR.[16] Nor can recognition in Member States be based on Article 36 Brussels I^{bis} Regulation,[17] since this provision requires a judgment given in an EU Member State.

Instead, provisions in national cross-border insolvency laws for recognition and relief in respect of foreign proceedings may, depending on the particular regime and the facts, be applicable. Outside of the EU, many such provisions are based on the UNCITRAL Model Law on Cross-Border Insolvency, which has been adopted in 60 states in a total of 63 jurisdictions.[18] Others copy the EIR;[19] still others are completely independent in their historical development.

Finally, private international law must also be taken into consideration. The main legal source for the recognition of the legal effects of restructuring-related decisions on the parties' substantive rights (eg deferral, reduction of claims or security rights, reduction of interest rates, etc) can be the Rome I Regulation,[20] at least when it comes to recognition in EU Member States, because there the Rome I Regulation is directly

et seq, [2.126] et seq; Jennifer Payne, 'Cross-border issues' in *Schemes of Arrangement. Theory, Structure and Operation*, 2nd edn (Cambridge, CUP, 2021), ch 7 (pp 344–75); Christian Pilkington and Will Stoner, *Creditor Schemes of Arrangement and Restructuring Plans*, 3rd edn (London, Sweet & Maxwell, 2022), ch 11.

[14] A similar approach is taken in Art 1(2) Hague Convention on the Recognition and Enforcement of Foreign Judgments in Civil or Commercial Matters (*cf* below n 67). In other jurisdictions, 'private international law' may be used as an umbrella term for all rules on these legal fields, including those of cross-border insolvency and civil procedure law.

[15] Although certain English proceedings never fell within the scope of the Regulation, be it because they were never included in Annex A to the EIR, or because the proceedings were listed in Annex A but are capable of being invoked on both insolvency and non-insolvency grounds, with only the former falling within the Regulation's scope. See *Re Marann Brooks CSV Ltd* [2003] BCC 239; Kristin van Zwieten, 'Article 1 – Scope' in Bork and van Zwieten (above n 11) para [1.38] et seq.

[16] For an overview of post-Brexit recognition, see Jamie Murray-Jones, Luke FitzGerald, Miryam Farrelly, Craig Montgomery, Joseph Clarke and Darrin Carey, 'How Are the English Courts Adapting to Post-Brexit Challenges?' (2023) 20 *International Corporate Rescue (ICR)* 79–84 at 80 et seq; Kate Stephenson, 'Addressing Post-Brexit Limitations of Cross-Border Recognition of Restructuring and Insolvency Proceedings in Europe' (2021) 18 *ICR* 1–6; Kate Stephenson, Zoe Stembridge and Ann-Kathrin Ziegler, 'One year on: has Brexit been as "hard" as imagined?' (2022) 19 *ICR* 3–9.

[17] Regulation (EU) No 44/2001 of the European Parliament and of the Council of 12 December 2012 on jurisdiction and the recognition and enforcement of judgments in civil and commercial matters (recast), OJ of 20 December 2012, L 351/1.

[18] *cf* https://uncitral.un.org/en/texts/insolvency/modellaw/cross-border_insolvency/status (accessed 13 June 2024).

[19] An example is the German cross-border insolvency law in §§ 335 et seq InsO.

[20] Regulation (EC) 593/2008 of the European Parliament and of the Council of 17 June 2008 on the law applicable to contractual obligations (Rome I), OJ of 4 July 2008, L 177/6 (Rome I Regulation).

applicable, which also holds true in relation to third countries.[21] In Non-EU Member States, national private international law may be a relevant source.

This very brief overview reveals the difficulty of making general statements on the recognition of English restructuring processes outside the UK. Whether recognition is possible or not depends very much on the applicable national law of the state where recognition is sought. As national laws can differ greatly, it may well be that the restructuring is recognised in one country but not in another. I will now explore the legal frameworks in more detail.

IV. Recognition under Cross-border Insolvency Law

The first way to recognise restructuring is to apply cross-border insolvency law. However, it is true that restructuring proceedings and insolvency proceedings are very different in nature: the former are more debt-focused, the latter more asset-focused.[22] It is therefore by no means self-evident that cross-border insolvency law also covers reorganisation proceedings. Rather, this must be explained in more detail based on the relevant norms.

A. UNCITRAL Model Law

In many jurisdictions, the national cross-border insolvency law is shaped after the UNCITRAL Model Law on Cross-Border Insolvency. In the following analysis, it is assumed that the applicable national law corresponds to the text of the Model Law (ML), although in practice there are divergences.

Article 15 ML provides for the recognition of a 'foreign proceeding', not expressly of 'insolvency proceedings', but it follows from the subject matter of the Model Law and the definition of 'foreign proceeding' in Article 2(a) ML that it deals with the recognition of insolvency proceedings. Many authors have explored the question of what insolvency proceedings are, and what characterises and defines them.[23] The analysis in this section will not deal with this question at some general or conceptual level, but rather focus on

[21] Compared to the Rome I Regulation, the EIR is narrower in scope (since it is restricted to proceedings listed in Annex A for debtors with their COMI in an EU Member State) and it principally applies to regulate inter-Member-State relationships only (with the relativisations described by the CJEU in Case C-328/12 *Schmid v Hertel*, ECLI:EU:C:2014:6, [2014] 1 WLR 633).

[22] See on this extensively Madaus, 'The Cross-border Effects of Restructurings' (above n 10), at 479 et seq, who (at 482 et seq) therefore pleads for a new framework for cross-border restructurings under private international law in accordance with the *lex causae*.

[23] For examples, see Horst Eidenmüller, 'What Is An Insolvency Proceeding?' (2018) 92 *American Bankruptcy Law Journal* 53–72; Thomas H Jackson, *The Logics and Limits of Bankruptcy Law* (Cambridge MA, Harvard University Press, 1986; and Washington DC, Beard Books, 2001); Stephan Madaus, 'Leaving the Shadows of US Bankruptcy Law' (2018) 19 *European Business Organization Law Review (EBOR)* 615–47 at 620, 623 et seq; Riz Mokal, 'What is an insolvency proceeding? Gategroup lands in a gated community' (2022) 31 *International Insolvency Review* 418–73; Bob Wessels, 'What is an insolvency proceeding anyway?' (2011) (4) *International Insolvency Law Review* 491–510.

the specific question of what is meant by 'foreign proceedings' in the Model Law, and how English restructuring proceedings relate to this definition.

The term 'foreign proceeding' is defined in Article 2(a) ML as

> a collective judicial or administrative proceeding in a foreign state, including an interim proceeding, pursuant to a law relating to insolvency in which proceeding the assets and affairs of the debtor are subject to control or supervision by a foreign court, for the purpose of reorganization or liquidation.

From the perspective of a recognising state, English restructuring proceedings are not domestic but 'foreign' proceedings, However, it must be examined in more detail whether they are also proceedings within the meaning of this definition. I will answer this question for the restructuring plan in Part 26A of the Companies Act 2006 (UK),[24] the scheme of arrangement in Part 26 of the CA 2006,[25] and the stand-alone moratorium in Part A1 of IA 1986. For this purpose, five elements must be considered.

(i) Judicial or Administrative Proceedings

First, Article 2(a) ML requires judicial or administrative proceedings. That can easily be affirmed for schemes of arrangements and restructuring plans, since both need a convening order (sections 896, 901C CA 2006) and the sanctioning of the arrangement by the court (sections 899(1), 901F(1) CA 2006) and are therefore judicial proceedings. This is not so clear for the moratorium. On the one hand, the directors have to file the relevant documents with the court (section A3(2) IA 1986). On the other hand, a decision of the court is not necessary if the company is incorporated inside the UK (section 436(2) IA 1986, section 1044 CA 2006), since, in this case, the moratorium comes into force simply by filing the necessary documents with the court (section A7(a)(1) IA 1986).[26] However, Article 2(a) ML does not require a court decision. As the English Court of Appeal explained in *Stanford International Bank*, it suffices that the proceedings are subject to court supervision,[27] which is the case with the Part A1 moratorium, since the actions of the monitor and the directors are challengeable in court under sections A42 et seq IA 1986. Hence, a judicial procedure can be established here as well.

(ii) Pursuant to a Law Relating to Insolvency

Second, the proceedings must be conducted pursuant to a law relating to insolvency. It has been suggested that this prerequisite is met if the proceeding in question is regulated in insolvency law, ie in legislation that is called 'Insolvency Act' or similar.[28] However, that does not get to the heart of the matter, which does not depend on whether the

[24] Companies Act 2006 (CA 2006).

[25] For an overview, see Tim Lees, Michelle McGreal and Ellen Choi, 'Schemes of arrangement and their international effectiveness' [August 2022] *CRI* 124–26; see further above n 13.

[26] This is different for overseas companies, where a court order is required (ss A5(4)(a), A7(a)(3) IA 1986).

[27] *Re Stanford International Bank Ltd* [2010] EWCA Civ 137 at [15].

[28] *Re Hydrodec Group Plc* [2021] NSWSC 755 at [47].

respective proceedings are governed by insolvency law in some formal sense, but on whether they are factually linked to the insolvency of the company. Thus, function carries more weight than form.[29] As a consequence, it is not fatal if the proceedings are regulated by company law, provided they are connected to the debtor's insolvency,[30] and equally it is *not* sufficient if the proceedings are regulated in insolvency law but not connected to the debtor's insolvency.[31] On the other hand, it is not required that the debtor is already substantively insolvent. It suffices that the proceedings aim at protecting the distressed debtor from becoming substantively insolvent. As the Model Law's Guide to Enactment puts it: it is intended 'to refer broadly to proceedings involving debtors that are in severe financial distress or insolvent'.[32] Hence, Article 2(a) ML covers preventive restructuring proceedings as well.[33]

Against this background, it is generally recognised that scheme of arrangement proceedings – although impending or actual insolvency is not required in Part 26 CA 2006[34] – are insolvency-related proceedings within the meaning of Article 2(a) ML provided they are aiming at removing or preventing the company's substantive insolvency.[35] In contrast, 'solvent schemes' that do not seek to restructure the financial affairs of the company are not recognisable under the UNCITRAL Model Law.[36] The same distinction must be made here as between voluntary liquidation and liquidation in insolvency proceedings. Restructuring plan proceedings under Part 26A CA 2006 are beyond doubt within the scope of Article 2(a) ML, since section 901A(2) of

[29] Irit Mevorach and Adrian Walters, 'The Characterization of Pre-insolvency Proceedings in Private International Law' (2020) 21 *EBOR* 855–94 at 871.

[30] *Guide to Enactment and Interpretation of The UNCITRAL Model Law on Cross-Border Insolvency* (above n 9), at [73].

[31] According to some judgments, this prerequisite is met if liquidation proceedings were commenced on grounds that included insolvency, even though, in the particular case, the proceedings were based on other grounds (eg that it was just and equitable to wind up the company) without establishing the company's insolvency; see *Chow Cho Poon (Private) Limited* [2011] NSWSC 300 at [51]; *In re Betcorp Ltd*, 400 BR 266 (Bankr D Nev 2009); *Raithatha v Ariel Industries PLC* [2012] FCA 1526 at [41]; *Re Stanford International Bank* [2010] EWCA Civ 137 at [15]. See also *Re Ascentra Holdings, Inc (in official liquidation)* [2023] SGCA 32, where the Singapore Court of Appeal held (at paras 32 et seq) that foreign proceedings concerning companies that are neither insolvent nor in severe financial distress are included, as Art 2(h) of the SG Model Law, deviating from Art 2(a) UNCITRAL Model Law, refers to 'a law relating to insolvency or adjustment of debt'. However, this view should not be followed, as recognition is only dependent on whether the proceedings address the company's actual or impending insolvency, but not on whether they *could* have addressed this but did not actually do so.

[32] *Guide to Enactment and Interpretation of The UNCITRAL Model Law on Cross-Border Insolvency* (above n 9), at [65].

[33] *cf Re Gategroup Guarantee Limited* [2021] EWHC 304 (Ch) at [95]; Mevorach and Walters (above n 29), 870 et seq.

[34] On this, see Reinhard Bork, *Rescuing Companies in England and Germany* (Oxford, Oxford University Press, 2012) at [8.18].

[35] See *In re Avanti Communications Group PLC*, 582 BR 603 (Bankr SDNY 2018); *In re Agrokor DD* [2017] EWHC 2791 (Ch) at [68], [74]; *In re Cell C Proprietary Ltd*, 571 BR 542 (Bankr SDNY 2017); *Re Syncreon Group BV* [2019] ONSC 5774 at [28].

[36] *Re Sturgeon Central Asia Balanced Fund Ltd* [2020] EWHC 123 (Ch) at [5] et seq; *Guide to Enactment and Interpretation of The UNCITRAL Model Law on Cross-Border Insolvency* (above n 9), at [73]; Chan Ho Look, 'England' in Chan Ho Look (ed), *Cross-Border Insolvency: A Commentary on the UNCITRAL Model Law*, Vol 1, 4th edn (Woking, Globe Law and Business, 2017), at [178]; Mokal (above n 23), at 442. The *Equitable Life* decision of the German BGH referred to above (text to nn 2–5) cannot be used in this context, because it concerned German cross-border insolvency law rather than the UNCITRAL Model Law; see below at section IV.B.(i).

CA 2006 requires expressly 'that the company has encountered, or is likely to encounter, financial difficulties that are affecting, or will or may affect, its ability to carry on business as a going concern'. As for the Part A1 moratorium, in my view, the Supreme Court of New South Wales in *Hydrodec* was wrong to consider this an insolvency-related proceeding simply because it is regulated in the IA 1986.[37] This does not suffice. However, what does make the proceeding eligible to fall within the scope of the ML is that the directors (supported by a statement of the proposed monitor regarding the rescue prospects), must submit a statement that, in their view, 'the company is, or is likely to become, unable to pay its debts' (section A6(1)(d) and (e) IA 1986) in order to access the moratorium, which proves that the Part A1 moratorium is also sufficiently insolvency related.

(iii) For the Purpose of Reorganisation or Liquidation

Third, the proceedings must be conducted for the purposes of reorganisation or liquidation.[38] This is indubitably the case with insolvent schemes and restructuring plans,[39] but it is also the case with the moratorium. According to section A6(1)(e) IA 1986, the proposed monitor has to submit a statement that, in his or her view, it is likely that a moratorium for the company would result in the rescue of the company as a going concern. It follows indirectly from this that the purpose of the moratorium is to facilitate the reorganisation of the company[40] and therefore meets this requirement of Article 2(a) ML.[41]

(iv) Collectivity

The next prerequisite to discuss is collectivity, as the definition in Article 2(a) ML requires expressly collective proceedings.[42] The term 'collective' must be interpreted as opposed to 'individual'. According to the Guide to Enactment, it 'is not intended that the Model Law be used merely as a collection device for a particular creditor or group of creditors'.[43] This seems to create a problem for schemes of arrangement and restructuring plans, since both make it possible to restrict the arrangement to a specific group

[37] See above n 28.

[38] On this prerequisite, see *In re Agrokor DD* [2017] EWHC 2791 (Ch) at [100]; *In re British American Insurance Company Limited*, 425 BR 884 (Bankr SD Fla 2010); *In re Global Cord Blood Corporation* 22-11347 (DSJ) (Bankr SDNY Dec 5, 2022); *In re Millard*, 501 BR 644 (Bankr SDNY 2013); *In re Oversight and Control Commission of Avanzit SA*, 385 BR 525 (Bankr SDNY 2008).

[39] *cf* s 901A(3)(b) CA 2006 which provides that 'the purpose of the compromise or arrangement is to eliminate, reduce or prevent, or mitigate the effect of, any of the financial difficulties'. See also, albeit for Art 1 EIR, *Re Gategroup Guarantee Limited* [2021] EWHC 304 (Ch) at [115].

[40] For details, see Kristin van Zwieten, 'Mid-Crisis Restructuring Law Reform in the United Kingdom' (2023) 24 *EBOR* 287–315 at 296 et seq.

[41] *Re Hydrodec Group Plc* [2021] NSWSC 755 at [49].

[42] On this prerequisite, see recently *In re Global Cord Blood Corporation* 22-11347 (DSJ) (Bankr SDNY Dec 5, 2022) and on this case Arthur Rosenberg and Emily Rothkin, 'Recent Decision Clarifies What Kind of Foreign Proceedings Can Access Chapter 15' (2023) 42 *American Bankruptcy Institute Journal* 28–29, 66.

[43] *Guide to Enactment and Interpretation of The UNCITRAL Model Law on Cross-Border Insolvency* (above n 9), at [69].

of creditors[44] and to leave all other creditors' rights unaffected. However, on closer inspection, the restriction to one or some creditor groups does not make the scheme an individual collection device. On the contrary, the affected groups are restricted rather than supported in collecting their debts. It is therefore generally recognised that it is not required by Article 2(a) ML that the foreign proceedings concern *all* creditors.[45] It suffices that the proceedings affect certain creditor groups collectively, even if other creditor groups are not included at all. As the Guide to Enactment puts it: 'A proceeding should not be considered to fail the test of collectivity purely because a class of creditors' rights is unaffected by it'.[46] Hence, scheme of arrangement and restructuring plan proceedings are collective within the meaning of Article 2(a) ML.[47] This applies all the more to the moratorium. Indubitably, the opinion of the Supreme Court of New South Wales that the moratorium is collective because it is likely to result in the rescue of the company as a going concern[48] does not quite 'hit the nail on the head' (because it boils down to the conclusion that all restructurings are collective). However, the moratorium is nonetheless collective, since its effects as provided for in sections A18 et seq IA 1986 affect all creditors (insofar as they are not excluded from its scope by statute[49]), not only a certain group of creditors.[50]

(v) *Control or Supervision by a Foreign Court*

Finally, control or supervision by a court is necessary and the court must be a foreign court, seen from the perspective of the recognising state. This can be established for all three of the English restructuring proceedings. In this respect, it is not detrimental

[44] For amendments to shareholder rights in a restructuring plan, see *Re Smile Telecoms Holdings Ltd* [2022] EWHC 740 (Ch) and on this case Charlotte Lamb, James Maltby and Tom Astle, 'Smile Telecoms: New Part 26A Mechanism Used to Exclude Out of the Money Classes from Voting on Restructuring Plan' (2022) 19 *ICR* 79–82; Craig Montgomery, Katharina Crinson, David Bor, Frank Clarke and Sharon Tong, 'Smile Telecoms restructuring plan sanctioned: time for challengers to "step up to the plate"?' [2022] *CRI* 75–78; Kate Stephenson and Thomas Jemmet, 'Smile Telecoms: English Court Approves First Restructuring Plan to Disenfranchise Out-of-the-Money Stakeholders and First to Compromise Shareholders in a Foreign Company' (2022) 19 *ICR* 140–42; further *Re Smile Telecoms Holdings Ltd* [2022] EWHC 387 (Ch) and on this case Will Snowden, Katharina Crinson and Craig Montgomery, 'Smile Telecoms: second restructuring plan provides a number of firsts – debut use of s 901C(4) and compromise of members' rights in an overseas company' [2022] *CRI* 8–11.

[45] Of a different opinion is Eidenmüller (above n 23), 53 et seq. However, this opinion is too narrow, would even exclude some national liquidation laws, and is not compatible with the *Guide to Enactment and Interpretation of The UNCITRAL Model Law on Cross-Border Insolvency* (above n 9).

[46] *Guide to Enactment and Interpretation of The UNCITRAL Model Law on Cross-Border Insolvency* (above n 9), at [70].

[47] *Re Smile Telecoms Holdings Ltd* [2022] EWHC 740 (Ch) at [60]; Mevorach and Walters (above n 29), at 871. See also, albeit for Art 1 EIR, *Re Gategroup Guarantee Limited* [2021] EWHC 304 (Ch) at [110]. In contrast, see Eidenmüller (above n 23), 65 et seq, 70.

[48] *Re Hydrodec Group Plc* [2021] NSWSC 755 at [47].

[49] Bizarrely, this holds particularly true for financial creditors; for criticism, see van Zwieten, 'Mid-Crisis Restructuring Law Reform' (above n 40), at 302 et seq, and Natalie Mrockova, Chapter 8 in this book; see also Reinhard Bork, 'Pre-insolvency moratoria – a legal comparison' *European Insolvency and Restructuring Journal* (online) *(EIRJ)* 2021-9, 1–12 at 11 et seq.

[50] See Bork, 'Pre-insolvency moratoria' (n 49 above), at 7. For the converse constellation (recognition of a Singapore moratorium in England) see *H&C S Holdings Pte Ltd* [2019] EWHC 1459 (Ch) and on this case Jennifer Meech, '*H&C S Holdings Pte Limited*: Singapore's New Moratorium Goes Global' (2019) 17 *ICR* 62–63.

that they are conducted as debtor-in-possession proceedings,[51] because this does not change the fact that a review by the court takes place. Further, potential control (upon the application of an involved party)[52] and control at the end of the proceedings, or through an Insolvency Practitioner who is controlled by the court, will suffice.[53] This prerequisite does therefore not cause any problems in the present context. The scheme of arrangement and reorganisation plan proceedings are controlled by the court at least when handing down the sanctioning decision, and the moratorium is under the supervision of a monitor (sections A35 et seq IA 1986)[54] who is an officer of the court (section A34 IA 1986) and whose actions can be challenged before the court (section A42 IA 1986).

(vi) Interim Results in Relation to the Threshold Question

In sum, all three restructuring proceedings meet the requirements of Article 2(a) ML and are therefore recognisable as foreign proceedings under national cross-border insolvency laws which are based on the UNCITRAL Model Law. Recognition, in practice, will be subject to the public policy reservation.[55] Moreover, recognition is merely the threshold for accessing certain provisions of the Model Law concerning relief in respect of foreign proceedings; it certainly does not follow from the fact that proceedings are recognised under (a national version of) the Model Law that the effects of those proceedings under the foreign law will also be extended to the domestic territory. As explained below, much of the relief for which the Model Law provides is discretionary and subject to limitations.

B. Other National Cross-border Insolvency Laws

The legal situation can be even more difficult under other national cross-border insolvency laws that are not based on the UNCITRAL Model Law.[56] There are mainly two reasons for this.

(i) Inclusion of Restructuring Proceedings

First, although most of these laws require a foreign insolvency proceeding to enliven provisions on recognition, it is unclear whether restructuring proceedings are included, because the applicable definition of 'insolvency proceedings' may be narrower than the definition supplied by the Model Law. In Germany, for example, section 343(1)

[51] *Guide to Enactment and Interpretation of The UNCITRAL Model Law on Cross-Border Insolvency* (above n 9), at [71], [74].

[52] *In re Agrokor DD* [2017] EWHC 2791 (Ch) at [79]; *Re Hydrodec Group Plc* [2021] NSWSC 755 at [48].

[53] *Guide to Enactment and Interpretation of The UNCITRAL Model Law on Cross-Border Insolvency* (above n 9), at [74].

[54] See for this aspect *Re Hydrodec Group Plc* [2021] NSWSC 755 at [48].

[55] Art 6 of the ML.

[56] For recognition of a restructuring plan under the doctrine of comity in South Africa, see *Re Smile Telecoms Holdings Ltd* [2022] EWHC 740 (Ch) at [97].

sentence 1 InsO provides for automatic recognition of foreign insolvency proceedings. Whether restructuring proceedings are covered or not, is subject to debate.[57] The Bundesgerichtshof has recognised proceedings under Chapter 11 of the US Bankruptcy Code[58] but has denied recognition for a *solvent* scheme of arrangement.[59] The latter judgment was not only reasoned by reference to the lack of any connection to the debtor's insolvency (a position in line with the analysis above), but also by reference to the fact that the scheme affected not the entirety but only a certain group of creditors and was therefore not collective, which is regularly the case not only in proceedings for schemes of arrangement but also in Chapter 11. It seems fair to say that the two decisions are not completely free of contradiction.[60] However, given that public restructuring proceedings of the EU Member States which require the debtor's likely inability to pay debts are listed in Annex A of the EIR and are thus insolvency proceedings within the meaning of the EIR, it would come as a surprise if restructuring proceedings under Part 26A CA 2006, which are now recognised as insolvency proceedings in England,[61] would not be recognised as insolvency proceedings under § 343 InsO.[62] It remains to be seen how the Bundesgerichtshof will decide this question in the future.

(ii) Further Conditions

Secondly, many national cross-border insolvency laws contain additional prerequisites for recognising foreign insolvency proceedings. Even under the Model Law, it does not suffice that the proceedings are 'foreign' proceedings within the meaning of Article 2(a) ML, since foreign proceedings are only recognisable under Article 17(2) ML if they are foreign main or non-main proceedings within the meaning of Article 2(2)(b) and (c) ML. German law is another a good example of a jurisdiction with additional prerequisites. Under section 343(1) sentence 2 No 1 InsO, recognition is to be denied if the courts in the state in which proceedings were opened lack jurisdiction under German law. Following the so-called 'mirror principle', German law, in a unique approach, requires the foreign court to have international jurisdiction, yet not according to that court's own law but under the rules of German law. In order to determine international jurisdiction,

[57] A good overview is given by Peter Mankowski in Ernst Jaeger, *Insolvenzordnung*, Vol 9 (Berlin, de Gruyter, 2020), § 343 at 11 et seq. The issue received some attention in *Re Project Lietzenburger Strasse Holdco SàrL* [2024] EWHC 468 (Ch) at [123] et seq and [133] et seq, where there were two conflicting expert reports from German professors Christoph Thole and Dominik Skauradszun. While Prof Thole assumed that English restructuring plan proceedings were insolvency proceedings within the meaning of § 343 InsO, Prof Skauradszun took the opposite view. The expert opinions are published (albeit in German); see Dominik Skaurdszun, Jeremias Kümpel and Johannes Schröder, 'Zur fehlenden Anerkennungsfähigkeit eines englischen Part-26A-Restrukturierungsplans in Deutschland', *Zeitschrift für Wirtschaftsrecht (ZIP)* 2024 (45), 665–75; Christoph Thole, 'Zur Anerkennungsfähigkeit eines englischen Part 26A-Restrukturierungplans in Deutschland', *Zeitschrift für Restrukturierung und Insolvenz (ZRI)* 2024 (5), 790–94.

[58] BGH, 13.10.2009 – X ZR 79/06, NZI 2009, 859 at [8] et seq.

[59] See n 2.

[60] *cf* Thole (above n 57), ZRI 2024, 790, 793.

[61] See above n 33.

[62] It has been rightly observed by Ruiz and Hertz, Chapter 2 of this book (at fn 69) that, in this respect, the decision in *Re Gategroup Guarantee Limited* [2021] EWHC 304 (Ch) (above n 33), although German courts are obviously not bound to the opinion of the High Court of England and Wales, has facilitated recognition as an insolvency procedure abroad.

it must be examined whether a court in the foreign state would have jurisdiction for the decision to open proceedings if section 3 of the German Insolvenzordnung were applicable there. Consequently, the international jurisdiction of the foreign court is to be affirmed on the basis of the mirror principle if the debtor's centre of independent economic activity is in the state where the decision to be recognised was made. If there is no such centre of activity, the debtor's general place of jurisdiction in the state in which the proceedings were opened is decisive; in the case of natural persons, this is the place of residence; in the case of legal entities, it is the location of their registered office. Hence, schemes of arrangement or restructuring plans for companies with their COMI in Germany cannot be recognised at all – either as main or as secondary proceedings – because for such companies, under German law, only German courts have international jurisdiction.[63]

V. Recognition under Cross-border Civil Procedure Law

From an EU perspective, recognition of restructuring decisions under cross-border civil procedure law can only be considered where their classification as insolvency proceedings is denied. Otherwise, cross-border insolvency law takes precedence, due to respective carve-outs in most cross-border civil procedure instruments. These exclude insolvency and analogous matters from their scope.[64]

With respect to the application of EU cross-border civil procedure to English restructurings, neither the Brussels I^{bis} Regulation nor the Lugano Convention[65] is applicable, since the UK is no longer a Member State of the EU[66] and is not a party to the Lugano Convention. The UK has meanwhile signed the Hague Convention on the Recognition and Enforcement of Foreign Judgments in Civil or Commercial Matters,[67]

[63] This has always been a topic in relation to the UK, as English courts tend to favour a low jurisdictional requirement (*cf* above at n 57). However, they also need to be satisfied the restructuring plan will have substantial effect in relevant jurisdictions abroad (see Ruiz and Hertz, Chapter 2 of this book, also at n 21). This dovetails with the observation above (at section II.) that recognition is primarily about the legal *effects* of the restructuring process.

[64] For Art 1(2)(b) of the Lugano Convention (below n 65), see *Re Gategroup Guarantee Limited* [2021] EWHC 304 (Ch) at [85] et seq, and Stephenson, Stembridge and Ziegler (above n 16) (2022) 19 *ICR* 3 et seq. For discussion of the *Gategroup* judgment, see (supporting) Mokal (above n 23), at 448 et seq, and (criticising) O'Dea (above n 13), at [2.256] et seq; further Mark Fennessy, Mark Fine, Nicholas Jupp and Alexander Andronikou, 'Gategroup: What's the Fuss About?' (2021) 18 *ICR* 182–85; Kate Stephenson, 'Gategroup: UK Restructuring Plans Are Insolvency Proceedings; Classes Split' (2021) 18 *ICR* 98–101.

[65] Convention on jurisdiction and the recognition and enforcement of judgments in civil and commercial matters, OJ of 21 December 2007, L 339/3. The Lugano Convention is an agreement parallel to the Brussels I^{bis} Regulation between the Member States of the European Union and Ireland, Norway, and Switzerland. For the scope of application on proceedings commenced pre-Brexit, see Rodrigo Rodriguez, 'Recognition of Schemes and Restructuring Plans in Switzerland and under the Lugano Convention' *EIRJ* 2023-1, 1–27.

[66] For pre-Brexit solvent schemes, see the overview by O'Dea (above n 13), at [2.100] et seq.

[67] Convention on the Recognition and Enforcement of Foreign Judgments in Civil or Commercial Matters, OJ of 14 July 2022, L 187/4; in force since 1 September 2023.

which, according to its Article 1(2), renders the Convention applicable in relation to other Contracting States. However, the Convention does not apply to 'insolvency, composition, resolution of financial institutions, and analogous matters' (Article 2(1)(e) Hague Convention), which calls into question the applicability to restructurings. Hence, only national cross-border civil procedure laws can be considered.

In relation to national cross-border civil procedure rules, the same issues arise as with national cross-border insolvency laws.[68] For example, in Germany, section 328(1) No 1 Zivilprozessordnung[69] provides for recognition of foreign judgments unless 'the courts of the state to which the foreign court belongs do not have jurisdiction according to German law'. Again, the 'mirror principle' would hinder the recognition of schemes of arrangement or restructuring plans for companies with their COMI in Germany, because the general venue of companies is defined by their registered seat (section 17(1) ZPO).

Apart from this, recognition under civil procedure law does not seem to be the appropriate means for securing the effectiveness of a restructuring. During the UK's membership of the EU, English courts struggled significantly with the application of the Brussels I^{bis} Regulation, particularly regarding jurisdiction and recognition.[70] However, it is doubtful whether this Regulation is fit for resolving the problems of jurisdiction and recognition of schemes and restructuring plans. As regards jurisdiction, the reference to 'claimant' and 'defendant' in many provisions of the Brussels I^{bis} Regulation does not fit the circumstances in a scheme proceeding in which the company is an applicant rather than a defendant. As Mr Justice Zacaroli put it in *Gategroup*,

> rules which allocate jurisdiction by reference to the domicile of each creditor, or the legal nature of each creditor's claim, or by reference to bi-lateral contractual provisions with different creditors, are as inapposite and impractical in the context of Part 26A proceedings, which are premised on the financial difficulties of the company, as they are for traditional insolvency proceedings.[71]

As regards recognition and enforcement, the commercial imperative is more about recognising the effects of the scheme (eg reducing the creditors' claims) than about enforcing the sanctioning order per se,[72] which is more or less a requirement for the scheme effects coming into force[73] and not a judicial command which needs recognition and enforcement. In other words, cross-border civil procedure law is inept in the context of recognition of restructurings. I could not agree more.

[68] See above at section IV.B.

[69] Code of Civil Procedure, English text available at: https://www.gesetze-im-internet.de/englisch_zpo/ (accessed 4 January 2024) (ZPO).

[70] Examples are *Re DAP Holdings NV* [2005] EWHC 2092 (Ch) at [14]; *Re Lehmann Brothers International (Europe)* [2018] EWHC 1980 (Ch) at [171] et seq; *Re Magyar Telecom BV* [2013] EWHC 3800 (Ch) at [28] et seq; *Re Rodenstock GmbH* [2011] EWHC 1104 (Ch) at [35] et seq; *Re Van Gansewinkel Groep BV* [2015] EWHC 2151 (Ch) at [37] et seq; see extensively on this matter, O'Dea (above n 13), at [2.100] et seq.

[71] *Re Gategroup Guarantee Limited* [2021] EWHC 304 (Ch) at [100]; see also Payne (above n 13), at 355 et seq, 362 et seq.

[72] *cf* above at section II.

[73] This is why restructuring plans can be characterised as 'court-assisted contracts', see Madaus 'Leaving the Shadows of US Bankruptcy Law' (above n 23), at 624 et seq.

VI. Recognition under Private International Law

If neither cross-border insolvency law nor cross-border civil procedure law supports recognition of restructurings, private international law can be helpful.[74] This was first used in *DTEK* by Sir Alastair Norris, who relied on a report written by my colleagues Christoph Paulus and Peter Mankowski.[75] In short, this opinion refers to Article 12(1)(d) Rome I Regulation which provides that the law applicable to a contract by virtue of this Regulation shall govern (among other things) the various ways of extinguishing obligations.[76] Hence, where a contract is governed by English law, English law would also govern the extinguishing effect of an English scheme of arrangement.[77] In this way, neither the scheme procedure nor the scheme decision as such, but rather their amending effect on the claims of the creditors as regulated in the scheme, would be recognised. They would be accepted as being extinguished under private international law provided that the legal relationship between the company and the concerned creditors is governed by English law. However, as regards Germany and many other Member States of the EU, this is still subject to debate and has not been decided by courts so far. This holds particularly true for cases where the applicable law has been changed to English law shortly before or even during the restructuring proceedings.[78] Further, amendments to shareholder rights[79] are not covered by the Rome I Regulation due to the scope restrictions for company law matters in Article 1(2)(f) Rome I Regulation.

VII. Summary

In all, my findings can be summarised as follows. Recognition of English cross-border restructuring proceedings is relatively easy in jurisdictions that have adopted the UNCITRAL Model Law on Cross-Border Insolvency, since they can be characterised as foreign proceedings within the meaning of Article 2(a) ML. The legal situation can be more difficult under other national cross-border insolvency laws that do not mirror the UNCITRAL Model Law: first, because it is often unclear whether these laws cover

[74] Extensively on this aspect Payne (above n 13), at 361 et seq; *de lege ferenda* Madaus, 'Leaving the Shadows of US Bankruptcy Law' (above n 23).

[75] *Re DTEK Energy BV and DTEK Finance Plc* [2021] EWHC 1551 (Ch) at [37] and on this case Mark Fennessy, Sunay Radia and Alexander Andronikou, 'The Restructuring of DTEK Group: A Challenge to the International Effectiveness of a Scheme of Arrangement in a Post-Brexit Era' (2021) 18 *ICR* 331–32; see also *Re Obrascón Huarte Laín SA* [2021] EWHC 1431 (Ch) at [86]; *Re AGPS BondCo PLC* [2023] EWHC 916 (Ch) at [331] et seq. and on this case Kate Stephenson, 'Adler: English court approves contested restructuring plan' [2023] *CRI* 83–90; the appeal decision did not consider this topic in detail, see *Re AGPS Bond Co PLC* [2024] EWCA Civ 24 at [223] et seq (*Re Adler*).

[76] For non-contractual obligations, the same follows from Art 15(h) Rome II Regulation (Regulation (EC) No 864/2007 of the European Parliament and the Council of 11 July 2007 on the law applicable to non-contractual obligations, OJ of 31 July 2007, L 199/40).

[77] See also Ruiz and Hertz, Chapter 2 of this book at fn 22.

[78] Examples are *Re APCOA Parking Holdings GmbH and others* [2014] EWHC 3849 (Ch) at [227] et seq; *Re Algeco Scotsman PIK SA* [2017] EWHC 2236 (Ch) at [58]; *Re DTEK Finance BV* [2015] EWHC 1164 (Ch) at [15] et seq; *Re Jain International Trading BV* [2021] EWHC 1812 (Ch) at [6].

[79] *cf* above n 44.

restructuring proceedings, and secondly, because they contain provisos for protecting the international jurisdiction of their own courts. In the latter case, cross-border civil procedure law is mostly no help. However, as a last resort, recognition under private international law can be a solution.

However, even under the Model Law, the recognisability of schemes of arrangement and restructuring plans is only a first step. It should not be overlooked that even if the restructuring proceedings are recognisable, Article 20 ML only provides for automatic effects of the recognition decision to a very limited extent. Anything beyond this is at the discretion of the court, in accordance with Article 21 ML – and is therefore difficult to predict, since national courts take different views as to the interpretation of Article 21 ML – and subject to the adequate protection provision in Article 22. This is particularly the case because the Model Law largely preserves the ability to open local proceedings in competition to the foreign ones, including local restructuring proceedings. This contrasts significantly with the EIR, which, in the case of main proceedings, provides for an automatic and complete extension of the decision's effects as long as the EIR does not provide otherwise[80] and no secondary proceedings are opened. In this respect, the point made at the beginning of this chapter – that there is a difference between recognising a foreign decision as such and allowing for the effects of a decision as provided by foreign law to extend into the domestic territory – matters much less under the EIR than outside it. Under the Model Law, the fact that restructuring proceedings are recognised as foreign proceedings is only the first step towards establishing whether a stay provided in that process, or a compromise sanctioned under it, will be effective in relation to assets and creditors abroad.

[80] Exceptions are available in Arts 8–18 EIR, which may be obstacles to smooth restructurings. In particular, this holds true for Art 8 EIR which exempts rights *in rem* in respect of assets situated outside the state of opening from the effects of insolvency proceedings. On this, see van Zwieten in Bork and van Zwieten (n 15 above) [0.55].

11

The Lure of English Proceedings: Forum Selection from the United States to England

ANTHONY J CASEY*

I. Introduction

The English Scheme of Arrangement[1] and the more recently adopted English Restructuring Plan[2] offer appealing alternatives to Chapter 11 of the United States Bankruptcy Code. A large US-based firm seeking to restructure its debt might use one of these alternatives to bypass the Chapter 11 process by initiating English court proceedings. Once an English court approves the proposed scheme or plan, the debtor can enforce its provisions in the United States through Chapter 15 of the Bankruptcy Code.[3] Although the use of English proceedings as an alternative to Chapter 11 by US-based debtors remains largely theoretical – with the one[4] major example occurring in 2019[5] – the lure of the manoeuvre is likely to increase for several reasons.

First, the costs of Chapter 11 continue to rise relative to the cost of alternative proceedings. Second, various legal developments in the United States – including a recent Supreme Court ruling prohibiting non-consensual third-party releases,[6] an appellate court ruling restricting the ability of debtors to initiate Chapter 11 proceedings,[7] and

* The Richard Weil Faculty Research Fund and the Paul H Leffmann Fund provided generous support. I thank Kelly Bu, Kate Gross, Roland Kim, and Emma Lotts for their excellent research assistance.

[1] See Part 26 of the Companies Act 2006.

[2] See Corporate Insolvency and Governance Act 2020 (CIGA 2020) (adding Part 26A of the Companies Act 2006).

[3] 11 USC §§ 1501–1532.

[4] See Jones Day, 'Cross Border Restructuring Case Study: syncreon' (21 November 2019) available at: https://www.jonesday.com/en/insights/2019/11/cross-border-restructuring-case-study#:~:text=Looking%20Ahead%3A%20Syncreon's%20reorganization%20is,been%20recognized%20under%20the%20CCAA ('Syncreon's reorganization is widely considered to be the first-ever use of an English scheme of arrangement to restructure debt issued by a U.S.-based global enterprise').

[5] See *In the Matter of syncreon Group BV and syncreon Automotive (UK) Ltd*, Court File No CV-19624659-00CL; and *syncreon Automotive (UK) Ltd*, Lead Case No 19-11702-BLS (Bankr D Del 2019).

[6] See *Harrington v Purdue Pharma LP*, 144 S Ct 2071 (2024).

[7] See *In re LTL Mgt, LLC (LTL I)*, 64 F 4th 84, 93 (3d Cir 2023).

continued pressure on domestic venue shopping[8] – are likely to reduce the attractiveness of Chapter 11 relative to viable alternatives. Third, as Professors Paterson and Walters have pointed out, Chapter 11 proceedings are rigidly overinclusive relative to English scheme and plan proceedings.[9] Finally, the adoption of the Corporate Insolvency and Governance Act 2020 (CIGA 2020), with its addition of a cross-class cramdown option,[10] has significantly broadened the scope of cases in which English proceedings provide a viable alternative to Chapter 11.

Meanwhile, the path to securing English approval and United States recognition of a scheme or plan remains broad. English courts have demonstrated their willingness to preside over proceedings related to foreign enterprises as long as the necessary formalities have been followed and nothing in the scheme or plan plainly prejudices one class of creditors.[11] United States bankruptcy courts, for their part, have also demonstrated a broad willingness to recognise and enforce the results of English proceedings as long as the English court was satisfied with its own exercise of jurisdiction over the case and accorded a minimum of fair process to the claimants, which they almost always will.[12]

The lure of English proceedings has received little academic attention until recently.[13] Josh Macey and I explored the topic in February 2021, noting:

> [I]n many cases, the English scheme of arrangement now represents a viable alternative to the American bankruptcy system, and over the past decade, a number of companies have chosen to use an English scheme of arrangement to restructure their debt instead of chapter 11, with the first United States headquartered business doing so in 2019.[14]

The topic has received increasing attention since then,[15] and interest has ramped up significantly in the wake of the ruling of the Supreme Court of the United States in *Harrington v Purdue Pharma* in June 2024.[16]

[8] See below at section V.B.(ii).

[9] Sarah Paterson and Adrian Walters, 'Chapter 11's Inclusivity Problem' (2023) 55 *Arizona State Law Journal* 1227, 1290.

[10] See CIGA 2020; see also Kristin van Zwieten, 'Mid-Crisis Restructuring Law Reform in the United Kingdom' (2023) 24 *European Organization Law Review* 287 (providing a detailed description of the reforms included in CIGA 2020 and their effects); Jennifer Payne, 'Debt Restructuring in Transition' (2023) 139 *LQR* 101.

[11] See below at section VI.A.

[12] See below at section IV.C.

[13] Practitioners took note of the possibilities implied by the recognition order in the *syncreon* case in 2019. See, eg, Jones Day, 'Cross Border Restructuring Case Study: syncreon' (n 4); Mark Lawford and Andre J Wilkinson, 'syncreon's Financial Restructuring Implemented by Landmark English Schemes of Arrangement With Parallel Chapter 15 and CCAA recognition' (1 October 2019) available at: https://eurorestructuring.weil.com/cross-border/syncreons-financial-restructuring-implemented-by-landmark-english-schemes-of-arrangement-with-parallel-chapter-15-and-ccaa-recognition/.

[14] Anthony J Casey and Joshua C Macey, 'Bankruptcy Shopping: Domestic Venue Races and Global Forum Wars' (2021) 47 *Emory Bankruptcy Developments Journal* 463, 468; see also Oscar Couewenberg and Stephen J Lubben, 'Good Old Chapter 11 in a Pre-Insolvency World: The Growth of Global Reorganization Options' (2021) 46 *North Carolina Law Review* 353; Bruce A Markell, 'Domestic Entities as Chapter 15 Debtors: A Possibility?' (July 2021) 41(7) *Bankruptcy Law Letter*.

[15] See, eg, Bruce A Markell, 'The International Two-Step: Recognizing Domestic Chapter 15 Reorganizations' (2024) 98 *American Bankruptcy Law Journal* 1; Paterson and Walters (n 9).

[16] See n 6 above, and section V.B.(i) below.

And so, this chapter explores in more depth the possibility of United States debtors migrating to English proceedings. It looks at the likelihood of such a migration, identifying various factors that could push the trend up or down, the type of cases in which debtors are likely to make the trip, and the possible effects that would be felt if such a trend materialises.

II. Background: Venue and Forum in the United States

A. Venue within the United States: Chapter 11

Venue options for Chapter 11 proceedings in the United States are quite broad. The relevant statute allows a firm to file in any federal district in which its 'domicile, residence, principal place of business, or principal [United States] assets' are located, or in which an affiliate has a pending bankruptcy case.[17]

The affiliate provision essentially allows a debtor to file in any district. The firm can create an affiliate – even on the eve of filing – with its domicile, principal place of business, or principal assets in the desired district; initiate Chapter 11 proceedings for the affiliate in that district; and then initiate proceedings in that district for all other relevant entities. The only meaningful constraint on such venue shopping is the bankruptcy court's discretionary power to transfer a case to another district 'in the interest of justice or for the convenience of the parties'.[18]

B. Venue for Global Cases Coming to the United States: Chapter 15 and Chapter 11

As one court put it, '[T]here is "virtually no formal barrier" to having federal courts adjudicate foreign debtors' bankruptcy proceedings'.[19]

Formally, section 109(a) of the Bankruptcy Code requires – for Chapter 11 and Chapter 15[20] – each debtor[21] to have at least a domicile, place of business, or some property in the United States.[22] That requirement has been interpreted

[17] 28 USC § 1408. The statute's location requirement must be met for 180 days before filing or for the longer portion of that 180 days than any other location. Ibid.

[18] 28 USC § 1412.

[19] *In re Globo Comunicacoes e Participacoes SA*, 317 BR 235, 249 (SDNY 2004).

[20] On its face, the language of section 109(a) plainly applies to all chapters of the Code. Nonetheless, the circuit courts are split over whether to apply the provision in Chapter 15. Compare *Drawbridge Special Opportunities Fund LP v Barnet (In re Barnet)*, 737 F 3d 238, 247–48 (2d Cir 2013), with *Al Zawawi v Diss (In re Al Zawawi)*, 637 BR 663, 668–70 (MD Fla 2022).

[21] See *Bank of America v World of English*, 23 BR 1015, 1019–20 (ND Ga 1982).

[22] 11 USC § 109(a).

liberally.[23] For example, in several courts, 'a professional's retainer in a U.S. bank account satisfies the "property in the United States" requirement'.[24] Similarly, claims by a debtor against a parent entity's bank account in the United States would qualify.[25] Thus, the main threshold question is not whether a foreign debtor can file in the United States, but which US district is the proper venue.

(i) Chapter 15 Venue

The venue rules for Chapter 15 cases are broad. A debtor (through its foreign representative) may initiate a Chapter 15 proceeding in any district where it has its principal place of business or its principal United States assets, if such a district exists.[26] If no such district exists, the debtor can initiate proceedings where an action is pending against it. If there is still no relevant district available, in the last instance, the debtor may bring the case in a district that is consistent with the interests of justice.[27]

(ii) Chapter 11 Venue for Foreign Debtors

The venue rules for a foreign debtor to file a US Chapter 11 petition are equally permissive. Just as with domestic cases, the debtor group need only have one affiliate with domicile, principal place of business, or principal United States assets located in the district. Once that affiliate presence is established, all other debtor entities may file in that district under the affiliate-venue provision.

Thus, it has become commonplace for a foreign-based business to initiate Chapter 11 proceedings by way of affiliate venue. For example, in recent years the bankruptcy court in the Southern District of New York was the chosen venue for the Chapter 11 proceedings of GOL Linhas Aéreas Inteligentes SA (a Brazilian company); LATAM Airlines SA (Chile and Brazil) Philippine Airlines, Inc (Philippines); Avianca Holdings SA (Columbia); and Grupo Aeroméxico, SAB de CV (Mexico). Meanwhile, the bankruptcy court in the District of Delaware hosted WOM SA (Chile); and Corp Group Banking SA (Chile). And the bankruptcy court in the Southern District of Texas was the venue for the Chapter 11 proceedings of Condor Inversiones SpA (Chile).

The upshot of these rules is that virtually any foreign debtor can find its way into a United States bankruptcy court under either Chapter 11 or Chapter 15. Just as with domestic filings, the courts retain some discretionary authority to abstain from hearing the case, but the US courts have certainly demonstrated a willingness to serve as a forum for international restructuring cases.

[23] See *In re Northshore Mainland Services, Inc*, 537 BR 192, 200 (Bankr D Del 2015) ('Courts construing the "property" requirement of § 109(a) to foreign corporations and individuals have determined that the eligibility requirement is satisfied by even a minimal amount of property located in the United States'.).

[24] *In re Avanti Communications Group plc*, 582 BR 603, 612 (Bankr SDNY 2018) (*Avanti*). Other courts have reached the same conclusion. *In re Yukos Oil Co*, 321 BR 396, 401–03 (Bankr SD Tex 2005); *In re Global Ocean Carriers Ltd*, 251 BR 31, 39 (Bankr D Del 2000).

[25] *In re Global Ocean Carriers Ltd*, 251 BR 31, 39 (Bankr D Del 2000).

[26] 28 USC § 1410.

[27] ibid.

III. United States Enforcement

The discussion so far has been about whether a case can proceed in a US court. More important for the foreign debtor is whether the US courts will provide the desired relief.

When a foreign debtor files for Chapter 11, the desired relief includes an enforceable plan of reorganisation as well as intermediate procedural remedies such as the automatic stay and preliminary injunctions. The debtor may plan to seek recognition of the plan in its home country or in other jurisdictions where it has assets, operations, or creditors. In some cases, however, enforcement by a US court might be sufficient to achieve compliance abroad.

This can be true even when the debtor's assets are located mostly abroad, as long the creditors against whom enforcement is sought are subject to – and take seriously – the injunctive power of the US courts. Given the size of the United States economy, this condition is often met. Indeed, one particular attraction of US proceedings is that in many cases there are several assets and parties with connections to the US jurisdiction who are, therefore, subject to US enforcement.

For example, when a US court issues an order prohibiting a creditor from taking action in a foreign jurisdiction, the enforcement mechanism is the court's power to punish the creditor in the United States, often through a finding of contempt. A debtor who has no presence in the United States might safely ignore the prohibition and penalty. A creditor with US assets or operations, on the other hand, will be within the reach of the court enforcing its orders. The creditor who has interests or activities in the United States is, thus, unwilling to violate the US order abroad.[28] In this way, an injunctive order from a US court can bind the actions of a creditor even regarding assets located in another jurisdiction.

The same dynamic can play out when a foreign debtor seeks Chapter 15 recognition of a proceeding from another jurisdiction. The debtor wants a US court order prohibiting stakeholders from violating the terms of the foreign proceeding in the US and abroad.[29] Such an order puts the US enforcement power behind the foreign proceeding. In this way, US recognition increases the cost to creditors of violating the terms of the foreign proceeding. It effectively extends the domain of the foreign proceeding to cover all creditors that have a presence in the United States.

With that foundation, we turn now to English proceedings and to the willingness of US courts to grant orders of recognition and enforcement to those proceedings.

[28] For example, in the case of Corp Group Banking, the US court enjoined creditors for initiating certain proceedings in Chile. While the creditors objected to the court's order, they ultimately complied without the involvement of any enforcement mechanism in Chile. Order Enforcing the Discharge Injunction Under the Debtors' Chapter 11 Plan of Liquidation, *In re Corp Group Banking, SA*, Case No 21-10969 (Bankr Del), Dkt No 1013; see also, Anthony J Casey, 'The Curious Case of Corp Group Banking and the Problem of Private Criminal Enforcement' (January 2024) available at: https://papers.ssrn.com/sol3/papers.cfm?abstract_id=4746560.

[29] Chapter 15 recognition of a foreign main proceeding provides an automatic stay with regard to any property and any debtor in the United States, including extraterritorial actions that could affect that property or that debtor: 11 USC § 1520; *In re JSC BTA Bank*, 434 BR 334 (Bankr SDNY 2010). The court also has the power to issue further protection and injunctions to enforce the provisions of the foreign proceedings: 15 USC § 1507 and 1521. For recognition of non-main proceedings, there is no automatic stay, but the court may grant appropriate relief. Ibid.

IV. The English Proceedings in Brief

A. The Scheme of Arrangement

A scheme of arrangement is a mechanism that can be used to restructure debts under English law. Schemes are authorised under Part 26 of the Companies Act 2006. Like Chapter 11, scheme proceedings are available to solvent and insolvent debtors alike. The scheme is a fairly quick process, usually involving relatively fewer judicial court proceedings than Chapter 11 and often reaching completion within a few months. It is particularly useful for purely financial – as opposed to operational – restructurings. In those cases, the scheme allows the debtor to reach an agreement with the supermajority of a class of financial creditors and use the scheme to bind any holdouts within the class. Specifically, schemes require a majority in number of creditors and 75 per cent in value of classes affected within the scheme.[30]

B. The Restructuring Plan

In 2020, the Corporate Insolvency and Governance Act added the option of a restructuring plan, which expanded the available relief within streamlined English proceedings. In many ways, a restructuring plan is like a scheme of arrangement. But there are several important differences. For example, businesses must meet a financial-difficulties requirement to qualify.[31] A restructuring plan also provides the added features of cross-class cramdown and an the option to request a 20-day moratorium.[32] Thus, a debtor who reaches a deal with a class of creditors (by a vote of 75 per cent in value of that class) can bind a dissenting class by showing that the plan leaves that class no worse off than it would be under the 'relevant alternative'.[33]

This addition of cross-class cramdown broadens the scope of English proceedings considerably, bringing it closer to the scope of Chapter 11 proceedings. And it does so without adding considerable procedural hurdles or other costs.

C. Broad Recognition

As Judge Glenn of the Southern District of New York has noted, 'Schemes of arrangement under UK law have routinely been recognized as foreign proceedings in

[30] Part 26 of the Companies Act 2006 (n 1).

[31] CIGA (2020 (n 2) at s 901A(2).

[32] See generally Jennifer Payne, 'An Assessment of the UK Restructuring Moratorium' available at https://papers.ssrn.com/sol3/papers.cfm?abstract_id=3759730.

[33] CIGA 2020 (n 2) at s 901G. For a cross-class cramdown to be approved, the court must be satisfied no members of the dissenting class are made any worse off than 'they would be in the event of the relevant alternative'. Ibid. And the accepting class must be one that 'would receive a payment or have a genuine economic interest in the company, in the event of the relevant alternative'. Ibid. Like Chapter 11, approval of a restructuring plan requires a horizontal and vertical comparison of treatment among classes and a justification for treatment that does not distribute value *pari passu*. See, eg, *Re AGPS Bondco plc* (*Re Adler*) [2024] EWCA Civ 24.

chapter 15 cases'.[34] It would be an exceptional case for a United States court to deny recognition to an English scheme of arrangement. And while the restructuring plan has only been around for a few years, US courts have already granted recognition in the first two restructuring plans brought before them.[35]

Importantly, Chapter 15 recognition of foreign proceedings is broad enough to encompass provisions that would have been prohibited in Chapter 11.[36] While Chapter 15 allows a court to deny recognition of a foreign proceeding when doing so would be 'manifestly contrary to the public policy of the United States',[37] this exception has generally been reserved for extreme procedural inadequacies.[38]

V. The Appeal to US Debtors

A. The High Costs of Chapter 11

The appeal of English proceedings to US debtors is largely a function of the burdens and costs of Chapter 11 proceedings. Chapter 11 is already the most expensive insolvency (and pre-insolvency) regime in the world, and the costs continue to increase. Attorneys' rates and the total fees billed in large Chapter 11 cases dwarf the rates and fees charged in other jurisdictions.[39] In addition, the robust procedures required in Chapter 11 often take longer than a comparative English proceeding aimed at the same outcome.

The fact that many foreign debtors file in the United States suggests that the high cost is often worth it, but that won't be true in all cases. There is likely a tipping point at which the relative cost-benefit tradeoff begins to favour alternative forums. I turn to the major factors influencing that tradeoff in the remainder of this section.

B. Costly Legal Developments for Chapter 11

(i) Third-party Releases: The Purdue *Effect*

Speculation over US debtors using Chapter 15 has increased dramatically in the wake of the ruling by the Supreme Court of the United States in *Harrington v Purdue*

[34] *Avanti* (n 24) at 613 (citing over a dozen cases recognising schemes of arrangement).

[35] See *Virgin Atlantic Airways Ltd*, No 20-11804, Order Granting Recognition and Related Relief, Docket # 37 (3 September 2020); and Provisional Relief Order, Docket # 17 (17 August 2020); PizzaExpress Financing 2 PLC, Order Granting Petition for (I) Recognition as a Foreign Main Proceeding, (II) Recognition of Foreign Representative, and (III) Related Relief Under Chapter 15 of the Bankruptcy Code (4 October 2020) No 4:20-bk-34868, Docket # 25 (Bankr SD Tex).

[36] See *Avanti* (n 24); *In re Sino-Forest Corp*, 501 BR 655 (Bankr SDNY 2013).

[37] 11 USC § 1506.

[38] *In re PT Bakrie Telecom Tbk*, 628 BR 859, 887 (Bankr SDNY 2021) (denying recognition in the absence of even a 'rudimentary record' to support 'the procedural fairness of the underlying process'.).

[39] See Kenneth A Rosen, 'What Does Chapter 11 Really Cost?' (20 April 2016) *Bloomberg Law*, available at: https://news.bloomberglaw.com/bankruptcy-law/what-does-chapter-11-really-cost (discussing the various fees associated with filing Chapter 11).

Pharma LP.[40] In short, the Court ruled that non-consensual non-debtor (or 'third-party') releases are no longer available in Chapter 11.

The use of third-party releases is common in restructuring and insolvency proceedings around the world. As part of a large (or 'global') settlement, the debtor will seek an order restraining creditors from pursuing claims they have against non-debtors such as affiliate companies, officers and directors, equity holders, potential co-obligors, and insurers. In exchange, and as part of the global settlement, these non-debtors often provide funds to the estate for the benefit of the creditors.

In *Purdue Pharma* – a case involving mass torts related to the production of the opioid drug Oxycontin – the debtor sought releases of claims against the members of the Sackler family, who had owned and controlled the business before it filed for bankruptcy. In exchange, the family agreed to pay around US$6 billion into the estate. This money was to be used to establish various funds to pay the claims of victims and other claimants. Thus, the Sacklers were released from their liability and the claims against them were channelled to these funds. The claimants were offered a chance to vote on whether to accept this settlement.[41] While the overwhelming majority voted in favour of the settlement, a small fraction (less than 5 per cent) of the claimants voted against it.[42]

The question posed to the Court was whether those non-consenting claimants could be forced to accept the deal. The Court answered that question in the negative.[43] Notably, the ruling in *Purdue Pharma* reaches beyond mass tort bankruptcies. The Court ruled that non-consensual releases of direct claims against non-debtors are categorically prohibited in Chapter 11 cases.[44] This ruling will apply even to cases where a small group of financial creditors is dissenting from a deal that releases cross guarantees among affiliates.[45]

Practising lawyers were quick to note the possibility of evading the broad effects of *Purdue Pharma* through Chapter 15 recognition of foreign proceedings. The ruling in *Purdue* made clear the deep divide between the US and other countries in their approach to non-debtor releases. In jurisdictions like England, such releases are considered commonplace.[46] And so, within weeks of the decision, practitioner articles and firm memos proliferated, exploring the possibility that US debtors would bring their cases to England to get releases approved and then seek Chapter 15 enforcement.[47]

[40] *Harrington v Purdue Pharma LP*, 144 S Ct 2071 (2024).

[41] ibid at 2708–80.

[42] See *In re Purdue Pharma LP* (*Purdue* Lower Court), 633 BR 53, 107 (Bankr SDNY 2021).

[43] *Purdue Pharma* (n 40) at 2087–88.

[44] ibid.

[45] The Court left a few questions open. For example, it did not rule on the legality of releases in cases where the claimant is being paid in full. It also left open the use of releases for claims that are derivative of liability of the debtor. But direct claims – such as tort claims or claims for guaranties – against a non-debtor can no longer be released without consent or full payment.

[46] See, eg, *Avanti* (n 24) at 618 ('[T]hird-party non-debtor releases are common in schemes sanctioned under UK law, particularly for releases of affiliate guarantees of the debt that is being adjusted by the scheme.').

[47] See, eg, Ola Antly and Miriam Peguero Medrano, 'Chapter 15 Loophole? Implications of the Ruling in Purdue Pharma on Recognition of Foreign Non-Consensual Third-Party Releases' (July 2024) *INSOL International Technical Paper Series No 65*, available at: https://www.insol.org/getmedia/3096b116-524f-4834-ae30-5bdc821f24dd/Chapter-15-loophole-implications-of-the-ruling-in-purdue-pharma-on-recognition-of-foreign-nonconsensual-third-party-releases.pdf; Rahem Connelly, 'Purdue Pharma and the Future of Nonconsensual Third-Party Releases in Chapter 15 Cases' (July 2024) available at: https://www.pillsburylaw.com/en/news-and-insights/purdue-pharma-nonconsensual-third-party-releases-chapter15.

While it is too soon to gauge the full potential for evasion, a few observations are in order. First, cases involving financial creditors are distinct from those involving tort claimants. It is likely that English proceedings will continue to be available for US companies seeking to restructure financial debts if they shift their Centre of Main Interest (or COMI) to England.[48] Now that US courts may not use releases to bind holdouts when it comes to claims against affiliates (including claims for loan guarantees), US debtors will look for an alternative that allows releases. English proceedings offer exactly that.[49] For tort cases the situation is murkier. As discussed below, it is far from obvious that the English and US courts would approve global forum shopping in those tort cases.

(ii) Good-faith Filing: The J&J Effect

In *LTL Management LLC*, the United States Court of Appeals for the Third Circuit introduced uncertainty about the financial conditions required for a debtor to initiate Chapter 11 proceedings.[50] The case involved lawsuits against Johnson & Johnson (J&J) and its subsidiaries, claiming a link between Baby Powder and ovarian cancer and mesothelioma. J&J attempted to put a newly-formed subsidiary into Chapter 11 to resolve these lawsuits.

Claimants challenged this manoeuvre, arguing that the subsidiary had filed its Chapter 11 petition in bad faith. The appellate court agreed and dismissed the case.[51] The sole basis for the decision was that the subsidiary was too solvent to justify using Chapter 11. The Court held that Chapter 11 proceedings are not filed in good faith if the debtor cannot show 'immediate' financial distress.[52] This holding created uncertainty about what is required of a debtor to take advantage of Chapter 11. Indeed, at the

html; Madlyn Primoff, 'Psst, Need a Non-Consensual Third Party Release After the Supreme Court's Purdue Decision?: Consider a Non-U.S. Proceeding Plus Chapter 15 Recognition' (2 July 2024) *Freshfields*, available at: https://blog.freshfields.us/post/102jbq3/psst-need-a-non-consensual-third-party-release-after-the-supreme-courts-purdue; Michelle McGreal et al, 'Purdue Pharma Bankruptcy Ruling Sidesteps Chapter 15 Implication' (10 July 2024) *Bloomberg Law*, available at: https://news.bloomberglaw.com/us-law-week/purdue-pharma-bankruptcy-ruling-sidesteps-chapter-15-implications.

[48] Under the UNCITRAL Model Law on Cross-Border Insolvency, a debtor is supposed to initiate main proceedings in the jurisdiction of its COMI. But a debtor can shift its COMI on the eve of filing. See Anthony J Casey, Aurelio Gurrea-Martínez, Robert K Rasmussen, 'A Commitment Rule for Insolvency Forum', *European Corporate Governance Institute – Law Working Paper No 754/2024*, available at: https://papers.ssrn.com/sol3/papers.cfm?abstract_id=4704029. A COMI shift is generally accomplished by establishing a debtor entity with its registered offices in a forum. That entity can serve as an anchor for a restructuring that encompasses all affiliates within the debtor's enterprise. COMI shifts are economically meaningless transactions. The rules of COMI thus consume resources without meaningfully constraining forum shopping. That is why I have advocated for a new rule governing insolvency forum. See ibid.

[49] The court in *Avanti* (n 24) at 606 explained the challenge of restructuring a case without the ability to release such guarantees: 'Without releasing those guarantees, it would be difficult to restructure the debt because the collective assets and earnings of the group are needed to support the restructured debt without the risk of some creditors that hold the guarantees separately reaching the assets of the affiliates, endangering the ability of the group to meet its restructured debt obligations'.

[50] *LTL I* (n 7).

[51] ibid.

[52] ibid; see also *In re LTL Mgt LLC* (*LTL II*), No 23-2971, 2024 WL 3540467 (3d Cir July 25, 2024) (dismissing the second Chapter 11 bankruptcy of LTL Management on similar grounds); *In re Aearo Techs LLC*, No 22-02890-JJG-11, 2023 WL 3938436 (Bankr SD Ind June 9, 2023) (dismissing the Chapter 11 bankruptcy of 3M's subsidiary Aearo Technologies on similar grounds).

current moment, there is a deep division among US courts about what a debtor must show to establish that a case was filed in good faith.[53]

If the Third Circuit immediate-financial-distress test is adopted more broadly, it will make Chapter 11 more costly. Any single creditor can bring a motion to dismiss a case, arguing the absence of financial distress. These motions are likely to produce costly litigation at the outset of a significant number of cases. In contrast, there is no financial distress requirement for a scheme of arrangement.[54] Thus, a debtor negotiating a single class restructuring might take these cases to England, fearing that a single holdout could challenge a bankruptcy filing in the US.

(iii) Domestic Venue Reform

Chapter 11 venue rules are controversial. Over the last four decades, academics have debated their propriety,[55] and Congress has considered various statutory reforms.[56] These reform proposals have not been adopted, but neither have they been fully dismissed. And so, the debate continues.

In recent years, the issue has become even more salient, and calls for reform have gained steam. A confluence of events has drawn the attention of the media as well as Congress, who have railed against the use of Chapter 11 to reach settlement in mass tort cases. One of the primary targets of their criticism has been the debtor's ability to choose its bankruptcy court.[57]

Most notable were the criticisms of Purdue's decisions to file its case in the courthouse in White Plains, New York. At the time, filing in White Plains meant the case would be assigned to one specific judge. This practice was labelled 'judge shopping' and was criticised by academics,[58] journalists,[59] and Members of

[53] Compare, *LTL I* (n 7) at 93; with *Carolin Corp v Miller*, 886 F 2d 693, 700–01 (4th Cir 1989) (requiring objective futility and subjective bad faith in order to grant a motion to dismiss for lack of good faith); *In re Premier Automotive Services, Inc*, 492 F 3d 274, 279 (4th Cir 2007) (same); *In re Bestwall LLC*, 605 BR 43, 48 (Bankr WDNC 2019) (applying *Carolin* to deny a motion to dismiss in a 'Texas Two-Step' case); and *In re Piazza*, 719 F 3d 1253, 1271 (11th Cir 2013) (applying a totality-of-circumstances test to determine whether a case was filed in good faith).

[54] For a restructuring plan, there is a requirement that the company 'has encountered, or likely to encounter financial difficulties' that affect its going concern value. CIGA 2020 (n 2) at s 901A). This is likely a lower threshold than the Third Circuit's requirement of immediate financial distress.

[55] See Casey and Macey (n 14) at 472–74 and fn 37.

[56] See, eg, Proposed Bankruptcy Venue Reform Act of 2021, available at: https://www.congress.gov/bill/117th-congress/house-bill/4193.

[57] See, eg, Proposal for the Ending Corporate Bankruptcy Abuse Act of 2024 (ECBA 2024 Proposal), available at: https://www.whitehouse.senate.gov/wp-content/uploads/2024/07/ALL24352.pdf.

[58] See, eg, Adam Levitin, 'Judge Shopping in Chapter 11 Bankruptcy' (2023) *Illinois Law Review* 251; 'Submission of a Proposal to Adopt a Rule to Require Random Case Assignment for Mega Bankruptcy Cases' (19 January 2024): https://aboutblaw.com/bcnl; Robert Lawless, 'Bankruptcy Venue Shopping Breaks Perceptions of Judicial Fairness' (26 June 2024) *Bloomberg Law*, available at: https://news.bloomberglaw.com/us-law-week/bankruptcy-venue-shopping-breaks-perceptions-of-judicial-fairness; Michael Waldman, 'End "Judge Shopping"' (20 March 2024): https://www.brennancenter.org/our-work/analysis-opinion/end-judge-shopping.

[59] See, eg, Dave Zucker, 'Why Did Purdue Pharma File for Bankruptcy in Westchester County?' (20 September 2019) https://westchestermagazine.com/life-style/why-did-purdue-pharma-file-for-bankruptcy-in-westchester-county/; Robert Lawless, 'Bankruptcy Venue Shopping Breaks Perceptions of

Congress.[60] While the criticisms of judge shopping in the Southern District were overblown, they ultimately resulted in procedural change, requiring all major Chapter 11 applications filed in the district to be distributed among all Southern District bankruptcy judges regardless of which courthouse the debtor chose.[61]

The above-mentioned bankruptcy filing by a subsidiary of J&J as part of a structure intended to settle mass tort cases has also been criticised. And a group of Senators responded to the filing with proposed legislation that includes a provision deeming a case to be filed in bad faith 'if the court determines that the debtor manufactured venue'.[62]

Finally, the rise of the Southern District of Texas as the leading hub for large Chapter 11 cases and the resignation of its most prominent bankruptcy judge amid allegations of ethical violations has added fuel to the venue-shopping fire.[63]

These calls for reform could, ironically, lead to an increase in global forum shopping. Debtors often venue shop for good reason, seeking experienced courts with efficient procedures. If debtors worry that US filings will be funnelled to less experienced courts, they will look for alternatives. Put simply, the harder it is for a debtor to choose a venue within the United States, the more likely a debtor is to go elsewhere. Josh Macey and I explored this theme in 2021, noting that proposed domestic venue reforms could encourage debtors to look for more flexible global forums.[64] We noted,

> Cutting off access to judges that specialize in large chapter 11 cases would make chapter 11 – which is generally more costly than foreign proceedings – less attractive. At some point, those costs will not be worth it. The same debtor who was willing to bear those costs in the Southern District of New York may not be willing to do so in a less predictable [US] venue.[65]

While no major venue reform has yet taken hold, there is mounting pressure in the minds of debtors and their lawyers who evaluate the alternatives to Chapter 11.

Judicial Fairness' (26 June 2024) *Bloomberg Law*, available at: https://news.bloomberglaw.com/us-law-week/bankruptcy-venue-shopping-breaks-perceptions-of-judicial-fairness.

[60] See, eg, 'Sherrill Applauds Renewed Measure to Stop "Judge Shopping"' (13 March 2024): https://sherrill.house.gov/media/press-releases/sherrill-applauds-renewed-measure-to-stop-judge-shopping; Mattathias Schwartz 'Senate Leaders Look to Curb "Judge Shopping" but in Different Ways' (10 April 2024) *New York Times*: https://www.nytimes.com/2024/04/10/us/judge-shopping-senate-schumer-mcconnell.html.

[61] Modification in Assignment of Mega Chapter 11 Cases (22 November 2021): https://www.nysb.uscourts.gov/news/modification-assignment-mega-chapter-11-cases.

[62] See ECBA 2024 Proposal (n 57).

[63] See, eg, Creditors Rights Coalition. 'Special Feature: Venue Reform in the Spotlight' (2023) available at: https://creditorcoalition.org/special-feature-venue-reform-in-the-spotlight/; see also, Letter from Academics to the Chief Judge of the United States Bankruptcy Court for the Southern District of Texas, available at: https://blogs.illinois.edu/files/7000/1905560292/220995.pdf (urging the court to adopt reforms aimed at reducing domestic venue shopping); Ronnie Greene, et al, 'How Kirkland Uses Court Shopping to Get an Edge in Bankruptcy' (6 August 2024) *Bloomberg Law*, available at: https://news.bloomberglaw.com/bankruptcy-law/how-kirkland-uses-court-shopping-to-get-an-edge-in-bankruptcy (casting a negative light on domestic venue shopping).

[64] Casey and Macey (n 14).

[65] ibid at 493–94.

C. Overinclusivity

Finally, as Sarah Paterson and Adrian Walters pointed out, Chapter 11 has an 'inclusivity problem'.[66] It is difficult in the United States to restructure one class of creditors without putting the entirety of the debtor's operations into bankruptcy. As a result, an attempt to restructure one class of debt triggers procedural rights for all creditors and counterparties. A creditor who will not be affected by the ultimate deal may extract value by bringing procedural objections along the way.

English schemes of arrangement and restructuring plans, on the other hand, provide what Walters and Paterson refer to as 'selective corporate restructuring'.[67] The unaffected stakeholders are left outside of the proceeding, and the affected creditors can negotiate in a streamlined environment.

In the J&J case discussed above, the debtor attempted to replicate selective restructuring by creating a new debtor that isolated liabilities from operations. It used a divisional merger under Texas law to split its subsidiary into two companies – an operations entity and a liabilities entity. To ensure creditors were not disadvantaged by the transaction, J&J included a funding agreement guaranteeing that liability payments would be backed by the same assets that were available before the divisional merger.[68] The liabilities entity, LTL Management LLC, then filed for bankruptcy.

This manoeuvre is pejoratively referred to as the 'Texas Two-Step' and has produced significant backlash. Litigants have challenged it in court, journalists have criticised it, and Senators have proposed legislation to prohibit it in the future.[69]

These attacks are unfortunate. The Texas Two-Step is a mechanism for reducing Chapter 11's inclusivity problem and facilitating selective corporate restructuring. Indeed, the Texas Two-Step essentially mimics the process of a scheme of arrangement. It puts one group of creditors into a restructuring proceeding, allows them to vote on the proposed outcome, binds holdouts within the class if a supermajority of the class agrees to the deal, and allows all other creditors to remain unaffected by the process.

If measures to prohibit the Texas Two-Step are implemented, they will reduce the options available in Chapter 11. Debtors will, in turn, seek alternatives through foreign proceedings like those in England that provide selective restructuring.

D. CIGA 2020

Finally, as noted above, the enactment of CIGA 2020 significantly expanded the options available in English proceedings. The ability to achieve cross-class cramdown brings those proceedings somewhat closer to Chapter 11. While the proceedings are not

[66] Paterson and Walters (n 9).

[67] Sarah Paterson and Adrian Walters, 'Selective Corporate Restructuring' (2021) available at: https://papers.ssrn.com/sol3/papers.cfm?abstract_id=3924225.

[68] For a fuller description of this process see Anthony Casey and Joshua Macey, 'In Defense of Chapter 11 for Mass Torts' (2023) 90 *University of Chicago Law Review* 973.

[69] See ECBA 2024 Proposal (n 57).

identical and the CIGA restructuring plan is not available to all debtors, the new options it provides do increase the appeal of English proceedings for debtors looking for viable alternatives.

VI. Potential Limitations

English proceedings followed by Chapter 15 recognition as an alternative to Chapter 11 have been used by debtors outside of the United States and once by a US-based debtor. There are, however, limits to how far the English and United States courts will go in tolerating forum shopping.

A. Limits in English Courts

English courts are quite liberal in exercising jurisdiction over debtors with foreign operations – even where the debtor has shifted its Centre of Main Interest (or COMI) to England on the eve of the scheme proceedings. One English court, in approving such manoeuvre, noted, '[T]here can sometimes be good forum shopping'.[70] Still, there are limits. Another court has explained that it is not a 'rubber stamp' and will consider 'all matters relevant to jurisdiction and the exercise of its discretion'.[71]

One might expect that courts will look more closely at cases where the debtor has created an artificial COMI for the purpose of initiating proceedings. But if the debtor can argue that it has done so to achieve the most efficient restructuring and has not disadvantaged any creditors, then the English court may take the cases even where the connection was created on the eve of filing. For example, the High Court in *Codere* noted,

> [W]hat is being attempted is to achieve a position where resort can be had to the law of a particular jurisdiction, not in order to evade debts but rather with a view to achieving the best possible outcome for creditors. If in those circumstances it is appropriate to speak of forum shopping at all, it must be on the basis that there can sometimes be good forum shopping.[72]

This reasoning has been characterised by some as suggesting that extreme forum shopping may be tolerated without strong pre-existing connections to England. All that is required is a COMI shift that establishes a connection, if the purpose of the shift is to benefit the creditor group as a whole.[73] Indeed, if the governing law of underlying agreements is changed to English law, the *Gibbs* rule might even dictate that England

[70] *Re Codere Finance (UK) Ltd* [2015] EWHC 3778 (Ch).
[71] *Re Global Garden Products Italy SpA* [2016] EWHC 1884 (Ch).
[72] *Re Codere* (n 70).
[73] See for example, Reorg Research, *Scheme Analysis: Over 75% of 2016 English Schemes Applicants Were Foreign Issuers; Predictability, Targeted Cramdown Potential Attract Global Companies* (2016) available at: https://reorg.com/articles/scheme-analysis-over-75-of-2016-english-schemes-applicants-were-foreign-issuers-predictability-targeted-cramdown-potential-attract-global-companies/.

is the only acceptable forum, regardless of other connections between the debtor and England.[74]

Still, I suspect that English courts will examine eve-of-filing connections more closely when the pre-existing connections are more tangential. And so, English courts will take cases where US debtors are seeking a financial restructuring supported by the majority of affected creditors.[75] There is considerable doubt, however, about whether they will accept cases where the primary claims being restructured are Unites States tort claims. There is no precedent, and a US mass tort case may test the English appetite for foreign cases.

A debtor might argue that the tort victims' rights are not impaired by the move to the English forum. With a supermajority of claimants on board, the debtor might argue that the claimants will be better off with the deal being put before the English court. After all, the settling claimants benefit from an English proceeding that binds the few holdouts, especially when the same deal is now impossible to achieve under Chapter 11. Such argument would be consistent with the logic behind *Codere* and the idea of 'good forum shopping'.

Still, English courts are unlikely to ignore the fact that (1) there is no substantive connection to England; (2) tens or even hundreds of thousands of claimants are in the United States; and (3) these particular creditors may have less familiarity with global legal proceedings and have had less direct participation in pre-scheme negotiations than a typical financial creditor.

More cynically, one might predict that English courts will decline to take these cases so as to prevent backlash. Exercising jurisdiction over a United States mass tort case after a COMI shift could get the attention of US courts or legislators. That could provoke a protectionist response (such as legislative amendments to Chapter 15) potentially threatening the recognition of English proceedings in other cases, including financial cases involving US debtors or even those involving all non-UK debtors.

This prediction assumes – as critics of forum shopping often do – that courts have an interest in attracting cases to their jurisdiction.[76] It also assumes that a United States Court, or perhaps Congress, would find fault with an English court exercising jurisdiction over a US mass tort case where the debtor is evading a ruling of the Supreme Court of the United States. This is certainly plausible, as a case of that sort would likely attract attention from journalists in the same way that domestic venue shopping has.

A United States court might simply decline to recognise that particular case.[77] But the court's reasoning could go further and establish a rule prohibiting recognition of all English proceedings that follow an artificial COMI shift. This would call into question the recognition of even those cases where the debtor has shifted its COMI to England from a jurisdiction other than the United States.[78]

[74] *Antony Gibbs & Sons v La Société Industrielle et Commerciale des Métaux* (1890) LR 25 QBD 399.

[75] See, for example, *syncreon* (n 5).

[76] The incentive for such behaviour would likely be an interest in building the local legal market.

[77] Or Congress might introduce legislation to prohibit recognition in such cases.

[78] US courts currently recognise foreign proceedings after a COMI shift when the shift is viewed as furthering a successful restructuring: *In re Ocean Rig UDW Inc*, 570 BR 687 (Bankr SDNY 2017).

…y to come from the bankruptcy courts.[79] But a district … well announce such a blunt rule.

…ly to welcome a significant portion of – but not all – US … e-of-filing connections to the forum. The hardest line may … ructuring debts owed to financial creditors and the ones … to US tort victims. Cases involving operational creditors – … on and receive less political attention than mass tort victims – are n… border and be subject to case-by-case analysis.

B. Limits in the US Courts

As noted above, US courts almost always recognise and enforce English schemes of arrangement. Thus, the baseline assumption is that courts will recognise the English proceedings in the absence of extreme circumstances. From there, one can infer that an English proceeding restructuring the financial debts of a US-based firm will be recognised and enforced in the United States.

This is probably true even when the English proceedings include non-debtor releases of the type prohibited by the Supreme Court's ruling in *Purdue Pharma*. US courts routinely recognised English proceedings involving non-debtor release before *Purdue Pharma*, even while noting the possibility that such releases might be prohibited in Chapter 11.

One court summarised the US position this way:

> [P]rinciples of enforcement of foreign judgments and comity in chapter 15 cases strongly counsel approval of enforcement in the United States of the third-party non-debtor release and injunction provisions included in [Foreign] Orders, even if those provisions could not be entered in a plenary chapter 11 case.[81]

None of that has changed. *Purdue Pharma* does not imply in any way that non-debtor releases are contrary (much less 'manifestly contrary') to United States public policy. Indeed, the Bankruptcy Code expressly allows non-debtor release in asbestos cases.[82] It is implausible that the Supreme Court of the United States would hold a practice explicitly adopted by Congress in all asbestos cases to be 'manifestly contrary the policy of the United States' in other cases. Relieving any doubt, the Court in *Purdue Pharma* further explained,

> Someday, Congress may choose to add to the bankruptcy code special rules for opioid-related bankruptcies as it has for asbestos-related cases. Or it may choose not to do so. Either way, if a policy decision like that is to be made, it is for Congress to make.[83]

[79] If it did, those courts would be subject to wide criticism, as US bankruptcy courts have regularly presided over Chapter 11 cases involving primarily foreign enterprises. See Adrian Walters, 'United States' Bankruptcy Jurisdiction over Foreign Entities: Exorbitant or Congruent' (2017) 17(2) *Journal of Corporate Law Studies* 367, 397.

[80] Or the Supreme Court in the unlikely event that one of these cases ended up there.

[81] *In re Metcalfe & Mansfield Alternative Investments*, 421 BR 685, 696 (Bankr SDNY 2010).

[82] 11 USC § 524(g).

[83] *Purdue Pharma* (n 40) at 2087.

That passage is not consistent with a view that these releases are man
to the public policy of the United States. And so, US courts will not categor
recognition of foreign proceedings that include non-debtor releases.[84]

Still, in particular cases, a court may find the circumstances around forum shoppi
suspect. Where a court thinks a US debtor has invoked English proceedings solely to disadvantage creditors, it may deny recognition. This is most likely true when the debtor has no ties to England, is primarily restructuring the claims of US tort victims, and has no other apparent explanation for the decision to bring the case in England.

Finally, it is worth noting one other open question regarding recognition of English restructuring plans. The restructuring plan structure allows for cross-class cramdown. But unlike Chapter 11, it has no Absolute Priority Rule, which requires objecting classes of creditors be paid in full before any junior classes recover any value.[85] Thus, while the English case law on restructuring plans is nascent, a restructuring plan might allow shareholders to retain their interest while forcing an objecting class of creditors to accept less-than-full payment.

A plan with that structure would be strictly prohibited in Chapter 11. But it remains to be seen whether such a plan is enforceable under Chapter 15. No US court has directly examined whether a violation of the Absolute Priority Rule is manifestly contrary to the public policy of the United States. My intuition is that it is not. But if any bankruptcy rule is considered sacred enough to trigger the public policy exception, it is likely the Absolute Priority Rule.[86] To take it one step further, Professors van Zwieten and Ellingsæter explain in Chapter three of this volume that English law has effectively adopted a rule that leaves priority to the discretionary design of courts.[87] This creates foundational uncertainty about distributional entitlements that might independently make it difficult for a US court to recognise a proceeding under Chapter 15.

VII. Conclusion

Forum shopping can be good or bad. Debtors sometimes choose a forum based on the efficiency and expertise of the courts. Other times they choose based on perceived advantages for certain stakeholders. There are various rules that a jurisdiction can adopt to facilitate good forum shopping while limiting the bad.[88]

[84] At least one US court already granted recognition to a foreign proceeding that included non-consensual non-debtor releases after *Purdue Pharma*: *In re Americanas SA*, Case No 23-10092, Docket No 75 (Bankr SDNY July 22, 2024).

[85] See generally Douglas G Baird, 'Priority Matters: Absolute Priority, Relative Priority, and the Costs of Bankruptcy' (2017) 165 *University of Pennsylvania Law Review* 785.

[86] The Absolute Priority Rule should have no claim to such reverence. There are other priority rules that are equally coherent and efficient. See generally Anthony J Casey, 'The Creditors' Bargain and Option-Preservation Priority in Chapter 11' (2011) 78 *University of Chicago Law Review* 759. But it is not unthinkable that US courts would get this wrong.

[87] See Kristin van Zwieten and Sjur Swensen Ellingsæter, 'Rules of Priority in Restructuring Procedures' Chapter 3 of this volume.

[88] See Anthony J Casey, Aurelio Gurrea-Martínez, and Robert K Rasmussen, 'A Commitment Rule for Insolvency Forum' (2024) *European Corporate Governance Institute – Law Working Paper No 754/2024*, available at: https://papers.ssrn.com/sol3/papers.cfm?abstract_id=4704029; Casey and Macey (n 14).

In this chapter, the analysis is more predictive than normative. Forum shopping will happen. The US bankruptcy market has largely ignored competition from jurisdictions abroad, but that is changing. The possibility of US debtors going abroad has received increased attention in recent years, especially in the aftermath of the Supreme Court's decision in *Purdue Pharma*. This chapter has explored the likelihood of such a trend and how it might play out.

In closing, the reader should note that England is not the only jurisdiction that might compete with the United States for restructuring cases. Several other jurisdictions, including Ireland, The Netherlands, and Singapore are potential contenders offering a similar alternative. More aggressive jurisdictions are also likely to join the competition and take specific actions to attract large debtors. Meanwhile, developments in the United States are likely to reduce Chapter 11's appeal. It will be a long competition, but England and other jurisdictions have gained considerable ground in this opening round.

INDEX

www.ingramcontent.com/pod-product-compliance
Ingram Content Group UK Ltd.
Pitfield, Milton Keynes, MK11 3LW, UK
UKHW020845290926
15470UKWH00004B/1570

9 781509 978380